THE FUTURES
OF CHRISTIANITY

THE FUTURES OF CHRISTIANITY

by

David L. Edwards

HODDER AND STOUGHTON
LONDON SYDNEY AUCKLAND TORONTO

British Library Cataloguing in Publication Data

Edwards, David L.
  The futures of Christianity.
  1. Christianity
  I. Title
  200   BR121.2

  ISBN 0 340 40742 5

He who goes out weeping bearing the seed
shall come again with gladness
bringing his sheaves with him.

Psalm 126:6

CONTENTS

FOREWORD BY THE ARCHBISHOP OF CANTERBURY

What is the state of Christianity today? What can it offer for the future? I am often asked these questions and always feel the inadequacy of my answers. Such questions require us to look at the experience of Christianity in various parts of the world and at its role in different societies, cultures and histories. We need to be familiar not only with our own, but with a wide range of expressions of Christianity. And we need to make a judicious appraisal of the heart of the Christian faith, as well as of its religious and secular alternatives.

Charting a future course for the Church is difficult and demanding, and I for one am grateful to David Edwards for his impressive synthesis of a mass of material, and for his ability to identify common themes. He writes from within a distinctively Anglican tradition and does not try to hide his own particular perspective. But his breadth of knowledge and sensitivity to other approaches will make this a compendium of universal and enduring value.

As Christians we need to cherish our past, look honestly at the present, and peer into the future with a hope grounded in a mixture of realism and expectation. The Provost of Southwark guides us with scholarly authority and personal conviction, and offers an antidote to the twin dangers of easy complacency or defeatist pessimism which mar so much discussion of these questions.

ROBERT CANTUAR
November 1986

PREFACE

I am deeply grateful to those who encouraged me to write a book discussing the developments in worldwide Christianity which seem most significant for its future. I have been struck by the diversity, so that I write about Christianity's *futures*. But there is only one essential Christian faith, which unites or could unite the diversity. I do not wish to claim that this 'essential faith' is identical with my own way of perceiving Christianity, so that I have found it necessary, before exploring the Christian world in the 1980s, to visit the world of the Bible and the world of the early Christian centuries. I have tried to find there the answer to the question, 'What is Christianity?'; to see what is the faith which really has united Christianity as millions upon millions of Christians have known it; to listen to the communion in diversity which, I think, Christianity can keep in its many futures. I hope that others will find it worthwhile, as I have certainly found it, to attempt to see these developments in the past, the present and (possibly) the futures as a whole, even if only in outline and subject to the many limitations of my knowledge, insight and eloquence. For a good many years now I have written an article or two almost every week on current events and new books and I am grateful, specially to the *Church Times*, for that opportunity. But something is gained by trying to stand back in order to see the complete picture, even if one's eyesight is defective.

In particular I thank the archbishop of Canterbury and the bishop of Southwark for encouragement; Sydney Evans, then dean of Salisbury, and the other trustees of the St Augustine's Foundation, who sponsored the project by offering in 1982 to fund some international travel; Samuel van Culin and others who made my independent task easier by associating it unofficially with the work of the Anglican Consultative Council; the General Theological Seminary, New York, where I studied and listened; the many people who guided me in journeys which, however incomplete, took me from the library of the World Council of Churches to a glimpse of a jungle in Sarawak; friends who commented on my drafts, and among them Marcus

Braybrooke, Henry Chadwick, Kenneth Cragg, William Frend, Mark Gibbs, Adrian Hastings, Daniel Jenkins, Lesslie Newbigin, Edwin Robertson, John Stott, W. W. Simpson and Mary Tanner; my colleagues in Southwark Cathedral, particularly Peter Penwarden and Gerry Parrott, who generously accepted the absences from the busy life of this London church of the priest who is rightly supposed to be the servant of all; my daughter, Helen, and my secretary, Susan Cowdell, who typed and retyped these pages; and my wife Sybil, without whom . . . Not the least of her contributions are the facts that she spent many years among Africans and – alas, far more briefly – accompanied me to India.

I am very much an Anglican. I am of course specially interested in the Anglican contribution, but it is characteristic of the Anglican communion that I have been encouraged to range much more widely than Anglicanism. This has involved some study of a considerable variety of historical and theological literature published in recent years and I hope that some fellow readers may be helped by the lists of books in the notes. However, since this book is not offered as a work of scholarship I have restricted myself to recommending books in English and I have made no attempt to be comprehensive in treatment or bibliography. It would have taken too much space to give the names of the publishers, but enquiries in a good library or bookshop will show that most of the books were distributed at the time of publication both in the UK and in the USA. Where the place of publication was outside those countries, I have mentioned it. I have found myself specially indebted to the publishing programmes of Orbis Books (sponsored by the Catholic Foreign Mission Society of America, which received me with a gracious hospitality at Maryknoll) and the SCM Press in London (of which I am a proud ex-editor). Biblical quotations are usually from the New English Bible, by permission of the Oxford and Cambridge University Presses. Finally I thank my editor David Wavre, David Mackinder who edited my text for the printer, and the other staff of Hodder and Stoughton. Knowing that their predecessors had published my *Religion and Change* in 1969, they never flinched when I told them that I wanted to write about still more changes.

Michaelmas
London, 1986   David L. Edwards

1

A YOUNG FAITH

What's past is prologue

Christianity is young and if it lasts for as long as humanity is expected to last on this planet it has futures of at least two thousand million years ahead of it. If there is to be a nuclear war, presumably among the survivors will be people included among, or descended from, the people, perhaps as few as a thousand million or perhaps more, who are Christians in one sense or another in the mid-1980s – and they will rebuild the church. If our civilisation is preserved from suicide but natural disasters lie ahead (ice ages, for example, or the melting of the ice at the poles), it can be expected that such disasters will not obliterate a Christian community which already in the 1980s is worldwide. If the progress of civilisation, now science-based, is continuous as the more optimistic kind of science fiction predicts, presumably the Christian church will continue to be a part of the input although it will change profoundly along with the rest of human society. It is, of course, a matter of faith, not knowledge, to believe that the powers of death will not prevail over the church, but the story of the first two thousand years is repeatedly a story of ordeals overcome. There is good reason to think that 'what's past is prologue' – Shakespeare's words so splendidly carved on the National Archives building in Washington. We are the primitive church. All our theology is immature. All our organisations are experimental. Almost all our spirituality, or our thinking about the problems of society, has been at its best adolescent.

The psychology of youth has always been the character of this faith. The theologians call it eschatological. They mean that the 'last things' will be the things that matter most – and have not yet arrived. The Christian Bible stops before the end. The Old Testament breaks off with the tormented question: Will God's promises be fulfilled? Almost the last words of the New Testament are words of longing: 'Come, Lord Jesus!' The prayer has been recorded in the Aramaic spoken by Jesus himself and the first Christians: '*Marana tha*' (1 Corinthians 16:22). And the history of the church to date has always been a history of the hope that the church's greatest days are still to come, when 'the gospel shall be preached to all nations'; when 'the fulness of the Gentiles shall be gathered in and all Israel saved'; when the church shall be made glorious 'like a bride adorned for her husband'; when the universe itself is to enter upon the liberty and splendour of the children of God. Such hopes have arisen repeatedly, transforming realities which were far from glorious. The letter to Hebrews in the New Testament more or less equates faith with willingness to look forward and therefore to endure. Knowing that the call to discipleship is a call into the future, Christians have never forgotten how a man clinging to the past was told: 'Let the dead bury their dead!' 'A Christianity which is not totally and utterly eschatology has nothing whatsoever to do with Christ': it was the youthful Karl Barth speaking, but he had a point.

However, most Christians have not claimed a knowledge of exactly what lies in the future. The prophets whose visions are among the chief glories of the Hebrew scriptures were often right when they functioned as 'forthtellers', discerning the consequences of present attitudes – but they could be wrong as 'foretellers' of detailed events. The earliest gospel gives as the cautious teaching of the Lord himself: 'about that day or that hour no one knows, not even the angels in heaven, not even the Son; only the Father' (Mark 13:32). Nor is the impression left that Jesus knew exactly what the world would be like in the future. His question is reported: 'When the Son of Man comes, will he find faith on earth?' (Luke 18:8).

In the gospels are to be found other sayings, and whole parables, where the theme is the urgency of the crisis created by the beginning of the arrival of the kingdom of God, and the evidence suggests that Jesus shared the hope that 'there are some of those standing here who will not taste death before they have seen the kingdom of God already come in power' (Mark 9:1). Much of the rest of the New Testament reflects the early Christian expectation that history was going to end soon with the *parousia*, the 'second coming', of Jesus in glory. Much of that expectation is still maintained by many Christians in the twentieth century AD. For them, the proper understanding of the authority of the Bible is such that they take (for example) the book of Revelation more or less literally as a forecast. They may be confident in expecting the 'rapture' of the saints on earth to heaven and the 'millennium' of perfection on earth for a thousand years. But in the New Testament there is no evidence of a profound and widespread breakdown of Christian faith when it became clear that the apostles and many others were going to die before the arrival of 'the kingdom'. The church in the second half of the first Christian century, when the gospels were written, preserved much of the original sense of intense urgency but there was also the awareness or hope that the harvest grows slowly, that the tree gently spreads its branches so that the birds of the air may nest in it, that 'all men' will be drawn as the church preaches to 'all nations'. The book of Revelation ends with the vision of the kings of the earth bringing the wealth and splendour of the nations into the holy city. And in the subsequent history of Christian faith, the enthusiastic expectation that the 'second coming' of the Lord will come quickly and precisely as predicted in one or other passage of the Bible has become a minority belief. So far as most Christians are concerned, the Bible's pictures of the coming 'kingdom' can be treated as visions of destiny rather than as forecasts of the next few years. They can be interpreted as 'myth' – as elaborately magnificent poetry conveying faith, hope and courage to Christians under temptations and persecutions. Most Christians have accepted the prospect that history is likely to be a long process and have been content to leave the future largely veiled. That kind of agnosticism has marked people who nevertheless are glad to belong to the church and who know what one theologian (Wolfhart Pannenberg) means when he calls the church 'the community of the end time'.

Twentieth-century theology has paid much attention to the problem of how the glory of those visions of the 'end things' can be related to the probability that history will continue year after year. What today is the cash value of the eschatology of the New Testament? What do these pictures say to us, who still seem chronologically far away from the 'end time'? No clear consensus has been reached. But in so far as agreement is emerging out of a long and large debate, it may perhaps be expressed somewhat like this.

To believe in the God revealed in Jesus is to believe that history will end in 'the Day of the Lord' – a way of speaking about the fulfilment of God's purposes which are the purposes of redeeming love. Meanwhile each crisis in history, public or personal, brings a little judgement by God on the evil which resists those purposes; in Greek *krisis* means 'judgement'. As it is experienced, the crisis often seems all-important and all-decisive. And it may indeed be the end of one 'world' and the beginning of another; in the twentieth century during and since 1914, many 'worlds' have ended. But it does not follow that God is in as much of a hurry as man is. In his sight, a thousand years are said to be 'as one day'. It is his will, it seems, that people should respond to his purposes freely. With this end in view he gives them space and time. He gives them a future which must be the interplay between his power and their freedom. Such a future is still undetermined by him or by any other force – and therefore it cannot be predicted in detail. And the Christian who holds on to this vision of God's loving sovereignty, who sees also God's condemnation of evil, who receives the gift of time as a sign of God's fatherlike mercy on the undeserving, and who prepares to enter the future, is taught by the example of Jesus himself to be as patient as the God whom he worships. Albert Schweitzer's theory (advanced by less celebrated scholars before him) that Jesus died hoping that his self-sacrifice would persuade, enable or even force God to bring about the 'end of all things' immediately is not convincing. It ignores the basic character of the faith of Jesus which gives birth to the hope of Jesus. This is the faith of Gethsemane, which does not attempt to give God orders or to force his hand. Jesus, it seems, hoped that the end of the evil in the world around him was near. But as he faced his final conflict sweating in anxiety, he freely obeyed the Father who retains his own freedom: 'Your will be done!' This is the faith which enters the dark future in trust, not knowledge; which treads the way of the cross into Easter. And every Christian who has trodden that way knows that it is a road both disillusioning and rewarding, a life both dying and rising.[1]

It is in this agnostic faith that the Christian takes part in the discussion sometimes called 'futurology' but better known as 'futures thinking'. The solid, intellectually respectable, basis of this discussion was expressed unpretentiously by Edward Cornish when President of the World Futures Society: 'educated guesses about what might happen in the coming years after studying current trends'. To think about such possible developments with as much care and objectivity as possible, with or without the aid of computers, is a healthy exercise of the mind – and may help us to take wiser attitudes to what is going on around us. 'Futures thinking' of this sort has itself been one of the constructive movements developing in this century. It has a longer history, of course, but what matters most is that beginning in the optimism of the twentieth century's early years, this movement of excitement about possibilities has again and again opened eyes which otherwise would have been blinded by tears over the unfolding century's tragedies. As the avalanche of technical change has speeded up in recent years, the widespread discussion of 'alternative futures' has helped to spread the sense that humanity is challenged rather than doomed by its technology; that it is possible to examine resources and options rationally and creatively, sometimes even changing behaviour in the light of warnings. But the history of thought about the futures does not encourage any belief that we are capable of getting the details right. Too many outcomes have not come out. Even if we sensibly restrict ourselves to the implications of what is already taking place, and even if we limit our curiosity to the few years remaining before AD 2000, foresight is not easy. Prognostications of a Doomsday which cannot be avoided litter the history of the future. In retrospect they often seem comic. Intoxicated predictions of a Utopia staffed by Supermen are also plentiful. The harassed humans who look back on them often find them tragic, with perhaps the weary joke that 'the future is not what it used to be'. Cicero remarked to the Roman Senate that no soothsayer should be able to look at another without laughing.

So this book is being written by a Christian who finds a special incentive for some modest 'futures thinking' in the teachings of Christianity. The futures (Christians believe) will be under God's sovereignty – but the futures cannot be controlled, or in detail anticipated, by any futures-thinker. If we study current trends, that may make our guesses about the futures 'educated' and perhaps our responses to current problems will be a little more understanding – but no foresight or insight within our capacity will be other than human.

In my own education of study, travel, listening and thinking, I have found two themes growing ever larger in my mind. One is the theme of diversity. It has been estimated that in the world in the mid-1980s there are at least 1,500,000 Christian congregations. They are served, it is said, by about 3,750,000 professional ministers or other workers; they have a corporate income of very roughly £50,000 million (or $75,000 million) a year; they distribute about forty-three million Bibles a year; they read, or at any rate are offered, more than twenty thousand periodicals and more than twenty thousand new religious books a year; and they are divided into more than twenty thousand denominations. Although about two thirds of the world's Christians are either Roman Catholics or Eastern Orthodox, even in those great churches there is nowadays no uniformity. So this diversity in church life is a fact which will not go away. And my 'educated guess' is that any unity will have to be found amid this astounding diversity, denominational and regional, temperamental and institutional, within a world population which already in AD 1986 includes five thousand million different people.

But another theme has also gained power in my mind the further I have probed. It is the conviction that a Christian communion including all this diversity is possible although it must be conceived in a way that is genuinely open to the variety and the change. Too often Christians seeking 'unity' have attempted to retreat to some narrow formula in theology or to return to some legendary golden age in the past. The truth about the Christian past teaches what is possible. In the Christian scriptures, in the early Christian centuries and in the experience of the modern churches, there is immense diversity with jewels as well as trash in abundance. But there is also one very precious pearl. The shared experience of the God embodied in Jesus Christ unites Christians in the 'fellowship of the Holy Spirit'; in valuing the Bible, baptism and the eucharist and therefore an ordained 'ministry'; and in producing the authenticating fruits, the Christlike character and the Christlike action. The challenge to the Christian who thinks about the futures is to imagine a communion based on the realities of this unifying experience and big enough to cover the diversity now seen to be inescapable and now welcomed as the will of an imaginative Creator.

Am I in some way being false to the spirit of Christianity if I stress these two themes of *diversity* and *communion*? I do not think so. For I find that these themes run through the Bible and the very early Christian centuries.

Hebrew beginnings

Christianity at first seemed to be one Jewish movement among many. Although Christians have often fallen for the temptation to call the Jewish religion in the first century of our common era formal, narrow, legalistic, sterile or fossilised, the truth recovered by modern scholarship is very different. Judaism was then bursting with life. The religious energy of the Jews attracted many converts ('proselytes') and was expressed untidily in rivalries between groups stressing one or other element in Israel's heritage.

About 1200 BC 'Hebrews' – *hapiru*, people living beyond the margins of civilisation – appeared out of the wilderness, joined forces with landless labourers already in Palestine, and overthrew the ruling class of the Canaanite civilisation which had been in possession. Canaanite holy places were now associated with the Hebrew patriarchs Abraham, Isaac and Jacob who, it was told, had in dimly distant days believed promises from their God, Yahweh, about a good future in this land. And the rules and customs – religious, hygienic, social and moral – which were binding these tribesmen together were associated with the great figure of Moses the lawgiver, who in the much more recent past had been the leader of a group escaping from slavery in Egypt. In a book published some six hundred years after that exodus, a creed was set out for recital by a farmer coming to present the first fruits of the harvest to Yahweh: 'My father was a homeless Aramaean who went down to Egypt with a small company and lived there until they became a great, powerful, and numerous nation. But the Egyptians ill-treated us, humiliated us and imposed cruel slavery upon us. Then we cried to Yahweh the God of our fathers for help . . . and so Yahweh brought us out of Egypt with a strong hand and outstretched arm, with terrifying deeds, and with signs and portents. He brought us to this place and gave us this land, a land flowing with milk and honey' (Deuteronomy 26:5–9). Among the deeds of Yahweh celebrated by these tribesmen was the immobilisation of the Egyptian chariots, sent in pursuit but bogged down in the marshes of the Red Sea. The stories told by these Hebrews were not always accurate history, but this grateful farmer's creed in Deuteronomy preserved a memory of a liberation which was real. It celebrated the beginning of the adventure of the diverse tribes now united to constitute Israel.

We have met a tribal religion – or rather, the religion which bound together a federation of tribes. Anthropologists and sociologists are familiar with the phenomenon. But what has been astounding about this particular tribal religion has been its spiritual fertility. The creed of those Hebrews has been important to large sections of mankind up to our own time – not only to Jews but also to Muslims and to Christians who share the indebtedness of Jesus to the religion which was taught to him in Nazareth. Millions upon millions have been enriched by the Hebrew legacy – a legacy of temples and laws, a passion for social justice and a profoundly personal spirituality, God-intoxicated prophecy and humane wisdom, patriotism and supernaturalism.

Jesus encountered Sadducees, the group of aristocrats and priests who controlled the temple in Jerusalem. They were so conservative that they rejected any belief in immortality or resurrection: it was not authorised by the scriptures which they accepted. This was an un-romantic group, but behind it lay the work of the priests who had consecrated the unity of the tribes in the early days. Jerusalem was made the capital of these tribesmen after its capture by King David about 1000 BC. The first temple, virtually a royal chapel, built by David's son Solomon in alliance with King Hiram of Tyre, symbolised an agreement to move into what was then the modern world – a world of kings, commerce, fine buildings and elaborate rituals. After Solomon's death the political unity of the tribes could not hold: ten made up the northern state of Israel, leaving two to form Judah around Jerusalem. But despite efforts to provide an alternative religious centre in the north, Jerusalem and particularly its temple remained magnetic; and the magnetism survived through many centuries of exile. Here was the chief focus of the Jew's continuing sense of identity. The psalms in the Hebrew scriptures were the temple's hymn book. They have been treasured so highly because they voice the temple's spirit although its stones have been demolished, rebuilt, demolished, rebuilt, demolished, rebuilt, demolished and replaced by a pagan temple, Christian churches and Muslim shrines. The godlike king of the house of David was praised in highly idealistic terms which Christians have taken over to sing the praises of the saviour; and a link with the earlier egalitarianism of the Hebrews was preserved by the insistence that the king was raised above other men precisely in order to bring justice to the poor. So the community's life was sanctified. However, the psalms also show the temple to have been the scene of a fervently personal religious devotion. Whether in lament or celebration, in penitence or thanksgiving, the individual emerged out of the group in order to pray with the heart. This piety has outlasted the Davidic monarchy and countless other governments. It has also survived the end of the animal sacrifices which were the most conspicuous feature of the Jerusalem temple. It has inspired the devotions of synagogues all over the Jewish world – when the temple was no more, but Jerusalem as an idea still meant everything to every loyal Jew.

Without surprise we read that Jesus the Jew was deeply moved when he noticed a poor widow putting all her money into the collecting box in that temple. He compared his love for Jerusalem with a hen gathering her chicks, but he wept over the city because the temple's ideals had been betrayed. His action in overturning the tables of the moneychangers was a demonstration of his zeal that the temple should be the house of prayer for all peoples that had been intended; and it was probably this action which, more than any other, aroused the determination of the chief priests to see this troublemaker's life ended. He looked forward to a new temple in the new world. What can be seen to have come is a Christianity attaching great significance to its own temples, sanctifying many societies and housing the prayers of many individuals.

Jesus also encountered the Pharisees and other 'scribes' and teachers of the religious law. These were the exponents of the written 'law of Moses' and of the oral tradition interpreting its 248 positive commandments and 365 prohibitions. When the temple was destroyed by the Romans in AD 70 the unrivalled centre of Judaism became the law as taught by the Pharisees, as rabbis trained in the academy at Jamnia, in Tiberias or in the schools of Babylonia fashioned a religion based on the scriptures read in a synagogue, not on the sacrifices offered in a temple. And not many years passed before Christianity, too, became a legally minded religion.

Modern scholars have helped us to understand that the 'law of Moses' had strong roots in human history and a strong hold on human hearts. While some bits probably go back to Moses, and parts are rules for farmers about how to keep clear of the Canaanite fertility cults (Exodus 34:10–26; Deuteronomy 27:15–26), much of the legislation reflects the work of Israel's prophets. Spiritual giants such as Elijah proclaimed the power, holiness and demands of Yahweh. Israel's God – the God who had liberated and united these tribes, the God under whose rule all these 'brothers' were equal – would tolerate neither the oppression of his people by mere kings nor the corruption of their piety by the worship of mere idols. But it was not enough for the prophets to protest in Yahweh's name. In the Jewish tradition which surrounded Jesus, Elijah was associated with Moses because this passionate protest movement also gave birth to strong legislation. The collection of laws called by modern scholars the Book of the Covenant (Exodus 21:1–23:19) demanded a simple, strongly moral worship and a classless, humane fairness between fellow Israelites. When the northern kingdom was overwhelmed by the Assyrian empire, a more elaborate code of laws, decreeing far more severe measures against all heathen worship, was taken to Jerusalem and published in 621 BC, causing another religious revolution, this time under King Josiah (Deuteronomy 12–26). From material surrounding this 'second law' Jesus extracted the timeless commandment to love God with all one's heart, soul and might (Deuteronomy 6:5). When Jerusalem had been conquered by the Babylonian empire, a third large collection of laws was published, the Law of Holiness (Leviticus 17–26). This insisted on a stricter purity in the worship of Yahweh and a sterner enforcement of justice and equality between the worshippers. The code as we have it dates from a time when the temple had been reconstructed on a more modest scale and a small law-abiding community formed around it in Jerusalem – but the loftiness of these puritanical standards reflects the ideals of major prophets such as Ezekiel who had guided the exiles or Micah, Isaiah and Jeremiah, who had courageously announced their vision of

Yahweh's holiness while the original temple was still standing. Thus in days which made for despair their religious law became to the Jew a badge, symbolising what it meant to be a Jew – like circumcision for men and the strict observance of the Sabbath (Saturday) as a day of rest. And from the Law of Holiness Jesus took the commandment to love your neighbour (Leviticus 19:18), meaning originally the fellow Israelite. So Christians should not be surprised that Psalm 119 has preserved the intensity of the delight taken by the orthodox Jew in obeying the *Torah*, the 'law of Moses', thus assembled. He has kept the law out of love. It has seemed sweeter than honey. The gospels suggest that with this motive Jesus of Nazareth obeyed most of this law in its written form, although he rejected any wooden legalism and attacked additions appended to what was written (for example, the severe restrictions on the sabbath). Each sabbath found him at worship in a synagogue.

Luke gives us a picture of Jesus reading from the book of Isaiah in the synagogue at Nazareth. And Jesus was often welcomed as a prophet – as a man who would teach the people with fresh authority; who without fear or partiality would denounce the enemies of God; who would heal the sick in order to demonstrate the power of the living God to save his people now; who would cut through legalism in order to proclaim God's majesty and mercy. In Galilee at that time there were a number of such 'prophets' – teachers and healers with charismatic gifts. However, the gospels report that Jesus was hailed as the equal, even as the reincarnation, of a major prophet in the past such as Elijah. They also record that Jesus taught for some of the time in a style which recalled the most unusual aspect of the work of the major prophets. He interpreted the 'signs of the times', making sense of the present by proclaiming what would be the future results of the good or evil now being done by men. He challenged his contemporaries to examine their own age as they would examine the sky for signs of the weather or see in a budding tree evidence that summer was near.

When they called him a prophet, his contemporaries placed Jesus in a tradition of truly great men. With a courage seldom matched in the whole history of religion, Amos the shepherd and 'dresser of sycamore-figs' from the little village of Tekoa denounced the rich who lived at ease in the sophisticated capital of the north, Samaria. Or Jeremiah foretold the capture of Jerusalem by the Babylonians in 597 BC, urged the surrender of the city and the acceptance of exile, and understood all these disasters as God's just punishment of his people's sins. But their greater God towered above these great men.

Although the major prophets all had impressive personalities (for example, Hosea – a man faithful to his unfaithful wife, finding in that bitter experience the truth of God's faithfulness), it is significant that the greatest of them all was remembered for his teaching, not for his name. This was the anonymous prophet nowadays known as Second Isaiah, who had the courage to proclaim Yahweh as the creator of all and to greet King Cyrus of the Persians as his 'anointed' or *Messiah* (Isaiah 40–55). And the most amazing phenomenon in this whole story of prophecy is the determination of faithful Jews to preserve and collect such writings although they so often pour scorn and anger on the national leadership. The prophetic books became part of the Hebrew scriptures because their predictions of evil days seemed to have come true in the people's history; because their vision of Yahweh as the Lord of history, as the ultimate controller of events, seemed to have been justified by the very tragedies which had almost totally extinguished the Jewish nation. Second Isaiah had prophesied that the coming glory after the exiles' return would move all the nations to acknowledge the power of Yahweh. But not so! The world has been impressed because amid the ruins of their national hopes – amid the dry bones left by history's massacres – the Jews have repeatedly cried their 'Amen' and their 'Alleluia' to their mysterious, terrible, reigning God.

The prophets were all intensely patriotic men. But their vision of God was greater than their patriotism. 'Holy, holy, holy is the Lord of Hosts: the whole earth is full of his glory' (Isaiah 6:3). That vision of perfection led them to denounce their own people. Some even saw that this God cared for the distant Ethiopians and was responsible for the exodus of the hated Philistines from Crete and for the arrival on the Israelites' scene of the equally hated Syrians (Amos 9:7). He loved 'Egypt my people . . . Assyria the work of my hands' (Isaiah 19:25). The prophet Malachi dared to say that the worship offered by the priests in Jerusalem was inferior in comparison with the worship offered outside Israel. 'From furthest east to furthest west my name is great among the nations. Everywhere fragrant sacrifice and pure gifts are offered in my name', declared this universal God (Malachi 1:11). That may be merely a compliment to Jewish worship in Gentile lands; but it may also be interpreted as the endorsement of Gentile worship. And one way of understanding Christianity is to see it as the carrier of the prophets' message about the one real God to the ends of the earth.

Either in Palestine or in the *Diaspora* (dispersed amid Gentile communities), there were Jews very unlike the prophets. They had taken Jeremiah's advice to settle down in exile and to work and pray for the prosperity of their new neighbours – or, remaining in Palestine, they had welcomed the enrichment of foreign influences. Some were willing to adopt their Gentile neighbours' customs even if it meant disloyalty to their own religious traditions, but more often Jews retained the conviction that the religion of Yahweh emerged obviously superior from every encounter with another tradition. Some of the writings of this varied group are known by modern scholars as 'wisdom' literature, ranging from the world-weariness of Ecclesiastes to the sharp prudence of Proverbs; from Job's tortured and totally uninhibited eloquence about the problem of evil to the equally uninhibited celebration of the ecstasy of sex in the Song of Songs. The scholarly book Ecclesiasticus reconciled contemporary knowledge with pride in the Jewish heritage: its solution was that the God of Israel had established a perpetual covenant with men and revealed to them his decrees, far outside the confines of Israel (Ecclesiasticus 17:12). Beautiful short novels told of devout Jews who lived peaceably with their neighbours – Ruth the Arab girl who found a new faith and a new home, becoming the ancestress of King David; Jonah the refugee who had a vision of the mercy of God in the Assyrian capital, Nineveh; and Tobit, a model of piety in his family circle and 'buyer of supplies' to the imperial court in Nineveh. The climax of this tradition comes when a book of 'wisdom' celebrates 'a spirit intelligent and holy, unique in its kind yet made up of many parts, subtle, free-moving, lucid, spotless, clear, invulnerable, loving what is good, eager, unhindered, beneficent, kindly towards men, steadfast, unerring, untouched by care, all-powerful, all-surveying, and permeating all intelligent, pure and delicate spirits . . . She spans the world in power from end to end, and orders all things benignly' (Wisdom 7:22–23; 8:1).

Jesus is not said to have had much contact with Gentiles during his short period of public teaching and healing, but there are passages in the gospels which hint at the appeal which the message about him was to make to the world after his death. He admired the attitudes of some foreigners (for example, an officer in the army or a woman with a sick child) – and was admired by them. He interpreted the law of Moses with a bold freedom, infuriating the Pharisees. He can be understood, at least in part, as a teacher of 'wisdom'. He was not inappropriate as the founder of a religion which was to spread with its schools and colleges into all the continents; which was to censor and persecute, but was also to inspire great artists, scientists, rational thinkers and tellers of the truth about the human condition. Certainly this Jew from Nazareth became the most universal of all men when crucified.

There were also Jews so proud of their heritage that for them the only wisdom was the waging of a holy war. Other novels included in the Hebrew scriptures told of nationalist heroines – of Judith, a merry young widow who cut off the head of a drunken Assyrian general, and of Esther, a Jewess who preserved her piety as well as her beauty while queen at the court of oriental luxury and ruthless intrigue. More seriously, many prophets and other teachers of the people predicted the coming of a Messiah – a general who would be a worthy Son of David, matching King David's military triumphs. Indeed, the history of the Jews in the two centuries before the birth of Jesus displays patriotic pride at a time when the Jewish culture was being battered by Greek sophistication and Roman power. When a small Jewish state could be constructed, it was on a very firmly exclusive basis. When it collapsed, many ardent Jews sought even more exclusiveness, with a pure Israel within Israel. Thus John the Baptist called for a spiritual elite – Jews who would accept for themselves the rite of purification which the 'proselytes' converted to Judaism had to undergo. In the desolate region of the Dead Sea, near the site of his preaching, are the ruins of the monastery at Qumran where Essene monks pondered the meaning of the scriptures as they expected the imminent war of the Sons of Light against the Sons of Darkness. Obedient to the teaching of an anonymous Teacher of Righteousness, they rejected Jerusalem, its temple, its comforts and all its compromises. And other Jews defended their purity with violence. A few miles away one can climb to the spectacular ruins of the mountain fort of Masada, where the last of the Jewish rebels against Rome preferred suicide to surrender in AD 74. These rebels feature in the Christian gospels as the Zealots. At least one of the twelve apostles was a Zealot and so (presumably) were Barabbas and two bandits crucified with Jesus, who allegedly had claimed to be king of the Jews. The violence of the Zealots was plainly condemned by Jesus, but it was to be copied on a tragically immense scale by men who have claimed to be his followers – including, by a specially horrifying twist in the tragedy, massive violence against Jews. Often Christianity was to baptise nationalism.

However, many Jews who longed for the overthrow of heathen oppressors put their trust – as John the Baptist and the Qumran community did – not in human violence but in the miraculous intervention of God, who surely must send legions of angels to fight on behalf of his oppressed people. The literature called 'apocalyptic' preserves something of the passion of this hope and has often been studied and imitated by Christians. Books circulated in a well-recognised code. The date of the story being told was inserted into history and most of the story consisted of visions of the future. But this strange literature was not really about the past or the future, for the explanation of this code was that the people were being exhorted to cling to their hope in the present. In the Hebrew scriptures the book of Daniel has this character most conspicuously. At the time of the revolt led by the Maccabees, about 165 BC, this book spread the message that deliverance was coming. After the trampling of beasts as they crushed helpless victims (this was the procession of the empires through history), a 'son of man' (NEB, 'one like a man') representing the 'saints of the Most High' (the faithful Jews) was to be given 'sovereignty and glory and kingly power'. Such promises of supernatural help kept alive popular enthusiasm behind the idea of the kingdom of God. And enthusiasm of the kind that burst out when Jesus of Nazareth rode into Jerusalem in his brief moment of political popularity. As palms were waved, he was hailed as the Son of David. The revolutionary cry went up in words such as: 'Blessings on him who comes as king in the name of the Lord!' (Luke 19:38). Actually, the victories of Jesus were to be in the spiritual realm and were to be won by suffering. But they were to inspire with a fresh passion many hopes that by the action of God the kingdom of God would come 'on earth as in heaven'. And in many generations the belief that the current crisis was *the* crisis – the faith that after the ending of so many worldly hopes the End must come soon – was to help to give the followers of Jesus the necessary strength to endure.[2]

Jesus and the gospels

It is possible to recover much of the historical truth about Jesus of Nazareth, using the methods which honest modern students would apply to the investigation of any other prominent character in ancient history. Few serious scholars would reject any of the following propositions about the Jesus of history. He was crucified as a suspected rebel under Pontius Pilate, who was governor of Judea from AD 26 to 36 – although he had made a special point of befriending tax collectors and had urged collaboration with the occupying army (for example, when conscripted to carry a soldier's pack). According to John's gospel the date of his death was 7 April AD 30. Although he had been baptised and had received his own call to public work and some of his first followers through the holiness movement around John the Baptist, he claimed that a greater and more joyful event was taking place around him. Although he had worked as a carpenter in the obscure village of Nazareth, he was widely welcomed as a teacher and prophet. He performed many healings regarded as miraculous. Although the medical details of these cures cannot now be recovered, many of them can be understood in the light of our knowledge of the interaction of mind and body. They demonstrate the power of religious faith over the physical symptoms of disease, particularly skin diseases then understood as 'leprosy' and other diseases then understood as demon-possession. Jesus broke some religious laws because of human needs and he severely criticised religious leaders, both Pharisees and Sadducees, because they made it harder for the people to worship in simple sincerity and childlike trust; he was himself thoroughly a layman. Some hostile Jewish responses to him survive outside the Bible and belong to the first century. They describe him as one who practised sorcery and mocked at the words of the wise. He became the friend of the disreputable, teaching the unconditional love of God and man. He rejoiced over their penitence more than over the smug respectability of the conventionally pious. He announced that the kingdom of God was near, even 'among you' (Luke 17:21), by telling parables – short stories about one crisis or another already within the people's experience. Exercising his personal authority, he summoned and sent out messengers to his fellow Jews in Galilee and Judea. He singled out twelve to represent the twelve tribes of Israel, but the message he gave them was potentially for all mankind, since the kingdom of God would not be restricted to Jews. While hoping and expecting that the full coming of the kingdom of God was imminent, he disclaimed knowledge of the exact date and foretold great suffering for himself, his fellows and his people. He believed – finally, although not easily – that his cruel death, identifying him with criminals, lay within the purpose of God. After it his followers became convinced that on this as on other matters he was right, for he was their living Lord, able to save and lead them – although the exact character of the experiences which resulted in this conviction cannot be known by the methods of historical science.

The personality at the centre of these propositions has already fascinated an innumerable company of people, including many saints and geniuses. They, too, would exclaim: 'Did we not feel our hearts on fire?' (Luke 24:32). But it has never proved possible to put Jesus securely into one category. He had something in common with each of the movements of active religion among his people – and he had everything in common with none of them. He was a devout and clean-living Jew, and received his only education in the school attached to the synagogue at Nazareth. There is no record that he visited the sophisticated Gentile cities of Sepphoris and Tiberias, although the former was only four miles from Nazareth. Yet he was not an exclusive Jew; in a passage whose theme can be matched in the other gospels, Luke (4:16–30) tells us that in his sermon in the Nazareth synagogue Jesus listed foreigners who had received healing from Yahweh according to the Hebrew scriptures. It was not popular. He is also reported to have paid the temple tax and to have gone on pilgrimage to the temple; yet it is not said that he offered any sacrifice. In words quoted or misquoted at his examination before the religious authorities, he caused great offence by claiming that the kingdom which he was inaugurating as God's agent would be greater and longer lasting than the temple. He broke some religious laws – and kept others. He worshipped on the Sabbath – and declared that it was 'made for man'. He called Pharisees 'hypocrites' – and accepted invitations to dine with them. He spoke and acted as a charismatic prophet – yet was very gentle with individuals. He urged his hearers to imitate the holiness of God – but frequently had meals with prostitutes and swindlers. He prayed to his Father in deep humility – but claimed the power to forgive sins. He enrolled in his innermost circle Simon who had been a Zealot and Matthew who had been a tax collector. The most dramatic part of his message was that he expected the imminent end of the world as he knew it – but everything did not depend on that. Although he seems to have accepted the title of Messiah on some occasions, all the gospels except the fourth make it clear that he avoided any public claim since it was bound to convey the misleading impression that he wished to lead a rebellion. These gospels say that he referred to himself as the 'son of man' but they do not explain what he meant. Did he claim to be the 'Son of Man' of the book of Daniel – a supernatural figure rising in triumph to the throne of God the judge? Or did he mean what is meant when a speaker refers to himself as 'one'? Or did the phrase have different meanings on different occasions?

Since Jesus never wrote a book or even a letter that has survived, questions about him have often been answered by reliance on the 'apostolic gospel'. And certainly there was good news of which the apostles were messengers – good news about God's action in Jesus. But although it has been claimed that the apostles, who had been eyewitnesses, preached or wrote down the facts about the life and teaching of their Lord, agreeing with each other, and thus defined the

Christian church's faith, the real situation seems to have been more complicated. Although the apostles clearly had a high authority, very little is known about most of 'the Twelve' who were specially close to Jesus. Because the lists are different, even their names are sometimes uncertain. Paul, we know, claimed to be their equal although he had held aloof from the Jesus movement until about two years after its founder's death. He named Andronicus and Junias (some manuscripts give Junia, a woman's name) as 'eminent among the apostles' (Romans 16:7). Most modern scholars agree that he was the only apostle who wrote any part of the New Testament. The gospels of Matthew and Luke depend on the gospel attributed to Mark, who was not an apostle although he was a personal assistant to Peter and Paul. Eyewitness evidence is embodied in the gospels, but it reaches us edited. And the apostles cannot truly be said to have bequeathed to the church a detailed statement of the faith to be derived from the facts they announced. In *The Apostolic Preaching and its Developments* (1936), C. H. Dodd extracted a seven-sentence creed from the Pauline letters and the Acts of the Apostles: 'The prophecies are fulfilled, and the new age is unaugurated by the coming of Christ. He was born of the seed of David. He died according to the scriptures, to deliver us out of the present evil age. He was buried. He rose on the third day according to the scriptures. He is exalted at the right hand of God, as Son of God and Lord of quick and dead. He will come again as judge and saviour of men.' But to read this creed is to see that it is a mere outline which different New Testament documents fill in differently.

Almost all the evidence which we have about Jesus of Nazareth is contained in four gospels. This was a new type of literature, because it combined a collection of sayings and a collection of miracles with a narrative of the passion and death of Jesus, to form an artistic whole. And with its artistry each gospel painted a different portrait – a foretaste of the variety which was to enrich the interpretation of Jesus in Christian history.

The earliest surviving gospel is Mark's, apparently written about thirty-five years after the crucifixion. Towards AD 130 Bishop Papias recalled 'the elder' as remembering that it was Mark's work, based on Peter's preaching. If it was compiled in Rome soon after the martyrdom of Peter and Paul there (about AD 64), that origin accounts for its atmosphere. If it appeared elsewhere (Syria has been suggested), its background must have been a community facing a sharp ordeal. It is a call to personal devotion, humility, purity, poverty, self-sacrifice and the steady endurance of unpopularity and suffering. According to this

gospel Jesus experienced the very human emotions of pity, impatience, anger, exhaustion, surprise, ignorance and the fear of death. To
a stranger who paid him a compliment, he protested: 'Why do you call
me good? No one is good except God alone' (Mark 10:18). His last
words were agonised and agonising, wrung from him on the cross:
'My God, my God, why have you forsaken me?' (Mark 15:34). Yet
Mark was, so far as we know, the first man to write any document
which could start: 'Here begins the Gospel of Jesus Christ the Son of
God'. Amazingly his story was 'gospel' (good news) because it
proclaimed, 'The time has come; the kingdom of God is upon you'
(Mark 1:15) – and because it showed that the kingdom soon to arrive
in its full power was already conquering evil (in the shape of the
demons who caused diseases), sin and death. No wonder that so many
of those who followed Jesus at a breathless pace, including the
women who visited his empty tomb, were 'afraid'! Yet the blood of
Jesus sealed God's new covenant with his people, and 'if a man will let
himself be lost for my sake and for the Gospel, that man is safe' (Mark
8:35).

   All but a tenth of Mark's gospel reappears with minor changes in
Matthew's and about half of what Matthew adds is also in Luke's
gospel. But enough is Matthew's own – about a quarter of the whole
gospel – to enable us to see a portrait of Jesus which has been painted
so as to help Christians in a situation different from the background to
Mark. The author is accurate about Jewish customs and does not
explain them. He does not translate words from Aramaic, the dialect
which Jesus spoke. But he always uses the Greek translation of the
Hebrew scriptures (the Septuagint) and he writes better Greek than
Mark's. He refers to a report spread about by 'the Jews' after the
resurrection of Jesus. The impression that he stands on the frontier
between the Jewish and Greek worlds – probably in Syria – is
confirmed by the content of his gospel. According to it, Jesus fulfilled
in detail many prophecies in the Septuagint and did not come to
abolish the written law of Moses. 'So long as heaven and earth
endure, not a letter, not a stroke, will disappear from the Law . . .
Anyone who keeps the Law, and teaches others so, will stand high in
the kingdom of Heaven' (Matthew 5:19). Yet Jesus has come to
'complete', even to correct, that law: although 'your forefathers were
told' the law, 'what I tell you is this' (Matthew 5:21,22, etc.) In this
gospel are collected terrible denunciations of Jewish teachers – and
moral teachings given by Jesus to show what is the behaviour
appropriate in the kingdom of Heaven. There are five collections of
the sayings of Jesus, and these may correspond with the first five

books of the Bible attributed to Moses in the Jewish tradition. Writing at a time when the Jewish community is being reorganised around the Mosaic law after the temple's destruction – and is excluding Christians as heretics – Matthew writes for the community of the disciples and uses the word which in Greek is *ekklesia*, 'church'. Simon Peter's leadership has been 'the Rock' but there is so much equality that no one is to be called 'teacher' or 'father'. Here is a community bearing a heavy load, but it is sustained by great miracles, it is inspired by the standards of moral perfection set out in the sermon on the mount, and as it goes into the world it is assured that its only teacher, Jesus, is with it 'always, to the end of time'. It believes that 'all things are entrusted' to this Jesus – and 'no one knows the Father but the Son and those to whom the Son may choose to reveal him'. From him, it accepts a new moral law.

In contrast, Luke addressed both his gospel and its sequel, the Acts of the Apostles, to a real or imaginary reader with a Greek name, 'Theophilus' or 'lover of God'; and the theme is a journey into the Gentile world. He is vague about the geography of Palestine and not interested in Jewish controversies. His Jesus is often called 'Lord', a title which may imply no more than 'sir' but which was used with a much more exalted significance by Gentile Christians. This Jesus dies with confident words: 'Father, into your hands I commit my spirit.' He rises to lead his followers out of Jerusalem in joy, wonder, enthusiasm and a peace which survives the fury of mobs or shipwreck at sea – until Paul takes courage at seeing the Christians who have come to meet him from Rome. Although Luke is described as Paul's friend and doctor (Colossians 4:14), and Acts includes a travel diary about the adventures of 'we', neither the gospel nor Acts suggests that Luke has been profoundly influenced by Paul's theology except on the simple, crucial points that God forgives sinners freely and that the church is freely open to the Gentiles. He minimises Paul's conflicts with his fellow apostles. Paul is far more outspoken in his surviving letters, but Luke likes to think that 'the whole body of believers was united in heart and soul' (Acts 4:32). The third of his gospel which has no parallel in Mark or Matthew gives little emphasis to suffering under persecution. Instead it pays special attention to good Samaritans, to women in distress, to those who are poor and humble before God. It is lit up by a great beauty of universal appeal, for it is to Luke that the church owes its most deeply loved pictures of Christmas and Easter and the parable of the prodigal son. And Acts is an almost equally attractive book. It tells of many incidents which have never been forgotten because the telling of the story is so dramatic; and together these stories convey a very strong impression of energetic courage and infectious love as the church advances in the power of the Holy Spirit, appealing as the Lord Jesus had always appealed to foreigners, women and the devout. The emphasis in all Luke's writing is not on the conflicts of the martyrs but on the progress of the gospel; not on a new moral law but on the poetry of God's grace; not on organisation but on charismatic enthusiasm. At the beginning of Acts those who receive the Holy Spirit proceed to speak in many languages, so that the gospel of the new joy can be understood by all. It is not long before Peter is having a dream while he dozes on the flat roof of a house overlooking the harbour at Joppa (Jaffa). He sees the ships' sails; he imagines their strange cargoes; he learns that the world is clean; and he baptises a Gentile soldier.

The fourth gospel is again different. Nothing in it proves that its author used the other three, although it is agreed that he wrote after them, perhaps about AD 90. (A fragment of a copy made in Egypt about AD 110 has been discovered.) The identity of the author is an enigma. The gospel declares that 'the disciple whom Jesus loved' was the man 'who wrote it, and we know that his testimony is true'. But who are the 'we' who know this, and how much have 'we' added? About AD 180 Bishop Irenaeus wrote that John the beloved disciple 'published his gospel while he was living in Ephesus in Asia' and at points the author gives historical or geographical facts which seem to be at least equal to the evidence supplied by the other gospels. He brings Palestinian earth with him. But he also refers repeatedly, and it seems with a remote hostility, to 'the Jews' – and he thinks it necessary to explain that Passover is a Jewish festival and that 'Rabbi' means 'Teacher'. The most likely answer to these riddles is that here some followers of John the beloved disciple have recorded some straightforward history but mainly have registered the results of years spent listening in deep devotion to a voice greater than any sound – the voice of the eternal Jesus. Theirs has been a journey into 'true' life, into abundant and eternal life. To John, this is infinitely more significant than the journey from Jerusalem to Rome.

There is much evidence that the first Christians believed that Jesus continued to communicate with them after his death. The Revelation of John opens with messages to the seven churches of Asia from one who 'was dead' and is now 'alive for evermore'. The gospels offer interpretations of the parables of Jesus which seem appropriate to the situation of the early church, not of the original hearers. Matthew's gospel shows that Jesus did not teach his disciples to fast and did teach them that all divorce was against God's will; yet the sermon on the mount includes instructions about fasting and the permission of divorce after adultery. Matthew's gospel repeats (with a small variation) the saying of Jesus given by Mark: 'There are some of those standing here who will not taste death before they have seen the kingdom of God come in power.' And it gives no evidence that Jesus baptised or wanted his followers to baptise. Yet it includes passages which indicate a long mission to the world, and which may have been spoken by Christian prophets claiming to teach in the name of Jesus: 'Where two or three have met together in my name, I am there among them'; 'Go forth and make all nations my disciples; baptise men everywhere in the name of the Father and the Son and the Holy Spirit.' Luke not only refers to teaching by Jesus after the resurrection (for example, the interpretation of the Hebrew scriptures during the walk to Emmaus). He also relates that in a vision in Jerusalem Jesus told Paul, 'I am sending you far away to the Gentiles' (Acts 22:21). In Corinth 'the Lord said to Paul, "Have no fear: go on with your preaching and do not be silenced, for I am with you and no one shall attempt to do you harm; and there are many in this city who are my people"' (Acts 18:9–10). One night in Jerusalem 'the Lord appeared to him and said, "Keep up your courage; you have affirmed the truth about me in Jerusalem, and you must do the same in Rome"' (Acts 23:11). Whatever we make of such reports by Luke, Paul's letters show that he based his whole life on the experiences of having 'seen' the Lord after his death and of having been commanded by him to be an apostle to the Gentiles. On one unforgettable occasion, he recalled, the Lord's answer was: 'My grace is all you need; power comes to its full strength in weakness' (2 Corinthians 12:9).

The gospels all show the firmness of the Christian belief that the Holy Spirit continues the teaching work of the historical Jesus, whether or not Jesus is represented as still speaking. Mark, Matthew and Luke record John the Baptist's promise that Jesus will baptise 'with the Holy Spirit' and the warning of Jesus about 'blasphemy against the Holy Spirit'. Here are reflections of the importance given to the Holy Spirit in the Acts of the Apostles when the appearances of the risen Lord have ceased and the Holy Spirit has been bestowed at Pentecost. John has only to press the point further. For him, the work of the Holy Spirit is to 'bear witness' to Jesus, to 'call to mind' what Jesus had told the disciples and to show 'where right and wrong and judgement lie' by telling the truth about Jesus. The Holy Spirit is given on the first day of the appearances of the risen Lord, who 'sends' them in 'peace'. Just as Peter is commanded to 'follow' Jesus to and through death, so because of the Holy Spirit the disciples can now receive and obey the words of Jesus in a relationship which never will end, a relationship which is eternal life. Although no clear distinction was made between the works of the Son and the Spirit, the words of a modern Protestant theologian, Emil Brunner, seem to be a fair (if somewhat cool) summary of the teaching of the New Testament as a whole: 'If the Name "Father" designates the origin and content of the revelation, the Name of the "Son" designates the historic Mediator, and the "Holy Spirit" the present reality of this revelation.'[3]

The language of John's gospel has parallels with some Jewish literature (for example, the scrolls found near the Qumran monastery) but it is also of a kind that Greek-speaking Gentiles would understand. Here is no talk about the kingdom of God – except in the conversation with Nicodemus, when the real subject is spiritual rebirth. Here is no Jesus who discourages speculation about who he is, preferring practical obedience. On the contrary, the Jesus of John demands a response to his own clear claims. He reveals his glory in seven signs culminating in the cross and resurrection which will 'draw all men'. In speeches entirely different in style from the other gospels, he declares that he is 'the Son of Man, who came down from heaven', the Messiah, the Son of God, the bread of life, the light of the world, the eternal 'I am', the good shepherd willing to lay down his life for the sheep, one with the Father whom he makes visible, the resurrection and the life of believers, the conqueror of the world. If he is to respond in faith, a man or a woman must be born again, must drink of living water, must eat the flesh of Jesus (although John sees no need to tell again the story of the beginning of the eucharist). Outside the circle of those so transformed, there is darkness. But as the last speech of Jesus to his disciples declares, he makes them clean, he sets them his example of humility and love, he prepares a place for them in heaven, he enables them to do greater works than his own on earth, he sends the Spirit to stay with them for ever and to teach them everything, he remains united with his chosen friends as a vine is united with its branches, he fills them with a gladness which no one can take away and with a unity as close as his own union with the Father, he protects them so that not one of them is lost, he shares his glory with them. Although mention is made of belief in a general resurrection on the last day, already 'this is eternal life: to know you who are truly God and Jesus Christ whom you have sent'.

That summary of the fourth gospel comes in the midst of the 'high priestly' prayer of Jesus during the night before his death. The prayer in John 17 shows why as this gospel ends (apart from the epilogue in the present last chapter) Thomas says to Jesus: 'My Lord and my God!' – the title which the Roman emperor Domitian claimed for himself and attempted to make compulsory during his reign (AD 81–96). For Jesus is exalted by his Father as sovereign over all mankind. Before the world began he received the love and shared the glory of the heavenly Father, with whom he has always remained 'one' although he has come into the world and has completed the work given to him there. The true climax of this work is the strange glory of the cross, for 'I shall draw all men to myself, when I am lifted up from the earth' (John 12:32). The nature of the glory of Jesus before he came into the world is not explained, except in the prologue to the gospel (which many scholars think originated independently, as a hymn). There Jesus is identified with 'the Word' (in Greek, *Logos*). This would be an explanation, however incomplete, both to scripture-studying Jews accustomed to the idea of the Word (or Wisdom) of God and to educated Gentiles familiar with the philosophical idea of the *Logos* (Spirit or Reason) unifying the world. For Jews and Gentiles alike, the basic idea was of the Word as God's self-expression, but it was almost inevitable that God's self-expression should be personified when thinking and writing, so that the Word (or Wisdom) of God could often be spoken of as a distinct heavenly person and thus more easily identified with a human being. As John's prologue puts it: 'When all things began, the Word already was . . . what God was, the Word was.' The world owed its very being to God's self-expression, yet did not recognise the real 'light which enlightens every man' when God expressed himself in a human life or 'the Word became flesh'. We have here the beginnings of the later theology about the holy trinity, although 'God' is still distinguished from 'Jesus Christ' and there is no interest in philosophical definitions of the love between the two. What matters for John is that God and Jesus are of one life and love.

So John draws the curtain a little to show Jesus' eternal background as he sees it, particularly at the beginning and end of this 'flesh'. His gospel may be contrasted with Mark's, which begins more austerely with John the Baptist in the wilderness 'dressed in a rough coat of camel's hair' and which ends (in the manuscripts nearest to the original) with the women after the resurrection who 'said nothing to anybody, for they were afraid'. John's approach is closer to Matthew's, who begins Jewishly with the descent of Jesus from Abraham through David to Joseph but then dramatises the newness and worldwide appeal of Jesus. He relates the conception 'by the Holy Spirit' and the humble pilgrimage to Bethlehem (David's own village) of astrologers from the East. Similarly, at the end of this gospel Jesus appears on a mountain in Galilee and tells 'the eleven disciples' that 'full authority in heaven and on earth has been committed to me.' The prologue to Luke's gospel again locates the birth of Jesus within the circle of Jewish piety, but when Mary is told that 'the Holy Spirit will come upon you, and the power of the Most High will overshadow you' we sense a new beginning – a beginning which will be 'a revelation to the heathen' (Luke 2:32), 'to be proclaimed to all nations' (Luke 24:47). A hint about the universal significance of Jesus is also given when Joseph's family tree is traced from 'Adam, son of God'.

These are therefore very different gospels. (Even the family trees are different and, since they celebrate Joseph rather than Mary, may be older than the stories of a virginal conception.) Problems are raised by that fact. To some extent they have been recognised ever since Tatian attempted to harmonise the gospels in parallel columns about AD 150. But if we really accept what it means to have *four* gospels – four masters' portraits rather than newspaper photographs, four essays rather than tape-recordings, four narratives where history is recounted but also edited in order to convey a spiritual message – we are the better prepared to acknowledge that other traditions about Jesus were passionately advocated by other groups among the first Christians.[4]

The first churches

The church in Jerusalem was deeply Jewish. Although brief references in Paul's letters and the Acts of the Apostles are the only evidence surviving about personalities and events, the letters of James and Jude preserved in the New Testament may well represent some of the teaching given in this circle. It is a teaching which insists on the highest moral standards of Judaism but which includes little or nothing which is specifically Christian apart from Jude's references to Jesus Christ. Jesus, says Jude, has the readers in 'safe keeping' for eternal life. Under the pressures of paganism and persecution such teaching could be developed into a fierce emotion which showed what had always been implied in loyalty to Jesus. In the New Testament, the Revelation of John the Divine shows this development taking place in the churches of Asia Minor. There a prophet who has been imprisoned as a Christian writes of visions of the risen Christ. In barbarous Greek, but using magnificent images drawn from the

Hebrew scriptures, he foretells Christ's victory over the Roman empire. So Jesus has become 'the Lamb' who stands, with 'the marks of slaughter still on him', on the throne of God. Similarly, the letter to Hebrews (perhaps to Jewish Christians in Rome) uplifts the heart to contemplate Jesus as the Son who is the radiance of God's splendour – and the heavenly high priest who has made the perfect sacrifice, of himself. The least that Christians can do is to sacrifice their own selves in the faith which sees the invisible. Such documents may well present a more developed doctrine about Jesus than could have been found in the Jerusalem community – but they help us to understand how tough and how stern was this early Jewish Christianity.

Luke's narrative in Acts seems to incorporate some reliable evidence about a community which looked like a Jewish sect. In Jerusalem most of these followers of Jesus seem to have been regular and devout in their attendance at the temple. Their ranks included priests and Pharisees. They pooled their resources and thus were able for a time to live off the capital since they believed that 'the end of the age' was very near. Jesus they regarded as a 'man singled out by God' (Acts 2:22) – the servant of God, made Lord and Messiah. He was now in heaven but would soon return to Jerusalem to inaugurate a new world, of which the charismatic experience of the Holy Spirit was a foretaste. The coming miraculous salvation of Israel's twelve tribes was represented by the twelve apostles. Jesus would be given 'the throne of his ancestor David, and he will be king over Israel for ever' (Luke 1:32). There is no record of any missionary work done by any of the Twelve apart from Peter, whose absence from Jerusalem after AD 44 made it possible for the leadership of the Christian community in the city to rest in the firm hands of James, a brother of Jesus converted to his cause after his death. He was succeeded by a cousin of Jesus. The arrangement recalls the Caliphate or leadership exercised by the Prophet's descendants in Islam. The Gospel of Thomas, compiled after AD 100, still represents Jesus as saying that 'heaven and earth came into existence' for the sake of his brother.

There were, however, great tensions. An early protest against this community's exclusiveness came when a group of Greek-speaking Jews who had been converted complained that their widows were being neglected in the distribution of the common income. Seven additional leaders with Greek names were then appointed and one of them, Stephen, publicly attacked the temple and its officials, bringing about his own death by stoning. Beneath the narratives in Acts we can discern a growing revolt against the Jewish conservatism of the leadership, and the pluralism grew when the trouble which Stephen had caused brought persecution and 'all except the apostles were scattered over the country districts of Judaea and Samaria' – for the scattering of the Christians led to the conversion of rural Jews (many of whom would have had their own memories of Jesus), of Samaritans and even of a Jewish proselyte who had been on pilgrimage from Ethiopia. But the biggest challenge came after the conversion of Saul of Tarsus, who had watched Stephen's death. Claiming to be the equal of the Twelve in Jerusalem, giving the term 'apostle' the missionary meaning which it does not seem to have possessed before (for the Twelve had not led any mission to the countryside or Samaria), and even changing his name to 'Paul' to show that he now belonged to the Greek-speaking world, Paul insisted on the admission of Gentiles without circumcision or insistence on strict keeping of the Jewish religious law. Although Luke's eirenic narrative in Acts claims that an agreement was reached at a council in Jerusalem (about AD 48), Paul's agitated letter to the Christians in Galatia shows that he was far from certain that his convictions would prevail over the authority of 'the men of high reputation (not that their importance matters to me)' and the 'reputed pillars of our society' who adhered to the Jewish religious laws and demanded that all other Christians should do the same. Paul claimed that in the end James, Peter and John, then the joint leaders of the Jerusalem community, had agreed that his version of the gospel was permissible among the Gentiles. Even so, Peter went back to his old habits during a visit to Antioch. He refused to eat with Gentile Christians. Paul had to oppose him to his face. Now these Galatians were themselves being 'stupid' enough to allow interference from Jerusalem and the preaching of 'a different gospel'. And Paul is later found attacking 'sham-apostles, crooked in all their practices, masquerading as apostles of Christ' (2 Corinthians 11:13).

The gospel according to Paul resulted from the impact of the personality of Jesus on a man fantastically energetic, easily able to evoke both love and hatred, divided and restless in himself, both self-justifying and self-accusing, proud of the Jewish heritage into which he had thrown himself passionately while a young Pharisee, but possessed also by an imperious will with the ability to organise and by a world-vision – both of which qualities made him fully worthy to be a Roman citizen. He found in his devotion to Jesus as much inner unity and peace as he was ever to know before the death for which he longed. He was not particularly interested in details about the history of Jesus of Nazareth. He had been, as he put it, 'arrested' by the Jesus of Easter, the Christ of all the world. He was converted when he

suddenly realised, on the road to Damascus, that the Jesus who had
already fascinated him was to be met in the persons of his followers –
whom he was then persecuting. Although this appearance of Jesus
was in no way physical, Paul insisted that it belonged with the
resurrection appearances, making him an apostle. Blind for a time,
isolated for much longer, never claiming that his vision was complete
or his message non-controversial, he worked out for himself the
implications of this spiritual crisis.

Christ's coming meant a 'new creation' as the Christian became so
identified with the heavenly Lord that the union was – in a way both
mystical and moral – a sharing in the crucifixion and resurrection. The
church was now the 'body' of Christ. The Christian was chosen by
God for membership of that body; all that was essential was a faith
which meant a personal trust in God through Christ. It was like
acquittal in a court of law ('justification') or like liberation from
slavery by a ransom ('redemption'). In his early teaching – for
example, in his letters to the Thessalonians, probably written in AD 49
and AD 50 – Paul expected Jesus to return as judge within a few years.
Later he taught, as in his letter to the Christians in Rome, that this
judgement was being delayed in order that the conversion of some of
the Gentiles should persuade more of the Jews to accept Jesus as the
Messiah. He came to accept that he would die before the fulfilment of
God's purposes; and thus he wrote from prison to the Christians in
Philippi while still surrounded by controversy. He was very conscious
that before death man's knowledge of God could be only 'puzzling
reflections in a mirror'. But about one thing he was always sure after
his conversion. He had been captured by Jesus, made his willing
slave, and entrusted with a mission to make him known. His message
was that anyone – Jew or Greek or barbarian, free or enslaved, man
or woman – could be given the same experience by the spiritual power
of God. Anyone could enter the new life 'in Christ' if called and
willing. Anyone could discover a power which was greater than the
strength of any evil or the merits of any human righteousness or
success. 'To me,' he wrote, 'life is Christ.' He counted everything else
in his past 'so much garbage'. For 'what can separate us from the love
of Christ?'

We should not gain the impression that he felt free to invent
Christianity. We are told that the followers of Jesus were first called
'Christians' in Antioch and that Paul was originally a missionary sent
by the church in Antioch – an ethnically mixed congregation which is
said to have included in its leadership Simeon the Black, Lucius the
Libyan and Manaean 'who had been at the court of Prince Herod'

(Acts 13:1–3). To the Thessalonians Paul wrote about a tradition which he had 'passed on'. His first letter to Corinth shows that he did not attempt to invoke the authority of 'the Lord' for anything he wished to teach. Whether 'the Lord' taught him through traditions about the teaching given before the crucifixion or through later visions, what 'the Lord' said possessed for him a unique authority. When some of the Corinthians announced that they belonged to a Pauline party, he was horrified; and his feeling for the unity of all who were 'in Christ' was such that he took great trouble to organise financial aid for the church in Jerusalem, much of whose theology he detested. All were the Lord's. But everything in the gospel according to Paul has been made personal. He is sometimes profoundly interested in his reader; he is always intensely interested in himself; and above all he is interested in the Lord who has given all its meaning to the life of one who is 'in Christ'. Like John – that other mastermind of the early church – he has been driven by his experience to say that Jesus, while genuinely a man, is much more than other men.

All the evidence which we have suggests that for many years – indeed, for about fourteen centuries – after Paul's death few Christians shared at the same depth his experience of a totally transforming identification with the crucified and crowned Lord. Always he was respected; seldom was he fully understood. The note of puzzled respect is caught in a late document within the New Testament (2 Peter 3:16). But Paul did for Christianity something momentous. He made sure that its message would be available for reception and interpretation by people far distant from Galilee and Jerusalem. He was thoroughly a Jew; he never argued in non-Jewish terms; he told the Christians in Rome that his great hope was that the Jews would be led into Christianity by the example set by the Gentiles; and when he attacked the religion of fellow Jews, it was because it had failed to satisfy his own ardent, Jewish spirit. But the religion he preached could no longer be seen as a Jewish sect. Now interpreted in terms familiar to the Greek-speaking Mediterranean cities, it was potentially a religion capable of being expressed within all human societies.

This combination of an initial dependence on Judaism without a permanent restriction by it was of crucial significance. Bishop Stephen Neill, in his *History of Christian Missions*, pointed out that by the first century AD the Jews who were widely dispersed in the Roman empire had attracted many to their religion. Yet most of the Gentile 'God-fearers' held back from becoming Jews. They were dismayed by the insistence on circumcision and on many food regulations – and by the rebellious nationalism of Palestinian Judaism. It was this opportunity that Christianity seized. 'It was the presence of this prepared elite that differentiated the missions of the apostolic age from those of every subsequent time, and makes comparison almost impossible.' But the Christianity of the Jerusalem community, although it faithfully reflected many aspects of the teaching of Jesus of Nazareth himself, was too Jewish to fill the gap. Indeed, as Neill observed, 'it is hardly possible to imagine a setting or a doctrine less likely to serve as the starting-point for a religion that was to become the faith of all mankind'. Paul, the Jew who was also the universal missionary, was needed.[5]

Less exciting than Paul's spirituality, but more influential in the actual life of the church, was the development known as 'early Catholicism'. It is represented in the New Testament in letters which were attributed to Paul, and which almost certainly embody genuinely Pauline passages, but which are regarded by most modern scholars as being, in the form in which we possess them, reflections of a later situation. In those days it was not thought dishonest to put an honoured but dead teacher's name to a letter which was believed to say what he would have said had he been around to say it – any more than it was thought dishonest for Christian prophets to speak in the name of Jesus. These letters composed by Paul or Paul's followers include the high doctrine about Christ and the church addressed to the Ephesians and Colossians. Poetry about Christ pours out. 'He is the image of the invisible God . . . the whole universe has been created through him and for him. And he exists before everything, and all things are held together in him . . . Through him God chose to reconcile the whole universe to himself . . .' In Christ 'the complete being of the Godhead dwells embodied'. The secret of the church 'is this: Christ in you, the hope of a glory to come' – and so the church, Christ's body, 'holds within it the fullness of him who himself receives the entire fullness of God'. 'Pastoral epistles' or instructions about good order in the church are sent to Timothy and Titus. These letters (somewhat like the letters attributed to Peter) convey an atmosphere of steady loyalty to the church, its scriptures and its appointed leaders, in a tradition which can be inherited from grandparents. The morality of Christians must be such that even pagans admire it because it produces decent citizens, honest workers, good family life. 'We all know,' Timothy is reminded, 'that the law is an excellent thing.' The splendour of the vision of the kingdom of God, coming quickly in power and glory, has dimmed; but the proclaimer of that kingdom has become the proclaimed – and the church is part of his endless life. Here is the gospel according to the church.

The New Testament shows why Christianity was institutionalised in this manner, for it often refers to 'enemies of the gospel' who claimed the Christian name. Exactly what these enemies taught is usually not clear. Some, it seems, simply echoed the hardliners of Jerusalem who insisted on Gentiles becoming Jews if they were to become Christians. Some were enthusiastic revivalists, sure that the world was about to end. Others preached a more esoteric kind of 'knowledge' (in Greek, *gnosis*) and were the forerunners of the Gnostics whom we see rather more clearly in the second century. It is, however, impossible to reconstruct 'Gnosticism' as a system, partly because it was never systematic. Various teachers taught various kinds of spiritualism, some influenced by Judaism and some by Christianity. In the New Testament such 'knowledge' is attacked on several grounds. Claiming to be spiritual because the flesh must be evil, it denies that Jesus Christ is more than angel – that he 'came in the flesh'. Claiming to describe the supernatural world, it really consists of 'interminable myths and genealogies, which issue in mere speculation' (1 Timothy 1:4). Claiming to be a secret known by the elite, it encourages an arrogance which results either in unhealthy asceticism (looking down on the common man's physical needs) or in sheer licence (being superior to the common man's sober morality). 'These men draw a line between spiritual and unspiritual persons,' says Jude, 'although they are themselves wholly unspiritual.'[6]

It was, it seems, chiefly in conflict with Gnostic claims to possess true but 'secret' sayings of Jesus that the 'canon' (or agreement about the contents) of the New Testament was settled. For example, the second-century gospel of Thomas was excluded, apparently as being essentially Gnostic and unreliable. The need to fix the canon was demonstrated when in about AD 140 a leading teacher then in Rome, Marcion, issued a list accepting only an expurgated version of Luke's gospel and ten of Paul's letters (and excluding the entire Old Testament). The Muratorian Canon, probably drawn up in Rome some sixty years later, included the Wisdom of Solomon and the Revelation of Peter and excluded four of the books later canonised (among them the letters of Peter). But the Christians already possessed 'scriptures' in the shape of the Old Testament and, in the second letter attributed to Peter, Paul's letters are already treated as belonging to 'the scriptures' although it is admitted that they contain difficult passages causing controversies. The general acceptance of ten of Paul's letters, and of the whole gospels of Mark, Matthew, Luke and John took place in the second Christian century. Slowly and informally – for there was no council which decided the matter – agreement was reached between congregations which regarded themselves as orthodox to acknowledge twenty-seven books as having authority over the church because they were in one sense or another 'apostolic'. (The epistle to the Hebrews was held to be by Paul, Revelation by the apostle John and 2 Peter by Peter; these were the most disputed books.) The agreement was not finalised until the middle of the fourth century.

The church's attitude to the canon of 'the Old Testament' makes a roughly similar story. After the initial period almost all Christians relied on the Greek translation, the Septuagint, which finally included books which were not read in the synagogues (the 'Apocrypha' or 'Deuterocanonical' books). When during the reconstruction of Judaism after the fall of Jerusalem the orthodox rabbis agreed on their own canon of thirty-nine books (also without a formal council), these books were excluded. In the fourth century Jerome, who learnt Hebrew and translated the whole Bible into Latin, urged that the church should accept this Hebrew canon but the other books remained in Christian use. In the sixteenth century they were gradually but definitely excluded by Protestants. Four hundred years later the irritating problem of these books still hinders cooperation between Catholics and Protestants in the production of Bibles, although some 'common Bibles' have appeared.

Such, it seems, are the origins of the Christian Bible. The story which I have retold so briefly at least makes clear the great diversity in the origins. And now I concisely attempt to say what the significance of these scriptures appears to be.

The Bible is not infallibly true, containing no historical or moral mistake: that can be demonstrated repeatedly. If the men who wrote the Bible had intended to provide scriptures of that perfect character, presumably they would have produced a book looking much more like the all-holy Quran of the Muslims. Instead they provided laws, histories, poems, proverbs, novels, visions of the future, controversial letters and four gospels. Even the ten commandments and the Lord's Prayer are given to us in slightly different versions. Even the exodus from Egypt and the resurrection of Jesus are recounted to us in different stories. These many documents, written at different dates in different styles treating different materials for different purposes, can be studied as other books are studied, examining authorship, intention, style, use of older materials, connections with other literature, and so forth. But when so examined, the books of the Bible can be seen to possess an authority which does not depend on any unsustainable theory that they are 'without error'. In the words of

Bishop Lesslie Newbigin, for long a Christian missionary among Hindus and more recently a missionary among the secular English: 'I would want to speak of the Bible as that body of literature which – primarily but not only in narrative form – renders accessible to us the character and actions and purposes of God.'[7] For these books are almost everywhere the reflections of people's experience of the real God. Being human they are imperfect, but they provide glimpses of an incomparable value into the divine perfection. Nothing else which we can know is more important than these glimpses; and nothing else that life can bring is more significant than the offer to draw near to the joy glowing on these pages. These books belong to the real world and they show it by their variety and their flaws. But these books are also unlike other literature. They witness to the God who searches and demands – as in the story that, walking in the garden one cool evening, he confronted Adam. They witness to the Jesus who, walking, dying and resurrected on earth, is 'the Word behind the words'; for the many gospels are ultimately about that One. They witness to the power of God the Spirit by the uniqueness of their unfailing power to convey, in a great variety of epochs and cultures, the truths which they were inspired to convey. These books read us. In particular, they judge Christianity.

Developing churches

When Paul was executed, he cannot have thought it likely that some of the letters which he had dictated would become the sacred literature of Christian orthodoxy although their central theme – faith in God's grace freely given to the sinner who trusts in it – was to be blunted. This development could occur only because the prestigious Christian community in Jerusalem, which had never fully accepted Paul, lost its standing. It fled from the city as the Roman army began its seige of the rebel Jews' capital, probably in AD 68. As refugees its surviving members lived to lament the destruction first of the temple and then of the whole city. In the second century their faith's distinctiveness was preserved only in a small group of Christians who called themselves the Ebionites (or 'poor'), clinging obstinately to the observance of the Jewish law and the use of the Hebrew language and having their own heavily edited version of the gospels. Meanwhile in every Jewish synagogue a new 'benediction' was recited every Sabbath, cursing and excluding the Christian or 'Nazarene' heretics. The centre of the development of Christianity shifted decisively into the

Gentile world. None of the major teachers known as the fathers of the church was a Jew. Christianity's attitude to Judaism was to be marked by blind incomprehension, stupid arrogance and tormenting, murderous cruelty.

It was to be even more significant that the traditional Jewish practice of acknowledging many movements as all equally within the family of faith was rejected by the most influential Christians during this period of the church's formation. In the church a powerful new legalism emerged, confining the right to be called 'Christian' to believers judged orthodox by councils of bishops. Not only was Jewish Christianity now marginalised. Other 'heresies' were also to be eclipsed. This development stressed and expanded elements to be found within the New Testament, chiefly the high doctrine about Christ taught by Paul and John and the call for obedience to scriptures and leaders taught by the letters to Timothy and Titus. The oldest of all Christianity's documents includes a reference to those who 'in the Lord's fellowship are your leaders and counsellors' (1 Thessalonians 5:12). But the new emphasis on the authority of the official leadership marked a great change because other elements in the New Testament were either subordinated or ignored. The expectation of the imminent end of 'the world' (or of 'this age') was no longer central once it was realised that the apostles had died and Jerusalem had vanished yet history was continuing. Indeed, the empire was prosperous and peaceful. In the slower pace of mission, the disregard of intellectual questions to be found in, for example, Mark's gospel for martyrs was changed into the policy of encouraging the 'apologists' to outargue Jews, Gnostics and Christian heretics. This movement began within the second century with Justin the martyr in Rome and Irenaeus in Lyons, but its centre became Alexandria, already a place of learned dialogue between Jewish and Greek scholars. The high drama of miracle, riot and storm which had pervaded the Acts of the Apostles was changed into a policy of reliance on face-to-face conversations in the cities of the Roman empire and their satellite villages. The profound emotionalism of Paul's religious psychology was transformed into a demand for the acceptance of a 'rule of faith'. Christianity was becoming a matter of doctrines and beliefs. Simple creeds emerged in the main centres from questions and answers used in instruction before baptism. Probably many Christians refused to accept the new uniformity, but if so very little is known about them. When orthodoxy prevailed, steps were taken to destroy even the memory of scriptures and leaders judged heretical.

For practical purposes, the decisive move was the emergence of the bishop as the living authority in the city's Christian congregation and any suburban or rural offshoots. He it was who, as teacher or disciplinarian, brought constant pressure against opinions regarded as religious or moral errors – for example, against the adoption of one of the 'gospels' available which in fact taught Gnosticism under the guise of secret sayings of Jesus. On his way to martyrdom in Rome in AD 107 Ignatius, bishop of Antioch, wrote letters urging other congregations to obey the bishop as the representative of Christ, the heavenly high priest. He even told the Magnesians: 'Let the bishop preside in God's place.' Such teaching would have seemed strange in some churches. The *Didache*, a document probably coming from Syria about AD 100, shows an area where charismatic and travelling prophets and teachers still have most influence although it is added that the honour given to them is to be shared by 'bishops and deacons' who are to be elected locally. When about the same time Clement, who was responsible for the Roman congregation's correspondence, wrote a letter to Corinth pleading for an end to the innovations and disorders there, he did not mention any bishop either in Corinth or in Rome. Presumably he was the presiding presbyter in Rome. The first more exalted bishop of Rome known to history was Anicetus in the AD 150s.

Certainly the Ignatian style of control by a bishop has not clearly appeared within the New Testament. In the third letter of John we meet 'Diotrephes, their would-be leader' (another translation being 'who enjoys being their leader') – and we find that he is condemned as the man who has tried to expel from the congregation those who support John 'the elder'. The congregation in Philippi to whom Paul writes has 'bishops and deacons' but the Greek words probably mean no more than 'overseers and servants'. Neither bishops nor deacons are mentioned among the gifts of the ascended Christ listed by Paul (1 Corinthians 12:28). In Ephesians 4:11 the leadership still seems to be charismatic ('some prophets, some evangelists, some pastors and teachers') under the general direction of 'some apostles'. These functions – or some of them – have become definite offices in the congregations glimpsed in the (later) letters to Timothy and Titus. But since no 'elders' are mentioned along with the bishops and deacons, it can be assumed that the 'bishops' in these letters are virtually the same as the 'elders' called 'shepherds' in the Acts of the Apostles (Acts 20:28).

The main hint of things to come is given by the instruction that 'elders who do well as leaders should be reckoned worthy of a double stipend, in particular those who labour at preaching and teaching' (1

Timothy 5:17). And when the Revelation of John the Divine addresses messages to the 'angels' of the churches in the Roman province of Asia, the reference seems to be to human leaders. Eventually the need for leadership was supplied by the spread of the practice of appointing only one bishop in each local church. The practice seems to have become general during the second century – although, as with the 'canon' of the New Testament, no council decreed it. The whole emphasis was now on the preservation of the early Catholicism which was identified with the apostles' gospel against innovators such as the Montanists, a charismatic sect which repeated the prediction in the Revelation of John that the end of the world was imminent, that the Lord Jesus would come quickly. In North Africa the Montanists recruited Tertullian, then the church's leading theologian. Their spiritual strength was such that they were still a heresy to be reckoned with in the fifth century. But their enthusiasm now seemed a 'new prophecy' and the bishops resisted it successfully. In the main the church survived the departure from its ranks both of Marcion and of Tertullian, perhaps its two most brilliant sons in the second century. It preferred a secure network of steady leaders to the charismatic genius. It chose the bishops. At the end of the second century Irenaeus, Bishop of Lyons, put the main reason on record in his book *Against Heresies*. The bishops, he held, taught what the apostles had taught. The heretics taught what was new.

The emergence of the threefold ministry of bishop, presbyter (or elder) and deacon was further strengthened by being associated with an increasing emphasis on the sacredness of the sacraments over which the bishop presided. These sacraments were open to serious misunderstanding; thus baptism could appear to resemble admission to a secret revolutionary society and the charge that the Christians were cannibals arose from rumours about their treatment of bread and wine as the body and blood of Christ. But such rituals were not strange to the religious world in which the church now had its mission. Jews baptised converts; Gentiles were accustomed to initiation ceremonies and were specially impressed by the 'mysteries' of the fringe religions; many clubs held meals to deepen their fellowship. It cannot have seemed utterly odd that Paul taught that 'when we were baptized into union with Christ Jesus we were baptized into his death' in order that all might be 'one with him in a resurrection like his' (Romans 6:3–5). The dramatic repetition of the Last Supper of the Lord was already a matter of tradition when he wrote to the Corinthians, and was found to be a harmless gathering before daylight every Sunday when a Roman governor, Pliny, tortured some women deacons and reported their evidence to the emperor Trajan in AD 112. The sharing of the bread and wine was followed by a simple meal or love-feast. It had been an occasion of some disorder in Corinth and Pliny, while not finding it actually scandalous, included it in his general ban on private clubs where plots might be hatched against the state. The decline of this love-feast made the eucharist as the weekly act of worship by the baptised all the more solemn, although less communal.

In about AD 180 a pagan critic, Celsus, wrote a book (now only known through the Christian answer to it) in which he paid a reluctant tribute to the spread of Christianity. Essentially this strange new sect was, he was sure, contemptible; Jesus had been a bogus magician and the Christians' additions to Judaism simply made the Jews' nonsense more nonsensical. But this sect seemed to have achieved stability – and it preached dangerous nonsense, for it threatened the social order. It was being spread by evangelism among women, children, slaves and gullible people generally. Before the end of the second century Tertullian boasted that Christians were spread all over the empire: 'we are but of yesterday and we have filled all you have.' They were being martyred, but the blood of the martyrs was the church's seed. Before Bishop Polycarp was martyred in about AD 165, he told the proconsul that he would not revile the Christ he had served for eighty-six years. Nor would he join the mob's cry, 'Away with the atheists!' Christians, although they denied the divinity of the emperor and the reality of the pagan gods, showed by their disciplined worship and conduct that they had knowledge of God to offer to people not satisfied by the empire's combination of prosperity with fatalism. And they secured publicity by their courage as martyrs when emperors of Rome, alarmed by the growth of this empire of Christ, launched systematic persecutions.

What explains the establishment of Christianity as the official religion of the Roman empire some 250 years after the worried contempt of Celsus?

The correct answer to this question is surely that this faith, as it had developed since New Testament times, proved able to supply to the empire a spiritual foundation which no other religion could offer. It seemed obvious to most people that an empire needed a religion to secure the favour of God or the gods, to sanctify the social order from the emperor downwards, to teach morality and to console the despairing. It also became obvious to enough people that the religion needed could not be provided by the official mixture of the Roman and Greek mythologies about amorous and capricious gods and goddesses. In temples animal sacrifices were offered by priests often said to be corrupt, lazy or stupid; and there was ridiculous fortune-telling. Nor could the soul be satisfied by the official emperor-worship which merely worshipped the state – a state which quite often changed its rulers after civil wars. The fringe cults made a deeper spiritual appeal, but again relied on mythologies. Many were in practice for men only or for women only, and they failed to develop either a theology or an ethical code. They had various scriptures, but nothing to compare with the New Testament and no agreement about which books possessed authority. Philosophy did teach religion and ethics, but in too intellectual a style to inspire the average person; the Roman empire very seldom troubled to discipline even the most radically minded philosophers. Judaism had been discredited (except in the eyes of orthodox Jews) by the total failure of the Jewish revolts. Christianity, which had entered the Roman empire on the back of Judaism but had jumped off, remained available.

In contrast with its rivals, it developed a rational theology without ceasing to be popular. The pioneer in this process was Justin the martyr, the first 'apologist' to relate Christianity systematically with Jewish and Greek thought. He became a Christian in AD 130 but never ceased to believe that anything that had been 'said well' belonged to the Christian's heritage. The theology was expressed in terms of the Neoplatonic philosophy which was then the leading intellectual movement. This was a major adventure of mind and spirit, since the whole emphasis in Platonism was not on the active, angry, compassionate, saving God of the Bible but on the ascent – or, rather, the return – of man to the unchangeable God through various levels of eternity. Plato taught that eternity was more real than time, which was merely 'the moving image of eternity', and Platonism was a philosophy of the spirit – temporarily imprisoned in the body but in reality a spark of the divine fire. It was an estimate of humanity and divinity that appealed profoundly to a society full of change, confusion, coarse materialism and incredible religion.

The most distinguished teacher of Christian Platonism was Origen in the first half of the third century. (He it was who replied to Celsus.) He boldly declared that passages in the scriptures not easily reconciled with Platonism were meant 'morally' or 'spiritually', not literally – for example, the Old Testament stories of the creation and fall of man or the New Testament pictures of the devils and of hell. We cannot wonder that he was exiled from Alexandria to Caesarea and that the second council of Constantinople found it necessary to condemn his heresies some three hundred years after his death. Yet

Origen died because his health had been destroyed by prolonged torture. He was in a sense a Christian martyr, like Justin. This whole philosophical translation of Christianity, spectacular in its daring, still depended on the teaching and other work of Jesus of Nazareth, a saviour who was historical – as the redeemers in the Gnostic myths (or Mithras or Heracles) were not. Origen laboured as a biblical scholar and taught that in addition to the literal, moral and spiritual senses of the scriptures there was also an 'anagogical' sense, meaning that the scriptures could correspond with the eternal reality of God as Father, Son and Spirit. And this loyalty to the Bible meant that in the last analysis the church stood on the earth of Nazareth and Calvary.

The church thus grounded in the real world had much to offer to those without Origen's intellectual and contemplative tastes; to those who with Tertullian asked what Athens had to do with Jerusalem. The unchallengeable leadership of the bishops made for unity both within the congregations and between them, if necessary by formal councils – a unity which could not be matched by any rival religious body. Its superior organisation also gave the church financial strength: about AD 250 the Christians in Rome supported not only a staff of over 170 but also more than 1,500 widows and other needy persons. But it is not sentimental to say that the church's moral strength was its outstanding feature. Its teaching about the father-hood of the one God and about salvation in Christ followed by the gift of the Spirit implied a new dignity for women, children, slaves and the socially underprivileged in general – as Celsus had complained. In its own understanding of itself the church was a society basically equal although many social distinctions remained and may have grown with the years. (For example, women seem to have been allowed less prominence and powers of initiative than they had had in the con-gregations glimpsed in the Acts of the Apostles and in the last chapter of Paul's letter to Rome. But in the 380s a famous preacher, John Chrysostom, still found it necessary to complain that in the church women made too many of the decisions.) And the message of its scriptures, taught by the bishops and their assistants, dramatised by the sacraments, was backed up by a stern disciplinary system. It produced a moral standard which surprised. It preached not only the usual virtues but also self-control in sex for men and joy for the dying and the bereaved; so that a religion which could stretch the mind of Origen could also lift a young gentleman above vices and an old slave woman above despair. Christians fasted every Wednesday and Fri-day. And Tertullian quoted the pagan compliment about a more important custom: 'See how these Christians love one another!' 'The godless Galileans,' a pagan emperor complained, 'care not only for their own poor but for ours as well.' That moral standard and active love spoke louder than any words.

Then came the great triumph, followed by great tragedies.

The triumph was that the emperor Constantine became a Christian, pulling his empire after him. He was no saint and no theologian, but before a decisive battle in a civil war he saw a cross in the sky (possibly caused by the fall of ice crystals across the rays of the sun). The vision reinforced the thought which may well have been growing in his mind that the Christian minority – probably between a fifth and a tenth of the empire's population – preached the religion most likely to bring prosperity to him and to the empire. In AD 313 came the legislation known as the edict of Milan, granting freedom of worship to Christianity and all other cults (in that order). This was followed by fifty years during which the position of the church was transformed. It was a change as large as the earlier separation from Judaism.

Christians were now favoured by the imperial authorities. Fine churches were built at the state's expense (usually modelled on the *basilica* or hall of justice) and handsome gifts to them were encouraged. Multitudes – including many in areas where previously the church had made little impact – hastened to become Christians at least in name. Despite the equality implied in the gospel, it seems probable that in most places where it had flourished the church had been predominantly middle class, although this category then included the more educated and privileged slaves and ex-slaves. The art that has survived suggests a way of life that conformed, where conscience allowed, to the standards and tastes of middle class pagans. And while theoretically open to all, this had not been a society easy to join. The course of instruction given to recruits or 'catechumens' had, it seems, often lasted for three years; at least it had done in Rome. The 'conversion' of Constantine therefore made possible not only the widespread patronage of a distinctively Christian architecture and art but also the opening of the doors of the churches to the ordinary man, woman or child who possessed no extraordinary courage, self-confidence, patience or capacity to understand religious doctrine. The half-century after the edict of Milan witnessed the emergence for the first time of a Christian society which was wider than a network of congregations of saints or near-saints.

When Constantine founded Constantinople, also called Byzantium, as 'the new Rome', it was an effort on a sumptuous scale to create in the east an imperial capital, and an empire and a culture around it, which would be free of the decadence now associated with Roman paganism. The effort was not in vain: the Byzantine empire lasted until 1453 and the Eastern Orthodox churches which it established have kept their faith into our own time, often with great heroism under Muslim or Communist pressure or persecution. They have offered the faithful *Theosis*, Godlikeness. They have venerated icons on which the faces of the saints are Godlike; and many living faces have also mirrored a glory. In the west also, the collapse of the Roman empire was not a total disaster – thanks largely to the role of the Catholic church as the mother of a new Europe, transmitting and refining much of the old civilisation amid the barbarism. Constantine's conversion made all this possible. No doubt he was flattered extravagantly by Bishop Eusebius of Caesarea, his theological adviser who was the first man to write a serious history of the church and the first exponent of the ideals of Christian monarchy and statesmanship. But the anti-Christian renaissance which the last of the pagan emperors, Julian, sponsored in the 360s was brief despite an ingenious adaptation of many of the features of Christianity. After more than a thousand years of expansion and dominance, the religion of Rome was fragile. Constantine's decision was not inevitable – but once taken, it showed that the church was able to develop as paganism no longer could. Only one of these rivals had a future in her womb.

Many Christians have regretted this development. They would have preferred the church to remain free of the state's patronage, sheltered from worldliness by its unfashionable or criminal reputation and loved to the point of martyrdom by its comparatively few but deeply committed members. Such protests were made soon after the church's acquisition of its new status – and made heroically by new movements of hermits and monks in the Egyptian deserts and elsewhere. But once Constantine became determined to acknowledge the Christians' God as his patron, and to worship and reward that God by bestowing privileges and endowments on the church, it was not really possible for the church to make a grand refusal. Nor does it seem convincing for Christians to argue that more was lost than was gained by acceptance of the new emperor's wishes. There was surely gain in the beginning of the spiritual wealth of a public Christian culture and in the beginning of the moral value of the whole attempt to make society Christian. The enrichment brought to humanity can scarcely be imagined despite all the fame of the art, the literature or the statesmanship of 'Christendom'. But more important in Christian eyes must surely be the gathering of a flock now to be

counted, over almost seventeen hundred years, in very great numbers
– souls drawn into the church because the Christianisation of the
empire, however superficial, made it a bit less difficult to be a
Christian; because the new prestige of the church secured attention,
sometimes profound attention, for the church's scriptures and their
invitation to holiness. The conversion of a Roman festival, Satur-
nalia, into Christmas was typical. Those who condemn the church's
inevitable decision to accept the support of a Christian Caesar have
not weighed the losses which would have followed a consistent
decision to remain no more than a persecuted minority, had such a
decision been conceivable. Perhaps they have not noticed how later
generations of Christians under persecution have almost always
welcomed any prospect of peace, freedom and influence.

The epoch following the Constantinian revolution saw fine new
fruit on the tree of Christianity. The teaching of Ambrose, elected
bishop of Milan in 374, not only secured for the church a new beauty
in worship (for example, he introduced the regular use of hymns,
many written by himself). It also secured for the state a new subjection to the Christian conscience; thus Ambrose excommunicated the
emperor Theodosius I, who did public penance, after a massacre.
This emperor, so far from being permanently alienated by this
humiliation, made Christianity the only religion granted official
recognition in the empire (in 380). When on his death in 395 the
dominion of Rome was divided for ever into the Eastern (Byzantine)
and Western empires, the memory of Theodosius survived for legislation summing up the justice of Rome in a Christian setting. That
tradition was brought to a climax by the emperor Justinian, who ruled
the East in the middle of the sixth century. Justinian's own majesty
was displayed in a setting which suggested also a hierarchically
ordered heaven. All this was symbolised in the architecture and
mosaics of the church of *Hagia Sophia* (Holy Wisdom), the greatest
glory of a rich empire and still overwhelming in its beauty as a mosque
in Istanbul.

Leaders of the church in the East included the masterful Athanasius who began to shape the new orthodoxy by his book on Christ's
incarnation – and (later) Basil of Caesarea and his brother Gregory of
Nyssa, who defined full-blown Byzantine Christianity. Their influence had to be tested in the persuasion of 'ecumenical' councils of
bishops coming mostly from the Eastern empire and usually a little
less or more than two hundred in number. In such councils no bishop
was dominant by virtue of his office. Rivalry existed in theology as
well as in ecclesiastical politics between Alexandria and Antioch, and

gradually their honour was shared with old Jerusalem and new Constantinople. Since councils of bishops could overturn the decisions of previous councils, quarrelling churchmen frequently appealed to the emperor to take decisive action. However, despite these limits and tensions it was surely an advantage for Christianity that its leaders were able men, now free to confer together in public.

If one problem was the absence of any bishop who because of his office would be expected to preside over a council, a possible solution was appearing in the development of the bishopric of Rome. Before the close of the second century Irenaeus, bishop of Lyons, had written about Rome: 'It is with this church, on account of her more powerful origin, that every church should agree.' For in the West there was no other bishopric with Rome's prestige and wealth. Into the church of Rome Peter and Paul had poured, as Tertullian had said, their teaching as well as their blood. Rome's bishop could speak, in a sense which became more sharply defined as the years passed, with the voice of Peter, buried on the Vatican hill after his martyrdom. To be the church in the city which had ruled the whole Mediterranean world, and to possess the spiritual power which seemed to flow from the memories and bodies of Peter, Paul and other saints and martyrs, was to be in a position which strong-minded bishops could use for high purposes. The first such bishop was Damasus, elected in 366. He built up for the 'Apostolic See' (as it was now called) an almost imperial dignity, with churches which fully matched the splendour of the old pagan temples; he secured the reign of Latin for more than fifteen hundred years by ending the use of Greek in the eucharist in Rome and by commissioning his secretary, Jerome, to translate the Bible (the version known as the 'Vulgate'); and he prepared the way for his successor Siricius, a tough administrator, to exercise jurisdiction over the Western churches as 'pope' (father).

In the middle of the fifth century Pope Leo I was able to persuade Attila the Hun to spare a city protected by Peter and Paul. At the end of the century – by which time there was no Western emperor even pretending to rule – Pope Gelasius I explicitly claimed not to be bound by the decisions of any other bishops whatsoever. Although the Eastern bishops rejected the claim, and Western bishops of the stature of Cyprian, Augustine and Ambrose would never have accepted it, among many Catholics of the West the value of a Christian Rome in the maintenance of cohesion based on traditional beliefs seemed clear. A bishop was glad that he could get the correct answer to a problem from the one centre where efficiency and continuity could be relied on. In effect the pope had become the heir not only of Peter and Paul but also of the Caesars. But this was a practical rather than theoretical development long before the appearance in the eighth or ninth century of a forgery, the 'Donation of Constantine', granting to the living representative of Peter imperial powers and properties in Italy and the West. It was also long before the papacy claimed a religious infallibility. On the contrary, Pope Vigilius was excommunicated for heresy by the fifth ecumenical council (553) and Pope Honorius I by the sixth (681). Forged documents purporting to show that the early papacy had not been bound by the tradition of the church as expressed in the councils of the bishops were not produced before the ninth century (the 'Decretals of Pseudo-Isidore'). It was only in the eleventh century that Gregory VII, then locked in struggles with secular rulers, claimed to be the absolute monarch of the church and incapable of error, and only in the twelfth century that this claim was embodied in Gratian's canon law, quoting the forgeries as authentic. It was only in 1302 (in the Bull *Unam Sanctam*) that Pope Boniface VIII, in the course of his conflict with the king of France, aspired to jurisdiction over the whole of the creation and decreed that 'to be subject to the Roman pontiff is necessary for salvation'. At about the same time Thomas Aquinas more cautiously taught that questions of faith were to be 'decided by him who presides over the whole church'. But even in the Western church it was still possible for the conciliar movement to flourish at the end of the Middle Ages with a far greater emphasis on the bishops' councils than on the papacy, sadly divided and discredited. In 1870 papal infallibility was to be defined by a council (Vatican I) after considerable hesitation by the many bishops who thought the definition 'inopportune'. But such an extension of papal power could never have been anticipated in the days when the Roman church was honoured with far less precision as the chief centre of stability in a West becoming Christian. In those days the prestige of Rome was incontrovertibly one of Western Christianity's assets.

However, the triumph of Christianity quickly brought with it many tragedies.

One was the new power of the Eastern emperor to decide questions about Christian belief. 'Caesaro-papism' is an apt term for this power. The welcome given to this strange arbiter of theological controversies began with Constantine himself. No theologian, but a soldier who was as ruthless or as diplomatic as suited him politically, he played the decisive role in the council of Nicaea which he convened at his own expense in 325. He put forward the formula 'of one substance' (*homoousios*) which was almost unanimously adopted to explain the eternal relation of the Father and the Son in the trinity. His motivation was certainly not an interest in metaphysics. It was to secure unity in the church, in the belief that this achievement would gain from the church's God the blessing of unity in the empire – and with unity prosperity. Essentially the same motive drove many of his successors in the East to dominate bishops' councils and to attempt to settle theological disputes by intimidation or brute force. Theodosius and Justinian identified heresy with treason. And other rulers imitated them. In 384 a Spanish bishop, Priscillian, was in trouble as an enthusiast whose theology was unorthodox (it seems, in a Gnostic direction). Denounced by a fellow bishop as a protector of magic, he was executed on the orders of an emperor of the West, a usurper anxious to curry favour with the orthodox bishops. With him four priests, a poet and a widow were put to death. Just over seventy years after the grant of religious freedom to Christians, the state was being used to deny life to heretics.

Emperors might be defended on the ground that they represented the Christian laity, but another development in this period was the exaltation of the clergy, in theory and practice, far beyond anything known in the New Testament. In the congregations the eucharist was now 'celebrated' in a largely fixed form giving more prominence to the more richly dressed president – the bishop or a presbyter delegated by him. Inferior ministers became like courtiers to this almost royal figure. Candles, incense, gold, silver and marble added to the impressiveness. In the church of the Holy Wisdom in Constantinople a screen separated the clergy from the people and this innovation, at first criticised, spread into all the churches of the East. Another factor making for separation was the growing pressure on bishops and presbyters to remain unmarried, unspotted by lay lusts. It was in North Africa that the bishop began to be often called *sacerdos*, the Latin for 'priest'; and it was Cyprian of Carthage, who became a bishop within two years of becoming a Christian and was martyred in 258, who added a potent theory to this use of a word which did not necessarily imply any theory. He stressed the comparison between the Christian priests ordained by the bishop and the Jewish priests of the Old Testament. The bishop's authority was essential to the church's unity, as Ignatius and many others had already said. It was based on the bishop's guardianship of the tradition of the whole church beginning with the teaching of apostles, as Irenaeus and many others had already said. It could be conferred only by other bishops; early in the third century Hippolytus of Rome had made this clear.

But now, for Cyprian, the validity of the church depended on its regularly consecrated bishops being in a succession of rulers beginning with the apostles. And for Cyprian the priests ordained by the bishops offer in the eucharist the body and blood of Christ as the Christian sacrifice. Clericalism – the greater prominence of bishop and priest in the life of the church – was thus now accompanied by 'sacerdotalism', a higher doctrine of their religious functions. It was a new development in the church's self-understanding and it fed a rapid growth in 'sacramentalism', the placing of the sacraments at the very centre of Christianity.

Some of those who had been courageous under persecution – the 'confessors' – traded on the prestige of the martyrs in order to demand the exclusion or very severe punishment of those who had yielded, particularly the *traditores* (traitors) who had bonded over the scriptures for themselves. This rigorous and exclusive puritanism – which on the evidence of his gospel Mark would have found congenial – became a numerous sect in North Africa under the leadership of Donatus. It was 'schism', the cutting-off of oneself from the body, and great bishops such as Cyprian and Augustine fought it for the sake of a wider vision of the comprehensiveness of the 'Catholic' (universal) church. The Catholics were willing to use military weapons once the emperor could be persuaded to deploy them – and in the 340s the emperor agreed. It could be pointed out that the Donatists had themselves used force to express the grievances of the landless labourers. But the Catholics also used a spiritual weapon: a greater emphasis on the sacraments as effectively saving acts which depended on authorisation by the Catholic bishop but not on the feelings, faith or morality of those taking part. At first the validity of baptisms by schismatics such as the Donatists had been denied but now the view prevailed that a baptism was valid if administered with water and in the name of the trinity. The bishop of Rome was insistent on this principle, rebuking Cyprian's narrowness. The Catholic laity were becoming the recipients of grace conveyed by the sacraments which the priests administered – and, as Cyprian proclaimed, 'outside the church there is no salvation', for 'he cannot have God for his Father who has not the church for his mother'. Whatever we may think of this as a theological principle, we have to note that the Donatism which protested against it in a Puritan style was the kind of religion that many Christians in North Africa found more attractive than the institutionalised Catholicism of the Romanised upper class. At its peak the Donatist church was led by more than five hundred bishops. It was bluntly simple in its morality and proudly provincial in

Augustine

its ethos, using local languages and blessing the peasants' grievances. It seems to have remained popular until the arrival of Islam.

The development of the Catholic church in the West was decisively influenced by the invasion of Italy including the sacking of Rome by a barbarian tribe, the Goths, in 410. Soon after that the Roman legions left Britain and lost control of Gaul (France) and Spain. The Huns followed the Goths, and another group of barbarians, the Vandals, ravaged North Africa. With a stunning rapidity the Roman empire was disintegrating in the West, leaving the church as the strongest institution preserving civilisation. This was a period when many of the ablest sons of the aristocracy or products of the universities chose or accepted positions in the church, sometimes (as with Ambrose and his pupil Augustine) in mid-life. Against this background, it is entirely understandable that they should concentrate on refashioning Catholicism as an empire within the empire which was dramatically in decay; and it was psychologically inevitable that during this secular decay they should take a gloomy view of the human condition, in striking contrast with the optimism of Origen.

A response was made to this challenge by the genius of Augustine, who became bishop of Hippo in North Africa and a prolific writer. His *Confessions* told of the spiritual pilgrimage of a highly educated and sensitive seeker after truth, through Neoplatonism to a biblically based Christianity. His *City of God* pronounced a Christian judgement on the decline and fall of the Roman empire and on many other matters. Augustine never completely identified the Catholic church with the supernatural City of God, but he taught that it was the ark of salvation amid the world's storms. He analysed the sins in which he had himself indulged, giving sexual sins an emphasis for which there were few Christian precedents. Although he acknowledged that Catholicism blessed conjugal embraces, he still concluded that man's 'original' sin was transmitted, generation by generation, through the lust inherent in the act of sexual intercourse. The church, with its scriptures and sacraments, was God's offer of salvation to those believers whom he had chosen out of the 'damned mass' of sinful humanity. Their salvation depended on his choice, or 'election', and his grace, not on any good works of theirs; and Augustine waged a mighty and successful theological war against Pelagius, a teacher who was believed to have attached too great an importance to the human will to be good. Even outside the church, the 'tranquillity of order' in a just society depended on the suppression of many untranquil desires.

It was an analysis of society, of the human condition and of the soul that penetrated depths beyond the probe of any previous theologian since Paul and John. Long after Augustine's death in 430 his work was to provide not only an education but also an invitation to a life of converted dependence on God's grace. But there were elements in this magisterial theology which were to combine as a more sinister legacy to the future – the willingness to use psychological and military pressure to secure obedience to the church, meaning in effect the Catholic bishop; the insistence on the church's authority to expound the true meaning of the scriptures (although Augustine knew no Hebrew and not much Greek); the obsession with sexual sin, very much from a male angle and very unlike the attitude recorded in the gospels; a generally low view of human nature accompanied by an insistence on orthodox belief; the doctrine of 'predestination', which could easily slide from joy over God's saving grace into the belief that the mass of humanity had been damned by God himself to the everlasting torments of hell. Augustine always remained able to soar into the contemplation of the beauty and mercy of God. But in the hands of teachers without his spiritual stature, some ideas to which he gave his authority would grow into a variety of Catholicism (or of Protestantism) which made the institutional church all-important, which served the interests of the men in power, which despised the sinners who constituted the great human majority, which exalted orthodoxy high above goodness, and which pictured God as the Eternal Torturer.

Many of the laity in the chief cities of the empire, at least in the East, seem to have needed little persuading to turn out for demonstrations for or against a bishop or theologian involved in controversy. But it was another symptom of the church's sickness that the attention of the laity should be directed to personalities involved in disputes about the right philosophical definition of the inner being of Christ. Such controversies obscured the far more important challenge to the church to reconsider the relevance of Christ's spiritual and moral teaching now that the whole empire was becoming Christian. On the face of it, Christianity was being flattered by the popularity of rival theologians. Actually, however, the evidence does not suggest that the level of interest taken in this dispute was usually philosophical or spiritual. People were interested in people, places in places, mobs in chanting slogans, emperors in strengthening their political power. For a time theology was as popular as football is nowadays – but (like our football) not chiefly as a contest of technical skills which onlookers practised themselves. And when ruthlessly pursued to their conclusions, these 'theological' conflicts resulted in the use of

Roman power to enforce the acceptance of Greek philosophical solutions to mysteries which the New Testament had left mysterious. Inevitably those who for one reason or another disagreed with these solutions appealed to political rulers who might be able to defy or dislodge the prevailing political power. Thus the unity of the church, which those who defined orthodoxy claimed to be preserving, was destroyed. At the first council of the church where bishops from East and West were present in almost equal numbers – at Sardica (Sofia) in 343 – the Easterners, who had been lodging in the Byzantine imperial palace, walked out. They accused the Westerners of heresy and the Westerners, who now resolved that disputed questions should be submitted to Rome, matched them in the exchange of insults.

A lust for definition

Less than a hundred years after the crucifixion of Jesus, Pliny reported to the emperor that Christians sang hymns 'to Christ as to a god'. The fourth gospel was accepted by Christians as containing the actual words of Jesus such as 'my Father and I are one' – but even if that gospel had never been written, developing Christianity would have treated Jesus as more than a servant or prophet of God. The crucial factor was not the luxury of theological speculation but the evidence of Christian experience, from which the theology followed. For Christians claimed that the love and power of the Father were conveyed to them within their own experience by the love and power of Jesus, the Lord who they were sure was alive.

Communication with pagans was helped by being able to talk about a divine redeemer descending to earth, for that was an idea familiar in the myths about the gods appearing among men. But the basic belief in the utter uniqueness of Christ was not taken over from non-Christian sources. It was blood pumped from the heart of Christianity, so that the letter to Titus could without explanation use not only the normal formula 'God our Father and Christ Jesus our Saviour' (Titus 1:4) but also (at least in some manuscripts) one reference to 'our great God and Saviour Christ Jesus' (Titus 2:13). In his certainly authentic letters Paul was not prepared to call Jesus 'God' in a direct way, and a document as late as the first letter to Timothy is full of the doctrine that God 'alone possesses immortality, dwelling in un-approachable light'; that 'there is one God, and also one mediator between God and men, Christ Jesus, himself man'. But Paul had put Jesus in a position far higher than any other man's – for example, when he ended his surviving correspondence with Corinth: 'the grace of the Lord Jesus Christ, and the love of God, and fellowship in the Holy Spirit . . .' Indeed, he produced his own embryonic creed— 'there is one God, the Father, from whom all being comes, towards whom we move; and there is one Lord, Jesus Christ, through whom all things came to be, and we through him' (1 Corinthians 8:6).

John, Paul and the authors of the letters to the Colossians and to the Hebrews had all interpreted their experience of Jesus by using the picture of the 'Son' or 'Word' of God existing from eternity and becoming flesh. They had not given this picture any theological refinement, for what interested them was not speculation about eternity but the response of grateful faith and humble love. The Christians to whom they wrote were encouraged not to argue theologically but to imitate the humility of the one who had been rich and became poor; who had shared the divine nature yet had assumed the nature of a slave; who had been higher than the angels and yet, being tempted in a thoroughly human manner, had learnt obedience to his heavenly Father in the school of suffering, praying with cries and tears; who, made flesh and glorified by being crucified, had given believers 'the right to become children of God'. John had not made further use of the idea of Jesus as 'the Word' after his first chapter (or prologue), preferring the warmer idea of Jesus as 'the Son'. But now that the church had more security, sophistication and leisure in the Eastern empire it was inevitable that attention should be given by Christians with intellectual tastes to the work of constructing a theory. And tools for the making of a satisfactory theory seemed to lie to hand for, as Origen and Augustine had both appreciated, the Greeks' Neoplatonic philosophy contained a strong element of religious mysticism (seen at its most impressive in the philosophy of Plotinus). This tradition continued to feed the contemplation of the Christians' God even when the emperor Justinian (in 529) had forbidden the teaching of pagan Neoplatonism. It was distilled in writings published in 532 and falsely attributed to the Dionysius who had been converted by Paul in Athens – writings which had a great influence on later Christian mystics. For many hundreds of years the church's greatest minds were deeply stirred by the thought of what was possible if the wisdom of the philosophers could be allied with the gospel of the apostles, drawing out what the gospel implied. Through reasoning as well as through mysticism, the church could contemplate the reality of God. And through the right understanding of the glory of God as well as through holy living, Christians could 'come to share in the very being of God', as the second letter of Peter had myster-

iously promised (2 Peter 1:4). Humanity, freed from sin and ignorance by Christ, would return to the highest glory.

But who was, and who is, Christ? Arius, a priest of Alexandria
born about 250, and his followers were anxious to stick close to the
words of scripture and to safeguard the orthodox Jewish and Christian insistence on the unity of God. They therefore denied that the
Son was fully and eternally divine. They used a slogan: 'There was
when he was not.' For had not the New Testament (Colossians 1:15)
described Christ in a phrase which might be understood as 'the first
born of all creation'? And had not Jesus himself – frequently depicted
in prayer to God – declared: 'the Father is greater than I' (John
14:28)?

The reaction of many people, including devout Christians, standing outside this controversy may be that it is a dispute about mere
words. Is it possible to talk or think sense about time ('when he was
not') or persons (such as the Son, created but not yet human) in
eternity? The orthodox refusal to countenance any suggestion that
the Son was 'created' in eternity, followed by the agreement that he
was 'begotten', may also seem a play with words. If the comparison
between the eternal Father and a craftsman creating something is an
inadequate metaphor, so is the comparison with the sexual reproduc-
tion achieved by a human father. However, when it was fresh the
challenge of Arianism seemed deadly serious because it threatened to
reduce Christ to the status of a being who was neither God nor man.
He was not human in any ordinary sense because he had existed in
eternity before his conception as a human being. Indeed, through him
all the rest of creation had been created. But he was not fully divine
because he, too, was a creature – and that seemed to contradict the
essential Christian experience of prayer to him being answered.
Although the council of Nicaea which condemned Arianism in 325
adopted the philosophical expression that the Father and the Son
were 'of one substance' (*homoousios*), it is clear that the whole
emphasis of the assembled bishops was not philosophical but devotional. By 'substance' (*ousia*) they meant, as Aristotle had done in
his philosophy long before, what really is there – but by the *divine*
substance, they meant what is there to be worshipped. The Lord
Jesus Christ was 'God from God, Light from Light, true God from
true God . . . For us men and for our salvation he came down and
became flesh, was made man'. It was almost a hymn. And some such
words will often arise in the hearts of Christians who have the
experience that 'God was in Christ reconciling the world to himself' (2
Corinthians 5:19).

What seems tragically wrong about the development of theology after Nicaea is the unwillingness to stop with the rejection of the claim that Arianism was orthodoxy. Councils developed a habit of defining dogmas about the being of Christ and his eternal relationship with the Father – and also the habit of expelling as heretics any who dissented. Those who lost the debate often experienced persecution by the state.

One result was that theological movements which might have developed healthily were quickly branded as heretical – and, if they did not disappear, became more obstinate in isolation. Early in the third century Sabellius, a presbyter of Rome born in Libya, argued that 'Father', 'Son' and 'Holy Spirit' were names of the one God. His followers seem to have said more technically that there was only one divine substance (they used the Greek word *hypostasis*) but three activities (*energeia*), God as Father in creation, as Son in redemption and as Spirit in prophecy and sanctification. This position could be developed so as to claim that the Word of God was 'created' in eternity, or that God the Son had only a temporary existence, or that the activity of God in Jesus began only at the latter's baptism, or that this activity was no more than his activity in other prophets and miracle-workers. Tertullian alleged that teachers in this tradition 'crucified the Father and expelled the Paraclete'. Such charges were made against teachers such as Bishop Paul of Antioch, whose views were condemned by a council of fellow bishops in 268. The pagan emperor was persuaded to deprive him of his bishopric. But the tradition of simply stressing the activity of God through the man Jesus, without any theological refinements, had strong roots in the New Testament. So did the simple idea of the Spirit of God (or of Christ).

To express the more complicated statement which most of the bishops now wished to make about Jesus, new meanings had to be given to old words. It is worth going into some detail in order to see that phrases which later became standard, indeed sacred, in orthodoxy were at one time daring innovations, excused on the ground that Christian faith demanded new expressions.

The Greek word *hypostasis* was used only once in the New Testament, when it was affirmed that the Son was the stamp of God's own 'being' (Hebrews 1:3). Sabellius, for example, continued to use the word in this sense. Yet Origen and other Christian Platonists taught that the Father, the Son and the Holy Spirit were each a *hypostasis*. These innovators were influenced by the Neoplatonists' teaching that the One, the Mind and the Soul each constituted a *hypostasis* in the divine reality. Eventually this usage was accepted by the orthodox. *Hypostasis* was what the Father, the Son and the Holy Spirit each had, and by an innovation the term *ousia* was adopted to mean the divine 'being' or 'substance' – that 'nature' which the Father, the Son and the Holy Spirit had in common. But how could *hypostasis* in its new meaning be translated? The Latin theologian Tertullian used the word *persona*, but this alarmed the Greeks to whom it suggested their word *prosopon*, meaning an actor's mask. They insisted that the Father, the Son and the Holy Spirit are not mere masks of the one God – masks which do not express the fullness of God and can be discarded. Nor, of course, can the Father, the Son and the Holy Spirit be three people in the meaning of the word 'person' which has been normal ever since at the beginning of the sixth century Boethius defined *persona* as 'the individual substance of a rational nature'. It has always been an essential part of Christian orthodoxy to assert the unity of God, and a consequence has been an insistence that the operations of the three 'persons' of the Holy Trinity cannot be divided as we experience them. (The first and second 'persons' are both involved in creation, the second and third 'persons' in inspiration, etc.). For the most respected theologians, or 'fathers', of the church during its first four centuries, not even the 'person' of Jesus had that individuality which moderns in the Western world think is the essence of being a person. In the Platonic world of thought, humanity as a category seemed more real than any individual – so that it seemed possible and right to say that the Son assumed 'human nature' without being simply 'a man'.

In addition to these difficulties over the church's vocabulary there were more substantial problems. For it seemed necessary to answer questions which took orthodoxy further and further away from the simple necessity of expressing the human experience of God as Father, as Son and as Spirit; and during these controversies, vast damage was done to the communion of Christians.

If Jesus was the second *hypostasis* in the divine *ousia*, did he have a human spirit? The bishop of Laodicea, Apollinarius, who had eloquently denounced Arianism, thought he was being orthodox when he also denied this – only to be condemned for denying the full humanity 'assumed' by the Son and therefore denying the possibility of healing for all humanity. To those who reckoned themselves as truly orthodox, the human hope of participating in the divine nature depended on participation in the human nature which the Son had assumed. So they argued that it was of the utmost importance for the church to pronounce on what might seem to be a theological tech-

filioque

nicality. Whether or not they were right, they succeeded in suppressing this highly gifted theologian. Only fragments remain of the many books he wrote – and most of them survived by sheltering under other authors' names.

Was the Holy Spirit subordinate to the Father and the Son? Many New Testament passages pointed in this direction but when other theologians went down the road they, too, were condemned as heretical. At the council of Constantinople in 381 the orthodox doctrine became that the Holy Spirit was the fully divine 'Lord and Giver of life' and 'proceeded' from the Father. Yet even after that there were problems – for Western Christians, influenced by Augustine, added that the Spirit also proceeded 'from the Son' (in Latin, *filioque*). This addition to the creed started in Spain. It was intended to glorify the divine Son in opposition to the Arians. But from the seventh century onwards it increased greatly the difficulties of relationships with the Christian East, where the idea of adding to the creed was abhorrent, particularly since the Christians of the West had acted without consultation. To the East, the *filioque* clause seemed dangerous because the assertion that the Father alone was the source of divinity was what preserved the belief in the Holy and Undivided Trinity from being a belief in three gods. It also seemed dangerous because it seemed to deny the full divinity of the Holy Spirit. If the Spirit could be said to proceed 'from the Father and the Son', the Spirit might be no more than the love which united the Father and the Son who alone were truly divine, so that the doctrine of the trinity had been reduced to a belief in two persons. Or so it could be argued by Easterners who were anyway hostile to a unilateral move by the West.

Was the mother of Jesus rightly called 'Mother of God' or God-bearer, *Theotokos*? Nestorius, patriarch of Constantinople, mindful that Christ had two natures, answered that she was – but only if at the same time she was called 'Man-bearer'. He preferred 'Christ-bearer'. After much confusion the council of Ephesus condemned and deposed him in 431. It was alleged that Nestorianism meant belief that there were two persons as well as two natures in Christ. But the debate was influenced by the hostility of the patriarch of Alexandria and the pope of Rome to a highly active and talkative patriarch of Constantinople. Heresy could be alleged by churchmen who found it trying to be Nestorius-bearers.

Did Jesus have only one 'nature' (in Greek, *physis*)? This might seem to be the simplest interpretation of the gospels and 'monophysites' believing in one nature predominated in the theology of Alexandria. But the leading theologians of Antioch replied that Jesus united in one *hypostasis* two natures, divine and human – and they were finally pronounced orthodox at the council of Chalcedon in 451. A major factor in this controversy was the human nature of the Egyptians. They were not sorry to find that their own intellectuals were in disagreement with men who taught in Antioch, a foreign theological centre. They backed their own side. Since they already disliked the rule of the emperor Marcian, they saw no reason to cease to support Alexandria's theological position when he supported Antioch's. And since the ordinary Egyptian did not speak Greek, the superior merits of Antioch's exposition of Neoplatonic Christology did not have a wide appeal in Egypt.

The upshot of these agitations was a definition of orthodoxy which tried to do justice both to Alexandria's emphasis on Christ's divinity and to Antioch's on his humanity. That was the purpose of the Tome which Pope Leo I despatched from Rome to the East in 449 and of the definition which the council of Chalcedon adopted two years later. Despite resentment at the pope's claim that his summary of doctrine should not be examined, it was accepted as orthodox. Between them the pope and the council did, indeed, produce a finely balanced statement about Christ as 'truly God and truly man', consubstantial with the Father in Godhead and with us in manhood, made known 'in two natures without confusion, without change, without division, without separation'. But the Alexandrians' patriarch was excommunicated and deposed by the majority of the bishops. After that, the Alexandrians' communion with those who had prevailed at Chalcedon was terminated. The monophysites joined the Arians, Appolinarians and Nestorians in the category of 'heretics'.

It seems possible and right both to admire the theological skill of Chalcedon and to regret that Christianity was torn apart. Certainly theological disagreements over Greek philosophical terms were not the sole cause of the splits. Many an individual wanted to assert his individuality; many a church wanted to be independent or superior; many Christians did not wish to remain under the thumb of the Byzantine emperor; many did not wish to use Greek at all. But these divisive tendencies could now be made religiously respectable by quarrels over the details of orthodoxy in doctrine. Christians who wished to break off fellowship with fellow Christians now had a reason, or at least an excuse, because 'heresy' could be alleged. It could be claimed that what was at stake was faithfulness to the gospel.

It was a tragic development and a new one. For the insistence on detailed orthodoxy was far from early and far from inevitable. The creeds, despite their high authority, have a history which reflects a certain variety in earlier expressions of faith. The summary known as the Apostles' Creed originated as a formula recited by candidates seeking baptism in Rome during the third century. Although there is evidence that this Roman formula was widely used from the fourth century onwards, each centre felt free to decide the detailed wording of the tradition to be handed on at baptism. It was the emperor Charlemagne who in 813 picked on the version called the Apostles' Creed and did his utmost to make it compulsory throughout his empire in the West, for the sake of imperial unity. The legend that it was composed by the apostles dates from no earlier than the fourth century. The statement known as the Athanasian Creed has, like the Apostles' Creed, never been used in the churches of the East. Composed not by Athanasius but anonymously and probably around 500 in Spain or France, it asserts that if anyone does not keep the faith which it defines 'without doubt he will perish everlastingly' – although the Father is declared to be incomprehensible, the Son incomprehensible and the Holy Spirit incomprehensible (yet 'there are not three incomprehensibles'). The damnation of those not subscribing to all forty-two of this creed's doctrinal statements is difficult to reconcile with the teaching of Jesus. The creed known as Nicene, the only standard of belief which most branches of the Christian church have in common apart from the Bible, dates in its full form not from the council of Nicaea but from the council of Constantinople in 381. Although of course already familiar to theologically minded people, it was introduced into the eucharist in Constantinople only in 511, in Spain, Ireland and elsewhere later, and in Rome about 1014. The custom of reciting it in the eucharist began in Antioch early in the fifth century, among Christians who were judged heretical by the council of Chalcedon.

When we count up what was lost to orthodox Christianity by the failure to hold deviationists within its fellowship, we have to note that Arianism did not die quickly. The emperor Constantine, annoyed equally by this disruption and by the turbulence of the anti-Arian bishop Athanasius, wanted compromise. His theological adviser, Eusebius, suggested that the Father and the Son were 'of similar substance' (*homoiousios*). A later emperor, Valens, championed Arianism until his death in 378. He died in battle against the invading Goths, a tribe whose conversion was to be led by one of its own sons, Bishop Ulphilas. This great missionary translated most of the Bible into Gothic, thus founding the culture we call German – and he was an Arian. Almost all the barbarians who poured into the Western empire, when they embraced Christianity, remained Arians until further converted to Catholicism (often by force) in a process lasting to the end of the sixth century. It was not until a Catholic bishop baptised Clovis, king of the Franks, on Christmas Day 496 that it became clear that Arianism would fade from northern Europe. Even after that Charlemagne, crowned emperor in Rome on Christmas Day 800, was troubled by the need to suppress its remnants.

At the beginning of the sixth century an Arian king of Italy, Theodoric, established his capital in Ravenna, and the mosaics of churches built at his command still testify how close his religion was to orthodoxy. A great orthodox emperor, Justinian, and his consort Theodora soon added to Ravenna their own glorious art. But Theodora, a formidable empress, was a monophysite in her religious views and seems often to have pointed out to her husband that so, too, were the majority of his subjects who took an interest in theology. Certainly it is a fact that the church remained largely monophysite in Egypt, Armenia and Syria, despite all the persecuting efforts of emperors more single-minded than Justinian. One important factor was that the church in those areas did not usually speak the Greek of Constantinople. From Egypt this faith spread down the Nile to Ethiopia, where it greatly strengthened the presence of Christianity established by Bishop Frumentius early in the fourth century; and this faith dominated Ethiopian life, at least among the ruling Amhara people of the highlands, from the early 500s to the Marxist revolution in the 1970s. Ethiopian theology remained monophysite, and one of the other peculiarities of church life there was the adoption of many Jewish customs. But it is an impressive story. Similarly, the Copts of Egypt (who welcomed the Muslim invaders and joined them to repel a Byzantine army in 645) have retained their identity as a minority under incessant Muslim pressure over thirteen centuries. Although Gregory the Enlightener who planted Christianity in Armenia during the fourth century transmitted a monophysite form of the Christian light, the extraordinary persistence of the Armenian church through persecutions was not weakened by its continuing hold on this theology. The monophysite Syrians (called Jacobites after their great missionary, Jacob Baradeus) have similarly resisted absorption. From Syria this faith spread to South India and when the Portuguese landed in India in 1500 they found about a hundred thousand 'Syrian' Christians there – the St Thomas Church, so called after their belief that Christianity had been taken to India by the apostle Thomas. In the 1980s such groups still challenge the right of the adherents of the

Chalcedonian definition to monopolise 'orthodox' Christianity.

The Nestorians, while having no sympathy with the monophysites, also prospered – again in countries where the use of Greek was rare. Emigrating to the Persian empire, they secured the official recognition of their faith although the empire remained officially Zoroastrian; and by 630 they had eighty-three dioceses on Persian soil. Their missionary enthusiasm also spread a network of other bishoprics into Arabia, India, Turkistan, China and Central Asia. Their influence has been traced in the history of the development of Islam, Hinduism and Buddhism. They enjoyed the protection both of the Abbasid Caliphs in Bagdad and of the Tang dynasty in China, but other Muslim rulers of the former Persian empire were less tolerant and in 845 some three thousand of their monks were expelled from China as 'foreigners'. Even that was not the end of their astonishing story. What really doomed them was the series of exceptionally ferocious Mongol invasions which devastated Central Asia in the twelfth, thirteenth and fourteenth centuries. Although the Nestorians could on occasion influence, serve and even convert the Mongols, in the end they were almost everywhere obliterated. However, even in the 1980s they linger on as the Assyrian community, mainly in Iraq and the USA.

Such 'heretics' did not command much sympathy among the 'orthodox' Christians who remained loyal to Constantinople. On the contrary, writings thought to be sympathetic with Nestorius were condemned at the second council of Constantinople in 553 (despite an earlier attempt by Pope Vigilius to defend them) and all efforts at reconciliation with the monophysites came to an end with the condemnation of the formula that Christ had one will, monothelitism, at the third council of Constantinople in 680 (despite an earlier use of the formula by Pope Honorius). Even more decisive was the survival of Constantinople (Byzantium) as a rich and prestigious religious centre when Jerusalem, Antioch and Alexandria had been submerged by the tide of Muslim conquest. But huge damage was inflicted on Christianity when the sense of one church – one communion with one mission – was almost completely destroyed. And some of the damage can be observed in history. When the armies of Islam appeared, monophysite and Nestorian Christians already felt alienated from the Byzantine empire, just as the Donatists felt alienated from the Catholic west in North Africa. The fact that these 'heretics' had no wish to lay down their lives in the defence of Byzantium or Rome does much to explain the speed of the Muslim conquest. And after those conquests the prospects for Christian survival and evangelism were gravely weakened by Christianity's internal divisions.

It may be asked whether the completeness of the separation from 'heretics' was the necessary price of the defence of the true faith. In the centuries to come Eastern Orthodox theologians were often going to protest against the arrogance of definitions of doctrine by the Roman Catholic Church. Their complaint was not merely that the papacy aspired to powers that properly belonged only to ecumenical councils which, so far as they were concerned, had ended in the eighth century. They also lamented that the papally approved theology of Thomas Aquinas (who owed much more to the coldly reasoning Aristotle than to the mystical Plato) was overconfident of the precise grasp which the intellect could have on revealed truths if guided by the church. The Orthodox tradition, partly in reaction against the intellectual and legal overdefinition of dogmas in the West, now stressed that authority was to be found in the teaching of the Bible as a whole, interpreted by the fathers as a whole and received by the church as a whole. While the doctrinal formula of Chalcedon was certainly never contradicted, the emphasis was on 'doxology', the living worship of the revealed triune God, not on intellectual speculation.

Indeed, it was said repeatedly that theology must often be 'apophatic' or negative, safeguarding the mystery of the God being worshipped by declaring what words used about the mystery were wrong. John Chrysostom's name, one of the most honoured in this tradition, was honoured not least because he was the author of a book *On the Incomprehensibility of God*. In keeping with this line of thought, it could often be claimed that the ecumenical councils had only condemned the assertions of heretics who were overzealous intellectuals. More recently there have been attempts to move towards a reconciliation in the theological disputes by maintaining that the 'heretics', no less than the 'orthodox', had only been trying to safeguard the incomprehensible divine mystery against explanations which might mislead. Thus in 1967, in conversations between theologians from Orthodox churches (which accepted Chalcedon) and Oriental churches (which did not), it was agreed: 'Ever since the fifth century we have used different formulae to confess our common faith in the One Lord Jesus Christ, perfect God and perfect man.' After an expert examination of the issues at stake, a non-Chalcedonian theologian, a 'Syrian' Indian who has been a professor in the monophysite Church of Ethiopia, has shown that the theological barriers can be crossed if there is good will. 'The obvious conclusion,' writes Dr V. C.

Samuel, 'is that by defending the council of Chalcedon the Chalcedonian side did not really achieve anything for orthodoxy which the non-Chalcedonian side, while rejecting that council, had not all along maintained consistently as their doctrinal standpoint.' To this scholar, the theological issue 'was, at best, only one of expressing reservation regarding the language used'.[8]

Fortunately for the church, the tragedy of Chalcedon was never exactly repeated. Although controversies continued, there were to be no more major and permanent splits in the Eastern church justified by bitter quarrels over doctrinal details. In the centuries to come 'Eastern Orthodoxy' was to show itself capable of developing a strong bond of spiritual strength without the insistence on uniformity. The stress was to be placed on communion (in Greek *koinonia*, in Russian *sobornost*), not on legislation. The great succession of ecumenical councils claiming to make decisions for the whole Christian world was still accepted as authoritative but it came to an end in 787. During the next period much diversity was to be accepted. Although Greek customs were for a time presented as essential in the evangelism of pagan peoples (and that caused great difficulties in the conversion of Bulgaria), it was gradually acknowledged that departures from these customs might be allowed as Greek missionaries advanced into the Balkans and up the Dnieper and Volga rivers. Greeks such as Cyril and Methodius in the 860s, or the missionaries who responded to the call of Vladimir the king of Kiev in the 980s, were heralds of all the future wealth of the Slavonic and Russian Christian cultures in worship, art and life. Nor was this to be the limit of Orthodoxy's acceptance of pluralism. In the twentieth-century USA there exists a mosaic of Orthodox jurisdictions, each with its strong identity – not only Greek and Russian but also Albanian, Arab, Bulgarian, Romanian, Serbian and Ukrainian. So we may regret the failure of Constantinople's orthodoxy to recognise and embrace Egyptian, Syrian, Armenian, Indian or Chinese Christianity.

The best leaders deplored the tragedy, at least in the early stages. Severus, the formidable patriarch of Antioch who in exile in Alexandria organised the supply of new bishops and priests to serve the monophysite faithful, seems to have been utterly sincere in his anguish over the spiritual dangers of heresy and schism. In his own exile in Egypt, Nestorius pleaded that although he had taught that Christ's two natures were united by one will rather than by one *hypostasis*, he had never intended to lead a heresy or a schism. On the contrary, he accepted Pope Leo's Tome as a definition of orthodoxy. In the end pressures towards a permanent separation proved irresistible, being strengthened by emotions which later generations would call nationalist. But it seems beyond controversy that 'orthodox' and 'heretics' were spiritually and theologically impoverished when disagreement over the nature or natures or will or wills of Christ, or over the titles of his mother, was treated as a conflict touching the heart of Christianity. A dispute over theological details was taken as seriously as the church's earlier battle against those who would have accepted Caesar-worship or would have reduced Christianity to Gnostic spiritualism. The bishops' councils culminating at Chalcedon and Constantinople have much to teach us about how not to handle Christian diversity.

And even when we have counted what was lost to the spiritual life of the churches when their inevitable diversity was allowed to end in the isolation of the 'orthodox' from the 'heretics', we have still not reckoned the full extent of the disaster. Part of the picture is the fact of the religious appeal of Islam after the divisions of Eastern Christendom. Unlike the Mongol, the Muslim was not merely a brutally successful soldier. He was the product of an extremely powerful religious movement. About 120 years after the council of Chalcedon a boy was born in Mecca who grew up to be the Prophet of Islam. His genius as a political and military leader, welding the tribesmen of Arabia into victorious armies, was certainly important for the history of the world – but it is clear from his book, the Quran, that Muhammad had a genuine experience of God. His vision of God's unity, majesty and holiness was one of the peaks of all humanity's spiritual life and as he 'recited' his vision he was among the world's greatest poets. From a Jewish or Christian point of view it is tragic that such a man could not find satisfaction in one of the two great faiths which already taught much that he experienced as true about God. How near he was to this is shown by the fact that before 624 he made his followers turn towards Jerusalem when praying. But his first followers were in commercial competition with the local Jews, who anyway had little interest in the conversion of despised Arabs. His impressions of Christianity were scarcely more favourable. Its teachings were known vaguely to the Arabs through contacts with Syria and Ethiopia, but no attempt seems to have been made to found an Arab church or to translate the Bible into Arabic. The Quran speaks highly of Jesus as a virgin-born apostle of God and as a man whom God will vindicate on the last day, not blaming him for the corruptions introduced into his message by his followers. But as it reached Muhammad, the church appeared to have become another form of idolatry. It seemed to speak with great excitement of God having a son and a mother too, resulting in three divinities. And it seemed to be hopelessly divided about what its faith meant. The 'Surrendered' (Muslim) creed therefore became that Muhammad was a later and superior prophet, teaching the simple truth about the one God (Allah) in a perfect book which could never be corrupted. In the Quran (5:14) Allah pronounces his verdict on the disputes between the Orthodox, monophysite and Nestorian churches. 'We made a covenant with those who said they were Christians, but they have forgotten much that they were commanded. Therefore we stirred among them enmity and hatred, which shall last until the Day of Resurrection, when we shall declare to them all that they have done.'

Yet it would not be fair comment on the first four centuries of Christianity to conclude a brief chronicle on a tragic note. For Christianity was shown by the very diversity of its developments to possess an adaptable vitality that would be to its advantage in the centuries to come. Islam (a word which means 'Submission') was always to be committed to a belief in the perfection of the Quran, and from that belief was to flow a call for obedience to laws (the *Sharia*) definite and unalterable. In contrast, the Christian church did not begin as a complete society, let alone as an army on the march. In its origins it was ill-defined and materially powerless. Yet much fruitfulness was to come from the diversity which was first dramatised by the vigorous complaint of the Greek-speakers in the Jerusalem church that their widows were being neglected by the Jewish apostles. Before it was four hundred years old, Christianity had proved able to leave behind its Jewish origins, since not even the great diversity to be found within Judaism could contain it. It had shown its power to survive the disappointment of its belief in the imminent end of the world; to plumb the Pauline depths of the individual's psychology; to create a disciplined Catholicism which under scriptures and bishops was active in most parts of the Roman empire; to endure persecution and to take over the empire which had persecuted it; to embody the vision of the City of God as barbarians invaded the West; to inspire the religious and moral simplicity of the Donatists of North Africa; to be translated very strangely both into the empire of Byzantine and into the elaborate restatement of beliefs about Christ in terms of Neoplatonic philosophy; and to launch another great missionary expansion – this time to north, east and south and mainly through the work of churches condemned as heretical. The many tragic elements in the early history of the Christian church should not make us forget that its tragedies did not bring death. Flexibility helped it to live and expand. It grew like a tree. And a tree is a home to birds which sing, breed and fly. To a considerable extent the early Christian centuries fulfilled the prediction in the most Jewish of the gospels: 'Many, I tell you, will come from east and west to feast with Abraham, Isaac and Jacob in the kingdom of Heaven' (Matthew 8:11).[9]

ONE CHURCH'S EXPERIENCE

Catholic and Protestant

It seemed necessary to discuss the question, 'What is Christianity?' before exploring the futures of Christianity, and for me the best way to find an answer was to consider the history of Christianity in its biblical origins and in its first four centuries. If what Christianity essentially is, and is not, did not appear in that period, it never will appear. I have, I hope, demonstrated both that there was a great diversity built into the Christian programme from the start and that this diversity was not essentially incompatible with a communion, the fellowship of those who followed Jesus rather than defined him. The reader can now be spared any attempt to sum up the whole history of Christianity.[1] But it will, I believe, be helpful if in this chapter I move towards the futures by way of a short study of the experience of the denomination to which I belong – the Anglican communion.

I find myself loyal to this tradition partly because my life has given me so many reasons for gratitude to it ever since I was taken as a child to a little white church in a suburb of Cairo and particularly since I lived as a schoolboy in the precincts of Canterbury Cathedral. As a priest, I have worshipped and served in a succession of great churches which are ineffaceable pictures in my heart – churches of Oxford, Cambridge, Norwich and London. But I like to think that I have theological as well as sentimental reasons. I believe that there are in this tradition seeds of something far more significant than the mere perpetuation of Anglicanism. Readers who belong to other traditions may be interested to compare their own experiences, loyalties and hopes with this Anglican contribution. Certainly I should never wish to claim that the Anglican way into the future is the only road or the ideal road. Since Anglicanism's membership, which according to the maximum plausible estimate is about fifty million, contributes only a small fraction of the universal Christian community, any arrogant claim on its behalf would be pathetically silly. I am conscious that in the USA, for example the Anglicans (the Episcopal Church) have a membership of no more than about 2,750,000 – about forty-nine million fewer than the baptised Roman Catholics, twenty-two million fewer than the Baptists and eleven million fewer than the Methodists. The first essay in theology which I wrote was a little book called *Not Angels but Anglicans*. Almost thirty years later I am more maturely an Anglican but I am still unable to record any experience of Anglican perfection. However, this is the road which I know best, for it is my way. And while being (I admit) prejudiced, I want to say that in their far from perfect history Anglicans have begun to learn some lessons which all other Christians will need to learn some day, somehow. For those lessons indicate the road to communion in diversity in the Christian futures.[2]

Today nine tenths of the dioceses of the Anglican communion lie outside England and more than half of them are outside the Commonwealth of Nations which has succeeded the British empire. The most vigorous part of the Anglican communion – ebullient with joy, glorified by martyrdoms, expanding very rapidly – is African. The Anglicans (Episcopalians) in the USA are probably to be reckoned, if the size of their resources is related to the size of their membership, the best educated and the wealthiest denomination on earth, with a good record of concern for the poor. At the Lambeth Conference of Anglican bishops in 1978 a quarter of the bishops came from Africa – almost as big a proportion as came from the USA. I am very thankful for such facts. But much as 'Roman' Catholicism looks to Rome, or 'Lutheranism' to Martin Luther's German revolt against Rome, so the very name 'Anglican' indicates the centrality of England. The theological tradition of Anglicanism originated in a strange English experience. A little island which had belonged devotedly to the Catholic Church of the West became a largely Protestant nation without any complete break with its past. Out of an island's history which included intercourse between Catholicism and Protestantism, Anglicanism was born. And it is largely because that island acquired an empire which included a quarter of humanity that Anglicanism has become a church which includes people who are not English. An arrangement originally intended to be the national church of England, combining Catholicism and Protestantism because it was so thoroughly English, became an international denomination because these islanders mastered the world's seas. Their ships took their religion as well as their commerce overseas. There is a sense in which the most influential of all Anglicans was a country clergyman's son, Horatio Nelson.

The main theme of pre-Reformation English religion was the intensity of its pride in belonging to Catholic Christendom. Its membership was symbolised by its spiritual link with Rome – and the evidence taken as a whole suggests that after the outbreak of the Reformation right up to the end of the sixteenth century the majority of the population would have been glad of a solution of the religious problems that restored the Roman Catholic faith without the papacy's political and financial interference in the affairs of the nation. The organisation of the Church of England was preserved largely in its medieval shape, with bishops, archdeacons, cathedrals and parish churches performing many of their old functions under the royal supremacy and the parliamentary legislation. Equally or more important was the traditionalism of the Book of Common Prayer compiled (in editions of 1549 and 1552) by Archbishop Thomas Cranmer, who had a scholarly mind and a great gift for beautiful language. The Prayer Book attempted to achieve uniformity throughout the nation. It stressed baptism and the 'Lord's Supper or Holy Communion' (formerly the mass), trying to return to what Cranmer gathered were the practices of the early centuries; as he claimed, it was 'much agreeable to the mind and purpose of the old Fathers'. It turned the other daily services of the medieval church into Morning and Evening Prayer, although those services were now occupied chiefly by the recital of the entire psalter every month and by the reading of the whole Bible every year. It provided for the ordination of priests and deacons by bishops (although the forms of ordination have been rejected by the papacy as 'absolutely null and utterly void'). This continuity was essential if the national church was to have any hope of commending itself to a conservative people. When Elizabeth I resisted the attempts of the Puritans to move the church in a more decidedly Protestant direction, she was motivated not only by her own religious tastes but also by the politically shrewd conviction that Protestant preachers did not possess the hearts of her people. Nor was any other move to delete the Catholic elements from the Prayer Book successful, apart from a short period when the Church of England had been overthrown in a civil war. The thousand years when a Catholic England had been in communion with Rome had left their mark.

In 597 Augustine, the first archbishop of Canterbury, was sent as a missionary to Kent direct from Rome by a fellow monk, Pope Gregory the Great. He made a great fuss about the dangers facing him, but actually he was assured of a hearing because Ethelbert the king of Kent was married to a Frankish (French) Christian. The conversion of the tribes then occupying England – the Angles, Saxons and Jutes – was slow, with many open relapses into paganism and much half-hidden survival of pagan customs. The church had to be careful to adopt and adapt as many of these customs as possible – as, indeed, Pope Gregory advised Augustine – and the fact that care was taken to do this helps to explain why England became at least superficially Christian without a single martyrdom. Everything depended on kings agreeing to be baptised and to be guided by bishops. Christianity spread out from the royal courts through the baptism of the tribesmen and their families by the bishops or their assistants, the priests. The main spiritual appeal of the Christian message seems to have been the confident preaching about heaven and hell, but another powerful influence was exerted by this new religion's tactful embodiment of the superior culture of continental Europe. Anglo-Saxon rulers were aware of the civilisation across the English Channel through trade. When they became Christians, and presided over the Christianisation of their petty kingdoms, they were joining that civilisation as a part of the journey to heaven. In the twentieth century the spread of Christianity in Africa and in the centres of capitalism on the rim of Asia has been helped by similar ambitions.

The Catholicism of the bishops who led this mission was summed up in the belief that Peter of Rome held the keys to heaven. It prevailed over the Celtic Christianity which had developed in other parts of Britain and which, had it survived in strength, would have presented formidable problems to the new missionaries from Rome. In isolation from the centres of Western Catholicism after the withdrawal of the Roman legions, the British had grown accustomed to practices abandoned elsewhere (as in the method of dating Easter) and to some traditions which suited these islanders. The social unit was the tribe and church life had its centre in the monastery, the bishop being one of the monks. The clergy had few possessions, living close to nature and the people, but were great believers in miracles. Much attention was paid to the copying of manuscripts of the scriptures. These inspired obedience to some Old Testament laws (for example, food regulations) as well as to the New Testament's call to a self-denying holiness. Such a form of Christianity had proved able to take root in Wales, Cornwall and Wessex and to spread to Ireland and Brittany, but in most of England it either disappeared or went underground as the country was taken over by pagan invaders from across the North Sea. Augustine, very conscious that he represented papal Rome, insulted the Celtic bishops when he met them. He could afford to – since apparently there had been no Christian evangelism from Wales to reach the hated Anglo-Saxon settlers. Celtic evangelists trained in the Irish tradition did spread out from the holy islands of Iona and Lindisfarne and planted Christianity in southern Scotland and northern England. But at a small English synod meeting at Whitby in 664 the decision was taken to adopt Catholic, not Celtic, customs. For about nine hundred years Catholicism was to have no effective rival in England.

Anglo-Saxon Christianity, thus defined, gradually became the heart of a people's sense of identity. Its church life was united in itself, and united with the rest of Catholic Europe, while politically there were still rival kingdoms in England; and when the invasions of the Vikings overwhelmed all the kingdoms except Wessex, the revival of this religion was the centre of the rally led by King Alfred. This form of Christianity, thoroughly Catholic but also thoroughly English, flourished in the architecture and rich art of the churches which gradually covered the land, each the centre of a parish. It inspired both poetry and written codes of law, modelled on the legislation in the Old Testament. It put courage into heroes of faith and celebrated them as the minstrels celebrated the heroic warriors after banquets. It motivated a historian, Bede, who completed his *Ecclesiastical History of the English People* in 731. Producing also an assurance that Christian England had a mission to neighbouring lands, it led to heroic evangelism on the continent, repaying the papacy for sending Augustine by greatly enlarging the area of Catholicism. Willibrord the first archbishop of Utrecht and Boniface the first archbishop of Mainz were Englishmen. Alcuin, the true architect of the emperor Charlemagne's immensely influential religious and educational policy, came from York. The pagan and fierce Vikings were quietly converted to this faith when they, too, had settled in England. Cnut, who for a brief period made England the centre of a Danish empire, was a devout Catholic. So was the most renowned of his successors, Edward the Confessor, who founded Westminster Abbey. All this involved a certain distinctiveness in culture and organisation (not in faith), but the differences from the rest of Catholic Christianity were not so extensive as to lead to any long-lasting religious problem when William of Normandy had conquered England with the papal blessing in 1066. Twelve years earlier the division between Western Catholicism and Eastern Orthodoxy, already a virtually accomplished fact, had become final. But it is not accurate to think of Anglo-Saxon Christianity as deviating from the Catholicism taught in Rome to anything like the same extent as the Orthodox of the far-off East.

The papacy backed the Norman conquest of England because the

Normans were now as conspicuous as the ruthless patrons of an orderly church life as they had recently been troublesome as blood-thirsty pirates. In an amazingly short period of time the new colonial settlers built massive cathedrals and monasteries as centres for the reorganisation of the English church in line with current continental trends. And over the next four and a half centuries the building, rebuilding and decoration of medieval parish churches (of which some ten thousand are still standing in England in the twentieth century) testified how eager was the religion of the people, rich and poor alike, in country or town. Of the two first great poems in English, William Langland's *Piers Plowman* was devout while also indignant against injustice and Chaucer's *Canterbury Tales* echoed a robustly lay life but always in a setting of Catholic piety.

In the fourteenth century a radical movement, the Lollards, arose under the leadership of John Wyclif. Although originally a stirring in theological Oxford which some powerful laymen welcomed, it developed into a movement somewhat similar to the Donatists in fourth-century North Africa. It became identified with the grievances of the peasants. It attacked the growing wealth and power of the senior clergy. It questioned the development of the eucharist or mass into a ceremony in which – often without the presence of a lay congregation – a priest 'made' Christ by transforming the substance of bread and wine into the substance of his body and blood. It translated the Bible into English and encouraged lay people to read or hear it for themselves. More peacefully, a native English tradition developed in mystical prayer, reaching a climax in the direct apprehension of God as love by Mother Julian of Norwich. But the Lollards were driven underground and pre-Reformation English Christianity was never troubled by any other large deviation from the Catholic system or the orthodox creed.

There was no quarrel with Rome apart from the war waged by almost all the kings from William the Conqueror to Henry VIII against the efforts of the papacy to build up, under its tight control, an organisational and financial machine paying little or no attention to political frontiers. This war of words could lead to strong measures to defend the rights of the church or the crown; events included the murder of Archbishop Thomas Becket and the surrender of his kingdom to the papacy by King John. Eventually this war resulted in a tacit agreement to allow the king to choose the bishops (often his most trusted civil servants) and to veto any papal legislation or taxation which seemed contrary to his interests. In effect it was acknowledged that the extreme claims to universal lordship of popes such as Boniface VIII (1302) did not apply to England. Similar arrangements existed elsewhere in European Christendom. But this was a war limited by the existence of an unshakeable agreement with Rome in faith, persisting even while (between 1379 and 1415) Christendom had to live with the existence of two popes, one in Rome and one in Avignon. England, while achieving this limited degree of independence in ecclesiastical organisation, was often praised as a devoutly Catholic land. Its people delighted to build and endow glorious churches or to sing their carols as they danced after Christmas; and they were still doing this in the early years of the reign of the 'Defender of the Faith' (so called by a pope), Henry VIII.

The storm of the Protestant Reformation in the 1530s was therefore a sudden storm. At first the rejection of papal authority by a parliament which responded to the wishes of Henry VIII was inspired entirely by nationalism and anticlericalism, like the rejection of the pope and other foreign clerics in China in the 1950s. Patriotic Englishmen (it was proclaimed) could no longer tolerate the right of the papacy to frustrate the determination of the king to secure the annulment of his marriage and to marry Anne Boleyn in the hope of begetting a male heir. Nor could papal taxation, or the appeal to Rome in ecclesiastical lawsuits, be accepted any longer by a proud nation; or so parliament decreed. When the monasteries were suppressed there was surprisingly little opposition because it was claimed that no attack was being made on the monk's faith. But the storm of the Protestant Reformation in England raged more fiercely when it was gradually united with more genuinely religious disturbances on the continent.

The late Middle Ages had witnessed the intensification of personal piety associated with personal unease. This was due in part to the rise of the middle classes with their greater individualism. The success of the religious revolution led by Martin Luther in Germany was the success of a breakthrough in meeting this mood. The institutions of the church had become increasingly irrelevant to the deepest spiritual needs of many of the more sensitive Christians – and increasingly expensive. Some of the doctrines, in the forms that reached the general public, had become implausible – most prominently, the doctrine that the pope by an 'indulgence' could remit 'days' spent in the pains of 'purgatory' after death (in exchange for a cash payment) and the theory that the priest was a magician able to 'make' Christ in the mass (and therefore able to sacrifice him afresh in order to secure a favourable answer to a prayer suggested by a benefactor). The regulations of such a church had become to some souls a burden, as

the law of Moses had become a burden on the souls of some sensitive
Jews such as Paul. Like Paul, Luther (when already a monk) experienced a profoundly personal conversion to Jesus Christ and felt
liberated from guilt. He had found peace with God. He began to live
by a trusting faith, not by obedience to regulations, and he began to
believe that such a faith, not the righteousness which could be
reached by keeping laws, 'justified' (put right) the individual in the
sight of God. His faith was Pauline, that 'it is by his grace you are
saved, through trusting him; it is not your own doing. It is God's gift'
(Ephesians 2:8–9). When he articulated this experience in pamphlets, hymns and a whole movement protesting against the corruptions of Roman Catholicism, he found that he had inaugurated a
breakaway larger than any of the heresies of the fourth and fifth
centuries and more powerful in its theological and religious energy.
Despite all the efforts of Henry VIII to keep the Lutheran heresy out
of England, these essentially spiritual disturbances did cross the
North Sea and did meet a sympathetic reception, at first in a small
minority.

The story of English religion from the 1530s to the 1830s is, in the
main, the story of the growth of Protestantism. The growth was
affected by political disorders which decreased or increased its popularity. Thus under Henry VIII's son Edward VI, Protestantism was
identified with the brutal greed of the transfer of most of the church's
wealth into the pockets of the nobility and gentry and the brutal
rapidity of the abolition of many of the Catholic customs and appearances in the parish churches; and in the next century under Oliver
Cromwell, the Puritan variety of Protestantism came to be identified
with rule by the army, instability when that rule faltered and the
suppression of harmless pleasures. But on the Catholic side there
were similar or worse disasters. Under Henry VIII's daughter Mary,
Roman Catholicism was restored but came to be identified with
national humiliations and with the burning of Protestants; and under
his other daughter Elizabeth, loyalty to the pope meant agreeing that
King Philip of Spain had the right to dethrone England's queen.
When James II tried to restore Roman Catholicism clumsily in the
1680s it became finally clear that 'No popery' had become part of the
creed of almost every Englishman.

The growth of Protestantism in England was assisted by more
definitely religious movements, all flowing from the translation of the
Bible into English. A better version than the Lollards' was the joint
work of William Tyndale and Miles Coverdale in the 1530s. It was
improved in later translations culminating in the Authorised (or King

James) Version in 1611. A devastating commentary on a crucial failure of the medieval church is provided by the vast and transforming influence of these scriptures once they were liberated from Latin. Each reader or hearer took what he or she understood and confusion was inevitable. There seemed to be a need for a system into which the scriptures could be fitted – and that need was met by an import more coldly rational than Lutheranism.

John Calvin, who became the reformer and religious dictator of Geneva, worked out the first systematic theology to reject medieval Catholicism almost entirely. His most dramatic emphasis was on Paul's and Augustine's doctrine that God predestined his chosen ones, his 'elect', to eternal life, but he had less squeamishness than Paul, and even than Augustine, in also teaching that God predestined the bulk of the human race to hell. Christians who had been called and chosen by God were given the Holy Spirit and the holy scriptures; and they had a direct and reliable understanding both of the meaning of the Bible and of the certainty of their own election, thanks to the Spirit. The systematic interpretation of the Spirit's guidance was, however, proclaimed by the synod of Dordrecht in 1618–19, in five points popularly recalled by the acrostic TULIP – total depravity (of mankind in general), unconditional election (of the predestined), limited atonement (Christ died for the elect only), irresistible grace (saving the elect), perseverance (of the elect only, until they reach heaven). With all this, the elect were also given a motive to lead a confident, purposeful and inexhaustibly energetic life. Calvinism of a moderate kind (which usually refrained from the emphasis on hell) provided a theology which gained the adherence of most of the teachers of the Church of England. It was reflected on paper in the Thirty-nine Articles of Religion drawn up under Elizabeth I – and in human hearts as the Puritan movement created 'godly' commonwealths both in Oliver Cromwell's England and across the Atlantic in New England. One force operating against pure Calvinism in old England was the survival of bishops appointed by the crown and in effect the ecclesiastical agents of the government – while Calvin, appealing to the New Testament, had insisted on the equality of ministers whose main work was preaching. Another factor was the survival of a more positive attitude to the good works of man, summed up in the belief of the Arminians (who seemed heretics to the strict Calvinists) that Christ had died to save all. But despite these factors, the influence of Calvinism was what was chiefly in mind when the Church of England was customarily described as 'Reformed'.

The fervour of Calvinism was discredited by the damage done

during the civil wars of the seventeenth century, and when Charles II was restored to the throne of his ancestors in 1660 the bishops and the Book of Common Prayer were restored with him. There was now much more confidence in the 'high church' ecclesiastical party, treasuring the Catholic elements which remained in the Church of England. Others rejected all religious enthusiasms, and on the whole the eighteenth century as the 'age of reason'. But in the 1730s a revival of religious emotion began. It was led partly by Calvinists and partly by Arminians who did not deny the essential importance of the second birth, the heartfelt conversion. The pioneers were George Whitefield, supreme as a preacher, John Wesley, supreme as an organiser, and his brother Charles, supreme as a hymn-writer. In its early stages both Whitefield's preaching and the Wesleys' Methodism made most stir by crossing all parish boundaries and reaching large audiences in the open air, and in the end they drifted off into open nonconformity. But the broader movement which became known as Evangelicalism embraced many who remained respectable clergy and laity in the Church of England. The Evangelicals' emphasis was on the scriptures, rather than on the traditions of the church; on personal faith and on 'scriptural holiness', rather than on goodness understood as quiet and steady conformity to the standards of a Christian society; on conversion to Christ as one's personal saviour, rather than on the acceptance of the church as one's motherly guide from baptism as an infant; and on an understanding of 'saving faith' which emphasised supremely the self-sacrifice of Christ in dying as a substitute for oneself, thus appeasing the just wrath of God the Father against one's sin. By the 1830s this movement had become the main source of spiritual vitality in the Church of England and was able to secure major reforms such as the abolition of the slave trade and of slavery.

During that decade it began to be rivalled by the Oxford or Tractarian or Anglo-Catholic movement, announced from Oxford by a series of pamphlets, *Tracts for the Times*, reasserting the Church of England's Catholic heritage. The initial protest of the scholars who launched this movement – John Keble, J. H. Newman and E. B. Pusey – was against the danger that Parliament would take it upon itself to reform abuses in the church without regard to the sacred status of the bishops as successors to the apostles and of the priests as their ordained assistants. Many of those who responded to this call had already undergone an Evangelical conversion and the new emphasis on the Catholic structure of the church seemed no more than the proper completion of the old emphasis on the converted individual. But gradually the movement became a comprehensive alternative to Evangelicalism and in particular to Calvinism. When Keble had retreated from controversy to be a model parish priest in the countryside, and when Newman had left the Church of England because the logic of his own spiritual development seemed to point in the direction of the validity of the Roman Catholic development in the church's history, the leadership of the movement was left to Pusey. He once defined the holiness being sought in six points – 'high thoughts' of baptism and of the eucharist; bishops as 'God's ordinance'; 'the visible Church as the body where we are made and continue to be members of Christ'; the Catholic customs such as daily public prayers, fasts and festivals; 'the visible part of devotion'; and 'reference to the ancient Church, instead of the Reformation, as the ultimate expounder of the meaning of our Church'. Pusey encouraged the revival of orders of monks and nuns and the interpretation of the Bible in the light provided by the ecumenical councils and by fathers of the church such as Athanasius and Augustine. Churches influenced by this movement looked much more like medieval churches. If they were new their architecture was in style medieval or 'Gothic'; and if they were old, they were restored to what was thought to have been their medieval condition. Old or new churches often now had a stone altar at the end, rich vestments for the priest, an organ and surpliced choir, candles and stained glass windows. Confessions of sins were made in private to priests and 'retreats' or conferences deepened spiritual life. The medieval gatherings of representatives of the clergy known as the Convocations of Canterbury and York were revived in 1855–61; they had not met for business for more than a century, but the fact of their meeting encouraged the election of a House of Laymen (without powers) in 1886. This timid church was regaining its sense of identity, if necessary against the state. Above all, the eucharist was restored as the main act of worship. The Book of Common Prayer already provided scripture lessons for every Sunday and saint's day; and these were now used.

The high church and Puritan elements during the sixteenth and seventeenth centuries, and the later Evangelical and Anglo-Catholic movements, often seemed at total variance with each other theologically, but in practice their adherents were held together not only by their common quest for a holiness inspired by the Bible but also by their common acceptance of office or membership in the nationally established Church of England. It was once said that this church possessed a Catholic Prayer Book, Calvinist articles of belief and an Arminian (or middle-of-the-road) clergy. At least the little joke was a reminder of the church's comprehensiveness, a deliberate policy since the days of Elizabeth I. This policy was reaffirmed during the Victorian age by a series of decisions by Parliament and the Judicial Committee of the Privy Council – which still effectively exercised the supremacy secured by Henry VIII for the crown. Probably most active members of the Victorian church of England were, in one sense or another, Evangelicals, but one of the decisions taken by the state was not to maintain the imprisonment of Anglo-Catholic 'ritualists' which Disraeli had foolishly tried while prime minister; and Evangelicals under Queen Victoria had to accept this decision, just as the Puritans under Elizabeth I had been compelled to accept that queen's insistence on the preservation of Catholic elements in the Prayer Book.

So Catholic and Protestant elements were permanently, if uneasily, combined. Nor was this the total of the diversity within the Church of England.

Orthodox and liberal

Part of the history of the Church of England is the transition from an insistence on orthodoxy to an insistence on freedom in the expression of Christian doctrines. For long it was said – or silently assumed – that there was no need of a separate 'confession of faith' (to set alongside the great Lutheran and Calvinist confessions or the decrees of the Roman Catholic Council of Trent) because the Church of England simply believed what Bible-based and Catholic Christians had always believed. But more recently the approach has often been quite different. It has been argued – or assumed – that no 'confession of faith' could command sufficient agreement in this free church. Even a revision of the Thirty-nine Articles to reflect the changes in theology since Tudor times would be too difficult to be worth attempting. It is a significant change, from the position that an Anglican 'confession' is unnecessary to the position that it is impossible.

In Anglo-Saxon and medieval England there was very little interest in theological speculation which might lead to charges of heresy, although the universities when they emerged harboured some independent and daring scholars. At the Reformation there was acute controversy about the nature of the church, ending in the deaths of both Protestants and Roman Catholics executed in their hundreds for a combination of heresy and treason. But those who established the Church of England on its new foundation were anxious to assert their entire acceptance of the scriptures and of the 'fundamental' doctrines of the Catholic church. The new Prayer Book ordered the public reading of the Old and New Testaments every morning and evening and the recital of one of the ancient creeds at almost every service. Indeed, the accusation against the papacy was that it had added its own arrogant claims, accompanied by superstitious medieval doctrines, to this older body of teaching which constituted Christian orthodoxy. In doctrine the Church of England's attitude seemed to be 'the older the better' and its theologians repeatedly stressed their acceptance of the 'rule of faith' to be found in second-century writers such as Irenaeus or Tertullian. Such an attitude could suggest that this church was a Western version of Eastern Orthodoxy, but even more conservative. And to this day the Church of England has maintained its official loyalty to the scriptures, creeds and oldest traditions. Most of the clergy and regular churchgoers have probably always been content with a conservative faith, particularly as voiced in familiar hymns. One hymn-writer, Bishop Thomas Ken, expressed it before his death in 1711: 'I live and die in the holy catholic and apostolic faith, professed by the whole church before the disunion of east and west. More particularly, I die in the communion of the Church of England as it stands distinguished from all papal and puritan innovations, and as it adheres to the doctrine of the cross.'

However, the comprehensiveness of the Church of England has not only included those such as the Puritans or Evangelicals who wanted to add a new fire of personal conviction to the old faith. This church has also mothered and embraced many liberals. They belong to the tradition which first made a major impact on Western Catholicism in the Renaissance of the fifteenth and sixteenth centuries. Then scholarship revived with the wider knowledge of Greek and the spread of printing. Laymen asserted a freedom against the clergy, and there was in the air a new spirit of confidence in the powers of the human mind. The Renaissance never made a similar impact on Eastern Orthodoxy, then preoccupied by the struggle against Islam and devastated by the capture of Constantinople by the Turks in 1453.

The heirs of the Renaissance have done more than merely recover accurate knowledge of the scriptures and of the ancient traditions. They have in various ways questioned or rejected the authority of conventions in theology. This element in the church has been called 'liberal' because it has consistently pleaded for freedom in the interpretation of orthodoxy – freedom for the individual to appeal to reasoning from public facts or private experience. It has also been called 'modernist' because it has always advocated the updating of religious teaching in the light of new knowledge and experience, particularly in order that the essential truths in orthodoxy may be more appreciated by the laity living in the midst of the world which is 'modern'. And although the Church of England has never officially abandoned the orthodoxy on which it insisted in the sixteenth and seventeenth centuries, it has often encouraged the development of doctrine by the reinterpretation of orthodoxy. In practice there has been a liberty for experiments in modernisation which could be matched in none of the other fundamentally conservative churches largely administered by bishops and frequently reciting the Apostles' and Nicene Creeds. It is inadequate to say, as the constitution of the Church of Ireland said in 1870, that Anglicanism simply holds 'the faith of Christ as professed by the Church' and rejects all innovations 'whereby the Primitive Faith hath from time to time been defaced or overlaid'.

During the sixteenth century some influential teachers imitated the example set by Erasmus, the contemporary of Luther who had devoted himself to honest scholarship and had (gently) opposed all forms of enthusiasm. A Dutchman, he had spent some time in England. Richard Hooker, in his *Laws of Ecclesiastical Polity*, defended the Elizabethan settlement of religion against those Puritans who wanted the Reformation to be completed by the total acceptance of Calvinism. He argued that the Bible was never intended to provide a detailed pattern for church life, but that much could be left to the developments of history as approved by the authorities of the nation concerned. For example, it was theologically legitimate for England to accept a Prayer Book ordering the use of services adapted from the worship of the medieval church in accordance with the Act of Uniformity passed by parliament; and it was excellent that this Prayer Book encouraged dignity and beauty in speech and music. A high value was placed on laws which expressed and protected a whole national culture. Among the laymen of the Church of England thus established was William Shakespeare. Among its priests were John Donne and George Herbert, poets who brought a rich culture to the celebration of the divine love. Among its mystics were Henry Vaughan and Thomas Traherne, who eloquently found God in nature. For such men, religion was as large as life.

During the seventeenth century the Arminian movement developed this breadth of outlook. King Charles I patronised it. When Calvinist orthodoxy, which condemned it, had spent its force (after cutting off the king's head) many thoughtful Englishmen turned with relief to quieter, more tolerant, versions of Christianity. There was a movement of Christian Platonism, the contemplation of God in his eternal truth. There was a welcome to the rise of science; many of the founders of the Royal Society were clergymen. There was a stress on morality as prudence pleasing to God as well as to man. When in the eighteenth century the deists asserted that the truth about God was his remoteness from human affairs which ought to be conducted in accordance with secular common sense, defenders of the Church of England such as Bishop Joseph Butler attempted to defend its adherence to a more biblical view of God on rational grounds. In his *Alliance of Church and State* (1736) William Warburton defended the privileges of the Church of England on the ground that of all the English churches it was the most rational. In the nineteenth century the stress on integrity and kindness in personal relations to be found in the novels of Jane Austen was probably typical of the religion of most of the laity, and the mid-century theologian F. D. Maurice preached God's fatherhood and mankind's brotherhood, transcending differences of religious opinion and even class divisions (for he was a cautious kind of Christian socialist). To Maurice, 'liberalism' was repugnant like every other 'ism' or system of opinions held by an ecclesiastical party. As his authority he appealed simply to the Bible and to the Book of Common Prayer. But he had his own definite interpretation of the scriptures and the sacraments. To him, they were essentially celebrations of human unity under God. He addressed the laity.

At every stage of its history since the rejection of papal supremacy the Church of England has been under lay supremacy, whether royal or parliamentary. Indeed, under Henry VIII, Elizabeth I, James I and Charles I its most distinctive doctrine seemed to be the duty of obedience to the crown based on the doctrine that kings had a 'divine right'. Some of its finest clergy, led by the archbishop of Canterbury, became 'non-jurors' by refusing to swear allegiance to new monarchs when parliament had deposed James II. (One of them, Bishop Ken, thought that 'the doctrine of the cross' included the imitation of Christ's example of non-resistance to the state.) For much of the eighteenth century the Established Church was firmly controlled by the Whigs, the political party which then controlled parliament, although most of its clergy were high churchmen and Tories. In Victorian England this stress on the nation, and on the laity ruling it, was still the chief characteristic of the Church of England. It meant that the clergy seemed to be identified with the landowners and the owners of the factories despite many efforts to reach and serve 'the poor'. But a more positive result of this patriotic and lay character of the national church was a sympathy with current educated thought. The minds of the leading clergy and laity were shaped by the same schools and universities. When seminaries for the professional training of future priests developed, they were subsidiary to the universities.

Liberalisation led in 1865 to the Clerical Subscription Act, making it clear that clergymen were no longer required to assent to the literal sense of each and every one of the Thirty-nine Articles; and it could result in liberal opinions among men who were, or would become, bishops. For example, Charles Gore's contribution to a volume of essays, *Lux Mundi* (1889), startled conservatives because here was a trusted spokesman of Anglo-Catholicism (a future bishop and already the principal of Pusey House, Oxford) admitting that there were limits to what Jesus knew and that the Bible was not all infallibly true – admissions which would also have horrified the fathers of the church. That was liberalism in what Gore maintained were the 'outlying departments of theology'. Archbishop William Temple went further in expressing dissatisfaction with the fathers; he once described the council of Chalcedon as the confession of the 'bankruptcy' of Greek patristic theology. But such men retained most of the earlier confidence that orthodoxy would stand up. Even Temple, more liberal than Gore in his day, was later to appear remarkably conventional. As the twentieth century brought much more revolutionary change, and as the old English alliance of church and state disintegrated under the pressures of science, industrialisation and secularisation, a more militant group arose – the English modernists, who concentrated on the frank acceptance of the truths of science including the scholarly criticism of the Bible. The church seemed to have much to learn and the 'latitude' or freedom which had been demanded from the seventeenth century onwards now included the liberty to reject (or at any rate to be agnostic about) many or all of the miracles recorded in the Bible. The call was to return to the simple message and example of the 'Jesus of history', abandoning the complexities of later Catholic or Protestant theology. In response to this modernist challenge an Archbishops' Commission on Christian Doctrine was set up to study the diversity now within the Church of England's theological comprehensiveness and to seek unity. William Temple became its chairman. Its report, published in 1938, accepted both the Anglo-Catholic emphasis on the sacraments and the liberal stress on intellectual freedom.

However, 'modernism' – a movement closely similar to 'Liberal Protestantism' in Germany – declined when the horrors of the two

world wars taught a lesson not to be found in the modernists' books.
To be saved from rampant evil, humanity needed more than sound
scholarship and a belief in the goodness of God and of man. It needed
a transcendent, active, judging and saving God. The movement
known as 'biblical theology' or 'neo-orthodoxy' stressed that this
gospel of God gave a unity to the diverse books of the Bible – and put
a backbone into the church. The wars, among many other consequences, killed the optimism of the modernists, but something new
was born: Christian believers identifying themselves as a minority.
Since Anglo-Saxon times English Christianity had been supported, or
at least officially 'established', by the state and the surrounding
society – an attitude dramatised by the coronations of monarchs
continuously since Edgar in 973. Now the Christian minority was
becoming self-conscious and defiant, often finding its weapons in a
conservative theological armoury. But part of the problem was that
there was an unprecedented amount of confusion about the right
shape and message of the Church of England.

Since the second world war this church has not ceased to be in
ferment. Like many others around the world, it has seen a revision of
its 'Catholic' practices. Its worship has become dominated by a more
corporate understanding of the eucharist as the 'Parish Communion',
a service often using the modern English of the Alternative Service
Book (1980), and the regular private confession of sins to a priest has
dwindled. The spiritual energy has come mostly from the Evangelical
movement. This has flourished by being clear and decisive in a time of
confusion but it has largely abandoned both the Calvinism of the
earlier period and the fundamentalism of the Victorians' attempt to
defend every word in the Bible as being equally authoritative. The
greatest controversies have resulted from the intellectual challenges
which have come from the radical heirs of the modernists, insisting
that all past statements of Christianity were conditioned by the
culture of a society which has now disappeared. In 1963 a small book,
Honest to God by John Robinson, then bishop of Woolwich, boldly
questioned the adequacy of traditional ideas or images in the description of God. Later books by other theologians firmly rejected the
validity of the formula of the council of Chalcedon in the description
of Christ. The virgin birth and physical resurrection of Christ were
quite widely regarded as mythical, and in the 1980s the bishop of
Durham, David Jenkins, attacked these doctrines with a crude
vigour. Many openly abandoned the traditional claim that Christian
faith was 'necessary to salvation', stimulated by the presence in
England of some three million adherents of other religions such as

Muslims, Hindus and Sikhs. A few of the clergy (such as Don Cupitt, a lecturer in Cambridge) also abandoned any belief that there was a transcendent God able to save anyone. They were extremists – but the 1976 report of the Doctrine Commission on *Christian Believing*, together with its sequel *Believing in the Church*, showed that many beliefs or whole styles of believing previously condemned as unorthodox were held by members and teachers of the church with impunity. So did the 1986 statement of the House of Bishops on *The Nature of Christian Belief*, although the bishops also declared that corporately the church still 'upholds' the traditional beliefs. There was also a ferment of fresh thinking and controversy about ethical questions such as abortion, artificial conception and contraception, divorce, homosexuality or the legitimacy of deterrence by nuclear weapons. Despite the continuance of a stout traditionalism, the theme emerged that the only truly Christian morality was to do the loving thing in a given situation. And what was 'loving' might be what dismayed conservatives.

In previous generations those who were radical in theology or ethics would still have been largely content to use the Book of Common Prayer, but now there was a widespread move, acceptable to many whose beliefs remained conservative, away from uniformity in worship. In addition to the use of the official alternative to the Prayer Book, many groups met in homes or workplaces, not churches, and their atmosphere might be either far more conservative or far more radical than the official norm. In church services friendliness and warmth, which might include the exuberance of a charismatic joy, were prized above the old virtues of decency and order. In previous generations the authority of the state would also have held together the loyal sons of the Church of England, and bishops still sat happily alongside 'temporal' peers in the House of Lords. But now the democratic spirit of the times was acknowledged as representatives of the parish clergy and laity debated all matters they chose in synods. The General Synod secured the right to control worship and doctrine and the role of the prime minister in the selection of bishops was drastically reduced. Most members of the General Synod wanted reunion with Methodism and with the United Reformed Church, and the ordination of women as priests – but such moves were opposed with great determination by conservatives, particularly by those who were keen to be reconciled to Rome.

All these tensions added to the stresses, and there were many prophecies that Catholics and Evangelicals, orthodox and liberals, would not be willing to be fellow members of one church for much longer. But by the middle of the 1980s no expansion of comprehensiveness had proved fatal and no disruption had proved final. The traditional structures of the Church of England – most prominently, the places given to bishops and creeds – were still holding firm. Liberalism in its many manifestations had grown far beyond any liberty thought desirable in the sixteenth or seventeenth century. But it had so far been contained by a feeling of humility and tentativeness in its relationship with the convictions of orthodoxy – or at least by the agreement to worship with the orthodox using forms acceptable to them. And conservatives had so far not been so outraged or dismayed by the tolerance of radicalism as to leave the Church of England in large numbers. They had grown to accept a comprehensiveness which included Catholic and Protestant elements. They had been reluctantly willing to extend this principle (or was it the lack of principle?) to cover what in the old days would have been called heresy.

Inside this situation, if one shared the persevering loyalty of the active members of the Church of England, one could be impressed by the mixture of the willingness to debate and experiment and the determination to stay together. But the cold statistics of church membership, and of participation in the sacraments, were discouraging. To observers outside the situation, including Anglicans outside England, it could appear to be a scene of confusion and decline, reflecting similar changes in the mood of the English people and in their position among other nations. At least it could be agreed that in England church and state now resembled each other in *not* being a model to the world. Just as Western Catholicism had been reshaped around the Roman papacy after the collapse of the Roman empire, so Anglicanism would have to be reshaped after the end of the British empire. The question was: around what?[3]

The end of Englishness

The international expansion which created the Anglican communion largely followed the growth of the British empire, but it survived that empire's dissolution. The geographical spread brought out the tensions in Anglicanism more strongly, in lands where the authority of crown and Parliament was remote or non-existent; for the rival religious movements were no longer held together by the English state exercising its supremacy over the national church. Later, as the control exercised by London or New York through missionaries also weakened, it often seemed that it was an unanswerable question:

What did hold Anglicans together, apart from the force of habit? But its expansion into the world also gave this denomination more opportunities than ever before. Anglicanism became more vigorous in North America or in Africa than in England. It shared in the enrichment of the spiritual expansion of Christianity to include all the continents. It began to make its contribution to the emergence of a Catholicism which would be truly universal, an Evangelicalism which would present the whole gospel to the whole world, and an understanding of Christ which would at last begin to see his illuminating power as the light of the world. It was a development never contemplated by the men and the queen who had shaped the Church of England in Tudor times – but in keeping with their basic conviction that Christ and culture need not be at enmity.

The Preface to the Book of Common Prayer in its 1662 edition noted that a service for 'the ministration of Baptism to such as are of riper years, and able to answer for themselves' had also been added. It was needed partly because many had not been baptised as infants under the Cromwellian Commonwealth; and 'the growth of Anabaptism, through the licentiousness of the late times crept in amongst us', was lamented. But the service 'may be always useful for the baptising of natives in our plantations, and others converted to the faith'. So already under Charles II the leaders of the Church of England had been made aware that there would be religious consequences of the growth of the British empire. However, for many years no great attention was paid to the possibility that radically new forms of church life would be needed when the faith and order of the Church of England had been transplanted.

It was at first taken for granted that wherever Englishmen went for government, trade or settlement, their Prayer Book would be taken and worship held according to its provisions. Since the beginning of the thirteenth century Wales had been a part of the province of Canterbury and in the sixteenth century it accepted the new religious arrangements with little protest, but the establishment of the Church of England among the Welsh became increasingly identified with English colonialism – with the result that during the nineteenth century the majority of the population became nonconformist. In Ireland, too, the various Acts of Parliament reforming the church were applied with little trouble, but Englishmen were appointed to enjoy the revenues of the leading positions, the Book of Common Prayer was not translated into Irish and in 1801 the Church of Ireland was formally united with the Church of England, a union which lasted until its disestablishment in 1871. In reaction to this colonialism the majority of the population became definitely Roman Catholic during the seventeenth century. In Scotland the English influence was never allowed to become so strong, but the reintroduction of bishops in 1618 and the imposition of a Prayer Book in 1637 were due mainly to the initiatives of kings who had become essentially English. They were regarded as instruments of English control. Restored under Charles II, bishops and Anglican prayers were swept away in 1690, only a small minority of Scots remaining 'Episcopalians'.

The same pattern of Englishness may be seen in the Anglican aspect of the colonial expansion of England overseas. There was a chaplain from the Church of England on board when Sir Francis Drake circumnavigated the globe; another arrived in America with the first colonists who founded Virginia in 1607, and the Church of England remained 'established' in that colony until 1786; the East India Company included Anglican worship among the opportunities which it offered to those who traded in its service; and Richard Johnson was the humiliated pastor of the first convicts transported to Australia in 1788. But all these clergy and their congregations, in any part of the world, were left under the jurisdiction of the bishop of London until the consecration of Samuel Seabury as the first American bishop in Scotland in 1784, the English bishops having felt themselves unable to act despite the achievement of political independence by the American colonies. It is not surprising that the religious life of the American colonists was, on the whole, marked either by the strict Calvinism which had inspired the settlement of New England in defiance of the bishops and Prayer Book or by the later and more widespread cool religion of most of the founders of the American Republic who viewed God merely as the 'Author of Nature'. In 1800 there were only about twelve thousand Anglican communicants in the whole of the Americas. It was not until 1813 that official provision was made for entry into India of Englishmen going out for the purpose of 'enlightening and reforming' Indians. A bishop of Calcutta was then appointed to supervise the chaplains and (hopefully) to influence the missionaries. Previously it had been assumed that the English were in India to trade, not to govern or to enlighten. Although the East India Company had given some support to German Lutheran missionaries, the predominant motive had been a fear of offending the religious feelings of Hindus or Muslims while their country was being exploited.

The Society for Promoting Christian Knowledge (SPCK), founded in 1699, supplied libraries and schools for the American colonies as well as for English parishes, and the Society for Propagating the

Gospel in Foreign Parts (SPG), founded in 1703, concentrated on helping to finance 'an orthodox clergy in America'. But it was not until the nineteenth century that the Church of England developed anything like a worldwide vision. Even then, evangelism overseas was left to voluntary societies, each with its distinctive ethos. The SPG was now chiefly concerned to send missionaries out to support bishops. The Church Missionary Society, founded in 1799, was Evangelical – more eager to take on pioneering work, less eager to please bishops. The South American Missionary Society, founded in 1844, was so Evangelical that it had no inhibitions about converting Roman Catholics, and the Bible Churchmen's Missionary Society broke off from the CMS in 1922 because the latter was too liberal. The Evangelically minded Colonial and Continental Church Society (with various origins back to 1823) specialised in work in Canada and Australia. The Catholic revival developed its missionary outreach around the Melanesian Mission (1849) and the Universities' Mission to Central Africa (1858) as well as the SPG. Some missionary leaders saw the need to be more flexible (among them Henry Venn of the CMS), but on the whole these missionary societies kept control in their own hands and used 'natives' mainly as assistants.

In contrast with that pattern, the Protestant Episcopal Church in the USA formed its Board of Missions in 1835 and accepted responsibility for mission as a church, not leaving it to voluntary societies. The 1830s were a time when its confidence in its own future, feeble for many years after the trauma of independence in the 1780s, was at last firm. (The General Theological Seminary, New York, had been founded in 1817 by the first really impressive bishop of New York, John Henry Hobart. The more Evangelical Virginia Theological Seminary followed under the impetus of the equally energetic bishop Richard Moore.) It was impressive that, unlike the Baptists or Methodists, the Episcopal Church was not permanently split by the civil war of the 1860s – although one bishop, Leonidas Polk, fought as a general in the army of the southern states. The Episcopalians worked out the idea of the 'missionary district' or subsidised diocese whose bishop could sit in its own House of Bishops. The concentration, specially on the Catholic wing of the church, was an expansion on the swiftly moving frontiers in America itself, but mainly Evangelical missionaries often laid significant foundations for church life in China, Japan, the Philippines, India and the African diocese of Liberia and established a presence in South America. However, it took many years to reach the stage when it seemed right to coordinate this work with that of any English missionaries in the area and further years before leadership was handed over irrevocably to the local Christians. Meanwhile the Church of England had the greater opportunity because of its position as the established church of the 'mother country' of the very widely spread British empire.

But what was to be the status and constitution of a colonial church, if it was not to be a part of the 'established' Church of England? What message was it to preach, if it was not able to reproduce the complete symphony of the accents of the Church of England? And what lessons could it learn from North America?

The political rebellion of the American colonists did not immediately create any great difficulties in the redefinition of Anglicanism. The remoteness of the bishop of London from the colonies had contributed to a situation in which the Prayer Book was used by congregations which for the most part appointed and paid their clergy and did not expect from them any conspicuous leadership in spiritual or social matters. It seemed no great change that representatives of such congregations should appoint their own bishops and even the Parliament in Westminster soon accepted it. Church life continued to be conservative and gentlemanly in tone when in 1784–85 the 'Protestant Episcopal Church in the USA' was constituted as an autonomous body or 'province'; and so it remained for about a hundred years. In Canada the creation of new Anglican dioceses was at first the work of 'Loyalists' emigrating north from the rebellious colonies. For a time bishops could still be appointed by the crown and religious innovations were avoided; and it remained 'the Church of England in Canada' until 1955. But the numerical growth of the American and Canadian peoples inevitably increased the size and self-confidence of those Anglican congregations and dioceses and interest grew in the question: What was Anglicanism, now that the 'divine right' of English kings was so obviously no longer its most characteristic doctrine?

In 1865 the bishops in the eastern half of Canada asked for a conference of all the Anglican bishops in the world. The suggestion echoed a plea for a 'Pan-Anglican Synod' made by an American, Bishop Hopkins of Vermont, as early as 1851 but it caused some surprise and suspicion in England. It could not now be brushed aside because, as the Canadians pointed out, a doctrinal crisis had arisen in South Africa. One of the leading missionaries there, Bishop Robert Gray of Cape Town, was an adherent of the Oxford or Tractarian movement. Another, the more liberal Bishop J. W. Colenso of Natal, accepted some of the conclusions of the new German criticism of the Old Testament as literature and history. He felt under no obligation

to teach the Zulus that the whole Bible was the infallible word of
God. For this offence he was deposed from his bishopric by Bishop
Gray – who was overruled as having exceeded his powers when
Colenso appealed to the Judicial Committee of the Privy Council
(since both bishops had been appointed by the crown). Gray persisted in wanting to model Anglicanism in South Africa on the
disestablished but clearly orthodox Episcopal Church in the USA,
rather than on the Church of England. This crisis, combining theology with legal problems, resulted in the holding of the first of the
Lambeth Conferences in 1867. Seventy-six bishops met at the invitation of a worried archbishop of Canterbury, talked together and
decided nothing. The significance of this meeting was that at length
an organisation had begun to emerge which was an organisation
alternative to the crown in the never easy job of holding Anglicans
together.

Since 1867 the reduction of the Englishness of the Anglican
Communion, and its growth in spread and numbers, have been
continuous processes. Three years before the first Lambeth Conference an African, Samuel Crowther, had been consecrated as bishop
on the Niger. The experiment was regarded as a failure when
Crowther was an old man and an impatient new generation of English
missionaries had arrived in Nigeria – but, like the ecclesiastical
independence of the Americans in the 1780s, it dramatically set a
pattern of local leadership. This has been increasingly followed by
Anglicanism around the world. The church in Wales, separated from
the Church of England and disestablished in 1920, has achieved its
own spiritual life by being more Welsh. The experiences of the
Church of Ireland and of the Scottish Episcopal Church have been
similar, although the former has been a dwindling body and the latter
has remained small. The Episcopal Church in the USA and the
Anglican Church in Canada have displayed the pioneering vitality
which has often characterised Christianity in North America, for
example in the ordination of women priests. The Anglican Church of
Australia has faced greater problems, partly because its roots in that
vast island are not so deep. It achieved its own constitution as 'the
Church of England in Australia' no earlier than 1961 although the
first bishop had arrived from England in 1836; and twenty more years
were to pass before it was officially named 'the Anglican Church'. But
the Church of the Province of New Zealand, commonly called the
Anglican Church there, has been self-governing since 1857. The
Church of the Province of South Africa, with its constitution now
clarified, has combined Gray's sacramentalism with Colenso's social

concern and has become famous for its leadership in the struggle against apartheid.

The emphasis on local leadership has also been seen in the policy of associating dioceses in 'provinces'. That form of association can be of limited importance, as it is in England or the USA. But it can be very significant when the province coincides with a political, ethnic or cultural entity. Stable, if numerically small, Anglican provinces have been formed outside the historic areas of English settlement – in Brazil (1965), Burma (1970), the Indian Ocean (1973), Japan (1887), the Middle East (1976), Melanesia (1975), Papua New Guinea (1977), the Southern Cone of America (1982) and the West Indies (1883). Anglicanism is also represented in Sri Lanka, Cuba, Korea and South-east Asia, although it has not yet proved possible to incorporate such dioceses into provinces. But the greatest recent success of Anglicanism, apart from its North American growth, has been its rooting and growth in Africa. This has given birth to seven provinces – the French-speaking Burundi, Rwanda and Zaire (1980), Central Africa (1955), Kenya (1970), Nigeria (1979), the Sudan (1974), Tanzania (1970) and Uganda (1980).

What is Anglicanism?

Eleven Lambeth Conferences of bishops have offered their wisdom about the doctrinal basis of the Anglicanism which is now dispersed in twenty-seven provinces and almost 450 dioceses throughout the world. In addition some Anglican Congresses including clergy and laity have met for mutual encouragement and since 1971 the much smaller Anglican Consultative Council has provided another focus and forum. In the 1970s and 1980s fresh material, showing substantial agreements with Christians of other traditions, emerged out of bilateral dialogues held internationally between Anglicans and Roman Catholics, Eastern Orthodox, the Lutherans and the Reformed.

Anglicans are sometimes known by the name 'Episcopal Church', most conspicuously in the USA. This suggests the truths that they agree to recognise the oversight (in Greek *episkope*) of bishops and will not unite with churches which are not willing to have bishops consecrated in the 'historic' or 'apostolic' succession. Yet Anglicanism cannot be defined at all fully in terms of episcopacy taken in isolation. Although a harder line has been maintained by many Anglo-Catholics in the past, during recent negotiations about church unity it has been made clear that Anglicans do not insist on the theory to which non-episcopalians most object: namely, the making of episcopacy the essential ministry because Christ entrusted the priest-hood to the apostles, who transmitted it to the first bishops, who shared it with priests ordained by them and with their own successors up to the present. Indeed, most Anglicans who have considered the matter would say that such historical evidence as is available does not support such an interpretation of the first century. They would add that the experience of the work of ministers not ordained by bishops does not suggest that this work is ineffective or invalid. The value of bishops is seen much more in their positive work – in their pastoral care, spiritual leadership and guardianship of the essentials of ortho-doxy (however defined). But it cannot be said truthfully that Angli-cans have worked out a perfect answer to the practical question, 'What does a bishop do?' In England the diocese is large and elaborately organised, the diocesan bishop usually being supported by assistant bishops, a substantial staff and a magnificent cathedral; but most Anglican dioceses are far more informal, with far smaller numbers of clergy and regular communicants. In some provinces a bishop may be 'translated' from one diocese to another – but not so elsewhere. In England a diocesan bishop is appointed by the crown after an advisory process – but only in England. An archbishop or 'presiding bishop' may or may not have a diocese of his own, and this may or may not always be the same diocese. Within the diocese, the diocesan bishop may be somewhat withdrawn, perhaps because he is a scholar, perhaps because (in England) he is a member of the House of Lords. In other dioceses he is much closer to the clergy and people, often travelling long distances in order to share their often hard lives. In some dioceses the bishop controls the clergy closely and is the effective inspirer and leader in almost everything that happens above the humblest level of church life. In other dioceses he has to work far more democratically and the main power is kept in the hands of the lay 'vestries' in the local churches. Usually the bishop is expected to consult representatives of the clergy and laity in important matters. 'Synodical government' has increasingly been the pattern since the Americans adopted it in the 1780s and the English in New Zealand in the 1840s; the General Synod of the Church of England dates from 1970. But the relationship with the more personal style of episcopal government has not yet been clarified. It has become the practice in talks with other churches to emphasise that neither the Anglican communion nor a particular Anglican province provides the perfect model of episcopacy in action. That is a wise admission.

Part of the unity of the Anglican communion is to be seen in the
requirement of communion with the see of Canterbury. The Lambeth
Conference of 1978 spoke of 'the loyal relationship of each of the
churches to the Archbishop of Canterbury who is freely recognised as
the focus of unity'. The central place of the papacy in Roman
Catholicism offers a faint analogy. The comparison is not at all close,
since the archbishop of Canterbury claims no special powers in the
definition of doctrine and exercises no jurisdiction except in strictly
limited and almost entirely English spheres. But it may be agreed that
the Anglican communion does possess a theological and spiritual
character which is in some ways comparable with Roman Catholicism.

This character is moulded and sustained by its worship using the
Book of Common Prayer of 1662 or modern alternatives (such as the
American Book of Common Prayer of 1979) which in the main
remain close to that book's spirit. The attempt to reach uniformity
has long been abandoned; in 1897 the Lambeth Conference resolved
that 'liturgical uniformity should not be required as a necessity
throughout the Anglican Communion'. But the absence of uniformity does not mean the absence of identity. It strikes a visitor that the
Episcopal Church in the USA (for example) seems almost to court
controversy and to risk internal divisions by its willingness to espouse
the causes of minorities. Yet it is given a deep identity and a solid
strength by its flourishing tradition of liturgical worship. From Anglican worship, it has often been said (as by the Lambeth Conference of
1978), Anglican doctrine can be deduced. The Anglican theological
tradition combines the acceptance of the Old and New Testaments, of
the sacraments of baptism and the eucharist, and of the 'historic' (a
deliberately cool word) ministry of bishop, presbyter or priest and
deacon, with the acceptance of other knowledge, reason and experience as interpreted both by Christian tradition and by contemporary
science and scholarship. The worldwide dispersal of Anglicanism has
resulted in a greater awareness that the right answer to the question of
the Christian's authority is not simple. That authority, too, is 'dispersed' instead of being entirely concentrated in one infallible Bible
or one infallible teacher or group of teachers. Scripture, tradition and
reason are all considered as Anglicans look for authority when
struggling with questions. Here is a 'threefold cord'.

Different Anglicans understand these elements of authority differently and the tensions have shown up frequently in the process of
working out new Prayer Books. Not only are there disputes between
Anglican theologians and less noisy disagreements among the Angli-

can laity. Whole dioceses and provinces can differ from each other. Dioceses differ because they owe their foundations to different missionary enthusiasms; thus in Australia Anglican dioceses were unable to agree about the freedom to be allowed to each other with the result that the constitution of an Australian Church was under discussion from 1926 to 1961. Provinces differ because they face different challenges. Thus the Church of Ireland, or Anglicanism in South America, tends to be Evangelical in a predominantly Roman Catholic country, while in mainly Presbyterian Scotland, or amid the Dutch Reformed of South Africa, Anglicans are usually Catholic in emphasis. Since the USA is the most modern country on earth and one of the most mixed in ethnic origins, modernity bringing with it freedom and plurality in lifestyles is the challenge felt most keenly by American Episcopalians; while in more conservative societies Anglicans, too, are conservative. Such disagreements must be recognised. But it would not be true to say that Anglicans have failed to reach any agreement at all about the nature of the acknowledged authority which binds them together.

In 1886 the House of Bishops of the Protestant Episcopal Church in the USA, meeting in Chicago, accepted a suggestion which arose out of the passionate concern of a priest, William Reed Huntingdon, that in the bitter aftermath of the American civil war this church should come forward as 'the Church of the Reconciliation'; for Christian unity should be a model for national unity. The suggestion was that there should be a definition of the inherent parts of that sacred 'deposit' which was 'essential to the restoration of unity among the divided branches of Christendom'. The Chicago Quadrilateral insisted on '(1) the Holy Scriptures of the Old and New Testament as the revealed Word of God, (2) the Nicene Creed as the sufficient statement of the Christian Faith, (3) the two sacraments – Baptism and the Supper of Our Lord – ministered with unfailing use of Christ's words of institution and of the elements ordained by him, (4) the Historic Episcopate, locally adapted in the methods of its administration to the varying needs of the nations and peoples called of God into the unity of his Church'.

When the Lambeth Conference of 1888 made this the Lambeth Quadrilateral, it introduced two significant changes. The holy scriptures were said to 'contain all things necessary to salvation' (quoting the sixth of the Thirty-nine Articles) and to be 'the rule and ultimate standard of faith', but the simple description of them as 'the revealed Word of God' was not repeated; and the Apostles' Creed was added as 'the Baptismal Symbol' (thus unintentionally distancing Anglicanism from Eastern Orthodoxy). The Lambeth Conferences of 1920 and 1968 expanded the clause about bishops to take more account of ministers not ordained by them. Thus in 1920 the bishops paid a tribute to the 'rich elements of truth, liberty and life' in the 'great non-episcopal communions' but desired 'a ministry acknowledged by every part of the Church as possessing not only the inward call of the Spirit, but also the commission of Christ and the authority of the whole body'. They asked, 'May we not reasonably claim that the episcopate is the one means of providing such a ministry?' Many criticisms made by Anglican scholars would question, or at least refine, the description of the Nicene Creed as 'the sufficient statement of the Christian Faith'. But for a century the Chicago/Lambeth Quadrilateral has stood as an account of some indispensable elements in Anglicanism – and the modifications made in the wording have indicated the influence of those other elements which are specially valued by liberal-minded Anglicans. In 1982 the General Convention of the Episcopal Church in the USA endorsed an 'explication' of the Quadrilateral (printed in this book as the Appendix). It incorporates some of the key themes of recent theology into the pattern set out in 1886.

The theological situation resulting from this Anglican understanding of authority is often referred to as 'comprehensiveness'. The word can be attacked as implying many things including intellectual laziness among the clergy or control by laymen who are not really interested in theology. But the idea can be stated positively. It was so stated at the Lambeth Conference in 1968. 'Comprehensiveness,' the bishops said in one section of their report, 'demands agreement on fundamentals, while tolerating disagreement on matters in which Christians may differ without feeling the necessity of breaking communion. In the mind of an Anglican, comprehensiveness is not compromise. Nor is it to bargain one truth for another. It is not a sophisticated word for syncretism. Rather it implies that the apprehension of truth is a growing thing: we only gradually succeed in "knowing the truth". It has been the tradition of Anglicanism to contain within one body both Protestant and Catholic elements. But there is a continuing search for the whole truth in which all these elements will find complete reconciliation.'

It is often said that a church which has such a theological tradition lacks the cutting edge which only a simple faith can provide. To this charge, the sermon delivered by the present archbishop of Canterbury at his enthronement in 1980 was an Anglican reply. '"Speak out, condemn, denounce" is what is expected,' he said. 'But the throne of

Jesus is a mercy-seat. It stands firm against all the vileness of the world but it stands also for compassion. The way of Jesus means reverencing people whether they belong to our party or not. The strategy of Jesus means changing lives with love. That is a hard way and people tend to want it only in theory. The cry is "the Church must give a firm lead." Yes, it must – a firm lead against rigid thinking, a judging temper of mind, a disposition to oversimplify the difficult and complex problems. If the Church gives Jesus Christ's sort of lead it will not be popular. It may even be despised for failing to grasp the power which is offered to it in the confusions and fears of our contemporaries. But it will be a church not only close to the mind of Jesus; it will find itself constantly pushing back the frontiers of the possible.'

In what community can the truth of Christ, thus understood, be expressed? Here again, Anglicanism seems best understood as one contribution to growth into Christianity's futures. This appears to be the deepest interpretation of the Anglican experience whether one considers the human appearance of the church as one organisation among many or whether one looks at the church more theologically; whether one assesses the Anglican communion in the context of the social life of the different nations in which it works, or whether one views it in the context provided by the ecumenical movement with its dialogues between separated churches.

When an Inter-Anglican Theological and Doctrinal Commission first met in 1981, it was one of the occasions for experiencing the fact of social and cultural diversity in this international family of churches. It was reported that 'it quickly dawned on all of us that the Anglican Communion was far from being a monochrome affair. The Church of England had brought Christianity – and its own distinctive ways and style – to a wide variety of peoples and cultures. We ourselves, members of one rather small commission, came from South and North America, from Hong Kong, Ireland, Australia, and New Zealand, from Sri Lanka, the West Indies, and various sections of Africa – and, of course, from Britain. All of us shared – and in subtler and more pervasive ways than we were perhaps willing to admit – the theological, liturgical, and spiritual heritage of the Church of England. Yet to all of us it quickly became clear that, for the daughter churches of Canterbury, to be "Anglican" not only *could* no longer be, but in fact *was* no longer, a matter of being "English". In part, no doubt, this judgement did no more than record a natural consequence of the disappearance of the British empire. At a deeper level, though, it grew out of our recognition that the traditional Anglican understanding of the relations of Church and society and thus of the way in which the Church serves and represents the kingdom of God – is no longer viable in view of the changed situation of all churches, including the Church of England itself. In this way we were drawn to face openly the pluralism and variety which characterize our churches theologically as well as culturally: a pluralism and variety which the commission itself embodied.

'For if it is true that the situation of the Anglican Churches has radically changed, it is also true that their situations are very different. For some, the central problem was that of the cultural foreignness of Anglicanism – and indeed of Christianity – in a society with strong and mature religious traditions of its own. For others, the primary problem was that of the "establishment" style of Anglican theology and practice in settings where the burning issue was that of the economic and political oppression and degradation of the great majority of the population. For yet others, it was the issue of the disengagement of the Church from a culture and social order with which it had become all too thoroughly identified. And these different theological approaches, which had only this in common, that they were uniformly dissatisfied with the customary stance of Anglicanism on a wide range of issues having to do with the relation of church and society.'[4]

It is also true that the theological quest for Christian unity has shown how Anglicanism has become essentially a struggle to grasp a reality which in its fullness belongs to the futures. Anglicans have sometimes nursed the hope that their communion might be used as 'the bridge church', to bring about a reconciliation between Catholics, Orthodox and Protestants. At the height of the British empire the potential significance of Anglicanism sometimes seemed to have few limits and enough of this hopefulness survived in 1920 for the Lambeth Conference to issue an 'appeal to all Christian people'. It was a time of many hopes for reconciliation between the nations after the first world war. 'The vision that rises before us,' said all but four of the bishops, 'is that of a Church genuinely Catholic, loyal to all truth, and gathering into its fellowship all who profess and call themselves Christians, within whose visible unity all the treasures of faith and order, bequeathed as a heritage by the past to the present, shall be possessed in common and made serviceable to the whole Body of Christ'. The bishops then declared their willingness to sacrifice everything except the essentials for the sake of that wider unity, but it was commonly taken for granted by Anglicans that this worldwide communion now provided the nucleus of what was sometimes called 'the coming Great Church'; that around Anglicanism there would be 'the wider episcopal fellowship' leading into the greatness. Certainly many Anglican initiatives were taken in that optimistic spirit – by the Lambeth Conference itself, in England, the USA and elsewhere, and in the vital Anglican contributions to the early work on 'Faith and Order' which was adopted by the World Council of Churches. But outside the Indian subcontinent all negotiations for reunion following the 1920 appeal failed to come to fruition in the next sixty-five years. Ideas or schemes put forward, if they succeeded in appealing to non-Anglicans, alarmed one section or another of the Anglican family and resulted in voting which produced an inadequate majority. This pattern repeated itself so often that the conclusion was drawn that Anglicanism, being so deeply divided, was 'not unitable with'. Despite the brave words of 1920, and despite the enthusiasm of many of its leaders and members for processes such as the Anglican-Methodist unity scheme in England or the Consultation on Church Union in the United States, Anglicanism could not agree in practice on the terms of reunion. Too warm a welcome to non-episcopalians would offend Catholic Anglicans; yet too cold an insistence on episcopacy would offend Evangelical and liberal Anglicans. Too much generosity in response to unconventional theology would seem to compromise the orthodoxy of Anglicanism; yet too much stress on traditions would betray its liberalism. The success of Anglicanism in holding together Catholics and Protestants, orthodox and liberals, had inspired an ecumenical vision – for if Anglicans could bridge these gaps, why could not other Christians? But this success had barely concealed a continuing disunity which was bound to emerge once any change in the formula of unity was proposed. Thus Anglicanism's basic disunity now seemed to have become an obstacle to ecumenical progress. If this was the bridge church, 'no entry' signs could be detected at both ends. In the mid-1980s, the question was once again looking for an honest and realistic answer: What is to be the Anglican contribution to Christian unity?

A clue to the answer seems to be provided by the fact that Anglicanism does not claim to be the universally obligatory form of Christianity. Anglicans are seldom willing to 'proselytise' among fellow Christians. This church receives some recruits from other churches but it does not actively seek them. It has left the heartlands of Roman Catholicism, Lutheranism and Eastern Orthodoxy largely alone apart from its chaplaincy work using the English language. It has made no attempt to turn its communion with the Scandinavian churches, and with some indigenous groups deviating from Roman

Catholicism, into extensions of Anglicanism. It now has no branch in the Indian subcontinent, the Anglicans there having joined the Church of South India in 1947 and the Churches of North India and Pakistan in 1970. After the enforced withdrawal of Western missionaries, completed in 1950, political events meant the end of the 'Holy Catholic Church in China' – the name given to Chinese Anglicanism, which had been constituted an autonomous province in 1915. It was gradually submerged in the Protestant 'Three-Self Movement' and the China Christian Council, moving into a stage described as 'post-denominational'. The result is that Anglicanism as a denomination now scarcely exists in Asia.

In Latin America it is far from clear to everyone why Anglicanism should exist. Since the population is expected to increase ninefold within the twentieth century and since the Roman Catholic Church is supported by only about a tenth of the population in active membership (one reason being the very severe shortage of priests), the region can be regarded as wide open to every kind of Christian evangelism. It might be expected that Anglicanism would make a major contribution and it does seem to be true that its congregations are becoming more confident about their own mission and about their fellowship with other Anglicans. In a few areas the Anglican church is the only church known by converted 'Indians'. But on the whole, Anglicanism is not taken very seriously by other churches and is properly modest in its own claims. It has never been sure of its identity in a region where the Roman Catholic Church includes about eight tenths of the population in nominal membership and where about nine tenths of Protestantism originated in Pentecostal or fundamentalist versions of Christianity brought by missionaries from the USA. The problem is not only that conservative Catholics tend to regard Anglicans as Protestants and therefore as heretical. Nor is it only that conservative Protestants tend to regard them either as crypto-Catholics or as flagrant liberals. Nor is it only that by their very title – for which no substitute seems universally acceptable – Anglicans are associated with an England which has lost power, prestige and moral standing (while the alternative source of Anglican missionary work and theological training, the USA, is often hated). The fundamental problem was shrewdly stated in a report by an American sociologist, Dr Ivan Vallier, in 1962. He wrote: 'The question of Anglicanism's fit in the South American culture may be posed as follows. Are the English capacities to participate in subtle democracy, to compromise, to embrace empiricism, to provoke a humorous self-image, to handle things on one's own and to hold the old and new

in balance, congruent with the typical South American tendencies to
tolerate heavy-handed leaders, to view ideas as solutions in themselves, to stand one's ground and defend it with honour . . . right or
wrong, to glory in myth and non-empirical principles, to let things
take care of themselves, and to tolerate no middle ground, either
rejecting completely the old or standing completely aloof from the
new?' And similar problems surround tiny Anglican communities in
some other parts of the world.

It is significant that the Anglican communion, although it has been
served by a full-time 'executive officer' or 'secretary general' with a
small staff since the Lambeth Conference of 1958 authorised this
development, has not allowed the Lambeth Conference itself to
develop into a General Synod with the power to legislate. To do that,
this conference of bishops would have to acquire juridical powers
comparable with those of the Roman Catholic college of bishops
headed by the pope and seen at work in the Second Vatican Council
(1962–65), but despite some talk of the 'collegiality' of Anglican
bishops, no move has been made in that direction. Nor has it been
seriously proposed that representatives of the clergy and the laity
should be summoned, although that step would be necessary to fit the
Lambeth Conference into the general pattern of 'synodical' government in the Anglican Communion. Clergy and laity have been added
to bishops in the Anglican Consultative Council, as agreed at the
Lambeth Conference of 1968, but that body, in addition to being
excluded from power (as its very title emphasises), has been kept on a
small scale and a low budget. The contrast is striking with, for
example, the Lutheran World Federation – which has a staff of a
hundred in addition to the thousands employed in its worldwide relief
work. The Primates' Meetings have been a useful way for some
church leaders to keep in touch with each other and to identify
current issues; but despite some talk about the need for a 'tribunal',
these meetings have been too rushed and too modest to claim to be
more than meetings. A central training college (St Augustine's
College, Canterbury) and magazine (*Anglican World*) were launched
but not sustained. No large international conference has been held
since the Anglican Congress of 1963. And since the Lambeth Conference of 1978 it has been recognised that some Anglican provinces
would, and some would not, ordain women as priests. The conference was itself unable to do more than plead for mutual respect. And
the validity of the ordinations of the large numbers of women priests
in North America and elsewhere has not been acknowledged by all.
On the eve of the Lambeth Conference of 1988 it is a real question

whether all the provinces of the Anglican communion are fully in communion with each other.

So Anglicanism is still exploring its vocation and mission. But it has assets. It is equipped strongly for this exploration by its tradition of a balanced spirituality. 'The absolute heart of the English-Anglican tradition,' wrote Martin Thornton, 'is a constant attempt to synthesise these two poles: intellectual and affective, reason and emotion, corporate and personal, the head and the heart.'[5] The Anglican approach to theological problems does not avoid sharp controversies but has, on the whole, been marked by an agreement to appeal to tradition and to reason as well as to the Bible, and by a willingness to remain in communion even if there is still disagreement. Such international meetings as are held are, in this spirit, usually both lively and friendly. Although with a very patchy effectiveness, the Anglican provinces have recognised ideals of 'mutual responsibility and interdependence' since 1963 and of being 'partners in mission' since 1973. They have been willing to exchange manpower and encouragement, on however limited a scale, and have encouraged systematic intercession for each other. The growth of Anglicanism in some areas has been rapid, its persistence in other areas courageously obstinate.

It does not look like a church about to disappear, and one reason for the general failure of its reunion negotiations has been that many people are happy and proud to remain Anglicans. But this strange communion's origins are an inescapable part of its identity. Those origins include not only an Englishness which still to some extent limits it but also an English dream which forbids the erection of firm barriers around it. That is the dream of a united church ministering to a united people. Henry VIII, Elizabeth I, their Parliaments and their chosen bishops had no intention of founding one denomination among many. They had every intention of reforming the Catholic church in England so that it would embrace, and satisfy the consciences of, the whole of a Christian people. The language of the key Acts of Parliament, and of the Book of Common Prayer itself, makes this motivation abundantly clear, and it was worked out as a theological scheme (although this was never rigidly schematic) by scholars such as Richard Hooker. Now that Anglicanism has a role on a stage no narrower than the world, it seems probable that its vocation will not be fully obeyed, and its mission will not be fully discharged, until it has offered all that it could offer to the emergence of expressions of Christianity deeply rooted in all the world's regions and reaching the spiritual hungers of all the world's peoples. That would do for the world what the Church of England was meant to do for Tudor England. In other words, Anglicanism seems to have a history which will be fully understood only in the Christian futures. Some words written by Bishop Stephen Bayne in 1954 deserve to be remembered. They sum up a great deal of his influential teaching. 'The vocation of Anglicanism is, ultimately, to disappear. That is its vocation precisely because it does not believe in itself but it believes only in the Catholic Church of Christ; therefore it is for ever restless until it finds its place in that one body.'

In 1963 J. W. C. Wand, a great bishop of London, lectured to the Anglican Congress in Toronto. 'If I were asked to state in a single sentence the position of the Anglican Communion,' he said, 'I should say that it strives to give expression to the full teaching of the Bible as reflected in the age-long history of the Christian Church. This implies both faithfulness to the original foundation of the Church and a constant adaptation to changing circumstances.' The bishop went on to plead for 'a firm grasp of the principle of continuity which allows no essential break with the past or any departure from the lines laid down in our fundamental documents'. That was a warning which almost all Anglicans would echo when considering the limits to 'adaptation to changing circumstances'. But there is less agreement about what is 'essential' or 'fundamental' and Bishop Wand may be criticised as hinting at too much satisfaction with the way in which the Anglican communion 'strives'.

It seems that what Anglicans can offer to the Christian futures is something very unlike the uniformity which was attempted under the Tudor and Stuart monarchs of England. Anglicans have largely abandoned the Book of Common Prayer which was for long supported by every possible kind of legal and moral pressure in order to secure uniformity of worship. They have also abandoned their close alliance with a monarchical government or any other form of state power, apart from lingering remnants of the establishment of the Church of England – remnants which would probably be abandoned without much stress if there were to be a strong new vision of the church. Most Anglicans no longer feel committed to their sixteenth-century Articles of Religion, except in a most general way. Many do not even feel committed – even in a general way – to the English cultural tradition as a whole. There is no single theologian who has influenced Anglicanism as Aquinas has influenced Catholicism, or Calvin the Reformed churches, or Luther the Lutherans or John Wesley the Methodists. A comparison with the Eastern Orthodox shows that the 'fathers' of the church are more honoured than consulted by Anglicans. The scriptures, the creeds and the bishops are indeed prominent in daily practice, but these bonds of unity are subject to different interpretations. So Anglicans cannot persuade anyone that they have worked out a system to which all should submit. On the contrary, through many controversies it has become clear that Anglicanism is a spirit, not a system – and that it is a spirit which involves a willingness to recognise that no neat formula can contain the biblical and Christian fullness. For the futures, here is a small model which allows much diversity, theological and cultural, in order to welcome truth and reality, even at the price of being, or of appearing to be, untidy, confused and broken; and here is an experiment (often a failure) which is admirable precisely because, when at its best, it has never claimed to have reached all the answers.

A future archbishop of Canterbury, Michael Ramsey, wrote in 1936: 'While the Anglican Church is vindicated by its place in history, with a strikingly balanced witness to Gospel and Church and sound learning, its greater vindication lies in pointing through its own history to something of which it is a fragment. Its credentials are its incompleteness, with the tension and the travail in its soul. It is clumsy and untidy, it baffles neatness and logic. For it is sent not to commend itself as "the best type of Christianity", but by its very brokenness to point to the universal Church wherein all have died.'[6]

3

AMERICAN FUTURES

Across the Atlantic

There are, of course, two Americas. The USA (I reserve Canada for my last chapter) is so obviously the world's No. 1 nation – despite unease about Japan – that its inhabitants are usually known as 'the Americans'. With seven per cent of the world's population, they consume almost a quarter of the world's resources, as much as the entire developing world. And the other Americans, as we all know, are mostly worried not about keeping trim but about survival. In the 1980s there are more than 370 million Latin Americans, expected to be near 570 million in the year 2000. The average income is about a tenth of the US average and the average life expectancy is twelve years less. Writing amid the sordid agony of El Salvador's civil war, a local theologian observed about Latin America: 'the suffering of the present, not wonder, plays an active role in the process of understanding'.[1] And so the love of life is defiant, with death always near. One big reason why life often seems more colourful, more vibrant 'down south', is that life is usually much less sheltered by middle class securities, comforts and conventions than in most of the USA. The people are nearer to the soil, not hiding the raw emotions of despair, defiance and anger or the physical joys of survival and togetherness. They suffer and they celebrate with all the heart. The existence of God seems to be commonly taken for granted in Latin as well as in North America, but the question whether God *cares* is put by millions of very distressed people and it is one of the reasons why in comparison with North America the churches, where the clergy have traditionally preached a smooth doctrine of contentment under authority, have been poorly attended. A scholar in the USA has commented: 'Their question is not "How can we believe in God in the world of science?" but "How can we believe in a personal God in a world that denies our personhood?" '[2] That is a question which in Latin America has often been addressed to the Virgin Mother. And other immense differences have arisen from the contrast between the Protestant influence on the USA and this Catholic influence on Latin America which is epitomised in the cult of the Virgin. Catholicism, for long the sanctification (in the main) of a virtually feudal system, has recently been in the forefront of the struggle for 'liberation' in many Latin American countries – but it has been far less prominent in the history of the USA. To Thomas Jefferson it was 'monkish ignorance and superstition' being dispelled by 'the light of science'. Instead, the main tradition of the USA has been the 'American' creed as expounded by Jefferson – faith in the individual, in freedom and in equality; faith that the individual has the right to protest and the right to achieve. Because there are, of course, two Americas, perhaps the least that I ought to do when offering to analyse them is to do it in separate chapters.

But I have reached the conclusion that it does make sense to think of one truly 'American' Christianity. For here, in north and south, is a practical and popular religion. I offer a few thoughts organised around that single fact, which can perhaps be appreciated by a European who knows that his own continent has not recently been the scene of such popularity for religious things and people.

Latin American church life has always been practical, supplying the emotional needs of the people without too much regard to the caution of theologians. Under the feudal system, the people wanted to pray to the Virgin and the saints for supernatural help; and the priests provided the images. In more recent times, the people have been aroused to help themselves; and in a new generation the priests have assured them that God has inspired their liberating struggle. In the USA church life has always had the same practical bent. Protestant or Catholic, fundamentalist or liberal, ethnic or cosmopolitan, it has been about the happiness and success of the citizen and making the world, or at least the USA, a better place. In the Americas, north or south, religion has had to make itself useful to humanity – and in response humanity has been, on the whole, favourably inclined towards religion. In Latin America a Catholicism mixed with non-Christian survivals has been at the heart of the culture through four centuries, although only a minority has been regularly churchgoing. In the USA the churches have been more consistently democratic and have themselves become mightily popular. It is evident that its exodus across the Atlantic into the new world rejuvenated Christianity by undoing the work of the emperors Constantine and Charlemagne, who had made European church life an alliance of church and state based on power. Although strenuous and persistent attempts were made to turn the new world into a replica of Europe, it slowly became clear that American Christianity was going to be undisciplined by European standards – too superstitious or too revolutionary. Nowhere, not even in the midst of the devout Catholicism of Latin America or of Quebec, was a church to be established, supported and controlled by a state in a way that proved permanent. One result was the growth of denominations competing for popular support. However, this support has been forthcoming – and on a scale which astounds Europeans. In south and north alike the Americans – Catholics, Protestants and Pentecostals, Indians, blacks and whites, slaves and freemen – have often enjoyed their religion, believed its consolations, sung its songs and even loved its teachers. In the end, in both the Americas, Christianity has grown out of the commitment of people who have chosen – or, at least, have not been compelled to accept – one or other of its varied forms. No other basis for the churches was available. And this dependence on the public rather than the state has encouraged church leaders to take the side of the public. It has happened, in the end, even in Latin America. The American churches have put Bibles into the hands of the laity and therefore high explosive into their hearts. The American peoples, after learning the Bible's promises from their churches, have concluded that it is possible to liberate both the society from poverty and the individual from unhappiness. The translation of these promises into everyday reality has been full of struggle and disaster, but it was a Bible-feeding conscience, more than any other factor, that ended slavery in the Caribbean islands and in the southern states of the USA; that, from Independence to the Reagan years, inspired what was noblest in the 'American dream'; and that put bishops and preachers in the front of the recent beginnings of the long march of the Latin American masses. These developments have been clothed in many different languages, cultural, religious and political. But they have involved enormous numbers of believing and praying Americans. New hopes have lit up the landscape like the fireworks at a carnival. New futures have been growing like the corn on the prairies. Hymns from new churches have scraped the sky.

Liberation in Latin America

The story of Christianity in Latin America began in an atmosphere which was in important ways similar to the moral climate of the early colonisation of North America. Motives of personal profit and national aggrandisement were obviously dominant and it was a fact that the wealth of Latin America (supremely its silver) played a crucial role in the economic development *of Europe*. However, in a Europe still dominated by Christianity such ambitions were seldom expressed with a straightforward materialism. The blessing of heaven was confidently invoked on a movement which would spread both civilisation and the gospel. Many sermons and official declarations greeted the chance to build the church in the new world with a purity untainted by whatever was thought by that particular group to be the corruption introduced by European history. If earthly as well as a heavenly treasure arrived as a reward, this too could be explained within the language of religion. The Bible was quoted – plentifully by Columbus – as promising new riches to God's chosen people and their anointed king. Idealism, or at least hypocrisy, was frequent, so that not a few of those who crossed the Atlantic after Columbus regarded themselves as apostles of Christ – as he did.

The European colonists' favourable image of themselves survived the sight of indigenous peoples being battered by European guns, epidemics and drinks, reduced to serfdom, driven into small 'reservations' or (in the Caribbean islands) almost completely exterminated. A *conquistador* such as Cortes in Mexico or Pizarro in Peru would devoutly attend mass before a massacre, much as preachers in New England would lament the moral condition of the 'Indians' whose lands were being occupied and whose lives were being destroyed. For prominent in the much-cited Bible was the gift of the land of Canaan to the people of God, involving the massacre or degradation of its existing heathen inhabitants. Although in Latin America the defence of the rights of the 'Indians' by a few prophetic missionaries such as Bartolemé las Casas inspired some legislation, both the protests and the laws were largely ignored by the colonists and the general tendency of the Catholic church's local spokesmen was to bless the arrival of 'civilisation' and to overlook its devastations. Massacre, disease and overwork in the fields and mines reduced the original inhabitants from about eighty million in 1500 to about 3,500,000 in 1650. This was in a Latin America where the civilisations of the Mayas, Incas and Aztecs had reached a high standard of culture and where less technically advanced 'Indian' tribes had worked out a lifestyle, in community close to the earth, which on a reduced scale has been strong enough to survive into the twentieth century although under many great strains. The 'discovery' of Latin America by Europeans could better be called its rape – a term which has the merit of referring accurately to the circumstances preceding the births of many millions of Latin Americans of mixed parentage. It was small consolation to the victims of this combination of genocide with mass-rape that in 1537 Pope Paul III (in *Veritas ipsa*) gave his authority to an assurance that the Latin Americans were 'truly human beings' and therefore fit for the church's sacraments, although their idolatry deserved severe condemnation and punishment. The general complacency of Protestant preachers about the genocide of the 'Indians' in order to build the USA makes a roughly similar story.

Latin America diverged from North America because Catholicism as a triumphant religious and moral ideology supported the Spanish (or sometimes Portuguese) imperial crown. The long history of the reconquest from the Moors had left the Spanish (or Portuguese) monarchy as the focus of militant nationalism and as the chief instrument in the defence and propagation of the Christian faith and the Catholic church. Protestantism was to gain almost no foothold in such a kingdom. And when the kingdom – that, rather than any middle class – acquired an overseas empire, it was natural to think of the colonies as being directly under the control of the crown, in spiritual as well as temporal matters. The papacy not only bestowed its theoretical benediction on the new empires, as when in 1493 Pope Alexander VI divided up the new world between Spain and Portugal. It also agreed that the kings should appoint all the bishops, appropriate all the tithes (ecclesiastical taxes) and in general exercise through church councils which it convened almost all the Vatican's own jurisdiction. Moreover, the blessing of the Vicar of Christ seemed to be matched by a miraculous speed in the overthrow of heathenism. Ancient empires were rapidly conquered by a combination of force and diplomacy – and Christians saw the verdict of God in these spectacular triumphs. The subjects of these empires and more primitive tribesmen elsewhere were not slow to embrace Catholicism. The new faith was imposed by rulers who were ruthless. But it was also spiritually impressive, filling the vacuum left by the sudden collapse of the old cultures. Moreover, the Catholic church could console the disrupted by being strangely familiar. It, too, had impressive rituals and honoured priests. Under the robes of the Madonna – supremely, the Virgin of Guadelupe in Mexico (*la Morenzia*, the Brown Lady) – could creep many petitions which had been addressed to a fertility goddess. In the faces of the saints could be found substitutes for other ancient divinities. In the crucified Christ could be found an image of the people's own suffering. Although the new priests, virtually all white, could not marry, the appetites of white laymen were such that large numbers of *mestizos*, people of mixed blood, soon embodied a whole half-new culture, half Spanish (or Portuguese) and half 'Indian'. The half-Christian folk religion of this culture had no public rival – and its position was strengthened by the Inquisition's persecution of any deviants. It also quite easily imposed itself, at least superficially, on the millions of slaves shipped from Africa into the Caribbean islands, Brazil and elsewhere when too many of the 'Indian' Christians or semi-Christians had dropped dead.

Such empires and churches seemed secure until the beginning of the nineteenth century – and they were not ended by any action by, or on behalf of, the original inhabitants. Here as in North America, the revolutions which secured independence were the work of men of European descent who were already prospering and who resented taxes and controls. Latin America, more than 4,500 miles long and almost double the size of Europe, had been colonised by the *encomienda* system, copied from the earlier reconquest of Spain and Portugal from the Moors. Land had been granted on a lavish scale to a settler willing to convert and civilise the 'Indians'. An aristocracy had been founded. The new ports through which the trade of South America was channelled to the imperial bases such as Cadiz and Lisbon grew to provide a second source of social power and by the nineteenth century they had become the seats of a small middle class, the *criollos*, eager to end Spain's (or Portugal's) monopoly of overseas trade and also excited about the ideas of the Enlightenment associated with the success of the British and the North Americans. The expulsion of the *peninsulares*, the colonial administrators born in Europe, was usually led by these *criollos*. But there was no tradition of enterprise and participation by any large middle class or by artisans determined to better themselves. Without a broad basis, democracy as known by North Americans was impossible, although parliamentary institutions were erected as part of the Enlightenment's concept of civilised independence. South America continued to lose in the competition for immigrants from Europe to fill the empty lands. Although Brazil during the rubber and coffee booms, or Chile with its resources of nitrates and copper, or Argentina at the height of its exports of grain and meat seemed to offer prospects as good as Canada's or Australia's, there were never enough settlers to make Latin America a duplicate of North America and the big profits stayed in the hands of the few. The impact of Europe on the north populated it; the impact of Europe on the south exploited it.

An equally dangerous legacy of the colonial era was the lack of continental unity. This was a problem in North America, where Canada went its own way and the USA had to undergo the trauma of a civil war. But the USA survived as a nation (and annexed half Mexico). In contrast, Simon Bolivar's dreams of a United States of South America came to nothing. For some three hundred years the colonial authorities had prevented trade between the colonies, and the religious authorities had been equally successful in discouraging spiritual contacts which might be directed against the papacy or the crown. Such a subcontinent was easily carved up. In some places geography, in others the authoritarian personality of a leader (*caudillismo*), made for the emergence of Latin American republics still numbering twenty in the 1980s. The lack of economic and political unity in Central America and the Caribbean islands is particularly striking and disastrous.

Protestantism now added to the fragmentation. In the Caribbean the Anglican and nonconformist forms of English religion were introduced during the days of slavery, attracted and consoled the slaves (although handicapped by the slave-owners' suspicions), and remained attractive when slavery had been ended. The story of Protestantism in the rest of Latin America is different. There, religious pluralism was introduced only with the achievement of political independence and with the liberation of commerce. With the British and North American traders and investors came Protestant clergymen who gradually gathered fairly small local congregations made up of converts anxious to be 'liberal' in the European style. With some missionary work among tribesmen untouched by Catholicism, this accounted for some fifty thousand Protestants by 1900. The values taught were congenial to the middle classes: temperance, stable family life, education, hard work, commercial enterprise, parliamentary democracy. Such seed fell on some fertile soil, specially in Argentina, Uruguay and Chile, and by 1985 the Protestants of the historic denominations numbered about a million. The most successful Protestant evangelism, however, has come in the twentieth century from the Pentecostal churches such as the Assemblies of God, with a more popular message. By 1985 these churches had some nine million members. Unshackled by formalities and unhindered by too great an emphasis on puritan morals, this movement matched the spiritual authority of Catholicism by an enthusiastic reliance on the Bible and on the repetition of the miracles of the Bible. The offer to working people or the unemployed was not (or not at first) one of individual self-improvement. It was of rescue from disease and despair into a joyful and caring community of the converted. Pentecostalism might depend on an authoritarian pastor – *caudillismo* again – but more significant in the long run was the entrusting of leadership to preachers trained through many years as ardent laymen evangelising in the streets and homes of the people.

The Roman Catholic Church, already gravely weakened by the expulsion of the Jesuits, was for many decades left in disarray by the expulsion of its colonial patrons. The spread of Protestantism startled it, as did the atheism of the Enlightenment – and often it found it difficult to distinguish between these two innovations. Its manpower and finances declined just as the population began to grow and to be urbanised. In colonial times the church had become accustomed to the practice of leaving most of the peasants in the countryside without effective evangelism or pastoral care. They had been dispensed from the obligation to attend Sunday mass. The church had looked for support not to the people but to the state. Even its noblest missions (such as the Jesuits' protection of the Guarani Indians in fortified settlements in Paraguay) had been paternalist and therefore fragile (as when the crown and the papacy together suppressed the Jesuits in the 1760s). Now, with the political pressures favouring Catholicism removed, the numbers attending those churches which the clergy did staff sank, although the 'rites of passage' (baptisms, marriages and funerals), the main Christian festivals and pilgrimages remained popular. With no indigenous theology and little indigenous spirituality, the church's morale was low. It was rescued by the papacy, which encouraged the movement into Latin America of tens of thousands of foreign priests and nuns. Subsidies derived mainly from North American and German Catholics were transmitted through the Vatican. Theological faculties, seminaries, study centres, radio stations and periodicals were founded. Schools and colleges were opened to provide an education strongly coloured by traditional Catholicism, although these were in practice largely confined to the privileged. Student and youth movements sprang up. Lay movements such as Catholic Action were organised under the control of the bishops. Although imitating the communist 'militants', these concentrated on causes which could be regarded as the defence of religion and morals rather than of any specific political programme. Christian Democratic parties emerged in the 1940s, campaigning for moderate social reforms but leaving most of the wealth of the rich intact, and there was much emphasis on resistance to international communism. The Peronist movement in Argentina seemed to have a similar inspiration. There was talk of a 'new Christendom', often associated with the 'true humanism' of the Frenchman Jacques Maritain, marrying a conservative Catholicism with a cautiously liberal democracy. The church in the 1980s still shows the results of this rally. But the improvement of the church's position did not include a sufficiently radical approach to the people's problems. That would have been a fatal defect, had not another movement arisen.

This movement, 'liberation theology', corrected a theology shared by most Catholics and Protestants throughout most of the history of Christianity in Latin America: the understanding of the gospel exclusively as the offer of eternal salvation to the converted individual. Although both Catholicism and Protestantism in their different ways ministered to the economically successful, the emphasis was not on progress in this world. Although both Catholics and Protestants formed congregations and had inescapable relationships with wider communities, the main stress was not on corporate life in church and state. It was on the obedient and patient devotion of the individual. The predominant image in popular piety was of the tortured, impotent Christ whose sufferings had won heaven, or of the weeping Madonna with her silent child – and the human ideal was of the saint whose own self-denial and acceptance of suffering imitated the Saviour and the Virgin so pictured. Part of Christian morality was the distribution of charity by those able to afford it – but charity should relieve no more than the basic needs of the 'unfortunate' and it should always be subordinated to the main teaching that the individual ought to earn his daily bread by patient work. Poverty could not be avoided since God had so made the world – and it should not be resented, since it encouraged many virtues. Envy and covetousness were sins. Obedience to the authorities was an important part of the gospel. Here was a theology compatible with Fascism.

But by the 1960s bitterness about the failures in the economy was growing faster than any gratitude for foreign investments of foreign spiritual fellowship; and it was inspiring a hungry anger. The Christian Democratic or Peronist promises led mostly to disillusionment. So did the pledges of various other political or military regimes. So did the US-dominated Organisation of American States and the US-financed Alliance for Progress. Where there was dramatic industrial development, as in Brazil, the mass of the people did not benefit. The disappointment was due in part to the growth of the population. Yet that could not be the only explanation. In Latin America certainly much of the soil is poor (it is in mountainous areas or beneath the rainforests of the Amazon, which anyway cannot be destroyed without incalculable damage to the whole environment). But experts reckon that only about a quarter of the potentially arable land has been cultivated. Argentina, which has ideal farming land, has never had a population of more than fifteen to the square mile.

Many other countries could expand their farming safely if care was taken. The main problem has been – and largely remains in the 1980s – the ownership of three quarters of the cultivated land by a tenth of the population. The drift from rural poverty to the cities has produced cheap labour to the profit of a few employers, but to the people it has meant physically stinking *favelas* (shanty towns) in morally out-rageous proximity to the symbols of wasteful luxury. At the bottom of the heap, the 'Indians' feel alienated in their own land. The whole economic system seems to have no place for them apart from employment (far from guaranteed) as the cheapest labour. Their languages are scorned by governments and schools. Altogether it can be said that three quarters of the Latin American population have been pushed to the fringes. That explains why 'developmentalism' (*desarrollismo*) has become a word to be mocked. In the distribution of wealth between nations and between classes, the gap has actually been widened by 'development'. What has been developed, it seems, has been the profitability of US corporations.

In country after country, through many years, the privileged imposed 'order' on the angry and terror on the paralysed. In response guerrilla movements used violence with little effect apart from feed-ing the anti-communist propaganda of the 'national security' regimes. Power remained in the hands of 'those above' – an oligarchy depen-dent in the last analysis on force and the financial and even armed support of the USA. But beginning with the peasant revolt of 1910 in Mexico under the banner of 'Land and Liberty', the struggle never entirely ceased to find an alternative to this 'national security' and to put power into the hands of the people. Drastic, and if need be violent, measures seemed essential; measures which were indicated, however ambiguously, by the two words 'revolution' and 'socialism'. Cuba was the flashpoint. The last colony in Spain in the Americas, since 1898 it had been nominally independent but in reality it had depended on the USA, growing sugar and tobacco for export at prices fixed in the USA, with a people (barely noticed by the gambling and whoring tourists) sunk often in illiteracy and usually in poverty, and a government which was corrupt, cruel and ineffective even by this subcontinent's standards. Often-spoken revolutionary words took marching legs when guerrillas under Fidel Castro entered Havana on New Year's Day 1959. The sound was heard throughout Latin America.

The next decade witnessed the alignment of many Christian leaders with the hopes of the poor and therefore with 'socialism'. Once again movements originating outside Latin America were powerful. The historic Protestant churches were influenced by the World Council of Churches, which increasingly came to see its main role as the articulation of the sense of injustice and anger felt by the politically conscious Christians of the Third World. Some radical North American theologians, feeling profoundly guilty about their country's record of economic exploitation, encouraged the new protests. More significant was the effect of the Second Vatican Council on educated Catholics. In their months of meeting in Rome the bishops had both tasted and encouraged a new freedom of speech, a new emphasis on the authority of the Bible and a new concern about political, economic and cultural developments affecting humanity as a whole. The council's signal had been that the interest of the church in perpetuating a traditional piety must not be allowed to override the renewed conviction that the Bible's God demanded justice and liberty for all. It was a signal to the laity to discern the 'signs of the times' and to act with a new degree of independence, not subject to the detailed directions of the bishops themselves. It was, commentators agreed, a signal for 'orthopraxis' (right action) whereas previous church councils had been absorbed in the teaching of 'orthodoxy' (right belief). Encyclicals from John XXIII and Paul VI put the church behind 'development' but in terms which stressed (however imprecisely) the priority of the just needs of the poor.

One of the effects of the council permitted by the papacy had been the gathering of national or regional 'episcopal conferences' with uncertain powers but with the capacity to relate the insights of Vatican II to local problems. Nowhere in the world was there a conference with more courage than the meeting of the Latin American bishops at Medellin in Colombia in 1968. It responded with less than the usual caution of church leaders to a flood of radical protests and pleas; typical was the open letter from a thousand Brazilian priests about 'a murdered people, a plundered people'. The documents which the council adopted reinterpreted the traditional principle that peace is 'the work of justice'. They gave priority to the rights of the people to food, work and freedom and denounced 'a situation of injustice that can be called institutionalised violence'. 'We should not be surprised that the temptation to violence is surfacing in Latin America. One should not abuse the patience of a people that for years has borne a situation that would not be acceptable to anyone with any degree of awareness of human rights.' The bishops, coming out of a background of identification with the rich, now urged 'solidarity with the poor'. 'Christ, our Saviour, not only loved the poor but rather "being rich he became poor"; he lived

in poverty. His mission centred on advising the poor of their liberation and he founded his Church as the sign of that poverty among
men.' God the Father 'sends his Son in the flesh, so that he might
come to liberate all men from the slavery to which sin has subjected
them: hunger, oppression and ignorance – in a word, the injustice and
hatred which have their origin in human selfishness'. The bishops
gave reasons for the 'Christian preference for peace' rather than for
the counter-violence of revolution: 'the enormous difficulty of a civil
war, the logic of violence, the atrocities it engenders, the risk of
provoking foreign intervention illegitimate as it may be, the difficulty
of building a regime of justice and freedom while participating in a
process of violence'. They therefore hoped that 'the dynamism of an
awakened and organised community' would be enough. But in a
silence which echoed all over Latin America, arousing thrills of joy or
indignation, they did not proclaim that revolutionary violence was
always wrong – as the papacy had explicitly taught at the time of the
struggles for independence from Spain and Portugal.

Such words, although seldom specific, were very different from
previous failures of Catholic bishops to be in any sense the spokesmen
of the poor. (The record of such failures may be traced back to the
Donatist crisis in fourth-century North Africa.) They were very
different from the bland pronouncements of the previous meeting of
the Latin American bishops (in 1955). For all their ambiguity they
inclined further to the left than the middle-of-the-road wisdom of
Paul VI, who briefly visited Medellin for a Eucharistic Congress – the
first pope to set foot on any American soil. They were interpreted by
more cautious words as the conservative bishops rallied and enlisted
the Vatican's patronage. The conservatives warned that the church, if
it turned from 'popular' to 'political' religion, would end up by
blessing communism and atheism. But when the bishops met for their
third conference, at Puebla in 1979, it was finally made clear that the
'preferential option for the poor' advocated at Medellin could not be
totally undone. Indeed, it became part of a pattern of a much wider
and often more committed movement. Some priests became guerrillas, the most famous being Camilo Torres in Colombia. Others
became socialist politicians, most notably Ernesto Cardenal in
Nicaragua. Born in privileged backgrounds, Torres had been a
sociologist and Cardenal a poet. Some bishops, while thinking violence unwise in the circumstances, became consistently outspoken
radicals; among these, Archbishop Helder Camara of Brazil was
given a worldwide fame. Nuns, priests and bishops were murdered
because of their 'interference' in the brutal oppression of the people.

Probably as many as a thousand sacrificed their lives in this way in the 1970s and early 1980s. Among them Archbishop Oscar Romero of El Salvador, originally a very cautious pastor, was revered around the Christian world as a martyr.

Theologians published books, manifestos and articles which also reverberated. Gustavo Gutierrez, a scholarly priest in Peru, achieved a first synthesis and a programme in his *Teologia de la Liberacion*, which appeared in Lima in 1971. It was translated into five other languages – including an English translation published two years later by the Catholic Foreign Mission Society of America at Maryknoll near New York, a body which became the persistent sponsor of a flood of Third World theology. Although it soon won attention and admiration in many nations, 'liberation theology' continued to be earthed in the sufferings and struggles of Latin America. Although their training was academic and in contact with European and North American theology, these new men usually worked in seminaries or other institutions related closely to pastoral work – and were not reluctant to undertake literary tasks of a directly pastoral character. Such theology was usually aimed at social and religious needs that seemed urgent, and not addressed to a highly educated audience. It was indebted more to sociology than to historical research and its conclusions were political rather than philosophical. Since it largely ignored questions traditionally dividing Catholics and Protestants, it was in effect ecumenical and the welcome it received in (for example) the World Council of Churches came as no surprise. Many Protestants in Latin America have been suspicious of it, but the formation of the Latin American Council of Churches in 1982 seemed to indicate that there would be no complete polarisation between the pious and the political.

Names prominent in this 'new way of doing theology' (an epithet Gutierrez rightly claimed for it) have included those of Rubem Alves, the Protestant who has meditated on the possibility of messianic hope amid the 'captivity' of Brazilian capitalism and the escapism of his own Presbyterian church's fundamentalism; another Brazilian (but repeatedly in flight from the police), Hugo Assmann, a Jesuit who is an expert on Marxism and in the eyes of many too much of a convert to it; José Miguez Bonino, who more than any other has communicated the force of this movement to conventional Christians such as his fellow Methodists in Argentina; Leonardo Boff the Franciscan in Brazil, the author of *Jesus Christ the Liberator* among many other books, in 1985 silenced for a year after warnings from the Vatican; Ernesto Cardenal, poet, priest, pastor and (despite a papal censure) cabinet minister; Enrique Dussel, the historian and philosopher exiled from Argentina to Mexico; José Miranda of Mexico who has interpreted the fourth gospel as liberation; Jan Luis Segundo, the author of *Theology for the Artisans of a New Humanity* in five volumes; and Jon Sobrino, whose profound book on Christology was written amid the hell of El Salvador. A project for a series of forty volumes by three times as many theologians has been announced under the title *Mysterium Liberationis*. In the 1970s and 1980s no theological movement anywhere in the world has displayed more vigour or has won a more dramatically powerful influence.

Greater in its popular impact on Latin America, however, and a more effective answer to the reaction of the conservatives has been the success in setting up a very large network of Catholic *comunidades de base* (grassroots communities), with some similar Protestant groups. These are lay groups which meet sometimes for basic education, more often for Bible study – a purpose which includes the uninhibited discussion of personal and social problems in the light of the Bible, preferably leading to some agreed action. If a priest is present, he acts more as a consultant than as a director; he is there to elicit speech, not silence. This is a great contrast with the days when priestless peasants were urged to gather round a wireless which was broadcasting the mass. The aim is not to 'civilise', the word which was used to define the social mission of the church in Latin America right up to the 1960s. It is (to use a word invented by the popular educator, Paulo Freire) to 'conscientise'. In other words, these groups awaken the common people to their dignity as the children of God, to their rights and opportunities, to their ability to choose and to choose rightly.

These modest communities have shown how to fulfil the desire of the bishops at Medellin for a 'liberating education' which would free the masses to ascend to 'more human conditions'. They have shown in practice what talk about a 'church of the poor' means and what is learnt from finding 'Christ's presence in the poor' – for through these communities, as has often been said, 'the poor evangelise the church'. The numbers involved at any one time cannot be known precisely but run into many hundreds of thousands. Such a phenomenon is explicable only against the background of Latin American history, the shortage of priests coinciding with no shortage of keenly felt problems. Here is a setting of large-scale adherence to Christianity (if not of regular churchgoing) combined with the frequent absence of political agencies willing and free to ventilate the people's grievances. All these factors had to combine in order to give birth to a movement which in other circumstances might well not command such support among the laity – or clergy. It is a movement which, precisely because it is local and poor, has been widely admired since its first national conference (in Brazil in 1975). In 1985–86 a discreet struggle between the bishops of Brazil and conservatives in the Vatican ended for the time being in Rome's acknowledgement of the new reality.

All over Latin America the people have increasingly treated the Catholic church as their ally and spokesman. Inevitably the alliance has had bitter disappointments. In 1967 the killing of Che Guevara, the Cuban guerrilla who had attempted to arouse the peasants of Bolivia, dramatised the failure of that way of violence – a way which almost all the bishops and priests have always condemned as futile if not completely immoral. With the slogan 'Che lives' the attraction of the guerrillas' heroism has lingered on in some quarters; but the subsequent successes of the security forces made the failure increasingly obvious. Six years later the killing of President Allende of Chile also seemed to dramatise the failure of the parliamentary way to socialism. Allende had won the largest (although not the majority) vote in an election and had become the focus of many hopes, for example in a 'Christians for Socialism' conference. But inflation had reduced the economy to a shambles and he was overthrown in a conservative coup which depended only in part on support from the USA. The Pinochet regime which followed him was the most brutal in the subcontinent. After such deaths, which were matched in other countries, despair was the temptation of Latin American revolutionaries and progressives. However, in the 1980s hopes revived. The practice, or at least the pretence, of holding elections had persisted as a legacy of the liberal enlightenment in which the Latin American republics had won independence; and now in many countries (most dramatically in Argentina) politicians with programmes of reform were allowed to win elections and to replace military *juntas*. Brazil, the giant among these republics but under military control since 1964, acquired its first civilian president for twenty-one years – and he began a massive programme to give land to the peasants. In 1986 Chile was sending out signals that it might not remain the most prominent exception to this healthy trend. And all the time, through dark and brighter days, the churches (even in Chile) and their *comunidades* have been feeding recruits into a forward march which has been looking for convincing political leadership. Many observers have noted that the old generalisations about the Latin American character are becoming ever less valid. It is no longer plausible to say that resentment, distrust and pessimism are generally combined with irresponsibility modified by a taste for violence. Here in Latin America has appeared nothing less than a 'new breed of Christians'.[3]

People's churches in the USA

The central theme of the story of Christianity in the USA was stated by James Madison. 'The religion of every man must be left to the conviction and conscience of every man,' he wrote, 'and it is the right of every man to exercise it as these may dictate . . . It is the duty of every man to render to the Creator such homage, and such only, as he believes to be acceptable to him. This duty is precedent both in order of time and degree of obligation to the claims of civil society.' But no more than the French around the great lakes of Canada, or the Spaniards and Portuguese in Latin America, did the Englishmen who began the colonisation of the eastern seaboard of North America intend to start a free market in religion. Often the motive of financial profit was dominant, although the provision of chaplains and churches in familiar styles was a part of the civilisation which they took over with them. That seems to have been true of the English in Virginia, or of the Dutch in what was to be New York. And religious liberty was not the motivation of the Pilgrim Fathers and of other English Puritans who founded New England. What they sought was liberty for themselves to be Puritans. They wished to build a godly commonwealth where the pure gospel as they understood it could be preached faithfully and enforced to the limit of the magistrates' powers. Only those who could report the experience of conversion were to be church members; and only church members were to have political votes. 'A due form of government both civil and ecclesiastical' was to be the 'city upon a hill' which John Winthrop envisaged in his lay sermon on the *Arbella* in 1630 – and that was, in practice, the iron regime from which a dissenter such as Roger Williams had to flee six years later. But the little settlements of Rhode Island, founded by brave eccentrics such as Williams, were early homes of toleration. The larger and originally Roman Catholic colony of Maryland (1634), and the larger and originally Quaker colony of Pennsylvania (1682), also showed that a community – a very prosperous community in Pennsylvania's case – could be more tolerant than any of the rulers of Europe then found conceivable. The eighteenth century brought a check on this daring trend; the Church of England was established in Maryland, for example. On the achievement of independence the denominational problem was ignored in the constitution of the

United States ratified in 1789. But the First Amendment decreed that 'the Congress shall make no law respecting the establishment of religion or restricting the free exercise thereof' and in the states the privileges of establishment were withdrawn from the churches one by one, the last to be affected being Puritan Congregationalism in Connecticut (1818) and Massachusetts (1833). Pastor John Robinson, preaching in 1620 to those who were to cross the Atlantic in the *Mayflower*, had promised that 'the Lord hath more truth and light yet to break forth out of his holy Word'. In a development which would have bewildered Robinson, part of that light turned out to be religious freedom accompanying the separation of church and state.

It was only in the 1960s that this principle was fully accepted by the Roman Catholic Church (but a major influence on the Second Vatican Council was the thought of an American Jesuit, John Courtney Murray). This is understandable. For long many Christians took it for granted that in North America as elsewhere the Christian message should be accepted officially by the state and translated into the civil laws, as it had been all over Europe. At least it was assumed that part of the history of the church in any nation ought to consist of an agreed attitude to movements in politics and culture, an attitude voiced by accredited spokesmen. In return 'the church' would contribute powerfully to the unity of the nation – and would take care that its spokesmen usually spoke in support of the government. But little of this pattern, so familiar in European history, was to be seen in the USA. There the vision that prevailed was of the church as a gathered community of believers and worshippers, free from state control but also free from any strongly felt duty to shape a whole society. The story of the Christian response to current movements in politics and culture in the USA has always been a story of disagreement between Christians. No church leaders have ever been authorised as the official spokesmen of the Christian conscience of the American nation. The Christian church has been fragmented and often has been absorbed in its own congregational life or in evangelism narrowly defined. Fundraising from its own membership, rather than from politicians, has been its spur. Indeed, it has found it difficult to relate in any way to government and legislature. And many regrets have been expressed. Indeed, while the First Amendment has been treated as sacrosanct the conviction that the state still has a duty to uphold morality has remained very strong among American Christians. The Eighteenth Amendment (1919) prohibited the sale of alcoholic beverages throughout the USA and this 'great social and economic experiment, noble in motive and far-reaching in purpose' (so said

President Hoover) was not formally abandoned until 1933. Many states retained morally inspired restrictive legislation for another dozen or more years. Some counties still retain it in the 1980s. In 1954 the pledge of allegiance was amended to make it clear that the USA was 'one nation under God'. 'In God we trust' spelt out the same message on dollar notes. In the 1980s debates are freshly vigorous in response to movements (encouraged by President Reagan) urging severe restrictions on abortion and pornography and the restoration of prayers to public schools. But the paramount fact is that the popularity of the Christian religion which has produced these political consequences – and which has made almost every American politician a public advocate of Christian morality – has not relied on the Constantinian pattern of the patronage of the church by the power of the state.

It has relied on a great and continuing series of movements organised to reach, touch and hold 'hearts and minds'. Of course there has been much steady quietness in the worship of the churches and in the Christian lives of their members. The more prophetically radical elements in the membership have also frequently proclaimed that there has been much dull complacency. The 'suburban captivity of the churches' has been attacked in the twentieth century as vigorously as the formalism of colonial church life was denounced in the eighteenth; and in godly New England itself not many years of the seventeenth century had passed before the decline of the founding fathers' enthusiasm became the standard theme for the pulpit of every eager successor of Jeremiah. It seems fairer to say that this quiet type of religion, with its emphasis on family life, good citizenship and cultural self-improvement, has provided a home where enthusiasm could find rest. It has been a lake into which rivers could flow from the mountain tops of spiritual excitement. But a more unusual phenomenon in American Christian history is the succession of revivals in personal, heartfelt religion resulting in the expansion of churchgoing. The effectiveness of this evangelism appealing to the individual for a Christian and churchly decision has more than matched the support given to Protestantism by the northern states of Europe or to the Counter-Reformation by the Catholic powers. It has resulted in a recruitment with massive dimensions. Strong popular support for the churches is still indicated by the public opinion polls of the 1980s. 'The evidence,' impartial observers assure us, 'seems overwhelming that materialistic Americans have remained a God-fearing people despite all those "-ations" that are supposed by sociologists to cause a falling off of interest in religion: modernisation, secularisation, urbanisation and industrialisation. More than nine out of ten Americans say they believe in God and prayer; seven out of ten that they believe in an afterlife. Over a third describe themselves as born-again Christians. Over forty per cent reply Yes when they are asked by pollsters: "Did you, yourself, happen to attend church or synagogue during the past seven days?"[4] Many American clergy conclude after surveying the numbers before them on the average Sunday that the last figure, at least, is an exaggeration. But it comes from a Gallup poll in 1981 and if it is unreal the polite hypocrisy of a people is not to be ignored when assessing its real attitudes. If more people in the USA claim to go to church than do, it only goes to show that the theology printed on every dollar note has not got it totally wrong. Most of them like to give the impression that they trust in God. Moreover, a Gallup poll in 1982 reported that seventy per cent of Americans give money to churches or other religious organisations.

Moral and spiritual energy earned the churches' popularity. Recent historical research has shown that this energy was solidly at work in periods which previous historians had been inclined to condemn. When considering Massachusetts, for example, it is unfair to concentrate on the censoring rigidity of Puritanism; to many Puritans, religion was the chief meaning of a hard life and in their own way they enjoyed it. It is also unfair to concentrate on the hysteria about witches; that was short-lived. And when judging the more relaxed middle-eastern Atlantic colonies, where Anglican churches were more in evidence, it is unfair to ignore the evidence about the practice of religion. Attendance at church was far more popular than was the acceptance of the financial and other responsibilities of church membership. Religious energy was not entirely asleep in any of these areas before the Great Awakening of the 1730s and 1740s. But it is beyond question that the future was shaped by a Calvinist revival associated with the gospel of the 'new birth' and with the names of the giant preachers, Jonathan Edwards and George Whitefield. The Awakening restored dynamic movement to the inner life of the people and of the Christian church in the people's midst. It united the colonies as no previous development had done; and it gave them an unprecedented confidence that they were a people (why not a nation?) chosen by God for a thrilling new purpose. 'The supplying of the world with its treasures from America,' announced Edwards, 'is a type and forerunner of what is approaching in spiritual things, when the world shall be supplied with spiritual things from America.' The Awakening also ensured that in the future American clergymen

would be commonly judged not by their book-learning or contemplative piety or quietly pastoral sympathy but by their powers of
leadership expressed in spontaneous oratory, businesslike administration and charismatic fundraising; for only 'go-getters' could recruit
and sustain active communities. In denominational terms, the
Awakening showed that the future lay with the aggressively informal
Baptists and Methodists rather than with the more cultured traditions
although these were in the backgrounds of Edwards (a Presbyterian)
and Whitefield (an Anglican).

This revival influenced a white population of around a million in
1740. Its emotionalism distressed most of the better educated and the
great names associated with American independence (Washington,
Franklin, Jefferson) are not the names of men who had undergone
the 'new birth'. But later revivals with much the same character as the
Great Awakening avoided the development of the United States into
a society which would have been explicitly post-Christian. The deist
and democratic belief in a Supreme Being who commanded liberty
and the pursuit of happiness with other moral duties on which all the
religions agreed, but who did not intervene in human affairs, might
have developed into a negative scepticism. (The American influence
of Tom Paine's *Rights of Man* was a hint in that direction.) But any
such danger was averted by the spread of faith in the biblical God who
commanded holiness and righteousness and who emphatically did
intervene by pouring out the Holy Spirit on many revivals. 'The cause
of America is the cause of Christ,' exclaimed Robert Smith in 1781.
By 1840 Alexis de Tocqueville could observe that 'no country in the
whole world exists in which the Christian religion retains a greater
influence over the souls of men than in America'.

Christianity was now presented as the emotionally compelling and
transforming answer to the frequent strain and loneliness of life as a
farmer on the frontier towards the west or as an immigrant in an
industrial city. On the frontier preachers were as intrepid as any
pioneer and revivalists gathered and inspired 'camp meetings'. As the
cities grew, equally intense revivalist meetings were held either by
ordained enthusiasts such as Charles Finney or by businessmen such
as the early leaders of the Young Men's Christian Association.
America was on the move. This was the century when Joseph Smith
led the Latter-day Saints or Mormons into the desert of Utah with
their own new scriptures telling of Christ's own mission to America in
distant days – and when William Miller led the Adventists with their
eager expectation that Christ was about to come to America in
triumphant glory (it was at first said, within thirteen years of 1831). It

was a time of many small communities experimenting in a Utopian lifestyle and of new independent fellowships such as the 'Disciples', modelled directly on the New Testament by Alexander Campbell in 1811. In the southern states strong churches of slaves or ex-slaves flourished on their own. But it was also a time when doctrinally orthodox and ethnically European churchgoers were as enterprising as any of these groups. In the USA Christianity had become enthusiastic.

There followed the 'Benevolent Empire' – a host of new church colleges and of religious and philanthropic institutions such as the Bible Society, mainly Evangelical in inspiration. This empire did much to mitigate the human suffering inflicted by the new industries. It stretched overseas, as in the mission to Burma of the Baptist, Adoniram Judson, or in the larger invasion of China by a host of missionaries. Most of this activity could be matched in (for example) the England which was beginning to be Victorian. But unique to America was the scale of the churches' recruitment of immigrants, almost five million of whom entered the USA in the years 1830–60.

Many came from areas of Europe which naturally fed the Protestant churches – for example, Scandinavian immigrants were recruited by the Lutherans. But the numbers of Roman Catholicism suddenly swelled, first with Germans and then with the poorer and more priest-dominated Irish. It was the reversal of a Protestant near-monopoly which had been thought to be the character of North America since the earliest colonisation – and which had been reinforced by the conquest of French Canada and of Louisiana around the Mississippi, and by the expulsion of the Spanish from Florida, in the 1760s. For a time the new immigrants aroused a fierce anti-Catholic (particularly anti-Irish) prejudice; but these Catholics were, like previous waves of immigrants, absorbed quite rapidly into the American way of life and nationhood. On the whole they were happy to be thrown into the great melting pot. Within their new community – or, rather, communities, since ethnic divisions between Catholics went deep – there was controversy about the degree of Americanisation which would be compatible with Catholicism. Should democracy be welcomed in the state and practised in the church? Should all the nation's varieties of Christianity be admired? In the end the mainly Irish bishops won against the mainly German intellectuals. The ecclesiastical power was now with them rather than with lay trustees in the parishes, and the doctrine which they taught was taught also in a vast network of Catholic schools and colleges. But what could not be controverted was the need to be active in the human and physical construction of countless new parishes and other organisations. Often adapting revivalist techniques, clergy, nuns and laity all displayed an energy which made this 'nation of immigrants' partly Catholic (it is roughly estimated, four million out of a population of twenty-seven million in 1855 and about 26,500,000 out of a population of 122 million in 1930). The Vatican still had to thunder against 'Americanism' (as in the encyclical *Longinqua Oceani* of 1895) – but it did acknowledge that American Catholicism had ceased to be a 'mission' church, in 1908. In the USA the Catholic church had learnt how to compete.

Slavery had been an unsolved problem ever since the million or so 'Indians' inhabiting North America when the Europeans arrived had been wiped out or pushed out and tougher Africans had been imported forcibly in their many millions. The civil war of the 1860s was fought over the insistence on slavery in the cotton-growing southern states. It showed American religion to be divided as painfully as English religion had been in the 1640s – and only in the 1980s are the divisions being finally healed. As in Cromwell's England, in the American conflict both sides deeply believed that 'our God' was marching with their armies, while those who sought reconciliation (most notably Abraham Lincoln) also phrased their message in the language of religious idealism. But whereas in England lethargy followed the traumas of the seventeenth century until the Evangelical and Catholic revivals gathered momentum, in America the story of revivalism was continuous. Amid their disappointments after the abolition of slavery, the Negroes of the south found their souls anew through black churches (almost entirely Baptist or Methodist) unrivalled as community centres. Amid the often violent stresses of the accumulation of industrial wealth in the north, preachers continued to proclaim the American dream which was self-improvement in every sense; and the workers were not to be excluded. The denominations often gained financially from the patronage of capitalists, but a 'social creed' was adopted by the Federal Council of Churches in 1908 after more than thirty years of sermons along these lines in many pulpits. The demand for 'complete justice for all men in all stations of life', however naive, was a reminder that American Christianity had by no means sold its soul. Nor was it completely isolationist. By 1900 'the evangelisation of the world in this generation' was a slogan often heard among students.

In this atmosphere it often seemed that the heady predictions of prophets such as Jonathan Edwards were about to be fulfilled. American Christianity would (to use a word about which there was in

134   THE FUTURES OF CHRISTIANITY

that period little hesitation) 'conquer'. In 1885 Josiah Strong of the
Evangelical Alliance greeted the prospect that 'this race of un-
equalled energy, with all the majesty of numbers and the might of
wealth behind it – the representative, let us hope, of the largest
liberty, the purest Christianity, the highest civilisation – having
developed peculiarly aggressive traits calculated to impress its institutions upon mankind, will spread itself over the earth'. Five years later
Lewis Stearns declared even more candidly: 'Today Christianity is
the power which is moulding the destinies of the world. Just in
proportion to the purity of Christianity as it exists in the various
nations of Christendom is the influence they are exerting upon the
world's destiny. The future of the world seems to be in the hands of
the three great Protestant powers – England, Germany and the
United States. The old promise is being fulfilled: the followers of the
true God are inheriting the world.'
   From the 1870s onwards American Protestantism was, however,
split as fundamentalists battled against liberals to secure the right
response to the intellectual and moral challenges of modernisation –
challenges summed up in the Darwinian claims about the evolution of
man from lower animals and by the biblical critics' claims that the
Holy Bible was literature like any other book. Conservatives put up a
strong defence, which in the 'Bible belt' (the southern states and the
Mid-west) was generally thought to have prevailed against innovations. Elsewhere popular religion was also often conservative, simply
believing that the Bible was 'true'. Among Catholics – or at least
among those Catholics who spoke freely and publicly on theological
topics – the papal condemnation of 'modernism' in 1907 inaugurated
half a century of a strictly loyal conformity to the dogmas taught by
the hierarchy. Among Protestants strongly conservative movements
continued to arise and to sweep through the country – characteristi-
cally combining their conservatism with great promises. A development in this direction which went far beyond the bounds of the
Christian tradition was the 'Watch Tower' movement led by Charles
Russell and later called Jehovah's Witnesses; biblical texts were used
(or misused) as these witnesses watched for a new age. Another
unorthodox movement was Christian Science, founded by Mary
Baker Eddy. It was conservative in that it attacked modern medicine,
teaching the unreality of disease and other evils; and it was optimistic
in that it promised that its adherents would find health and success
through Mrs Eddy's new 'science'. But within the more orthodox
Christian territory there was a fresh stirring of the Adventist fascina-
tion with the biblical prophecies of the end of the present age,

ushering in the millennium of glory ('dispensationalism'). A vastly influential textbook in this field was *Scofield's Reference Bible*, first published in 1909. There was also a new wave of emphasis on the supernatural cleansing and healing of the heart in the 'second blessing' after baptism (the 'holiness' movement). A revival at Bethel Bible College in Topeka, Kansas, in 1900–1901 was the beginning of the mighty Pentecostal movement, rejoicing in 'baptism in the Holy Spirit' and in the gift of 'speaking in tongues'. The Church of the Nazarene (1908) and the Assemblies of God (1914) brought together many congregations of such believers. This whole conservative Protestant tendency was summarised afresh in a series of twelve paperbacks entitled *The Fundamentals* and published (with large subsidies by two Californian millionaires for extensive publicity) in 1910–15. It was the origin of the popular term 'fundamentalism'. Psychologically what was crucial was the faith in Jesus Christ as the personal 'Saviour and Lord', a faith associated with what was understood as *the* biblical doctrine: trust in Christ's perfect sacrifice as the sufficient payment of the penalty due for sin and trust in his virgin birth, physical resurrection and physical second coming as guarantees of his divine uniqueness. But it was maintained that faith so defined also involved a straightforward belief that the Bible was 'entirely trustworthy' or 'inerrant' in what it said about science, history or morals as well as in what it said about salvation. Fundamentalists were convinced that if they admitted one error in the scriptures the whole structure of their faith must collapse. Provided that they maintained the 'integrity' of scripture along with the firm moral standards based on scripture, their lives would be radiantly victorious and they could 'rescue the fallen' who were still wallowing in the evils of the present age.

It might be expected that old-fashioned religion of this kind would merely succeed in setting up a rearguard action in a retreat from triumphant modernity. And indeed liberalism did often seem to be prevailing. Although in 1923 a conservative theologian, J. Gresham Machen, published *Christianity and Liberalism*, contrasting the two creeds and inviting the liberals to take the logical step of leaving church, eventually it was he who left the ministry of the Northern Presbyterian Church. However, seventy years after the publication of *The Fundamentals* this tradition of 'Bible-believing' Christianity was alive and growing – whether expressed in large denominations such as the Southern Baptists or the Missouri Synod Lutherans, in congregations of the historic denominations which still stood out against the prevailing liberalism, in loosely organised networks of independent congregations, or in 'parachurch' movements. It was growing faster than the group of denominations which had become 'liberal' in their acceptance of modernity. The question which Harry Emerson Fosdick had asked expecting the obvious answer in a famous sermon of 1922, 'Shall the Fundamentalists win?', had to be asked again.

Here was a phenomenon as striking, and to many observers as puzzling, as any other feature in the history of the USA, but some explanations can be offered. They all suggest that the liberal denominations would have continued to make statistical progress had they not been burdened by handicaps which no one could have predicted before 1910. These handicaps meant that while more or less liberal congregations continued to be gently attractive to many Americans, the effective recruiting campaigns among those untouched by this quiet church life were almost always conducted by conservatives most of whom used the self-designation 'Evangelicals' and some of whom did not object to being called 'fundamentalists'. Many of them were narrow-minded, uncultured, brash – but they had the conviction and the energy. And their opportunity came.

The liberal Christians' acceptance of modernity usually took the form of believing that the God whose chief characteristic was love for all as revealed in Jesus was successfully accomplishing his purpose in the evolution of humanity towards harmony, prosperity and perfection, his most effective weapon being the spread of knowledge and of idealism (going together) through education. The kingdom of God hailed in this 'social gospel' had to be worked for, but it seemed particularly close to the Americans and Europeans who had built history's richest and best civilisation. Lavish church buildings were among that civilisation's many glories and from them extensive crusades could be launched to conquer the evils remaining in society. But this evolutionary optimism was shattered first by the great war of the 1910s and then, in a disaster which hit Americans harder, by the great economic depression of 1929 and the 1930s. The 1920s were probably the most secular decade in all the history of the USA. When in 1929 Robert and Helen Lynd published their famous study of the American way of life encapsulated in Muncie, Indiana (*Middletown*), they noted that 'in theory, religious beliefs dominate all other activities in Middletown; actually large regions of Middletown's life appear uncontrolled by them'. And in *Middletown in Transition* (1937) they reported that the gap between the churches and the daily life of the people had widened.

It is interesting to have the more recent judgement of a leading historian of the prolonged dream of a 'Christian America'. His view is that 'the Protestant era in American life had come to its end by the mid-thirties'.[5] In response, conservative movements, although en-joying little public esteem (they were for long identified with opposi-tion to alcohol and tobacco, to Charles Darwin's evolutionism and to movements of social progress such as President Roosevelt's New Deal), added numbers. They recruited among those who, particu-larly in rural areas, in small towns and in the states of the 'Bible belt' saw no reason to identify themselves with the modern world – and also among more sensitive souls seeking a spiritual security which the modern world could no longer offer. Even in the mainly modern-minded and liberal denominations the 'neo-orthodoxy' expounded by theologians such as Reinhold Niebuhr now stressed sin, revelation and redemption. It won influence among some of the educated as a far more convincing analysis of the human condition.

A recovery of the nation's prosperity and proud confidence took place during the 1940s, encouraged by the successful war. This recovery tended to restore the prosperity and confidence of the liberal Protestant denominations. The enemies were then clear – the cruel Japanese, Hitler, Stalin; and it seemed equally clear that the American crusade against these evil men had a religious and moral inspiration. Did not Eisenhower himself entitle his account of the war *Crusade in Europe*? Scepticism about the value of religion, defined very broadly, seemed dangerously un-American. Did not Eisenhower often say so? Church membership, perhaps half the total population in 1940, had climbed to over sixty per cent by 1955. But there was still much unease. Three of the most influential preachers all had messages which did not assume that the nation was happy. Fulton J. Sheen offered peace of soul through the acceptance of the faith and ethics of the Roman Catholic Church; Norman Vincent Peale offered peace of mind through 'positive thinking'; and the much more intellectual, and therefore much less popular, Paul Tillich offered a religious philosophy of 'Being-itself' as deliverance of the isolated individual from an age of anxiety. And even such messages had foundations which, as later developments showed, could be shaken. Sheen's Catholicism was not nearly so stable as it looked. Peale attracted Americans who now needed to be told to think positively amid the problems. Tillich's subtle theology could be reduced, in a harsher mood, into the admission that 'God' – or at least the strongly personal, intervening God worshipped by traditionalist Catholics and Protestants in more confident days – was 'dead'. And in the long term, some of the most significant religious developments in these 'Eisenhower years' were the beginnings of definitely Evangelical movements which offered less vulnerable answers to the anxieties afflicting many Americans. Young Life, Youth for Christ, Campus Crusade for Christ and the Navigators were all founded in the decade 1941–51. Their common characteristic was that they offered a stronger religion – a simpler faith, a warmer fellowship – than the liberal Protestant denominations. So they recruited effectively for congregations and movements of the type that was represented either by the (proudly fundamentalist) American Council of Christian Churches founded in 1941 on the basis of 'no co-operation, no compromise' or by the more inclusive National Association of Evangelicals constituted in the following year.

Then the 1960s and the 1970s tore the nation apart almost to the extent seen in the civil war a hundred years before. The manufacturing industries began to seem unable to provide mass employment, or even to produce goods without unacceptable damage to the environment. Lakes were dying through pollution and the farmers were destroying their own topsoils. The blacks and the young angrily demanded rights. The voice that most clearly articulated the moral content of the American dream was the voice of the black leader, Martin Luther King – and he was murdered. The most hopeful voice in politics was President Kennedy – also silenced by an assassin. The war in Vietnam turned out to be neither just nor victorious. The crusade against communism came to a halt and American involvement in the world's affairs suffered one criticism or humiliation after another. Richard Nixon disgraced the presidency. On most of these political issues the leaders of the liberal denominations took courageously definite positions, in keeping with world opinion, and protests for civil rights or against the war often united Protestants, Catholics and Jews – but many Americans reacted to the confusion by turning to other movements.

They might turn to a conservative teaching of religion and morality. These were years when Billy Graham was the best-known and best-loved religious leader in the nation. He embodied a religious world which also produced a vast number of radio and TV programmes and evangelistic organisations. While avoiding the dishonesties and the worst crudities of his revivalist predecessors, and while being willing (as they had not been) to cooperate with the churches, his spiritual message was essentially the same gospel as theirs. That reassured many. His city 'crusades' and his continuous ministry implied affirmation of the American way of life, for his own style, famous since 1949, was sincere, positive, well-advertised, happy to be large-scale but aimed at the true happiness of the individual. Or if preachers such as Billy Graham did not appeal, Americans might react to the political confusion by turning back to unworldly values older than orthodox Christianity. These were years of enthusiasm for nature, for nature's protection from pollution or exhaustion by industry, for the natural glory of the healthy and beautiful body, for the raising of consciousness by meditation which did not seem to involve anything alarmingly supernatural. The motorcycle or Zen Buddhism – or, it was claimed, a combination of the two – could take a new American generation away from the discredited world of smokestack industrialism and of the middle classes in their grey flannel suits, back on the journey over the frontier into the 'New Age'. And with its inexhaustible vitality American Christianity proved that it could join this 'counterculture' which was a new American dream. The hippies who with their flower-power were the gentle standard-bearers of the movement were matched by first-century-imitating 'Jesus freaks'. Non-Christian cults which found inspiration in Eastern mysticism were rivalled by new Christian sects which also offered a direct access to God. The use of drugs spread – but so did the answer that the highest excitement was the enjoyment of God through his gift of charismatic powers.

In the 1980s the nation's wounds began healing. A new industrial revolution promised new jobs and new wealth through the magic of high technology. Despite continuing unemployment many blacks and young whites became upwardly mobile in earning power. A more successful presidency restored national self-confidence, partly because there were to be no more Vietnams. Once again Americans felt good and walked tall. But the new mood was largely a return to the old American philosophy of self-help within a nation providentially isolated from the world's stresses and there was now little talk of a 'great society' to be constructed at home or abroad. Public opinion had moved away from the period when the main denominations had influentially rallied to political crusades and world leaders such as Roosevelt and Eisenhower. Now, in a daring union of religion and technology, the moral philosophy of America was reinforced by preachers on Sunday morning TV. Some of these were explicitly to the right of the Republican administration, claiming to be the voice of the 'moral majority' in ultra-conservative politics. Or they might be explicitly in the tradition of past preachers of an ultra-conservative religion. But the most popular of them avoided political and theological controversy. They encouraged people who were often (despite the public rhetoric about American strength) lonely and frightened. They affirmed the great simplicities of faith in God and in oneself. Under the American system or non-system of broadcasting, they could in return ask for financial support from viewers. This was forthcoming in substantial amounts, indicating the gratitude of millions for this ministry which might be a comfortable alternative to churchgoing, a heartening supplement to it, or (for a minority) an attractive door into it.

If enquirers went to church, they might well find that the congregation was committed to strict standards in belief and behaviour; for example, members might be expected to tithe, giving back to the Lord a tenth of their incomes. And such congregations drew many into their fellowship. A widely noticed and accepted book of 1972, analysing this movement before it reached its crescendo, was entitled *Why Conservative Churches are Growing*. Its author was a Methodist, Dean Kelley. His denomination was one of the places where American Christians asked themselves whether liberalism had enough to offer the people. Liberal churches, unlike the 'electronic church', made financial demands without offering health, happiness and prosperity in the simplicity of the most popular preachers. And liberal churches, unlike the conservative congregations, made demands on time and loyalty without offering a fellowship so warmly embracing that it could be a second family. With all this in mind Dean Kelley had originally suggested to his publisher that his book should be called *Why Strict Churches are Strong*. By the 1980s there were in the USA more than 450 Evangelical colleges and seminaries, fed by some eighteen thousand 'Christian' schools with about 2,500,000 pupils outside the state's educational system. This constituency supported almost three hundred periodicals and more than three thousand bookstores. Some polls have suggested that some twenty per cent of all the citizens of the USA over the age of eighteen identify themselves as Evangelicals.

Thus an outline of the history of Christianity in the USA up to the 1980s might conclude that conservatism had the future before it. Many North Americans would say so, thinking that the broadly conservative magazine *Christianity Today*, established in 1956 and soon overtaking the liberal *Christian Century* (what a nostalgically evocative title!) in sales, might as well have been called *Christianity Tomorrow*. But in the mid-1980s there are significant pointers to the possibility of other morrows.

Change has been sweeping through American Catholicism, into which a fifth of the population has been baptised. In the years 1945–60 the Catholic numbers doubled but the effect of the Second Vatican Council (1962–65) was statistically disastrous for Catholic activities (as contrasted with nominal membership). Thousands of priests abandoned their calling and seminaries emptied. In the parishes the clergy had far less authority. The regularity of attendance at mass, the practice of confessing sins to a priest, lay organisations and parochial schools – all slumped. In the twenty years from 1954 to 1974 weekly attendance at mass fell from seventy-eight per cent of all Catholics to about fifty per cent. During a visit Pope John Paul II was scandalised to find himself the target of feminist protests by nuns. Confidence in Catholic doctrine has also suffered many blows. Polls have suggested that only a minority of Catholic laymen now think the pope infallible and that most married couples are untroubled in conscience as they passionately disobey his teachings on contraception. The style of much American Catholic theology has often become almost as disturbed and critical as in the liberal Protestant denominations. In spirituality the emphasis has been on a fresh personal involvement – as in the charismatic revival, which has drawn heavily on the style of the Pentecostal churches and has filled some of the gap left by the downgrading of some traditional symbols which had been the focus of popular piety. There has also been a new courage in controversial political topics, shown in long statements by the bishops on nuclear weapons and on the economy. The immediate effects of these changes of emphasis should not be exaggerated, since under the patronage of bishops (all appointed by the Vatican) much conservatism has remained official in the USA's 175-or-so dioceses. But the long-term effects must, it seems, amount to a less authoritarian version of the religion of the Americans who identify themselves as Catholics in communion with Rome (in the 1980s, about fifty-two million).

Americanisation is clearly a strong trend all through the complex world of the churches – and in human terms it has been brought to a head by the trend, increasing over many years, for American marriages to cross the barriers between the religions and ethnic communities. Catholicism has been acknowledged generally (although still not universally) as patriotic; the decisive recognition was given in 1960 through the election of John F. Kennedy.

Protestant bodies have also felt themselves being swept into the mainstream of American life. Even the Eastern Orthodox churches, while still divided ethnically, participate in the life of the National Council of Churches. The black churches have remained in many ways movements of protest against the mainstream. Yet a black Christian leader such as Martin Luther King, in life or death, could stir the consciences of many millions of white Americans. Great efforts have been made by whites (including rulings by the Supreme

Court, presidential initiatives and Congressional legislation) to satisfy the blacks' grievances over education, voters' registers, access to amenities and economic prospects; and the black churches have been agencies through which members have advanced their social and economic position, like the churches of the white immigrants in earlier years. With all its limits, the movement towards the equality of white and black is a potent example of Americanisation, the move out of the ghetto. It matters: in the 1980s sixteen per cent of the population is black. And now Hispanic and Asian immigrants are beginning to repeat this traditional process. In the 1980s, almost a quarter of the population has no ancestral connections with Europe.

So what is 'America'? Can this 'nation of immigrants' agree on its aims? The liberal denominations are often criticised by conservatives for being absorbed in political issues rather than in spirituality and evangelism; and for a time their drooping membership statistics could be used as evidence by their critics. But the leadership has remained convinced that the application of the Christian gospel to national and international problems must have priority over narrower concerns and in due course the membership statistics have shown some signs of recovery. It is true that there has been a limited switch within these churches from political controversies back to spirituality and evangelism, but it also seems to be the case that many of the American people do not object to churchmen taking an interest in their society's problems. Even many Americans who are firmly conservative in religion recognise that Americanisation must involve serious thought about the great moral issues in public life. For most conservatives, these issues are causes different from the leftward-leaning agenda of the World and National Councils of Churches. Their enthusiasm is given to 'pro-life' issues such as the resistance to abortion and drugs and the defence of the traditional family against pornography, promiscuity, cohabitation without marriage and easy divorce. At times, indeed, there has seemed to be a very wide gap between the perceptions of 'liberal establishment' which takes counsel together in the National Council of Churches and those of the 'moral majority' which is marshalled in growing organisations often led by avowed fundamentalists such as Jerry Falwell. Thus the liberals leap to the defence of 'human rights', 'equal rights' (for women and men) and 'welfare rights'; they seek gun control at home and arms control internationally; they oppose the death penalty; they support the United Nations and the conservation of nature and of energy. None of these causes usually appeals to the conservatives – who greatly resent the liberals' preference for 'civil liberties' (in the separation of church and state) when asked to support what seem obviously good causes such as the use of simple prayers to God in the public schools. But some Evangelicals, like some Roman Catholics, are as outspoken as any of the liberals in their attacks on militarism and unrestrained capitalism, proclaiming that these are the poisoning evils in the nation's life. Widely organised as Evangelicals for Social Action, dramatically radical as the Sojourners Community publishing a hard-hitting magazine from the nation's capital, they, too, deserve attention.

In the nation as a whole, the collapse of tradition and authority seems more significant than any conservative backlash; and one of the victims of change is for many the authority of the Christian tradition. The American people, while strikingly favourable to the churches and willing to profess their trust in God, are on the whole undeniably materialist. They have usually isolated themselves from the hunger and agony of the world. They have tended to judge their own fellow citizens by their material success. They have accepted an economic system which is harsh on the unfortunates. They have tolerated violence by their appetite for bloodshed on TV and by extremely permissive gun laws. They are often also permissive in their sexual conduct, after a liberation which would have utterly scandalised their ancestors. And they have sheltered behind a nuclear wall of terror. Intellectually, the battle has often seemed to be going against Christian belief, at least in its more conservative forms. University and college teachers (specially the social scientists) tend to want to keep their distance from the churches unless they work in the church-related or Evangelical institutions. Non-Christian religions have gained many adherents, whether these are immigrants loyal to ancient, inherited faiths or rootless enquirers seeking spiritual homes in new cults. The whole pressure of education is to increase sophistication and scepticism despite all the counter-trend making for folksy simplification, and it is significant that many conservative Protestants, specially recent college graduates, have renounced the old prejudices – anti-black, anti-Catholic, anti-homosexual, anti-Semitic. They have also moved away from much in the old puritanism; they may 'take a drink', 'smoke pot' or 'have sex' before marriage, although with far more self-discipline than their secular contemporaries. A Hollywood actor remarried after divorce (wisely) and not a frequent churchgoer or a total abstainer from alcohol has been the political hero of the Christian right in the 1980s. Agnosticism about traditional creeds and morals is in the air in many places although it is still unwise to be too public about it. There is a tendency to secularisation which challenges the churches of the USA in ways not totally unlike the problems of the churches in a much more heavily secular continent – Europe, the subject of a later chapter.

The number of Americans who are willing to describe themselves as 'born again' Christians is impressive. But it seems to be generally agreed that, to be a Christian, it is not enough to have been born (or naturalised) as an American. The convert has to enter a new family, the Christian community, which is smaller than the nation and larger than the natural family, and which demands a spiritual transformation. The individual has to make a deliberate, costly choice – and has to choose something different from a journey of the heart back to the frontiersman's childhood or the immigrant's homeland. For two hundred years after the 1730s it was possible to believe that what the American people needed in order to claim their Christian heritage for themselves was 'revival'. In this independent and often rebellious daughter of European Christendom, an existing but dormant faith had to be brought to vigorous, active and infectious life which would be thoroughly American yet also related to American Christianity's European origins. Sermons and hymns often appealed to memories of mothers' knees and green fields, trying to reach a believing innocence which still seemed to lie at the heart of the adult's life. And it worked. Faith was revived. The churches recruited. The American people was 'a religious people whose institutions presuppose a Supreme Being'. So Justice Douglas of the Supreme Court declared in 1952. But as the twentieth century moves towards its close, there is less talk about an essentially conservative 'revival' even in circles where the word has belonged to a treasured inheritance. As a new age begins and is almost everywhere known to be beginning, with the USA Protestant but also Catholic and Jewish, Christian but also Buddhist, Muslim and Hindu, religious but also secular (Justice Douglas made no secret of the fact that he was not personally religious), with the people certainly not conservative in most of their moral attitudes, the revival of an old religion cannot be enough. Despite the success of the Evangelical and other Christian movements, it must be ominous for the churches that Gallup polls reported that the proportion of Americans saying that religion was 'very important' in their lives fell from seventy-five per cent in 1952 to fifty-three per cent in 1980. Other studies of public opinion show that youth in the USA in the 1980s, while more God-conscious than its parents, respects the churches less. It seems that the decisive challenge will lie in the dialogue of the churches with a fast-changing modern or post-modern culture. New responses, as energetic as any of the revivals in past years, will be needed if Christianity is to continue to play the central role in the USA which the Great Awakening made its privilege.[6]

Linking the futures of the Americas

In this new age it will surely be important that the Christians of both the Americas should consider the problems and opportunities of their societies in a new way. To suggest that is not to say that it would be good to see a 'Christian' political and economic policy agreed in detail. It is, on the contrary, fortunate that it is utterly impossible to imagine any such agreement. One of the most valuable lessons taught by the history of Christianity in the Americas is that the spokesmen of religion ought to be kept at some distance from the leaders of political movements. Politicised religion becomes corrupt; religionised politics becomes fanatical. But the Christians of both the Americas do share a responsibility for considering together the great issues which are then passed to politicians and economists for detailed recommendations. They can build up concern and support. Up to the present much has been lost by the restriction of any such common concern to minorities. In Latin America, in the churches as elsewhere, the general tendency has been merely to denounce the USA for interference except in those privileged minorities where Uncle Sam is admired as the patron. In the USA, many Christians have been among those contemptuous or bored about 'banana republics' and alert only to the dangers of communism. These popular prejudices place great obstacles in the way of any creative discussion of the crisis. Yet the crisis does present a very great opportunity to be creative. If handled rightly, Latin America's fate to be the neighbour of the USA could be its unique advantage over Africa and Asia – and the USA's assistance of Latin America in its hour of need could be one of the finest things in history. A far better future can be created if only prejudices can be examined and shallow slogans replaced by a determination actually to change the situation in a way that really does benefit men, women and children. For the sake of the peoples – to give them food and jobs rather than words – the discussion of Latin America's future needs to be liberated from the rhetoric of Marxism. If the human factor is to be fed into the calculations, the USA's future needs to be considered at a level which goes deeper than the technical wizardry which so far has been the main topic of conversation in 'futurology'. And Christians could find in their shared faith a special reason to care deeply about the people and therefore to care realistically about the facts.

When the liberation theology of Latin America became accessible through translation to Christians in other regions, it often seemed naively Utopian. It was criticised by conservatives in the Vatican for concentrating on dreams of an earthly paradise to the neglect of hopes of heaven. Essentially similar reactions came from those Evangelicals who understood the gospel of salvation as primarily the offer of eternal glory to the converted individual, the world being left in darkness. Many Protestants who prided themselves on their greater sophistication, and who spoke less confidently about heaven or salvation, now included a 'Christian realism' as a part of their equipment for life in the real world; and they reckoned that the Latin Americans had been deceived by political illusions. In particular (and in an unusual agreement) all these Christians were now unimpressed by the Marxist promises which seemed to have enthralled Latin America's leading theologians. They warned that revolutions claiming to be quick advances into Utopia had been followed in real history by new and more ruthless tyrannies, by self-perpetuating elites and by corrupt and inefficient bureaucracies. They pointed out also that Marxists, while glad enough of the support of religious bodies before the revolution, have tended when in power to show their contempt for the 'opium of the people'. The spread of atheism through education and propaganda, the exclusion of practising members of churches from public life, many kinds of petty harassment, the closing of churches and other religious institutions and ruthless persecution – these have been the actual sequels to the applause with which Christians have surrounded the early promises of the Marxist brand of idealism. Any thought about worldwide Christianity would show that hundreds of thousands of the churches' most dedicated clergy and laity have been killed during the twentieth century under communist governments – whether as outright martyrs for their faith in deviation from the new national ideology or as 'subversives' identified with various struggles for freedom under the dictatorships which have invoked the sacred name of the proletariat. To all these realities in the Marxist Utopia, Latin America's 'Christians for Socialism' seemed blind. Appropriately, it was a Polish pope who claimed the highest authority to open their eyes.

The replies given in Latin America denied that heaven had been forgotten – but they still put it in the background, defending the priority given to the prophetic denunciation of rampant injustices on earth. Such replies could appeal to the authority of the large sections of the Bible. Whatever else may be said about religious people who talk about heaven while withholding their just wages from the poor, it cannot be said that their religion conforms to the Hebrew and Christian scriptures. The replies to foreign criticism also denied any intention to endorse the brutalities of Stalinism or even the ugly side of Maoism. 'Socialism' was never defined in exact detail by these theologians, who usually had not attempted to become experts in economics or politics, but all the definitions offered stressed that 'socialism' would be democratic. It would be the liberation, not the suppression, of the political, economic and cultural energies of the people. In the ill-fated Czech term of the 1960s, it would be 'socialism with a human face' – and that face would be Latin American. That implied the continuing or increased freedom and prominence of Christianity. If some descriptions of that goal seemed Utopian in style, the only motive had been to win imaginations away from enslavement to the necessity of the existing order. And there, too, an appeal could be made to the Bible, where hopes which do not 'make sense' liberate hearts and wills from despair.

What are we to make of this debate?

The USA has prospered mightily under an economic system which has been supported, or at least accepted, by the overwhelming mass of its people, even by most of the poor: the system of wealth-creation by capitalism. That system's record of performance is superior to anything on view in any socialist country. Although in practice the US economy has been dominated by giant corporations, public opinion persists in showing where its own heart is by calling this system 'free enterprise' and by welcoming predictions that the new stage of the Industrial Revolution will bring back the supremacy of the small workshop and even enable Americans to earn good livings without leaving a home which will be an 'electronic cottage'. With an equal or greater passion the people hold dear their freedom of speech and their power to overturn governments by 'one person, one vote'; and this freedom is valued with a fierce intensity by minorities who oppose the dominant economic or cultural system. Among conformists and rebels alike, anti-communism is the almost universal creed and even the word 'socialism' is highly suspect. None of this has made for ready sympathy with a Marxist or semi-Marxist understanding of liberation. It is therefore easy to present Latin America to public opinion largely in terms of an anti-communist crusade. And in the business community, where there is a sharper awareness of Latin American realities, it is easy to be influenced solely by some very realistic thoughts – that the rate of return on Latin American investments is far higher than in the domestic market, that imports from the dependent south are cheap, that exports to a non-industrialised Latin America get high prices. The only question seems to be: For how long will the USA be allowed to get away with it?

On the other hand, the cry for justice now so prominent in Latin American life, including religion, must arouse echoes in many North American hearts. As we have seen, the history of the USA has included many phases of high expectation that the kingdom of God on earth was near, perhaps just over the horizon in the movement to the west or just around the corner in the industrial city. The Declaration of Independence was, in the eyes of those who framed it, the proclamation of a new age for mankind. The 'social gospel' of the liberal denominations in the nineteenth and twentieth centuries was Utopian. So was the supernatural millenarianism of the fundamentalists who reacted against such worldliness. So was the protest movement of the 1960s, in defence of 'doing what comes naturally' against militarism and industrialism. The conservatism of the 1980s, while certainly not idealistic, has been highly confident about the ability of 'Americans' to combine doing good with doing well. Many phases in the 'American' tradition have left legacies which encourage many in the USA to listen with sympathy to the hopes and fears of Latin America. It is supremely important that they should go on listening.

They need to listen because the USA's 'last frontier' – the supreme test of optimism, the supreme challenge to determination, ingenuity and skill – lies not on the moon, or anywhere else in space, but south of the Mexican border. There two thirds of all the people with a true title to be called 'Americans' live in conditions which pose obvious dangers to both the Americas. The illegal immigrants who cross the border in large numbers – and who are sheltered by thousands of law-abiding churchgoers in the USA – are ambassadors with a message.

It would not be right for an ignorant foreigner to get involved in the controversial intricacies of US economics. But as they consider the tasks which will confront President Reagan's successors, perceptive commentators often stress that there are sound economic and political, as well as moral, arguments in favour of putting much more purchasing power into the pockets of the poor both within the USA and overseas. If automated machines are going to pour out vast quantities of goods, it will not be merely sentimental to say that new markets will have to be discovered for them – and adequate new markets cannot be created merely by the rich consuming even more. If less manpower is going to be needed in that industrial production (and in the USA white-collar workers have outnumbered blue-collar workers since the 1950s), the danger will increase that a large section of the people will be alienated from society. If US farmers are going to grow more and more food, if the US population does not grow proportionately in its purchasing power, and if other countries cannot afford US prices, the farmers are going to have to accept prices so low that high debts will overwhelm them – as is already happening in the 1980s. Already in the 1980s the poorest three fifths of the population receives only one third of the total personal income. A fifth of the population under eighteen is below the poverty line and half of all black children are raised in poverty. Unemployment remains stuck at around seven per cent of the work force. The frustrations of the elderly meant that crimes committed by them increased by forty-eight per cent in the period 1978–83. Computers and other machines which are transforming both jobs and bargaining positions in industry, to the further detriment of unionised labour, are at the same time creating a society which is more fragile than ever before because more open to paralysing sabotage. The media which are moulding the millions into one viewing (and sometimes reading) public are at the same time showing that public how the privileged live, so that every flaunting of affluence can become an incitement to envy and violence. The growth of crime, including violence against the person, is the obvious writing on the golden wall of the USA's high tech economy. And many of the USA's potential rebels are Hispanics, for in the 1980s there are more Spanish-speakers in the USA than in Central America.

The case for putting more money into the pockets of poor people outside the USA sounds strange to most of the citizens of a nation which tends to suspect that laziness lies at the bottom of other people's problems. But the case can be made convincingly if made carefully. It is not being suggested that food should be given as aid, except in emergencies: that would only reduce the incentives of Latin America's (or of other regions') own food-producers. Nor is it being suggested that financial aid should be lavished on every government which would like it: some nations to the south do not need it and some of those which can prove a need for it also need watching because of the proven record of corruption and waste. But some measures which would aid Latin America and other regions can be justified in hard-headed terms. Indeed, already some of the desirable moves have been made. Many tempting suggestions made in order to protect US industries and agriculture against foreign competition by tariff walls and import quotas have been resisted and more could be renounced without ruining the US economy. Sensibly, there has been awareness of the dangers of retaliatory trade wars which would wreck US exports. Foreign debts have been rescheduled in order to make possible repayment without bankruptcy and the exchange rate of the dollar has been checked and altered in the interest of international trade. It would be in keeping with the logic of such wise moves if there were to be more sensitivity in the USA to the need of Latin American governments to control the operations of US corporations and to the desirability of funding some projects which would be keys to economic growth, meaning among other things that in future there would be a bigger market for US exports. Such projects include the development of science and technology and the building up of the agricultural and industrial infrastructure.

The only long-term solutions to the Americas' problems seem to be a wider spread of purchasing power within the USA and greater equality in the economic relationships between the USA and other countries. It will be realism for future US governments to make sure that their own poor are not too poor to buy and to assist the growth of Latin American and other economies to become more equal trading partners. The great precedent here is the superbly imaginative, generous and well-rewarded Marshall Plan, which was essential to the reconstruction of Western Europe after 1945. But another precedent is the fact that year by year in the 1970s and 1980s the Soviet Union has been kept alive by grain grown in the USA. That grain has been sold, but the price has been subsidised by the US government. Had it been the consistent policy to use military and economic strength solely in order to resist the expansion of communism's 'evil empire', presumably the Soviet Union could have been left to starve.

More familiar to the US public – and equally formidable as an intellectual case – is the argument from geopolitics. Already Latin America costs the US taxpayer massive sums because its instability, actual or potential, is held to be one of the dangers justifying a defence expenditure in the region of $300,000 million a year. But some of this money would be better spent on reducing the causes of unrest. To put it crudely, the best way to keep communism out of the Caribbean is to let more sugar into the US market at a fair price; the best way to drink to the cause of democracy in Brazil is to pay more for a cup of coffee; the best way to make the Latin American peoples one's friends is to show that one can help their progress, not their repression under a system rejected by their hearts and consciences. The days when President Theodore Roosevelt could build the Panama canal by his 'big stick' and announce that 'chronic wrongdoing' elsewhere in Latin America would require 'intervention by some civilised nations' (in 1904) are over. Despite small-scale interventions in the 1980s, militarily the turning point came with the failure of force to sort out the Dominican Republic in the 1960s. Psychologically the decision was made when public opinion in the USA adopted the doctrine 'No more Vietnams'. After that trauma, it became the real situation that it was the USA that feared dramatic action by its neighbours – for example, the repudiation by Latin American governments of some of the vast loans which the US banks had been pouring into their countries at greedy rates of interest ever since the 1930s. Yet Latin America could become a more equal trading partner for the USA, bound by innumerable links of mutual advantage. In 1982 a US government report to the president (*The Global 2000 Report*) predicted on the basis of the far from revolutionary trends then prevailing that by the end of the century the level of economic performance (GNP per capita) would be three times higher in Latin America than in Africa or Asia. It also demonstrated that the USA would not be ruined if it gave economic assistance to its neighbour, since the level of its own economic performance would be seven times higher than Africa's or Asia's. The alternative to cooperation in prosperity would, however, be likely to bring disaster to the USA. All the signs are that the opportunities still open in the 1980s to Latin American governments which are more or less acceptable to the USA will not be permanent. And not only the security of the massive US investments and loans is threatened. If the poverty of the masses is allowed to deepen and if the USA is seen as indifferent to their plight, it is certain that they will turn to Marxism as the people of China turned. A Latin American variety of Marxism in power may be as independent of Moscow as China is, but that cannot be guaranteed. Indeed, the probable scenario is that the Soviet Union would secure many bases within the American hemisphere. That would be the nightmare which successive US presidents, in minor crises, have striven to avoid. In 1823 the Monroe Doctrine established the principle that non-American interference in Latin America would be interpreted as a threat to the USA. It was a realistic doctrine.

But the economic and political arguments are not the only arguments in favour of a response by the controlling forces in the USA to the poverty of their own people and of Latin America's. There are also moral arguments. Not for nothing did Virgilio Elizondo, Director of the Mexican-American Cultural Center in San Antonio, Texas, entitle his presentation of the case *Galilean Journey* (1983). The poor in Latin or North America are despised, as the Galileans were despised nineteen centuries ago. But Abraham Lincoln echoed a teacher from Galilee when he declared that a nation divided into slave and free 'cannot endure'. The Union would not have become the USA we know had not slavery – which Lincoln himself in many moods felt to be a permanent institution – been abolished. Nor would the USA have been the land of the free had the free not been brave enough to end the tax-free tyrannies of the capitalists who amassed fortunes like robber barons in the early years of industrialism, creating what was virtually a new form of slavery. The USA is a democracy or in its own estimate of itself it is nothing. Just as the American democracy could not survive half-slave and half-free, just as it could not survive without a New Deal for the poor, so it will not be able to survive the futures if it has to contain a bitter, poor but muscular minority, black, Hispanic and other. The ghetto will explode. Nor will the American democracy's image of itself, already badly dented by the moral disaster of the Vietnam war, survive if it is seen that Latin America is being allowed to slide into despair, chaos and communism when it could have helped progress to prosperity at an affordable price and without a military involvement. The nature of the US involvement (or aloof non-involvement) in Latin American affairs constitutes a threat to the health of the nation comparable with the menace of the drugs so plentifully smuggled in from the south – for a nation can be poisoned by action or inaction which is in its own eyes immoral. Already in the 1980s this moral concern has received a sharp focus in the protests of many American Christians against, for example, the Reagan administration's emphasis on merely military measures to 'stop communism' in Nicaragua. These protests contrast with the acquiescence of the churches in nine previous US interventions in Nicaragua (dating back to 1853) and in the US participation in the overthrow of the Allende government in Chile in 1973. Plainly Latin America's problems will not be killed off by throwing dollars at them. But firing bullets will also not be enough – partly because some of these bullets will wound or kill the self-respect of the USA, a nation which, whatever its external or internal critics may say, has always had an image of itself as being on the side of justice and freedom throughout its own territory 'from sea to shining sea', and throughout the world.

Vital parts of the realistic hope for Latin America can be called 'socialism' if that word, used by a myriad of groups, appeals. It means reducing expenditure on armies and armaments. It means greater cooperation between states with a similar social and economic philosophy, in a new movement towards the United States of Latin

America. And it means making it no longer necessary for an army to be armed to the teeth against its own people. It means taking the hands of a few landlords and capitalists off the levers of economic power for the good reasons that they underpay their workers, gain unreasonable profits and invest too much abroad. It means uncorrupt, detailed and sustained government action against the exploitation of cheap labour and cheap raw materials to the unfair profit of companies based abroad. It means breaking the monopolistic power of these multinational corporations and ending their control over Latin America's own resources. It means stronger negotiation in international bargains, including bargains with bankers and the international financial organisations. It means more finance for public education and health care, for housing and social services, for job training and income maintenance. It means taxing the rich so that the poor may survive. Whereas in North America and Western Europe the wealth creation of capitalism has trickled down to the benefit of the bulk of the population, in Latin America the gloomy predictions of Marx have come true: the rich have become richer, the poor poorer. That process can and must be reversed by measures more radical than any which the 'popular' governments of the 1930s and 1940s – Peron's in Argentina, for example – proved willing to take.

The challenge of urban poverty is inescapable. In the USA much – although not enough – has been done to cure the cancer cells constituted by the deprived and violent sections of the great cities (which are markets for drugs grown in Latin America). But already in the 1980s almost half of all Latin Americans are living in urban areas, mostly in poverty. In the year 2000 the world's two largest cities are expected to be Mexico City and Sao Paulo. Between them they will have more inhabitants than the United Kingdom. The comparatively small Rio will have more than twice the population of Greater London. When expanded on this scale, the already terrible contrast between the slums and the luxurious quarters, now to be found in many Latin American cities, will surely be ended one way or another – by reform or by revolution. If the cities are to be rescued peacefully, it must be by the growth of jobs; in the 1980s employment in manufacturing gives jobs to no more than fourteen per cent of Latin America's labour force. But China and India both teach that it is impossible to improve conditions in the city unless there is a check on migration from the countryside. It is obviously self-defeating to confine reforms to the cities if after some improvements these cities are to become even more powerful magnets attracting new millions of the landless, the indebted and the hungry. Something in the right direction can be done by government controls on migration, but the problem of the cities has been shown to be insoluble unless the economy of the countryside is made more viable. And China and India show that rural poverty is not an unconquerable mountain.

In Latin America as in China and India, the need to stop the urban drift by rural renewal is dwarfed only by the need to grow more food in order to avert famine in city and countryside alike. Most experts do not despair about the possibilities. The world output of grain doubled in the years 1950 to 1985. The cautious staff of the World Bank has declared its conviction that during the ten years after 1985 the world's productivity could grow by six per cent each year. But the experience of many countries has demonstrated that farm workers need the incentive of personal profit if they are to work hard and efficiently. They need many things from governments (despite the caution of the World Bank). They often need resources more powerful than their own if technical education is to be given, if electricity is to work the pumps and light the homes, if water, fertilisers, tractors, pesticides and improved seeds are to be made available, if credit is to be obtainable at affordable interest rates until the harvest comes, and if the produce is to be stored safely and marketed. But (as the World Bank urges) what they often need most is an end of government interference in the market – for food prices should not be kept artificially low by politicians seeking urban support at the cost of rural profitability. Above all they need to be allowed to help themselves. At the beginning of the day it has to be the farm worker who gets up for work. He wants to work for profits and on soil in which he has a direct, personal share. His sweat has to be the holy water which makes the land prosper. He wants to feel that the earth into which his sweat drops is *his* land (and preferably also the land of his ancestors), securely owned or leased. Thus a 'socialism' which wants to feed people cannot safely 'collectivise' the farms except in providing collective services to meet the needs of the people of the farms – services which may include the ultimate ownership of the land leased to the people. All these things are true in Latin America, as throughout the world.

Nor can a Latin American 'socialism' which needs the products and the jobs of a growing industrial sector afford to place itself under a large central bureaucracy which would be out of touch with local markets and slow to adapt to change. Nor can it afford to isolate itself from the USA, which together with Japan seems likely to remain for a long time the world's chief fountainhead of industrial research and investment. Aid from the US government has so far brought little except disappointments to the Latin American peoples. Too much of it has strengthened military forces which could then control domestic politics; too much of it has ended up in the pockets of the rich; too much of it has been wasted. But some aid makes long-term sense. And some trade makes sense in development which benefits the peoples. The multinational corporations under largely US ownership are vigorously attacked by Latin American progressives, including churchmen, and it is clear that it is absolutely essential for Latin American governments to impose many more controls on their operations. But it is equally plain that it is in the interests of the Latin American peoples to provide a reasonable return on some US investment; for that is the quickest road to competitive modernisation. Similarly, while nonessential imports should be restricted it is in the peoples' interests that foreign currency should be earned by some export of crops and industrial raw materials. It has been misleading to regard Cuba as the model for Latin American progress (although Sir Thomas More's *Utopia* was located in that island, in 1516). Before Fidel Castro's revolution Cuba was virtually a US colony – but largely because of unrelenting hostility by the USA, its economic problems since then have made it accept the role of a virtual colony of the Soviet Union, dependent on prices which are artificially high for its exports of sugar and artificially low for its imports of oil. Such Soviet favours could not be bestowed on many other countries. The reality of the situation is that other Latin American nations, if they attempt to sever all links with the USA, will find themselves sliding into non-Utopian problems.

An urgent responsibility facing governments throughout Latin America is to work out precisely which connections in aid and trade are genuinely to the mutual advantage of the two Americas. And one urgent task facing churches in both Americas is the encouragement of that undramatic process, rather than the rhetorically exciting, but ultimately sterile, war of words between anti-communism and anti-Americanism. It needs to be said loudly that if the aim is to put food into the bellies of Latin Americans and up-to-date machines into their hands, it is cruel madness either to be oversimple when defining the necessary 'development' or to be sweeping when condemning it. In the Americas more than anywhere else in the world, the churches have the power to shape the futures by influencing public opinion to face realities – an influence which can end up in the election of a government. That is why this task is morally urgent.[7]

Religion in the Americas

So cooperation for prosperity could produce better economic and social futures despite the obvious problems. But what could be the religious futures in the two Americas? As a European who is therefore semi-detached, I offer a few notes towards an answer.

The liberation theologians of Latin America are surely right to be concerned about economic and social conditions. However, they are themselves open to criticism for a tendency to despise popular religion. They are dismayed by the superstition of the masses – by the preference for spectacle over study, for procession over prayer; by the rivalries between miracle-working local Virgins; by the obsession with Christ's sufferings as suggesting the only alternative to a miracle from heaven; by many aspects of folk-Catholicism including its aesthetic vulgarity and its profitability to the higher clergy; by the syncretistic mix of folk-Catholicism with the African religion of the slaves (debased into *Voodoo* in Brazil, the Caribbean islands and elsewhere); by the anti-intellectual fundamentalism of the Protestants; by the hysterical emotionalism of the Pentecostals. But these theologians can be accused of a lack of sympathy with their own people – the very people whose economic liberation they have advocated at such risk to themselves. Popular religion was described by Marx as the 'heart of a heartless world'. It has provided an escape for the imagination from poverty, disease and early death into a rich world of the spirit shared by ancestors and neighbours. It has been enjoyed and has, in times past, accounted for the laughter amid the tears of life. And as change sweeps over traditional societies, religion still offers its consolations as an oasis of stability and as a warmly human community in a new world which seems impersonal. That has, of course, been the North American experience. Elements in popular religion, Latin or North American, certainly are sub-Christian. But precisely because it belongs to the people it deserves to be treated with a respect which does not come naturally to critical intellectuals. If it is the calling of intellectuals to criticise, for Christian intellectuals that vocation will one day involve a careful attention to folk-Catholicism, Protestant fundamentalism and other popular religion.

Professor Harvey Cox paid tributes both to the liberation theologians and to the popular religion of Latin America, finding in both phenomena clues to the 'post-modern' theology needed by North America. In his bestseller of 1965, *The Secular City: Urbanization and Secularization in Theological Perspective*, he enthusiastically urged Christians to greet what was liberating in modernity as symbolised by the North American city. He has never abandoned that welcome to greater opportunities for ordinary people, but in later books he has also greeted the revival of interest in spiritual life and in the simple joys of the body amid nature. For example, in *Turning East* (1977) he was sympathetic with the new interest in Hinduism and Buddhism. Now in *Religion in the Secular City* (1984), pulling all these themes together, he has praised the Christian leadership of the liberation of the Latin American poor, particularly in the *comuni-* *dades de base* – and also the Latin American *fiestas* with their celebration of the joy of life. His conviction had grown that modernity (in its theological expression, 'liberalism') was being replaced by a less industrial, intellectual, individual and inhibited lifestyle, by a conviviality more in keeping with the real needs of human nature. This conviction had, indeed, given him some sympathy with the fundamentalists of the USA. But he now observed that the examples provided by Latin America are healthier, because more full of respect for humanity and more affirmative of humanity's full freedom and joy under God.

—See p.125

This analysis seems to be essentially right. Religion must relate to the society around it, and share the responsibility for that society's advance – but after being valued so highly for centuries in the Americas, it is not likely to wither away in post-modern times. It will remain not a creed imposed by the state but an affair of the heart and a social reality, providing images which will be thought (or felt) to illuminate the mysteries surrounding human life, resources which sustain life's battles, and fellowships which help life to be a celebration. Religion will still be there – but will be affected, as so often in its history, by changes in society. And much popular religion will be slow to change. Traditionalism is often given more, not less, appeal in religion when the changes in society are disturbing and threatening. But as education expands over a wider range in society and over more years in most people's lives, religion seems bound to become, however slowly, more intelligent. Its officers will not be obeyed blindly, its doctrines will not escape scrutiny, the patronage which the churches can provide will not seem so necessary to the poor. And many religious people are going to welcome the challenge of change. They will not be displeased by the opportunity to innovate in religion when they earn their livings by being adaptable at work.

So, being popular in all those senses, religion is likely to be still very diverse in the Americas. The division into denominations is likely to remain the general pattern. It will be a long time before the gaps between Catholic and Protestant in Latin America can be bridged –

and before the Christians of the USA lose their fear of being controlled by the authorities of a superchurch in a New York sky-scraper. The dream of a Protestant monopoly in the north, or of a Catholic monopoly in the south, or of a complete ecumenical union, seems to have little or no future in it. And there will still be great contrasts between 'progressive' and 'conservative' religion within Catholicism and Protestantism alike, because people will continue to differ in their willingness to see religion changed along with society. The importance which some will attach to the preservation of tradi-tion or stability will be matched only by the passion with which others put first truth or relevance in terms understood by their contempor-aries in the science-based society. Yet it seems likely that there will be some convergence as well as much diversity, for some trends affecting all the churches are already gathering force. Underlying many of these trends is the reality that the churches are becoming more thoroughly American. Europe is rapidly losing its prestige, not least because its churches give the impression of being marginal, confused and unenthusiastic. And migration from Europe across the Atlantic is no longer a flood. The exile's nostalgia for European church life – or at any rate for European church architecture and styles of worship – has shaped much of the history of Christianity in both the Americas. It is a dwindling pressure.

A refusal to allow the control of its theology and its life by people who do not know the problems increasingly marks the Catholic church in Latin America. Unless the local leadership adjusts itself with a radical courage and speed to the pressures for change now building up, the African phenomenon of a multitude of independent churches will be reproduced. But there is little reason to think that such a development is inevitable. Historic loyalties to Catholicism are stronger in Latin America than in Africa (and in Africa most of the independent churches have walked out of Protestantism, not Catho-licism). Moreover, this already popular church is becoming steadily more Latin American in its leadership. In the future the churches of North America and Western Europe are highly unlikely to continue to export many priests. Their clergy will be needed nearer home if anything like the present ministry (of one priest to about 850 Catho-lics in North America and of one to a thousand in Europe) is to be maintained. One response may be insistence by the Latin American bishops on the ordination of large numbers of men who are not celibate and not trained in European theology. The alternative would be to make Catholicism a lay movement (if 'movement' is not too strong a word) with only occasional contact with a priest. Already in the 1980s there are about seven thousand Catholics to one priest in Latin America and inevitably few of these are regular churchgoers or close students of the clergy's teachings. If the present patterns in the priesthood continue, in the year 2000 Latin America will have some ten thousand nominal Catholics to one priest. Thus it may be predicted with confidence that the day of the domination of Latin American Catholicism by a professional, celibate clergy looking overseas for inspiration will soon be over if it is not already ended.

Another pressure making for change in response to Latin American realities will be the need to accept artificial birth control. As with the need for more local clergy, this will be the case whatever the Vatican may or may not say. The trends of the period 1950–2025, as known in the 1980s to be irreversible, are producing a growth of some seven hundred million in the population. Both in the Vatican-dominated hierarchy and among the liberation theologians, who are disinclined to have too many fights on their hands at the same time, there has been a conspiracy of silence about the necessity of contraception. Meanwhile most of the laity have seen no great harm in having many children. As in Africa or India, those children have seemed cheap to feed and clothe and easy to use in the fields or on the streets; many of them have been expected to die in infancy or youth, and few of them to spend many – or any – years in school; and the sons that survived have been relied on to support their parents in old age. But as these conditions alter it will not be possible to evade for ever the problem of too many mouths. Mexico showed the way. In twenty years, from 1960 to 1980, its population did almost exactly double, but the free provision of contraceptives was in 1974 made a constitutional right.

If the worst economic consequences of population growth can be avoided by a combination of economic advance, the availability of contraception and the self-interest of parents who will no longer want large families, the fuller stomachs and fuller minds of the laity will mean a fuller syllabus for any teacher of Christianity. The criticism of the Bible and of the church's traditions by science and scientific history will have to be faced if educated people are to be persuaded. More positively, the tradition of Latin American piety will have to be developed with a greater concern for the spiritual growth of the free, intelligent individual and for those sufferings which are the human condition whatever the political and economic system. The life of the spirit – no longer reduced either to conformity to ecclesiastical rules or to participation in a political struggle, and no longer having in its centre either the consolation or the awakening of people who are helplessly poor – will have an opportunity to advance to a richness already to be glimpsed in some Latin American poetry and fiction and heard in the *Nueva Cancion* (New Song) movement. In a subcontinent linked with both cultures, human liberation could become a theme handled with the profundity of Europe's masters of prayer as well as with the wisdom of North America's teachers of pastoral psychology.

Religion in both the Americas, whether or not it remains traditional in its doctrinal basis and in public activities such as worship, seems likely to become more and more positively humanistic in its ethics and its counselling. So far this tendency has been most noticeable in the zest of preachers and laypeople in the churches of the USA for one or other of a long series of movements in popular psychology. That enthusiasm can be mocked as the absurd adoption of a series of fads memorialised on the shelves of any paperback shop, where the 'how to be happy' books usually outnumber the books on how to cook and even those on how to be fit. But the pursuit of happiness is surely not entirely hostile to the spirit of Christianity. At least in some of its expressions, it defines 'success' in terms of the healing of people, their restoration or entry to the life combining peace, health, harmony, prosperity and joy, for which the Hebrew term is *shalom*. In that way the American concern for the 'human potential' recalls the interest taken by Jesus in the healing of body and mind; an interest to which religious laws are subordinated since 'the Sabbath was made for man'. The stress is on the power of faith, which accounts for the tone of optimism – and that, too, is close to the recorded work of Jesus. In particular the stress is on raising despised minorities – most recently the blacks, the Hispanics, the homosexuals – and on releasing women from taboos imposed by centuries of male dominance. That also is in keeping with the gospels, where Samaritans are treated equally and women accompany Jesus freely, talk with him as naturally as do men, are loved and cured by him, and witness his resurrection. During my last visit to New York, I thought that probably no activity undertaken by the city's very numerous and busy churches was more Christian than a meeting which the Episcopal Church arranged in order to make known the medical and spiritual resources available to the victims of Aids, an epidemic which less compassionate Christians could interpret simply as God's way of punishing homosexuals.

Some trends in North American life, and in the life of the more fortunate in Latin America, suggest that this stress on the 'human potential' is one of the things that will grow. The new industries are likely to depend on energy from the fission or fusion of atoms, from the sun and the wind, from deep in the earth or moving water, and from sugar. But they will equally depend on information controlling production and distribution through the microprocessor. The human consequences of these changes have been predicted by many analysts with an encouraging amount of agreement. Women, it is expected, are going to compete for jobs with fewer handicaps because more families are going to be small. For women and men alike a sound basic education and up-to-date training are going to be the tickets to personal prosperity, and governments are going to be under great pressure to sponsor better education for all children and all adults. In very large numbers people are going to change their jobs more often and to experience spells of being unwaged, so that governments are also going to be made to arrange dignified unemployment benefits, and there is going to be a great demand for everything that helps to fill leisure agreeably. Working hours are going to be shorter and manu-facturing or administrative work, being less brutally repetitious, will make demands on intelligence, responsibility, cooperativeness and adaptability rather than on physical stamina. People who will no longer be crushed by work will want more entertainment, more sport, more cultural activities, more opportunities to swap skills with neigh-bours and to give unpaid service to the community. Many goods will be mass-produced by automated machines in order to get low prices, but most of the employment is likely to be in small businesses which can be, in one sense or another, communes. Computerisation will make it possible to adapt standard brands to suit the personal tastes of customers prepared to pay extra – and more people will be able to pay that. But there is also likely to be a spread of the small shops or street markets selling hand-made goods because in a more affluent society person-to-person contacts and craftsmanship are still going to be valued. It is not necessary to subscribe to the naive optimism of some predictions which underplay the problems of unemployment and poverty in order to agree that for most people life is going to present more, not fewer, opportunities. What can be looked at as the Reagan revolution in the 1980s was based on the fact that the poor on whom the Democrats had concentrated had become a minority – in the case of unionised labour, a comparatively small minority. Simply, people with money felt that it was time that the government did something for them; and that category included many people far removed from the traditional image of the Republican capitalist. And the popularity of a president in his seventies emphasised another trend of increasing significance. People are going to live longer, more actively. They will have votes as well as voices. They are going to get more attention for their psychological as well as physical needs. Youth had better look out.

What will these changes mean for the churches? Certainly they will mean that the churches will have to deepen and sharpen their contributions to the public debate about the significance of the continuing transformation of society; otherwise they will be guilty of helping to leave these changes out of human control. That responsibility must involve speaking up for the poor. And certainly these changes will mean that, with more leisure, people will have more time in which to be unhappy and to mess up their private lives. So the churches will be needed for counselling and for their sustaining fellowships. But the churches will also be needed to provide more of a vision of the potential glory of humanity in communion with God. Freed to a considerable (not complete) extent from the drudgery which has burdened all previous centuries, people are going to be able to live humanly.

In this context, Catholicism in the USA seems likely to become much more confidently American and therefore humanist. Its universities, colleges and seminaries have already ceased to propagate a dogmatism opposed to the mainstream of American intellectual life. The appearance and the activity of the parish church demonstrate an escape from a foreign-looking ghetto. What used to be a definitely Catholic culture in the USA has been diluted – but is able to flow more easily into the life of the rest of a science-based society. The control exercised by the Vatican over the dioceses through the appointment of their bishops (and through detailed directives to these appointees) is already out of keeping with the spirit of the nation – for the public life of the USA consists largely of the reverberations of the system of democratic election. Similarly, the personal control of finance and property by the diocesan bishop is out of keeping with the emphasis given elsewhere so constantly on the accountability of public officials and trustees. And in an age when more and more is being asked of the laity in any active parish, it will become less and less acceptable for the parish priest to keep the sole executive authority in his hands. Although lay Catholics have usually accepted this inherited pattern of church government out of loyalty to a religion which seemed hierarchical through and through, changes are now visible. It is an age of guitar masses for the young, of a demand that the laity be given the wine as well as the bread at the mass and of the use of lay men and women as 'sacramental ministers' distributing the bread and wine and as parish administrators. Informal meetings are taking place in homes and they bear some resemblance to the Latin American grass-roots communities. There are already many signs of a wish to restrict interference by the Vatican and to see a mature, educated, responsible laity actively involved in building up an American church. These may be the beginnings of an American Catholic appendix to the Declaration of Independence.

Catholicism in the USA's futures is likely to be involved once again in the traditional process by which disadvantaged immigrants work their way up the competitive ladder. Now it is the turn of the Hispanics. They will want a North American version of the liberation theology of the south, whatever warnings the Vatican may issue. The most effective warning to the US hierarchy in this connection has already been issued within the USA – for many Hispanics, feeling that their ancestral Catholicism does not fit into their new struggles and opportunities, have been turning to Pentecostal and other Protestant churches.

To many whose economic needs are satisfied or at least not painfully dissatisfied, the relationship between the sexes is the most emotive topic. The entire culture of the USA is already saturated by the philosophy of the pursuit of happiness through sex and as the nation enjoys more leisure it seems likely to give even more attention to this topic. Similarly it is proclaimed that the sexes are equal. Catholicism is now affected because the Vatican-enforced insistence on celibacy for all candidates for the priesthood (apart from a handful of recruits such as married ex-Anglicans) has already been a major factor in the sharp decline in the number of candidates. The army of nuns – in the past vital to the Catholic strategy in parishes and schools – has also diminished and, when staying at its posts, has become more feminist than is liked by the men of the Vatican. The pressure for the ordination of women to the priesthood has begun to grow, particularly among nuns, and already women ministers distributing the preciously consecrated bread and wine are often to be seen at mass in the parishes. And there are likely to be far-reaching consequences of an existing fact: the vote of the Catholic laity where (to them) it matters most, in the marriage bed, has gone overwhelmingly against acceptance of the Vatican's ban on the artificial control of births. It is clear from many opinion polls that the papal encyclicals condemning such contraception offend the moral sense of most of the married, to whom the sexual act is important – indeed, sacred – primarily as the strengthening of love between equal partners, not as the procreation of children. It has been noted by scholars and laymen alike that the encyclicals cannot appeal to any scriptural teaching or long tradition in the church and that the appeal which is made to 'natural law' is philosophically questionable. A similar, although as yet less powerful, feeling has grown against the exclusion of remarried divorcees from the church's sacraments. When marriage is regarded as a love affair between equals, its breakdown has to be provided for – and the USA has provided for it in a very high divorce rate, most divorces being followed by second marriages. People who regard themselves as the victims of these new social customs usually do not feel guilty enough to give an inner assent to excommunication. And it is a reflection of the layman's lack of respect for the clergy's official position on these and other ethical questions that the average Catholic in the USA no longer accepts any obligation to confess sins privately to a priest. The layman asks: Does the priest know what a sin is?

It is not to be expected that Americanisation with consequences of this nature will be accepted calmly throughout the Catholic church in the Americas. Traditionalists will put up a stout fight and the only reason why their defeat may be predicted is that in the period 1960–85 changes which, at least initially, dismayed the conservatives have been widely accepted. And since American Catholicism will undergo these traumas, often reacting negatively, it is not to be expected that the scope for Protestantism will be lessened significantly for a long time to come. On the contrary, continued growth may be expected for Pentecostalism, which offers a genuine alternative to any church where the professional clergy have the authority to uphold the tradition. Because Protestantism has so often before made its adherents more prosperous, this movement is likely to become more educated and more truly democratic, meaning a growth away from fundamentalism and the *caudillismo* of authoritarian pastors. Already in Latin America a middle class Pentecostalism has emerged. And in North America for many years to come, Protestantism – whether Pentecostal or 'mainline' – is likely to continue to carry the main burden of the Christian mission in a society subject to many of the influences which have already made Europe largely secular; for in response to that immense challenge, Protestantism will remain free to experiment in organisation and message. The question is: What Christian unity will be compatible with this diversity?

In the USA the Consultation on Church Union, proceeding at a leisurely pace since Eugene Carson Blake preached his boldly visionary proposal in 1960, is not likely to result in a union comparable with the mergers between corporations in the business world. *The Plan of Union for the Church of Christ Uniting*, published in 1976, proposed the inclusion of congregations of different traditions in 'parishes' which would meet together regularly for celebrations of the eucharist. The ministers would form teams in which resources would be shared and major decisions taken in common. There would be bishops coordinating these teams, and the coordinators of 'regions' would virtually be archbishops. Such proposals were far too radical to win acceptance in any of the denominations. But some ethnic or other sociological divisions between churches in the USA have already begun to lose their meaning. In the period 1925–80 nearly seventy 'united' churches were formed out of two or more denominations. A significant example was the United Church of Christ, resulting from a union between Congregationalists with ultimately English roots and the Evangelical and Reformed Church which had been founded in the USA by Germans. The Orthodox jurisdictions, still divided according to national origins, are slowly moving together with the prospect of one day forming a single communion which will be truly 'the Orthodox Church in America' – already the title of a denomination of about a million members (roughly a quarter of the whole). Plans for the union of three Lutheran churches, and the covenant relationship into which Lutheran and Episcopal churches have already entered, have thrown bridges across divisions resulting from German, Scandinavian or English origins. At the same time the leadership of these denominations has seen the need to rethink the goal of the ecumenical movement, abandoning earlier dreams of a single Protestant church. The new aim is a 'communion of communions' to include both the contributions of Catholicism and Orthodoxy and the continuing protest of Protestants against monolithic uniformity. In 1980 it proved possible for the Consultation on Church Union (still involving ten denominations) to issue a revised 'theological consensus' including an agreement that the threefold ministry of bishop, presbyter and deacon was desirable. In 1984 it sent out a document, *In Quest of a Church of Christ Uniting*, which proposed a 'covenant' between denominations with local councils to give it teeth. It is not dead.

There seems to be no reason why the activity of evangelists outside the historic denominations should diminish in the future that can be foreseen. On the contrary, the development of technology will put more devices into the hands of evangelists willing to use TV to spread the message and computers to register its responding recipients. But counteracting this influence will be the sheer abundance of the messages aimed at consumers by the new communication machines – and the abundance of the opportunities of those subjected to this barrage to spend time and money or other 'leisure' pursuits. Consumer resistance as the market becomes more crowded will mean that the sky is not the limit for the 'electronic church'. And another obstacle to the expansion of unsophisticated versions of Christianity, preaching fundamentalism or a simple moral 'uplift' even when the latest technology is used, will arise from the growth of the education on which the technology must rely. People trained to the challenges of the new industries, in a society where everyone at work will be in some sense a manager, are going to be less likely to accept the appeals of authoritarian preachers without examination. And people whose minds have been expanded by science are not likely to find a permanent spiritual home in a narrow or shallow religion. Obviously here, too, change will not be quickly spectacular – but the slow and steady movement may well be into those denominations which have kept room for the educated and the questioning and which offer worship in which the sensitive can take part without blushing. Already a denomination such as the Episcopal Church receives many laity and clergy from churches which seem to offer less to the educated. Presbyterians or the United Church of Christ (Congrega-tionalists) are reckoned more sophisticated than Methodists and that can be an attraction. And the liberal United Methodist Church benefits from the work of evangelists cruder than its own ministers. The liberal, cultured and respectable denominations often do not hold their own young people and do not impress people with no background of strong church affiliation: they are not sufficiently positive and demanding. But it is reckoned that some forty per cent of American Protestants switch churches during the course of their lives. Most of these moves are, in social and cultural terms, 'upward' – and that is a big reason why the liberal denominations have survived and are likely to carry on surviving.

In the USA in the 1980s there are, it seems, over four hundred thousand local churches. Whether liberal or conservative, they are likely to remain the backbone of the nation's Christian life. They will be valued all the more in an age of greater leisure as places where people can get together and enjoy themselves. But the people attached to them are also likely to continue to enjoy some opportuni-ties to worship. The corporate nature of Christian worship has been a theme so prominent in the twentieth century that it seems unlikely to be forgotten in a hurry. The displacement of the Latin-mumbling priest in Catholicism, matched by the dethronement of the Bible-bashing preacher in Protestantism, is not going to be reversed. Nor will there be any reversal of the great movements which have made the Bible available to the Catholic and Protestant laity in easily understandable translations, with scholarly but popular study aids and through groups for the discussion of the meaning.

However, it can be expected that the dominance exerted over the strategy of the churches in the 1980s by the Bible-based and clergy-controlled congregation will be modified in ways which will enlarge the opportunities open to the laity. Christians will want to pray more, help more and celebrate more, in activities both smaller and bigger than the local church.

I have already ventured the prediction that if Latin America escapes the worst social disasters which in the 1980s remain possible, its leading Christian teachers will take a greater interest in spirituality, in the hunger of the soul which can be fed only in solitude or in quiet companionship. The interest in Asian ways of spirituality which has been so widespread in the USA is already beginning to be matched by a greater stress on the 'interior' life, fed by prayer and meditation, drawing on the resources of the Christian tradition. The individual or the small group will want to deepen this knowledge of God. But small groups will also want to tackle the continuing problems of society. The lay movement constituted by the Latin American *comunidades de base* will grow. So will the church groups in the USA which do something about that nation's psychological and social problems – the club for the lonely, the centre for the rejected, the action group to help the neighbourhood. And the large-scale Christian events in both the Americas – whether 'pilgrimages' or 'crusades' or 'protests', whether addressed by the pope, by Billy Graham, by Martin Luther King, by some lesser speaker or by music – have shown how such rallies can attract and influence many thousands who are unwilling to go to church Sunday by Sunday. More events of this kind will be launched and welcomed. Religious seekers and innovators, as they become more educated and more prosperous, will stress the individual and small group, but their imaginations will also be stirred by spectacles, skilled oratory, choirs and crowds. Since it will remain a practical and popular religion, Christianity in the Americas will need cathedrals made up of the living flesh of gathered Americans.

Those are a few guesses by a visitor who has been educated and impressed by some contact with American Christians and their books. But what is really interesting is not to guess about the future shapes of the churches and other religious movements. It is far more important to ask what will be the Christianity preached to the souls of peoples. The answer which I have reached is that, if it is to be strong (and why after all that history should it not be strong?), it will be a

Christianity able to inspire the peoples of the Americas with a strong vision of their meaning as individuals and as societies.

Latin American Christianity, whether Catholic or Protestant, has so far been largely a response to life seen as tragedy. Its symbols have been offered as a consolation for the hardness of daily existence and they have appealed because in this presentation the central figures of Christianity gaze out of a world of suffering – the dependent Child, the sad Mother, the dead Lord, the martyred saints. Of course people could never be content to be entirely passive. The paradox of the traditional Latin American character, often noted, was that people rose from their knees to confront tragedy – but in a style which is illuminated more by the great novel of Cervantes than by the gospels about Jesus Christ. There was the reaction of Don Quixote – the romantic gesture, the brief and doomed escape into fantasy. And there was the reaction of Sancho Panza – cynicism, fatalism, nihilism. There was also, of course, a great deal of violent self-assertion. *Caudillismo* was the cult of the leader who could be given absolute authority because he promised to take care of things – whether as a general turned dictator or as a parish priest or as a Pentecostal pastor. *Machismo* was the cult of the man as the household dictator, with more muscle than brain. But the Christ who would lead his followers into an active and strangely conquering life, transforming the personality by love and the society by justice, was not so often offered and not so often honoured. If he was celebrated as the saviour, the most popular occasion was Good Friday. If he was presented as Christ the king, as in the colossal statue overlooking Rio, he was kept on the mountain top, away from the very ugly realities of a city of institutionalised injustice. That is the Latin American Christianity that Latin American Christians are rejecting. In its place they seek a Christ who will move down into the city and liberate them to build a Latin America freed from the sense of doom – an Easter Christ. In the nations which they have begun to reconstruct the poor are being lifted out of degradation, the peasants and the women are being encouraged to speak with dignity, the despairing are being given a faith which makes tragedy an empty tomb. And that must involve a religious revolution. 'The central question in Latin America today', begins a recent discussion of *The Idols of Death and the God of Life*, 'is not atheism. The central issue is linked neither to the connection between atheism and secularism nor to the crisis that marks the West European modern age. The central issue is *idolatry* – a worship of the false gods of the system of oppression.'[8] And many Latin American Christians already have the courage to ask whether among these false gods are some of the images that have dominated their own churches. That question need not result in the Protestant action of sweeping away all the images. For most Latin American Christians, it is far better to relocate the images within the biblical gospel of liberation, in an Evangelical Catholicism.

Christianity in the USA, in all its many varieties, has largely been seen as a relationship between the individual and God. In the 1830s de Tocqueville popularised the word 'individualism' when discovering this culture which he reported to fellow Europeans who would share his own surprise. In a shrewd study a century and a half later, Robert Bellah and other sociologists have assessed the gains and losses produced by this enduring individualism. Liberty, self-esteem, self-expression and self-reliance have beyond doubt aided the pursuit of happiness, and the best side of 'the American way of life' has been the willingness – often courageous while battles were being fought – to give civil rights, equal opportunities and genuine respect to groups which in other nations would have been treated as second-class citizens because they belonged to religious, ethnic or sexual minorities. But that is not the whole story. 'Americans tend to think of the ultimate goals of the good life as matters of personal choice,' these observers write. 'The means to achieve individual choice, they tend to think, depend on economic progress. This dominant American tradition of thinking about success does not, however, help very much in relating economic success to our ultimate success as persons and our ultimate success as a society . . . Freedom is perhaps the most resonant, deeply held, American value. In some ways, it defines the good in both personal and political life. Yet freedom turns out to mean being left alone by others, not having other people's values, ideas or styles of life forced upon one, being free of arbitrary authority in work, family and political life. What it is that one might do with that freedom is much more difficult for Americans to define . . . Our American traditions encourage us to think of justice as a matter of equal opportunities for every individual to pursue whatever he or she understands by happiness. Equal opportunities are guaranteed by fair laws and political procedures – laws and procedures applied in the same way to everyone. But this way of thinking about justice does not in itself contain a vision of what the distribution of goods in a society would end up looking like if individuals had an equal chance to pursue their interests.'[9] And the rest of the world would add – and frequently shout – that this concentration on the freedom and the rights of the individual in the USA has not been accompanied by any sufficiently strong sense that most members of the human race, who have not the privilege of being 'Americans', still have their dreams of freedom and often their convictions that a world system economically and militarily dominated by US power is foully unjust. Despite all the noble words which have come out of the USA during the twentieth century, and despite some noble actions, the rest of the world gets the impression that to most citizens of the USA foreigners are a distant nuisance. So the world has not yet seen an 'America' whose deeds would match its rhetoric in its awesome responsibilities as the leader, and potentially the nuclear destroyer, of the world.

The supreme challenge to the Christians in the USA in the period into which they are now quickly moving is to work out, and to spread, the answers to these questions, reversing the privatisation of religion which is here the equivalent of Europe's more thorough secularisation. They can draw strength from their history – from the long tradition of the idea of a 'Christian America' based on personal integrity, hard work and a glad commitment to a family; from the struggles to secure the rights of a great succession of minorities, including the slaves and the industrial workers, raising up one group of immigrants after another; from the idealistic internationalism of the liberal Protestants in their heyday; from the Catholic bishops' courageous teachings on social justice; from the volcanic explosion of protests against dehumanisation in the 1960s and from the later conservative backlash against a permissiveness which if taken to its logical conclusion would destroy what remains of 'Christian America'. Here are at least fragments of answers. But this history also provides many warnings. From the Puritans of the seventeenth century to the fundamentalists of the twentieth, some Christians have been too inclined to interfere with the freedom of their neighbours. The reaction of the majority has been such that prayers in schools are forbidden and guns are sold with very lax controls. Too often the spokesmen of the churches have oversimplified national and international problems. They have repeated the slogans of 'big government' or 'small government' without seriously asking just what in an imperfect world, with or without budget deficits, a US government can do. (Many churchmen failed to see the point either of the swing to the left under Roosevelt in the 1930s or of the swing to the right under Reagan in the 1980s.) In international affairs they have adopted the simplicities either of unrealistic pacifism or of uncritical crusading. (Many US churchmen, whether isolationist or interventionist in their comments on US foreign policy, have failed to see just how different – often, how much nastier – the rest of the world is.) Shining examples abound in the Christian heritage of the USA. But no model which the past can provide is fully adequate to guide the discharge of responsibilities in the futures.[10]

4

ROOTED IN AFRICA AND INDIA

A sacred world

About forty million years ago, before the continents took their present shape, India was a part of Africa. Still the average African and the average Indian have one experience in common. They live in a sacred world, defined by traditional religion.

Hundreds of millions of villagers – and most townsmen – feel that nature is alive because God (the Supreme Being however conceived) is alive; that God is the origin of all that can be seen, and of invisible spirits also; that man, too, is a spiritual being; that his existence has meaning, for he can aspire to be 'with' or even 'in' God; that under God human life is life-together, for to be human one must belong to a family and a community; that the family or community is a religious group; that the duties of its members are best taught by religious traditions; that the living who perform their duties are not left completely unrewarded; that the dead are not completely dead. In this sacred world of African or Indian religion, life has a vitality, smiling and singing, which often seems absent in 'developed' societies. A European cannot help feeling that the weather often helps, for it is easier to be happy when warm. But there are deeper explanations. Man is here in touch with nature; with the great mystery surrounding his existence; with his own unconscious where the enduring, life-enhancing myths and rituals have been born. Coming down to earth from the realms of Jungian psychology, the visitor observes that the family and the village are strongly supportive as life proceeds in its traditional, religiously sanctioned, pattern. The African or Indian, although often poor, is rich because he belongs. In many ways he is more privileged than, say, the European because the sunshine of a sacred, traditional world warms his spirit.

But other aspects of this world are more difficult for visitors to envy. Traditionally God has been seen with many faces. These are his (or its) 'names and forms', as educated Hindus say, or they are the faces of his messengers and executioners in Africa. In the myths and rituals of the peoples these faces have become gods with characters attractive or terrifying, good, bad or morally indifferent, and the religion of the people has become mainly an attempt to secure the favour of these gods by petition or magical manipulation. The sanctions of traditional religion have been used to hold in subjection millions needed to do the dirty work for the privileged. Their fate has been decreed by gods or spirits in Africa; in India, by the inflexible operation of the law of *karma*. Traditional religion has also lent its authority to many customs of family life or of agriculture which have to be rejected, or at least questioned, by modernised people – for the 'sacred' customs have encouraged the exploitation of women, the suppression of all originality, gross inefficiency in agriculture and the fatalistic surrender to disease and early death. The horror of African and Indian religion expressed by many of the early Christian missionaries can be understood. Nor is it hard to understand why many Africans and Indians, when separated from the traditional influences of family and village (in a city, for example, or in a foreign land) cease to worship traditional gods.

Although it is being reshaped by many modern influences, and although a few anti-religious voices have been raised (Pandit Nehru's was one), this largely remains a sacred world, for good or ill. When long ago India left Africa and collided into Asia, the Himalayas erupted from the collision – and the religiosity of the average African or Indian is still divided by a barrier as high as any mountain from the secularisation which to the north covers religion like a blanket of snow.

Of course there are economic, cultural and religious contrasts between Africa and India, so much so that Africans and Indians have often heartily disliked each other. Such contrasts can be seen in the history of European colonialism. When the Europeans entered India, they entered a civilisation which had flourished for thousands of years while their own continent was barbaric. They were seeking 'loot' (an Indian word). To them, despite the establishment of some forts and trading or victualling stations, Africa was for close on four hundred years the land that lay along the seaway to the treasures of the East. It seemed almost as inhospitable as the surrounding ocean. But permeating every part of the rich civilisation of India, religion possessed public festivals, domestic pieties, temples, scriptures and theologies as elaborate as anything in Europe. Generations of traders and rulers respected the strength of this religious tradition sufficiently to leave it alone. When eventually India was opened up to Christian legislators, school teachers and missionaries, the hope that it would be Western-ised rapidly did not last long. Not only did Indian soldiers mutiny. European scholars now took pride in interpreting India's three main religions – Hinduism, Buddhism and Islam – to a modern world which was impressed. The international prestige of Indian religion has been raised further in the second half of the twentieth century. Thousands of pilgrims from the West arrive in India every year to seek enlighten-ment at the feet of *gurus* or at least to discover what a religiously inspired society looks like on the streets and in temple precincts. Many more who feel dissatisfied with their own Christian or post-Christian society stay at home and admire extracts from Indian holy books or experiment with Indian *yoga*. Recruits have been won, so that the chant of *Hare Krishna* is heard in the cities of Europe, transcendental meditation appeals to some of the secularised British or Swedes, and the Vedanta Society flourishes in California. In contrast, Africa was until recently regarded by most Europeans as savage. It was 'the dark continent'. Very little trouble was taken to understand its religion or culture. Its religious leaders seemed mere 'witch doctors'. It took a long time for European Christians to admit that it was wrong to enslave Africans, and it is estimated that they shipped about thirty million of them to the Americas. Black men were often thought to be the perpetually cursed children of Ham (Genesis 9:20–27). Or it could be asked whether they were fully human.

In the twentieth century the economic contrasts between Africa and India remain – but there has been a very great change in the expectations of the Christian churches. Despite enormous problems India has made economic progress; in the 1980s it has been exporting grain and is among the top ten of the world's industrial nations. In contrast, many African states experience or fear famines and the local poverty inflames the local resentment when Indian shopkeepers prosper in Africa. So in economics old patterns reassert themselves: India is respected, Africa inspires pity or fear. But for the churches, things are very different. The rapidity with which Christianity has won converts from Africa's disintegrating tribal cultures during the twentieth century can be compared only with the speed of the conversion of Latin America in the sixteenth. David Barrett, a missiologist with a long experience of Africa, has estimated that there were about ten million Christians in Africa in 1900 and about thirteen million more in the still largely colonial continent in 1950. Thirty-five years later there were, he thinks, about 191 million and he expects about 324 million in the year 2000. Many other experts would reduce these estimates – for example, Franklin Littel in *Britannica World Data* for 1985 puts the Christian population of Africa at a bit over 147 million – and accuracy is plainly impossible. (Who counts as a Christian, in whose eyes? And how can exact figures be reached when the administrative systems of both governments and churches work under such difficulties?) But it is agreed that the growth in church membership has been spectacular and has shown no signs of slowing down. In 1985 the Vatican estimated that Catholics in Africa, some two million in 1900, now numbered some sixty-seven million and were growing by at least two million every year. The fact that when a government takes a census more Africans claim to be Christians than appear on the churches' rolls is also a tribute to Christianity's prestige, like the claims to piety made in public opinion polls in the USA.

In India the churches have not known such success. Their membership has grown from about 2,500,000 in 1900 to about twenty million in 1985. Although the wider influence of the teachings of Christ has also grown, in a government census fewer Indians register themselves as Christians than the churches expect. These figures have to be considered in the context of India's population growth, from about 230 million in 1900 to 685 million in 1981 (the numbers being of those living within India's present frontiers). If there are to be as many as thirty-four million Indian Christians in the year 2000 (as David Barrett expects, with sixteen million 'crypto-Christians'), they will be one small element in a population of about a thousand million. So far in the twentieth century, the Hindu element in the population has declined only slightly and the decrease seems to be due mainly to the discouragement of the remarriage of widows by Hindus but not by Muslims. Approximately eight Indians in every ten are Hindus.

However, it remains true that Africa and India have much in common as fields for Christianity – because religion is everywhere so significant. The questions which potential converts ask are not usually political or economic. They are about the difficulty of abandoning the local religious community. African tribalism has dominated the background from which Christians are expected to break free and naturally Africans ask how complete the break must be. The same question is raised in respect of 'Hinduism', a word invented to refer to the luxuriantly unsystematised religion of India. (Muslim conquerors became conscious of what was beyond the river Indus and therefore 'Hindu' – and Europeans later thought that it must be an 'ism'.) Because most of the conversations into which they are summoned are usually about the implications of allegiance to a religious community whatever government may be in power, the leaders of thought in the African and Indian churches have taken a different approach from Latin American colleagues who preach the supreme importance of revolutionary action in politics and economics. 'Liberation' in Latin America is the exodus of a whole people from slavery. But to Africans it tends to mean liberation from control by malign gods, evil spirits or human enemies (in particular from witchcraft). For Indians, too, 'liberation' often has a religious content. Devout Hindus belong to a tradition which seeks liberation from the world itself, for to live in the world is to belong to a scene of ignorance and suffering. It has also to be said that many Indians want to be liberated from Hinduism, seeing it as a prison which makes sure that they are ignorant and do suffer. So in its African and Indian evangelism Christianity has had to say what it offers in terms of religious liberation.

Christians in Africa and India are, of course, acutely conscious of their peoples' poverty. The majority of them are poor themselves. The most articulate of them often want the churches to take a lead in protests and experiments with a passion to reduce that poverty, and they are likely to give that urgent concern for desperately needed development a much higher priority than the intellectual, elitist dialogue on religious topics. But everyone knows that spirituality is a real force in these societies where social reformers (and even soldiers or lawyers in government) have to function as preachers if they are to be acceptable leaders. Since Africa and India remain soaked in believed and practised religion, to care about their peoples is to care about their piety. A report of a conference in New Delhi in 1981 stated the challenge clearly. 'An attempt to express the Christian faith in traditional Indian symbols, generally Brahmanic, with strong emphasis on contemplation and great indifference to social change, is paralleled by a liberation theology that, prompted by its concern for the poor, strives to articulate the experience of the people's struggle for liberation without looking for an Indian "language" to achieve it. These two trends, which surface at every theological meeting in India, have as yet failed to meet. Yet it is only at their meeting point that a genuinely Indian theology of liberation will emerge.'[1] The situation is essentially the same in Africa.

In such a context, the churches' biggest problem is often how to persuade others that Christianity is no longer the white man's religion. Apart from ancient (but non-missionary) churches in Egypt, Ethiopia and South India, the only Christianity surviving on any considerable scale in these vast areas in 1900 had been introduced by missionaries associated with European traders or colonists. Since all

Africans or Indians had to belong from birth to a community defined in religious terms, they assumed that the incoming white man, however ill-behaved, was a Christian; and some of them became Christians because for one reason or another they were willing to live under the white man's influence and protection. Conversion meant a total rejection of their own 'heathen' society. It often included a new name given in baptism and sometimes a physical move into the 'mission compound' or Christian village. Unless a whole village or clan accepted Christianity, few of the converts were people with large stakes in the societies they had abandoned. Virtually they were refugees.

When colonialism ended during the forty years from 1945, the churches in Africa and India experienced immense problems as they moved away from such colonial origins. The new national governments have expanded the scope of the state, gradually taking over many church-related schools, colleges and hospitals which previously had seemed as important as the activities of the gathered Christian congregations. These governments arouse loyalties never given to the colonial regimes. They are often corrupt (and in Africa brutal), but the leaders of the churches are caught between their moral obligation to denounce such evils and a natural desire to exercise their patriotism – and their prudence. And church leaders always have to struggle for an answer to the question: What is the right shape for the church in these new nations? These Christian communities in Africa and India have often been valued precisely because they gave more of an opportunity to be in contact with the modern world – and many of those converted to Christianity had many reasons to feel alienated from the local 'heathen' world. It can be suspected that those who urge that Christianity should now become less Western and more African or Indian are dragging such converts back into a world which they hate. This suspicion is not eased when some of the loudest enthusiasts for the 'indigenisation' of the church are Westerners. Even where no such emotions are expressed, many links with churches in other countries are valued. Missionaries and grants seem vital and even All-Africa, All-India or All-Asia Christian organisations owe much to foreign training, encouragement and subsidy. English, French, Portuguese or Latin has to be used to communicate, for Africa speaks about two thousand local languages or dialects and India about four hundred (fourteen being recognised as major languages in the constitution). International forms of worship are respected and loved by those accustomed to them. Above all, there is loyalty to the gospel which the missionaries brought, together with the fear of 'syncretism' understood as a cowardly compromise with the worship of idols and devils. But all the time another pressure is strong – the pressure to bury all remnants of the colonial past; to be free, responsible and adult as Christians of a new age; to be proudly African or Indian. It is likely to be the stronger pressure.

The problems involved in making the churches African or Indian cannot be solved easily. What is most striking is that the problems have been tackled, in one of the most difficult transitions Christianity has ever made. Indeed, these Christians of Africa and India have been successful to a degree which before 1945 few thought likely or even possible. In the 1980s it is generally agreed that the futures of these churches depend on their ability to make sure that African or Indian Christianity is rooted firmly in the local soil. And it is also usually agreed that the energy for this great task is arising.

The planting of Christianity in Africa

In contrast with Brazil, Africa towards the end of the eighteenth century had almost completely forgotten the missionaries who had accompanied the Portuguese explorers and colonisers in the fifteenth, sixteenth and seventeenth centuries. The first black African to be a bishop (a son of a king ruling around the Congo river) had been consecrated in 1518 and the first white missionary to be martyred had been killed in 1561, some six hundred miles from the mouth of the Zambesi. But the small congregations had never grown substantially and the priests sent out from little Portugal had in the end been defeated by disease and by their association in the Africans' minds with the horrors of the slave trade. The modern planting of the church in Africa began only when Christians had separated themselves from that trade – but had thrown themselves into a movement which was to end in a new wave of colonialism.

From the 1790s onwards Christian ex-slaves liberated in the Americas were settled in Sierra Leone and Liberia and began some evangelism. They were followed in West Africa by white Anglican or Protestant missionaries – and, from 1843 onwards, by Roman Catholics, mostly French. Other missionaries won converts in Madagascar – converts who multiplied into a large Christian community despite almost thirty years of persecution. Fanning out from the little settlement at the Cape of Good Hope, Protestant missionaries also made contact with the peoples of Southern Africa, and from Zanzibar they penetrated into East Africa. The first major thrust of the Catholic missionary movement began in 1878 when Bishop Lavigerie's White Fathers set out for Tanzania, Uganda and West Africa. Ten years later King Leopold of Belgium, now misruling the Congo basin, began to invite in large numbers of Belgian Catholic missionaries and to give them the monopoly of subsidised education (which lasted until 1946). A similar position of great privilege was given to the Catholic church in the Portuguese territories. Neither the British nor the French colonial authorities ever gave any single group of missionaries such open support, but when the Berlin Conference of 1884–85 regulated the European scramble for African colonies the patronage of missionaries was established as a proper part of respectable imperialism. It was repeatedly claimed that what was being spread was 'Christian civilisation'. A minority of the missionaries criticised their patrons for the exploitation of the 'natives', but the dominant fact was that, outside Ethiopia, Christianity almost always reached Africa south of the Sahara as part of the impact of the Europeans.

Despite the power of the emotions which surface in much discussion, it is not yet possible to reach any final judgement about the advantages and disadvantages of colonialism in Africa. The missionaries and administrators often loved the people they served and did the best they could with their resources. They brought education to preliterate peoples. They were crusaders against disease, if not against poverty. They had a high prestige and they often earned it. But criticisms there must be – and one is that the African was systematically patronised. The colonial mentality which had ended in the Americas by 1825 did not begin to end substantially in Africa until the 1950s. Ghana's independence was the first political move, in 1957, and the Portuguese empire was not dismantled until 1974. Only in the 1950s did the Roman Catholics and Anglicans set up hierarchies of bishops in West Africa with real independence. After the death of Samuel Crowther in 1891 no African was appointed an Anglican diocesan bishop for another sixty years. In East and Central Africa, Africanisation was even slower, while in South Africa it is notoriously not complete in the mid-1980s. In all Africa the Roman Catholics had only one black bishop in 1950. Fifteen years later, when there were about twenty-seven million Roman Catholics in Africa led by about fourteen thousand foreign missionaries, the black priests numbered only about a thousand. It was always explained that the churches were promoting Africans faster than governments or businesses, and that there were too few 'civilised natives' fit for promotion. But such arguments revealed that the African churches were being modelled on non-African patterns and that the ability of their potential leaders was being tested by non-Africans with non-African expectations.

In that colonial era the churches functioned to the great benefit of many Africans; for example, in 1923 there were some six thousand church schools in British Africa when the government schools numbered about a hundred. But the churches founded by the historic denominations had not yet become spiritual homes where Africans could be themselves and lead each other. One result was a shortage of clergy. In Kenya in the 1970s fewer than a hundred of the seven hundred priests serving about seven million Catholics were Africans. Another result was the suppression of African ideas. In the early 1980s it was still possible for the Vatican to discipline Emmanuel Milingo, Archbishop of Lusaka, who had attracted vast popularity as a healer and exorcist in a style familiar to readers of the Acts of the Apostles. He was silenced by an enforced move to Rome as a reminder of the realities of ecclesiastical power. Another, much larger, reminder was the refusal of official marriage to all Catholic priests – a refusal contrary to the whole African emphasis on the family and crippling to the supply of priests. Some similar attitudes could be found in the Anglican and Protestant churches, an example being the excommunication of members who maintained the very long African tradition of polygamy while others whose conduct was much more anti-social in most African eyes were allowed leading positions. In all the main churches European ideas were being imposed and this psychological empire lingered on even when the colonial flags had been lowered.

African traditional religion was severely shaken by the effects of European commerce and colonialism. The new traders sold goods which were exciting in comparison with the implements of the timeless lifestyle of the village. The new schools brought in a new world of knowledge to challenge the village's customs. The new hospitals and clinics were more effective than the herbs and incantations of traditional medicine. The new towns and mines were beginning to disrupt the old pattern of subsistence-farming on ancestral land. Yet the churches controlled by the missionaries simply had too few missionaries to feed the flock. Although the mission schools did great work, often the result was that Africans educated by a church used that church in later years for occasional worship. On that basis, the acceptance of that church's religious and moral teachings might not be very profound. And the expansion of the system which won these converts presented great financial problems. Missionaries had to be housed and salaried or priests and nuns had to be maintained in conditions thought to be appropriate for Europeans. School teachers and village catechists had to be paid (at lower levels). Many buildings had to be built and repaired. Accounts had to be kept, partly because the need for subsidies from overseas was never-ending. The historic denominations when they had established their mission stations with an outreach to nearby villages often found it impossible to produce the manpower and money which seemed needed for the evangelism of Africans whom the system did not cover – in remote rural areas or in the growing towns.

The vacuum was filled from various sources. In West, Central and East Africa, Islam attracted many converts as an enthusiastic brotherhood with leadership which, whether or not it was African, was at least not white. As a result, in the 1980s the number of Muslims in the whole of the continent seems to be about the same as the number of Christians. However, there was also a revival of heartfelt religion and strict morality experienced within the historic Christian denominations. It was not controlled by the missionaries. A Protestant 'revival' movement began in Rwanda in the 1930s and spread throughout East Africa, leaving behind essentially lay fellowships of prayer. Basically similar was a movement among Catholics in the Belgian Congo beginning in the 1950s, creating the *jamaa* or spiritual family which took as its model the love between Jesus and Mary. From overseas there arrived a wave of 'faith' missions. Mainly coming from the USA, Scandinavia and Britain with its white dominions, Protestant or Pentecostal missionaries began a less formal and institutional style of evangelism in Africa at the end of the nineteenth century. From the 1950s onwards they have multiplied in what has been called the 'Evangelical scramble for Africa'. These evangelists have sometimes been Baptists (conspicuously in Zaire). But mainly they have belonged either to new denominations such as the Adventists or to interdenominational (and usually also international) societies such as the Africa Inland Mission, the Sudan Interior Mission, the Africa Evangelical Fellowship or the Regions Beyond Missionary Union. They have opened up innumerable churches but not so often schools or clinics, and in those churches they have preached a simple faith. The emphasis has been on miracles rather than on modernity. This approach, first seen in the Christian world when the revivalists fed many emotional needs in the USA, has met a considerable response in Africa.

Where the response has been large and enduring, however, both the revival movement and the imported new churches have faced many of the same problems as the leadership of the historic denominations. The central issue has been Africanisation: how far should the prayer life of the new fellowship take an African form, and how far should the gospel of the new faith mission encourage a distinctively African response? An enthusiastic response has been given to radically new denominations, mostly small and often ephemeral, which have answered such questions by being thoroughly African from the start. These churches were at first called 'separatist' but are now known as 'independent' or 'indigenous'. In South Africa and Nigeria they had been present since the last years of the nineteenth century and they have been strong since the 1920s. In many – although not all – African countries they have grown to add a fifth element to the pattern of Catholic and Anglican, Protestant and Pentecostal. Ever since the publication in 1948 of Bengt Sundkler's *Bantu Prophets in South Africa* (a study of the movements which have used religiously the suppressed talents of the Zulu people), they have been the subjects of careful and sympathetic research. And ever since the publication twenty years later of David Barrett's *Schism and Renewal in Africa* it has been known that almost all these movements had a common origin: the availability of the Bible in the local language. Like the European Protestants in the sixteenth century, large numbers of African Christians, once they had that access to the Bible, ceased to respect, or to depend upon, alien religious officials. It was not necessary for them to be able to read the Bible themselves. They trusted their own prophets to do that.

'Bible-believing' evangelists in the USA have often insisted on independence; and William Booth, the founder of the Salvation Army, could not be content within the Methodism of Victorian England – the Methodism which had begun because John Wesley would not be limited by the conventions on which Anglican bishops insisted. But it is a pointer to the religious sensitivity and creativity of Africans that many thousands of such independent denominations have flourished. They had two famous precursors, the African equivalents of Wesley and Booth. In 1913–14 a layman from Liberia (originally a settlement for ex-slaves from the USA), William Wade Harris, made a preaching tour of the Ivory Coast and Sierra Leone. His background was partly Methodist and partly Anglican, but he preached a very simple message of reliance on the one God instead of fetishes (idols), on the Bible instead of human knowledge, and on healing by faith instead of modern medicine. He was quickly deported as a disturber of the colonial peace and reduced to obscurity before his death in 1929, but his was the most effective evangelistic campaign that Africa has ever seen and the existence of the strong Harris Church is among his many memorials. In 1921 a Baptist layman, Simon Kimbangu, conducted a similar mission in the lower Congo. It lasted for six months. Sentenced to life imprisonment by the Belgian authorities, he died in prison thirty years later. His followers were persecuted and rent into factions, but were reorganised by his sons after his death. In the 1980s the largest independent church in all Africa is the Church of Jesus Christ on Earth through the Prophet Simon Kimbangu, with some six million members and membership of the World Council of Churches.

These militantly independent denominations, the spiritual homes of perhaps thirty million men, women and children, are very varied. Some denounce polygamy, alcohol and dancing. Some, however, accept such practices, and others frowned on by the missionaries, as parts of the African way of life. Most of their pastors lack theological training, and some are undiscriminating in the defence of African traditions, so that they can be attacked as 'syncretistic' or 'post-Christian'. But on the ground there is a clear division between the groups which are Christian and those (far fewer) which are not. All the Christian churches acknowledge Jesus Christ as Lord and pray to his Father with an enthusiasm which they attribute to the Holy Spirit. Excited by a sense of crisis and guided by visions and dreams, they believe in the power of prayer to heal disease, expel devils and perform other miracles; and they criticise the missionaries for concealing the importance of these things in the Bible. Scope is always given to African leadership, often including leadership by women – and often producing splinter groups when the authority of the founders has been disputed. Although their background was usually Protestant, these groups have spontaneously developed 'high church' practices. Many use colourful vestments and ritual dances in worship led by impressively entitled clergy. Many have 'Zions' or holy places where, under the guidance of the founder and his (or her) assistants, believers sick in body or mind can come for healing like the Catholic pilgrims to the shrines of saints. Some of these 'Zionist', 'spiritual' or *Aldura* (praying) groups come as close to missionary-defined orthodoxy as seems possible without sacrificing independence. The most orthodox can be called 'Ethiopian' because they value the example of the Ethiopian Church in maintaining a proudly African version of Christian orthodoxy with a strong Old Testament flavour. Such churches have found it difficult to collaborate with the less orthodox independents.

Because all Africa's churches were founded either by historic denominations imported into the continent during European colonialism, or by foreign or African evangelists with strong personalities, they have never found it easy to unite. And they have not often found unity desirable. There has seemed to be plenty of room in the continent for evangelists and pastors from many backgrounds who needed little if any cooperation. The situation was helped in Africa (as in India) by the 'comity' agreements between the main Protestant missionary societies, dividing up the field between them. When lay Christians have found their existing denominational allegiance inconvenient – on marrying, for example, or after moving to a town, or having been impressed by a new prophet or pastor – they have seldom hesitated to change churches. In recent years national and local councils of churches have worked to develop cooperation as part of the international ecumenical movement, and they have been channels through which aid has flowed from churches outside Africa. But plans for formal church unions have aroused little real interest. In Nigeria in the mid-1970s, for example, a proposed merger of Anglicans and Methodists was abandoned under threats of legal actions by aggrieved congregations and, instead of uniting, the Methodists reorganised themselves under bishops, archbishops and a patriarch. The Catholic church was never involved in the plan, partly because it has been specially identified with the Ibo people – and with the abortive attempt to break away into an Ibo nation, Biafra, in 1967–70.

In Kenya, where almost three quarters of the population are Christian (as compared with half in Nigeria), a similar diversity has been accepted after the failure of moves towards a formal unity. Here, as in Nigeria, the Anglicans are the second largest church but they are almost rivalled by the African Inland Church and surrounded by many smaller Protestant bodies – and they are heavily outnumbered by the Catholics. A similar pattern (although with fewer Protestants) exists in Uganda, where in the past divisions between Catholics and Protestants had a strong political significance; a pitched battle was fought between them in 1892. In Zaire, where about ninety-five per cent of the people are Christian, President Mobutu's dictatorship, determined in the 1970s to Africanise and to control, failed to impose unity on the churches. In addition to the Catholics, the Kimbanguists and the Greek Orthodox, it had to register a Protestant federation, *l'Eglise du Christ au Zaire*, with some eighty constituent churches or *communautés*. In such countries under present circumstances few church leaders would put their energies into free negotiations of further unions.

However, it seems probable that in the Christian centuries which lie ahead in Africa changes in society will encourage the churches to change their own patterns of activity. A great deal of tumultuous history was crowded into the thirty years from 1955 and it is inconceivable that the future will be stable. So something (however short and inexpert) must be said about the context of church life in economics and politics.

The population of Africa is expected to grow from about 220 million in 1950 to about 1,540 million in 2025 and the problems resulting from that development have aroused wide and passionate concern and discussion – for example, in the special session of the United Nations in 1986. Already in the 1980s about half the population is under fifteen – and already about a hundred million Africans suffer from malnutrition. In Kenya, for example, there is already a shortage of cultivable land, causing the drift to the appalling slums of Nairobi. The famines in the Sahel, Ethiopia and Sudan have concentrated the horrified attention of the world on the effects of poor rainfall when the soil has been mismanaged. Drought was a problem over many centuries, but now whole peoples have starved because their numbers have increased without any growth of their understanding of better methods of birth control, agriculture and cattle-raising. The forests, rivers and soil have been misused in frantic but ignorant struggles against famine. Outside that crisis area, there has been much complacent conservatism in reliance on traditional farming methods believed to be producing more or less enough food. Yet Africa's ability to feed itself has declined since about 1965, and its own governments seem to be partly to blame. A comparison between the improvement of agriculture in Indonesia with the record of another oil-producer, Nigeria, makes a sad contrast. State Marketing Boards have often kept food prices artificially low, discouraging the farmers in order to please the urban consumers who are nearer to the politicians. In pursuit of an urban idea of modernisation, money which might have strengthened agriculture has been spent on the kind of imports, including food, that towns welcome and, favouring imports rather than exports, exchange rates have been overvalued. Too much reliance has been placed on the (often taxed) export of 'cash crops' which suited the economies of the colonial powers but which have been far less profitable in years when world commodity prices have slumped; Ghana's cocoa is an example. Natural resources have not been conserved; for example, wood has been used recklessly, specially since kerosene became expensive, without insistence on replanting trees. Little use has been made of the solar power which pours down on the continent. The land has not been used to the full; only about six per cent of Africa's land surface is under cultivation, and even when the desert and the jungle are left out of the reckoning it is generally thought that more of the soil could be cultivated. The green revolution which has brought such benefits to India (for example) through improved seeds, irrigation, pest control and storage has not yet been effectively brought to Africa. Governments have sought 'security' by spending on the army and the police rather than the farmers. They have not held themselves aloof from the corruption and casualness which have poisoned business life and one result has been that the arrangements made with transnational corporations exporting crops or minerals have not sufficiently favoured Africa. It is, of course, true that outsiders have done too little to help. Even the advice of the thousands of expatriate experts to be found in Africa has often taken too little account of African realities, physical and psychological. Transnational corporations have exploited local weaknesses and banks that have advanced loans, often without real need, have demanded unrealistic rates of interest to compensate for the lack of security. Richer governments have done little to help solve the admittedly complex problem of stabilising commodity prices at levels which give a fair profit to the actual producers. They have made much of their 'aid' but often this has been tied to projects resulting in jobs for the 'donor' countries but not at the top of Africa's own realistic priorities. Communist countries have not even pretended to offer aid without strings. The European Community takes a pride in its Lomé Conventions providing some access to its market for the products of French and other ex-colonies – but without any unreasonable 'sacrifices' it could do far more to make Africa the colossal trading partner which it could be, with enough purchasing power to absorb European manufactures. It could cease to impose high tariffs on the import of food which Africa could grow more cheaply and it could cease to subsidise exports in competition with Africa's. The rich non-Communist nations which have made such a fuss about helping in Africa's emergencies could easily do more. At the end of 1984, the year of Africa's worst food crisis, they had some 157 million tonnes of surplus grain expensively stored. (It was the result of their policy of massively subsidising their own farmers – a policy which contrasts with the usual African attitudes.) Africa needed no more than three million tonnes to fill its empty bellies.

That is a very long catalogue of problems – and it is not complete. But every one of these problems could be reduced, if not solved, by human effort and Africans can do much to help themselves even if outsiders remain unprepared for 'sacrifices'. Nature has not yet come to the end of its offers to the African peoples: the fertility of Uganda despite appalling governments is a dramatic illustration. Since the fact is that while an immense population is unavoidable an immense economic disaster could be avoided, in the last analysis economics is controlled by politics. There is a lesson for Africa in the economic history of China since 1978. The growth in Chinese agricultural productivity (the output of grain has increased by an average of six per cent a year, compared with 2.6 during 1957–78) has not been due to any large increase in the use of chemical or other inputs. It has been the reward of government decisions to give farmers more incentives in marketing. And there is another lesson in the success in the mid-1980s of a number of African nations, arresting the decline in output by the adoption of policies which have been welcomed by farmers and economists.

In Africa Marxism has stiffened the revolutions necessary to topple the feudalism of Haile Selassie in Ethiopia and the colonialism of the Portuguese to the south. It has also won some other victories. But it seems unlikely that it will be Africa's freely chosen way into the future any more than it will be Latin America's. There will be 'socialism' in the sense that governments will be expected to be tough with rich capitalists and multinational corporations, but state ownership of the land is entirely contrary to the African tradition of ownership by the family or the tribe and the nationalisation of the major industries would run up against the problem of the shortage of efficient administrators. So what is to be the 'African socialism' which has often been discussed? His Arusha Declaration of 1967 made Julius Nyerere, for long president of Tanzania and always a devout Catholic, the moral teacher of Africa – and he alone of African leaders had the courage to denounce Idi Amin's atrocities in Uganda openly. His encouragement of the simple life, and of self-help and cooperation in the enlarged village, may well be the best way for nations such as his own, where his philosophy has won widespread – although not universal – acceptance. But it is questionable whether this philosophy is so relevant to countries such as neighbouring Kenya (called by him a 'man-eat-man' society) where the modern sector of the economy is larger.

What 'socialism' means positively in the African context is the 'togetherness' of 'familyhood' about which Nyerere and other prophets have spoken. If socialism in that sense inspires the rulers of tomorrow's Africa, it ought to be possible to achieve more continental unity. Kwame Nkrumah, the first president of Ghana, had a dream of a United States of Africa. Since his fall in 1966, that dream has not been revived. Nor did Leopold Senghor's idea of a Federal Republic of French West Africa bear fruit. The far more modestly conceived Organisation of African Unity has concentrated on maintaining the old colonial frontiers against other African nations and against tribal rebellions. Various calls from conferences for African cooperation in development have remained little more than words. But as in Latin America, many of the lines drawn on the map years ago do not correspond with economic realities. Traditionally nomadic peoples suffer from these artificial frontiers – but so do others. Free trade between the nations and collaboration in appropriate industrial development make much more sense. One of the lessons which Africans – and Europeans – most need to learn is that India's economic progress has been made possible by its union as one republic. Already there have been some impressive examples of the acceptance of short-term losses by African states for the sake of each other, as when Tanzania sacrificed itself in the overthrow of Amin's tyranny in Uganda, and Mozambique in the overthrow of white supremacy in Zimbabwe. Such truly African acts of statesmanship arouse the hope that leadership matching Africa's needs will arise and will transcend the present divisions into nations which owe their frontiers to colonial map-makers.

So what churches would be appropriate in an Africa which could prosper if . . . ?

One important answer, constantly stressed by many church leaders, is that the membership of the churches will have to care more about the general welfare of their societies. So far, the churches' record has been far from dishonourable. In a continent where most Christians have naturally been interested chiefly in their new religion, and where governments have almost always enforced a one-party rule, it is remarkable that the leadership of the churches has so often been the only, or the main, source of public and reasoned criticism of the policies of the current president. Where corruption has been rife, the churches have almost always had honest leaders – and where the rulers of the state have been remote, rushing by in large cars surrounded by security men, the leaders of the churches have been closer to the needs of the people. Here are foundations for a stronger contribution to 'nation building' and to wider unities in the years ahead.

As a part of that contribution, unity will remain on the churches' agenda despite the difficulties already noted. Small independent churches will have to combine if they are to train and pay a more educated clergy capable of ministering to a more educated laity and if they are to evangelise beyond their own small circles of listeners. The cooperation already achieved in support of the Bible Society is a pointer to this future. And the cooperation may not stop short of actual reunions as the causes which drove the charismatic founders of independent churches to rebellion are forgotten. A numerous and famous independent church founded in Zambia in the 1950s by a prophetess, Alice Lenshina, has declined in a way which may suggest the future of many such groups. But the churches' ties with the countries which sent out the missionaries will also be slackened. Those who peer into the future have to note the rejection of the French and Portuguese plans to 'assimilate natives' as being offensive to African dignity. It has been a feature of African society that long politeness can suddenly erupt into a violent insistence on independence, much to the surprise of the authorities. The white settlers in Kenya were amazed by the savagery of the Mau Mau rebellion among the Kikuyu in the 1950s, and Catholic and Anglican bishops by the determination of the Christians among the Luo people who formed large independent churches in the 1960s. The Catholic bishops in Zaire were unprepared for the outburst of the demand for 'authenticity' which led to the struggle between church and state in the 1970s and church leaders in Ethiopia were stunned by the suddenness of the overthrow of the imperial government and much else in 1974. American Protestant missionaries flooding into Africa in the 1980s have been dismayed to experience the vigour of anti-Americanism. That pattern of African protest is likely to be repeated within the historic denominations as well as on their fringes. In the All Africa Conference of Churches, inaugurated in 1963, there has been open, if premature, talk about the need to declare a 'moratorium' on all foreign missionaries and financial aid. Among Catholics there has been little talk of that kind – but there has been a keen interest in 'All Africa' meetings and, particularly among the bishops, a keen sense of African dignity.

Such pressures will in due course create new organisations of African Christians. It would be entirely unrealistic to expect the construction of a single, tightly controlled African church. But it would also be unrealistic to expect divisions imported from overseas to be permanent. It has always been a source of grief and anger to some of the most thoughtful of Africans that Christianity has preached a message of love and peace but by its denominationalism has introduced fresh divisions, sometimes splitting up families and villages. A deep feeling for African Christian unity, in a continent which has always stressed the togetherness of the community, is likely to be expressed in ways that cannot be predicted in the 1980s. What may be prophesied confidently is that African churches united or divided according to African realities will work under African leadership – and will work together in ways which will suit Africa in the opinion of Africans.

It also appears probable that Christianity will become more thoroughly African in its beliefs. Nothing can stop the colonial period disappearing into history. By the year 2000 only a small minority will remember it at all. If, as is possible, Africa avoids the economic disasters often predicted, self-confidence will help it to resist cultural influences from outside. But if a starved and diseased Africa becomes once again a continent full of pain, its religion will still be different from the religion of Europe. 'You can and you must have an African Christianity', so Pope Paul VI declared in Kampala in 1969. He qualified his blessing. He was referring to 'the language and mode of expressing this one Faith', not to any substantial deviation from the religion taught in Rome. He declared: 'an adaptation of the Christian life in the fields of pastoral, ritual, didactic and spiritual activities is not only possible, it is even favoured by the Church . . . Indeed, you possess human values and characteristic forms of culture which can rise up to perfection such as to find in Christianity, and for Christianity, a true superior fulness.' But it may be doubted whether the Africanisation of the future will be restricted to such 'adaptation', stopping short of theology and church discipline. In many fields this continent can be expected to develop its own version of Christianity's young faith, as in the days when the Donatist peasants of North Africa rebelled against Catholic Rome or when the Christians of Egypt separated themselves from imperial Byzantium.[2]

Towards an African Christianity

As a non-African tries to assess the most significant trends in a growing volume of discussion about Christian beliefs in an African context, one simple change of policy that is already taking place is seen as essential. Africans must never be forced to choose European Christian names. There will, no doubt, always be many Africans who will prefer their children to have names found in the Bible, and there may be some Africans who admire non-Africans sufficiently to want their names to be adopted into African families. But a name is in itself a sacrament and Christianity must not be thought to demand the abandonment of all that an ancestral name can mean. The African Christian can participate in the meaning of baptism, the dying and rising of Christ, without the total rejection of the rock from which he was hewn. He can revere Christ as the 'great Ancestor' without ceasing to respect the ancestors of his tribe, village and family.

Another change already being accepted is similarly essential. Africans must never again be forced to accept European or North American ways of worship which they find meaningless or superficial. Many Africans will continue to value many customs imported into their continent and in particular middle class Africans, earning their living in an essentially international world of business, administration and education, will often find it natural and helpful to worship as Europeans or North Americans do. But Africa had a very rich religious tradition before the arrival of Christianity and it is surely right that some practices which seemed strange or offensive to the early missionaries should now be baptised into Christian use, somewhat as customs developed by the Canaanites contributed to the worship in the temple in Jerusalem or as customs of pagan Europe were taken over by Catholicism.

Europe and North America have a particular reason to appreciate the power of African music, in that the music of African slaves in the southern states of the USA not only made their own spiritual survival possible but also greatly enriched the music of the white man. The rhythms which come naturally to almost all Africans, in instrumental music, singing, swaying, clapping and dancing, deserved to be used, not suppressed, when Christianity provided better themes for celebration within Africa. This music is sacramental because its delight is believed to express the joy of the relationship between the Creator and the creature and because its harmony enacts the unity of the Creator's children. Religion in Africa has always been sung out and danced out rather than thought out; and although the advance of education will increase its intellectual content, African Christianity will have no reason to be ashamed if music remains its most characteristic expression. In the few years since the end of colonialism, already sounds which are new but also old have been heard in the Christian praise of God throughout the continent. The desire of African Christians to be faithful to the teachings of the Bible and of the great Christian saints is best fulfilled by the composition of strong new hymns using the images of Africa to voice the praises and prayers of orthodoxy.

Other elements in traditional African worship have been resisted by some missionaries – and for reasons which have gone deeper than their unfamiliarity with African worship. For example, Protestants brought with them the tradition of wearing black and white when leading worship, or in everyday clerical dress, in protest against the rich garments associated with the evils of Catholic 'priestcraft'. But African religious leadership has traditionally clothed itself in many colours to symbolise its life-enhancing potency and many African Christians in the independent or historic churches have happily revived this tradition. The early missionaries also brought with them an ingrained suspicion of alcohol. In Europe and North America temperance in drinking had often been the habit that, more than any other, had enabled wages to be spent on the necessities of the family – and by Protestants temperance was often thought to mean prohibition. In the Catholic church wine was usually accepted, for it had been an integral part of the culture of the Mediterranean world (including the world of the Bible), but beer was less familiar. In traditional Africa there were very strong social pressures against drunkenness and the neglect of a family, but communal beer-drinking (for example, after a funeral) was a custom with a high moral and religious content. The Christian churches have slowly come to take a more positive attitude to this tradition. Indeed, the question has often been raised whether wine and bread made of wheat really are essential to the eucharist in a culture far more familiar with beer and maize. (When the Kimbanguist church in Zaire at last agreed to adopt the eucharist, previously identified with the white missionaries, it still refused to use bread and wine.) It seems to be a question for Africans to settle.

As the emphasis has shifted from the Christianity of the missionaries to the Christianity of the villagers, problems have been raised which again seem to call for decisions by Africans. One is the problem of how to combine the tradition of strong leadership with the tradition of consultation. The old social system of Africa usually revolved around the chief or king, but this leader was expected to keep in step with the wise men of the place and could be removed if he got out of step. In tribal religion there was much respect for the holy man, soothsayer or healer whom the incoming missionary viewed with distaste as a mere 'witch doctor'; but he, too, was expected to conform to the expectations of the people whose modest offerings provided his livelihood. He was not separated from his fellow villagers by education away from home or by celibacy.

In Christian Africa since the 1950s chief-like bishops have been prominent. This can be observed even in independent churches where control by missionary bishops had been repudiated and even in historic denominations (such as the Lutherans or the Methodists) where episcopacy had not been given any theological emphasis. And

Africans, when made bishops, have often been grander in their personal style than their European predecessors. In the Anglican church the diocese has tended to become the bishop's family, diocese has differed from diocese, and there has been resistance to the development of national and provincial structures. The same tendencies can be observed when Catholics still under the authority of Rome begin to prefer the authority of the local bishop. The high episcopalianism which inspired the theology of Cyprian on the northern shore of Africa in the third century remains congenial. But this need not mean dictatorship – for the authority of the African bishop is increasingly being set within the authority of the African consensus. When the congregation meets at leisure, or when the parish council or the diocesan synod debates an issue at length, it is in the African tradition of the *palaver*, an activity less formal than the Western machinery of democracy but usually more effective in reaching agreement. And if Africans who are educated or who feel spiritually gifted are not to withdraw from church life, they will not be content simply to take orders from a bishop or other leader. The contribution of leaders such as bishops has been seen at its best in the work of men such as Bishop Christopher Molekwa, who has spearheaded the movement among Catholics in Tanzania to set up 'base communities' for Bible study, open discussion and informal prayer on the same lines as the communities of Latin America; or in the initiatives taken by a number of Africa's enthusiasts for agricultural training and for 'theological education by extension'. Bishops can enable the people to be themselves.

On the whole missionaries from a Catholic background, despite the handicaps imposed on them over many years by the insistence that they should do as the Romans do although very far from Rome, seem to have understood the African better than the pioneers of Protestantism. They have valued ritual, symbolism and mythology. They have honoured angels and saints. They have encouraged prayers for the dead. All this has appealed to people who have traditionally valued religion as ritual which gets or keeps the living on good terms with the 'spirits' and particularly with the ancestors who are the 'living dead' while they are still remembered by the living members of their families. Catholics have been in general more favourable to 'native' customs and a touch of 'paganism' has not alarmed them unduly. However, it has become increasingly obvious that the general 'pro-life' stance of Catholicism has had one major defect in African eyes. For so far the Roman Catholic bishops of Africa have upheld the teaching of the papacy that priests cannot be married or female, and so far enough African men have accepted celibacy as a legal requirement for the shortage of priests not to seem intolerable. But as the numbers of Catholics in Africa grow, and as the numbers of foreign missionaries decline, a crisis appears inescapable. Already many Africans and many missionaries who long to see Catholicism advancing even more vigorously all over the continent have protested against the denial of marriage to priests – a denial which was never made in the early centuries of Western Catholicism, which has never been attempted in Eastern Orthodoxy, and which in Africa has resulted in a shortage of priests so great that it has been impossible to offer a regular priestly ministry to the Catholics outside the more privileged congregations. In practice village Catholicism, presided over by the catechist or another layman, has not normally been the religion of the mass; and in practice stable, loving, sexual relationships between priests and women have often been encouraged by the congregations. The contribution made by the officially recognised clergy wives of the Anglican church has been a factor compensating for that church's past identification with colonialism. Clerical marriage seems bound to be a part of African Christianity. However, even in Anglicanism there has so far been no widespread pressure for women priests. The African tradition greatly honours prophets and healers believed to have been entrusted with unusual spiritual powers, and many women in that category are remembered with veneration and love, but it seems probable that many years will pass before the admission of women to positions of formal leadership is widely demanded.

The sphere in which African Christian women have already taken the lead is the life of prayer. Thousands of Catholics have become devoted nuns. Many thousands of others have formed groups which have stayed together for regular praise and intercession within the village or the town. The tenderness of women, and their understanding of other people's emotional needs, have flowed out in quiet petitions to God. The strength of this feature of African church life (whether independent or historic) has also been a reminder that the African usually values prayer from a heart more than prayer from a book. One reason why African Catholics and Anglicans have so far been slow to insist on the use of definite African liturgies (despite some very promising experiments) seems to be that to most Africans no words printed in a book have entirely the same value as extempore conversation with God and with each other, unless that book is the Bible.

It is natural for the African to pray for healing. Many studies of the independent churches have shown how often they have attracted by their healings. This tradition does not exclude medicine; the medicine man of the traditional village used herbs and the doctor with Western training is usually valued very highly. But deep in the African mind is the conviction that health comes from God and can be restored through penitent prayer and the mediation of men and women to whom God has given healing powers. To the African it seems obviously true that the person is a unity – neither a 'mind' or 'soul' imprisoned in a body nor a body which can be treated without any regard to psychology. From this belief follows a 'psychosomatic', not rigidly compartmentalised, approach to the healing of the person – an approach which is beginning to be congenial to Western medical thought. Less easy to reconcile with the cultures which have produced scientific medicine, or with Christianity, are the traditional African convictions that disease usually has one or other of three causes – the just wrath of God or the gods against sinners, the anger of ancestors against those who have offended (for example, by neglecting rituals), or sorcery by enemies. It has, indeed, often seemed that a head-on collision with such ignorant superstition is the only course open to the faithful African Christian; for Christianity is committed to the beliefs that God is love and that evil is conquered – and the victory of the loving Christ over evil, including any spirits, has been right at the centre of Christian experience in Africa. In particular the person-alisation of evil in strange women who are then denounced as 'witches' and cruelly persecuted has been seen as a great evil in itself. But the recent revival of exorcism in Western churches has been a reminder that it can 'work' for those who believe in it – and those who do believe in it can justly claim that the Bible is full of exorcism. And recent Western medical thought has stressed the importance of harmony with the group which threatens or supports the individual. It will be a challenge to all the African churches, as they place much more emphasis on the restoration of health to the person in the community, to explore this whole mystery with the aid of biblical, Western and African insights and techniques.

To the African, 'I am because we are' (as John Mbiti has put it). That is why African Christians are so interested in the Old Testament's frequent insistence that a tribe, clan, village or family has a corporate personality which can be praised or found guilty. The African often surprises the European or North American by being willing to take time over establishing or strengthening personal relationships. A job or a journey often seems to be valued as an opportunity to get to know, or to know more deeply, a friend – and the practice of using one's fellow men as mere instruments in some achievement is condemned with a profound contempt. African friends can exchange token gifts of their own blood, or can proudly hold hands when walking in public. They make the ideals of friendship surviving in other cultures seem anaemic.

The strength of African family life is also a wonder to visitors. Europeans and North Americans often reflect that their own lives have been tragically impoverished by the decline of the family in their societies – and that the destructive effect of modernisation on the African family is another tragedy, to be countered where possible. Traditional family life in Africa had the great weakness that it reacted with horror to the unusual – to twins or to questioning youngsters or to adults with unusual temperaments or sexual natures. But it had great strengths. It took a pride in children, rejoiced over their births and held them in a loving discipline up to adulthood. It accepted the importance and cleanness of normal sexuality but strictly regulated relations between the sexes in the interests of stable family life, the detailed customs varying from tribe to tribe. It looked after the sick and the old without aid from any other institution. A marriage was always thought of as an alliance between the two families which had arranged it or consented to it. That has been the significance of 'bridewealth', the transfer of cattle (or sometimes of other valuables) as compensation to the family which was losing the bride's services. This custom is increasingly losing its force, for it has imposed heavy burdens on young men, it has seemed to put too commercial a value on young women, and it has caused the rearing of cattle with attention to numbers rather than quality. Missionaries and African church leaders have often criticised it; it has seemed to be a way of selling girls. But it showed no wisdom in the missionaries when they introduced wedding services which took almost no account of the families of the bride and groom. As African Christians have delighted to point out, the stress on families, their internal unity and their coming together in the wedding feast, pervades the Old Testament.

It is in this context that the problem of polygamy is most usefully considered. The missionaries came from societies in which monogamy, with chastity before it, was taken for granted as an essential part of Christianity and of civilisation. It was not only because their own marriages were often an important part of their personal religion (how many courageous 'missionary ladies' accompanied their husbands to Africa!) that they were moved so deeply by the apostle Paul's comparison of Christ's love for the church with a marriage. They knew that Jesus had declared that husband and wife became 'one flesh'. Therefore they condemned polygamy without hesitation. Many tens of millions of African men accepted the new discipline as the Christian teaching. They either drastically changed their own attitudes to marriage or agreed that they could not belong to the full fellowship of the church while practising polygamy. In that case, not only were they not admitted to holy communion while alive; their bodies were usually not admitted to church when dead. And countless African women have been grateful for the insistence of the churches that they were entitled to the exclusive and lifelong love of their husbands. The rejection of polygamy has been the distinctively Christian contribution to the advance of women in Africa to an equal dignity. Clearly it is not going to be abandoned and ought not to be abandoned. But it is becoming equally clear that the penalties for polygamy can be relaxed without abandoning the principle of monogamy, somewhat as in the West the penalties for divorce are being relaxed. The spread of the desolating plague of divorce is much slower in Africa than in North America or Europe, but it seems to be inevitable that many marriages will break down irretrievably, that Christians will be involved in these tragedies, and that even those who have deserted their ex-spouses will not be excommunicated for ever. Is less compassion to be shown to a man who has taken a second wife, without sending away the first wife and often with her positive agreement, usually not chiefly because of lust but in order to have children or to provide for widows or to get the work of the house and farm done? Here is another question for Africans, but fortunately the problem seems likely to grow less important. Modernisation makes men feel less dependent on using the privilege of polygamy and (where there is no family farm) less able to afford it; and it makes both first and potentially second wives less willing to accept an arrangement which must be humiliating. The experience of Islamic countries also shows this.

His immediate family is, of course, not the only group to which the African belongs from birth. Loyalty to the family, expecting support by it, extends to the whole clan and the whole tribe. The elaborate initiation ceremonies of the clans have been more than circumcisions. They taught or reminded young men and women about their roles as adults, including their delights and duties as sexual partners and the parents of families. The traditional skills and responsibilities of workers and neighbours were passed on. The young men were given opportunities to display their strength and courage, and the young women their beauty, agreeableness and fertility. The early missionaries were so full of the importance of baptism (followed by confirmation in the Catholic and Anglican traditions), and put such energy into starting European-style schools, that these ceremonies were regarded merely as initiations into 'heathen' religion. There certainly was a non-Christian religious element in the old initiations, as there was a brutal element – and as women gain dignity probably female circumcision will arouse disgust. But much discussion by Africans has shown that it would be a tragedy for Africa if no use were to be made by Christians of other elements in the tradition of educating young people for life. Other areas of the world are the poorer for the comparative weakness of their equivalents. And the challenge to the Christian churches to cooperate in training the young people of the neighbourhood, and in influencing the religious and moral education in the schools, is one of the most powerful factors making for a degree of Christian unity amid the prized variety.

But what will be the African vision of God communicated to new generations? The question may be put more intellectually by asking what will be the character of a theology both truly Christian and truly African. By the 1980s it has become possible to study a considerable body of literature in English and French debating this question. The literature includes radical pleas by theologians with affinities to the left-wing intelligentsia of the West – and cautious notes sounded by Catholic or Evangelical conservatives. But no African Christian theology which will be worthy of the traditions which have prepared for it will be mainly intellectual. African religious thought before the arrival of Christianity was expressed in vivid proverbs, not in abstract philosophy. Christian thinking in Africa has been dominated by practical considerations. Its heroes have not been professors. They have been evangelists, women and other healers, the many martyrs. The Christian theology now needed is a theology covered with the red dust of Africa.

The traditional African sense of the presence of divinity in nature is being challenged by the explanation and exploitation of natural processes by science and technology. To the degree to which they are modern-minded, Africans are beginning to experience the world as a place to be understood and used by the human intelligence without reliance on supernatural forces and without fear of them. Although this is a transformation of attitudes which will not be completed for many generations, what Western scholars call 'animism' – the traditional vision of nature as a battleground between good and evil spirits – does seem to be doomed. So far, however, the challenge of modernity has produced little outright scepticism about the reality of God, for the African sense of that reality seems to be almost an ingredient of the African soil. Africans have gone on believing in the goodness of the Creator through many natural disasters such as epidemics and droughts; under the scourge of the slave trade and under the humiliations of colonialism. They are not going to give it up because of what comes out of Western laboratories or lecture rooms. In the depths of the African mind will remain an awareness of the 'One who has no equal', the 'One who needs nobody', the 'One who fills all things', the 'One who gives life', the 'Chief of Chiefs', the 'Wise One', the 'Great One', the 'One who is there'.

Early anthropologists, like early missionaries, often concluded that Africans had little belief in this Supreme Being. Africans usually seemed to be 'polytheists', believing in many gods and worshipping many 'fetishes', although some tribes were thought to have no religion at all. Certainly there has been a great variety in the religious beliefs and practices of Africa's tribes and it is understandable that some anthropologists should deplore any attempt to suggest that there is one such thing as 'African traditional religion'. However, recent studies have frequently shown that behind the fear of spirits or the worship of divinities there is among most African peoples a traditional belief in the Creator who made everything including the divinities at the dawn of time. 'No one', runs an Ashanti proverb, 'shows God to a child'. Many African myths tell of the insults which persuaded God to withdraw from much contact with the world of men, the world he had made. He can, however, still be prayed to – and often is, addressed with 'praise-names' which express in pictures the belief that he is all-powerful, all-knowing and all-holy. It is deeply significant that the song that has become known as the African national anthem can be translated as 'God bless Africa'. This very long tradition of the worship of the Creator is one reason why so many Africans have turned to Islam. And the essence of the Christian message to Africa is that in Jesus, the 'Great Ancestor' supreme above all ancestors, the Creator has come in blessing, the 'Rain-giver' has given himself. From this, everything Christian follows.

There was in African traditional religion little of the intense thirst for God to be found in (for example) the Hebrew psalms; John Mbiti has described this religion as 'pragmatic and utilitarian rather than spiritual or mystical'. But since God is now said to be close, it makes much more sense to desire him. There was little sense of personal sin as a failure to love God, for God was thought to have broken off contact because of some insult delivered by bad ancestors. But since God is now said to have revealed his holy love in the Christ who was crucified by men's wickedness, it becomes urgent to repent. There was little sense of the future and little faith that the Creator was directing the course of one's own history or the history of one's society. But since God is now said to have revealed his power in raising Jesus from defeat and death, a belief in his providential care can be born. Although immortality was taken for granted, it was traditionally believed that the dead focused their attention on the living and that their greatest hope was to be reborn among them. There was no sense at all that they improved their position by dying. But now the hope of 'resurrection' into a share in the divine splendour can arise from the Easter faith and it becomes possible to think of the dead as being in a 'heaven' which means the life of God.

But Christianity also declares in Africa that the life of God is not remote from the sufferings of mortals. Traditionally there was in Africa little understanding of misfortune or disease except as an evil caused by bad spirits or, through sorcery, by bad people. Now, since God is believed to have been embodied in the Christ who suffered, it has become possible to regard the 'One who is there' as the fellow sufferer, afflicted in all humanity's afflictions including the afflictions which cannot be explained. In the New Testament it is an African, Simon of Cyrene, who carries the cross of Jesus to Calvary and becomes the father of the Alexander and Rufus known to the readers of Mark's gospel (Mark 15:21). And it is another African, a high official from Ethiopia, who is converted to Christianity when he has been reading the book of Isaiah and has asked Philip about the song of the suffering servant. ' "He was led like a sheep to be slaughtered; and like a lamb that is dumb before the shearer, he does not open his mouth. He has been humiliated and has no redress. Who will be able to speak of his posterity? For he is cut off from the world of living men." "Now," said the eunuch to Philip, "tell me, please, who it is that the prophet is speaking about here . . . ?" ' (Acts 8:32–34). The answer comes that the sufferer is Jesus and that the African can be baptised into the fellowship of his sufferings. Responding to this vision, much African Christian art finds the strange glory of God in the agony of the man on the cross.

In 1975 the Catholic bishops of Zaire issued a new order for the celebration of the eucharist, in a boldly African style. It had been approved by the Vatican for use by small groups, without publicity, as an experiment for a set period. But in fact it has been used widely and enthusiastically. In this service may be heard many of the themes emerging from discussions and experiments all over the continent. Before the service, which usually lasts two hours, the ancestors of the congregation and the saints of the church are invoked: 'be with us'.

Strangers are named and applauded. The priest and all his assistants are also named, and as they enter (in African dress) they dance. During the joyous chant of the *Gloria* the people clap and dance and fragrant materials are burnt on a small fire. After the biblical readings extempore songs reinforce their message. The sermon is full of proverbs and people are free to applaud or to comment. An act of penitence covers all sorts of sin, not merely the sins of the individual; 'as an insect sucks the blood . . . so wickedness holds us in its grip'. The bread and wine are brought up with a dance: 'gifts of God, they also come from the fields and from human labours'. Then thanks are offered to 'you, our Father; you, the Sun which one cannot gaze at . . . you, the Master of life; you, the Master of all things'. God is praised through Jesus Christ. 'Through him you created the river Zaire, the streams, brooks and seas, and all the fish living in them. Through him you created the woods, the plains, the savannas, the mountains and all the animals living in them. Through him you created all the things we see, and all the things we do not see.' And so these Africans recall that Jesus Christ reconciled humanity to the Father by the self-sacrifice of his suffering.[3]

The planting of Christianity in India

When Portuguese missionary work had spread out from Goa, for a time it seemed that Catholicism might quickly take on a thoroughly Indian character and flourish in its new soil. The 'Syrian' Christians on the Malabar coast who proudly claimed the apostle Thomas as their founder, but who had been monophysite before falling under Nestorian influence from Persia, were persuaded to acknowledge the pope during the very years, in the sixteenth century, when the papacy was losing half Europe. The Jesuit Roberto de Nobili, who arrived in Madurai in 1605, began to evangelise in a manner both Catholic and Hindu, using the Sanskrit and Tamil languages. (This was more than the St Thomas Christians had done; they had always kept their Syriac liturgy, but otherwise had settled down as one caste among many.) But in the 1650s a rebellion against interference with their customs took most of the St Thomas Christians back into independence. A bishop who had been consecrated by the Nestorian patriarch of Babylon had fallen into the hands of the Roman Catholic authorities in Goa and had been burnt as a heretic. The papacy which had blessed such activities of the Inquisition eventually rejected the suggestion that the liturgy and theology of the European Counter-Reformation had to be modified in India. And the suggestion now seemed far less important within India, for the high caste Hindus on whom de Nobili had set his heart rejected his gospel. It seemed novel, foreign and exclusive however carefully it had been wrapped in Indian expressions. Very few were converted permanently. Missionaries mainly French and Italian carried on the work within the limits set by Rome; and in 1662 many of the 'Syrian' Christians returned to their allegiance to the papacy. But the larger hope had gone out of Indian Catholicism.

Moreover, the Protestant island of Britain gradually reached across the seas to become the dominant colonial power in India. Nervously avoiding any interference with 'native' customs, the East India Company appointed a few chaplains, permitted a few Lutheran missionaries, had to tolerate the arrival of the English Baptist, William Carey, in 1793, and could not resist the decision twenty years later to revise its charter so as to favour 'religious and moral improvements'. The new, more idealistic, attitude of England towards India involved paying an Anglican bishop of Calcutta with assistants, encouraging missionaries of many denominations, and forbidding some Hindu practices such as the burning of the widow on the husband's funeral pyre. It also involved the teaching of modern knowledge to the Indian elite in the English language through colleges and schools staffed by Christians. For a time it was hoped that at least the highly educated Hindus, and members of lower castes or tribesmen anxious to cooperate with the British as liberators from an oppressive Hindu system, would respond by seeking baptism in large numbers. Yet this dream, too, was doomed. Soon after the completion of the British conquest of the country, the 'Indian Mutiny' of 1857 showed that the conquest had been superficial. Direct rule by the imperial crown was imposed; the administration was raised to high standards of integrity; more British missionaries arrived and mission schools were extensively subsidised; but beneath the good works, the splendour and the arrogance of the British *Raj*, the feeling nagged that it would not be permanent and that Hinduism would outlive this intrusion. Although the logic of this feeling would have dictated the rapid Indianisation of the churches being founded, in India (as in Africa) 'native' leaders were judged to be 'unreliable' by European standards. Not until 1912 was an Indian (Azariah of Dornakal) made a diocesan bishop by the Anglicans – and for many years he was left as a solitary, although richly creative, leader. The Roman Catholic Church was also firmly under non-Indian leadership, but its priests and nuns who were in plentiful supply made converts by personal contact and began to recruit Indian colleagues, so that by 1900 it had about a million more Indians regularly at its altars than did the Anglican church (which had about four hundred thousand). The other Protestant missions had a baptised membership of about half a million. The definitely Christian element in the population probably amounted to little more than 1.5 per cent. At least three quarters of it had resulted not from individual conversions but from the movements of groups such as the fishermen of the southern tip of India or the tribesmen of the hills of Assam on the frontier of Burma.

Ninety years after the 'Indian Mutiny' the British quit India. A new nation was born after a bloody separation from its twin, the Islamic nation of Pakistan. In 1947 it seemed likely that its economic problems would result in famines which would be far more costly in human life than the horrifying riots accompanying independence. It also seemed likely that the imitation of Britain's parliamentary democracy would be unable to stand the strains. Yet the first forty years of independent India have not fulfilled the gloomiest prophecies. Problems there have been, indeed. There have been local famines; there has been destitution in the cities; disease, hunger and death have been as familiar as their little fields to many peasants. The growth of the population has meant that more than half of it remains below the poverty line (without a minimum diet for moderate activity as defined by the central government) and some sixty-four per cent are illiterate. About forty per cent of children die before they reach the age of five. There have been many angry tensions between linguistic and other communities and between the states and the centre. Nehru's espousal of socialism ran up against the problem – familiar in Africa – that efficient and honest politicians and civil servants are not very plentiful. Indira Gandhi's problems were dramatised both by the period when she governed by emergency powers and by her assassination by Sikhs. Her son and successor inaugurated 1986 by a brave speech denouncing widespread corruption, incompetence and selfishness. And the image of a nation preaching peace to the world has been damaged by the long quarrel with Pakistan. But there have been many signs of progress. The improvement in agricultural productivity and the industrialisation (including nuclear power) have been so successful that the world can no longer believe that all Indians are by 'temperament' unable to cope with modern opportunities. Since independence the average expectation of life at birth and the proportion of the population that is literate have both doubled. And unlike Africa, India has remained a democracy with free elections – the largest democracy in the world. Unlike Africa and Europe, it has achieved a federal union surviving the massive pressures of communalism.

In 1947 it seemed likely that Christianity would shrink as a nationalist Hinduism expanded. Yet despite the agitation which Hindu nationalist movements had conducted since the 1870s, India did not become Hindustan. Enough Muslims remained in it, alongside enough Christians, Buddhists, Sikhs, Parsis, Jains, tribal religionists or sceptics, and enough Hindus of the lower castes, or animist tribesmen, resented the inferiority imposed on them by the predominant religious system, for the republic to be constituted a 'secular' state. The government is forbidden to subsidise any religion or to discriminate in its favour, while every citizen has 'the right freely to profess, practise and propagate religion'. When in 1979 this right seemed to be threatened by a bill against 'conversions' before the Indian parliament, Christians were foremost in the protests, on the ground that it is a human right to be converted if fairly persuaded, and were effective. In the mid-1980s it is surely significant that the able and popular prime minister of India is an agnostic married to a Christian. And the Indian churches have renewed themselves. Shortly after national independence the Church of South India (CSI) was formed by Anglicans, Congregationalists, Methodists and Presbyterians (after discussions which had begun in 1919) and by the 1980s the CSI had a membership of about two million. The numerically smaller Church of North India, including Baptists and Brethren, was formed in 1970. The long-established National Christian Council has included groups such as the Methodists of American origin or the Lutherans of German or Scandinavian origins who have so far refused to join these unions. In 1976 the Evangelical Fellowship of India celebrated its silver jubilee confidently. The Catholic church was for long, on the whole, pietistic in a European style, but the All India Seminar at Bangalore in 1969 introduced a revolution in the spirit of the Second Vatican Council. The Vatican approved the introduction of Indian postures, gestures and rites of purification into the mass, and by the 1980s the use by devout Catholics of Indian traditions in spirituality, including music, dance, drama and meditation, was becoming widespread. The new energy was a factor in a growth to a membership of about twelve million. In some districts, Kerala, Goa and Chota Nagpur being the largest examples, a popular Indian Catholicism is large-scale.

Since the 1960s the Indian government has often made it difficult or impossible for missionaries from overseas to enter the country. The chief motive has been disapproval of aggressive fundamentalists, Muslim or Christian, who cause trouble and arouse Hindu counter-attacks, but the policy has helped to make the leadership of the churches almost entirely Indian. Financial aid from overseas is still wanted by the churches, particularly in the support of hospitals, colleges and schools and in development projects, and among Catholics a loyalty to Rome persists; for example, it caused the acceptance of a veto on the idea of a National Pastoral Council (including priests and laity) which the bishops wanted. But there is increasing resentment at any attempt at control from overseas. The report of the 1983 meeting of the Indian Theological Association (in Nagpur) was entitled *Searching for an Indian Ecclesiology* and it left the impression that the leading intellectuals of the Catholic church were bursting with impatience about the Vatican's 'colonialism' and advocating an approach close to that of the liberation theologians of Latin America.

Realists must be cautious. Not even the outlines of a united 'Church of India' can be seen in the 1980s: and it may well be that the complex diversity of India will always prevent any complete union, just as it has prevented a monolithic Hinduism. The CSI and CNI cannot persuade the Protestants of North-east India (where Baptists predominate) to follow their examples. Nor can they achieve union with Lutherans and Methodists who value moral and financial support from overseas more highly. Nor can they unite with the Mar Thoma Church which is a 'Reformed' part of the Syrian Christian community formed under Protestant influence in 1875. The other Syrians, now some three million strong, are divided between the Syrian Orthodox and Roman Catholics who treasure the Syrian rite (with a smaller St Thomas Evangelical Church formed in 1974). Half the Indian priests and three quarters of the sisters in the Roman Catholic Church are Syrians, but there are tensions between such Catholics and those of the Latin and Malankara rites. More than half the Indian Christians seem happy to be in communion with Rome and almost half seem equally happy to be out of that communion. These Indian churches are by now sufficiently deep rooted that they tend to regard themselves as mainly hereditary minorities within India's larger life. Some of their members have been willing to appeal to the secular courts in order to get their own way in church affairs. Litigation, usually over the possession of property after the departure of foreign missionaries, has been a plague afflicting the CSI and CNI. Nor is it easy to predict that the churches' baptised membership will grow on anything like the African scale. Recently the numerical results of great and costly campaigns by Evangelical organisations –

for example, the Every Home Crusade – have been more disappoint-
ing in India than elsewhere. Again and again optimism about the
churches' prospects in India has been falsified as Hinduism has
proved its power to persist and to absorb – a reaction much more
dangerous to Christianity than any militant revivalism has been.
Hinduism has no creed and for it there is no such thing as heresy. It is
possible to be a Hindu monotheist, a Hindu pantheist or a Hindu
atheist. It is therefore fairly easy for a Hindu to accept what he
understands and likes of Christianity. But he is unlikely to become a
Christian, for Hinduism, as it calmly teaches the traditional *dharma*
(religious duty) of the family, caste and village, seems to be part of the
atmosphere of India, suffocating or glorious according to taste. Rare
courage or desperation is required for a Hindu to break away from
that heritage. For this reason the influence of Christianity on India
has always been difficult to quantify statistically. In the mid-1980s
many who remain Hindus are willing to discuss religion with Christians, to listen to Christian broadcasts or to read Christian literature.
The more articulate among them may belong to one or other of a
considerable number of fairly small movements which are partly
Hindu and partly Christian, the largest being the Subba Rao movement in Adhra Desh, or they affirm many Christian values through
Gandhian thought and social service. But to be baptised is to 'ruin
one's caste', to 'betray one's people'.

However, realism about Christian prospects in this endur-
ingly Hindu society must also include the observation that (like
Americanisation or Africanisation) the process of the churches'
Indianisation is growing. It surfaces in the discussions about education and medicine. In the years of dominance by missionaries a
great network of schools, colleges and hospitals was created, using
European methods, and then angled towards the elite using the
English language. The network is still needed, for standards in other
colleges and schools can be low and there is only one medical doctor
to every seven thousand Indians. But it is also felt widely that the
maintenance of this vast machine has been absorbing too much of the
attention of the clergy and key laity. In particular it is felt that too
many of the schools, colleges and hospitals have reached too few of
the people because they have demanded (and needed) fees. The
Jesuits and other Catholic religious orders have courageously decided
to make the institutions under their control less elitist, while in the
CSI pressure to make its many institutions 'people-orientated' has
grown. At the same time pressure has been building up for the
development of more deeply Indian congregations. Many in the

churches seek to escape from the limits of their own institutions and from the rigidities of their organisations (all modelled on European structures) into the life of the people. They want Indian Christianity to be at home in the 'culture' – an abstract, intellectual word for the living reality of the poverty, the dirt, the heat, the rain, the traditions of devotion and the occasionally soaring spirituality of the three thousand or so communities and tribes which constitute flesh-and-blood India.

Of course there are problems. When in 1975 the Vatican put a stop to the inclusion of some extracts from the Hindu scriptures in a specifically Indian mass, it echoed the conservatism of most Catholics. M. Azariah, the General Secretary of the CSI, has written that 'indigenization is a subject more and more debated and less and less implemented – and in fact unthinkingly resisted by the rank and file of the Indian Church'. As in Africa, this resistance is inspired by a deep sense of loyalty to the teachings of the Catholic or Protestant missionaries. By accepting these teachings, Christians received salvation and understood it, as taught, in terms which go right back to Paul: 'What has righteousness to do with wickedness? Can light consort with darkness? Can Christ agree with Belial or a believer join hands with an unbeliever?' (2 Corinthians 6:14–15). Many Christian families broke away from a Hinduism from which, for one reason or another, most of them already felt alienated. Many of them have naturally been suspicious of proposals to take them back into heathen, alien societies which they rejected and which rejected them. Instead, they have preferred to take pride in conforming to the models recommended by the missionaries. In practice, that has usually meant remaining in separate denominations: and they have not been unaware of the grants which could still be expected from overseas (from the Vatican, for example) if their familiar identities were preserved. In answer to these feelings, it is surely wise to expect and accept the indefinite continuation of many European or North American elements in Indian church life. Yet the arguments against the status quo are compelling. Sometimes in the towns Indian Christians assure the visitor that talk about the Indianisation of Christianity is a fad which interests only a few intellectuals. But actually what is under discussion is popular religion. Even in the days when congregations in the towns obeyed the missionaries and felt obliged to struggle to reach their standards, Christians in the villages, where they existed, remained in most ways very like their neighbours. If allowed, they took part in many of the traditional festivals and other practices of their communities. The power of 'Mother India' was only a little less if the whole village or caste had become Christian in one of the 'mass movements'. In the 1980s it is becoming increasingly obvious that Indian Christians must follow 'the Christ of the Indian road' (the phrase is owed to one of the greatest of all American missionaries, E. Stanley Jones) if they are to meet the Indian masses in the villages and the slums. M. Azariah has written: 'Riven by rampant and antagonistic communal sections, our poor people are entrenched in lethargy and inertia, cowed down into a culture of silence, condemned to a religiously sanctioned sense of fatalism and resignation.' Such words are a reminder that the Indian people, for all their disbelief that change is possible, their proud patriotism and their strong communalism, are often far from content with the way things are. In a country with a baffling mixture of conservatism and radicalism, they are surprisingly often willing to look at something new – provided it does not mean that they become foreigners in their own land.

M. Azariah is one of those, both Protestants and Catholics, who urge the need of Indian equivalents of the *comunidades de base* of Latin America, responding to conditions which are in some ways similar – a shortage of clergy, and a laity that needs to gain confidence in itself and to discover for itself what is the Christian message amid poverty and exploitation. Already there have been some brave groups of this kind, most actively in the communist-ruled state of Kerala where left-wing Catholicism has been strong for some time. But it was a major blow to Christianity when the great leader of the ex-untouchables, B. R. Ambedkar, became a Buddhist, declaring that Christianity was not the best alternative to Hinduism since it had done little for the uplift of his people. The condemnation was not entirely fair: the churches brought schools and modern medicine and more recently have poured money into development projects. But it is fair in the sense that churches did not sufficiently awaken the aspirations of the poor in the light of the Bible. Thus if this movement is to spread in India to dimensions at all comparable with the Latin American phenomenon, there will have to be new attitudes in the churches. The leaders of the churches will have to make a Gandhi-like 'option for the poor'. The clergy who are the missionaries' successors will have to let go of much of their control of docile flocks. And two challenges will have to be met which do not arise so sharply in nominally Catholic Latin America. In many areas Christians of different churches will have to collaborate. In all areas Christians will have to welcome the opinions and serve the needs of definitely non-Christian neighbours. In short, a revolution in church life will be needed if Indian Christianity is to play its full part in the necessary transformation of Indian society. Already many of the clergy and educated laity have produced a small flood of books about the problems of society – often along lines very similar to the analysis of Latin American society by radicals there, using a Marxist analysis. The National Biblical, Catechetical and Liturgical Centre and the Christian Institute for the Study of Religion and Society, both in Bangalore, have been models of prophetic activity through seminars and publications which have slowly influenced the churches. But as those institutions in Bangalore fully recognise, this intellectual achievement now needs to be matched by a similar energy in mobilising the average Christian with their neighbours. It was a helpful start that in 1978 Catholics and Protestants came together (for the first time in Indian history) for a creative conference in Bangalore on the plight of the Christians of the 'scheduled' (lowest) castes. No change can be made overnight in India. But in due course the growth of a Christianity rooted in the soil may be expected to produce new forms of church life, more thoroughly Indian and therefore transcending divisions which arose in Europe.

Towards an Indian Christianity

A mere visitor who attempts to enter the active discussion about an Indian Christian spirituality and theology must be modest. How can a stranger appreciate (for example) the depths of devotion which are present if an Indian addresses to the Father through the Christ who is present in the Spirit the ancient, mystic words *om*, *tat*, *sat* – as was proposed in 1972 by the liturgical commission of the Catholic church? But even a visitor can see a few things, and one is the fact that in India images and lives are far more important than words. Eight Indians in every ten live in villages. Two in every three cannot read any writing, let alone a theological book in English. Here lies one of the advantages of Catholicism, with its visual and dramatic richness, its ability to bless both popular piety and advanced mysticism, and its strong corporate sense. It seems clear that few Indians are going to renounce their heritage of the world's most luxuriant religious mythology (with, on the usual reckoning, some 330 million deities) in order to embrace an austerely Protestant religion of Bible and sermon. The pictures of the gentle, suffering Christ and his pure and beautiful mother, already seen in India very widely outside as well as inside churches and Christian homes, convey the Christian visions of manhood and womanhood more powerfully than any printed or spoken theories can. To remove the shoes and to prostrate the body can be the most eloquent penitence; oil lamps, incense and flowers can be the most heartfelt petitions; painting, architecture, sculpture, music and dance can say more than a creed. It also seems clear that Catholicism's use of festivals and pilgrimages, and its practice of keeping churches open for prayer, rest and casual conversation, give it an advantage over the Protestant reliance on the congregation assembling Sunday by Sunday. Marian shrines such as may be found within India at Velankanni can remind Protestant visitors of Hindu temples – and in India that is a point in their favour, although many Catholics are among the Christians who want to see the popular appeal preserved without the superstition. It is probable that many Indians who wish to worship God through Christ will always find it easier to do so privately, or by dropping into an open church as into a temple, or on special public occasions, rather than by regular congregational worship – an idea unknown to orthodox Hinduism. It is imperative that the churches should make far more imaginative provision for such people. Appealing far more effectively than anything copied from Europe or the USA, that would be evangelism in India.

Hindu festivals and pilgrimages are often scenes of excitement, releasing the frustrations of a hard daily life, celebrating the naturally good things such as light or harvests. But it is significant that the family matters much more than the temple to the average Hindu. By the family Indians are taught from childhood to be gentle. The tenderness with which they usually treat animals – and with which the Jains treat midges – they usually extend to each other despite the tensions which can explode into appalling violence because fuelled by overcrowding and poverty; and they are tender also to their gods. Among Christians, Pentecostal heartiness has not been welcomed in India as it has been in the Americas and in Africa. Silence is thought to be as charismatic as any ecstasy. The churches are therefore wise to lay great emphasis on quiet family prayers as a substitute for the Hindu domestic devotions. As in Africa, praying mothers and grandmothers can make a specially important contribution. Another development which meets the Indian tradition of spirituality is the growth of the *ashram*, the family-like group which lives together (not often permanently) in order to pray in peace and to learn from a *guru* who is believed to have an unusually deep experience of God. During and since the 1950s Christian ashrams have begun to be established with the blessing of the churches. Although the churches have hesitated more about this, the most interesting of them have made much use of Hindu, Muslim, Sikh and other non-Christian scriptures in addition to adopting a very simple lifestyle and a practice of open hospitality in accord with Indian customs. As the level of education rises in India, it would be intellectual suicide to abandon the Christian colleges which have earned their prestige since Alexander Duff, a young Scot, opened his college in Calcutta in 1830. There the clergy can be trained, the Christian laity equipped for the modern world, and many thousands of Hindu students given a glimpse of Christian values. But as laboratories for tests which are vital to the making of an authentically Indian Christianity, the ashrams are potentially as important as the colleges. For here is a land with at least ten million wandering holy men (*sannyasin*). Every village has its priest and its shrines. More than any other nation in the world, it is the land of God-consciousness.

This Indian Christianity is likely to develop with significant differences from African Christianity. In India despite many recent stirrings of protest there is no tradition of basic human equality. It is significant that the African socialising ritual of beer-drinking has no equivalent and that initiation ceremonies have normally been confined to the boys of the highest castes. It is true that the householder has traditionally been expected to pursue wealth and pleasure as well as religious merit, but the absence of material prosperity has been accepted as the working of the justice of *karma* and the renunciation of a worldly lifestyle has been regarded as earning the most merit under this unchangeable law. Although some Hindu scriptures and sculptures are lustily erotic, the grandfather who renounces home to live with his wife in a forest hut is praised, and the old man who renounces even marriage to live as a wandering beggar is honoured still more highly. Sharing with Africa the custom that marriage brings together families rather than individuals, the Indian variations reveal that less dignity is given to the woman. Child marriage used to be common although it is now prohibited in theory. Traditionally the bride's family, not the groom's, has produced the payment cementing the union, and there are still cases of brides being burnt to death if their families have failed. Polygamy has not been widespread and is now illegal, but in Hindu tradition the wife was firmly subordinated to the husband in every way, so that the widow's condition was pitiable and death at her husband's funeral (now abolished) seldom had a pleasant alternative. 'Widow remarriage' was made legal only in 1856. Daughters still cannot perform the all-important ceremonies at a funeral, when a correct cremation is believed to assist a better reincarnation. In no area of Indian life was the work of the Christian missionaries more appreciated in the long run than their defence of women and girls against male exploitation. An essential part of the Christian message to India has proclaimed the spiritual equality of all women and men. The most urgent challenge to the Indian churches is to relate that message to contemporary conditions by word and practice.

Although the religion of Indian peasants may be called innocently superstitious – and even in the towns astrology is often taken very seriously – Hinduism is far more sophisticated than African tribal religion. Its tradition of religious philosophy is at least as rich as Europe's and is unmatched anywhere else. In such a country the churches have all been handicapped by the origin of most of their members in castes which traditionally had no access to education. These were the people who had little to lose by ceasing to be Hindus and when they became Christians they proved themselves able to take advantage of the schooling provided by the missionaries, to the extent of qualifying themselves for responsible (rather than exalted) jobs, at first under their colonial masters who might appoint them because they were fellow Christians. They and their descendants were left with a taste for administration and litigation, so that it can be said that India's churches have been run more efficiently and more honestly than is normal among Indians but also with at least the normal amount of quarrels and lawsuits. What has too often been lacking has been the courage to meet the adherents of other religions at a deep level, whether in religious dialogues or in organised social service or (as is far more likely) in informal conversation and caring.

No outsider should underestimate the intellectual difficulty and spiritual cost of the encounter with Hinduism. An influential Roman Catholic priest, Raymond Panikkar, the son of a Hindu father and Spanish mother, has written: 'Knowledge is not enough . . . Only mutual love overcomes that egocentric position of knowledge. When I love, I go out, I give up, I am the guest, I am no more at home, I am received and possessed . . . The real Christian encounter with other religions requires a very special asceticism, the stripping off of all external garbs and forms to remain alone with Christ, with the naked Christ, dead and alive on the cross, dead and alive within the Christian too who dares such an encounter with his non-Christian brother.' Less scholarly Indian Christians often feel acutely the difficulty of arguing about religion with Hindus who are superior to them in caste – and often also in spiritual development. And whether or not they are educated most Indian Christians are conservative because they believe that to be essential to the defence of their faith.

Their consciences drive Catholics and Protestants alike to resist all changes in worship or doctrine which are said to be aimed at making Christianity 'more Hindu'. In the background is always the fear that Hinduism will take over Christianity as, in India, it once took over Buddhism. To a professor of economics I quoted the title of a recent pamphlet by a bishop of the Church of South India (Sunder Clarke): *Let the Indian Church be Indian!* 'No,' he replied. 'Let the Indian Church be Christian!' But the easiest way to begin the necessary renewal is to acknowledge that both Christianity and Hinduism have changed in the past in response to the realities of India. On neither side has there really been an 'eternal religion' deserving defence against any suggestion of change in the present or any future.

The Christianity which was brought to India by the Counter-Reformation as interpreted by the Portuguese, or by Protestantism as understood by the British, was different from the gospel which Thomas the companion of Jesus had brought if he was in fact the apostle to India – and different from the doctrines of the Syrian Christians who have preserved the name of Thomas. And the fact that Hinduism has changed over some thirty-five centuries is the great historical fact behind the presently immense variety of the 'names and forms' of God; for Hinduism has adopted new 'names and forms' in order to absorb the traditions of new peoples. The *Rig Veda*, the hymns sung by the priests of the Aryans who began the conquest of the rich Indus valley about 1,500 years before the birth of Christ, celebrated the deeds of many local gods who have subsequently lost their prominence. New gods and new beliefs (such as belief in the reincarnation of souls) were added as the Aryans conquered and mingled with the earlier Dravidian inhabitants who were incorporated into the social system as the lower castes. Gradually local heroes such as Krishna or Ram came to be regarded as incarnations of the superior God (Vishnu) and popular hymns were encouraged. Although the Upanishads written from 600 BC onwards were more mystical, their teaching was not systematic. That is demonstrated by the profound differences between the religious philosophers of medieval India. The Hinduism of the Brahmin priests, with their elaborate sacrifices and aloof superiority, has been challenged by Jainism over some 2,500 years and has in particular absorbed from that source the doctrine of *ahimsa*, non-violence. It had to come to terms with Buddhism – a movement born in India some five hundred years before Christ which inspired emperors and countless humbler Indians before it began to decline in the seventh century AD. Thus the great theologian and reformer Sankara was deeply influenced by a

Buddhist teacher, Nagarjuna. No sooner was Buddhism eclipsed in
its homeland than Islam began to influence North India, its rulers and
its peoples; for example, it converted Nanak, the fifteenth-century
founder of the Sikhs, to a passionate belief in one God. At the same
time the Brahmins had to respond to an internal challenge – the
devotion to a personal God in the popular religion of South India.
And they did respond, as in the theology of Ramanuja. No sooner
was the Mughal empire in decline than Christianity arrived in its
modern shape, revitalising Hinduism by arousing movements of
social and intellectual reform from early in the nineteenth century
into the present day. It is only when both Christians and Hindus fully
admit that neither has inherited an unchanging, always perfect,
system that it becomes possible to discuss which parts of these
heritages must change in order to answer contemporary challenges
and which parts have lessons to teach living Indians.

The easiest part of Christianity for Hindus to appreciate is the
moral teaching of Jesus when this is associated with the simple idea of
God as the Father of all. In 1820 a Hindu scholar and reformer who is
often referred to as the morning star of Indian nationalism, Ram
Mohan Roy, published an exposition of *The Precepts of Jesus: The
Guide to Peace and Happiness* which inaugurated a great tradition,
acknowledging Jesus as the teacher of active love for all on the basis
of love for the loving God. Millions of Hindus have not only acknowledged the supreme importance of such teachings; they have also
stressed only those elements in their own heritage which are similar,
in particular interpreting in this way the *Bhagavad Gita*. This tradition has included no less a figure than Gandhi who laid down his life
for it. It has inspired many Hindus to be loving in their personal
relationships, to be active in works of charity and to base their own
lives on prayer to God as Father. To most Christians this understanding of Christianity is inadequate and it is, indeed, only one strand in
the New Testament. But if Gandhi's *Sarvodaya* (the welfare of all),
an idea explicitly linked with the teaching of Jesus as well as with
Indian sources, is agreed to be common ground between those
Indians who have accepted baptism and much larger numbers who
have not, it would surely be immensely foolish as well as uncharitable
for Christian spokesmen to be always insisting on the inadequacy of
the simple doctrine of 'God the Father and man the brother'.

The wisest of the Indian Christians (M. M. Thomas is an example)
have been eloquent in defence of the idea of India as a 'secular' state.
In practice that means not that the nation is irreligious but that the
religious factor is not considered when the state guarantees civil

rights. The traditional caste system and the other customs of Hinduism are not enforced, and the contrast with the Islamic basis to
national life in Pakistan or Bangladesh is great. The Indian state and
Indian public opinion are certainly not hostile to religious bodies
which explore spiritual motivations for the service of fellow men. On
the contrary, any movement which hopes to appeal to the masses in
India has to honour religion. A respect for the spiritual life, if not for
religious customs, is constantly stressed in the 'socialist humanism'
which is the most influential non-religious ideology. Nehru, the chief
architect of the 1950 constitution of the secular republic of India, was
personally an agnostic – but was too shrewd to disparage religion
openly. The Soviet Union is still valued as an ally for many purposes –
but seldom as the teacher of atheist communism. The communist
parties of India are vehemently criticised by some radicals who point
out that their leaders belong to the higher castes. They argue that the
mere importation of Marxism from the Soviet Union does not meet
the needs of India. Fundamental among these needs, as they see
them, is the abolition of the Hindu caste system. They draw much
inspiration from China, but they are also glad to welcome allies
among non-Hindu religious believers and they make a point of
promising religious freedom in their ideal society. Thus both those
who defend and those who attack the caste system have to give the
religious factor a central role in the life of India.

Christians have often felt that an agreement with modern-minded
Hindus about the importance of love and spirituality in a free society
may be shallow. Unless Hinduism is changed radically, there must be
a continuing disagreement about the nature and destiny of man.
Hinduism has certainly had its own idea of human dignity. In a
famous passage in the Upanishads, a young man is told: 'The whole
world has *that* for its soul. That is the Reality. That is the Self. And
thou art that, O Svetaketu!' But only a small minority of Hindus has
ever believed in the dignity of each individual as the child of God.
Indeed, from a very early date right into the twentieth century AD,
Indian life seemed to rest securely on the foundation of the generally
accepted belief that it was reasonable and moral to divide society into
castes varying greatly in earning power, respectability and touchabil-
ity. Each caste was supposed to eat by itself and to marry into itself.
Many millions were left to rot as outcastes. It was a society which
radicals have often compared with Fascism – and which certainly
leaves the poorest in more degraded conditions than apartheid has
done in South Africa.

The division was theoretically justified by the belief that in previous existences people had been dutiful in different degrees, each building up his or her tally of *karma* (action) by which the destiny of each will be determined and earning after death reincarnation in a higher or lower caste or in a ghost or animal. Such beliefs have had enormous advantages. They have made every Indian know his or her place in society, within the family; there has been little of the modern European sense of purposeless isolation. They have helped countless people to endure miseries – for these miseries did not seem meaningless or unjust or final. It has been believed that merit earned in one life by the doing of one's duty would be rewarded in the next incarnation. The dying and the mourners have been consoled by the idea that death is only an incident in the very long drama of the soul's immortal life. It is illuminating to ask what Gandhi got out of the *Bhagavad Gita*, two thousand years old and modern Hinduism's favourite scripture. On the face of it, it seems strange that he, a campaigner on behalf of the 'untouchable' outcastes and a teacher of non-violence, should love a scripture which exhorts a warrior to do the duty of his caste by fighting in a civil war. But Gandhi drew from the *Gita* the idea that everyone, whatever his or her caste, must be dutiful in a spiritual light – and must be detached from all temporary disappointments or worldly lures, knowing that the soul cannot die. Nowadays he is often regarded by modern-minded Indians as a Utopian dreamer, but by these teachings he replanted Hindu nationalism in soil where it could draw sustenance from Hindu spirituality.

The Hindu division of society into castes has often appeared to be as eternal as the gods believed to insist on its maintenance. And many Christians have been among the Indians accepting it. Over many centuries the Syrian Christians did not recruit from the lower castes. To this day they are virtually a caste by themselves. In the seventeenth century Roberto de Nobili thought that a truly Indian Christianity must accept caste divisions. When the first Protestant church to be designed by a missionary was built in Tranquebar in 1706, a railing was provided to divide the higher and lower castes and for a century that was accepted as normal. In the twentieth century Evangelicals have often restricted a congregation to the members of one caste or tribe, on the principle that if a church is to grow it must be a 'homogenous' or 'monoethnic' unit. Elsewhere in Indian church life caste is often a half-hidden factor, like tribalism in Africa. It may not be talked about openly, but it tends to shape ecclesiastical politics.

It is worthwhile to pause over the argument that if it is to grow Indian Christianity must come to terms with the caste system. As put by (for example) Donald McGavran in his *Understanding the Church in India* (1979), that argument is thought-provoking. The Christians who have argued most vocally that congregations must disregard caste or tribe completely have almost all been people who have made good in the cities. In business or the professions they have felt closer to the international outcry against 'racism', to the central government's pressure against 'separation', and to the internationalism of the Vatican or the World Council of Churches, than to the traditions of the villages. Often they have used the English language as the medium of their worship and even of their thinking. From such circles most of India's church leaders have been recruited. But it seems that the 'one by one' way which may succeed with often rootless city people is unlikely to make a much bigger impact on the wider population. In India's three thousand ethnic groups, so far only about twenty have seen a major (and only about fifty a minor) movement into Christianity. In many rural areas only one Indian in a thousand, or one in ten thousand, has been baptised. In the majority of villages no church has any visible presence at all. It is surely realistic to expect that if Christianity does spread in India on anything like the African scale it will do so by arising largely within the system which divides the population into castes and tribes; and it seems right not to be too alarmed even if this process does produce a rash of 'independent' churches as in Africa. Certainly in the past the numerical expansion of the main churches has come about chiefly when whole families, villages or larger groups agreed to become Christians, so that life could continue with the minimum of further traumas – and even in the cities Christians newly arrived from the villages have naturally tended to look for a congregation speaking the language and preserving the habits of 'our own people'. The recognition of the way India is, in these ethnic realities, seems a necessary part of the Indianisation of Christianity. If it means one church for the village and one for the ex-untouchables outside it, the situation may be no more immoral than the coexistence of largely middle class and largely working class congregations in any Western city. If it means marrying only within one's caste, or treasuring only one's tribal stories, that is no more than is usually done by Christians around the world. What is against the Christian conscience is not the acceptance of social divisions but any practice by which the members of one group totally exclude, exploit or despise the members of another group. It is perfectly possible to be rooted in one's own group and yet acknowledge the unity of that wider fellowship which is the body of Christ as a foretaste of the unity of humankind.

Yet in this century the caste system is under an attack greater than any known since it was instituted. Traditional occupations are disappearing. Work often involves close contact with people of other castes. More people are eating together at stalls or in restaurants and are even marrying outside the caste. Villagers move into towns and cities where it is much more difficult to maintain the old barriers. Indians high or low jostle each other in the streets. They travel to other countries (which in the old days automatically meant becoming an outcaste). They study together. All the time the central government strives to uphold the idea of human equality – for in 1950 the constitution announced that 'untouchability is abolished' and allowed the state to discriminate in favour of the 'scheduled' lower castes, for example in educational opportunities. In the courts justice is not supposed to take account of caste. Radio and newspapers present human situations without much reference to caste except when reporting caste conflicts disapprovingly. Indian pop culture, spread by the world's most flourishing film industry and by the beginnings of mass TV, presents a diet of romantic love, ambitious effort and melodramatic violence, all dissolving traditions. All these influences support the noble proclamation of the Indian constitution that 'all citizens irrespective of religion, race, caste, sex and place of birth shall enjoy equality before the law and no disability shall be imposed on them in any respect'. So the official theory about the 'scheduled castes' echoes Gandhi's term for the outcastes – Harijan or 'children of God'. But about two hundred million Harijan still know the gap that exists between theory and practice. In practice discrimination against the lower castes in employment or housing is common. It is assumed that the leadership in most spheres of the nation's life will be drawn from the higher castes. The rich are able to quieten their consciences about the poor by the reflection that the poor are poor because of an eternal, divine law. Marriage between castes, still rare, can lead to very ugly scenes. What is common is conflict between the workers' castes within the Hindu system (the Shudras) and the ex-untouchables (the Dalits). So as the Harijan begin their long march to equality, it seems clear that the ideology of the caste system will not change much, whatever may be decreed by governments, unless basic beliefs change.

Beliefs are changing, however slowly. Just as the modern media constantly depict individuals who carve out their own destinies, so modern realism concludes that the dead are dead and that the living are not the dead come back. And many Indians ask whether it is intellectually or morally satisfying to attribute all sufferings to misdeeds in a previous life. It has been widely questioned whether Gandhi deserved to be murdered because of karma accumulated in existences before he was born, and the appeal of the example of Mother Teresa in caring for dying destitutes picked up on the streets of Calcutta points to an unease with the ideology which claims that their sufferings are their fault. The rigidity of the caste system with its supporting theory of reincarnation cannot be counted among the features of Hinduism which are likely to retain their prominence in the centuries to come. In the India which came to birth in 1947, there was a Christian element in the British liberal, democratic tradition which was chosen as the ideology of the new nation. In the India which is now quite rapidly changing, the Christian witness that all castes are 'one in Christ', with a consequent equality in every part of the life of the church, is of supreme importance. It is a witness given in more than words. Nine tenths of India's Christians have entered the fellowship of the church from the 'scheduled castes' or 'scheduled tribes'. And the church is challenged to be truly casteless – an ideal not yet reached – by the government's attitude that those who have become Christians do not need the compensatory benefits which others of the 'scheduled' may receive. Although Christians protest against this policy (which is not in the constitution), they recognise that for many years the churches have given opportunities to the lower castes through education and through the life of the congregation. Many respected church leaders (M. Azariah is one example) are Dalits.

Leaders of Indian Christianity who have been active in the struggle for social justice have often also stressed the need to struggle against some ancient Hindu beliefs.

Although India has produced far more complex civilisations than Africa's, people belonging to other cultures often notice with amazement that the sense of historical time has been largely absent here too. Rich societies have been forgotten until modern archaeologists have unearthed their ruins. Religious stories have had only the vaguest, if any, connection with secular events. Thus Krishna, the *avatara* or incarnation of God most popular among thoughtful Hindus in the twentieth century AD, may have had some basis in history, but the legends about him, drawn from many sources, are what matter to the spiritual life and these legends are cheerfully undated. Other Hindu deities must be classified as entirely mythological once the classification is made, but the lack of a link with the solid earth of history has seldom worried orthodox Hindus. This is because in traditional India, as in traditional Africa, the movement of time is not linear (progressing through history towards the future) but circular (rotating like the annual cycle of nature). That world-view comes naturally to peoples who live close to nature and who feel that they belong to nature along with the animals but who seldom experience history being made. It does not come so naturally to peoples who have experienced the astounding technical and political changes of the twentieth century AD. All over Asia, including India, modernity has awakened the millions in city, town or village to a new lifestyle. It has filled time with meaning.

It has also taught the importance of the material world and of its improvement. Indeed, the need to feed the poor dominates many modern consciences – and the poor are not to be fed by religious words. Traditionally Hinduism taught that the world was *maya*. This teaching can be interpreted to mean that the world is a reality dependent upon the greater reality of God; that the world can never entirely satisfy the moral and spiritual senses of humanity; and that therefore the world should never enslave the conscience or the soul. When so interpreted, it corresponds with a long Christian tradition of 'contempt' for the world. But the doctrine of maya has often been understood to say that the manifold world is a mere illusion, to be abandoned before there can be any significant spiritual growth, and that the things of the world are nothing but handicaps in the soul's ascent to enlightenment and liberation. The doctrine has been illustrated by saying that the 'reality' of the world is like a man imagining that he sees a snake in the twilight when what he is actually looking at is only a coil of rope. Although its own scriptures show Hinduism to be a religion able to counsel the man or woman who is preoccupied by the duties of the home or by the responsibilities of the world's business, the attraction of an escape from the world has been undeniably powerful and it is this escapist tradition that many Hindu reformers (Aurobindo is one example) have attacked as being the enemy of modern progress. They have found much in Christian activism to applaud and copy. They have also seen dangers in the Hindu tradition that nature and history alike are only *lila*, the play or dance of the gods without any moral purpose. Many of the legends of Krishna portray him as unimpeded by morality, like Yahweh in many of the stories in the Hebrew scriptures. For example, he sports with the *gopis* (milkmaids) at Vrindabad by hiding their clothes when they bathe and demanding that they approach him with hands touching over their heads – conduct which has with some difficulty been interpreted as a parable about the divine demand for the discarding of all selfishness. Less obviously charming is the prominence of the male and female sexual organs in the sculpture of many a Hindu temple, suggesting that what is being worshipped is the sheer fertility of the life that springs from the divine seed. And more disturbing still to many thoughtful Hindus, as well as Christians, is the frequent portrayal of God with the faces of animals (including a snake or a rat) or with human faces which are terrifying and disgusting. The face of Kali the goddess, Shiva's consort, is the face of death and destruction and in the past human sacrifice was offered to her. This variety in portraits of the Godhead springs out of the conviction that feeble man has to worship the overwhelming power in nature, whether or not that power seems moral or beautiful.

Indian Christian thinkers who favourably evaluate the 'modern' and even the 'secular' point out that behind the modern movement is to be found the influence on Europe and North America of the Jewish and Christian tradition which makes history sacred and the material world sacramental. Obviously there are many tensions between modernity and all religious traditions. But as these Indian Christians stress, some religious ideas are compatible with, and have even inspired, some modern or secular ideas. Time matters to the Christian – as to the Jew or the Muslim – because God has acted in time. The world is 'charged with the grandeur of God' because it is his good creation. History has meaning because in history the world is improved, because it is hoped that the 'kingdom of God' will come on earth as in heaven. In particular the Christian believes that the Creator is deadly serious about the world which he loves. For the Christian, the supreme symbol is not that God dances in a circle but that, in his Word, he is nailed down before he goes forward.

God in India

In the end there must be explicit talk about God in this dialogue between Christian and Hindu. The integrity of Christianity demands it. So does the Indian religious appetite. In India, this is talk which sooner or later is likely to baffle all enquirers except those who because of birth or adoption have known, loved and joined the Indian quest for the vision of God (*darshan*) over many years. But some simple impressions by a student and visitor can be recorded.

The pressure within Hinduism to stress the unity and holiness of God is already very great – and is the only force likely to move Hindus into a position where the Christian vision of God can be shared. Sankara, Ramanuja and other giant figures in the interpretation of the Hindu scriptures (although not Madhra) agreed in affirming the ultimate unity of God. This has been a constant theme of educated Hinduism's reply to the stern monotheism of Islam. Many modern exponents of Hinduism (Vivekananda and Radhakrishnan being the most famous) answer the criticism of Christian missionaries and of Western philosophers by repeating that Hindus are not idol-worshippers. But some Christian – or Muslim – criticism can appeal to plain facts. In the whole of India there exists only a handful of temples to Brahma (the Creator). Almost everywhere the name of the deity worshipped seems to compete with other names by the vigorous profusion of art, myth and ritual in a particular tradition. There seems to be a distinction between Shiva and Vishnu which is more than the distinction between the perceptions of the one God in South and North India; their characters have been different since their first (and inconspicuous) appearance in the *Rig Veda*, the one as a storm god and the other as a sun god. It matters whether or not the deity is 'the Mother'. On the ground Hinduism is in practice polytheism outside the small minority of reflective intellectuals – and in India there often have been, and often will be, ardent spirits who denounce polytheism with the fierce anger of the Hebrew prophets and of many Christian teachers and martyrs. Ram Mohan Roy, for example, wrote that he was 'disgusted with the puerile system of Hindu idolatry'. But another possible reaction is to trust more calmly that the ancient vision of the unity and holiness of Brahma will prevail over all the traditions which trivialise or degrade Hindu worship. Many Hindus besides Ram Mohan Roy have longed for that.

For Hinduism already has within it many teachings which can be revered when working out an Indian Christian understanding of God. These can often seem to be contradictory teachings – a phenomenon not unknown in Christianity. Of the two dominant figures in medieval Hindu theology, Sankara in the ninth century AD pursued the logic of *advaita*, 'non-duality' in the Godhead. His mind came to rest in 'the One without a second', *Brahman*. He loved to quote the answer which Varuna gave his son: 'That from which all beings originate, that by which they live, and that to which they return: desire to know that, for that is Brahman.' That ultimate reality is *nirguna*, without qual-ities, and the human mind which works by making distinctions cannot comprehend the mystery. 'How can the Knower be known?' Yet the *jiva* (finite spirit) purified by *yoga* (self-discipline) and *samadhi* (deep concentration) can reach a knowledge which is better than any intellectual analysis – a knowledge which is union. 'He who knows the supreme Brahman becomes Brahman himself.' The *Atman* (the essential when all egoism has vanished) can be united with that perfection as salt is united with the river and the river with the sea, or as the jar is broken and the space in it is united with all space. With a different emphasis Ramanuja, who was born in the next century, spoke of the One as *saguna*, with qualities, and as *Purushottama*, the Highest Person. Not only could Brahma (the Creator) be understood as *sat*, *cit*, *ananda* (pure essence, pure consciousness, pure beatitude). There was also a vision of Ishvara, the personal and active God as Lord of nature and history; and there could be *bhakti marga*, the way of devotion, a person-to-person adoration in love, in time and also in eternity. Indian religious literature has for many centuries been full of sublime expressions of the love of God and although Sankara's philosophy is the more widely admired by educated Hindus, the devotion which Ramanuja praised – and which Martin Luther's contemporary Caitanya stirred into new life – is still burning in the temple, ashram or home of the twentieth century AD. Near Madras I saw a dance of tender adoration of the child Krishna. It was the most beautiful and moving nativity play that I have ever experienced.

Christian scholars have already been serious students of the Hindu witness to God for over a century and they have brought many treasures to the attention of all who share their sense of awe. Sankara's pointing to the ultimate reality as 'the One without a second', beyond our seeing or imagining, corresponds with much in the Christian scriptures and mystical tradition as well as with that element in Western philosophy which speaks about 'the Absolute'. His promise that the spirit of man can be so purified of selfishness that it becomes capable of the vision of God, and even of union with God, also matches much that was taught by the Greek and Latin fathers of the church and by Christian theologians such as the sixth-century Syrian monk who wrote under the name of Dionysius – or Thomas Aquinas. Did not John the Evangelist see that the Son is 'one' with the Father and that the disciple can be 'one' with the Son? Ramanuja's delight that the One is not less than personal corresponds with the reality known in Christian devotion. So does his insistence that even in the ultimate union of man with God there remains a distinction between the glory of the One and the glory of the human person. But no description of God is adequate; and that is the truth in the Hindu cry of *neti*, *neti* ('not that, not that'). God the Creator has been seen both by Hindus and by Christians to be 'Being-itself' or 'the Ground of Being', the womb of the world, the essence of everything that merely exists, 'sun-coloured beyond the darkness' as in the *Bhagavad*

Gita – all that, but also the Person who can be known by love deathlessly. It is no loss either to Hindu or to Christian theology when it is admitted that the human attempt to see God has to use both personal and impersonal categories; has to be, as Bishop John Robinson taught after an admiring visit to India, 'two-eyed'; has to use words such as Being, Consciousness and Bliss as well as images such as Father, Son and Spirit.

If the Vaishnava tradition in Hinduism is right to say that Brahman is capable of developing a 'form' without ceasing to be perfect, then it becomes possible to think of Brahman as the Creator; and if Brahman is in some sense personal (without implying the limitations of human personality), then it becomes possible to consider the claim that the Creator expressed his love in the life of a person in history. It is not necessary to hold that an avatara or incarnation of God must be aloof from the sordid sufferings of real human history (it is believed that Vishnu was incarnate in a fish, a tortoise and a boar before incarnation in a human hero). Indeed, the claim to be an avatara of God has been made by many Hindus on behalf of Buddha, of Ramakrishna who died in 1886, and of Gandhi. Jesus has also been revered widely, often as an avatara. It was no accident that Vivekananda founded the Ramakrishna movement, still a strong missionary force in Hinduism, one Christmas Eve. Gandhi wrote about Jesus that 'the lives of all have, in some greater or less degree, been changed by his presence, his actions and the words spoken by his divine voice'. To this day Gandhi's followers often treasure a picture of the crucifixion as their most precious symbol of the 'Truth and Love' which to them reveal the divine.

It is surely understandable that Indian Christians – not only foreign missionaries – have often resisted the interpretation of Jesus as an avatara. They have in mind the Hindu practice of paying compliments, and even devotion, to many religious figures. In that tradition the character of the ultimate reality of God is never revealed, since Krishna, Buddha, Jesus, Ramakrishna and Gandhi are all equally praiseworthy, equally divine and equally indecisive. The New Testament and the whole tradition of the church make it clear that if one is to be a disciple or Christian one must regard Jesus as more challenging and commanding than this. The Christian holds that Jesus Christ was right in the essentials of what he taught about the Father; that his life, death and strange victory disclosed the Father as the Father has not been disclosed elsewhere in nature or history; that he is not a dead teacher but the living Lord whose presence and power can be experienced; that he is of universal significance. But it seems possible and right for the Christian to use the idea of the avatara. That idea is no more dangerous than was the idea of Jesus as the Messiah, a Jewish general who would miraculously defeat and abolish all Israel's many enemies. What is for the Christian true in the Indian tradition is that God has revealed himself in many prophets and saints, as well as in Jesus, and has in another way revealed himself in the beauty and power of nature including animals, and is always revealing himself to the open heart. That truth can be the Hindu way into the encounter with Jesus, his unique demand and his unique offer; for it is the truth that God comes to meet man.

In the nineteenth century an English theologian, Bishop Westcott, predicted that it would take an Indian to write the most profoundly understanding commentary on the fourth gospel. In the twentieth century the beginnings of an Indian Christology (*Kristvidya*) have begun to fulfil that prophecy. The wisest of the Indian Christians have seen that Jesus indeed has the authority claimed for him in the fourth gospel – but it is the authority of self-sacrifice, of selflessness, because mysteriously the heart of the life of Jesus is his union with the Father and his union with the disciple. That life, once seen and handled in history, continues from age to age and in eternity, so that Jesus can always be heard speaking. As he writes what he hears from Jesus, John repeatedly records the Christian experience of being, through Jesus, glorified. And now many Christians have begun to interpret this experience in the language of India. They have found in the man of Nazareth the incarnation of God that India seeks through its *bhakti* (devotion) for its *moksha* (liberation). In him is the *dharma* (righteousness) of God. And when Jesus is so understood – not only by scholars but also by people able to touch the hearts of illiterates, such as the singers of the Tamil Christian devotional lyrics – Hindus find it a little less hard to hear his call to discipleship. India's question is the question of Nicodemus in the fourth gospel, for it comes from the oldest among all the world's higher religions: 'How is it possible for a man be born when he is old?' But if Hinduism can be renewed in its depths by the encounter with Jesus, India's response may be that of the apostle Thomas: 'My Lord and my God!'[4]

AMID ASIA'S FAITHS

Christians in Asia

More than half of humanity lives in Asia, and the proportion is growing. And Asia is the home of great religious faiths. That is why the question of Christianity's failure there is so important.

'Asia,' says the leading Catholic missionary Walbert Bühlmann (a Swiss friar who became secretary general of the world's Capuchins), 'is the most religious of the continents. All the great world religions have their cradle here . . . Visitors from the West are surprised and impressed by the intensity of the religious atmosphere which they meet at every step. This is so, whether we go into the innumerable mosques, temples and pagodas with their magnificent traditions of art and culture or among the masses of pilgrims who show their faith with flowers and lights, with their bows and lifted hands or squatting in profound recollection. It is felt too when we are in contact with individuals in their homes, in the streets or even in air-flights . . . At the same time – this is the great mystery – Asia is the least Christian of all the continents.'[1]

Actually, Fr Bühlmann knows the explanation of this 'great mystery' perfectly well – and he has often expounded it. The same explanation has been given by many Catholics, Protestants and Orthodox as well as by many people who are not Christians, out of their own experiences of Asia. I shall state it in the plain words of a veteran Catholic monk, an Englishman who has given his life to India. 'It is certain that the peoples of Asia will never accept Christianity in its present form,' Bede Griffiths has concluded. 'Five centuries and more of missionary activity have shown the futility of the attempt. Christianity remains for the people of the East a foreign religion, moulded by the Western mind.'[2]

Such verdicts are fair comments on the history of a religion which was born in Asia but became alien to it. The armies of the Mongols and the Muslims obliterated Asia's ancient churches (with small exceptions) and when Christianity returned in strength it was carried by Western traders and colonial rulers (with the exceptions of the Himalayan countries, Thailand and Korea). So for all its talk about love it seemed to be the creed of people who were arrogant, grasping, brutal, sexually diseased, hard-drinking and prone to personal and national quarrels. The attitude of these intruders to the cultures around them – often cultures richer than their own – was a combination of ignorance with arrogance; and the contempt was justified only because they had more powerful weapons of war. They announced that all the ancestors revered all over Asia, in their uncountable millions, had gone to hell. They added that all the continent's present inhabitants would go the same way unless they accepted the salvation brought to them along with military defeat and commercial exploitation. In contrast, Asia's religions were inherited from centuries of piety, morality and culture; their message was one of harmony with nature and the neighbour, through self-discipline; they were built into the fabric of every village and family in its daily life; they satisfied both simple devotees and advanced mystics; they were, on the whole, calmly tolerant of each other; and their temples, teachers and books became all the more sacred as the societies treasuring them fell under Western dominance.

The foreignness of Christianity has remained its greatest handicap in Asia. The final struggles against Western colonialism stimulated the revival of non-Christian religions. To be patriotic in Burma or Sri Lanka meant, it was often said or shouted, being Buddhist; in the Middle East, Pakistan or Indonesia, being Muslim; in Israel, being Jewish; in China or Vietnam, being communist. And since the often messy end of the European empires, Christianity has been compromised by the neo-colonialism of the USA. Americans dropped atomic bombs on Asians (and Nagasaki was the only city of Japan to contain a sizeable number of Christians); Americans supported the notorious Fascism of the Marcos regime in the Philippines, the only Asian country to be nominally Christian; Americans devastated Vietnam, where French missionaries had built up Asia's second largest Christian community; Americans were allied with the Shah before Iran became the home of the Islamic Revolution. It is surely no great mystery that the religion associated with Europeans and Americans had by the mid-1980s only about 140 million converts (so David Barrett estimates) or about 104 million (the *Britannica World Data* figure) in an Asia inhabited by some 2,700 million people.

There are, however, signs that in Asia Christianity is at last beginning to be thoroughly Asian – and not only in India. I have stood in Hong Kong and Singapore marvelling not only at the skyscrapers but also at the vitality of the churches, social service projects, Bible schools, seminaries and study centres. Hong Kong's Christians, about an eighth of the population, have a good record in social responsibility and support more than six hundred churches. In the years 1970–85 the Christian element in Singapore increased from two to twelve per cent. Most of these churches still seem to be foreign to the Chinese or Malay culture, but on those extraordinary islands they attract because, while being actively concerned about the needy, they embody the values of modernity, education, health and confidence. They have boomed as humane parts of the general capitalist boom. In these rare situations such a kind of foreignness is no handicap. And there are some signs that in the future, when Hong Kong and Singapore will presumably be integrated more closely into the rest of Asia, these churches may have grown sufficiently under local leadership to be able to appeal as thoroughly Asian churches – although the Asia to which they belong and speak will of course be a continent which has accepted many modern values. One day, will these privileged islands become radiant centres of Asian Christianity's mission? Will they be for Asia what Iona once was for Scotland and the north of England, what Zanzibar was for nineteenth-century East Africa and what Macao was for East Asia in the years of the Portuguese sea-empire? Will they spread a vision – as one was spread to 'the churches of Asia' from the island of Patmos in the first Christian century?

When Chinese sovereignty over Hong Kong is resumed in 1997, an often disgraceful chapter of Christian history will be closed. It is notorious that the island became a British base at the time when the Chinese empire was being forced to open itself to imports including opium from India. By 'unequal treaties' beginning in 1842 many Chinese ports were in effect detached from China; in these 'concessions' Chinese laws did not have force and often Chinese people were not allowed to reside. Christian missionaries were conspicuous among the 'foreign devils' who entered the country through these ports and who, even when they had penetrated inland, could invoke the protection of their own consuls. Although they were seldom in any simple way the 'running dogs' of imperialism of later communist propaganda, it was inevitable that the missionaries should offend the Chinese who had so long been unfamiliar with foreigners. A further tragedy was that when one of the peasant revolts against a weak empire – the Taiping rebellion – included local Christian elements (however independent and unorthodox), the rebels were crushed by imperial forces led by a Christian mercenary, later to acquire further fame as General Gordon of Khartoum.

For a century most of the Christians in China remained under the influence of missionaries whose manner of arrival had been so unfortunate. Earlier Franciscan and Jesuit missions had shown far more respect for the Chinese and their ways; indeed, the letters of Matteo Ricci, a pioneer who died in 1610, had been one of the first beginnings of the European cult of *Chinoiserie*. But the work had been almost totally abortive, partly because a papal encyclical of 1704 disastrously forbade Christians to take part in any family ceremony which could be interpreted as ancestor worship; and now in the Catholic church the whole emphasis was international, the Latin mass being the great symbol. Most Protestant missionaries avoided contact with Catholicism and even used a different word for 'God' (*Shen*, Spirit), and their emphasis was on saving the Chinese from the hell where their ancestors were being tortured everlastingly. Hudson Taylor, the greatest of the Protestant missionaries, was driven on by the thought of how many Chinese were going to hell every minute. Converts could be sneered at as 'rice Christians' because they so often depended on Catholic or Protestant missionaries for charity, employment and protection from mobs or courts. Most were illiterate but often they or their children could rise socially through an education which made it seem that they, too, were foreigners.

At the time many earnest Christians thought this the only possible style of mission. The isolation of China from the rest of the world had made its religion seem impenetrable – and much of that religion has subsequently been condemned by most of the Chinese. It has indeed been easy to criticise the conservatism of the Confucians based on the rigid power of the bureaucrat and the father; the escapism of the Buddhists; the superstition and magic of the Taoists and animists. Chinese religion had moulded a society at once conceited, immobile and, in the experience of most of its members, squalid. Famines were frequent, diseases unchecked, the brutalities of warlords and bandits unpunished. It was natural for the Christian missionaries to seek to detach their converts from that China. It was also natural to hope that Europeans and Americans, then at the height of their self-confidence, could use their manifest advantages to deliver China from such evil. One of their motives was compassion. But looking back, almost all Christians have seen that this whole approach to China was tragically arrogant. It restricted the deep appreciation of traditional Chinese culture to a small minority of Christians – those who had the sense to see that the good side of Confucianism was its stress that life is communal; that the good side of Buddhism was its encouragement of the quiet contemplation of realities beyond change; that the good side of Taoism was its vision of the *Tao*, the ordering, harmonising and integrating principle in nature and life; that even popular Chinese religion had its good side, or at least its pathetically human side, in that amid poverty it sought prosperity. Unlike other Asians the Chinese had not usually put their deepest emotions into religion; they had expressed those in poetry, painting and friendship. But China's culture, for all its corruption, could have been used as a preparation for the gospel.

Instead, the missionaries' attack on a corrupt religion was interpreted by many of the 'natives' as contempt for all things Chinese. A practical people, more conscious of society and history than of the threat of hell to the soul, produced a reaction of great anger against such an intrusion. So the Boxer Rebellion which murdered some thirty thousand Christians closed the nineteenth century of the Christian era. Even then, the missionaries were not yet doomed. Although some of them accepted the enforced payment of an indemnity for the rebellion (paid until 1949), others saw the need for the Chinese churches to be 'self-governing, self-financing and self-propagating'. It was widely hoped that even if still under leadership by foreigners, or at least under direction from Rome and other centres outside China, the Christian influence would regenerate this vast, sick society.

Sun Yat-sen, who founded the republic of China in 1911, had been baptised as a student. Other Christians from Chiang Kai-shek downwards were prominent in the Kuomintang which attempted to hold the republic together during its long struggle against the invading Japanese. A network of churches, colleges and hospitals financed from abroad seemed to be impressing at least the Chinese elite, and large tracts of land were bought up by the missionaries and farmed by their converts. At the height of their activity there were almost ten thousand Catholic or Protestant missionaries in China and the churches grew. The Catholic church, about 1,200,000 in 1900, numbered about two million more in 1949. In the same period the Protestants grew from under 450,000 to about 1,300,000. But Christianity, baptising a bare one per cent of the population, was still thought to be foreign and the suggestion that it would regenerate China was not strengthened either by the failure of the 'Christian' powers to protect China against Japan or by the growing corruption and incompetence of the Kuomintang. Increasingly the Chinese intelligentsia turned to communism, which at this stage meant the example and support of the Soviet Union.

The Japanese imprisoned or expelled all missionaries found in the territories they conquered. When the communists had 'liberated' the land it became clear that no mission from overseas would be tolerated. In 'accusation meetings' Chinese Christians were attacked for allowing themselves to be the dupes of missionaries and thus of imperialists. Some of the accused persevered bravely in their full and public acceptance of the gospel and lifestyle which the missionaries had brought, enduring humiliation, ostracism, imprisonment, torture and death. Others, whether or not they remained Christians, were more anxious to demonstrate their patriotism and their hope that the communists would end the humiliating miseries of their nation. In 1950 a government-inspired but widely supported Christian manifesto made it clear that all foreign missionaries must leave. The exodus was complete by 1952 apart from those who stayed behind in prison. And then the communists in control demonstrated that their remaining objection to the 'foreign religion' was to its religiosity. The independent churches which had already thrown off missionary control – such as the 'Little Flock' led by the great evangelist, Watchman Nee – were liquidated. Almost all the institutions of the main denominations were taken over and their pastors were subjected to gruelling courses of Marxist indoctrination. Finally – as it seemed – every church building in China was closed. During the Great Proletarian Cultural Revolution of 1966–69, masterminded by the Gang of Four, persecution was violent as gangs of Red Guards had liberty to destroy all that smacked of any religion.

Such events posed a cruel challenge to China's Christians. Catholics who wished to continue the mass (in Latin) in public had to renounce the papacy's jurisdiction – not surprisingly, since under Pius XII the papacy seemed to be completely identified with anti-communism and with the Kuomintang government-in-exile in Taiwan. In 1957 the Patriotic Catholic Association was formed and next year Chinese bishops were consecrated without reference to Rome. Most of the Protestants – a category now definitely including Anglicans – were quicker and more thorough in their acceptance of the new day. Many of the most educated among them had already been thinking in Marxist categories long before the communist triumph. With about four hundred thousand signatures on their manifesto, they organised the existing Three-Self Movement on a more formal basis in 1951. Although some Catholics remained loyal to the papacy and some Evangelicals refused to support the Three-

Self Movement, these appear to have been minorities. The pressure to conform was too great; and it was not only the pressure of fear. Nobler emotions were aroused by the slogan 'Love country, love church!' Having made this submission the 'patriotic' Christians hoped to be allowed a place in communist society – until the Red Guards came. Then everything that was religious or even 'old', even the Three-Self Movement, had to die.

The wonder of Chinese Christianity is that there has been a resurrection. The turning point came in 1976, the year of Mao's death and the arrest of the Gang of Four which included his widow. It was then acknowledged that although Communism had many achievements to its credit there had been no 'great leap forward' into prosperity but rather a plunge into the destructive chaos of the Cultural Revolution. What the people of China now needed was 'modernisation' – but not in the style advocated by the Red Guards. Maoism, once the cult of an almost divine and certainly infallible helmsman, had ended in a disillusionment almost as great as the spiritual collapse of China's Japanese invaders. China had to join the modern world through technical education and through a degree of diversity in freedom, which involved as a minor feature the civilised tolerance of any lingering religion.

Now it could be seen that the Christian movement had survived. And although it had been without open churches, full-time ministers, public meetings, literature or even Bibles in adequate supply, it had grown because ordinary Christians had impressed their neighbours. Christianity has continued to grow under the 1978 Constitution which promised the protection of the state for 'legitimate' religious activities. Catholicism seems to have kept a baptised membership of around three million although it has been handicapped by its retention of the Latin mass, the scarcity of priests and the long interruption of relations with the Vatican. More is known about the more vigorous Protestants (who customarily still speak of Catholicism as 'another religion'). They describe their situation as 'post-denominational', but what this will mean when a new generation takes over from the present ageing leadership is not clear. In 1980 the China Christian Council, made up of the national and provincial Protestant leaders, was reconvened with the government's blessing. Its officers usually say that the numbers in the congregations registered as affiliated to it are about three million, but this may be an underestimate intended to avoid alarming the government. It has been allowed to print Bibles and even to encourage the flow of some money from overseas to welfare and educational projects through the Amity Foundation.

Some foreign observers believe that there are millions of Christians who are not registered as supporters of this 'patriotic' Catholic or Protestant leadership. Some optimists even speak of tens of millions, but without solid evidence. There certainly are Christian fellowships which meet secretly in houses, but being totally isolated from contemporary theology and without full-time leadership, their beliefs may be Catholic or Evangelical in a conservative style, or may blend Christianity with traditional Chinese religion; and their numbers cannot be known. All this makes for an uncertain future. But concerning both the 'legitimate' churches and these underground groups, the simple truth has been spoken by Bishop Ting, the Anglican who became the first president of the China Christian Council: 'Through their sufferings the churches in China have become more Chinese – a fact which has made more Chinese people willing to hear what Christianity has to say to them.' And that is the most significant fact to be weighed in any guess about the future of Christianity in a population which is already, in the 1980s, about a thousand million – about a fifth of humanity.

A considerable number of American missionaries, when expelled from China, escaped with the Chiang Kai-shek government to the previously remote and backward island of Taiwan. Church life there grew rapidly on this anti-communist basis amid a new capitalist prosperity. Growth slowed down in the 1970s but in the 1980s the Christians constitute some seven per cent of the population – about half a million people. A pointer to the future in the longer term is provided by the courage of the Presbyterian church – the largest on the island, at work since 1865 – in defending the interests of the native islanders against the influx of more sophisticated Mandarin-speakers from the mainland. And another clue is given by the fact that about a third of the island's Christians belong to independent churches rejecting all the main denominations. While Taiwanese Christianity has been heavily influenced by foreign missionaries, it is significant that this island has produced the scholar who more than any other has shown the world in recent years what theology looks like in Asian dress, Choan-Seng Song. He has related the Christian message not to the Confucian classics or the Buddhist scriptures but to stories and poems which spring out of the everyday life of the people.

In South Korea the Christian movement has thrust deep roots into the life of the people. This country was never invaded by Europeans. Catholicism reached it from China in 1787 and was severely persecuted, for this was the 'Hermit Kingdom' and Catholicism was heavily foreign. Protestants arrived in the 1880s, mainly from the USA, after

the overthrow of the Hermit Kingdom by the Japanese. They identified themselves with the Koreans (for example, by translating the
Bible into the people's language) and built the country's first modern
schools, universities and clinics. They were usually simple in their
own faith and held aloof from politics and the intellectual life – but
they had started a movement which would penetrate the whole
culture. They won many converts, whose own faith was tested,
sometimes to the point of martyrdom, as the hated Japanese colonial
regime (1905–45) became increasingly oppressive and attempted to
enforce the state religion, Shintoism, including the worship of the
emperor. But right from the beginning Christians were in the forefront of nationalist protests. Since the expulsion of the Japanese,
Christian missionaries have been allowed back into South Korea but
have been little needed – because the country's own Christians have
been so active, sending out their own missionaries (for example, to
Europe) and energetically serving their own people abroad (for
example, in the USA). Korea is the only Asian country where
Christian clergy are not in short supply. And no other nation in the
world sees Christian evangelism which is so effective.

In part the churches' success is due to the alliance of Christianity
with modernisation and prosperity – here as in Hong Kong, Singapore or Taiwan. The appeal of this alliance is strengthened by the
contrast with North Korea. There the communist regime is brutal and
relatively unsuccessful in economic terms. No church is open and
some two million Christian refugees had fled south before the war
between North and South Korea ended in 1953. The Christian
remnant that survives has to keep a very low profile. It is understandable that the bulk of South Korean Christianity is conservative in faith
and anti-communist in politics.

But some of the influence of Christianity has been due to the
courage of some Christian spokesmen in standing up to the ruthlessness with which South Korea's own governments have sacrificed all
other considerations to the cause of economic progress. 'Diabolical
acts against humanity' were denounced in a declaration of 1973 and
the struggles continued against the military regimes under presidents
Park and Chun. This identification with the people has meant that
there has been an expansion not only in the numbers attending church
services (and the numbers in the capital, Seoul, are staggering) but
also in involvement in causes which discontented non-Christians
value. Minjung ('people') theology has developed through the 'action
groups' of the Urban Industrial Mission, through the poetry and
dramas of Kim Chi-ha with his vision of 'the kingdom of God in the

Eastern Sea', through the relevant exposition of the Bible by preachers and writers, and through witness to Christ in interrogation centres, court rooms and prison cells.

Since the 1940s Protestant numbers have doubled every ten years and the growth of the Catholic church has been almost as dramatic. In the religious census of 1980 the Christian element in a population of over forty million was almost a quarter. Sober observers can predict that within the next half-century it will become the majority. They point to the weakness of the religious alternatives. Before the 1880s Confucianism was the official creed of the elite and a much more primitive animism the religion of the people. Buddhism attracted the spiritually minded. But none of these old faiths was able to put up a convincing response to the rapid modernisation of the country. Nor has South Korea's only systematised 'new' religion, *Dong Hak* ('Eastern Thought', founded in 1860), been able to rival the influence of Christianity. Picking up from traditional animism its word for 'God' (*Hananim*, 'Spirit of Heaven'), Christianity seems able to fill the religious vacuum.

In the Philippine islands, where the population in the 1980s is about fifty-five million, the whole culture was for long as much Latin American as Asian. This bit of Christendom was fundamentally a bit of Spanish colonialism, and at the beginning of the twentieth century, when the USA obtained control, this was still in theory a Catholic country apart from the Muslim five per cent. It has largely remained like that despite the deep cultural change involved in the switch from Spanish to English as the most prestigious language ('from the convent to Hollywood' is the standard joke). But the neglect or exploitation of the Filipinos by the higher clergy was so scandalous that a protest surfaced amid the brutal civil war of 1898–1906 during which the islands were annexed by the USA. The Philippine Independent Church was formed and attracted about a quarter of the population including many of the parish clergy. This nationalist body soon found, however, that it could not keep control of the parish churches and therefore could not retain a large following. Its clergy were poorly trained and low in morale; in isolation its theology increasingly deviated from orthodoxy; and other independent churches emerged as splinters and rivals. But the PIC was strengthened from the 1940s onwards by association with American Episcopalians (Anglicans) and in the 1980s these and other independents with a Catholic background account for some fifteen per cent of the population. (Protestants are little over five per cent.) The main Catholic church was for long kept by the Vatican under foreign control, in the belief that Filipinos could not be trusted; thus the archbishops of Manila were all foreigners until 1949. This leadership on the whole supported both American rule until independence in 1946 and then the anti-communism of the emerging strong man, Ferdinand Marcos. In return it was supported. In the 1980s those who compare the Philippines with Latin America note the great wealth of the Filipino church, the prestige of its clergy and the ability of its schools and colleges to attract – and, it seems, to influence – the children of the elite.

The main strength of Christianity in the Philippines has, however, been in the spectacular renewal of Catholicism. Here as in Latin America, the church was gradually awakened to a new spiritual life by international movements such as the *Cursillos de Christianidad*. A bolder interest in society's problems was focused by Catholic Action. And the church has found its own salvation in the deeply impressive courage with which its best bishops, priests and laity took the lead in arousing and sustaining the 'people power' which in the end over-threw Marcos, accomplishing something which the opposition in South Korea has not yet (1986) managed. Not all the clergy have shown this courage – and there has been a shortage of clergy of any sort, accounting for a continuing dependence on American mis-sionaries (who have often been radical). But the moral leadership given originally by an outspoken meeting of the priests and nuns who were superiors of religious orders in 1971 was after many hesitations developed by Cardinal Sin and most of his fellow bishops. When that cardinal called out a million people to surround the rebels who were being threatened by tanks, it was decisive; and the bloodless triumph over Marcos during Lent in 1986 opened up the way to an Easter for church and state. The aspirations of the most creative Filipino Christians were well summed up during a theologians' conference in 1981: 'They want to find true Christianity, without western trappings. They want to extend personal Filipino values to the social realm, expanding self-esteem to self-reliance, clan-centredness to mutual co-operation, familial closeness to national consensus, regionalism to patriotism, and smooth interpersonal relations to solidarity with humankind in viewing the world and social structures with a liberated consciousness.'[3]

Indonesia has one of the largest and poorest populations in the world, with more than 165 million people speaking about 250 lan-guages, it is a nation of more than thirteen thousand islands. Its name means merely 'Indian islands' and the central fact about it is that it is seeking a new identity, with the national motto 'Diversity becoming unity'. Its churches are growing – and they began to grow at the present rate when Christians participated in the anti-colonial struggle, memorialised as Christians and Muslims lie side by side in the Heroes' Cemetery in Jakarta. It was significant for the future that this struggle had its centre in Java, where the leading freedom fighters were *abangan* (not purely Islamic). Independent Indonesia was not born in an Islamic revolution.

When the Dutch had expelled the Portuguese from East Indonesia in the 1640s, for long they sponsored no substantial missionary work. When that developed during the nineteenth century they kept a tight control through state subsidies, so that in 1942 the conquering Japanese found 428 Christian ministers on the civil service's payroll. There had already been some church growth (for example, among the exceptionally able Batak people on Sumatra), but not much. Most of the growth of the Christian element in the population – from about one per cent in 1900 to about a tenth in the 1980s – has taken place after the final defeat of Dutch colonialism in 1949 and the establishment a year later of the Council of Churches in Indonesia with an aim to establish 'one uniting Christian Church'. In the exciting but dangerous struggle for independence, the Christians lived down the charge that they were pro-Dutch and there was another surge of converts when the Sukarno dictatorship ('guided democracy') came to an end in the mid-1960s. After an attempted coup hundreds of thousands of communists (real or alleged) were massacred by militant Muslims. In the end military rule, allied with business interests, was imposed. Christians had not joined in the violence and now the churches seemed to be havens of security and calm. The subsequent emphasis on economic development has been too materialist to satisfy the soul of a still intensely religious people and so Christianity's opportunity has not ended. The military government under President Suharto, while lavishing subsidies on the institutions of the world's largest Muslim community, has resisted the demands of the Muslim fundamentalists and has recognised other religions. It has permitted citizens to belong to the Protestant and Catholic churches or to 'Hindu-Buddhism'. It has also tolerated the independent Christian churches and in 1978 recognised the 'new religions' which mix elements of Islam and Christianity with the ancient animism and with the Hindu and Buddhist traditions (dominant for a thousand years before Islam took over in the fifteenth and sixteenth centuries AD). But atheism has been prohibited because of its association with the hated Communists. Faith in God had for many years under Sukarno been honoured as one of the *Pancasila*, the five pillars on which the

Indonesian nation was said to rest; but the elimination of the Communist Party made the recognition of 'religion' less vague. Since 1965 everyone has had to declare adherence to a particular religion.

This legal situation has worked to the advantage of Christianity. If previously a nominal Muslim, an Indonesian may well be dismayed both by the many regulations of orthodox Islam and by the many gods of 'Hindu-Buddhism' and the 'new religions'. Feeling 'not at peace' (a much-used expression), he will be looking for something modern but monotheistic and he may find that in Christianity. Inevitably many who have joined the churches have been Christians in little more than name. But spiritual enthusiasm has also been evident (as in Java, where more than two million converts were made in the six years 1965–71). Among the Protestants there has been much activity in the evolution of truly Indonesian styles of worship, art and theology. Among Christian intellectuals there has been a 'double wrestle' – to understand Christ and to understand Indonesia – and Christian political parties have been formed as contributions to national 'development'. The Catholic church has been comparatively conservative, but there are centres of renewal and of dialogue with neighbours such as the Trappist monastery of Rawa Seneg. Catholics have specialised in an educational network and it is a comment on their special appeal to one section of the community that their schools are often known as 'Chinese schools'. If in the years ahead the educational efforts of Protestants and Catholics can concentrate on training church members in an understanding of the gospel, both biblical and local, both spiritual and patriotic, a more thoroughly Indonesian church is likely to have a growing influence within a nation which is struggling to be modern without ceasing to be religious.

As in Indonesia, the Christian element in the population of Sri Lanka seems to be about a tenth. It has not experienced much growth in recent years; on the contrary, it can give the impression of being a conservative community, clinging to a religion brought by missionaries in colonial days. But in parts it, too, is making a creative response to a nation in crisis. On this very beautiful island the very unlovely poverty was partly caused by waves of colonialism – Portuguese, Dutch and British – all leaving behind them not only churches but also estates and factories where workers have ever since been shamelessly exploited. Another legacy of colonialism was the increase of the (mainly Hindu) Tamil element by the arrival from India of workers for the tea estates, resulting in communal riots from 1943 onwards. The leadership of the struggle against British colonialism was in the hands of the Buddhist monks, but since independence in 1948 many

Catholics and Protestants have shown an active concern for the continuing inequalities in society – and have been uniquely able to defend the rights of Sinhalese and Tamils, Buddhists and Hindus, alike. Christians were to be found amid the supporters of Mrs Bandaranaike's Marxist-inclined government in its periods of power. Since her fall in 1977 many leading Christians have shown either by their advocacy of radical indigenisation in the worship and life of the churches, or by a more politically conscious identification with the poor, that their patriotism is not less than the Buddhists'. Protesting against the predominant conservatism of the Catholic church (which far outnumbers other Christians), a Jesuit, Aloysius Pieris, has summed up the message: 'To regain her lost authority, the Asian Church must abdicate her alliances with power. She must be humble enough to be baptised in the Jordan of Asian religiosity and bold enough to be crucified on the cross of Asian poverty.'[4]

Although Christianity has thus flourished (within limits) in China, South Korea, the Philippines, Indonesia and Sri Lanka during the absence or decline of European or American power, any temptation to oversimplify the lessons to be learnt can be checked by a glance at the difficulties of the churches in other Asian countries. In Japan, for example, the churches have been conspicuously less successful than in Korea. In the mid-1980s only about three per cent of the Japanese describe themselves as Christians and the numbers of churchgoers are much smaller. The Catholic church in Vietnam has had a far more tragic history than the church in the Philippines. When the French colonists were expelled in 1954 about half the faithful and three quarters of the clergy fled from North Vietnam, only to be shattered again as the Americans were driven out of the south. Although the Catholic authorities report a growth from three million in Vietnam in 1954 to four million some thirty years later, many of the priests are still at the stage of being 're-educated' by the communist government and all of the bishops have to be extremely cautious. Buddhism has proved virtually impregnable in Thailand and in Burma. In Thailand, which was never colonised, Christians have been one in a hundred, or fewer, throughout the twentieth century and have been drawn almost entirely from ethnic minorities. In Burma (decolonised in 1948) the Christian five per cent is made up almost entirely of tribesmen in protest or rebellion against the firmly Buddhist central government. Under Islam the churches are far less free and far less active in 'West Malaysia' (Malaya) than they are in Indonesia; and in 'East Malaysia' (Sarawak and Sabah) their growth is among tribesmen who resent Islamic rule. In Pakistan the churches include between two and three per cent of the population. In Bangladesh the Christian element is no more than 0.5 per cent. In these parts of Asia which are both Arab and Islamic, the churches also constitute a tiny minority (apart from the resilient Coptic Church in Egypt) – and few Jews become Christians.

Yet it can be said honestly that in the second half of the twentieth century AD Christianity has begun to be at home in Asia. It has made a strong appeal in two situations – where it is associated with the entry into a prosperous modernity and where it is linked with the protest of an ethnic group, or of the poor, against an alien or ruthless government. In many places it has shown great courage, it has been sincerely patriotic, and it has outlived its colonial image. It seems that the Asian peoples are becoming more inclined to regard these churches as acceptable neighbours. It is conceivable that numbers could be multiplied in countries where, in the 1980s, the churches are still very small. And all over the continent a thoroughly Asian Christianity could at last begin to work effectively in the area of life where, at least potentially, it is at its strongest. If no longer seen as a foreign religion, it could make its response to Asia's religious quest – and many more Asians might find that response attractive and persuasive.[5]

Sharing the way of the Buddhists

Asia is cluttered with priests, temples and the other paraphernalia of religion. But Asia has heard many eloquent protests in the name of spiritual simplicity. Such protests occur within Hinduism, as the yogi thirsts for absorption into the ultimate reality, Brahman; so that Hindu scriptures speak of 'the unseen Seer, the unheard Hearer, the unthought of Thinker, the unknown Knower'. Simplifying protests are more conspicuously characteristic of Buddhism, or at least of its *Theravada* (Way of the Elders) form. Statues of the *Buddha* or *Tathagata* (Enlightened One), colossal and serene, are in contrast with the gaudy and convoluted flurry of Hindu temples. If instructed by Buddha's original message, the believer seeks absorption into the selflessness and no-thingness of the ultimate state, *Nirvana* ('Blown-out') or *Sunyata* ('Emptiness'). Instead of petitioning for earthly blessings, he turns to what Buddha promised: 'there is an unborn, an unoriginated, an unmade, an uncompounded'. And these protests in the name of simplicity are certainly characteristic of the Muslim's adoration of the one God and of the Jew's worship of the Lord who alone is 'holy, holy, holy'. A European in an aeroplane at the end of a

Siddhartha

visit to India had a vision of the unity of these spiritual searches. It came to him that the 'roar of the Boeing rising over Delhi into the stratosphere decodes the origin of Indian spirituality, of *Vedanta* and the *Upanishads*: either perish in this cauldron of suffering, this flaming world of birth, growing pains, business, dissolution, death, or rise above it! A few men, desperate but lucid, endowed with high intelligence, saw this only escape, constructed themselves spiritual Boeings, turned the switch, and contemptuous of all lethal dangers, disregarding the laws of gravity, lifted themselves through layers of pollution, through blankets of cloud, into the limpid transparency of silence, into Wisdom and Compassion'.[6]

Siddhartha who became Buddha was born (about 563 BC) into the warrior caste and into the family of Gautama, in a small state in the foothills of Nepal. He was the contemporary of the prophet, unknown to us by name, whose teachings form the central portion of the book of Isaiah. Somewhat as that prophet proclaimed a vision of God as the Creator of the whole world, well able to take care of Jews exiled far from their temple, Siddhartha attempted to detach Indian religion from its dependence on the Brahmin priests and their sacrifices and from its imprisonment in the caste system. He was evidently not alone in this radical rebellion against the basic Hindu conventions; the stories about his life are crowded with other hermits, rival teachers and loyal disciples. But he was the Teacher who by his own prolonged and painful efforts discovered the 'middle way' between self-indulgence and self-torture, and who trod that way to an enlightenment which gave him an authority unique in the history of Asia. Showing the qualities of a very great leader, he devoted the forty (or so) remaining years of his life not only to the contemplation of the light he had glimpsed but also to the instruction of other men and women, whatever their caste. However, he was unlike the prophet of the Jewish exiles in one vitally important respect. He dismissed as unimportant not only the ritual sacrifices of the priests but also their traditions about the divine creation of the world. He did not encourage any devotion to God or gods. For this reason he has sometimes been greeted by twentieth-century atheists as a colleague.

At least he may be described in modern terms as a psychologist. His sole mission from the great Benares Sermon onwards was to teach a therapy which others could adapt in ways which they found helpful to themselves, so that the enlightenment which he had found under the Bo tree could be theirs. The wisdom of this teaching can be appreciated by watching its practical effects not only in the lives of twentieth-century Buddhists, Eastern or Western, but also in great societies of the past where Buddhism was made the basis of a whole civilisation – in India under the emperor Ashoka in the third century BC, in China under the sixth-century emperor Wu-ti, in Japan under the prince regent Shotuku (converted in about AD 600), in Thailand (then Siam) under the king who welcomed the technical knowledge of the nineteenth century AD, Mongkut. In Sri Lanka, Thailand and Burma, where Theravada Buddhism has been dominant for many centuries, violence is not unknown – spectators of Thai boxing know that – but the peaceful kindness of the people is more typical. The wise serenity of the exiled leader of the Tibetan Buddhists, the Dalai Lama, has made a very favourable impression worldwide. The large-scale acceptance of Buddhism by the outcastes of India in the 1950s under their leader, B. R. Ambedkar, was a massive tribute to this tradition – although most 'untouchables' who had become Christians remained in the churches and some others returned to the Hindu fold. 'Buddhism,' Ambedkar wrote, 'presents itself as the only possible religion for all men in the new world which the peoples are to build.' Another striking tribute to Buddhism may be found in the spread all over the West in the 1970s of a philosophy which has checked the cult of unlimited economic growth. For example E. F. Schumacher, author of the widely influential *Small is Beautiful: Economics as if People Mattered* (1973), was a Christian who often acknowledged his debt to Buddhism. Countless Buddhists have disciplined the natural passions, have been admirable members of families and nations, and have been gentle to strangers as well as neighbours, to all nature as well as to animals. They have produced art of the highest beauty, expressing the humanism of self-conquest through portrayals of the peace of Buddha all over Asia and sketching a delicately beautiful nature-mysticism in Chinese and Japanese paintings and poems. Buddhism believes that it is possible for humanity to break through into a life which is on a different level from the life of the everyday ego with its unhappy greed. This humanism resounds in the daily vow chanted by Buddhist monks:

> Sentient beings are innumerable;
>   I vow to enlighten them.
> The passions are inexhaustible;
>   I vow to extinguish them.
> Buddha's teachings are immeasurable;
>   I vow to master them.
> Buddha's way is endless;
>   I vow to follow it.

Much of this contribution to the betterment of human nature can be appreciated without getting involved in anything specifically religious. Indeed, one of the factors explaining the great appeal of a mainly Japanese movement, Zen Buddhism, in the secularised West has been the contempt of that movement for all religious authorities and doctrines. The first teachers of Zen (or *Chan*) in medieval China repeated Buddha's own dismissal of the surrounding religion – but were radical enough to include Buddhism's own temples, scriptures, philosophies and doctrines of 'merit' in their mockery. More recently in the USA and Western Europe Zen has been imported eagerly as a technique of the spiritual life untainted by any religious tradition. Yet it is plainly false to the genius of Buddhism as a whole, as this has been exhibited in the history of Asia, to connect 'Buddha's way' too closely with the atheistic humanism of the West. Not only has Buddhism often functioned happily within a popular religion which offers a traditional system for obtaining miraculous blessings in response to petitions. The Teacher, who rejected that kind of religion with contempt, himself analysed the human condition in profoundly religious terms. He would have been horrified by some aspects of the Zen tradition of so-called 'Buddhism' in Japan – the flippancy about religion, the cynicism about rational argument, the use of 'consciousness-raising' to increase military or industrial efficiency. His vision of life was summed up in the story that in the prime of youth he saw a very old man, a very sick man and a corpse, and with utter seriousness gave himself to the search for a better end. He taught the noble, but slow and painful, 'way' of right understanding, motive, conversation, conduct, livelihood, effort, awareness and concentration. He taught it gently but persistently, with authority and with love, because it would lead to liberation from the craving which binds the ego to what is impermanent, unsatisfactory and full of sorrow. The paradox that strikes an observer from the West is that while Nirvana is not 'God', for Nirvana is not worshipped, the goal of Nirvana inspires a religious way of life.

It is because Buddhism has this religious dimension that it has been able to produce its northern or *Mahayana* (Great Vehicle) version. It is possible that this movement was influenced in its early stages by Christian preachers in East Asia, the Nestorians, but the Great Vehicle can be traced back to Buddhism's early Indian period. It could get started because Buddha himself had been in many ways Christlike. He had lifted his hearers above selfish passions by what he had been as well as by his words. He had set before them a goal which involved the radical denial of the ego. He had shown great compassion for human weakness. He had left behind a 'refuge' to gather and train those who would accept the discipline – the *Sangha*, the community of monks dependent on the generosity of the laity. Inspired by these elements in the Teacher's example and going beyond them, the Great Vehicle has been able to contain a great wealth of sophisticated religion in many ways comparable with the religious wealth of Christendom. Here may be found fine temples, large monasteries, chanted mantras, painted mandalas, elaborate metaphysical systems woven by philosophers, equally elaborate books of instruction in the spiritual life, fantastic mythologies about saviours and demons, and scriptures eventually translated into many languages. On such a vehicle millions could reach the promised land – a Nirvana now conceived in a more positive, and therefore more popular, way. In particular Buddhism has become a personal devotion to the *Bodhisattva*, the enlightened being who out of compassion postpones entry into Nirvana in order to teach and save humanity. Thus interpreted, Buddhism is no longer the advice to the individual to liberate his own Buddhahood. It is a message about a saviour, a Bodhisattva whose name can be recited tens of thousands times a day. In the twelfth century AD a Japanese monk, Honen, founded a cult of complete dependence on a Bodhisattva, a legendary Indian prince who came to be called Amida and who would bring his devotees into the 'Pure Land' of perfection. One of his successors, Shinran, developed this cult in such a way that 'Pure Land Buddhism' has often been compared with the Pauline or Lutheran understanding of Christianity: apparently it offers salvation by grace through faith. And in this rich Mahayana tradition there is also found the expectation of *Maitreya* ('the Compassionate One'), a Buddha who is to become incarnate in the future for humanity's salvation.

But the resemblance between this tradition and Christianity should not be exaggerated. Christianity claims to be founded on the human embodiment in actual history of the One God who is both 'holy' (which implies transcendent) and loving. In contrast, the stories told about Bodhisattvas such as Amida, or about Buddha himself in his five hundred incarnations before he was born as Siddhartha, have no firm anchorage in history. To the Buddhist this does not matter, for history does not matter in comparison with the timeless or with the 'here/now' through which the timeless is entered. But Christianity cannot, it seems, afford to lose its anchorage in the world of real events and real changes. And an even more basic contrast arises out of the response to the question: What is the character of the one God? To Christianity this is the question demanding the commitment of a disciple in life or in death, imitating the Christ who was consumed by a passion to 'do the will of the Father'. To Buddhism it is an unimportant, even a meaningless, question. Thus Buddhism has felt comfortable both with a popular religion which worships many gods and with a philosophy which denies that there is any god at all. In all its richly varied tradition, the respect shown to Buddha himself has never been allowed to develop into devotion which would treat that historical figure as 'mediator between God and man'. Any such development would contradict everything known about him. Although his teaching does not seem to have been written down for many years after his death, it is clear enough that the Teacher's message was 'work out your own salvation', 'be each one of you your own island'. And essentially this salvation was deliverance from the prospect of endless reincarnations (*samsara*). Detachment from suffering (*dukkha*) would come through detachment from impermanence (*anicca*), and the key to detachment from impermanence was the knowledge that there is ultimately no real self surrounded by other realities (*anatta*). 'There is no one who is miserable – but misery truly exists.' The disciple who knew this would, Buddha promised, become imperturbable, as unmoved by sorrow as by joy, ready for the final extinction of the components which had been falsely thought to constitute a self. It was a teaching (*dhamma*) intellectually incompatible with any promise of salvation by divine grace in response to prayer, despite the practice of many Buddhists. In this teaching, history was not a drama in which God was revealed and active; history was a prison to which the teaching offered a way of escape. Compassion was not supremely a reflection of the character of the ultimate reality, the eternal God. It was the willingness to teach others how little personal existence mattered. It has to be said that Buddha's message was a teaching far from identical with the faith, derived from belief in the incarnation of the One God in Jesus, that 'God is love'.

It was also a teaching incompatible with any belief that each human life is unique. Buddha, although he rejected most of Hinduism, retained what had become one of its central convictions: the belief in the reincarnation of almost every human life in a succession of other lives, human or less. His therapy was a cure for that disease. But the whole pressure of modernity is towards the uniqueness of the individual – preferably a happy uniqueness, for modernity is about self-improvement, but at any rate a distinctive individuality, for the whole understanding of personality is of a life which begins with a birth (although heredity and environment strongly influence it) and ends with a death (unless some sort of personal survival of death is

accepted on religious or psychic grounds). Modern-minded Buddhists – or Hindus – often interpret the belief in reincarnation to mean
that the individual influences other individuals by his or her conduct,
with an influence which lasts beyond that individual's death; which is
obviously true. But Buddha's message was different, far more striking and far more vulnerable.

Many developments have added to the pressures of modernity,
strengthening the sense that the individual is presented with one life
between birth and death, a life which can be good if only the self is
exerted as well as purified. Disease and poverty can be conquered.
Old age and death can be postponed and eased. 'Small is beautiful' to
Asians who could never be at home amid the standardisation and
impersonality of industrialism as it has been known in the USA and
Europe. But Asia has often willingly learnt from the prosperity of
Americans and Europeans that poverty is ugly. And it has learnt that
Asians, too, can be prosperous: Japan, Taiwan, Hong Kong, Singapore and even India set tempting examples. So more Asians have
more reasons to be cheerful about the everyday world. They leave the
advanced Buddhist beliefs and practices to the monks, often referred
to as the 'third sex'. Many young men acquire education and 'merit'
by temporary enrolment as members of the Sangha, but a lifelong
renunciation of pleasure and worldly achievement is not for them.
Nor is the renunciation of love and family life. In Mahayana Buddhism many of the monks have relaxed the discipline and marriage is not
unknown. Throughout the Buddhist world lay life often proceeds in
disregard of the traditional 'five precepts' which include prohibitions
of sex outside marriage, meat-eating and violence. And wherever
Buddhists study science and technology – on a very large scale in
Japan – they have to turn away from a religious tradition which has
denounced 'attachment to understanding' as well as attachment to
the flesh because it has seen the material world as essentially not
worth understanding. Burma seems to be the only Buddhist country
where in general the people prefer tranquillity in the Buddhist
tradition to higher living standards and it is questionable whether
Burma will remain isolated for much longer. 'Modernisation', the
new creed of China, seems to be winning.

It has sometimes seemed that the sturdily materialistic element in
the mind of Asia is going to turn to Marxism on a very large scale.
There are, indeed, some reasons for thinking that Marxism can
recruit quite easily from Buddhism. Both creeds advocate self-
discipline and self-sacrifice and have proved capable of inspiring a
whole society with some ideals which are nobler than greed and

violence. Both creeds reject the Hindu division of society into unalterable castes. These similarities have been stressed by Chinese and Vietnamese Buddhists and it is understandable that Marxist elements were incorporated into the 'Buddhist socialism' propagated by U Nu in Burma in the 1950s (although he was not a communist). But the history of Marxism in Asia has been less impressive than its promises. Communist governments have had to come to terms with realities unknown to Marxist theory – peasants grow more when they work for themselves in families; businesses also flourish more when run for profit instead of by bureaucrats; economic advance involves Western technology and that in turn involves some contact with Western ideas; people do not welcome an insensitive onslaught on their traditions including their spirituality. All this has been learnt with much pain in the recent history of China. In the mid-1980s the history of Tibet or of Vietnam under communism seems to suggest that the lessons still need to be learnt. And the history of Cambodia, where the Khmer Rouge regime broke world records for total cruelty and futility, exterminating about a third of the population, will take a lot of forgetting by those who believe that Marxism holds the key to Asia's problems. The overwhelming fact about Asia's experience of Marxism is that it proves that this doctrine, unless very substantially revised, is incompatible with Asia's very long tradition of profound respect for the spiritual quest of the individual in the setting of the family. A continent which has been fascinated by the idea that the soul can ultimately be 'blown out' in eternal perfection is not attracted by the idea that a citizen's life should be blown out in subservience to an all-powerful but not all-competent bureaucracy.

Asia in the 1980s wants to be modern in its own way. It is emerging out of the phase when the negations of anti-colonialism and anti-Americanism have been the dominant emotions. It is interested in the possibility of acquiring what suits it from North America and Western Europe, now that it feels itself to be on terms of human equality. Wherever there is a factory or even a shop, a TV set, a newspaper or even a transistor radio, there is this interest in the modern world of the West. And in this new period Asian people may become more interested in hearing the message of churches which, although now thoroughly Asian, cannot conceal that they were mostly founded by Americans and Europeans. It seems possible, even probable, that in the future more Asians will welcome Christianity as a religion which is profoundly spiritual yet also capable of flourishing in a modernised world; which is international but not entirely foreign; which teaches that the world is good because created by God; which celebrates the action of God in the history of the world; which proclaims the dignity of each Asian person as a child of God.[7]

A more Christian Japan?

Japan may become a country where a Christianity rooted in Asian soil blossoms. The gospel arrived in 1549 in the shape of a Catholicism led by Francis Xavier and other heroic Jesuits but identified with the new European traders – and so with a threat to Japanese integrity and pride. After sixty-five years of promising growth a very cruel and systematic persecution began. Thus was the official view enforced: Japan's religious needs were to be satisfied by a mixture of Buddhism for the spiritually sensitive and the worship of nature-spirits and ancestors, *Shinto* (the way of the gods), for the people. But Buddhism has been in retreat ever since the nation began to modernise in the 1860s. At first Shinto returned as the state religion, but it was discredited in the 1940s along with emperor-worship and militarism. The surrender in 1945 was a profoundly traumatic acknowledgement that the history which the Japanese had turned into an object of worship had collapsed in defeat and disgrace.

Post-war Japan has not found a satisfying religion. It is often said that in the period of rapid economic growth after the end of the American occupation (in 1952) the national religion became the cult of material prosperity. But that seems to be a very superficial assessment. The great concern over the pollution of the environment by the new industrialism has been matched by worry over the pollution of Japan's spiritual legacy – a tradition of simple dignity and gracious beauty, despite all the cruelties which had disgraced the period of militarism. The radical students' protests against the construction of airports in the late 1960s, or against the Osaka exhibition in 1970, dramatised the power of this 'green' feeling, which has continued to be felt by broad segments of Japanese society in quieter days. Perhaps half of the population (of some 120 million) may now be described as 'non-religious Buddhists', with some adherence to a family tradition but no personal belief. About ten per cent do not have even that minimal affiliation to a religion. Many are in occasional contact with a variety of religions. There is a joke that the average Japanese is dedicated as a baby at a Shinto shrine, has a largely secular education, is given a Christian-style wedding in a secular hotel, displays a Confucian-type loyalty to family and firm, is refreshed after overworking by a bit of Zen meditation, enjoys some contact with the Tao of traditional China through the tea ceremony, the rock garden, flower-arranging and ink-painting, and is buried with Buddhist rites. But being dissatisfied with the old religions, Japan experiments. Thus the largest of the new religions, *Soka Gakkai* (the Value-creation Society), has attracted about ten million active adult adherents to its modern version of Buddhism. Here is a country almost as full of new religions as of new technological devices; a book about Japan in 1967 was entitled *The Rush Hour of the Gods* (by Neil McFarland). And the Japanese are curious about Christianity's claims. The Japan Bible Society reports the sale of over a million complete Bibles a year. It is commonly agreed that Christian influence has played a large part in the growth of the attitude that if any kind of religious belief is tenable in a modern society it is belief in one God, not in the many gods of Shintoism or in the Bodhisattvas. And Christian ethics are admired. Often young people who have turned away from all religious bodies including the churches because they despise the failures to live up to ethical ideals (the 1940s have not been forgotten and not entirely transcended) are attracted by Jesus and are aware that Jesus can be followed in a Christlike way. What they need – if a European may be forgiven for repeating it – is to see more Japanese doing this.

So far, however, the churches have found it hard to increase their baptised membership. Altogether they are supported by about 1,250,000 adults but the number of people of all ages who think of themselves as Christians seems to be twice that number or more. This is because Japanese Christianity has been shaped largely by schools and colleges founded by foreign missionaries. As such it has been respected by a very clever people well known for their passion for education and for their immense success in learning from foreign models; and students seeking a faith can sometimes find one through the Christian sponsorship of their education. But such origins have made for fragmentation into many denominations either derived from missionary work or reacting against it. Only a minority belongs to the largest denomination, the *Kyodan* or United Church of Christ, a Protestant merger formed (under government pressure) in 1940 and in the post-war years rent by dissensions. And despite much justly renowned social work the churches have never reached the whole Japanese people in such a way as to invite them into membership. They have been mainly urban and well-educated, and have worshipped in foreign styles. They have been strangers in the land.

The Japanese churches' hope is that these origins may be diminishing handicaps in the most urban, educated and cosmopolitan society on earth. The economic miracle of Japan since the 1950s has produced a proper self-confidence in the nation – and admiration for this achievement is beginning to replace the bitter memories of Japan's colonial wars elsewhere in Asia. And so the possibility arises that a Christianity flowering on Japanese soil could give religious leadership to Asia. Kanzo Uchimura, who at the end of the nineteenth century founded *Mukyokai* or 'Non-church' Christianity in protest against the missionaries, was inspired by a dream. He saw a heavy dew falling on Mount Fuji and flowing to east and west until the whole earth was covered by this divine purity. Mukyokai, consisting of Bible-studying groups and individuals, has remained elitist – one in the disastrously large number of small Christian movements. But more could be expected from a Japanese church which would turn to its own people and to other Asians with more unity and humility and in the kind of faith that was seen in the Japanese equivalent of Francis of Assisi – Toyohiko Kagawa, who died in 1960. In Brazil, where there are some eight hundred thousand Japanese, about half of them have become professing Christians.

An Irishman who made an extensive study of Asian Christianity was in 1981 'inclined to feel that Japan holds most promise, despite the poor formal response so far. There comes a point at which a country cannot accept the techniques and trade of another society without absorbing the basis of its ideas. Japan has tried more than most to do this for a full century, but is reaching the stage where, as the post-war literature demonstrates, the compromise is wearing thin. While it is true that the secularism and materialism of the modern West may satisfy many, there remains a strong vein of spirituality and a traditional prejudice against egotism.' This observer noted 'the almost fashionable status of Christianity, whether as personal faith or as a talking point amongst the intelligentsia'.[8]

If we ask what a thoroughly Japanese version of Christianity would look like, we can examine Japan's new religions. They make a point of accepting science and technology, knowing that in no other way can Japan earn its living. For example, their organisations are proudly computerised. Yet beneath the modern surface they adapt some ancient Japanese traditions. They develop colourful rituals and provide classes for cultural activities, responding to a people which is artistic as well as technical. They provide opportunities to meet in small groups and to receive counselling about emotional or practical needs, responding to a people caught up in traumatic changes. They encourage meditation, which the Japanese have known to be an aid to self-improvement ever since the warrior class imported the Zen techniques from China in the twelfth century of the Christian era. So they discharge the age-old task of Japanese religion, which is to enable people to live in this world in inner tranquillity and social harmony. All these characteristics of the new religions could be copied by the churches – and to some extent already have been (for example, in the telephone counselling service). And the churches could add what other religions, old or new, cannot provide: a profoundly convincing commentary on the crisis of a nation humiliated in war, painfully transformed in peace, and still needing to come to terms with the rest of the world.

Among the many theologians already produced by Japan's Christian minority, the one with the most important message for Asia seems to be a scholar who before going to be a professor in New York was a missionary in Thailand and the head of a college in Singapore. Kosuke Koyama experienced the air raids which devastated Japan in 1942–45. Having been born into a Christian family, he struggled to find a religious meaning in this terror. He saw that Shintoism was no answer; it was not enough to say that this horror was a punishment for not obeying the emperor or the ancestors. Nor was it enough to escape from the crisis by a retreat into nature or into the contemplation of Nirvana. 'Calmness' was not an adequate response to the physical and moral ruin of a society. This deeply agitated patriot had to ask what had caused the war now ending so terribly. He concluded not that individuals who had been killed in the air raids had failed to acquire 'merit' but that the society which they and millions like them constituted had succumbed to evil. In particular they had embraced the idolatry of emperor-worship and the wickedness of a cruel militarism. So these evil cities were being judged by the just wrath of God. But to picture the divine judge as being simply and exclusively angry was impossible for a man who knew and loved Japan. As a student Kosuke Koyama was helped by his teacher, Kazo Kitamori, who was in his turn indebted across four centuries to Martin Luther – and across longer ages to Jeremiah and other prophets of Israel. Kitamori wrote a book, *The Theology of the Pain of God* (translated into English in 1966). He saw that the wrath of God is no ordinary anger. It is the anger of a Father whose love has been betrayed. It is therefore full of agitation and pain – not the 'calmness' admired in Japanese tradition. But God yearns to forgive, to redeem and to construct. Fiercely he loves Japan – and all humanity – and that is why he suffers until his purposes are achieved.

As a religious symbol, the crucifix always looks odd in Asia. It is unpleasant, undignified, harshly angular and colourless. No attempt to beautify it can obscure its commemoration of a tragedy in history. It depicts a death which is in complete contrast with the peaceful entry of Buddha into Nirvana (a condition well described as 'a state of everlasting, radiant smiles with nobody smiling'). But for a Japanese Christian this cross shows the strange compassion of God himself. Thus in his three books on Jesus published in the 1970s, the distinguished novelist Shusaku Endo concentrated on the theme of the weakness of the crucified Lord. Other Japanese Christians have the same message. For them, God judges evil; his love is holy. But God, they believe, suffered in Jesus – and he suffers in all the agonies which his children undergo, including those which they have brought on themselves. And his love has the last triumphant word because it is gladly prepared to suffer. An Asian Christianity which would honour and practise all that is noble in Buddhism, but also be as practical as Japan's new religions, might be organised rather like Soka Gakkai but with more colourful temples and with more ceremonies of the Catholic type. If it had at its heart the gospel about the suffering Father's active love, it might spread from Japan with a spiritual strength and splendour powerful beyond anything yet seen in Asia.[9]

Sharing the house of Islam

Muhammad, who became the Messenger of God and the Prophet of Islam, resembled Siddhartha who became Buddha in that both men swept away many gods, yet inspired people to build fine lives and fine civilisations. In the mid-1980s Islam comprises over 550 million people according to *Britannica World Data*, some three hundred million more than Buddhism. And after a period of apparent defeat by the West it is resurgent. In the mid-1980s about fifty nations claim to be Islamic. Some were created precisely in order to be Islamic, as when Pakistan was torn out of the mixed societies of Bengal and the Punjab. Some governments immensely rich from oil revenues have given large subsidies to fellow Muslims. In a very different style the Islamic Revolution which erupted in Iran at the end of the 1970s, and has been envied by fundamentalists or revivalists in many countries, has been a reminder of the massive spiritual energy still to be found in this tradition. And the spread of Islam by Muslims who are not oil-rich and not revolutionary is a phenomenon no less important and probably far more enduring. There are between 150 and 190 million Muslims in Africa, about eighty million in India, about thirty million in the USSR, about twenty million in China and about eight million in

Western Europe. Even in the USA there are almost two million. Mosques, schools, bookshops, festivals, neighbouring families and fellow workers now quietly spread the message of the Prophet in many of the world's cities. Prayer mats are unrolled in airports. A spiritual wealth which will last longer than the oil is possessed by the house of Islam.

Christian congregations meet in many places where Islam predominates and in many more where Islam is present, but the difficulties which they experience in communicating with their Muslim neighbours are very great. On the Christian side there is a long history of a largely negative view of Islam. The Eastern Orthodox have reacted in bitterness of spirit to the humiliation or obliteration of great churches including the churches of Asia Minor addressed in the New Testament, the churches of North Africa which so enriched the Christianity of the early centuries and the ecumenical patriarchate itself in Constantinople, now become Istanbul. In the Balkans and in Greece Orthodoxy became the religious dimension of the national resistance to Muslim conquest. Western Catholicism also had traumatic experiences. It saw Muslims sweeping up through Spain into France and through the Balkans to the gates of Vienna (for the second time, as recently as 1683). It became committed to the crusaders' armed invasion of Palestine because Muslim control of the Holy Places seemed intolerable. The declaration that there was no salvation outside the church, proclaimed by the Lateran Council in 1215, was originally a defiant response to Islam. The great oceanic voyages sponsored by the Portuguese and Spanish monarchies were also a response, because the Muslims blocked the way to India. Under many Muslim rulers Christians were protected and used if they paid a special tax, but they were forbidden to seek converts and the theory of Islam, seldom enforced, has been that apostates should be put to death. In modern times Islamic states insist that should a Muslim become a Christian – a rare occurrence – there must be assurances that the conversion is not due to material inducements. So a church under Islam becomes accustomed to life as a minority tolerated because inconspicuous. Its membership is almost entirely hereditary. The temptation is to be suspicious of strangers in the congregation, for they may mean trouble. This has generally been the character of even the largest Christian community in the Islamic world, the ancient Coptic Church in Egypt.

On the Muslim side there is a long tradition of hostility to any questioning of the perfection of the Prophet and of the book dictated to him by the angel Gabriel, the Quran. This is not only true of

Muslims with little education such as the industrial workers and their families encountered in Western Europe. Intellectuals, too, are reluctant to criticise. A sympathetic American scholar commented on the limitations of Muslim liberalism in 1957, twelve years before the return of the Ayatollah Khomeini from exile to Iran unleashed the full power of the revival of fundamentalism. He wrote: 'Such liberalism as has been achieved – whether primarily of external or internal source, whether primarily in ideas or in activity – has not yet been formulated in such a way as to envisage its dynamic truth within the central structures of Islam. It has not been set forth in such a way as to be theoretically compelling to a Muslim as such; nor incorporated in practice – specifically related to worship – as to give religious power to those intellectually persuaded. The liberal leaders of society have been but little provided with a religious base appropriate to their life and thought . . . The consequence has been not only their inability to communicate their vision to others, but also in times of stress they have not had the necessary courage and integrity to fight for it themselves.'[10]

So far from agreeing that the message of Muhammad needs to be supplemented, Muslims have often claimed that this 'Seal of the Prophets' was the 'Comforter' whose coming was predicted in the New Testament. His 'glorious message' seems to be far superior to Christianity in every way, not only as a more recent revelation but also as the restoration of the purity of the faith of Adam, Abraham and Moses, contrasted with the plainly irrational and idolatrous beliefs that God has a son and a mother (so that there are in effect three gods) and could be killed on a cross (so that he is not eternal) – beliefs which almost all Muslims sincerely think are held by Christians. Islam is often said to be the only pure monotheism and the only rational religion. It is also extolled as an ethical system all the better for being definite and practical, not demanding superhuman sanctity. And Muslims produce many reasons for believing that in practice Christianity has failed to inspire even ordinary decency. Memories of the brutality of the medieval crusaders are still alive. More recent memories are of British and French colonialism and of American neo-colonialism, accompanied in the imperialists' own countries by what seems to be moral anarchy – the flaunting of sex outside marriage, widespread addiction to drugs including alcohol, the rootlessness of the young, the general sense that life has no meaning. It is possible to project, in contrast, an image of Islam as a brotherhood of believers pure in their worship and clean in their living. When defects are admitted, it can be claimed that the trouble lies in the fact that

Islam has been colonised and corrupted by the 'infidel West' – and that the main hope of humanity lies in the growing freedom of Muslim peoples to be thoroughly Islamic.

Christians may, however, hold an alternative hope. For when not put on parade in order to impress 'enemies' Islam is, like Christianity, full both of diversity and of self-questioning. In the heyday of British imperialism some Muslim intellectuals appreciated the liberal side of the British tradition and began to attempt to reconstruct Islam in the context of modernity. Their efforts recalled earlier modernisations. Medieval theologians incorporated into Muslim orthodoxy the logic of Aristotle and current science before their Christian equivalents did. Indeed, Islam has had great periods which may be called liberal. In the fifteenth and sixteenth centuries of the Christian era the civilisation of the Ottoman empire was more sophisticated and tolerant than Europe, and the civilisation of the Mughal empire in India spread its faith peacefully to Indonesia without the entanglement in colonialism of the Christian missionaries to East Asia. In the twentieth century Islam has often had a tolerant attitude to local customs, whatever its theory might seem to dictate. In West Africa and Indonesia most conspicuously, but also elsewhere, Islam has in practice accepted magic and animism. (The Quran is treated as a magical talisman, the name of God is invoked magically, much attention is paid to angels and devils and the belief in God's predestinating control of events becomes fatalism about all that happens.) In Afghanistan Islam has adopted the harsh customs of the Pushtun tribesmen. In the Indian culture, on the other hand, there has been a rich development of spirituality and mysticism and often a gentle willingness to live on good terms with non-Muslim neighbours. (It seems likely that the Sufi movement, so creative and influential in Muslim spirituality, originated in Indian influence on Persia.) In the Soviet Union and China Muslims have largely accepted communism as establishing the framework of society but have kept alive a fervent religious faith. And elsewhere, even if beneath the appearance of unyielding pride in their heritage, many Muslims have quietly adjusted themselves to a Westernised modernity.

At present in many countries – in Egypt, for example, or Turkey, Tunisia, India or Indonesia – there are considerable numbers of Muslims who are educated, modern-minded, steadily prosperous and in no way fanatical. They deplore the insensitive secularisation of Turkey in the 1920s – but also the brutal fanaticism of Iran in the 1980s. They support the refusal of their governments to bow to the aggressive fundamentalism of the Muslim Brotherhood. Quietly they seek to worship and obey God while sharing many of the attitudes and customs of their contemporaries in the West. They ask, for example, what is wrong with a glass of beer – and what is right with an unspiritual religion of any kind. They do not aspire to be theologians and they do not want to be troublemakers by causing unnecessary offence to their neighbours, but it seems reasonable to believe that in due course – when Islam feels less hurt and confused by the impact of the West – their liberalism will be expressed more publicly and systematically in modernising theology and social thought. For example, it can be expected that the devout students of theology in al-Azhar in Cairo (the oldest university in the world), who in the 1980s still accept a medieval curriculum, will in the future wish to come to terms with the newly introduced secular studies which other students pursue. And alongside this educated elite can be found many millions, less fortunately placed, whose acceptance of the harsh restrictions of Muslim conservatism cannot be taken for granted as either heartfelt or permanent. In particular many women resent all that is implied when a marriage is arranged by the families, when the wife is thereafter supposed to be in *purdah* (behind a 'curtain'), when the black veil is imposed and few good jobs or educational opportunities are opened for competition with the men, and when divorce or polygamy is easy for a man.

The conservatives usually seek the enforcement of the 'whole system of Islam' by law (*Sharia*), with special courts. This medieval system is based on the Quran, about a tenth of which is legislative, reinforced by the *Haddith* (sayings and acts of the Prophet) and the *Sunna* (the 'path' of the Prophet's earlier followers). It includes food laws; all meat must be slaughtered ritually and the pig is never to be eaten. A flogging with eighty lashes is prescribed for the consumption of alcohol. Theft is to be punished by the amputation of a hand or foot. The whole development of modern economic life is challenged by the absence of any concept of 'corporate personality' of a company – and by a clear prohibition of *riba* or usury, usually interpreted as forbidding all interest on capital although profit-sharing after risk-taking and a charge for banking services are allowed. Such laws present obvious challenges to 'liberalisation' or 'modernity'. But private property is the will of God and it is assumed that the inequalities of wealth will be ironed out by compulsory almsgiving. These are traditions which present difficulties to Islamic socialism. Traditionally, too, all images of human beings are prohibited because they are temptations to idolatry; yet ultra-orthodox Muslim states stick photographs of their leaders on postage stamps, on portraits for display in offices, and even on placards to be waved in processions. Any modern idea of the equality of the sexes has been denied by restrictions on women which are all claimed to be 'Islamic', by the right of the Muslim man to have up to four wives and slaves including concubines (although he must make equal provision for all wives and treat any slaves humanely) and by the ease with which he may dismiss a wife by divorce. Although in the Quran adultery was (like fornication) punishable by a hundred lashes, it was later made a capital offence by stoning to death. Obviously much of this Sharia law had praiseworthy motives in its original setting – sobriety, hygiene, honesty, compassion, modesty, chastity, the rearing of children. The sex laws, for example, were made for a society in which women had to be protected by marriage but outnumbered the men (tribal wars were frequent). Adultery was viewed with horror because it disrupted the family – but had to be testified by four male witnesses, who were to be flogged severely if their accusations were shown to be false. And obviously non-Muslims cannot point to any great success in their own societies in solving all these problems. However, many Muslims who rightly take pride in many aspects of their own civilisation find it difficult to accept all the details of this legislation as equally and permanently essential to obedience to God. For example, many Muslim women notice that the Quran nowhere insists on the veil (*hijah*), which has become the symbol of severe restrictions. Originally the veil was a custom among some Byzantine and Persian ladies. It was taken over by Muslims long after the time of the Prophet.

Even practices which are called the 'pillars' of Islam are being reinterpreted. The law of prayer five times a day can be very difficult to keep in the circumstances of modern life and can, in any case, seem too formal; so that the practice of praying only three times a day, which was all that was required in the Prophet's lifetime, is now widely acceptable. The law of the fast throughout the month of Ramadan, from sunrise to sunset, was taken over by Muhammad from pagan Arabia, as was the compulsory pilgrimage to Mecca at least once in a lifetime (the *Hajj*). Like the daily prayers these duties have given countless Muslims a sense of spiritual unity in devotion to Allah, but they can be resented or ignored if Ramadan falls in the summer and is a burden on industrial or office workers, or if the pilgrimage seems an unreasonable demand to make of people who may live thousands of miles from Mecca. Already some humane arrangements are acceptable: feasting after nightfall during Ramadan is allowed and even encouraged, and only those able to afford it and free of domestic obligations need make the pilgrimage.

Similarly questionable among the other customs of Islam is the insistence on Arabic in all public readings of the Quran and public prayers – at a time when the Arabs constitute only about a tenth of all Muslims. It can seem very strange to Indonesians, for example, when 'religious education' means the recital of Arabic. And among sensitive Muslims there is embarrassment about the whole tradition of the *Jihad*, the holy war against unbelievers. It can be interpreted as meaning spiritual warfare or as solely justifying defence against aggression. But Muhammad clearly encouraged his followers to fight in battles which were bloody and not at all clearly defensive, and in the twentieth century the idea of the holy war has been used by Muslims to justify ruthlessness in armed conflicts between Arab states, in the mass-murder of communists in Indonesia and in the cruelty of the Islamic revolution in Iran.

Probably it will take many years of argument and experiment to work out what will be the probably diverse social structures of a modern or post-modern Islam. Towards the end of the twentieth Christian century the disagreements of Muslims are more striking than their successes in this endeavour. Thus a modern Islamic state may accept most of capitalism (as in Saudi Arabia or the Gulf states) or most of socialism (as in Indonesia or Algeria). It may even embrace communism (as in South Yemen). It may regard as 'fanatics' and 'enemies of the state' those who campaign for the full Sharia system (as in Egypt or Morocco). Or it may be deeply divided in response to this challenge (as in Pakistan or Sudan). Or it may enforce the system by terror (as in Iran). It may make polygamy illegal or its rulers may encourage it by their examples. It may subjugate or liberate women. In a number of countries undue conservatism or liberalism may cost a Muslim very dear. And it has to be said that in the AD 1980s the political unity of Islam remains largely a dream. Libya has been at war, open or covert, with all its neighbours. The Islamic revolution in Iran is feared – probably more than anything else in the world – by the custodians of Islam's central shrines in Arabia. Muslim slogans are chanted on both sides as Iran and Iraq wage war on each other with great savagery. Not even a shared hostility to Israel could translate the rhetoric about the 'Arab nation' into reality. Not even commitment to Islam could hold the two halves of Pakistan together as one nation. So Islam has not escaped Christianity's problems. It finds it hard to be a brotherhood politically.

It is, on the surface, an all-embracing ideology. Islam's dating of years begins not with Muhammad's birth but with his escape to

Medina, where he could begin to dominate his own community (in AD 622). Its reverence for the Quran is similar to the Christian's for Jesus; since AD 850 it has been Muslim orthodoxy to believe that the Arabic words of the Quran (some 120,000) were not created but existed in their unalterable perfection eternally, as the 'speech of God'. But many Muslims hold nowadays that not every part of the tradition is equally authoritative. They may recognise that the Quran reflects the development of the Prophet's life (if not later developments), and it has always been acknowledged that a later command abrogates an earlier one. Taking more of a risk, some Muslims dare to say that not all parts of the Quran are of equal spiritual significance. A few have even said that not all parts were really revealed by God to the Prophet. With more confidence it is often agreed that the Prophet's legislation, although codified by AD 850, still leaves some room for interpretation by the art of *fiqh* (jurisprudence). And it is highly significant that there has been no Muslim equivalent to the papacy. Originally Islam was led by the *Khalifah* (Successor) but from about AD 750, Muslims challenged each other about who should hold an office which was more political than religious. Since the murder of Uthman in AD 656 there has been a division between the Sunnites (majority) and the Shi'ites – most of whom look for the miraculous return of their twelfth *Imam* (Leader), last seen alive in the 870s. While waiting they give a power to their clergy which he Sunnites deplore. The last remnants of the Caliphate held by the Ottoman sultans were abolished during the secularisation of Turkey, in 1924, and since that date the recognition of the overlordship of any of the leaders of the Muslim movements or Islamic states has been impracticable. If it becomes clear that Islam does not prescribe any one social structure, legal order or political leader, the hope grows that its abiding strength will be seen to lie in morality and spirituality. Its legal and political arrangements have been, like the Quran itself, imperfect because human – but that fact does not contradict the truth of the essential, exultant cry heard across Islam, from where the Atlantic washes Guinea to where the Pacific washes New Guinea: *La ilaha illa Allahu*, 'There is no deity but God.'

In the 1980s of the Christian era the fact that Islam is in turmoil, spiritual as well as political and economic, is plain to the world. It is equally plain that the reassessment of Islam is approaching the spiritual through the social questions. Not the nature of God but the content of God's law for society seems to be what is commonly debated. More strictly theological conversations between Muslims and Christians are very rare and, when held, tend to be disastrous if either side is at any stage indelicate. Yet as Muslims reassess their societies, the religious foundations cannot entirely escape review. Different ideas about God underlie many of the arguments about the need to legislate according to the letter or spirit of the Quran. And once the religious question is raised, the question of Christianity follows. In some predominantly Muslim countries the question may be put by the existence of a sizeable Christian community, but almost everywhere in the Muslim world those who discuss the content of the law of Allah are aware of Christian criticism. They are usually resentful – but can quietly respond in their own way. And even if the intention is to restrict the debate to the content of the Quran, the question of Christianity arises. For in the Quran there are many references to Christians, some of them favourable – and Jesus is praised in terms inferior only to the praise of the Prophet himself.

The spiritual radiance of the Prophet's vision of the one holy God did not produce infallibility about the contents of the Jewish and Christian religions. On the contrary, mistakes here suggest one more question mark to put against the doctrine of the uncreated perfection of the Quran. Muhammad is traditionally believed to have been illiterate. Whether or not this can be a totally accurate classification of a man who had been a successful merchant, in so far as he was the author of the Quran it is beyond dispute that his knowledge of the Hebrew and Christian scriptures was imperfect. Many passages are lively expansions of the biblical narratives, suggesting that this amazing man was a novelist, particularly fascinated by the encounter between Moses and Pharaoh. But for no historical reason Abraham is said to be willing to sacrifice Ishmael (not Isaac) at Mecca (not Moriah), and Mary the mother of Jesus is the 'sister of Aaron'. It is also said that the Jews 'did not kill him, did not crucify him; it was made to appear to them' that Jesus was killed (4:157–9). Although the exact meaning of the Arabic is uncertain, most Muslim commentators explain that a substitute was crucified. Although it is said that after his apparent death 'Allah lifted him up to his presence' (and most Muslims believe that Jesus was 'assumed' into heaven with his body as well as his soul), the precise Christian claims about the resurrection are ignored. He is called the Messiah, his return as judge is expected, and his virgin birth attests his status, but 'Jesus is like Adam in the sight of Allah' and the title 'Son of God' is denounced as an example of *shirk*, the unforgivable sin of associating a creature with Allah in worship. Similarly it is thought necessary to deny the alleged Christian teaching that Mary the mother of Jesus is a goddess. It is also alleged that 'the Jews say Ezra is the son of Allah' and that they and the Christians 'worship their rabbis and their monks as gods'. The defence of this misunderstanding of the Bible is that the Jews and Christians have corrupted the scriptures originally revealed to them. But human errors by Muhammad seem a more probable explanation – unless some modern Western scholars are right to deduce from the literary and archaeological evidence that the Quran was compiled at a date considerably later than the death of the Prophet and includes many passages originating in disputes between Muslims, Christians and Jews.

These are not mere debating points, for more than accuracy about history is being asked for as Muslims are challenged to develop their response to 'Isa' the Son of Mary. Jesus is often praised in the Quran as a 'prophet' and 'apostle' (Sent One, *Rasul*). He has been called by impeccably orthodox Muslim theologians a 'word of God' and a 'spirit of God'. The Quran itself speaks of 'God's word which he put into Mary and a spirit from him' (4:171). Paradoxically, it is crucial for Christians to insist that this Jesus, so highly honoured, really was crucified. For the admission that he was rejected, betrayed, deserted, killed and buried would be for Muslims the admission that prophets and other servants of God do not always succeed in the eyes of the world; that it may be the will of God that they should triumph while failing and preach while dying; that out of such agonies the faith may rightly arise that in a good man's suffering is embodied the patient love which is the very being of God; that Muhammad Iqbal was wrong when he wrote that 'in the knowledge of death we are better than God'. The essential message of the cross of Jesus to the Muslim is that prayers to *Al Rahman al Rahim*, 'the Merciful Lord of Mercy', are not idolatry when addressed to the Word of God who knew death. And much can be found in the history of Islam which prepares the Muslim to receive the gospel. The tradition that God has ninety-nine 'most beautiful' names is close to much in the scriptures of the Jews and the Christians. So is the dedication of the Sunnites to the ideal of universal justice and equality under the Creator regardless of tribe, nation and race; not for nothing is it claimed that the head of John the Baptist is buried in Damascus. The Shi'ite veneration of the martyred Ali and Husain (the Prophet's cousin and grandson, killed in disputes about the Caliphate) is not far from Good Friday. The passion of the Sufis for union with Allah in love is close to the heights of the Christian saints' spirituality. And the devotion of all Muslims of all schools to the person of the Prophet, while stopping short of the Christian worship of Christ, can prepare them to understand how for the Christian the best name of God is a man's name. There is common ground between Christianity and Islam – and it is holy ground.

In the future Christians and Muslims will not be able to ignore each other's existence. Nor, if they are praying and thinking people willing to acknowledge all truth, will they rest content with the defences which the two religions erected against each other when embattled. Christians have already begun to accept Muslims as fellow believers in the one true God and to appreciate the strengths of Muslim piety and morality. Such were the affirmations of the Second Vatican Council in AD 1962–65 and of various dialogues with Muslims in which both the Vatican and the World Council of Churches were involved in the 1970s. The question is whether it can be acknowledged from the other side that the Christian, too, can be in some sense *Muslim* ('surrendered to God'). An achievement of such dialogues as have occurred is agreement that the thrust of the New Testament, no less than of the Quran, is to teach the unity of God, and that the doctrine of the trinity is misunderstood when it is understood to teach anything that contradicts that simple creed. Christians will always maintain that their trinitarian faith in the Son and the Spirit arises not out of idolatry but out of the experience of God's nearness – and the Quran says that God is nearer than a man's jugular vein. Neither religion intends to be idolatrous; not Islam when it receives the Quran as the Speech of Allah and not Christianity when it rejoices in the power of the Holy Spirit and when it accepts Jesus as the Son or Word of God. If that common intention can be mutually recognised, the way may be open for Christians to give thanks for what Allah has done through the Prophet's magnificent book and through the innumerable Muslim saints. And the positive attitude to Christians expressed in chronologically early passages of the Quran may return after many tragic centuries. 'The most friendly of men towards the believers', it is said at one point (5:82), 'are those who say "We are Christians"; that is because among them are priests and monks, and they are not proud.' If they were more humble, Christians could be made welcome to pray, to learn and to teach within the *Dar al Islam*, the household of those who obey Allah (the name of God already used by all Arabic-speaking Christians), the Sovereign, the Master of the Worlds, the Sustainer, the All-knowing, the King of Truth and Justice, the Constant Giver, the Lord of Daybreak, the Very Loving, the Merciful Lord of Mercy.[11]

Christians and Jews

It is, however, Judaism that presents the sharpest challenge to Christianity as the conversations now begin between the great religions born in Asia. This is not because the Jews are numerous or actively missionary. The earliest mention of the 'Hebrews' is an ancient Egyptian inscription which announces that they have been destroyed. Their history has often discouraged the Jews from having large families – and they have lost many of their number to privation, to disease or to massacre. In the Middle Ages there were probably only about a million Jews, in AD 1800 only about three million. The great growth which took place in Eastern Europe during the calmer nineteenth century of the 'common' era ended in the Holocaust under the Nazis. More recently Jews who have reached middle class living standards have kept their families small in order to maintain those standards. There are about seventeen million Jews in the world in the twentieth century but it is known that most are not orthodox. In the USA, for example, where most Jews now live, weekly attendance at synagogue declined from twenty-seven per cent of all Jews in 1955 to some sixteen per cent twenty years later. In the state of Israel there are about 3,500,000 Jews, about half the number in the USA – and it is usually reckoned that some three quarters of Israelis are *chiloni* ('secular') rather than *dati* ('religious'). Conversions to Judaism are rare and are usually connected with mixed marriages.

Nor is it the case that there is great pressure on the Christian churches to cater spiritually for Jews. In the state of Israel the Christian community numbers only about eighty-five thousand and the great majority of these are Palestinian Arabs in families which were Christian before the state of Israel was formed in 1948. A strict Israeli law against proselytisation, passed in 1977 but never fully activated, would no doubt be enforced if Christian evangelism were to look like persuading many Jews to formally renounce their ancestral faith. Small Christian missions carry on work among Jews in Israel and elsewhere but they have had little recent success. During the nineteenth century many Jews accepted baptism. Some became Christian evangelists but usually this Christianisation represented assimilation to the intellectual 'enlightenment' and the prosperous civilisation of Western Europe and the USA. The distinctively Christian-Jewish culture of the first century did not reappear.

Nor is it the case that theological conversations between Christians and Orthodox Jews are frequent and enthusiastic in Israel or anywhere else. Dialogues do take place between Christians and Jews who are for the most part 'liberal' or 'progressive', in the USA and elsewhere; I have taken part in some. But they quickly find that it is emotionally painful and intellectually bewildering to begin to uncover the causes of the separation and hostility of nineteen centuries. Outside the courteous dialogues of scholars, ignorance and prejudice are still powerful. The virus of anti-Semitism continues to be a threat to which Jews are acutely sensitive and few Jews wish to study at any depth a religion which persecuted their fathers. When neighbours and colleagues who are Christians and Jews get along with each other, or work together in humanitarian causes, it is usually on a human, rather than an explicitly religious, basis.

The sharpness of the Jewish challenge to Christianity is caused by the fact that, for the intelligent, Judaism by its sheer existence makes inescapable the problem of Christianity's relationship with other religions which seem permanent. It is impossible to read the Christian scriptures or to sing the Christian hymns without being aware of the church's claim to have taken over all that was best in the religion of the Hebrew prophets, of the psalmists and of Jesus. The church is self-styled the 'New Israel'. Yet Judaism has refused to die – even when, century after century, Jews were penalised, hounded, forcibly converted and legally or illegally murdered by the Christians who had grown impatient with the poor response to their theological arguments. After such a history Christians with any sensitivity are bound to ask themselves whether the lesson to be learnt is that the God of Abraham, of Isaac and of Jacob never meant Judaism to die. But having asked this, Christians must meet another paradox. At the very time when Christians are beginning to repent of past arrogance towards the Jews, many Jews are asking themselves what their future is. As a people they have survived. It seems a miracle. But for what purpose have they survived? All over the Jewish world there is great interest in the ceremony of *Barmitzva* in which at thirteen years of age a boy becomes a man through becoming a 'son of the commandment'. But parents know that this man is likely to ask, 'Which are the great, enduring commandments for Jews?' It is a question to which the followers of Jesus of Nazareth ought not to be deaf – and it is a question matched as young Christians confront their own tradition. Thus the Christian-Jewish dialogue raises questions which pierce both religions to the heart.

The dialogue can make no progress without a complete confession of Christian guilt. Obviously the Nazis who after subjecting them to mental and physical torment murdered about six million Jews, then about a third of worldwide Jewry, were not believing Christians.

Obviously Christianity was better represented by the few Christians who incurred great risks or sacrifices in order to rescue Jews from the Holocaust. And obviously that colossal iniquity was brought about not by theoretical anti-Semitism alone but by a combination of many historical forces – the flight of impoverished Jews into Western Europe from persecutions in the Russian empire; the defeat and prolonged humiliation and economic ruin of Germany, resulting in the search for a scapegoat to bear the blame; the fanaticism of the Nazis which led to the determination to achieve the 'final solution' of the Jewish question although other problems were visibly defeating them. Yet Hitler and almost all those who carried out his orders had been baptised in infancy. They were never excommunicated by their churches. They were confident in relying on the indifference or support of the many Germans who must have known about these atrocities. The historical forces which were the immediate causes of the Holocaust had been preceded by centuries of anti-Semitism. In 1543 Martin Luther's tract on *The Jews and their Lies* echoed the vilest medieval propaganda. Foul libels, such as stories about child-murder or cannibalism, had been very widely believed. Riots and massacres had been countenanced or commanded by Christian rulers. Jews had been forced into unpopular professions and had then been expelled penniless. And very few Christian consciences were troubled – for it was taught in church that the Jews were being justly punished for 'killing God'. The New Testament itself seemed to condemn the Jews. Passages of Paul's letters suggested that the Jewish religious law brought nothing but enslavement and misery, and in the gospels could be read heated attacks on Pharisees, priests and scribes. Most modern scholars attribute at least some of the fierceness of these attacks to the gospel-writers rather than to Jesus, remembering that the gospels were written in the very period when church and synagogue were being divorced. But Matthew 25 was a diatribe against Jewish 'blind guides' who did everything for show, overlooked the demands of justice, mercy and good faith, were 'brim-full of hypocrisy and crime', stopped men entering 'the kingdom of Heaven' and made converts who were 'twice as fit for hell as you are yourselves'. The same gospel reported the fateful Jewish cry: 'His blood be on us, and on our children!' (Matthew 27:26). The fourth gospel was also used in anti-Semitism. Although in that gospel Pilate is the only Gentile to speak to Jesus, who declares that 'It is from the Jews that salvation comes' (John 4:22), yet Jesus is condemned by Pilate in order to satisfy the Jews (John 19:16). 'The Jews' – a phrase which occurs about seventy times – are told that 'your

father is the devil and you choose to carry out your father's desires'
(John 8:44). All the Jews' teachers before Jesus were 'thieves and
robbers' (John 10:8). It is a history which must make all Christians
with open hearts and minds profoundly ashamed, for it is clear that
the church's history and even the church's gospels have been
poisoned by the great evil of hatred for the religion and the race that
gave Jesus birth, nourished his soul and supplied his audience. This
history resulted in a Jewish tradition which until recently avoided
even naming Jesus – and it still makes the idea of conversion to
Christianity unthinkable for almost all Jews. 'I am a Jew,' said the
religiously agnostic Isaac Deutscher, 'by force of my unconditional
solidarity with the persecuted and the exterminated.'

What is not unthinkable is the possibility that the future of Judaism
may be different from its past.

Recent Jewish discussion about this future reflects the intensity of
the spiritual crisis created by the Holocaust and the birth of the state
of Israel. It has been conducted with a very impressive combination of
energy, self-involvement, integrity, realism and learning, despite the
frequent pleas of the experts about the indifference of the Jewish
public. The contrast with the level of discussion in Buddhist and
Muslim circles is thought-provoking. The number of books dealing
with this theme is remarkable when one considers how few Jews there
are to support the literary industry and when one reflects that
between the second and the nineteenth centuries there was very little
uncertainty about what it meant to be a Jew. After the suppression of
the Jewish revolts against Rome, the reorganisation of Judaism
around the synagogue and the Torah taught there (with 'fences round
it', as was said) was so thorough that the variety of Judaism in the time
of Jesus was subdued. Charismatic prophets were distrusted and
discouraged. Both Sadducees and Zealots were silenced. The Essene
monks perished along with many dreams of the rapid dawn of the
messianic age. The revolts also wrecked hopes that Judaism would
prosper peacefully in the Greco-Roman world; Philo, the contemporary of Jesus who worked out a Platonic interpretation of the Hebrew
scriptures in the synagogues of Alexandria, was virtually forgotten by
Jews. There was no systematic Jewish theologian before Saadia in the
tenth century of the common era and when the greater Maimonides
appeared he, too, was suspected by his fellow Jews. No longer was
Judaism in any form allowed to be a missionary religion, as it has been
when Matthew's gospel could declare that the Pharisees 'travel over
sea and land to win one convert'. Instead the task of the Jewish
community became survival in obedience to the God who had

revealed his will for it in the Mosaic law. This law was codified and interpreted in the Talmud, which was finally edited in two versions in the fifth and sixth centuries AD as *halacha*, authoritative direction for the walk of the Jew through life. At the same time a vast quantity of *haggada*, or commentary on the scriptures, was assembled. The revival of mystical and charismatic movements, when it came, was kept well within these fences. But the debate which began when nineteenth-century West European Jews sought emancipation from any physical or mental ghetto has within a hundred years destroyed Jewish uniformity.

Indeed, it has often seemed that the experience which provoked and intensified this debate will end by destroying at least the religious identity of Judaism. Particularly in the USA many Jews have thrown themselves with great effect into business or into the aesthetic or intellectual life of the age, often maintaining little or no observance of the religious traditions which were sacred to their forefathers. The modern world has been shaped by the influence of largely secularised Jews such as Marx, Freud and Einstein – just as it has been enriched artistically by Jewish musicians, painters and novelists and materially by Jewish scientists and captains of industry and commerce. Equally impressive, in its way, has been the energy with which Israeli Jews have done all the normal work of a modern state. They have shown courage both as farmers and as soldiers, contending against great odds. The revival of Hebrew as an efficient modern language, as suitable for technology as for poetry, is only one of their achievements. It is entirely understandable that both Israelis and their fellow Jews who subsidise them from the USA and elsewhere are inclined to think that this defiance of all enemies, using secular methods which the world recognises and admires, is the only answer to the tragedies of the age when the Jewish community was defined in terms of religion. Often at the end of a visit to the museum of the Holocaust in Jerusalem the visitor is reminded that then the Jews had no effective friends and no weapons of their own – but now Israel's army strikes fear into the hearts of its neighbours. The Star of David, worn as an armband on Nazi orders in order to attract the contempt of Europe, is now at the centre of the Israeli flag. It flies over the tanks in the desert and over the armed settlements near the Jordan.

Yet robust and aggressive secularity, relying in the last analysis on money and firepower, does not seem to be the final answer to the question of Jewish identity. For Jews cannot escape all connection with their religion. What binds the Jews of the USA together is support for Jewish charities including Israel – and what binds Israel together is an ideology with a religious element. Orthodox rabbis, salaried by the state, have been given a prominent position in the life of the nation (in family law, for example). Bible study as history is included in the state's school system, the main religious festivals are national holidays, the traditional dietary regulations are observed in hotels and restaurants, and about half the population, while relaxed about the detailed commandments in their own lives, goes to synagogue occasionally, perhaps once or twice a year. I recall an Israeli who said to me: 'I don't know whether God exists – but I know he gave us this country.' It was a touch of Israeli humour, no doubt, but serious politicians, whether or not they personally adhere to the religious traditions, can never forget that their very existence in the leadership of a sovereign state is justified most easily by the argument that here is the land promised of old and in perpetuity by God to Jews. The quiet which descends on the nation every *Shabbat*, with all public transport stopped, speaks eloquently of all this. And so does the mixture of protests passionately complaining that Israel has become a nation too like other nations.

Some of these protests insist that the state ought to be enforcing rigidly the teachings of the most conservative rabbis – and ought to expel, or firmly subjugate, all Muslims remaining in *Eretz Israel*. But other voices are raised to say that despite the spectacular victories of 1948, 1967 and 1973, Israel has lost its soul when it has ill-treated the Gentiles; that the 'racism' which is widely ascribed to Israel should be particularly abhorrent to Jews who have emerged from the Holocaust; that nationalism should not be the creed of this unique nation which after great suffering is meant to be 'a light to the nations' (Isaiah 49:6); that militarism cannot be a long-term security. Such voices are reminders of the high idealism to be found along with other elements in the Zionist movement which over half a century prepared for the establishment of the state of Israel in 1948. The founders of Zionism were sometimes secular and sometimes religious in their inspiration, and the division has continued among idealistic Israelis, for example in the communes or *kibbutzim*. Some seek a secular and democratic state, perhaps in a Middle Eastern federation, and particularly since the Arab birth rate is far higher than the Jewish that vision probably implies the reduction of Judaism to a minority creed. Others (Martin Buber was among them) seek a religious renewal within a Judaism which would remain the heart of Israel but which would be passionately concerned for God and man and for their love rather than for Israel and the survival of traditional Judaism. Either form of Israeli idealism, secular or religious, would retain a peaceful, cooperative and securely recognised state as, in the words of the Balfour Declaration of 1917, 'a national home for the Jewish people' without prejudice to the 'civil and religious rights' of non-Jews. To expect that is to expect a miracle. But it is already surprising that the state of Israel was born and has survived. It is the land of great miracles.

What would be the shape of the Jewish religion which might unite and purify Israel and the Diaspora? That is now a question to which no answer is obvious. No Sanhedrin exists as a religious focus for world Jewry, nor is one contemplated. Judaism has no common creed and Jews seem to have no intention of producing one. Of the thirteen essential 'principles' which the medieval Maimonides discerned in the Jewish faith, and which have never been rivalled in their authority, nine are shared by Christians and Muslims – the existence, unity, non-physicality and eternity of God, who alone is to be worshipped, who had spoken by the prophets, who knows and judges the deeds of men, and who will raise the dead to eternal life. The remaining four principles clearly need restating to accord with modern knowledge, practice or expectation – 'that Moses comprehended more of God than any man in the past or future ever comprehended or will comprehend and became included in the order of angels . . . and no defect whether great or small mingled itself with him'; 'that the whole of this Torah found in our hands this day is the Torah that was handed down by Moses and that it is all of divine origin'; 'that this law of Moses will not be abrogated . . . and that nothing will be added to it or taken away from it'; 'that we should not find the Messiah slow in coming . . . and that there will be no king of Israel but from David and the descendants of Solomon exclusively'.

In the USA, where rich universities, seminaries and foundations can act as patrons of rival movements within religious Judaism, at least four answers have been given very publicly. The Reconstructionists, whose first notable spokesman was Mordecai Kaplan, have sought to rebuild Judaism without most of its religious heritage and in particular without belief in a creator; and naturally they have been little organised. The Reform movement, originating in nineteenth-century Germany, has deliberately abandoned many Jewish customs in its 'temples' (how many has varied from place to place and from time to time) in order to emphasise the religion of the prophets of ancient Israel, a religion strongly monotheistic and ethical. The Conservatives have preached much the same religious message but have in general tried to maintain Jewish customs (with the strictness of 'observance' again varying, from synagogue to synagogue and from individual to individual). The Orthodox community has venerated the Talmud in its entirety and has also adhered to highly traditional doctrine – or at least the Orthodox rabbis have done so, with many Orthodox laymen being far from orthodox in practice. The Conservative compromise has had the widest appeal, but both the Reform and the Orthodox movements include some thirty per cent of organised American Jewry.

Elsewhere in the Jewish world Orthodoxy is far more powerful, and the chief division – with economic and linguistic roots – has been that between the Ashkenazim (originally from Germany, Poland, Russia and other areas of Eastern Europe), the Sephardim (originally from Spain and Portugal) and the Jews from Arab lands. In Britain, for example, 'Liberal' or 'Progressive' synagogues do exist and are served by distinguished rabbis, but Orthodoxy remains the main expression of the community, and the Chief Rabbi is the man in the public eye. In central Europe, where many Jews were more or less liberal in the 1930s, the remnants left after the Holocaust tend to be self-consciously Jewish and that most readily means Orthodox. In Israel few synagogues deviate from Orthodoxy. The early settlers tended to come from the ghettos of Russia and Poland, with an admixture of modernised and secularised pioneers from Germany. The *Aliyah* ('Return') after the Holocaust was in an atmosphere which made it natural for the new state to put considerable legal powers into the hands of the Orthodox rabbis. After independence the main influx was from traditionalist Jewish communities in the Arab lands – again beneath a largely secularised middle class of European origin. But there are signs that the strength of Orthodoxy may not last. Martin Buber, although internationally famous and influential as an exponent of the Bible and of Jewish mysticism, found in Israel no synagogue with which he could identify. Many young Israelis feel with him and vote with their feet against Orthodoxy. Another great Jewish scholar, Gershom Scholem, has said: 'If you ask me today whether – in the light of all that has happened in the last fifty years – I believe that the Jewish future lies in the traditional Orthodox framework, my answer is no . . . I think there will be a crisis of birth or a crisis of passage into oblivion; time will tell.'[12]

It seems probable that as the Holocaust recedes into history the very honourable argument that Jews must conserve all their ancient customs in order to keep faith with the martyrs will gradually lose much of its urgency. It also seems probable that if Israel is recognised by its Arab neighbours, grants the rights of Palestinians to its citizenship or to their own 'national homeland', and no longer has to bear its presently crippling burden of defence expenditure, prospering Israelis will acknowledge the rights, the feelings and the beliefs of the Arabs inside or outside their national frontiers. (Visitors who notice how alike Jews and Arabs often look sometimes think that one day the American pattern of mixed marriages may be reproduced.) To acknowledge the realities of the situation will be to admit that, just as Jews have been prevented by the enormous mass of cruelty which they have experienced from taking the moral claims of Christianity seriously, so it has been inevitable that Arabs whether Muslim or Christian should react with a bitter mockery to the noble sentiments of Jewish teachers about justice and compassion. The Palestinians, who had no share in the evil deeds of Europe, have been driven from their ancestral land. (Only six per cent of the land of British mandated Palestine had been purchased by the Jewish Agency by 1948.) In exile they, like the dispersed Jews, have been forced into an unnatural and miserable way of life, excreting bitterness. Jews – as many of them declare – will have to confess to, and atone for, their sins of arrogance and violence in relation to Arabs. It is no less necessary than the Christian penitence to which they are themselves so abundantly entitled. If Jews do not see this light, Israel will increasingly be treated by the world community as South Africa (Israel's ally) has been treated – and, whether or not Israel can survive in isolation, in the Jews' own hearts the last act of the tragedy of the Holocaust will be the triumph of the racism of Hitler. In the public arena of politics, the last act may be nuclear war.

Judaism is wider than the state of Israel and clearly the problem facing Jews who seek the renewal of their dispersed religion is similar to the spiritual problem of Islam in the modern age. A fabric of halacha and haggada, of law and interpretation, which has seemed seamless and more precious than any cloth of gold, clothing many generations including many martyrs, originating in the revelation of the eternal God, has had to be examined in order to see what is wearable by modern people. But Judaism already contains in its ranks many who are convinced that this examination, however painful to conservative instincts, has become both necessary and possible. Most Jewish scholars now accept the findings of international scholarship about the composition of the Bible and many openly draw the conclusion that Moses was not the author of all the legislation which bears his name. After that step it is not too difficult to say that neither was God the author of every detail. Almost all experts in the Jewish religious law accept that it has changed, even if only by 'interpretation'. Not only have the Reform, Conservative and

Liberal or Progressive movements adopted customs such as men and women sitting together in synagogue; not only are lambs no longer eaten at Passover; not only are milk and meat sometimes taken together; not only have other dietary regulations often been found not practical. In weightier matters where the teaching of the Hebrew scriptures is unambiguous, laws have been allowed to lapse by highly respected Orthodox rabbis. No proposal to restore the Jerusalem temple with its animal sacrifices has been taken seriously. Slavery and polygamy are no longer accepted. The death penalty is no longer enforced for the prescribed crimes (including the attitude of 'rebellion' in a son). Usury is no longer prohibited. Nor is the sale of land in Israel. If the liberalisation of Islam is now possible, the further modernisation of Judaism seems inevitable. It would be contrary to this religion's own tradition of change for its forms to remain either fanatically medieval or militantly nationalist in the twenty-first century.

As Judaism is rethought, the question about history's most famous Jew becomes inescapable.

Already in modern Israel, in the USA and some other countries some Jewish scholars have developed the insights of a few of their predecessors (such as Joseph Klausner or Claude Montefiore) who before the 1940s expressed a sympathetic admiration for Jesus as a Jewish rabbi. Klausner, for example, although he held that 'Judaism is a national life' and lamented that 'Jesus came and thrust aside all the requirements of the national life', paid a tribute to '*the* moralist for whom, in the religious life, morality counts as everything . . . In his ethical code there is a sublimity, distinctiveness and originality in form unparalleled in any other Hebrew ethical code; neither is there any parallel to the remarkable art of his parables.' As I have already noted, it has been fairly widely recognised that those passages in the gospels which attack 'the Pharisees' or 'the Jews' may be editorial additions made when the separation of Christianity and Judaism was causing most stress. Or they may be examples of the prophets' hatred of religious hypocrisy and corruption, Jewish targets being the only ones available to Jesus. There are many parallels within definitely Jewish literature. All this tendency can result in is a portrait of Jesus as a liberal Jewish rabbi somewhat like his contemporary, Hillel. Yet it has also been acknowledged, by Jews among others, that the letters of Paul, which readers happy with Judaism have always found disconcerting, reflect the most profoundly personal form of the Christian experience, for here is the life of the spirit 'in Christ' through a rebirth after a radical renunciation of all worldly supports and standards; so that even here is something which Jews can respect. It has been granted that the repeated Christian attempts to find predictions of the coming of Jesus in the Hebrew scriptures were more than a mere collection of ridiculously artificial interpretations of the texts. They were also attempts to locate him in his native soil, for the son of Mary was the child of the Hebrew world and the Jews' scriptures were his. And some interest has been taken in Christian theologians' attempts to restate trinitarianism so as to bring out the fundamental monotheism. In scholarly dialogues between Jews, Christians and Muslims it has been repeatedly and gladly affirmed that the basic intention of all three religions is to love the one God with all the heart, mind and soul. The era has ended when so profound a scholar, and so sensitive a soul, as Martin Buber could declare that Christianity and Judaism were essentially 'two types of faith' (as he did in his book of that title, translated into English in 1951) – the one being the cold acceptance of formulae, the other being warm fidelity to God.

Christians, too, have learnt to listen – and not only to the truth of their guilt in the appalling history of anti-Semitism. It was a symbolic act of great significance when in 1972 Pope Paul VI solemnly declared that the Jews were not guilty of the death of Jesus. Increasingly Christians have recognised that the sins of 'the Jews' denounced in the gospels are in reality sins which mark humanity, including Christian humanity. And increasingly it has been sensed that the survival of the Jews is a part of the purposes of God. The strongly Jewish elements in the origins of Christianity are now appreciated. So are the words which Paul wrote to Rome: 'they were made God's sons; theirs is the splendour of the divine presence, theirs the covenants, the law, the temple worship, and the promises . . . God has not rejected the people which he acknowledged of old as his own . . . For the gracious gifts of God and his calling are irrevocable' (Romans 9:4; 11:2,29). And it is appreciated that both the religious law on which orthodoxy insists and the existence of Israel to which nationalism is committed are parts of the precious Jewish instinct that obedience to God involves a society, not only an individual. No criticism of Jewish obstinacy is fair if it forgets this motivation. And if in our time Christians around the world are being more 'prophetic' about social injustice, the debt to the prophets and lawgivers of ancient Israel should never be forgotten.

If considerable numbers of Jews are ever to forgive and join the Christian church – at present a remote possibility – it seems probable that more congregations will be needed which keep alive the best of these Jewish traditions. The precedent of the Jerusalem church living traditionally around the family of Jesus in the first century of the 'common era' could be followed and the small-scale experiments now linked in the Hebrew Christian Alliance could be developed. But a change of attitude on the part of Christian and Jew alike is far more important and urgent than this possible revival of the distinctively Jewish element in the diversity within the Christian church. What is most needed is a shift of emphasis away from the survival or expansion of the church as it is, or the survival of the Jewish community as it is, to the question of the character of God and of his activity in the world. And it is when one considers how 'religion' in Israel, in the rest of the Middle East and in the rest of the world is customarily regarded as hereditary membership of a community – Rousseau called religion *une affair de géographie* – that one sees what a revolution it would be if this wider vision of God at work in the whole of humanity could be shared by multitudes.

The first eleven chapters of Genesis, before Abraham arrives on the scene, have always been available as a starting point for an attempt – Jewish, Christian or other – to understand the dialogue which the one real God conducts with humanity. The language of picture and drama puts before us the divine creation of a 'good' universe, that of a planet that is like a garden; the human choice of evil – the evil which 'masters' when brother kills brother, and which has overwhelmed the earth on which man's 'thoughts and inclinations were always evil'; and, despite all this, the love which God has for man, as unceasing as the seasons, 'for in the image of God has God made man'. Even before God makes a covenant with Noah and all his descendants (that is, with all humanity), we can read of the continuing diversity and conflict between the peoples, the 'babble' of languages which frustrates the hope of building a tower 'with its top in the heavens'. But the human babble did not deter God. He 'came down' to see the 'city and tower which mortal men had built' – and he pulled down the evil in it. The pride of man was confounded as the peoples were scattered into many languages which cannot understand each other (a perfect description of the communalism of the Middle East). But no great faith – certainly not Judaism – has thought this the end of the story of how God 'came down'.

Such an analysis of the human condition is both mythological in form and profoundly true, for it presents truths experienced generation after generation – and never with more pain or hope than in our time. Its vision is an ocean deeper and a world wider than the defence of the claims and regulations of a religious community – Jewish,

Christian, Muslim or other. It places the mass murder of the Jews in the Holocaust within the universal tragedy of man's inhumanity to man. But it also prepares for the Christian gospel that God (without compromising his holy unity) 'came down' into this tragedy in the life of a Jew who was crucified. To the Christian, the suffering of Jesus suggests that God has been present, to the end and beyond it, with and in the Jews who were persecuted by Christians, with and in the Jews consumed by the Holocaust, and with and in the exiled Palestinians.[13]

Christ and the religions

'From now on,' Professor Cantwell Smith has written, 'any serious intellectual statement of the Christian faith must include, if it is to serve its purpose among men, some sort of doctrine of other religions. We explain the fact that the Milky Way is there by the doctrine of creation, but how do we explain the fact that the Bhagavad Gita is there?'[14] And if these words are the fruit of the long experience and reflection of a Harvard professor in the USA, contributing to a debate which has been raging in Christian theological circles at least since Ernst Troeltsch raised the question in a forceful book in 1902, the question is absolutely inescapable for any thoughtful Christian living amid Asia's great faiths. Nothing can be more important for the future of Asia's churches than that the question should be answered.

In 1964 Pope Paul VI established the Vatican's Secretariat for Non-Christians on the basis that 'for those who love the truth, discussion is always possible'. Twenty-one years later a meeting of representatives of more than twenty international, interfaith organisations near Bath in England urged the establishment of a World Council of Faiths. It was suggested that it would be an appropriate way of celebrating the centenary of the first organised meeting of representatives of the world religions, the World Parliament of Religions in Chicago in 1893. Certainly there have been many encounters between thoughtful adherents of humanity's great faiths since that initiative was taken at the end of the nineteenth century. I have had the enriching experience of living and working in an area of England which is definitely multiracial, multicultural and multireligious and being a member (and the honorary secretary) of the London Society for the Study of Religion, an interfaith fellowship of scholars founded by Baron von Hügel in 1904. If the twenty-first century is to pursue the progress made in mutual understanding, this 'wider ecumenism' of interfaith dialogue will have to be developed systematically by a neutral organisation not entirely unlike the World Council of Churches. At present there are many problems in this field (including the prominence of the widely distrusted Unification Church, the 'Moonies') – but slow progress does seem to be possible.

What hopes would Christians bring to the work of a World Council of Faiths?

It has become clear that experience has falsified two theories which appealed to many Christian theologians in the years before these encounters of minds and hearts became common. One theory was that all non-Christian religions were from first to last evil – and were at their most dangerous in their highest aspirations to reach God without the benefit of God's revelation, salvation and grace. In the heroic mission which took Francis Xavier from India to Japan during ten years of the sixteenth century, the preaching always assumed that Asians worshipped devils. In the no less heroic theology with which Karl Barth rallied European Protestants against Nazism and the 'German Christianity' which supported the Nazis, the self-revelation of the true God was proclaimed as the 'abolition' of man-made 'religion' which was always essentially resistance to the revelation. But many Christians who have met other people's living faiths on Asian soil, like most scholars who have studied the scriptures of these faiths, have come to see that such sweeping condemnations of the religious beliefs of the majority of the human race resulted from ignorance if not from arrogance. The theory that apart from 'the one and only true religion' (so described by Karl Barth) human religion is always demonic or idolatrous cannot be sustained by Christians whose eyes and minds are open after experiencing the goodness and prayerfulness of non-Christians. It is better to say with the International Missionary Council at Jerusalem in 1928 that 'we welcome every noble quality in non-Christian persons or systems as further proof that the Father, who sent his Son into the world, has nowhere left himself without witness' – and with the Second Vatican Council (*Nostra Aetate*) almost forty years later that the church 'rejects nothing of what is holy and true in these religions. She has a high regard for the manner of life and conduct, the precepts and doctrines which, although differing in many ways from her own teaching, nevertheless often reflect a ray of that truth which enlightens all men.'

But experience also denies the theory that all religions are essentially the same and, being the same, are 'true' with minor variations due solely to social and cultural conditions. Even my brief study of some of the great religions of Asia has been enough to show that the faiths teach many different beliefs. To the Buddhist, liberation from further rebirths is infinitely more important than any question about the existence of gods. To the devout Muslim, Jew or Christian, on the other hand, nothing matters ultimately except surrender and obedience to God, who alone judges the one life between birth and death. To pretend that such religions 'teach the same thing' is to insult them profoundly by claiming that all that they really mean to teach is a view of life so vague that practically any interpretation of it by creed, code or cult is equally valid. To mix them together in what is virtually a new religion, and a very superficial one, is to fall into 'syncretism' which offends all who are aware of the depths of the different religious traditions. Even if the 'essence' of all religion is defined more precisely as 'mysticism', it is still insulting to the mystics not to notice the difference between those who adore the God who is greater than they (or the whole of the creation) can ever be and those who seek to realise the divinity already within them (and, many add, within the world around them). It can be expertly argued that there is not one mysticism; there are at least two, philosophically labelled 'theism' and 'monism'. Therefore in any encounter between religions it belongs to the dignity of the subjects being discussed, and to the dignity of the people discussing them, to acknowledge that questions of truth are at stake and that 'conversions' are possible as people brought up in one religious tradition think that more truth is to be found in another.

The existing unity of the religions is to be found in experiences, not in the interpretations of these experiences. Sympathetic studies and observations always find in all the religions 'peak experiences' in which people glimpse a glory which is more than the everyday. Here is Rudolf Otto's 'tremendous and fascinating mystery'. The historian Arnold Toynbee found everywhere in humanity's records evidence of an experience: the meaning of the world is not contained simply in itself or humanity, but lies mysteriously in the 'presence' of the 'Absolute Reality' in the world, so that good living requires any human being to be no longer self-centred but in harmony with what is felt of this 'presence'. The psychologist Carl Jung found everywhere in the world's religions the great 'archetypes': light conquering darkness, life coming out of death, salvation and wholeness coming out of consecration and sacrifice. And the Christian who is not ignorant or arrogant has to say that all this is experience of God, inspired by God as a response to the reality and activity of God. God is known everywhere. From one end of the earth to the other, from one end of history to the other, there is what Paul Tillich termed the 'general revelation' of God to humanity. This truth is contained in the Hebrew pictures of God's self-disclosures to Adam and to Noah, long before Abraham became the father of 'the faithful'. There are similar teachings in the Quran. The New Testament, although certainly concentrating on the urgency of personal faith in Christ and on the dreadful consequences which follow if Christ is deliberately rejected, teaches that the good God is revealed through nature and through human nature with its inbuilt sense of what is good. God gives 'all nations' clues to his own nature in the kindness he shows: 'he sends you rain from heaven and crops in their seasons, and gives you food and good cheer in plenty' (Acts 14:17). All the peoples can 'seek God, and, it might be, touch and find him; though indeed he is not far from each one of us, for in him we live and move, in him we exist' (Acts 17:27–28). In every nation any one 'who is godfearing and does what is right is acceptable to him' (Acts 10:35). 'All that may be known of God by men lies plain before their eyes; indeed God himself has disclosed it to them. His invisible attributes, that is to say his everlasting power and deity, have been visible, ever since the world began, to the eye of reason, in the things he has made' (Romans 1:20). 'Everyone who loves is a child of God and knows God' (1 John 4:8). Accordingly Christians are to fill their thoughts with 'all that is true, all that is noble, all that is just and pure, all that is lovable and gracious, whatever is excellent and admirable' (Philippians 4:8). Those who, prompted by their own consciences, give food to the hungry, drink to the thirsty, hospitality to strangers, clothes to the naked or kindness to the sick and prisoners, are everlastingly blessed (Matthew 25:31–40). When in the 1960s the Second Vatican Council gave thanks for much that was true and holy because of God in the great non-Christian religions, and when more radically scholars such as Professor John Hick declared that Christianity needed a 'Coperni-can revolution' in which all the religions would be seen in relation to God, like the planets circling the sun, they were echoing the central message of the New Testament, as also of the scriptures of Jews and Muslims. They were also echoing Jesus. 'Christ crucified' preached not himself but God the Father and himself as the Father's servant. When Paul, for whom 'to live is Christ', pictured the end of history it included the subordination of the Son to the Father in order that God may be everything to everyone (1 Corinthians 15:28).

Because there is this unity in the basic experience of all the religions – a unity which Christians interpret as the general experience of God, responding to his general revelation – it is natural that the adherents of a particular religion, which to them is a 'special revelation', should be glad to recognise what they believe in what others believe. Thus Hindus traditionally recognise the validity of other ways of prayer, involving other 'names and forms' of God, in their fellow Hindus – and such generosity of spirit can often be matched in religious traditions outside India. This generosity can leap across the barriers which exist between the religions. Many Hindus have been generous to the 'names and forms' used by non-Hindus. Many Buddhists have found elements of Buddhism present wherever there is truth or compassion. Many Muslims have gladly acknowledged that Allah has been worshipped and obeyed outside the Muslim world. Many Jews have been content to say that their religion is the obedience demanded by God from only a tiny minority of humanity. Many Christians, holding with the American theologian W. S. Coffin that 'to believe that God is best defined by Christ is not to believe that God is confined to Christ', have been glad to find traces of their own most loved doctrines and practices in the other great religions – and non-Christians have similarly greeted some aspects of Christianity. Christ can be regarded by Christians as the 'crown of Hinduism' or as the fulfilment of all that is best in Judaism (or in Buddhism or Islam), just as he can be interpreted by non-Christians as an incarnation of Vishnu, as a Buddha or as a great Jewish or Islamic prophet. Indeed, sometimes in recent dialogues between representatives of humanity's great faiths there has been something of a competition in showing which religion is the most broad-minded in paying tributes to others.

But it does not seem that the best way in which Christians can express this correct recognition of the sacredness of all human religion is to regard other religions as 'stammering' versions of Christianity and to view their adherents as 'anonymous' or 'potential' Christians. Such phrases have proliferated in Roman Catholic theology since the Second Vatican Council, most notably in the work of Karl Rahner. They have an ancient tradition behind them; in the second century Justin the martyr and Clement of Alexandria honoured good Greek pagans as 'Christians' in some sense. Even the far from liberal Tertullian wrote of the 'naturally Christian soul'. Even the anti-Protestant council of Trent spoke of pagans who could be baptised 'through desire'. Even the predominantly conservative Pope John Paul II teaches: 'Man – every man without any exception whatever – has been redeemed by Christ, and because with man – with each man without any exception whatever – Christ is in a way united, even when man is unaware of it, Christ, who died and was raised up for all, provides man – each man and every man – with the light and strength to measure up to his supreme calling' (*Redemptor Hominis*). Even

Karl Barth came to hold that the Christian gospel is addressed to every man as 'a creature ordained to know and realise his membership of the body of Christ'. Such teachings can be linked with the Bible, where God whose Wisdom or Word 'became flesh' also speaks that Wisdom or Word in the whole of creation. 'All that came to be was alive with his life, and that life was the light of men' (John 1:4).

But dangers arise when what unites all the religions is equated with a 'Christ' who now has no firm anchorage in the history of Jesus of Nazareth, as when we are informed by a distinguished Indian Christian, Raymond Panikkar, that Christ is 'a living symbol for the totality of reality: human, divine, cosmic'. So, he suggests, 'the name above all names – the Christ – can go by many historical names: Rama, Krishna, Ishvara, Purusha, Tathagata'.[15]

To people who are not Christians these claims, in intention generous, can sound like arrogant denials of their right to be themselves; thus Jews have never welcomed systematic attempts to demonstrate that they were being merely blind in failing to see the revelation of 'Christ' throughout the 'Old Testament'. To many Christians all this can sound like a heretical denial of the need to 'receive' the Word made flesh by yielding allegiance and becoming childlike if one is to be a Christian (John 1:12). Similar problems arise when some Buddhists speak of Buddha, or Muslims of Muhammad, in ways which have little or no obvious connection with the historical figure; or when they speak of 'Buddhahood' in every man or of 'Islam' in every prayer to God. They, too, offend both the adherents of other religions and most members of their own households of faith. It is surely more illuminating, as well as more courteous, when the adherents of different religions can agree that their founders offered different teachings – but that all are related to the one ultimate reality (called 'God' by English-speaking Christians). The paths up the mountain are different, although there is only one highest peak. The planets are different, although there is only one sun. In the second Christian century Irenaeus saw it clearly: 'There is but one and the same God who, from the beginning to the end and by various dispensations, comes to the rescue of mankind.'

It also seems dangerous to stretch the meaning of belonging to 'the church' so far that the whole of humanity is included provided only that people follow the light given by reason and conscience.

The sympathetic Christian will understand the motive behind such a theology, which during the 1960s became characteristic of Roman Catholic thinkers as well as of liberal Protestants. The motive is to say that God saves many or all of humanity – with or without baptism or the deliberate 'confession' of a correct Christian faith. In the 1440s the council of Florence decreed that 'those not living within the Catholic Church, not only pagans, but also Jews, heretics and schismatics, cannot participate in eternal life but will depart into the eternal fire prepared for the devil and his angels unless before death they have been added to the flock . . . No persons, whatever alms-giving they have practised, even if they have shed their blood for the name of Christ, can be saved, unless they have remained in the bosom and unity of the Catholic Church.' In contrast, the Second Vatican Council (in *Lumen Gentium*) could teach that 'those who through no fault of their own do not know the gospel of Christ or his Church, but who nevertheless seek God with a sincere heart, and, moved by grace, try in their actions to do his will as they know it through the dictates of their conscience – those too may achieve eternal salvation'. So in a tradition which had authoritatively declared that 'there is no salvation outside the church' the escape from past bigotry has been through an extension of the meaning of 'church' so that the conclusion may be 'no salvation outside Christ', Christ being understood as the Light shining in all the world. But the many ingenious ways of pursuing this charitable line of thought do not persuade non-Christians that they ought to be classified with the baptised. Although it can always be said that non-Christians do not truly 'know' Christ or his church, it has become a fact about the non-Christian world, including Asia, that the church is very widely visible, so that many hundreds of millions of thoughtful and moral non-Christians alive at any one moment have consciously decided *not* to be baptised or *not* to remain committed to the life of the church. They want their decisions to be taken seriously by Christians. And many Christians want to insist that the church is a community 'called out' (the Greek *ekklesia* means precisely this). To them, belonging to the church is a visible reality of daily life. And they find very great meaning and value in that reality.

It seems that the correct Christian way of recognising the relationship between God and the majority of humanity is to say that just as there is a general revelation, so there is a general salvation. With his sovereign freedom God graciously gives his help and his eternal welcome to all who sincerely seek him, including those who seek him by their loyal adherence to non-Christian religions. In that sense these religions are 'ways of salvation', although the phrase is much disliked by many Evangelical Christians as well as by many Catholics.

It has become clear that the whole Christian church has much to learn even about its own 'way of salvation' through the non-Christian religions of Asia. The Hindu can teach the Christian how the life of a nation which is poor in material terms can be rich in spirituality – and how the life of a soul can end in union with the Ultimate Reality. The Buddhist can teach the Christian how meditation can bring release from triviality, from the lusts of the flesh and the eye, and even from suffering. The Muslim can teach the Christian about the unity and majesty of God and about the brotherhood of believers. The Jew can teach the Christian about the faithful courage required of the people of God. And all can teach the Christian, disgraced by so much arrogance and by indifference to the suffering of Asia and in particular of the Jews, what it means to be forgiven because people 'do not know what they are doing'. The psalmist long ago complained: 'How could we sing the Lord's song in a foreign land?' (Psalm 137:4). But Asia is the Lord's land where Christians have for too long refused to listen, preoccupied as they have been with singing a foreign song. Today and in the future Christians must take off Western shoes in the presence of Asian spirituality.

What, then, is the uniqueness of Christ as Christ is known by that unique community, his church? As the encounter between the religions of the world, particularly in Asia, has grown in breadth and depth, there has been intense reflection and eloquent discussion. And there has been controversy. Often it has seemed that the unique Lordship of Jesus Christ is being denied by liberal Christians, Catholic or Protestant; that by this denial they are surrendering any claim to be Christians in the sense of the New Testament; and that therefore the cause of Christian evangelism must be entrusted exclusively to those who would deny that men such as Buddha or Muhammad have revealed anything of God or saved their fellow men from anything evil. But conclusions which would destroy the uniqueness of Christ and of the Christian church do not follow inevitably from the glad admission that God, the Father of all, has bestowed revelation and salvation upon his children who walk in the ways of non-Christian religions. It can still be said that Jesus Christ, the figure of history and of spiritual experience to whom the New Testament bears witness, is 'revealer' and 'saviour' in a way that is utterly unique. Salvation can be found elsewhere, for God is the merciful God of all – but no other saviour can be named in the same breath, for this one saviour's teaching, life, death and victory were the self-expression of the God who so saves because he so loves. No other teacher in the history of the world has claimed to reveal what he claimed to reveal, or to be the Father's agent in the sense that he claimed. And no other founder of a religion has had quite the same transforming impact long after his death, justifying his claims. It can and should be gladly acknowledged by Christians that the one God is like the sun around which all the world's religions, including Christianity, revolve like planets. But a special kind of life can be made possible by the sunshine on one of the planets.

The significance of Jesus Christ is not fully understood, particularly since Asian experience of him and Asian thinking about him cannot yet be said to be mature. But already it can be seen that the basic Christian experience is of being liberated by him from all that alienates the individual from God. The Christian who responds to Jesus as the embodiment of the peace and joy of God, as Brahman or Tao made flesh, feels to the full God's 'amazing grace'. And the response has its focus in the Christian's response – however expressed – to the crucifixion and resurrection of Jesus. That mystery is seen as the supreme manifestation of God's compassionate, patient, forgiving and triumphant love. Out of this response to the dying and rising Jesus arises a new vision of God (God is love), of what man is (man is meant to be Christlike) and of where history is going (history, despite its tragedies, is moving towards the kingdom of God, which is the kingdom of personal love and social justice because it is family life in obedience to the will of the heavenly Father). And that vision is clothed in all the poetry of the New Testament, which celebrates in this light God's purpose for humanity and the universe. The Christians who make this response and share this vision – whether they are few or many – are the 'little ones' of God, mysteriously used for his great purposes; the 'salt' and 'light' of the world despite their often gross imperfections. They know the saviour who is the Son of the Father – or, as Paul Tillich put it in less traditional language, they know 'the appearance and reception of Jesus of Nazareth as the Christ, a symbol which stands for the decisive self-manifestation in human history of the source and aim of all being'.[16] While conscious of the glories of the other religions born in Asia, they rightly say that no other name can be named which brings salvation *of this sort*; that no other way *to this end* is so true or so alive. Since the human condition is marked by 'ignorance' as the Hindus say, by 'suffering' as the Buddhists say, by 'idolatry' as the Muslims say, and by 'rebellion' as the Jews say, it is not easy to know that God is real and near, transcendentally holy but endlessly loving. No one comes to know God *as Father* with anything like the intimacy with which the historical Jesus knew him – no one, that is, except those who through the spiritual power of the living Jesus have been drawn to put their trust in him as saviour.[17]

6

IN SECULAR EUROPE

The secularisation of Christendom

It has often been predicted that Europe will become completely secular and that the rest of the world will end up like it. And Nietzsche, who in 1882 famously celebrated the 'death of God', was surely right to call it the most remarkable of all events or expected events. For secularisation on the European scale is without precedent or parallel. I have, I hope, shown in previous chapters that although religion is being challenged everywhere in the modern world, the phenomenon referred to by talk about the 'death of God' is still foreign to the main traditions of both the Americas, of Africa and of the Asian masses. There the continuity with the religious centuries is far more noticeable. Whatever worldliness or wickedness may mark the daily lives of people adhering nominally to the communal religion, whatever criticisms of that religion may be uttered or muttered by a sceptical minority, and whatever moral or other failures by the leaders of religion might justify those criticisms, in general religion has been honoured. God, gods, heaven or Nirvana can be said to be there, even if in the background; and individuals, tribes, peoples and civilisations have been inspired, sometimes dramatically. The reason why in so many languages there is no word exactly equivalent to the English 'religion' is not that religion has been unimportant. It is that religion has not been separate. The activities called 'religious' have been taken for granted as part of daily experience. Worship seems as natural as eating or sleeping. Indeed, the secularisation of modern Europe has been a startling contradiction of Europe's own traditions. Historic monuments, art galleries and libraries instruct Europeans endlessly that it was here that Christianity achieved its greatest triumphs in its first eighteen hundred years. Countless Europeans were 'Christians' at least in the sense of being horrified by the possibility of being called Jews, Muslims or infidels; and to this day many Europeans interpret 'not Christian' as meaning 'not moral'. Europe was Christendom.

The contrast is great with the present European reality. There are in Europe excluding the USSR almost four hundred million people who are in some sense Christian, and in the USSR almost eighty million. But the public philosophy of the Soviet Union and of Eastern Europe is atheistic and in Western Europe, although explicit and firm atheism is in a minority (according to a 1981 Gallup survey of nine nations, a minority of no more than five per cent), regular church-going is also in a small minority, scepticism is widespread and neither politics nor daily life is often profoundly influenced by the teaching of the churches. It is understandable that many observers are convinced, whether cheerfully or gloomily, that whether or not 'God is dead', the sickness of the European churches and their creeds is terminal. And it can also appear inevitable that the ice burying these churches will one day cover the other continents. Already the societies which are most like Western Europe – the USA and Canada, the middle classes in South America, Australia – include strongly secular elements (so that it may well seem artificial to make this chapter on Europe the place where I discuss secularisation). On a smaller scale almost all countries in the world include these sections in rebellion against the dominant religion and usually the most secular groups are the modernised groups closest to Europe (which is my reason for linking Europe with secularisation in this book). Religion is more likely to be openly and thoroughly rejected by intellectuals in contact with European science, philosophy and culture and by the Marxists who adhere to an ideology which still bears many marks of its European origins. The attitudes of such creative minorities may gradually become the general tone of their societies. If the God worshipped by Christians seems hateful or ridiculous, intelligence-insulting or oppression-symbolising, paternalist or boringly improb-able in Europe, the eventual eclipse, even the disappearance, of all religion in the world becomes a possibility however hard it may be to imagine either the time-scale or the consequences of such a trans-formation of humanity.

Meanwhile fewer intelligent European Christians have felt any obligation or right to become missionaries to other peoples. Such missionaries, preaching Christianity in 'heathen' but deeply religious lands, have often been told that they were running away from the greater challenge of their own continent's secularisation. It is certain-ly the case that Christian evangelism overseas has been handicapped by the awareness of the 'heathen' that the average European has lost any vivid sense of God and any religiously based sense of right and wrong. And it is clear that Christianity will not profit greatly if its boisterous growth in the Americas and Africa, and its arrival to settle in Asia, turn out to have been temporary phenomena, to be terminated by the impact of a secular Europe as a human body is killed by the spread of a malignant cancer.

Of course the intensity of secularisation varies from one section of European life to another. Religion can be popular when it can be used as the badge of a group which is fighting a materially stronger group. Whole peoples can think of themselves in religious images when they are struggling to retain their identity against great empires, as the Greeks did when surviving the embrace of the Turks and as the Romanians and Poles do in the days of Soviet imperialism. In the 1980s the Catholic church in West Germany (for example) is conservative for the most part, and rich, because it is seen as a bulwark against the communism which has overrun East Germany. In Ireland Catholicism has been the badge of hostility to English colonialism – and in the province of Ulster, Protestantism has been the badge of hostility to Ireland's Catholic majority. Welsh or Scottish nationalism, in cultural rebellion against London, can be expressed religiously. Belgians who insist on speaking Flemish (which is less smart) are more likely to be Catholics than the French-speakers, and Norwegians in the rural north are likely to be more devout than the citizens of Oslo. Defiant provincialism among Bretons, the Basques, the Bavarians, the Slovaks and the Croats can be attached to the churches of that province which keep alive the old traditions. Conversely, where a dissident group exists but no church is available to represent its interests, that group may become more secular than the group which dominates the society. In Spain and Portugal the south is less devout than the more developed north. This seems to be because this area was under Muslim control until the latter part of the fifteenth century and, when reconquered for Christianity, was divided into large states with a landless peasantry (like Latin America); but the Inquisition and other pressures enforced a rigid orthodoxy so that there was no possibility of a free church forming in the south and only recently have the Catholic bishops developed any sympathy with 'socialism'. In Czechoslovakia, the battle of the White Mountain in 1620 resulted in the imposition of Catholicism by the Habsburg dynasty on the provinces of Bohemia and Moravia, previously in the main Protestant; but this imposition was inevitably associated with Habsburg imperialism and no religious reply to it could be made easily within a patriotic framework, for the lingering Protestantism became heavily German. In contrast, Slovakia has remained comparatively religious. The most secular countries in the Balkans are Albania and Bulgaria. In neither was Christianity identified with nationalism. In the former the Orthodox church was heavily outnumbered by Islam. During the centuries when Bulgaria was under Turkish occupation the church was not fully a focus of national sentiment, because it was controlled by the almost equally hated Greeks. These are only a few of the historical factors to be remembered when assessing the geography of Europe's secularisation.

The position of religion in a generally secular Europe can also be affected by the question as to whether the prevailing religion used to be Protestant. In countries where the Catholic clergy wielded great power and enjoyed considerable wealth until recently, a more secular generation rebels by militant anticlericalism and atheism, but the part of the population that remains loyal to Catholicism tends to be regular in attendance at mass (at least once a month) and may be willing to support Catholic political parties, trade unions or leisure clubs. In a poll in France, for example, eighty-three per cent of adults declared themselves 'Catholics' in 1976 – but the history of anticlericalism has been strong and bitter. In Italy the proportion of 'Catholics' is even higher – and the communist vote has been the largest in Western Europe. In Spain a poll taken in 1986 suggested that almost half the population claimed to be practising Catholics – but hatred of the clergy was a big factor in the civil war of the 1930s and has not entirely disappeared. In traditionally Protestant countries, on the other hand, religious practice may be low, and ecclesiastical interference in secular activities may be resisted, but there is likely to be a wider acceptance of some rites of the church, some role for the clergy in society and some respect for Christian morals. In Britain it is usually reckoned that only between ten and fifteen per cent are 'regular' churchgoers and on an average Sunday church attendance is much less. About five per cent of the population adhere to religions other than Christianity. Yet the Churches of England and Scotland remain 'established' by the state and 'religion', mainly biblical, is taught in the state's schools. In Sweden only about three per cent of the population can be found in the National Church Sunday by Sunday. But 94.5 per cent are registered at birth (not necessarily baptised) as members of that church. Almost as large a number is confirmed in adolescence and throughout adulthood is willing to pay church taxes which support the clergy and church buildings. The educational standard of the clergy (who are employed by the state as registrars) remains high. When in 1979 the government proposed the separation of church and state, which it claimed would reflect the realities, the General Assembly of the church did not produce a majority in favour of the idea. There was no public outcry. The average Swede in the 1980s still seems to regard his or her membership of the Church of Sweden as an aspect of citizenship.

The concept of secularisation also needs to be nuanced in order to take account of differences of age, class, gender and environment. In Europe, as elsewhere, young people scoff at the consolations of religion more lightheartedly than people who are nearer death. Educated people are more explicitly and argumentatively antireligious (or religious) than manual workers. Men tend to be less devout, or at least to have less time for religious activities, than women. The level of urbanisation also seems influential. On the one hand, rural life untouched by urban sophistication can be pagan. People can live close to their animals emotionally as well as physically, and the religious element in their lives can be a mixture of superstition, magic and local pride (which may be expressed in enthusiasm for a local saint or a local Virgin), particularly where no village church is active as a centre of Christian life. On the other hand, urban life untouched by a village's sense of a rooted community can seem godless. Almost everything seen is man-made and a sense of awe before the mysteries of nature is confined to the occasional sunset. If workers have recently arrived in a city, or if their housing is in high-rise flats, or in some other situations, there can be little or no sense of community. City life can make the blackened, illmaintained, cold and empty church seem as remote as the farm that has been abandoned. The easiest ground for the church is soil which is affected neither by rural remoteness nor by urban rootlessness. In an affluent suburb or a small town a church may be valued as a place where people can make friends, secure good influences on their children, enjoy music, be public-spirited and receive encouragement when dejected. There are flourishing churches in Europe (as in the USA) which are social centres for good neighbours, but they are usually given their numerical success by favourable environments. A map of France can be drawn dividing the population into more or less equal halves. In one half more than forty-five per cent of the parish receives Easter Communion, and such parishes are mostly in three great clusters – in Brittany and the north-west, in Alsace, Lorraine and Franche-Comté, and in the centre. The parishes which are indifferent to their churches are mostly found in the heavily secularised capital, in a broad strip which runs through all of France from the north to the south-east, and in a bloc to the south of the Massif

Central. Faced with these facts, French sociologists have been industrious and somewhat successful in producing explanations based on the history and economy of the area.

Secularisation has not always kept up the same speed. For example, in Europe the process slackened in the thirty years after 1930 because the evil forces of Fascism and Nazism had become so obviously nightmarish that many Europeans turned back to the idea of a Christian civilisation as the inspiration of the resistance, of the war effort and of post-war reconstruction. In the late 1940s and the 1950s, over much of Europe, the churches were the institutions whose prestige had been least damaged. The power of evil had carved through the universities, for example, like butter. This was the heyday of 'Christian Democracy' in the politics of Western Europe. A new factor was that in Eastern Europe cardinals became, astonishingly, popular heroes, for they were the symbols of resistance to the imposition of the Stalinist brand of communism. A roughly similar, although so far smaller, return to religion began in the 1970s when the materialism associated with economic growth was checked by the quadrupling of oil prices, the subsequent inflation and the stricter monetary policies of alarmed governments. Considerable numbers, in Europe as elsewhere, lost faith in a secular Utopia. Some found faith in one or other of the religious traditions; of these, most looked in the Bible for the 'oil of gladness'. Others at least showed a new respect for religion.

So secularisation is not to be thought of as a spread of ice which cannot be resisted or slowed down. And even when the ice seems to be overwhelming the churches, it is found that human nature remains in some sense religious. I shall be discussing some of the alternatives to the churches as ways of expressing some of the religious instincts which continue to influence Europeans. Surveys show that Europeans turn to private prayer and even have mystical experiences in surprising numbers. They often seem to think that their own lives cannot be explained in terms that are purely scientific – that 'God' or 'fate' or 'luck' has a role. It may therefore be better to speak not of a complete secularisation, but, rather, of the religious sense in a new phase, when it escapes from definition and control by the churches. Sociologists have suggested the terms *'laissez faire* religion', 'privatised religion' and 'invisible religion'. Or the religiosity which cannot be eradicated from humanity may be harnessed in the service of a highly visible institution with a philosophy the very opposite of *laissez faire*. The Communist Party has been a kind of church with its own sacred scriptures, heresy hunts, saints, martyrs, hymns, palaces of culture and youth movements. It has even produced its own initiation, wedding and funeral ceremonies. Thus Holy Russia has been made to follow the Red Star and to worship in the Kremlin instead of Bethlehem, and the Communist Party guides the people's morals in a sternly puritanical style, crusading against vodka and against more Western influences which make for 'decadence'. In Hitler's Germany National Socialism fought communism by becoming another quasi-religious movement, demanding human sacrifice to its idols. In less demonic forms nationalism elsewhere has been happy to employ the emotions of religion. Many national anthems invoke or enlist God as a super-patriot.

Nevertheless there is an indisputable reality, and an inescapable challenge to all Christians, in European secularisation understood as a process by which explicit religion becomes private, problematic, marginal and, in the end, eccentric. The desire to use churches to fly the flags of nationalism or provincialism will decrease if the churches are empty. As religion is thought to be mere superstition, it ceases to be respectable to have children baptised or a marriage blessed in a church. Even secular funerals may become socially acceptable when religious faith is dead. The afterglow of churchgoing, in fond memories of hymns and so forth, will fade as nostalgia becomes oblivion. The religion of the churches, if not believed in, will not be available to serve as a rallying point against social evils or for the spiritual life. And once factors delaying secularisation are removed, the process may accelerate rapidly. It was ominous that once the post-war prestige of the European churches had been eroded in the mid-1960s, their statistics fell rapidly and did not stabilise (at a much lower level) for about ten years. Everywhere a decline was recorded in baptisms, confirmations, weddings, funerals and regular attendance by children and adults. (In France ordinations fell from 779 in 1948 to just under a hundred in 1977.) The process of secularisation should be explained in its many nuances, but it should never be explained away by attributing the decline of religion (or its persistence) entirely to factors less serious than those which are indicated by the phrase 'death of God'. For when taken to its conclusion secularisation is a process by which God, once taken for granted by a society as the greatest reality, comes to be seen by the majority as the greatest illusion.

The process has been so dangerous to European Christianity because the rejection of the Christians' God has had both intellectual and social aspects. Christianity, if it had not been so widely regarded as untrue, could have been accepted without too close an examination and used by many people seeking a radical change in society – as it has been in Latin America. If the churches had not become so widely unpopular, the intellectual criticism of their doctrines could have remained the interest of a fairly small number – as has been the situation in the USA. It has been the combination of intellectual rejection with unpopularity that has constituted the disease, often thought to be fatal, of Christianity in what used to be Christendom. And it is necessary to ask why secularisation combining these factors in a unique intensity has occurred in Europe of all the continents. In a society where religious myths have little or no connection with rationality, and where religious rituals are conducted by priests with little or no motive to prefer rationality to magic, modernisation which brings with it the rational investigation of nature and the rational discussion of problems by equals easily damages traditional religion – as can be observed all over twentieth-century Africa or Asia. But since Christianity as taught in Europe spoke about nature as God's creation and about human nature as being Godlike in its rationality, the rise of science and democracy might be expected to avoid any great conflict with the spokesmen of religion. Or at least science and democracy might have been welcomed by the churches sufficiently to secure for Christianity that degree of popularity which it has not lost in the Americas.

The paradox which requires explanation is that, of all the civilisations in history, the Christian civilisation of Europe was the one that gave birth to modern science and democracy – yet it turned its own children into murderous rebels. It is a paradox much discussed by those theologians who are interested in society and by those sociologists who are interested in religion. And a part of the explanation, as it has emerged out of many studies, is that European Christianity carried with it, in its heart (the gospel), some of the seeds of secularisation.

When it had been expounded afresh in terms of Greek philosophy, the churches' official doctrine became as rational as it was possible for a religion to be. Thus Thomas Aquinas could teach a system of interlocking arguments answering almost all the questions about heaven or earth that seemed significant in the Middle Ages. Europe's ancient universities were founded primarily in order to nourish theology of this sort – theology as the 'queen of sciences'. In the sixteenth century the Protestant theology of Calvin was a coldly logical scheme; in the seventeenth century the Lutheran brand of Protestantism, originally a volcanic explosion, cooled down into a reasoned orthodoxy; in the eighteenth century the Enlightenment spread a very cold light of 'reasonable' religion. This theological rationality prepared the way for the whole later development of European intellectual life, including the 'rationalism' which totally rejected Christianity. The natural and social sciences also developed out of the medical and legal studies which were encouraged in the universities of the Middle Ages. In the seventeenth century, when modern science first became a substantial movement, almost all the scientists announced that they were exploring the world through microscope or telescope in order to understand and glorify the 'Author of Nature'. Nature was to be studied alongside the Bible – and in its way, nature was as sacred as the Bible. It was God's creation, clearly reflecting God's own orderliness, beauty and infinite power and skill, although it was not itself divine and therefore could be examined without irreverence. This welcome to science by Christians may be held to have prepared the way for the total rejection of God by atheistic 'scientism'. Many of the pioneers of modern democracy appealed to the Christian idea of the basic equality of all humanity under the one heavenly Father. In their own far more democratic style they developed the emphasis present in the medieval church on the duty to consult within a community – including the 'parliament' (*parlement*, talking place) of representatives of landowners and urban businessmen. In the nineteenth and twentieth centuries the thorough acceptance of the principles of democracy has been advocated by many European Christians on Christian grounds; but here again, such benevolence did something to prepare the way for atheism – in this case, the atheism of communism.

Such a summary of European thought would be accepted in principle by most scholars although they would be entitled to complain about its brevity and crudity. The problem is how to interpret this history.

It can be argued that European Christianity, because it encouraged rationality, science and democracy, was ultimately self-destructive. On this analysis the Christian mythology was useful for some centuries while these eggs were being hatched but could be safely discarded once it was seen that rationality, science and democracy were fullfledged and perfectly able to flourish without any religious protection or patronage. That is, of course, the verdict reached by those secular humanists who take any sympathetic interest in the story of Europe's Christian heritage. And I have been particularly interested in a theological movement which has agreed with that non-Christian verdict to a considerable extent. In the 1940s a German theologian, Dietrich Bonhoeffer, became dissatisfied with attitudes characteristic of the 'Confessing Church' of which he was a leader – the fellowship which resisted Hitler and his ecclesiastical supporters. He came to think that there was too much concentration on the survival and integrity of the church as a religious organisation. His *Letters and Papers from Prison* (in English, 1953) sketched a vision of a world which would be 'religionless' after 'coming of age' and which would be able to understand only a 'secular' or 'worldly' presentation of the gospel. Bonhoeffer's tentative ideas were developed by a number of other Christians who greeted the secularisation of the post-war period as preferable to centuries of superstition and oppression. They were convinced that the beliefs and organisation of the church would have to be changed radically if Christianity was to survive. I was the publisher who in 1963 brought out *Honest to God* by John Robinson, the little book which more than any other got these ideas talked about in the English-speaking world. I edited *The Honest to God Debate*. One of my predecessors as editor of that publishing house (the SCM Press), Ronald Gregor Smith, wrote a number of books developing the argument with considerable subtlety. One was called *Secular Christianity* (1966). And I am still convinced that Europe's churches do need to change radically in response to justified criticism, as I hope to show. It seems sound to argue that if man is Godlike in his mental and spiritual powers, if the universe is God's good creation, and if all people are God's children, the encouragement of freedom ought to be given to rationality, science and democracy – and it seems to follow that the clergy, who are professionally inclined to be unreasonably dogmatic and narrowly moralistic, ought not to be allowed to control all intellectual and social activities. If what is meant by 'secular Christianity' is humble Christianity, I still welcome it. But I have reached the conclusion that Christianity cannot be regarded as uniquely favourable to 'secularisation' in any wider sense, for it always has been essentially a religion of humility under God. If it did hatch the eggs which developed into thoroughly secular rationality, science and democracy, it never intended to do so and the true parents of those eggs must be found elsewhere. I have also learnt fully that secularisation is not in practice always the triumph of truth and love hailed by enthusiasts including some theologians. Like every other human phenomenon it is ambiguous. It can be the defence of truth and love against the clergy. But it can also develop into a demonic evil by removing all the restraints which have been placed on human folly by belief in God. If 'God is dead', iniquity can be placed on the throne. The imprisoned Bonhoeffer, a deeply devout saint who was hanged by the Nazis in a year which saw millions of other deaths caused by their iniquity, thought that he could safely assume that the evil in some kinds of secularism was obvious. Instead of attempting to repeat what all his friends knew to be true, he struggled to express to them thoughts which were more surprising – and less likely to be censored.

A stress on the lay or worldly elements in the total life of a society – in a 'culture' – has by no means been unique to Christianity. Other religions have had their own reasons for acknowledging the 'profane' and its merits. The attempts of some anthropologists to suggest that primitive man is 'pre-logical' because entirely dominated by religion or magic have been discredited by closer study. Primitive man, if he is to survive primitive conditions, has to observe nature very keenly and to be shrewd and efficient in using nature's resources. A primitive society's customs can often be explained logically by reference to practical considerations. And a more advanced society apparently controlled by religion often makes sure that no religious expert is allowed to interfere with the layman's robust zests for survival, for profits and for the pleasures of the flesh. The histories of African tribal religion, Hinduism, Buddhism, Islam and Judaism could all be expounded as illustrating the power of secular values. It would not make sense to argue that European Christianity created an area uniquely favourable to secularisation because here the clergy had uniquely *little* power to control or to discourage the laity's interests.

On the contrary, the most important explanation of the secularisation of Europe seems to be that in this continent the clergy had a uniquely and excessively strong position – and abused it with arrogant folly. The history of Europe made it possible for a philosopher and historian such as Bertrand Russell to judge that 'the churches, everywhere, opposed for as long as they could practically every innovation that made for an increase of happiness and knowledge here on earth'.[1] He exaggerated. For eight years I was a canon of Westminster Abbey. My daily experience of that great national shrine showed me how a church can still do much to inspire and preserve many things that increase knowledge and happiness in the life of a nation. That record, now more than nine hundred years long, could be matched in many places in Europe. Later, when I was dean of Norwich, I knew well that an ancient and very beautiful cathedral can be the symbol of a prosperous and mainly rural community. But I also know from my experience that now the popularity of Westminster Abbey and Norwich Cathedral, and of similar churches throughout Europe, depends substantially on their attraction to tourists seeking contacts with history and permanence, rather than on their specifically religious role. Many Europeans seem to think that Christianity belongs to the past because the churches belonged to the opposition to progress, much as Bertrand Russell said.

When I was dean of King's College Chapel in Cambridge in the 1960s, I often reflected on the gap between most members of the college and that magnificent church, perhaps the most superb building in England, the unstinted offering of the glory to the God of Lancastrian and Tudor kings of England and of a superbly talented multitude of craftsmen in stone, painted glass and carved wood. As was to be expected of a community both youngish and intellectual in twentieth-century England, the college was for the most part absent from the worship still offered every day in the chapel, although the chapel choir was usually regarded as one of the best in the world. The chapel's construction had been started by King Henry VI in order to praise God – and in order to impress young men who might be tempted to heresy: they would be well advised to agree with the clergy officiating in such a building. But early in the twentieth century the college around this chapel became known for a humanism in which Christianity had little or no place, the most famous names in this connection being those of J. M. Keynes and E. M. Forster. In the 1960s the building spoke to most of the young people around me, and to most of their teachers, of an objectionable attempt to control their predecessors. The soaring majesty of King's College Chapel seemed to them impressive, no doubt, but as remote as the pyramids of the Pharaohs.

In the 1980s I have found myself in a very different society, working in a cathedral in an area of London which used to depend on docks and factories now closed. In the nineteenth century Southwark was a scene of poverty, disease and crime, to be glimpsed in the novels of Dickens. The area as I have known it is sustained by more activity by central and local government than the Victorians thought possible, but it knows the miseries of unemployment and hopelessness, with much loneliness, particularly among the pensioners in old age. There are many single parent families and there are racial tensions. The small groups of people who support the local churches, often with an impressive quality of life, are in principle anxious to do what they can to serve the neighbourhood. But the churches do not seem to belong to this working (or ex-working) class society.

Middle class Cambridge and working class Southwark are very different places. But what I have met in both is the secularisation of Europe. I have lived as a clergyman in a society to which the churches are alien and I have felt it.

The blunders of Europe's churches

As we trace the intellectual and social sources of the secularisation of Europe, we can see at point after point that the arrogant folly of the clergy was decisive. More than anything else it was to blame for the bitterness of Christianity's internal divisions, for this religion's strange identification with militant nationalism, for its equally strange identification with old science shown to be false, for the Roman Catholic Church's quarrel with modern democracy and for the alienation of all the churches from the new industrial proletariat.

Some of the best minds of Europe saw what would be lost if the religious tradition was to be utterly defeated. They pointed to ways in which Christianity could still be believed. In the eighteenth century, for example, Bishop Joseph Butler in his *Analogy of Religion* granted that although religion should be as rational and prudential as possible it must always depend on the basic decisions of faith. But he pointed out that this applied not only to a 'revealed' religion such as Christianity, but also to a 'natural' religion about a non-interfering Creator, which the deists of his day were seeking to promote as an alternative to the message of the churches. Indeed, all morality depended on beliefs which could not be proved true; 'probability is the guide of life'. The Edinburgh philosopher David Hume laughingly concluded that all the decisions of faith were so illogical that they were indeed 'miracles' – and that the decisions of morality similarly depended on 'passions'. But Immanuel Kant replied with a far more profound account of religion than Hume's. He summed up his life's work: 'I have found it necessary to deny knowledge in order to make room for faith.' He agreed that the existence, attributes and commands of God cannot be known by 'pure' reason and that the 'Absolute' is inconceivable by the mind of man. But he was equally emphatic that 'practical' reason commanded morality, understood by him as the duty to act in a way which could become universal. In practice this would mean the command of the New Testament to love one's neighbour as oneself and Kant disagreed with none of the usual Christian interpretations of that command. 'Practical' reason also required, in order to suggest morality, belief in the freedom of the will to achieve goodness, in immortality to reward goodness, and in God as the source of the human desire for goodness. The 'starry heavens above' still suggested the existence of the Creator – and for 'practical' reason, the 'moral law within' clinched the matter.

Among the German Protestant theologians who in the nineteenth century became the intellectual leaders of Christianity (although

their popular influence, even in the churches, was limited), Friedrich
Schleiermacher interpreted religion as a feeling – the feeling of
absolute dependence on God. 'Cultural despisers' ought to acknowledge that it arose everywhere in humanity. And Albrecht Ritschl
understood Christianity to be essentially 'the moral effects of
the life, passion, death and resurrection of Christ'. The emphasis
common to both these theologians was on religion as intuition – as an
act of the whole person, not as assent to clear Catholic or Protestant
dogmas, not even as the literal acceptance of the words of the Bible.
Similar passages can be quoted from the work of Catholic-minded
theologians (for example, Cardinal Newman), although there they
were mixed with very different, and more prominent, teachings about
the necessity of assent to dogmas.

Some Christians were eloquent in describing how religious 'dependence' was felt and what values were inspired by it. In England
S. T. Coleridge taught that faith was a way of life, a deeply personal
form of reason fed by the 'imagination' which unified experience
rather than by the 'understanding' which coldly dissected experience
for the sake of 'utility' – and his advice to any who hesitated about
Christianity was: 'try it'. A greater poet but lesser thinker, William
Wordsworth, did try it and came to rest in it, having drunk deep in the
religion of revolution and in the calmer religion of nature. For him,
only the God of Christianity could answer the questions posed by
tragedy and death, the 'sad music of humanity'. In Denmark Sören
Kierkegaard wrote about faith as the individual's 'leap' amid uncertainty, the leap which responded to the mystery of God. His Danish
contemporary Nikolai Grundtvig, a great educationist, defended the
decisions of many to believe more traditionally and to constitute a
national church, the centre of a whole 'folk'. In France other prophets
(Félicité Lamennais was among them) proclaimed that the cause of
the church was the cause of the people. Protestants and Catholics
alike could turn from their old quarrels in order to say that trust in
God, and so in life, was the faith which would inspire and energise a
modernising nation. In Russia Dostoevsky, who had been converted
to Christianity in prison, similarly saw faith in deeply personal but
also popular terms. Christians were those who, in response to Christ,
opened themselves to each other's freedom, guilt and suffering,
laying aside as insoluble many problems about the meaning of life as a
whole; and Christianity, so understood, was the soul of Russia.
Another Russian novelist of giant stature and tormented personality,
Tolstoy, pictured the wounded Prince Andrei looking at the sky from
the battlefield, wondering whether to pray. He made to himself and

to the mystery around him a statement which sums up this whole religious movement: 'Nothing is certain, except the nothingness of everything I can conceive, and the majesty of something I cannot understand.'

Such Christians had an effect on thoughtful people which is still strong towards the close of the twentieth century. Although many church leaders and theologians disapproved of them as men who were only half-Christian, at least they outlined the shape of a Christianity which could be understood within the society and culture of modern Europe. With all their limitations they were honest, they were profound and they thought that they were expounding the gospel of Christ. But more influential as a reaction against secularisation, over many years, was horror at the excesses of the French Revolution. Not for the first or last time, the most effective argument for basing morality on Christian faith was the behaviour of people who considered themselves to be entirely liberated from that faith.

At first the new worship of 'Reason and Liberty' in France seemed a blissful dawn to many eyes. But in the 1790s the revolution's cruel destructiveness discredited its replacement of Christianity, and its image was not restored when its official religion became the cult of the 'Supreme Being'. Within France about half the clergy remained anti-revolutionary, enjoying much support, and elsewhere all over Europe the governing and middle classes turned back to the churches in alarm. Thus Napoleon, who took France over from the revolutionaries, concluded a concordat (treaty) with the papacy; in England a sober Evangelical piety and morality became almost fashionable; and elsewhere in Europe Catholicism revived. In the spiritual life of the continent the predominant movement was now Romanticism, which encouraged escape from the artificial towns into nature, from superficial logic into the heart, and from a plainly reasonable form of religion into mystery and often (in practice) into nostalgia for the Middle Ages. The 'age of reason' had been turned into the 'age of feeling'. Thus inspired, the European churches displayed immense energy over much of the nineteenth century, as innumerable church buildings still testify.

Yet by the end of the century there were many signs that all the energy of this Christian rally was dying down without having accomplished the reversal of secularisation. In the next century, our own, the kind of religion that can be referred to by the names of the national monarchies – Napoleonic or Bourbon, Victorian or Habsburg – was to seem as remote as the Middle Ages.

One main reason for the defeat of European Christianity has been that its identification with nationalism has been too close. We have already observed that even towards the end of the twentieth century churches can be popular as the sanctuaries of nationalism. But on the whole the churches' subservience to nationalism has been both excessive and disastrous. It is no accident that so much of the church history of Europe can be divided into periods labelled by the names of kings and queens. During the sixteenth century Christendom was torn apart by the Protestant Reformation, a movement which was partly a religious renewal. In the Middle Ages the church had organised a piety which, while financially advantageous to the clergy, had left many of the laity feeling remote and even alienated from God. A vacuum existed which was filled religiously. But the Protestant Reformation was also a political protest. Luther's religious revolt was sponsored by some of the German princes because they resented the wealth of the clergy and in particular the financial greed of the papacy. The Tudors made England officially Protestant because Henry VIII and Elizabeth I asserted their authority against the power of the papacy and incidentally confiscated the large estates of the monks and the bishops. The city of Geneva fell under the religious and moral rule of Calvin because it preferred that regime to control by the local bishop. Even in countries where the Roman Catholic faith prevailed, the clergy were now ruled by the crown – as in the Spain of Philip II or in the France of the cardinals Richelieu and Mazarin who were the monarch's men. The massive humiliation of the clergy by the national monarch in reaction to their medieval arrogance was the central theme in the history of most Protestant and Catholic lands; and in the history of Russia Peter the Great placed the Orthodox church under his royal heel.

This nationalism was religiously intolerant because the monarch believed himself to be possessed of a God-given right to decide what his subjects were to believe (in the Latin, *cuius regio eius religio*). As Protestantism arose and as the Catholic Counter-Reformation gathered strength in reply, strenuous attempts were made both to establish religious uniformity within the nation and to impose the national creed on other nations. Thus the imposition of Catholicism on Bohemia – a process which had used violence since the burning of John Hus in 1415 – was matched to the north by the aggrandisement of Protestant Sweden, and the Thirty Years War between Catholic and Protestant (1618–48) ruined Germany. Civil wars between Catholics and Protestants devastated sixteenth-century France. The power of the Catholic monarchy over the whole nation was then re-established by ex-Protestant Henry IV, but the toleration of

Protestants was ended by Louis XIV. The 'revocation' of the edict of toleration in 1685 signalled the ruin or exile of the most economically valuable section of the French people, the Huguenots. In countries which became mainly Protestant, such as England, the strong arm of the state was used not only against 'papists' who might be traitors but also against Protestants whose beliefs differed from those favoured by the authorities – and great damage was suffered, for example in the English civil wars ending in 1660. It can be said in defence of all the intolerance that here was a tragic mixture of political and military energy with religious seriousness – but it is easy to understand why in the eighteenth century so many Europeans turned with relief to the enjoyment and improvement of this world, distrusting 'enthusiasm' or fanaticism, preferring a religion which derived a calm sense of security, of duty and of charity from the pure light of belief in an orderly and benevolent Creator who could be believed in reasonably. This was the religion of 'the Enlightenment'. Because it subjected the Bible itself, as well as all the churches, to the test of 'reasonableness' (as in the thought of John Locke in England or Christian Wolff in Germany), it often seemed too humanistic, not religious enough, in comparison with warmly emotional movements such as Methodism in England and pietism in Germany. It was often denounced by orthodox Christians, including prominent theologians in our own century (for example, Karl Barth). Certainly it was too unemotional to be in touch with the depths of Christian feeling and it could lead to the denial that God had acted in Christ (as in the deist and Unitarian movements, which were examples of the abandonment of essential Christianity in a European kind of syncretism). But it was better than the darkness of wars and persecutions; and usually it was intended as a version of Christianity, not as its contradiction. It was at its best in the architecture of Wren and the music of Mozart.

When a consecrated nationalism again brought ruin to Europe – in the war of 1914–18 – the simple religion and morality of the Enlightenment seemed impossible as an alternative. There were many reasons for this, of course. The creed of the Enlightenment seemed too intellectual to the age of feeling. But another reason was that it seemed too complacent to the 'age of science' which arose during the nineteenth century; for the new science was widely understood not as a revelation of the goodness of an orderly and benevolent Creator but as the disclosure of a harshly godless universe. The sciences of geology and astronomy showed that in the universe time was very much longer than simple Bible-believers had thought, and space very much vaster. Biology showed that man, dwarfed by these immensities, had evolved from other animals, and Darwin was not alone in asking whether the religious thoughts of such an animal could be trusted. The laws of nature seemed unbreakable: there could be no human progress except by discovering and keeping them. But in nature the supreme law seemed to be the survival of the fittest, which meant the survival of the most cunning and the most ruthless. The world-view which many educated Europeans formed as a result of nineteenth-century science seemed to leave no room for Christianity, not even for the religion of the Enlightenment. For a time it offered the prospect of unlimited progress through the extension and application of scientific knowledge. But for the most sensitive Europeans there was often at the heart of the new vision a despair about the absence of God and the feebleness of humanity; and in that way the age of science prepared for the 'age of anxiety' which was to come after the worst fears of the pessimists had come true in the great wars.

No doubt the new science would have been in tension with the old religion, whoever had been the spokesmen of the religion. But the bitterness of the conflict between European Christianity (as interpreted by many churchmen) and science does not seem to have been necessary. Its origins lay in the Renaissance of the fifteenth and sixteenth centuries, when the pope was usually so much involved in the culture of his time that he was best known as a patron of the arts and as an Italian politician engaged in wars between nations and city states. There was in principle no reason why a papacy whose style was so sophisticated should seek to defend the account of an earth-centred universe taught by Ptolemy, a scientist in Alexandria in the second century AD. Later, educated Europe did homage to a scientist who researched in Cambridge during the seventeenth century, Isaac Newton – and Newton was as interested in the Bible as he was in nature. There was in principle no reason why the Enlightenment which saw nature through Newton's eyes should be entirely blind to Christianity; and it was not. In the nineteenth century many of the great scientists were Christians, either in their early years only or throughout their lives. There was in principle no reason why the churches should not officially accept the new revelation of the Creator's work through evolution rather than through the instantaneous creation of different species. Darwin, although he found his own piety disappearing, was never willing to detach himself completely from Christianity. Both Newton and Darwin were buried in Westminster Abbey and the more perceptive of their Christian contemporaries welcomed their genius and their discoveries. Yet by the 1910s the folly of many of the clergy during the Renaissance, the

Enlightenment and the rise of science had made religion appear the enemy of realism, rationality and truth.

Europe's most prominent religious institution, the papacy, had inherited from the Middle Ages a legacy of the misuse of power. Medieval brutality had crushed the Albigensian or Catharist heresy (a revival of Gnosticism which seems to have attracted mainly because its preachers denounced the village priests and landlords). The Inquisition had been established to punish heresy by severe imprisonment, torture and 'surrender to the secular arm' – meaning death. It had been specially notorious in Spain, where many thousands of Christians who had not entirely renounced Jewish or Muslim ways were burnt. Now in further tragedies the Inquisition in Rome burnt the pioneer scientist, Giordano Bruno, in 1600, and in 1633 by the threat of torture forced Galileo to never again teach that 'the earth is not the centre of the universe, and moves'. In the eighteenth century the Roman Catholic Church seemed to *philosophes* such as Voltaire the enemy of thought – and it invited this description by many of its own pronouncements and practices. In the next century, when the fixity of the species in nature (on which Voltaire, for example, had insisted) was shown to be false, eminent clergy rushed into the scientific debate, pouring scorn on any idea that man might be 'descended from the apes', and many earnest Christians felt it necessary to claim that ancient Hebrew creation myths gave an accurate picture of the origins of this planet and its inhabitants. It now became possible to make the 'warfare of religion against science' the central theme in a history of European thought.

The nineteenth century, which might have been a time when religion and science could together inspire a spiritually and materially rich and stable civilisation, in fact witnessed a considerable backlash of organised religion against the advance of science. The Evangelical revivals in England and Scotland, strict Calvinism rebelling against the official Reformed Church in the Netherlands, and pietism among the Lutherans of Scandinavia and Germany were movements all to a greater or lesser extent tending towards a fundamentalism claiming that the Bible was totally infallible and that its miracle stories, in particular, were totally accurate. And in the same mood that inspired this Protestant rejection of science, a stand was taken by the leadership of the Roman Catholic Church against 'liberalism' or 'modernism'.

In 1864 Pope Pius IX issued a *Syllabus of Errors*. It attacked a number of current movements including socialism and societies to distribute Bibles, and at its climax denounced any suggestion that he (or any of his clergy) ought to reconcile himself 'with liberalism and with progress and with modern civilisation'. Six years later he and future popes were proclaimed by the First Vatican Council to be infallible when most solemnly deciding for the universal church a question of faith or morals. It has seldom been claimed that documents such as the Syllabus of Errors were infallible, but it was unfortunate that Pius IX's total rejection of the modern world showed the atmosphere in which the 1870 dogma of papal infallibility was proclaimed. It was an atmosphere in which piety could flourish, with an emphasis on purity amid worldly temptations and on submission amid suffering – the piety of the intensified cult of the Virgin Mary and the Sacred Heart of Jesus. But no answer generally thought convincing was offered to basic questions about the truth and relevance of Christianity in the new civilisation. Under the next pope, Leo XIII, a more constructive attitude was adopted. However, in 1879 this took the theological form of the total endorsement of the theology of Thomas Aquinas, who had died 605 years previously. The adoption of Thomism involved some patronage of scholarship and some encouragement of reasoning; and it allowed a certain scope both to 'natural' (for example, scientific) knowledge and to humanism. But it subordinated all these things to 'supernatural' knowledge. It glorified a 'revelation' which was understood as a series of intellectual propositions stated as dogmas in textbooks. Stirrings arose in the Catholic intellectual world which could not be contained within this framework – stirrings of interest in Protestant biblical studies, of emphasis on 'intuition' or 'action' rather than on intellectualism, and of reliance on historical 'development' (rather than on the claim that, for example, the mass and the papacy had been directly instituted by Jesus). But Pope Pius X, lumping all these various movements together, condemned 'modernism' in 1907. Any priests who would not take an oath against such opinions were prevented from teaching, and the leading 'modernist' clergy were excommunicated. Any hint of dissent from the papacy's definition of faith or morals therefore had to be highly discreet until the Second Vatican Council in the 1960s. The result was that Roman Catholic theology became a private world. Theologians had to submit their writings to censors who had a keen eye for deviations from orthodoxy. As late as 1948 the 'index' of books which the faithful were forbidden to read listed some four thousand titles or authors. As late as 1968 one of the most intelligent and scholarly of the modern popes, Paul VI, in his *Credo of the People of God* (issued without any formal consultation), seemed to brush aside scientific knowledge of the evolution of man. 'Our first parents', he taught, 'were constituted in believing and justice, and man had no experience of either evil or death.'

In Russia, the Balkans and Greece, where the National Church was Orthodox, the ecclesiastical hierarchy did not show even the Vatican's degree of interest in progress, liberalism and modern civilisation. The immense wealth of the Russian Orthodox Church in the nineteenth century has to be contrasted with the fact that the religious teachers of the literate were novelists and other lay writers. The spiritually minded peasants depended for their instruction on holy hermits, the *startsy*. The Russian Revolution of 1905, which secured the state's toleration of most (not all) Christians, compelled the bishops to notice the winds of change and a renaissance of religious thought began to be public, only to be aborted (or at least exiled) by another revolution twelve years later. But the Russian church had been completely subject to the tyranny of Tsars since the 1720s and had been willing to be used as the main symbol of the extension of Russian Tsarism – for example in the Ukraine, in processes which had included persecution. The church had also been terrified of any liturgical or doctrinal change which might provoke a conservative schism similar to that of the Old Believers in the 1660s. In general Eastern Orthodoxy exhibited nothing but ignorance or total hostility towards all the changes in Western Europe flowing from the Renaissance, the Enlightenment and the French Revolution. In reaction, the Russian intelligentsia was before 1905 predominantly atheistic.

All over Europe towards the end of the nineteenth century it could be seen that the educated were increasingly rejecting the restraints of the religion of the clergy. At the height of the respectability of the middle classes in Victorian England, in his essay *On Liberty* in 1859, J. S. Mill had voiced the new gospel: 'be yourself'. Now a new generation noticed that 'respectability' allowed the exploitation of millions of industrial workers – and of hundreds of thousands of women driven by poverty into prostitution. It questioned the subordination of wives and daughters and the pretence that sex was unimportant. It was repelled by the ugliness of an industrial society and by the conventionality of art. It turned instead to the gospel of the free intelligence, the sensual body and the intimate friendship – the gospel preached in English literature by the Bloomsbury set and, in a deliberately anti-intellectual rebellion, in the novels of D. H. Lawrence. Before 1914 educated Europe began a whole host of experiments in honesty.

But into this scene, where Christianity was challenged by science and by the wider mood of the new scepticism about all the dogmas and the conventions, there was suddenly intruded an event which no one had expected. It was an event created by the demonic power of nationalism, about which nineteenth-century liberals, enlightened and progressive, had been far too complacent. It was discovered that science had given lethal power to this demon. And after this, the dogmas and the conventions seemed to lie among the corpses.

The first world war was the great catastrophe. It did less physical damage than the second world war – but far more damage to Christianity. By 1939 Europe had become used to the thought that a great war might occur on this continent and all Christians in Europe argued, either immediately or in retrospect, that Nazism and Fascism were thoroughly evil and thoroughly deserved to be eliminated. Yet the churches had learnt by their experiences in 1914–18 not to attempt to enlist God totally in the war effort. Recognition was often given to pacifists; it was acknowledged that war was itself an evil bringing many tragedies; some criticism, or at least hesitation, about the conduct of war by the allied victors was allowed, as when some protests followed the obliteration of German and Japanese cities. Teaching about prayers for victory and safety was more sensitive. On the whole the European churches emerged from the second world war with enhanced prestige. But that could never be said about the earlier great war.

The disaster of 1914 struck Europe like lightning in a summer sky. Since the European nations involved had become heavily armed empires without losing the trappings of a 'throne-and-altar' Christian civilisation, it had seemed inconceivable that there would be a long-lasting and all-consuming war. Very little in the traditions of the European churches had equipped them for the spiritual crisis. They all hoped for a quick campaign led by gallant cavalry, only to find themselves torpedoed and adrift on a very cold sea. They all rallied to their flags patriotically, only to find that the flag of a simple patriotism was shot through by the prolonged savagery of a new kind of war. They all encouraged their members to pray for victory and safety, only to find that a cloud of poison gas obscured all the doctrines which had seemed bright in days of peace. Like a bayonet in the body of a soldier, the war thrust home the question of whether Christianity was more than the clothing on the flesh of national arrogance. The image of God as the super-emperor, omnipotently taking care of the people and causes for which churchgoers prayed, was left like a corpse stinking in the mud of the trenches. Of course not all the Christians in Europe had all these feelings at the same time. During the war many turned to genuine prayer in their distress and in the 1920s the churches' statistics often maintained the pre-war levels. But it was a war that did great damage to the old style of the churches' teaching that God was in control like the clergyman in his parish. In many parts of Europe it strengthened the existing tendency of the educated to be cynical about religious belief and confirmed the feeling of the workers that they were being used by bosses who, like the generals and their staffs behind the front lines, did not actually get killed. Europe's religious history now had a new symbol: after the bombardments, all that was left in a French or Flemish church might be a crucifix.

If Christianity had retained its hold on Europe, there might have been a widespread return to those elements in the religion which the crucifix symbolised. The message of Jesus was about peace and love rather than imperialism and the God who allowed him to die was not a God who was 'in control' in any simple sense. Post-1914 Christians have surely been right to attempt to work out an understanding of God that includes some kind of suffering and some kind of powerlessness; that sees him on the side of the conscript, not the emperor. That kind of Christianity had been glimpsed by Coleridge, Wordsworth, Kierkegaard, Lamennais, Dostoevsky and Tolstoy – all men of sorrow, acquainted with grief. Christianity might have attracted more attention than it did after 1914 had the crucified God been allowed to speak. As it was, most of the educated preferred to say that no God existed; that Europe's only hope lay in the science which, however, needed to be rescued – no one quite knew how – from the misuse made of it on the battlefields. It seemed that in the life of the emotions the only honest course was to despair and prepare for death unless one could conquer anxiety either in the pursuit of fleeting moments of pleasure or, among the more serious-minded, in a personal decision to be hopeful despite the evidence – the decision which was the essence of the new philosophy, or rhetoric, of 'existentialism'.

So far I have summed up the story of European secularisation in a way which says something (however little) about the changing feelings of sensitive people, particularly in the middle classes. But even that story, complex as it is, is not the whole story. I must also say something about the alienation of the churches from the 'common' people. Here the wars were not the only disasters.

The Roman Catholic Church was not as heavily involved as the Protestants or Orthodox in the follies and tragedies of nationalism. But it distanced itself from the good as well as the evil in the modern European nation – for through a series of blunders by its leadership, this church failed to throw its influence behind those who within the nations of Europe were trying to build up a just and humane society.

It treated democracy as well as science as an enemy; and it lost that war.

For example, in Spain the church became so identified with land-owners and capitalists that the Republican opposition to Franco's version of 'Christian civilisation' was militantly anticlerical, disgracing itself by many atrocities against priests and nuns during the very bloody civil war of 1936–39. Almost throughout his forty years of Fascist power the authorities of the church supported Franco, although towards the time of his death in 1975 there were movements indicating some detachment. But during the next decade even the memory of Franco seemed to be buried in the Valley of the Fallen near Madrid. The new democracy reversed Franco's prohibitions of political parties, of trade unions, of a free press, of contraception, of divorce and of every other sign of 'liberalism'. The modern history of Portugal is similar. The republic of 1910–26 was decidedly anti-clerical and the Catholic state that followed was decidedly Fascist. Only in the 1970s was the church identified with democracy.

In Italy the papacy resisted the formation of a state which would incorporate the large territories which had been under papal mal-administration. The belief that the pope could function without being also an earthly monarch was one of those modern errors condemned by Pius IX in 1864. The 'error' finally prevailed six years later when the French emperor withdrew his troops from Rome, but Catholics were not allowed to take part in Italian politics until 1919. Even then their Centre Party was not allowed to form a coalition with the socialists. When Mussolini gained power through the division in the anti-Fascist forces, the Vatican concluded a prestige-giving concor-dat with him (in 1929) – and was silent when he invaded Ethiopia. After the second world war the church's political influence was thrown behind the Christian Democrats, but its battles against mod-ernisation (for example, the legalisation of divorce) continued and continued to be resented. The new concordat of 1984 virtually ended the status of Roman Catholicism as Italy's official religion.

In Germany as in Italy, the Vatican did not really back a movement making for a modern democracy until the late 1940s. In the 1870s Bismarck, a moderniser although no democrat, gained much support for his brief *Kulturkampf* ('war in defence of civilisation') against the church. Although after 1918 the Centre Party was vitally important in the Weimar Republic, it was betrayed and abandoned when the Vatican concluded a concordat with the Nazis in 1933. It was only in 1937 that Pius XI denounced Hitler's 'war of annihilation against the Catholic faith' and it was only when his words were too late to make any practical difference that Pius XII publicly condemned Hitler's extermination of the Jews.

In France the Roman Catholic Church allowed itself to be largely identified with the reactionary monarchies of the Bourbons and of Napoleon III – and then with nostalgia for these 'legitimate' regimes. Despite some priests who endorsed Christian Socialism, on the whole the French church became the church of the well-to-do, of the old and of the devout who liked an emotional and authoritarian religion. So 'clericalism' seemed to be the enemy of the Republic. In 1905 the state, which had already forbidden all religious instruction in its schools, severed its connections with the church in an atmosphere of great bitterness. In a series of anticlerical signals to the people, state salaries for the clergy ceased, church buildings were taken over (although their use for worship was allowed), bequests to religious institutions were declared illegal, the clergy were made liable for conscription into the army, and religious orders were forced out of the country. By 1915 most marriages in France were being conducted by officers of the now secular Republic. By 1930 out of some thirty-five thousand parishes staffed in 1880, about ten thousand no longer had a resident priest. The first world war brought the two sides together to some extent, but it was not until its condemnation of the *Action Française* movement in 1926 that the papacy finally made it clear that it accepted the Republic. Meanwhile, to a large extent church and state had become two Frances, to match the two Spains and the two Italys.[2]

While the Roman Catholic Church was thus distancing itself from the most creative political forces in Western Europe, the churches of Eastern Europe remained full. But a 'criticism of religion' worked out in Germany proved to be a time bomb which would be exploded there and elsewhere by twentieth-century Marxists.

Marxism began in academic circles. There German Protestant scholars applied the new methods of historical investigation to the Bible. *The Life of Jesus Critically Examined* by David Strauss (1835, translated into English by George Eliot in 1846) was a dramatic start to the process of exposing the editorial touches in the gospels and eliminating the miracle stories; and later scholars such as Julius Wellhausen uncovered the origins of the Hebrew scriptures. Criticising much more than the literature of religion, *The Essence of Christianity* by Ludwig Feuerbach (1841) was translated into English, also by George Eliot, in 1854 – a recognition of its importance for Europe. It claimed that God was no more than a projection of a human fantasy into a universe which was in fact coldly indifferent to man's own best qualities – his rationality and love. Later Feuerbach dealt with the doctrines of non-Christian religions in a similar style, but in common with almost all Europeans of that age he regarded the Christian account of God as the summit of all religion, so that its conquest made all the other tasks of secularism relatively easy. Karl Marx was by no means the only European to think that with Feuerbach's work the 'criticism of religion' was 'complete', but more than any other it was Marx who popularised a theoretical and practical atheism.

Marx was so important because he was the great interpreter of the formation of the urban proletariat which began in Britain about 1760. People were both enabled to survive and condemned to live miserably by the new industries. It was a population explosion comparable with the twentieth-century growth in Latin America, Africa and Asia; in the period 1800–1910, the population of Britain quadrupled. Here was another disaster inflicted on Christianity by the arrogantly foolish clergy. They were very slow to take action when workers poured into the new factories from a countryside which was now overpopulated and 'enclosed' (without common lands). Even in the villages the churches were less secure than appeared on the surface. Much rural religion was older than Christianity, being the magical incantation of the powers making for fertility in the fields and in women's bodies or being a whole mass of superstitions. Much of the churchgoing was enforced by landlords and other employers and was tolerated partly because there was little else to do, but even so the recoverable statistics disprove the idea that everyone went to church. It was fortunate for the rural clergy that they depended so little on the free-will offerings of the people. From this reservoir of labour the factories and the urban trades recruited the 'hands' which they needed. The trades were usually very poorly paid and wages were also low in the factories since there was so much competition for jobs. During many years women and children competed with the advantage of having cheaper 'hands'. Saving was impossible. The new machines were owned by capitalists, small or great, who were all anxious for a quick profit in order to invest in more machines. Around the factories, the swollen towns were for long without adequate housing, sanitation, police, education or recreation and their huddled inhabitants did not have the right to vote for their rulers. The expectation of life was short but no alternative appeared apart from emigration to the Americas (to which some forty million Europeans crossed in the years 1850–1914).

Although many Christians thought the industrial towns satanic, the churches were slow to attempt any large-scale mission to this new world. Most of the clergy were locked in the rural churches and parsonages. Their minds seemed to be locked in the fear of 'the mob' and in the faith that the 'iron laws' of economics would eventually work for the good of all (or of most) only if there was no interference. It was believed that higher wages would make the new industries unprofitable. And their moral judgements seemed to be locked in middle class habits of thought. Thus they condemned drunkenness, gambling, pilfering, the lack of unity and discipline in a family, dirtiness of talk and body, the casualness of sex for money or for a moment of pleasure – but they did not condemn the social conditions which made such behaviour inevitable. They condemned Sunday amusements – but not the brutality of life on the other six days of the week. Or these were, with some reason, believed to be their attitudes. During the crucial years when the new proletariat was forming its view of an ugly world, church buildings were far from prominent and those that existed were not well attended; in 1851 a religious census of England showed that only thirty-six per cent of the population was in church on a typical Sunday.

By the end of the century the mission by the alarmed churches to the proletariat in Britain and the rest of Europe was substantial. The workers did not, on the whole, object, although there were some riots which wrecked churches (as in Paris in 1871 and Barcelona in 1909). There remained a vague belief in God – a belief active after a death when a religious funeral was thought fitting, or at other turning points such as New Year's Eve, or on such other occasions as the half-remembered culture of Christendom suggested. There was, too, a reluctance to see God or Christ mocked; thus in England the small atheist movement addressing the proletariat called itself by a new word, 'secularist' (while the middle class equivalent, less organised, was a term coined in 1874, 'agnostic'). But seldom did the workers find a church homely. When they did, it was usually because a Catholic church was a place where their old national identity could be affirmed amid a hostile environment. This attracted the Irish in England, the Flemish in France, Belgium and the Netherlands, the Poles and others in the German mines and factories of the Ruhr, and the Basques in Spain. Or a Protestant congregation could be a fellowship of workers led by a preacher who was able to inspire self-discipline and self-help. This accounted for much of the appeal of nonconformity in South Wales, of the Primitive Methodists in England and of various small 'free' churches in the rest of Europe. Normally the churches were seen as fortresses out of which the clergy and other middle class Christians emerged to 'do good'. The poor were invited to visit them in order to show gratitude or to solicit further favours. The priest could seem a cassocked policeman (it was Marx's phrase) and the slightly more favourable image of the church was the image of the patronising Lady Bountiful.

How could the alienation of the proletariat from all that made human life glorious be ended? To most of the workers this was a more important matter than the question of how its alienation from organised religion could be ended. And to many it seemed that the most convincing answer came not from the vague exhortations of preachers but from the socialists who insisted that the means of production must be placed under the workers' control. Many politicians recognised that the state must do more for the workers; conservatives such as Bismarck in Germany and Disraeli in Britain did. It was even acknowledged that working men, and perhaps women, must be given the vote. But only the socialists seemed willing to transfer economic power to the workers whose labour had, in the last analysis, created the wealth. Before 1914 it appeared probable that the leadership of the socialist cause would remain in the hands of men who, being pragmatists, were willing to welcome any changes and any allies likely to improve the lot of the workers. In 1875 the Social Democratic Party in Germany adopted a Gotha Programme which soothingly assured Christian supporters that 'a man's religion is his private concern'. In France Jean Jauvres was the spokesman of a tradition which thought liberty as important as equality or fraternity, and which believed in enlightened reasoning; so that here, too, socialism could attract progressive Christians. But the war of 1914 set the socialists of Germany and France at enmity with each other, and the internationalist and libertarian ideals of the Second International never recovered from the blow. That great war put the Marxists at the head of socialism, for it brought them to power over an area which in the end included the whole of Eastern Europe apart from Greece and Turkey. Christendom was going to be subjected systematically to a systematic form of atheism.

Communist pressures

Marx's background was the educated Germany that had produced Strauss and Feuerbach. He soon became certain that the claims of the New Testament, and of religion in general, had been exposed as false and it was not long before he became too bored even to discuss the subject. But his father, a Jew, had conformed to the wishes of the

Prussian state and for this reason the young Karl Marx had been baptised. There had even been a brief, boyish, acceptance of Christianity. That experience had been enough to give him some insight into the comforts of religion. In 1843 he wrote: 'Man makes religion, religion does not make man. In other words, religion is the self-consciousness and self-feeling of man who has either not yet found himself or has already lost himself again. But man is not abstract being squatting outside the world. Man is the world of man, the state, the society. This state, this society, produced religion . . . Religious distress is at the same time the expression of real distress and the protest against real distress. Religion is the sigh of the oppressed creature, the heart of a heartless world, just as it is the soul of soulless conditions. It is the opium of the people. The abolition of religion as the illusory happiness of the people is required for their real happiness. The demand to give up illusions about the people's condition is the demand to give up a condition which needs illusions.'

This splendid rhetoric has become holy scripture to Marxists, but it was inaccurate. In 1843 Marx had little first-hand knowledge either of the industrial proletariat or of the clergy. He knew enough to know that the workers were often miserable and the clergy often indifferent to their sufferings, but he went beyond his knowledge both when he predicted that the workers would soon develop both the power and the will to overturn the whole existing order of society and when he suggested that meanwhile the clergy were effective in keeping the workers quiet. In fact, in Marx's day the proletariat was a minority and not a very powerful one. And since the workers made little use of a religion which on the whole kept its distance from them, the clergy had little influence on them. Marx's famous exaggeration of their influence resulted from his general theory of religion. It was an illusion, as had been demonstrated by atheists such as Feuerbach – or so he believed. But it was very important – or so he thought at that early stage in his life. Its importance did not lie in arousing a determination to change social conditions – that he could not conceive. In the early 1840s religion seemed important to Marx because it gave a false answer to the real, and interesting, spiritual needs of an 'alienated' humanity. He recorded his musings in *Economic and Philosophical Manuscripts* not published until 1932 (and then obscurely).

The young Marx was a member of an intellectual group, the young Hegelians. They responded in various ways to the mastery of the Berlin philosopher, Hegel, who had worked out a vast system of thought. This was not based on Christianity; it concerned the 'realisation' of the 'Absolute' or of 'Spirit'. But many, including Hegel himself, thought it compatible with Christianity. Indeed, it became the officially favoured philosophy in the Prussian state which also supported Lutheran orthodoxy and morality. The young Hegelians, including Feuerbach and Marx, were intoxicated by the daring of this interpretation of the whole of history as a single process, but they rejected the conclusion that church and state were twin realisations of the Absolute. Unlike Feuerbach, Marx also rejected the concentration on what people thought about Spirit. He wrote: 'Life is not determined by consciousness but consciousness by life.' And again: 'For Hegel the process of thinking . . . is the creator of the real world, and the real world is only the external appearance of the idea. With me the reverse is true: the ideal is nothing but the material world reflected in the mind of man, and translated into forms of thought.' Accordingly it was vital that the ownership of the means of production should be put into the hands of the workers – and that a brief period of 'socialism' controlled by the state after the workers' revolution should prepare for the 'communism' which was the goal. But an element of Utopianism remained within Marx's materialism. The communist society would inscribe on its banner: 'from each according to his abilities, to each according to his needs'. In such a paradise there would be no shortages; no need to have specific jobs; no alienation of a man from his work, neighbours and circumstances. A man, he predicted in his *German Ideology*, could 'hunt in the morning, fish in the afternoon, rear cattle in the evening, criticise after dinner, just as I have a mind'.

In his later years Marx, now a settled atheist, showed no great interest in religious questions. But when Marxism secured power (in countries to which Marx had paid little attention), its governments often interpreted the right of a citizen to be religious privately to mean that any public expression of religious belief must be persecuted. This was because of one of the oddest facts about Marxism. Marx made the bitter joke that he was not a Marxist. He was a pioneering thinker with very high intellectual gifts, courageously outspoken and, although seldom charitable in his opinions of rivals, in his own way highly moral. His compassion for people condemned to live in a place such as the Manchester described by his collaborator Engels in the 1840s was genuine. Since his experience of political organisation was confined to his role in the agitations of the First International, he was not exposed to the corruptions of power. But his name and elements of his thought have been associated with the enforcement by very powerful and entirely ruthless governments of a communism which, still claiming that it was dragging the comrades along the road to an earthly paradise, displayed in practice more dogmatism and intolerance than any religion. These governments were to be deaf to the sighs of the oppressed under their cruelly iron rule.

Marxism secured absolute power, and was absolutely corrupted by it, through the small Bolshevik Party amid the chaos of 1917–21 in Russia. Lenin and other leaders of that group had in exile strengthened their belief that any cruelty was justified as the price of a new society. The collapse of the Tsarist regime after defeats in the great war gave them their opportunity to establish socialism through the 'dictatorship of the proletariat' – or, to be more precise, of themselves. In the vast territory now under their control the Orthodox church had been identified with the old regime and had great wealth and privileges, specially in education. It was inevitable that the Bolsheviks should move against it. Such a church was in some ways a model which they were glad to copy: it had accepted state control and sacralised it, it had taught an intense patriotism, it had encouraged Russians to think that they had a messianic purity and mission in relation to other people, and it had discouraged questions. But the Bolsheviks intended to secure a monopoly of influence over the people. Later the Communist Party would make sure of a monopoly of privilege. In their eyes there was no room for the church.

It was also inevitable that the leadership of the Orthodox church should be bewildered when freedom from Tsarist control was given so suddenly and as suddenly accompanied by orders to cease teaching the subordination to princes and landowners which had been the church's social message ever since the baptism of Vladimir, king of Kiev, about 988, had been followed by the voluntary or compulsory baptisms of large numbers of his subjects. Many obstinate bishops and priests were now shot and the minority willing to collaborate with the Bolsheviks was rewarded. The leadership of the church eventually saw that it, too, had to come to terms with the new government (in 1923) – but that did not exempt the church from persecution as soon as the government had sufficient strength. The victory of Stalin meant a policy of 'socialism in one country' through the forced collectivisation of the peasants, the rapid construction of heavy industry and the ruthless establishment of a tyranny. Trotsky's advocacy of concentration on international revolution, which might have led to collaboration with Christians for practical purposes, was brushed aside. The teaching of atheism in the schools and elsewhere was stepped up after the formation of the League of Militant Godless in 1925. The intimidation of clergy and congregations, who had to be 'registered' to be permitted, was increased after Stalin's Law on Religious Associations in 1929. Hundreds of thousands of Christians were killed. Every form of religious education, public or private, was banned.

This ruthless persecution was intensified when Stalin tightened his grip with the purges of his fellow communists; then relaxed when he needed the church's loyalty after the German invasion (for the Nazis cynically encouraged a religious revival in the area under their occupation); and resumed in 1959 by Khruschev, who was alarmed by the church's revival. Of almost twenty thousand churches still open, two thirds were now closed. Since Khruschev's fall in 1964 there has been little or no slackening in the pressure to stop any religious activity which could be called 'anti-Soviet'. 'Religious associations' have often been limited compulsorily to the membership of twenty, made the legal minimum in 1929 – and have often been penetrated by KGB agents. Each parish of the Orthodox church has been brought under the control of a committee of three, which may include nominees of the KGB. The church has always thought of itself as patriotic; after the war it cooperated with the state in the enforced conversion to Orthodoxy of many hundreds of thousands of Catholics in the Ukraine. And it is a church whose self-understanding is that priests celebrate the 'divine liturgy' in the presence of devout believers. That was what made many expect the state's persecution of the church to be completely devastating. In 1914 there were about fifty-one thousand parish clergy in about fifty-four thousand churches; in 1980, about six thousand clergy in about 7,500 churches. In 1914 there were about a thousand monasteries and in 1980 about twenty; in 1914 more than thirty-seven thousand parish schools and in 1980 none.

After this immense destruction of everything material that had supported piety, the position of Christianity in the Soviet Union remains full of dangers. Certainly the Orthodox church has survived the persecution far better than could be expected when terror suddenly replaced many centuries of privilege. It is estimated that there are between fifty and seventy million Orthodox believers in the 1980s, in a population of about 265 million. But it is equally true that other Christian groups have survived and grown, to an extent inconceivable until recently. Some of these groups inherit religious loyalties from pre-Soviet days of national independence, most notably the Lutherans of Estonia and Latvia and the Catholics of Lithuania, but in the other Soviet republics the Baptists, Evangelicals, Pentecostals and

Mennonite Brethren have all put on strength as alternatives to Orthodoxy. They are all represented on an All-Union Council which tells the government that it speaks for about half a million baptised adults. The real figure is probably far higher; the council does not wish to alarm the government. Many unregistered sects and meetings are known to exist in defiance of the government, so that the total strength of the movement of Christian dissenters seems to be between five and ten million. If the large Muslim population and the religious Jews are included, it seems that between two and three out of every five inhabitants of the Soviet Union continue to believe in God after seventy years of communist power. That is an amazing fact about the contemporary world. There is, however, an obvious possibility that the definitely atheist element in the population – often reckoned to be about a quarter in the 1980s – will grow if the state continues over a long period to deny to the churches any possibility of instructing the young formally and any possibility of renewing their own life and thought through honest public discussion under trusted leadership.

The secularisation of Eastern Europe was proceeding before 1945 in those sectors of its life which were becoming modernised and therefore westernised, but its increase outside Poland has connected with political and military realities. It has been one of the effects of the installation of communist governments dependent (at least in their first two decades) on the power of the Red Army. Much of the 'socialist camp' in Eastern Europe still constitutes the Russian empire, the only empire surviving in the world of the 1980s. Throughout this region, even in nations which have now somewhat distanced themselves from the Soviet Union, atheism is taught in the schools. It is spread by the media (if only by the absence or scarcity of religious programmes on TV and radio). The children of believing families are liable to be penalised in the competition for places in higher education and for the better jobs, and adult believers often have to watch their steps. And the churches are handicapped as they try to respond to these pressures. In places they still undergo an open and systematic persecution or have good reason to fear its return.

Any statement critical of the government, or of the society it is creating, may be declared treasonable or 'counter-revolutionary'. Or the handicaps may be more subtle. Church leaders may themselves become content to concentrate exclusively on public worship and private prayer, refraining from any speech or action which could be interpreted as hostile to the state or even as attempting to rival the state's provision of education and social welfare. Or the churches may think it to their advantage to identify themselves with a nationalism which, while popular because it is anti-Soviet, is also to a greater or lesser extent alien from the actual development of the nation because it is hostile to socialism or at least nostalgic. At its extreme this last tendency was represented by those Catholics who in the 1940s and 1950s tried to keep the church mentally in the world of the land-owners – a 'feudal' world (as Marxists would classify it) in which the church had been prominent. All such handicaps have hindered Christianity from engaging freely and creatively in the life of a society which appears to be irreversibly socialist. In particular they have prevented the development of a detailed dialogue with Marxism, for the temptation is for Christians simply to declare, without any subtlety in argument, that they are against 'atheism' but for 'peace' and 'justice'. Marxism and Christianity are then regarded as two utterly different and totally irreconcilable philosophies which never-theless largely agree on practical aims for society. That is the public attitude of the official church leadership in the Soviet Union and in several other Eastern European countries. It avoids many awkward but vital questions.

In some ways this kind of separation between church and state brings benefits to the churches. In Eastern Europe the association of communism with Russian imperialism encourages popular support for churches which are by far the strongest carriers of the traditional local culture. These churches may be the only places where people may speak aloud about great matters in a language which does not echo the current line of the Communist Party. Thus in Poland, where a thousand years of Catholicism were celebrated massively in 1966, there are only about two million self-identified communists in a population of about thirty-five million. In contrast the Catholic church, despite the devastations of the war and its later conflicts with the communist authorities, doubled the number of its clergy and churches between 1937 and 1980. In Romania the Orthodox Church is in a similarly strong position statistically and is stronger educa-tionally. It came to terms with the communist government during the second half of the 1960s. In both national churches there are active movements for a Bible-based renewal ('Oasis' in Poland and 'the Lord's Army' in Romania). In East Germany half the population still belongs to the Federation of Evangelical Churches, with whom the government reached an understanding in 1978, and this half is content to pay a church tax (a proportion of the income tax) which the government collects. These churches maintain an extensive network of hospitals, clinics and social service centres. In Hungary the bulk of the population is at least nominally Christian – almost three quarters of it Catholic, the rest Lutheran or Reformed. Church and state patched up their quarrel in the 1970s so that 'goulash communism' could be matched by socialist Catholicism. The government's relations with the Protestants had improved earlier. In the 1980s it is only in Bulgaria and Czechoslovakia that restrictions as severe as those in the Soviet Union are still enforced in the churches. And it is only in Albania – a tiny country, so isolated that it does not in any way acknowledge the Russian hegemony – that all public religious activities have been forbidden.

However, the East European churches are not complacent and have no reason to be. The backing given to atheism by governments in effective control of the economy, of public life and of the police has reinforced the secularising trend which would no doubt have been powerful anyway. Thus a census in Bulgaria in 1962 reported that seventy-eight per cent of those over sixty-nine were religious believers but only twelve per cent of those between eighteen and twenty-three. Although this figure was disputed, it was suggested that the Orthodox element in the population had been reduced from some eighty-five per cent in 1939 to twenty-seven per cent. In East Germany the proportion of the population declaring itself to be 'without religion' increased from eight per cent in the 1946 census to about forty per cent in the census of 1974. In the 1980s less than a fifth of babies born are being brought to baptism and there is a severe shortage of clergy. In Hungary similar problems are experienced. Even in Romania there are pressures from the state – for example, limiting the numbers accepted for training for ordination.

The Yugoslav government has recently been cautious in its dealings with the churches provided that they stay out of politics. It needs national unity, particularly since it combines a moderate Marxism with a definite refusal to be a satellite of the Soviet Union. The statement in the constitution that 'the manifestation of religion is free; it is the personal affair of each individual' therefore has more substance than in some other communist countries. But in the popular mind the churches tend to be regarded as backward-looking. This explains why Tito persecuted them almost as savagely as other communist rulers until his change of policy in 1953. Orthodoxy has been identified with a Serb conservatism which has been nostalgic for the days of the monarchy. Catholicism has been linked with a Croat separatism which was in the 1940s embodied in an infamous government installed by the Nazis; such memories only began to die down with the death of Cardinal Stepinac in 1960. These Yugoslav churches seem to be gaining new life but their problems are not over now that their persecution has ceased. The country around them is, like many another nation under communist rule, at least as secular as Western Europe.[3]

European futures

It used to be expected that this long process of secularisation in Western and Eastern Europe would be generally interpreted as liberation, so that most Europeans would unite to celebrate intellectual and social freedom. But in fact the twentieth century has been a time of far more complex reactions in Europe. Certainly few think that there could, or should, be a return to the past. For most people, life is now materially better than it was for Europeans at the beginning of this century. But it is not often felt that this century has brought happiness. In Eastern Europe there is a profound sense that the communist governments are clumsily out of tune with the national traditions and ideals. In Western Europe there is a similar feeling that the free market – the City of Man as understood by capitalism and individualism – is spiritually inferior to the national glories commemorated in history and in much backward-looking fiction. In comparison with other continents, on the whole Europe looks to the past for its sources of pride. It has been marked by a failure of nerve about the future ever since it became clear that the 1914 war was going to last longer than a few months. To Europeans, it often feels as if the civilisation of Christendom has died or is in a terminal illness – and there is no confidence that it can be replaced. This century is the age of self-criticism often amounting to self-condemnation; of anxiety often ending up in despair.

Serious literature, film-making and play-writing have become predominantly concerned with the search for meaning and with the doomed defiance of the many forces which crush human values. Any note of optimism has been rare. More popular entertainment has been the only field apart from sport in which heroes have been admired. The popular media have often grabbed attention by the exploitation of sex and violence, encouraging a new barbarism by suggesting – even more forcibly than the serious artists – that European man is indeed King Lear's 'bare forked animal'. And the widespread despair or cynical scepticism about the human condition has not died down with the disappearance from the scene of monsters such as Hitler and Stalin, who cast off all the moral restraints of civilisation and mesmerised millions into obedience. It has persisted while peace has been preserved by nuclear weapons and while material living standards have risen for the employed. Obviously this mood has had many causes but a major factor in the failure of nerve is commonly agreed to have been the decline of the religion which gave Europe most of its ideals. The prophets of doom have included Max Weber, who analysed more profoundly than any other sociologist of his time the exclusion of modern Europe from the 'enchanted garden' of traditional religion and its entry into the 'iron cage' of rationality. Before his death in 1920 he was fearful of the future, as if predicting the rise of Hitler. 'Not a summer's bloom lies ahead of us,' he warned, 'but rather a polar night of darkness and hardness.' Another early twentieth-century sociologist, Emile Durkheim, coined the word *anomie* to describe the loss of the sense of belonging and purpose that results from the disintegration of a commonly accepted moral law. Like his predecessors in the foundation of sociology, Saint-Simon and Comte, he hoped that the 'science of society' would itself provide a new moral code in due course. But he interpreted religion as the celebration and enforcement of the unity of a society and he could not be confident that in this function it had yet been replaced. He sensed the developments which lesser sociologists have analysed in detail – the change from organic communities to artificial associations, from supportive families to profit-making firms with limited liability, from inherited status to bargained contracts, from tradition to efficiency. He made a study of the individual's exhibition of anomie in extreme cases – suicide.

'From the religious point of view,' an Italian sociologist, Sabino Acquaviva, has more recently written, 'humanity has entered a long night that will become darker and darker with the passing of the generations, and of which no end can yet be seen. It is a night in which there seems to be no place for a conception of God, or for a sense of the sacred, and ancient ways of giving significance to our own existence, of confronting life and death, are becoming increasingly untenable. All the motivations for religious behaviour and for faith persist – the need to explain ourselves and what surrounds us, the anguish and the sense of precariousness. But man remains uncertain whether somewhere there exists, or ever existed, something different from uncertainty, doubt and existential insecurity.'[4]

A British sociologist, Bryan Wilson, has been a stern critic of attempts by Christians to minimise the accelerating secularisation in post-war Europe. But he published in 1982 some reflections about the disadvantages of this process – and his tone is thoroughly European. 'All is far from well with the operation of contemporary society,' he wrote. 'It is clear that an increasing proportion of people are disturbed by the facelessness of modern bureaucracy, by the impersonality of relationships, and (despite elaborate entertainment and recreation industries) by the sense of boredom that is felt in the manning of the rational technical social system. The social problems of modern society grow at an alarming rate, even though the specific incidence of these problems may vary from one society to another. The growth of crime, of vandalism, and of neurosis and mental breakdown; the growing disruption of marriage; the increase in various types of addiction, whether to drugs, alcohol or gambling, and the incidence of personal isolation, loneliness and suicide all provide a commentary on the points at which the rational social organisation apparently fails.' He observed that 'modern society rejects religion on intellectual grounds, and fails to see what the cost might be in terms of the emotional assurance that men need in order to live'. He reckoned that 'men will be unable to remake the world we have lost' but found some hope in the thought that some 'religious endeavour' has been effective 'at the margins and in the interstices, and principally in the domain of private life . . . in allowing some men, at least, to transcend the present discontents, and in producing, by way of the dissemination of dispositions of goodwill and commitment, that salt of the earth that is necessary to sustain the social order'.[5]

Has Christianity any realistic hope greater than this prospect of surviving in a few private lives on the margins of a secular Europe? Will it become a little candle flickering in Weber's 'polar night of darkness and hardness', in Acquaviva's 'long night that will become darker and darker'?

Before we can begin to answer we must contemplate, however briefly and tentatively, the likely future of Europe apart from religion. This future is often expected to be bleak and some Christians are happy to be pessimists because of their faith that Europe's general collapse will make it seek consolation in the arms of the church. But on an unprejudiced analysis of the facts it seems more probable in the mid-1980s that there will be prosperity – if war can be avoided, if technology can attract enough support, if it can be used humanely and if the new industrial development can come to terms both with the physical limits of the environment and with the needs of the poorer nations of the world. And it seems clear that all these conditions could be met.

The European Community has bound twelve nations of Western Europe together – and, despite their continuing squabbles and their habitual cynicism about themselves, it has given them solid reasons to hope. Their belief in human rights, however imperfect, has given them a spiritual unity, acknowledged in 1949 by the creation of the Council of Europe with its Convention and its Court of Human Rights. Their belief in democracy led to the first direct elections to the European Parliament thirty years later. Their awareness that modern technology demands investment and sales on a continental scale led to the creation of the Common Market on the basis of the Treaty of Rome in 1957. It is encouraging that they have been sufficiently consistent to keep their membership open to proud but now poorer nations such as Greece, Spain and Portugal. Obviously the chief aims have been economic. The corporate economic strength of the European Community (which produces as much as the USA) has encouraged its member-nations first to protect their farmers by the Common Agricultural Policy and then to begin to turn to subsidising the renewal of the decayed industrial cities. And that is realistic. Neither rural nor urban poverty can be forgotten – not even in Western Europe. But it is also encouraging that there has been an acknowledgement of the threats posed by industrialism both to the natural environment and to human values, so that all over Western Europe the spokesmen of the 'green' movements are listened to, particularly by the young; and there is an awareness, however inadequate, of the needs of the non-industrialised nations, building on (while denouncing) the old colonial connections. For example, the sales of the Brandt Commission's reports, *North-South: A Programme for Survival* (1980) and *Common Crisis* (1983), have been far larger in Europe than in the USA. In comparison with the USA (or Japan or the growing economies of Asia) the West Europeans have become less willing to work and to innovate for the sake of material rewards. There are limits to the sacrifices they are prepared to make, for they do not 'sincerely desire to be rich' in the style of their American or Asian competitors. Their attitude may be laziness and it may prove their undoing if they cannot build a modern economic base sufficient to sustain their remaining material expectations. But it is equally possible that the West Europeans will work well enough and innovate well enough and – knowing that 'enough is enough' in material goods – will be better equipped to enjoy the unpaid work and the leisure which the new technology will make possible for all and compulsory for many. Europe seems to have within its grasp not the prospect of the highest material standard of living but the possibility of being the bit of the world where life is lived most richly.

If the development of industrial technology is producing a prosperous economic community rather than war within Western Europe, it also seems to be the case that the development of military technology has made war between NATO and the Warsaw Pact improbable, because despite their posturings both sides know that a nuclear war would leave no victors. In Eastern Europe it will be natural for trade and cultural contacts with the West to grow, and also for the 'socialist camp' to move towards its own union to match the European Community. Clearly much will depend on the attitude of the Soviet Union. But it seems probable that the Russian empire will gradually be dismantled, like all its predecessors in history. It will not be replaced by a return to the 1910s or to the 1930s. East German Protestants, for example, accepted the reality of the long-term separation of their society from the capitalist West when they set up their own Federation of Churches in 1969. Yet to accept the continuation of socialism does not necessarily involve the acceptance of Soviet control or of the Soviet model – which will itself change.

The rulers of the Soviet Union, whose attention will be concentrated mainly on the economic development of their own continent-sized country, will probably not be willing to pour unlimited resources into the unending support of iron regimes in Eastern Europe. They will instead base the security of their frontiers on nuclear and post-nuclear weapons. Behind this shield they will try to satisfy the needs of their own peoples for better housing, more varied food, more attractive consumer goods, and a richer culture. They will also have to come to terms with the anti-Russian sentiments of the smaller republics where the majority of the population of the Soviet Union now lives. In particular they will have to acknowledge the strength of Muslim traditions in the south. Anything like capitalism or democracy in the Western pattern is totally out of keeping with the traditions of the peoples now constituting the Soviet Union – including those Muslims. But it does not seem probable that vigorous peoples will always tolerate the form taken by state control since the 1920s (and essentially maintained despite the de-Stalinising moves) – domination by Moscow, inefficiency in local administration and the attempt to control every detail of economic and cultural life by the employment, and ruthless use, of a vast police force.

The third volume in the standard history of *Main Currents in Marxism*, by Lesek Kolakowski (1978), is entitled *The Breakdown*. Not only has international Marxism been completely split by the bitter quarrels of its two leading powers (with China accusing the Soviet Union of 'revisionism' and of its own kind of imperialism, and with the Soviet Union attacking both Maoism and its replacement).

During the post-war reconstruction the communist vote in Western Europe has steadily declined and since about 1963 (when in Italy Pope John and Palmiro Toggliati began to talk the same language) the whole tendency of 'Eurocommunism' has been away from imitation either of the Soviet Union or of China. There is a similar tendency in Eastern Europe, although restrained by Soviet power; and from within the Soviet Union widespread cynicism about Marxist-Leninism is very frequently reported. This philosophy is no longer plausible if presented as the only scientific understanding of man, his history, his society and his encounter with nature; too many facts cannot be fitted into its rigid framework. Nor is Marxist doctrine convincing if claimed to be the only key to economic progress; General Secretary Gorbachev has repudiated that claim almost as boldly as the leaders of post-Mao China. Marxism has also lost credibility as the only possible inspiration of true service to the workers and peasants. As Sartre said, there is a sense in which 'Marxism stopped' with the October 1917 revolution, for Marxists in power sent too many millions to prison or to death and became themselves overprivileged and corrupt. It is possible that the vast state apparatus which bears the name of communism will retain power for many years to come. But it is also possible that its overstretched control will crack and, having cracked, will crumble rapidly; and ever since Khruschev's denunciation of Stalinism in 1956 that development has seemed more likely.

The two Europes now developing will, it seems, be like the two Americas in that one will be a capitalist society modified by 'social democracy' and the other will be socialist (or nominally communist) but with a freer market in goods and ideas. But both Europes will owe their economic foundation to high technology and efficient agriculture – and this similarity between the two social systems will have profound psychological effects. No more potential Hitlers or Stalins will be able to argue that their ruthlessness is necessary because without it their nations would have no hope of escape from poverty. Rulers, whether or not they are 'democratic' in the West European sense, will have to be seen to be on the side of the ruled. In the factories and on the farms machines will do much of the work which in the nineteenth century brutalised the European masses. Already in the 1980s the proletariat sullenly manning the factories is disappearing into history, following the ragged army of agricultural labourers. Now the threat to the worker often comes not so much from the individual capitalist or landlord as from a corporation with many shareholders or from the state itself – and the great new injustice is long-term unemployment. But the hopes which encourage the Americas are valid also for Europe. These problems can be conquered if workers who are also citizens are allowed to participate in decision-making at every level and if a humane use is made of the wealth which can be produced if managers and technicians regard themselves as fellow workers. In this field Yugoslavia has much to teach the socialists – and West Germany can teach the capitalists. Jobs can be created by public expenditure. Work which is not highly technical, and therefore not highly paid, can be encouraged by public policy, for example by not taxing low incomes. Leisure can be filled by public education, including a much more creative use of television. Ideas are already in the air which could be brought down to earth, to make a Europe which would no longer feel itself to be in irreversible decline.

So the continent where science and democracy were born could at last begin to enjoy what they can achieve. And having glimpsed this possible fulfilment of the best hopes of Europe's revolutionaries, we can at last attempt to answer the question whether this continent, as it recovers its nerve after many tragedies, is likely to become completely secular. Or can a recovery of European religion freed from the misuse of their power by the clergy provide what Bryan Wilson called 'the emotional assurance that men need in order to live'?

Churches and alternatives

Superstition and magic will, no doubt, survive. Many twentieth-century Europeans are superstitious, repeating rituals (often with a joke) and accepting (or half-accepting) beliefs which go back to the dark centuries before the continent became nominally Christian. The prominence of horoscopes in newspapers and magazines is public proof of this. Magic is also accepted more widely than appears on the surface of European life, as is suggested by the appetite for material on witchcraft and the occult. But 'superstition' is a belief that survives in the teeth of the evidence. The higher religions of the world have claimed more than that. Magic is an attempt to manipulate supernatural powers to suit one's own desires, for example for crops and children. The higher religions of the world have claimed to submit to these powers in so far as they are holy and divine, worthy of honour by conscience and intelligence. Europe, if it is true to itself, will not allow superstition and magic to reign.

The 'sacred' (which may even be called God) will still be acknowledged in an 'invisible' religion far outside the churches. To say this is no more than to say that Europeans will remain human, for commitment to values and loyalties has always been what has given depth and flavour to human life. Of course many Europeans will continue to be lovers and parents. Marriage and the family will be 'sacred' although there will be more sexual freedom than in the past. And of course many Europeans will be fervent patriots, will love their neighbourhoods and (perhaps in fewer cases) their neighbours, and will have many experiences of the 'sacred' through nature, art and music. Many will be willing to sacrifice their own interests and appetites to these greater things. It was appropriate that it should be a distinguished novelist, Iris Murdoch, who set out this sense of the 'sacred' in her philosophical essay, *The Sovereignty of Good* (1970). But all this noble humanism need not mean the recognisable continuance of Christianity or of any other religion – for it need not entail any belief that human good really is sovereign over the evils so prominent in human experience. To Europeans in the Christian centuries, marriage and the family were sacred not only for the normal human reasons but also because love was an introduction to God. Nature was sacred as the creation of God; the arts were worship of God's beauty; humanitarianism served God's children; a country was loved with the faith that God watched over it. And by 'God' was meant a reality which transcended the self and the world; which was truly sovereign. If by 'God' is meant no more than human values and loyalties, or no more than a 'life-force' to be experienced in nature and history, then deep down this acknowledgement of the sacred is not religion but secular humanism. The question of European religion is likely to continue to include the question of the sovereignty of the God to whom Europe's churches were built.

It will not be enough that non-churchgoers should read religious literature, listen to religious broadcasts, or watch church services on TV. Literature has done a great deal to keep Christianity alive as an option for the peoples of the Soviet Union. Novels such as Dostoevsky's and Tolstoy's remain honoured classics of Russian culture and despite the censorship the profound religious element in the work of modern novelists such as Pasternak and Solzhenitsyn has not passed without notice. *Samizdat* (underground) literature has been circulated with a courage as well as a quality that could not fail to impress. The influence of books and journalism in Western Europe also spreads religious thought and activity – or so I believe, as a man who has given the best of his life to the writing, reviewing, editing or publishing of religious books. But it is obvious that there are limitations on the willingness of the Europe now emerging to absorb opinions from the printed page. The Soviet Union is among the countries where religious broadcasting has its influence, but particularly since European radio and TV seldom establish the direct link between the listener and the evangelist which is aimed at by the 'electronic church' in the USA, many investigations have shown that it is unwise to exaggerate this influence. Such broadcasting can keep alive and strengthen memories and loyalties formed by churchgoing and, when churchgoing is not (or does not appear to be) a possibility, it can spread knowledge of the Christian message. But the decision to embrace a religious vision of one's life and destiny almost always seems to require a face-to-face contact, as does a decision to change one's political views.

Schools are, of course, often the scene of face-to-face contact between adult Christians and a new generation. Except in communist countries where they are illegal, church schools attempt to provide a Christian atmosphere for the whole of education; and in some other countries religious instruction takes place in the state's schools. It is striking that most parents support this provision in Britain and Norway, countries where church attendance is conspicuously low. There has been an immense discussion about the purpose and effectiveness of this explicitly religious element in education, in church or state schools, within a largely secularised society. Many reports and conferences may be summarised by saying that the school, while it can provide information about religion and the subtler experience of encounter with religious teachers and school-fellows, cannot completely replace the home if that is secular or the church if that is unknown or unloved. Attendance at a church school in childhood does not have nearly as much effect on adult attendance at church as optimists such as Roman Catholic bishops have desired; and many are the complaints in worldwide Catholicism in the 1980s that the church has invested far too heavily in its schools. If teachers and children are basically cynical about the official religion, a church school is not likely to commend Christianity more effectively than a state school; on the contrary, it may present an easy target for rebellion. And in the state's schools if teachers have no real interest in them, school assemblies for worship and religious instruction may be quietly dropped from the curriculum although the law of the land still insists on them (as is the situation in Britain).

One stimulus to rethinking the content of religious education is that higher religions other than Christianity now have a substantial presence in Europe. The faithfulness of Muslim, Hindu, Buddhist and Sikh immigrants or 'guest workers' arouses European curiosity and

respect, and I hope that in previous chapters I have argued sufficiently that Christians should learn about and learn from these faiths.
But it is, I hope, not an example of Christian arrogance to say that
these religions teach beliefs which remain false and bewildering to
almost all Europeans – beliefs in divine spirits inhabiting nature and
in the supernatural powers of ancestors; beliefs in reincarnation and in
castes; the belief in Nirvana as the escape from the cycle of rebirths;
the belief that obedience to the Islamic or Mosaic law is essential. In
Europe respect for such faiths is likely to be much wider than
commitment to them. The question of God, as it confronts Europe, is
likely to retain a mostly Christian content.

New bodies, not necessarily damned by being called 'sects' and
'cults', have grown like mushrooms in Europe's religious vacuum.
Some spread westernised versions of Hinduism and Buddhism.
Others derive from the vitality on the fringes of North American
Protestantism – Jehovah's Witnesses, the Mormons, Christian Science and others. Some such as the Church of Scientology and the
Unification Church propagate a complicated and apparently up-to-
date mixture of Christianity, science and magic. Others more simply
offer a method of consciousness-raising or of encounter as the way
into a 'new age'. They have attracted converts by a style which may be
compared with Africa's less orthodox independent churches or with
Japan's new religions. They are intimate and warmly supportive
communities. They usually become a convert's second family and
they sometimes seek to detach 'those who accept the truth' totally
from the natural family. Their teachings always have at least the
appearance of being definite, confident and all-decisive: that is why
they seem to have a monopoly of truth. They usually give the convert
a sense of beginning a new life in a new light which deserves a total
allegiance. And they are not compromised by association with the
churches whose role has been so ambiguous in European history. But
they have many disadvantages if what we are seeking is the player of
the role of the inspirer of Europe. Their numbers are small and
membership in them seems often to be only temporary. There is no
possibility that they will become a united movement, for 'the truths'
which they propagate are contradictory. They are called 'sects'
because they purposefully cut themselves off from the mainstream of
European life and thought as well as from the historic churches. They
are all, by the standards commonly accepted by the educated in
Western and Eastern Europe, irrational. Since their religion rejects
the whole surrounding culture (although the membership may be, to
a greater or lesser extent, 'respectable'), they tend to be undiscrimi-

nating in their condemnations of it. In return they are portrayed by the media as cranks and they have enough customs which seem outlandish to give some substance to this charge. Governments, when they notice them, tend to think them insignificant or disruptive. At the extreme, Jehovah's Witnesses have been persecuted in the Soviet Union and elsewhere and have not had much public sympathy.

Some of these characteristics are shared by Christian congregations or 'house churches' in the Pentecostal and Adventist traditions which, as I briefly noted, arose in the USA. In Europe as in the other continents, these have flourished since the second world war. They recruit often (but not exclusively) from those who are not fully integrated into the surrounding society. Specially interesting and impressive, at the two ends of Europe, are the black churches which gather immigrants from the Caribbean in British cities and the secret meetings of Christians, usually workers and peasants, in the Soviet Union. But in Western and Eastern Europe such groups face special handicaps if they attempt to influence their neighbours on any large scale. Although their national traditions vary, most Europeans tend to take pride in their control of their emotions and in their rational and practical approach to life. They do not like to be thought uneducated or uncultured although their view of the peaks of civilisation may be mainly through a TV screen or through memories of some science picked up in school. The enthusiasm of the Pentecostals, with a literal acceptance of the Bible and a constant emphasis on the repetition of biblical miracles, tends to appeal only to those who, perhaps for temporary reasons, are in rebellion against this general attitude. In defence of these congregations it can be said that the Christian church was originally a Jewish sect, filled with enthusiasm on the feast of Pentecost. So it was. But chapter one of this book argued that the church appropriated a richly varied heritage from the Jews, including intellectual and social concerns; that its gospels soon reflected a variety of interpretations showing its appeal to many different temperaments in many different situations; and that without any major break with its past it came to be expressed in terms of Greek philosophy and Roman organisation, so that it could gradually become the religion of the majority in the Roman empire and in Europe. It seems improbable that these small groups of conservative Christians have within them a similar capacity for development while retaining their present distinctive characteristics. They reject modern society and expect to be rejected by it. Mostly they seem to recruit from dissatisfied members of the historic denominations, not from the secularised public.

Alongside these congregations and 'house churches' in the Pentecostal and Adventist traditions may be seen a considerable number of small communities and movements which are radical in their theological and political outlooks. These groups are impatient with the conservatism of the main churches and seek freedom to work out a truly contemporary lifestyle in Christian discipleship, without clerical control. Many of them concentrate on a single issue which is to their conscience and hearts of burning importance – justice for the Third World, for example, or the rights of women or of homosexuals. They gather unconventional but passionately committed Christians and feed them into what can be called the 'green' movement of protest, most notably in the Netherlands and West Germany. The disadvantage about most of these communities and movements is that their appeal is deliberately limited to people who share the same convictions. In practice their ability to hold together such enthusiasts is often also limited to a period when the cause seems specially urgent or a charismatic leader is specially active. Although such groups show how widespread among Christians is the longing for the renewal of Europe's churches, they are no substitute for that.[6]

But can the churches be adequately renewed?

Many who comment on the religious situation are sure that their effective renewal is impossible. Bryan Wilson, for example, is emphatic that 'in general, the Christian churches have engendered little that is new in many decades, except in a destructive sense, in the abandonment of old liturgies and the adoption, by way of replacement for them, of casual performances which imitate the ephemeral fashions of the entertainment industry of secular western society'.[7] Within the churches, however, the situation is often viewed more hopefully.

The Orthodox churches have kept their worship unchanged – and in a language which the laity do not understand – for reasons which Christians elsewhere respect for the time being. These are forms of worship loved by saints and martyrs as deeply in this century as in any previous age. They are holy with the holiness of costly and persistent devotion. Moreover, in the Soviet Union any proposals for change put forward by the present leadership of the Orthodox churches would be suspected by most of the worshippers as having been inspired by the state and they could not be discussed adequately because of the state's virtual prohibition of all religious activity other than the repetition of the existing liturgies. In other Eastern European countries the position is usually easier but here, as in the Soviet Union, the main popular appeal of Orthodoxy lies in its preservation of a pre-communist culture. The atmosphere is not one to encourage the questioning of religious traditions. But the survival of Christianity under communist persecution or pressure should certainly not be dismissed. The heroism of so many Christians in braving the hostility of the state is a phenomenon which could not have been predicted in the years when the church was under the state's censoring patronage. Old people often make up the majority in congregations – but in the Soviet Union those old people were young when atheist education was already compulsory in the schools. No less surprising is the interest taken in religion by young people who find the dishonesty and debauchery of Soviet society repulsive. For them the 'boring' creed – official but evidently false – is Marxism. Educated young people in the large towns may turn to the historic Orthodoxy and be patient with the Slavonic language of its liturgy – and to those who are not so patient, Protestantism is now often available.

In Western Europe the experience of the churches has been very different. Everywhere religious freedom has existed since the defeat of the Nazis and nowhere is it likely to be withdrawn. This has made Christian faith less intense and less courageous than in the Soviet Union, for it is less simple to confront consumerism rather than communism and general scepticism is harder to resist than official atheism. But theologians have taken advantage of this freedom and particularly in West Germany, the Netherlands and Britain have aroused a sizeable public reaction, whether enthusiastically in favour of the new explorations or indignant about changes to orthodoxy. The reluctance of theologians to deal in certainties has been assessed by a dispassionate observer as suggesting 'the greater tentativeness that might properly accompany greater subtlety. Indeed, there is much to be said for the proposition that the religious thinkers of post-war Europe have shown an intellectual vigour second to none'.[8] The spiritual vigour has, however, come mainly from a movement in many of the European churches which may be described as Evangelical or charismatic, marked by a simplicity of joy in Christian prayer and fellowship responding to a confident gospel. Many congregations in the historic denominations have proved that this atmosphere is not to be found only in the cults and sects. And both those who are interested in intellectual experiments and those who prefer religion to be heartfelt have often shown a strong sense of social responsibility. Church leaders and meetings have repeatedly debated the great issues of our time such as the threat of nuclear war, the protection of mankind's environment and justice for the Third World. Millions of members of congregations have expressed their concern over these

issues when an opportunity has been offered. No one will deny the
vigour of non-churchgoers and non-Christians in the 'green' groups
which protest on single issues such as disarmament or conservation
and which in some countries have made some impact as political
parties. But the churches have provided a network second to none in
the informed discussion of these daunting questions and in symbolic
action to challenge despair. In West Germany, for example, large
church meetings have given very serious attention to questions of
'peace' – and in Britain large church movements have thrown themselves into the fight against famine.

The Protestant churches have more easily been swept by the
excitements of theological, spiritual and social movements and controversies. But the biggest change is to be observed in the Roman
Catholic Church – which must matter for Europe, where in the 1980s
it can still muster almost a quarter of a million priests and more than
half a million religious sisters. The Second Vatican Council was
indeed, as Pope John XXIII desired, an *aggiornamento* (updating)
although its concerns were 'pastoral' rather than doctrinal and its
immediate consequences were to relax discipline and therefore to
decrease religious practice. But it was decisive for the future of
Catholicism when the dominant image of the church was no longer an
institution governed and defended by rulers and laws but 'a sacrament of intimate union with God, and of the unity of all mankind'. It
was a momentous change when new worship was authorised, no
longer in Latin and no longer isolating the priest – as advocated by the
liturgical movement, again chiefly in West Germany and France. In
this worship the emphasis has been on the reading and preaching of
the Bible and on the congregation's union with the crucified and risen
Lord. There is very little here of the 'ephemeral fashions of the
entertainment industry' which were all that Bryan Wilson could find
in church life.

This renewal of European Christianity, although in the 1980s far
from complete, has a thrust which may be discerned. It responds
seriously to a crisis which has no single cause and therefore can have
no superficial explanation. It responds by renouncing the arrogance
with which the clergy attempted to control those movements of
science and democracy which had sprung out of a Christian civilisation. The response develops the insights of the great Christian
prophets of the nineteenth century into the nature of religious truth as
awareness of the majesty of 'something I cannot understand', an
awareness which leads to a way of life. In Marxist terms, here is
honest 'praxis' – not the bogus claims of an intellectually systematic

ideology which in practice conceals realities. In this response most Christians have (however reluctantly) learnt to tolerate the differences in each other's approaches and have thoroughly accepted the principle of religious liberty, knowing that genuine religious belief can never be imposed by force or by legislation. After many controversies most Christians have also learnt that a spiritually powerful religion is possible without the pretence that the expressions of belief in past ages can be completely authoritative for the present – and without the pretence that the richness of human life can or should be forced into the confines of a dull respectability. After lessons which cost tens of millions of lives, Christians have learnt to hate war and to check their patriotism by the internationalism of their religion. And after lessons taught by communists among others, they have listened to what their own religion says about the divine demand for justice to the poor.

The churches have on the whole recognised that they have no longer the capacity, the duty or the wish to dominate Europe. The most intense faith to be seen in Europe arises out of the prolonged sufferings of the Christians of the Soviet Union – and it is faith which knows anguish, self-abasement and self-surrender. Met in prison camps or in very humble circumstances in what passes in the Soviet Union for freedom, this faith inspires others precisely through its humility. In happier conditions, the blessing given to religious liberty by (for example) the Second Vatican Council implies for West European Christians the glad acceptance of pluralism. In Europe's churches, this new attitude accepts diversity within the unity that is desirable and that can be achieved. The ecumenical movement has gathered strength in Western Europe, and in Eastern Europe Christians have more informally been glad to witness and suffer alongside each other. Europe's Christians know that it will not be possible in the foreseeable future to iron out all the differences between the Orthodox, Catholic, Protestant and Pentecostal traditions. Nor will it be possible for the clergy to discipline the belief and behaviour of the laity as in the past. The acceptance of pluralism also means agreeing that outside the churches many humanitarian and other movements serve the purposes of God. The state – even the communist state – is to be honoured and obeyed as a servant of God except when its decrees are manifestly so anti-religious or unjust that it is right to run the risk of anarchy rather than obey them. The churches do not even have a monopoly in the field traditionally called religious. What is described by the churches, as by the general public, as superstition and magic seems likely to diminish, but through the influence of science rather than through any new inquisition by the churches. Many ideas about 'the sacred' not prominent in the teaching of the clergy are going to remain prominent in the lay life of Europe. Religious ideas of many sorts are going to be propagated by books, broadcasts and schools. The great non-Christian religions are not going to be expelled from Europe. Many sects with little or no connection with Christianity are going to be free to recruit, and many Christian congregations with little or no connection with the main churches are going to hold their members by their unworldly enthusiasm. The message of the churches will be heard amid many other voices. It will be heard the more willingly, the more it is thankful for the liberty of those voices. Purified by suffering and humiliation, the voice of European Christianity is becoming the sound not of power but of prayer and love.

Christianity in the Americas, Africa and Asia is now hopeful because it is casting off the old Europe – its controls, its theologies, its styles. It is being made new by being made local. And now even in Europe there is Christian hope. In 1984 Roman Catholic bishops representing the European Bishops' Conferences met with Orthodox, Protestant and Anglican representatives of the Conference of European Churches. They met in Italy. The previous 'encounter' had taken place in France in 1978 and had been the first time that representatives of all the main European churches had met since, by solemnly systematising the doctrines of the Roman Catholic Church, the council of Trent (1545–63) had seemed to make Europe's religious divisions final. Now these church leaders gathered for their final act of worship in the cathedral at Trent. They agreed on a statement which noted that in Europe 'Christians can no longer rely on worldly power but are challenged to hear a personal and sincere witness'. And they declared: 'Our faith in the triune God revealed in Jesus Christ enables us to view even the continent of Europe with hope.'

It was a significant meeting, although barely a hundred strong. Since a Christian hope which includes 'even the continent of Europe' involves the readiness to accept Europe's new tasks, an effective contribution cannot be made until the churches are much more determined to end the shaping of their own lives by the quarrels of the past. We saw that in the USA there is very little conviction that the churches need to unite; cooperation is thought enough and history is not felt as a problem. As the United States of Europe emerges, however, and as socialist Eastern Europe moves into its own future, it seems obvious that the agenda of the future must be different from the agenda which in the past divided Catholic from Orthodox,

Protestant from Catholic and Protestant from Protestant. The most convincing sign that new tasks are being addressed seriously is the new collaboration of Christians in those tasks – which is why the ecumenical monastery at Taizé in France has attracted such great interest, particularly from young people who are fascinated by its total commitment to the gospel and by its ability to combine contemplation with a realistic concern for social problems. Obviously the churches, like the nations, of Europe are not going to be uniform. Indeed, the economic and political integration of Europe, Western or Eastern, has encouraged a healthy pride in the cultural tradition of nation and region. But it severely handicaps the European churches that they are so divided and weak in relation to problems which concern all Europe – and which do not concern other continents (not even North America) to the same extent. At present Orthodoxy is largely isolated from the rest of Christianity and its historic centres in Istanbul (Constantinople) and Moscow are severely restricted. Catholicism is dominated by the Vatican which has worldwide responsibilities, a long tradition of cool relations with the West European states, and a more recent record of hostility to communism. Protestantism has a focus in the World Council of Churches with its headquarters in Geneva, but the WCC is rightly absorbed in Third World problems. Interchurch representation at the headquarters of the European Community lacks both resources and a sense of direction. An interchurch response to the development of Eastern Europe is not organised at all. The Conference of European Churches concentrates on East/West relations but is little known. Educational programmes for the congregations are correspondingly weak – although it is, in outline, clear enough what is the vision of European Christianity forming in the minds of millions.

The church leaders meeting at Trent in 1984 based their hope for their ravaged and humbled continent on their common inheritance of faith. This faith was, for them, set out in the creed which had emerged from the councils of Nicaea and Constantinople in the fourth century. Such unity was precious to them, not least because at their meeting they experienced 'our inability yet again to share the one loaf and the one cup at the Lord's table'. They warned against any modernisation of the faith which might destroy the surviving remnants of unity: 'To abandon the tradition of the whole church in an attempt to reformulate the Christian creed could threaten the basic and indispensable unity and coherence of the Christian faith at all times and in all places.' But it seems that they were also uneasy about simply reaffirming the words of the fourth century and it is certain that had the laity of Europe's churches been more fully represented in their conference such uneasiness would have been very definite. As it was, these church leaders did not totally exclude the possibility of an agreed restatement of Christianity. 'Only a council in which all the churches could once again take part,' they said, 'would have the right to undertake a reformulation of the universal creed on the basis of the apostolic faith.' Heartened although also warned by that kind of official and cautious encouragement, we may consider the restatement of Christianity – knowing that it must address a Europe almost completely different from the heavily religious world known to the bishops who in past centuries met in Nicaea, Constantinople, Chalcedon and Trent.

Three areas seem to be vital in any such restatement. The intellectual basis of Europe has become scientific with supplements. The political basis of Europe has become socialist with modifications. And the moral chaos of Europe will not be ended without more agreement about sexuality. It is a pity that these burning issues were not on the agenda at Trent in 1984. For they are central to the hope that European Christianity will be adequately renewed.[9]

Christianity and the new science

During some thirty years of publishing and reviewing theological books I have been introduced to the controversies which surround the intellectual position of Christianity in Europe. My education has not been the mere gathering of knowledge about other people's beliefs and disbeliefs. I have continuously had to ask myself what I believe myself. And I find that I must believe as one who, however inexpertly, acknowledges the full validity of science as an outpouring of the Holy Spirit.

Science cannot destroy belief in God – unless the verdict of science is interpreted (as it still usually is in the atheist propaganda of communists) in terms popularised by crude materialists in the eighteenth and nineteenth centuries. Indeed, many of the discoveries of science have strengthened the faith of those already disposed to believe in God. The contemplation of the fireball which contained our universe in embryo some fourteen thousand million years ago is the furthest back that the human mind can reach (unless in the future science should confirm the intriguing suggestion that this fireball was the contraction of a previous universe). The 'big bang' beginning our space and time is capable of arousing religious awe, not least because as radio astronomy probes our universe traces of that explosion can still be detected. Amazingly, the gases thrown off by that 'bang' could make all of our universe, whose intricate orderliness can be penetrated by the mind of man down to the sub-atomic level where the elementary particles dance. That spectacle can still inspire a mystical sense of the orderliness of God – as it did for Einstein. Yet the 'indeterminacy' which these particles seem to have can also inspire a religious sense of the freedom to be found at many levels in the creation – a freedom which may be associated with the freedom of the Creator. The development of the stars and their planets still arouses wonder both because of the unimaginable size which the expansion of the universe has already reached and because of the immense variety of stable conditions which had to be combined if a life-supporting planet such as our own was to be created. The evolution on this planet of matter, inert or living, in a history of some four and a half thousand million years remains marvellous, specially now that our TV screens have contained the profoundly moving image of Earth filmed from the moon. And almost as incredible is the evolution of life from bacteria to people.

The spectacle of such a universe still arouses wonder, either the wonder of worship or the wonder of agnosticism – unless the spectator does not really see the mystery because his eyes have been blinded by religious or atheistic dogmatism. Throughout the realms of science humility is appropriate, for the progress made during the nineteenth and twentieth centuries in understanding the process of evolution has still kept before the minds of truth-loving scientists the fact that what is known is far less than what is not known. The reasons why the first few minutes of the history of our universe were astoundingly favourable to the eventual emergence of human life (the 'anthropic principle') are mostly not known. Nor is it clear whether the evolution of life up to *Homo sapiens* has been due to entirely random mutations in the genes, sometimes giving advantages in feeding and breeding, or whether these mutations are to any extent caused by the operation of a tendency in nature towards greater complexity or greater liveliness or more beauty or a higher spirituality. And it is possible that these mysteries will never be brought into the clear light of scientific knowledge; that not only we but also our descendants will never know.

It is possible to conclude from science that 'man at last knows that he is alone in the unfeeling immensity of the universe, out of which he emerged only by chance'. Such was the theme of, for example, *Chance and Necessity* by Jacques Monod (in English, 1972). But it is also possible to agree with Charles Darwin's belief at the time when he concluded *The Origin of Species* (1859): 'There is grandeur in this view of life, with its several powers, having been originally breathed by the Creator into a few forms or into me and that . . . from so simple a beginning endless forms most beautiful and most wonderful have been and are being evolved.' And the all-decisive choice between these world-views is very seldom made on intellectual grounds alone. Science by itself does not decide the all-important question. A scientist may be disposed to reduce the spectacle of the universe to the operation of physical laws imposing regularity and perpetuating improvement where there has been survival ('necessity'). Or he may reduce the universe to mere randomness ('chance'). Or (and this is far more likely) he may reduce it to a combination of the two. But if so, that reductionist scientist's mind has been disposed by his own experience, or by the atmosphere in the surrounding society, to be cynical about the significance of man's spiritual life with its intuition of glory. The religiously believing mind, which may be found in a scientist as in anyone else, believes because the whole person has already moved towards God, usually within a religious community and usually in a movement little influenced by intellectual arguments. This is one of the meanings of Hume's saying that 'reason is, and ought to be, the slave of the passions' and Wittgenstein's dictum that 'philosophy leaves things as they are'. A reasoning philosophy based on science can answer very many questions, to mankind's immeasurably great benefit – but it cannot answer the question about God out of its own resources.

The experience of Europe in the age of science repeatedly shows that belief in God can be overwhelmed by suffering. Amid the brutal industrialism of the nineteenth century, or the wars, persecutions and dislocating changes of the twentieth, Europe saw little of glory and many Europeans saw little of God. But in this period it is also observable that some Europeans have gone on trusting God and have found their faith becoming less shallow, sentimental and selfish. After all this atheists are entitled to say that the 'problem of evil' makes religious belief impossible for them, whether or not they would like to believe – and European atheists have said so unforgettably. In reply believers have had to admit that the will of the God in whom they believe is not done obviously in every occurrence. There may be in the creation a randomness which is essential as the source of novelty and therefore of progress – or there may be a tendency to decay, disorder and evil, the anti-creative force traditionally called Satan, the Adversary. Believers must humbly wonder. But believers can pray, like the dying Jesus, to 'my God, my God' when even he seems to have abandoned them. And they can find that God is there.

The experience which gives rise to faith in God is the experience of good. Why does anything exist rather than nothing? Why in this universe, in a limited time-span, have matter and life emerged against the probabilities? Why is there so much order and so much beauty? Why has 'spirit' – the human love of truth, beauty and goodness – come out of evolution like a rose out of earth and dung? Why do human beings, who are so frail physically, intellectually and emotionally, often find that they are mysteriously sustained, even in times of darkness? The experience of good may always be put in the second place by those whose tasting of life has been harsher – and it can and must always be expressed in symbols which many may misunderstand or ignore. If the Creator is within but also beyond our universe, he can never be described accurately in words or images taken from his creation. Even his personality, if real, is a feature of his reality greater than any human personality. If he is pictured as Father because he is believed to be steadily loving, caring and providing, aspects of the divine reality may still usefully be called She or It. If God's power is adored as 'almighty' or 'sovereign', it can also be loved as self-emptying or sin-bearing. If he rules in history as judge, he is also seen to suffer in history as victim. All language about him is incurably 'mythological' in the sense that it is the language of pictures or models or stories or poetry, suggestive rather than accurate. This includes the language of the Bible and of the churches' dogmas. In particular the creation myths in the Hebrew scriptures need to be understood as magnificent pictures in words, able to teach those who are willing to be taught. The lessons which they offer are about the ultimate meaning of the universe and of human existence; about God, the all-transcending origin of all that exists yet also the voice that reaches man; about man, placed amid delights yet weak, mortal, foolish and afraid. At no point do these myths compete with science or contradict truths taught by science. A. N. Whitehead well summed up both the difference and the similarity between theology and science. 'The dogmas of religion,' he wrote, 'are the attempts to formulate in precise terms the truths disclosed to the religious experience of mankind. In exactly the same way the dogmas of physical science are the attempts to formulate in precise terms the truths discovered by the sense perception of mankind.'[10]

Religious belief is usually formed within a religious community and that produces the tendency to give an absolute and exclusive validity to the community's doctrines and customs, with an arrogance which has brought ruin to European Christianity. In reaction the sociology of religion arises, sometimes claiming to reduce religion to the sense of belonging to a group. Science is also social. It, too, is transmitted in a community united by loyalties. It, too, can encourage loyalties which discredit it in the eyes of all who value humanity – as scientists feel acutely when in their hundreds of thousands they are recruited into the development of weapons of mass destruction or of industrial 'progress' which wastes resources on trivialities or destroys the environment. Yet at its heart religion including Christianity has always been the disciplining of the mind and spirit in the presence of what fascinates because it is mysteriously *there*, beyond the group. The fellowship of religion has always been the union of those who seek and serve a reality greater than themselves, greater than the surrounding society and greater than the religious community. Any god less than this is a mere idol. And the fellowship of science can introduce a science-based culture to the religious attitude, for scientists open themselves to instruction and correction in the hope of catching a glimpse of what is really *there* in nature. They are not dedicated to their personal ambitions or to any group. The one error that results in exclusion from their community is not to be dedicated to the truth. And since such is the dedication of the religious and scientific communities at their best, it does not seem over-optimistic to hope that in the centuries to come in Europe these communities will increasingly overlap. If religion and science can honour each other, Europe will profit. For Einstein's words are justly famous: 'Science without religion is lame, and religion without science is blind.' One sadness of Europe's history is that the blind have had enough power to lame those who could have walked while the lame have had enough strength to tear out the eyes that could have seen.

But the question of supernatural miracles has to be faced squarely. In a scientific culture all religious belief comes after the affirmation that the whole process of nature is one vast *miraculum* or marvel. As science has developed, so the awareness has grown in the minds of all the best scientists that what is understood is a fraction of what is unexplained and may be in principle beyond human understanding; so that the genuinely scientific mind is humble, never claiming to know all the truth, always glad to welcome fresh truth. When as a result of religious experience religious belief affirms that the Creator is greater than the creation as well as present and active within it, and when belief adds that the Creator is loving, the believer is likely to find nothing in true science which in principle forbids the claim that in his love God has performed 'miracles' which cannot yet be fitted into known scientific laws or regularities. But do miracles, which may be possible in principle, occur in fact? The believer needs to be reminded that the evidence for supernatural miracles needs to be far stronger than was thought necessary in the ages before humanity had reached even the present stage of understanding these laws or regularities. It has, indeed, been felt by many scientifically minded Christians that all miracle stories are pious legends or at least misinterpretations of natural phenomena. To such Christians it seems clear that the marvel at the process of nature is all that is needed and that miracle stories insult the majesty of the Creator by suggesting that he has to interfere in order to put right the process he created. On this view, prayer is essentially the contemplation of God and of the nature which God has made with all its regularities and in all its accidents. In no sense can prayer ever be asking for a miracle. God's action in the world is his action in creating the world as it is, but Christians of this sort find it very difficult, if not impossible, to believe in particular 'acts of God' which adjust or supplement the course of nature.

> It is surely tragic that in the history of Europe religious authority has so often been identified with the insistence that all supernatural miracles reported in the Bible or pronounced valid by the church must be accepted as having had a supernatural rather than natural cause. That insistence has alienated countless educated people from the churches, Catholic, Orthodox or Protestant. But it is surely possible to hope that in the future the European churches will recognise the freedom of thinking Christians. There will be the freedom to insist on the possibility of supernatural miracles since God is loving and God is free. There will also be the freedom to deny the probability that any particular story about a miracle is the best explanation of the actual event. And it seems unlikely that the churches will make much headway in a scientific culture until they have fully acknowledged this freedom of belief, along with the moral necessity of accepting what science can teach. In its first century the Christian church made obedience to the Jewish religious law optional for its members and only that decision enabled it to evangelise Europe. In the future the European churches, if they are to communicate the essentials of their message to a scientific culture, will have to make it clear that it is optional to adhere to ideas of creation and miracle which must seem to most members of that culture pre-scientific. Individual theologians who have expounded that argument may be criticised. There were defects in Harnack and the liberal Protestants; in Loisy and the Catholic modernists; in Bultmann the devout Lutheran with his insistence that the message of the New

Testament must be 'demythologised', and understood as personal and existential rather than semi-scientific, if it was to be communicated; in the radicals of the 1960s and later. But the essential argument running through all these inadequate theological movements is stronger than the defects of its champions. It is the argument that the Christian gospel can be heard by people who remain children of the age of science.

Conservative Christians are often deeply disturbed by the prospect that a Christianity kept strictly within the limits of science will be an option in the future. They may well be prepared to treat the creation stories in the Bible as myths which continue to throw a religious light on facts which we can know only through science. It is also probable that they will be willing to abandon the literal truth of some of the stories in the Old and New Testament of miracles which interfere with the course of nature, such as the instantaneous turning of water into wine; and they are likely to agree that many or all of the 'healing' miracles can be understood as faith-healing, showing the psychological roots of many diseases and the power of mind over body. Or at least they will probably allow that people who take these attitudes are fellow Christians. But they will insist that the definitely supernatural miracle of the physical resurrection of Jesus belongs to the essential gospel – and many will add the miracle that Jesus was conceived without a human father. To them, these miracles are not only central to the Bible in a way that the creation myths are not; they are also central to the belief that God is loving, active and victorious because sovereign. However, already in the 1980s many Europeans (and North Americans) who wish to be counted as Christians do take the view, in public or private, that the Christmas and Easter stories are in whole or part mythological. It will be important for the future of Christianity in a scientific culture to decide whether or not such people are Christians. My own hope is that the decision will be in their favour and I shall be personal in order to say why.

Having pondered the evidence for many years (and written about it more than once) I believe that the tomb of Jesus really was empty and that his appearance to his followers in a 'body' was more than a hallucination although also different from an ordinary physical body. I therefore do not think, as Rudolf Bultmann did, that what rose at Easter was the apostles' faith in the future. I derive my own faith in the future largely from an event in history, the resurrection of Jesus, which to me as to countless fellow Christians was a unique declaration of the glory of God's future amid man's sins and tragedies. But I have been persuaded by critical studies of the Easter narratives that they cannot all be accurate history in every detail; I am now sure that these stories as we have them have been coloured by the prayers of the communities behind the four gospels; and I cannot conclude that the evidence for the virginal conception of Jesus is as strong as the evidence about his resurrection, although the Christmas stories are as precious to me as to anyone else. This travail of mind and heart about the two most important miracle stories in the Bible has led me to the conclusion that, in a culture shaped by science, there should be freedom for the Christian to believe, to disbelieve, or to keep an open mind about particular miracles. When studying Christianity's encounter with a religious culture such as Hinduism, I reached the conclusion that there are two types of Christian response. The one is converted away from the surrounding society; the other turns towards it in glad affirmation. Similarly, for Christians in a science-based society there are two types of faith. This is a theme to which I shall briefly return in the next chapter.

Christianity and the new politics

During the years when I was the Speaker's Chaplain in the House of Commons in Westminster I saw for myself something of the response to the questions raised by socialism in national politics. Now in Southwark my home is in a working class district. So I have been taught something about Christianity and the new politics.

Christianity deals with questions which are not on the agenda of socialism or of any other political movement – questions about the ultimate meaning of the whole natural process, answered or not answered in accordance with a person's religious experience or lack of it. In dialogue between Marxists and Christians this truth has often been expressed by saying that Christianity raises its voice in the presence of death. To the person who is politically minded and nothing else, death is the end of all activity which is useful to society and it can be transcended only by the inspiration which a life may have given to the struggle of the new generation. But most people in Europe have found such a response to death coldly inadequate. It offers very little motivation to that vast majority which has little influence in political or economic affairs – and very little consolation to those whose hearts are broken by personal tragedies. It ignores the strength of the human feeling, which may be called an instinct, that any ultimate meaning which life may have is ultimate beyond death; that the last enemy is not the destructive power of poverty or of dissatisfaction with one's work. Many humanist atheists add to the socialist account the hope that, despite death, love and other personal values may be transmitted. Christians add the faith that death is not the end of the person's relationship with the eternal God. This faith gives a special meaning to all life, all work and all penultimate hopes. And the spiritual history of Europe in this century has proved that such a faith may be compatible either with socialism or with a wide range of other political convictions. It can be held by the unemployed, by industrial workers, by peasants, by the bourgeois or by the wealthy. The world known to politics can neither give it nor take it away. And in that political world, this faith cuts across the battles between individualism and collectivism, undermining their often chanted slogans. Bishop Lesslie Newbigin has put it well: 'From its first page to its last, the Bible is informed by a vision of human nature for which neither freedom nor equality is fundamental: what is fundamental is relatedness.'[11]

But that is not to say that socialism discusses matters of no interest to Christians. On the contrary, it remains morally necessary that the ideals which have inspired socialists should challenge those who have made an idol of 'market forces'. When discussing the USA, some consideration of these apostles of 'free enterprise' was inescapable. Their philosophy, dominant under President Reagan, has won a considerable following in Europe, not least in Britain under Margaret Thatcher's government. Commonly called monetarism, it advocates freedom for 'market forces' (i.e. the pursuit of private profit) apart from the provision of some government services within restrained fiscal limits. The belief behind this philosophy is, of course, that if given freedom these market forces will ultimately benefit the whole people; prosperity will trickle down. That belief has had special force at a time when (in Britain particularly) industry needed to end overmanning and to modernise its technology. Competition has been the most effective way of injecting more realism here. But monetarists need to be asked how they can be sure that the play of market forces will in fact create a society thought fair and enjoyable by enough of its members. As yet there are few signs of that happening. And there is a subsidiary question. If the answer is that the state will still take care of the disadvantaged and the unfortunate, compensating them in the interests of social justice or at least of social harmony, are the apostles whose public gospel is 'free enterprise' in fact conceding that the state must play a very large role? If so, should they not take more pride in what public expenditure can do? Should they not put high among their aims in wealth-creation their desire to increase public expenditure? There are many Christians and others on the conservative side of the political debate who ask these questions – and who point to the fact that no conservative leader has in fact cut public expenditure to anything like the extent that a harsh rhetoric suggests.

It does not follow, however, that the socialist critique of this idolatry of 'market forces' is in every respect convincing. On the contrary, the socialist tradition appears to have arrived at a cross-roads which must fascinate anyone who cares about the conditions under which humanity lives. As we have seen, this challenge to the socialist tradition is real in many parts of the world. But it is at its most intense in Europe, the continent of socialism's origins in the 1830s, of its most systematic testing in the history of communist power, and of its longest use on the banners of the Labour movement. All over Western Europe socialist or Labour governments have been over-thrown, or are seriously threatened, by the conservative alternative which offers greater economic efficiency. All over Eastern Europe there is confusion about what socialism ought to mean.

Traditionally socialism has had a simple creed. The aim is stated in the famous Clause IV of the constitution of the British Labour Party: 'To secure for the workers by hand or by brain the full fruits of their industry, and the most equitable distribution thereof that may be possible, upon the basis of the common ownership of the means of production, distribution and exchange, and the best obtainable system of popular administration and control of each industry and service.' That still seems the way forward to many militants. But it seems that increasingly socialists and others who share their concerns are asking whether socialism does not need a fresh set of agenda. What is the best way of organising the countryside? The answer is not always 'collectivisation'; on the contrary, agricultural production seems to flourish along with private ownership, although not large-scale ownership by landlords. The best way of running industrial or commercial enterprises – 'best' in terms both of efficiency and of the relationship between management and the shop floor – seems to depend on a variety of local factors. It is certainly not a problem to which the only answer that ever seems right is nationalisation. Nor does a workers' cooperative always seem ideal since a firm has to be profitable by selling to consumers what they want. And questions loom up which no longer assume that material wealth can be ex-panded infinitely so that the ambitions of all 'workers by hand or by brain' can be satisfied. How can an industrial or post-industrial society be so organised that it is sustainable in terms of consumption of the earth's resources, yet every man receives an income sufficient to support a family and every woman who wants it can get a satisfying job outside the home? Can full employment be restored – and if this is impossible (as seems very likely), can society afford to provide a decent minimum income for the unemployed? Can society afford to legislate for a minimum wage in paid employment and if that is impossible (as also seems likely), can the low paid be subsidised by the state? If wages are raised to levels fit for the citizens of rich societies, how can prices be stopped rising to inflationary levels – by competition, or by government action or restraint? If paid work is to be a privilege, should it be shared? Should overtime be made illegal? Should an earlier retirement age be made easier or enforced? Should the young be conscripted for civilian national service? How can leisure, voluntary or involuntary, be enriched and how can education for it be organised and financed? How can the growing numbers of the old be sustained with dignity? These are questions which Europe probably has the physical and intellectual resources to answer. But Europe does not yet know the answers. Here is an opportunity for the churches not to claim an economic or political expertise which plainly their spokesmen do not possess but to do all that they can – and it is still a great deal – to inspire and assist the necessarily long and difficult process of wrestling with the questions until the answers are found.

In the past Christianity seemed unable to rise to the challenge of socialism because not enough Christians were interested in the questions which socialists asked. In the 1980s that is no longer the case. But the churches have to admit that while they have encouraged a concern for 'justice and peace' in answer to the problems of the world, partly because of the challenge of the socialists, they have been less effective at training and releasing their laity to be active in the specifically European debates and experiments. In some countries the churches are afraid of upsetting their moneyed supporters, or the official circles in which church leaders want to move. In other countries they are afraid of upsetting the communists who are in power – and they know that hopeful dialogues between Christians and Marxists were crushed, along with much else, when the Soviet tanks rolled into Prague in 1968. In self-defence the Orthodox have developed a tradition of retreating into a private world of liturgy and piety. All over Europe the smaller groups have often felt that they have lacked the resources to tackle the big social questions. Despite the inspiration derived from the teaching about social ideals in successive papal encyclicals, the Roman Catholic Church has been bedevilled by the insistence of its bishops on attempting to control any practical involvement in politics in many nations. Between the wars in Europe 'Catholic Action' was explicitly an attempt to enlist the laity in varieties of social action approved by the ecclesiastical hierarchy. The defence was offered that this prevented the identification of Catholicism with partisan politics. Since 1945 the problem of the interfering bishop has been much less, but it has still sometimes been real; for example, the bishops of Italy and West Germany have favoured Christian Democratic parties, which have certainly been partisan. Only slowly has the Roman Catholic hierarchy in Europe as a whole learnt to leave the details of politics to the laity. In general it seems fair to say that there has not been nearly enough encouragement of the Christian laity to take part in politics at every level with informed consciences but with sufficient awareness of the corruptibility of local and national politicians not to adorn their controversial groups with Christian labels. The most substantial example of what needs to be done is the educational work of the courses for adults run by the Evangelical Academies and of the very large annual conference, the *Kirchentag*, in Germany. In the Church of England the General Synod regularly discusses careful reports on social problems. The British Council of Churches and other bodies representing European churches have similar functions, but most grass roots Christians are not involved in these high level meetings and are not aware of any wisdom that may emerge from them.

Thus the European churches are challenged to take part in the basic rethinking of socialism – and Europe, communist or capitalist, would find it in its interest to encourage the churches to bring new treasures out of the storehouse of the Christian tradition of social responsibility. But it would be wrong to end even the briefest of considerations of Christianity and socialism with a vision of political discussion groups studying socialism's new agenda theoretically. The great strength of working class religion, where it exists, is that it is severely practical. Many accounts of the religious attitudes of European industrial workers and their families are similar to accounts of the religion of Latin American peasants. (My own limited experience in a working class district confirms the impressions given.) The millions of people who are referred to as the 'workers' or the 'poor' cannot afford the luxury of religion that is speculative or devotional in any style not related to everyday problems. But they often have a deep belief in God as their Creator and helper and in a crisis they will often pray. They are also convinced that God is more interested in people's daily behaviour than in their Sunday churchgoing. Being 'Christian' to them is primarily being loving in practice towards family, friends, mates at work and neighbours. If all this is at the heart of true religion or is close to its heart – as, on the whole, the Christian Bible also teaches – then the workers and the poor have much to teach those with economic privileges. This religion will, however, be separate from the religion of the churches as run by the clergy and their admirers – unless the churches can sponsor activities which plainly are helpful to the kind of religion to which the poor adhere. Challenging examples are provided by the Latin American *comunidades de base*, where the poor themselves relate the Bible to their lives, and by the public acts of worship valued by working class Europeans in special situations, such as the Irish, the Poles and the Romanians. It remains for the European churches to give their enthusiastic backing to new experiments which can express and deepen a working class religion. If they could attract a larger following in religion, incidentally they would cut more ice when talking about the principles of politics.

Christianity and the new morality

Although any 'morality' which is not immoral has to avoid being obsessed by sex, a response to the new attitudes to sex and the family must be central to any honest consideration of the private lives of Europeans. Here, too, I have had my education – both as a pastor and as a member of a family which has had its share both of joys and of desolating sorrows. I do not write as a man aloof from the pleasures or the problems. I have married again after a divorce. I am therefore going to say a little about sex in order to discuss Christian morality.

Sexual ethics inspired directly by the teachings of Jesus and the convictions of faith should obviously not be abandoned by Christians merely to fit a change in moral or immoral fashions. But Christians are challenged because Europe, like North America, has certainly undergone a revolution in this sphere during the twentieth century. The chief cause has been the liberation of women from a pattern of society, many thousands of years old, which compelled them to attend exclusively to meeting the physical, emotional or snobbish needs of men, rearing children, cleaning houses and clothes, tending animals and working in the fields or in domestic industries. Now women have insisted that they, not their families, should choose their husbands. Contraceptives have enabled women to limit their families and machines have taken much of the labour out of housework. There has been much emphasis that women, too, are entitled to sexual pleasure. If unwanted or malformed babies are conceived, abortion has been made available – extensively in Eastern Europe, with restrictions in those West European countries which have legalised it. Many millions of jobs outside the home and the farm have been opened to women and in many industrial nations almost half the workforce, paid or unemployed, is now female. Women have entered management and the professions, although not yet in many senior positions. But the sexual revolution has also affected men. Slowly they are learning to treat women as equals – but also, on most occasions, unsentimentally. Contraceptives have made it possible for men to have the frequent sexual intercourse – before, inside and alongside marriage – which many men have always desired. While many men have remained faithful to their wives, the whole tone of European life has encouraged them to think of themselves as needing sexual satisfaction to be normal and healthy. The vast majority of women and men continue to get married at least once, but since marriage is now increasingly regarded as a partnership of equals based on sexual attraction and sustained by a continuous emotional intimacy – and since many married couples have to live together for a period as long as fifty years, much longer than in any other society on earth or in history – many marriages are held by one or both of the partners to have broken down irretrievably and on this basis in some European countries (for example, Britain) the divorce rate has reached the very tragic North American level. The availability of divorce from the state is gradually becoming universal throughout Europe despite the Catholic bishops' opposition. It is also increasingly recognised that many women and men of their own wills seek happiness outside marriage and also outside the traditionally austere lifestyle of celibacy. They may 'live together' or have non-resident intercourse with a partner of the 'opposite' or of the same sex and if they are reasonably careful to avoid giving offence they will experience very little social disapproval. Homosexuality, while usually regretted in those who are emotionally capable of the heterosexual pleasures, is also usually regarded as natural in women or men who are 'made that way'. Many magazines and films portray nudity in sexually provocative settings, and although public opinion is still hostile to child abuse and to some perversions such as sadism and bestiality, 'soft pornography' is generally thought to be a harmless source of pleasure. Masturbation, seen as a release of tensions, is also usually regarded as healthy. So are ways of heterosexual intercourse which used to be condemned as unnatural.

Obviously the revolution in attitudes just outlined has had many different causes and has aroused many emotional and moral responses. Anyone sensitive to the achievement of Christianity in establishing the dignity of women, men and children against the force of pagan practices will appreciate the motives of the conservatives in the European churches, who have resisted the revolution at every point. It is a fact that the sexual revolution has coincided with the secularisation of Europe and would have been impossible without the decline in the powers of the clergy. Many secularised people as well as many Christians are, however, now deeply worried about some developments. There is massive concern about the increase in the number of abortions, involving the sacrifice of embryos which are at least potentially human to the convenience of adults; about the divorce epidemic, inflicting cruel emotional damage on children as well as on wronged wives or husbands; about the pressure on women to coarsen their sexuality in order to keep men as friends; about the militantly 'gay' propaganda for homosexuality as a satisfactory alternative to marriage. And it is widely recognised that the often commercialised cult of sex – something very different from the life-giving role of sex in courtship and marriage – has been so prominent in modern European life partly because it has had to be a substitute for religion. Like religion, sex is a self-transcending activity. It gives meaning to life through the worship of a fascinating mystery. The ancients who worshipped sex-symbols such as the goddess Aphrodite knew this well; and not for nothing is the lingam or penis still a frequent symbol in Hindu worship. But religious believers have also known that the cult of sex is idolatry, can be demonic and brings innumerable tragedies. In the long run it does not satisfy the heart as does a faithful and loving relationship with God. It depends on human emotions which often become unstable, as one or other partner feels exploited or bored. Many films, novels and pop songs are true to life with their time-honoured and infinitely varied theme that sadness follows coitus.

It is obvious that such considerations must very seriously qualify the welcome which a Christian can give to the sexual revolution. Yet many Christians do welcome many parts of this revolution – and in Europe that welcome seems to rise from the great majority of Christians (of whatever denomination) born since 1950. In such a society the churches are in danger of alienating vast numbers of Europeans unnecessarily by insisting on moral and social customs which are not essential to the Christian understanding of sexuality. Innovators are clearly responsible for much of the moral chaos in Europe in the 1980s. But conservatives – whether Christian, 'respectable' or even Marxist – seem to be no less guilty if they identify 'morality' with attitudes which seem remote from the daily experience of what is real, alive and life-giving. The spokesmen of churches are guilty if they identify 'faith' with customs which most of their sexually active members have rejected after much conscientious thought as well as in conformity with the standards generally prevailing in the society around them. Yet it remains commonly agreed that sexuality ought to support love – and, among believers, that 'love is from God. Everyone who loves is a child of God and knows God' (1 John 4:7–8). It appears that what the European churches need, if they are to reduce the present gap between what their leaders say and what their members and the people around them do, is a profoundly conscientious morality which is about love. Here the USA has much to teach. Europe needs to be told that to be moral is to take the loving action in the situation that exists – and that in many many of the situations created by personal relationships under new conditions, the loving thing may be something which previous generations would have thought immoral.

Such a morality would not merely abandon the individual to make lonely decisions under the pressures of situations held to be without precedent. It would relate the central teaching of the Bible to situations which are commonly experienced although new to the past hundred years because they have been created by the multiplication of paid jobs for women, the invention of efficient contraceptives, the development of understanding of sexuality (heterosexual or homosexual) and the spread of the ideas of liberty, equality and personal communion. In the Bible are to be found a number of exhortations about sexual conduct and regulations, in the contexts of changing social situations. But they are to be found alongside a number of visions of pure love – and the central teaching of the Bible is that daily behaviour ought to be raised closer to the level of pure love, and by the grace of God can be. The regulations often reflect the down-to-earth needs of ancient Israel. Loyal wives were needed to breed obedient children who would cultivate the land and fight the enemies. The law in Leviticus therefore prescribes the death penalty for adultery, incest, homosexual practices and bestiality – and even for any man who 'reviles his father and mother' (Leviticus 20:9–21). But the visions are of a love in which heaven and earth are merged – as when Jesus lets the woman taken in adultery go free (John 8:1–11) or Paul moves from his exhortations to the wife to submit to the husband, and to the husband to love the wife, to a vision of the submission of the church to Christ who loves it as his own body, to the death. It seems clear that in every generation Christians need to connect human problems in all their psychological and social reality with the absoluteness of perfect love.

The problem of divorce provides an example which is sadly topical in Europe (and elsewhere). In the Bible, Deuteronomy permits divorce when a man 'finds something shameful' in his wife (Deuteronomy 24:1–4) and Paul when a Christian has a heathen partner who wishes to depart (1 Corinthians 7:12–16). In Matthew's gospel it is assumed that a man may divorce his wife for unchastity; and the concern of the evangelist is to stop other divorces (Matthew 5:31–32; 19:3–9). But even with this allowance to human nature, the vision of purity is so intense that it is said that a man who looks at a woman lustfully has already committed adultery with her in his heart (Matthew 5:27–28). And in Mark's gospel the vision is proclaimed that all divorce is against the will of God, for the husband and wife are meant to be one flesh (Mark 10:1–12). Specially since Paul gives a general ruling 'which is not mine but the Lord's' against all divorce before allowing an exception, it is almost certain that this strict teaching given by Mark (and echoed by Luke) is the authentic teaching of Jesus. If so, in this matter Jesus contradicted not only his contemporary, the liberal rabbi Hillel who permitted divorce on demand, but also Hillel's stricter teacher Shammai, who taught that only divorce after adultery was obligatory as being God's will. But it is improbable that Jesus intended to legislate in detail for a community existing long after his death. Indeed, this teaching on divorce was, we are told, given in the course of a debate in which Jesus refused to be trapped into breaking the law of Moses. Any interpretation of his vision by regulations was left to his followers. And it is neither surprising nor disgraceful that his followers have not been able to agree. In the sixteenth century Protestant Reformers reasserted the right of those rightly divorced to remarry – a right almost (but not quite) certainly assumed by Paul and Matthew. But for many centuries governments acknowledging a special relationship with the Roman Catholic Church did not make any provision at all for divorce and in the 1980s this interpretation of loyalty to 'the church's teaching' has not entirely disappeared.

A morality aiming to relate the biblical visions of love to the far from perfect situations now existing in Europe (and North America) can be stated briefly, although inevitably it is open to disagreement. It will rejoice that women are being given more options, for that is a more loving way of acknowledging their human dignity and their capacity to grow spiritually by making their own moral decisions.

Women are loved in the equality which is rightly theirs when they are free to decide whom they will marry, whether or not they want to work outside the home, and the number and timing of their children. Children, too, are loved when their births are arranged because wanted. Marriages are lovingly sustained by frequent and fearless sexual intercourse and contraceptives deserve a very grateful welcome because they make this possible. Most marriages in danger can be rescued, but experience does not always support the attractive theory that a marriage between baptised persons, once consummated sexually after the sincere exchange of vows, cannot be dissolved. Problems which Paul and Matthew faced in the first Christian century are not unknown in the twentieth: marriage partners are or become non-Christian, there is persistent adultery or conduct which is equally or more destructive. Accordingly it is against the conscience of most Christians in Europe in the 1980s to exclude divorced people from the church's love. And despite the still official Roman Catholic teaching, it seems to be felt by the majority that if such people marry again they should not be excluded from the church's communicant fellowship unless the circumstances are scandalous.

Heterosexual intercourse outside marriage always runs risks. It may cheapen sexuality; it may establish a pattern which continues after marriage with disastrous results; it may (still) cause a venereal disease or an unwanted pregnancy. But when it is chosen by unmarried partners as an expression of a genuinely loving relationship after taking due precautions against disease or pregnancy, it is less sinful than many other activities. Homosexual intercourse usually incurs a greater risk – of emotional damage when the relationship is broken off, of social disapproval (largely inevitable because of the deep human instinct to breed) and of disease. Particularly now that the nightmare of Aids is such a tragic truth, the real situation of homosexuals is not aptly described by the word 'gay'. But these, too, are the children of God, 'made that way', and they need and deserve the love of fellow Christians. More fortunately constituted Christians should not condemn them utterly even if they choose to express a loving and stable adult relationship physically. 'Respectable' married people probably commit greater sins. Nor should the experiments of youth be taken too seriously. That, at any rate, is what conscientious Christians in Europe often think in their assessments of themselves and their neighbours. For us, the tolerance of people in different life-situations has become an important part of morality.

After changing many of my youthful views, such is the morality to which I have been driven by Bible study, by experience and by observation. But I know as a pastor that it is possible for Christians to live healthily (with physical and emotional health) without sexual intercourse of any kind. I know Christians who keep themselves virgins before marriage and celibates if marriage is not for them. I know married Christians who 'forsake all others' in a maturing delight in each other – but who do not forsake hospitality and kindness. And I am sure that many Christians will live chastely and nobly like that in Europe's futures.[12]

Europe in the Christian world

I have traced the history of the secularisation of the continent that used to be Christendom, doing as much justice to its complexity as could be managed at this length. I have attributed it chiefly to the failures of the clergy to rise above nationalism, to understand science and democracy and to reach the industrial workers. The tale included many tragedies. I have, however, been cautiously optimistic about the economic and political prospects of Europe and in this context I have agreed with the suggestion that even in the field of religion a modest hope may be held – if the spokesmen of Christianity can both keep their faith and come to terms with the new challenges in science, politics and morality.

It has become usual for an argument which praises the vitality of the churches in the Americas, Africa and Asia to do no more than glance at Europe with contempt. The custom in conferences and books of this sort is to condemn colonialism utterly and to connect its lack of care for American, African and Asian realities with the total failure of the European churches to appreciate the realities around them. It is implied, or openly said, that Europe would never have gone secular if its churches had not been very wickedly blind to reality because blind to justice. It is assumed that the continuing ability of Americans, Africans and Asians to see the reality of God is the norm and that the secularisation of Europe is an unparalleled development which has punished this continent's churches for their complicity in much evil. On this analysis it will be good for Christianity that in the year 2025 Europe will constitute only about five per cent of humanity.

I have granted at various points that there is much truth in this diagnosis of the sickness of European Christianity. But there is no love in it and therefore it may be questioned whether it is a Christian verdict. My own position is, of course, not morally superior to the position taken by the many Christians of our time who have con-

demned Europe. But as a European I also notice the positive contribution to the progress of other countries made by colonialism. And I
see the redeeming features of the European churches' response to the
unprecedented and appalling difficulties created for them in their
own continent by the central challenges of the modern age – nationalism, science, democracy, industrialisation. I cannot be surprised that
the leaders of the churches often faltered or failed in response to such
challenges. (I observe that the leaders of non-Christian religions are
nowadays not always successful in their own reactions as these
challenges reach their countries.) I am prejudiced because I am a
European, but I cannot ignore the faith that has survived this
acid-throwing by European modernity. It has survived the unroman-
tic agony of doubt and the humiliation of the need to change one's
mind – as well as the persecution, subtle or involving torture and
death, which very powerful and very cruel governments inflicted
systematically. I believe that a faith tested and purified in these fires
still has something precious to contribute to continents where religion
has not so far been challenged so harshly. But if the rest of the
Christian world wants to receive from Europe's churches and other
Christian movements in the years to come anything but messages of
guilt and defeat, it will be to its own advantage if it can build a new
relationship based on mutual respect.

CHRISTIANITY TOMORROW

Lands of tomorrow

On the islands of the Caribbean and the South Pacific the churches are inclined to conservatism for many understandable and honourable reasons. They have impressive histories. In the Caribbean the Christian message has been heard against a background of slavery and poverty and the 'gospel music' of the Christians has moved many in many nations because it has sung of a spiritual liberation beginning when the slaves worked the sugar fields. Since the end of slavery the churches have continued to be prominent and the phrases of the Bible are echoed by the politicians. In the South Pacific ('Oceania'), at least in its eastern and central areas, whole peoples led by their kings were baptised in a movement recalling the way in which Europe was 'converted' – but it was a change both more rapid and more thorough than Europe's. The old image of Pacific missionary work, as one day providing food for cannibal feasts and the next day ordering the natives to wear trousers or 'decent' dresses, is surprisingly accurate – for it is the case that many of these peoples had practised head-hunting and cannibalism, and it is also the case that beginning with the adoption of the Christians' God by King Pomare before his victory in a civil war in Tahiti in 1815 the public life of many of the islands was shaped by the missionaries' teaching. Indeed, from the 1900s into the 1960s (when there were four thousand missionaries leading the churches amid these small populations), its achievement in the South Pacific appeared to be one of the greatest triumphs of the missionary movement in all the world. Here Methodism, for example, had the unexpected experience of functioning as the established church. And in the 1980s – when both in the Caribbean and in the Pacific the missionaries have at last handed over the leadership – these churches still often have large congregations. Migrants from the Caribbeans have taken their religious vitality to surprise Britain, and migrants from the Pacific cause a similar surprise in the similarly secular Australia. A Methodist minister from Dominica, Philip Potter, became the prophetically eloquent General Secretary of the World Council of Churches, on whose Assembly in Vancouver in 1984 Christians from the South Pacific made a memorable impact.

But these churches have not escaped criticism by their own members with the sharpest eyesight. It has often been said that since the end of missionary control clergy and churchgoers have tended to be too loyal to the maintenance of the inherited – which has usually meant European or American – patterns of church life. One of their problems has been whether to maintain admirable but expensive educational and medical work. Religion often seems to have become routine. There are complaints that emotion is repressed, worship is formal, preaching is theoretical, clothing must be smart, persons living in 'common law' relationships are not welcome, churchgoers are expected to stand aloof from the drinking and dancing which unite a community. Despite the cultural ties which still bind the peoples of the Caribbean to Africa, the churches have been influenced by the old European contempt for African traditional religion. In the Pacific the peoples, although obviously very shaken by the impact of modernity, are still shaped by cultural and religious traditions developed during the continuous human habitation of these islands over some forty thousand years; but the style of the churches is not yet thoroughly local.

The result is that many of the religious energies of these peoples now flow through channels other than the routine of the old or 'mainline' denominations. Energies may be poured into anti-colonialism. In the Caribbean the European powers, having virtually exterminated the original population (so that the name of the Caribs survives only in the sea), introduced millions of African slaves. Those who survived the sea passage experienced spiritual genocide – for example, by the prevention of normal marriage, which continues to have tragic effects, or by the deliberate rupture of tribal loyalties, which meant a rootless society. These slaves could not own property: they *were* property. They had no rights except by concession of their masters. Their very blackness was made the proof of inferiority. Their society was created precisely in order to be exploitable. Every step that seemed possible was taken in order to prevent it from becoming a community. When slavery was ended (partly because slave-grown sugar was now less profitable), the Caribbean islands sank into a poverty from which they have not yet recovered. Today the impact of the USA, most noisy in tourism, seems both inescapable and degrading and the terms of the trade which it has offered in the 1980s (the Caribbean Basin Initiative) have not been generous. In the South Pacific there was no experience quite so devastating as slavery. But ancient cultures were disrupted by the white man's intrusion; there was gross exploitation by foreign traders; imported diseases and alcohol took a toll worse than the worst of the cyclones; the Christian missionaries, although they were the sincere friends and often champions of the islands, seldom understood their culture at any depth. After the second world war the area has been used for tests of nuclear weapons by Americans and Frenchmen cynically unwilling to inflict such damage on their own peoples and territories, and Australia's new economic power is a quieter threat. The white visitors have viewed these islands as a paradise. Caribbean sunshine and rum pour down on tourists from the posters. In the eighteenth century Captain Cook seemed to have located the habitat of the noble savage in the South Pacific, and in the twentieth Margaret Mead listened with a gullible delight to tales of a trouble-free because disapproval-free adolescence in Samoa. A voluptuous ease is the continuing image, from Bermuda to Trinidad, from Hawaii to Tahiti. But often the white man has done what he could to turn the paradise into a little hell.

These familiar condemnations of colonialism are justified by the facts of history. Yet Christianity is not at its best when it is turned into a protest movement absorbed in the denunciation of other people's sins. Nor is it true to itself when it is reduced to a cult which looks back to an imaginary Utopia – as in the Rastafarian cult in Jamaica where the fallen Ethiopian emperor, Haile Selassie, has been idolised as the embodiment of the spirit of distant Africa. The futility of such fantasies was demonstrated in the fate of the 'cargo' cults which arose and flourished in Melanesia in the 1940s. The second world war brought heaps of strange new material and power to the Pacific islands. The founders of these cults watched – and then promised that, if suitably entreated, the ancestors would produce their own 'cargo' of good things, driving out the white intruders. But these movements have died down as modernity has made its less dramatic impact. Some 'Revivalist' churches resembling the African indepen-dent churches – Trinidad's Shouters, St Vincent's Shakers, the Etoists (the Christian Fellowship Church) of the Solomons – have retained much more of their Christian heritage and have had a longer life than the 'cargo' cults. There are also many Pentecostal congrega-tions which are definitely biblical in their doctrines. All these groups draw people by their handclapping, drumming, singing and praying, by their expectation of miracles and by their informal fellowship. But like the African independent churches they often suffer from a lack of stability – for example, when the leader's charismatic power is no more – and from a lack of education. As their members become more modern-minded, they tend to experience a need to choose between joining one or other of the duller churches and becoming secular. To many, neither choice is attractive.

The solution to problems which are symptoms of a profound spiritual crisis is not just to take more religion into these islands. A Jamaican theologian, William Watty, has commented: 'Today in the Caribbean, the air is thick and heavy with religion. The metre-bands are clogged up and congested with gospel. There is more religion in the Caribbean than there has ever been, and yet there is more brutality, more corruption, more barbarism, more crime, more filthiness, more violence. At the same time that we are besieged by one visiting evangelist after another, cocaine is spreading like wild-fire, top politicians are caught red-handed, we have had a political massacre, morals are breaking down, family life is going to pieces, the social fabric is coming apart, more and more people are thrown out on the scrap-heap of unemployment and we are on the threshold of massive social disturbance.'[1] What is needed, he argues, is the emergence of these islands' own Christianity. And essentially that is true about the South Pacific, although in its morals the region is probably more Christian than any other area in the world. What is lacking for the Pacific islanders, too, is a religion of their own, now that the missionary impact has killed or is killing their paganism. Like African Christians they want to celebrate before God with their whole bodies, with their own art and music – and the chief ways in which they experience the divine power are through nature and through family life (including ancestors and children). That is the 'Pacific way'. And if it could become the way of the Caribbean also, many of the tragedies referred to by William Watty would be overcome.

Some promising Christian responses are being made. Many Christians on these islands, inside and outside the main churches, have made their own personal response to Christ and through that experience have become dependent on the forms of European or North American Christianity. Slowly the separation of Catholics and Protestants is being bridged by the recognition that this experience of Christ unites. Through councils of churches and other contacts Christians are beginning to cross the seas between the islands – and racial, linguistic and cultural divisions which are at least as great – in order to respond together to the region's social problems. For example, the Pacific Council of Churches held its first Assembly in 1966 and ten years later was joined by the Roman Catholics in full membership. Through united theological colleges and other educational projects the future leaders of the churches are being trained to become also the spiritual and social leaders of their peoples. A forward-looking confidence is arising. Out of the mixture of beauty and poverty, out of the mix of races and languages and the political and denominational fragmentation, out of an ocean of problems, a Christianity belonging to the islands is being born.

Anyone who flies over Australia or New Zealand, Canada or South Africa, gets the sense that the economic opportunities are almost unlimited. And anyone who meets the peoples knows that the nations' history has scarcely begun in the 1980s. These are good countries in which to end a brief world tour, for here – as in the islands of the great oceans – the futures obviously matter more than any yesterday.

These churches of the 'old Commonwealth' came from Europe. They came through the self-sacrificing labours of many missionaries, full-time or lay, and the conservatism which developed was a tribute to such pioneers. These churches are monuments to the courage of the Jesuits, the other priests and the nuns who planted the French Catholic civilisation in the wilderness of Canada, defying torture if captured; to the almost equal courage of the Canadian Protestants who went with the people west to the Pacific; to the faith (however narrow) of the Dutch Reformed preachers and the Afrikaner men and women who put their Bibles and families on to ox-carts and drove into the unknown; to the undramatic determination of the Christians who refused to see their religion left behind in the British settlement of Australia and New Zealand. These churches are also monuments to the pastoral care taken of many immigrants who were glad to find in the snow, the bush, the strange city or the silent countryside a building, a congregation and a life that represented to them the best of the country they had left behind.

In the early days of conquest and settlement Europeans often said that these lands were invitingly 'empty'. Certainly it was the case that by European standards they looked, and still do look, underpopulated and underdeveloped; the population of Australia, an island almost as large as the USA, is expected to be still under seventeen million in the year 2000. When the white man arrived he seemed marvellous in the eyes of the indigenous inhabitants as well as in his own eyes, for people who had crossed oceans bringing with them at least some of the technology and culture of seventeenth-century France, eighteenth-century Holland or nineteenth-century Britain knew more tricks. These tricks could subjugate the Australian Aborigines or the Bushmen of South Africa who still lived in the Stone Age, or Canada's 'Indians' who were still hunters and trappers, or the Maoris of New Zealand who had largely maintained the way of life they had brought from the Polynesian islands almost a thousand years before. And the white man's religion seemed to be as magical as his gunpowder or his whisky. Inevitably when the white man read his Bible he found a mandate for his own aggression in the pages which exhorted the Hebrews to conquer and settle the promised land of Canaan. In particular the Afrikaners who trekked north from the Cape of Good Hope constantly exhorted each other as the successors of the chosen people led by God through Moses and Joshua – and as they fought the Zulus and other tribesmen very bloodily, they recalled the command of the God of the Old Testament that the heathen must be exterminated or enslaved. And the Old Testament was also available for use or misuse by Christians who 'discovered' other 'empty' lands, such as the British settlers whose treaties tricked the Maoris out of the ownership of New Zealand.

But it was inevitable that those early styles of white conquest, settlement and church-plantation should in the long run fail to satisfy the Christian conscience. The pioneers may have been heroes – but they were also rivals, often bitterly so. They competed for building sites, for state funds in their schools, for social status. The hostility between Catholics and Protestants in particular poisoned the life of the new nation, partly because it transmitted old hatreds between English and French (as in Canada) or English and Irish (as in Australia). When in the 1870s Education Acts took almost all the schools out of the hands of these competing churches, the rivalries and hatreds of Christians were among the factors that ensured that the education would be secular in Australia and New Zealand. In South Africa membership of the Dutch Reformed Church became the spiritual trek through which the Afrikaners escaped not only from the English but also from realities they could not live with – and, when the realities proved inescapable, the fantasy of a Christian civilisation uncontaminated by blacks became the spiritual laager in which they defiantly took refuge. And these rival denominations clung closely to the outward forms of the religion practised by their mother-churches in Europe. The vision of a new start in a new world, demanding the unity of Christians in response to the new challenge, was very slow to dawn.

When this vision did begin, it awakened guilt. Slowly Christians became troubled in conscience about the treatment of the 'natives'. The awakening came too late to stop most of the consequences of the white man's ruthlessness. In Tasmania, for example, the original inhabitants were shot down, often for sport, and exterminated. All over these vast territories lands which were ancestral and therefore sacred were thoroughly and permanently absorbed into the white man's farming or industry. It was a commentary on the identification of Christianity with white supremacy that the new religion was not extensively used by the 'natives' to express their own identity – apart from the black churches of South Africa (which, however, took some time to throw off white control) and the Ringatu and Ratana churches of the Maoris (which, however, did not permanently attract many). Not until the end of the 1970s did a powerful spiritual movement of this kind arise among the Aborigines of Australia. Not until the 1980s was it conceivable that a Maori, who happened also to be an Anglican archbishop, should become Governor General of New Zealand. But at least it became true during the 1970s that most of the churches were available as platforms for protests against racist exploitations of these lands' original inhabitants. Most famously has this been the case in South Africa. In all these countries the denominations imported from Europe are now ceasing to be clubs where memories of Europe could linger like the stale smell of exhausted cigars.

My second chapter outlined the process by which the Anglicans moved into self-government and escaped control by a bishop of London appointed by the British government. The Anglican church has also moved into life as a minority, with its practising or nominal adherents comprising little more than a quarter of the population in Australia, less than a tenth in Canada and less than seven per cent in South Africa. A roughly similar process has reduced the dependence of other denominations on European bases. For many years Catholicism in Canada deliberately preserved the religion of pre-revolutionary France. Priests were plentiful and powerful. Most of the educational and social work was in the hands of nuns or other agents of the church. It was risky and unusual to criticise openly the doctrines and morals taught by the clergy. The whole society was permeated by Catholicism. But the effect of the changes symbolised in the 1960s by the Second Vatican Council's stress on the freedom and dignity of the laity was to reduce the congregations, to cut ordinations sensationally, to lessen clerical influence in politics and to end the threat to Canadian unity posed by the Quebec independence movement. Canadian Catholics voted (with their feet or through the ballot boxes) that they wished to belong to a liberal church and a modern nation.

In South Africa, where tensions between ethnic groups were of course much greater, two rival declarations of independence were made. On the one hand, South Africa's Dutch Reformed Church, having supported since 1948 a government enforcing the doctrine of apartheid and having reunited in 1963 with groups which had previously walked out of it with the accusation that it was becoming liberal, had no wish to remain in fellowship with European critics. Accordingly it severed its links with the Reformed Church in the Netherlands. The cleavage was made final in 1978. It could not be avoided once apartheid was regarded by European Christians as a heresy, and these white South Africans had already walked out of the World Council of Churches (in 1961). On the other hand, most of the converts made by the Dutch Reformed Church among the black and coloured peoples gave many indications in the 1970s and 1980s that they now regarded the Afrikaner apostles of apartheid as their enemies, not as their evangelists. Their independence was a defiance of systematic oppression. Their leader, Allan Boesak, has expressed it in his book *Black Theology, Black Power* (1978) – and in powerful acts.

In Australia in the same period the Irishness of Catholicism became less pronounced. Its priests had never been allowed the power of the priests of Quebec, and the separation of the Irish Catholics from other Australians had never been as complete as the apartheid advocated by the Afrikaner preachers, but there had been a distinct identity, largely working class, nourished by the church schools and by the Labour Party. Now Australians of Irish descent are (like the citizens of the USA similarly descended) as prosperous, modern-minded and free-willed as any other social groups – and clerical control, looking to Ireland and Rome, is being replaced by an identity more lay and more local (as in the USA).

There is a similar distancing from European bases to be observed among the Christians whose heritage is, in English denominational terms, 'free church'. In 1925 the United Church of Canada brought together churches of this tradition (although not including the Baptists and some Presbyterians) and in 1977 the Uniting Church of Australia was formed on a similar basis. In New Zealand (as in South Africa) non-Anglican Protestants are strong but increasingly determined not to rely on old connections overseas. The formation in 1986 of a Conference of Churches in Aotearoa (the Maori name of the country) including the Roman Catholics may be highly significant for the future. A dialogue between the United Church of Canada and the Roman Catholic Church ended in a report similar to words spoken together after many other conversations: 'We assert that we are one community of faith despite splinterings and schisms that have marked our churches over many centuries. In short, what unites us is more profound than what divides us . . . We pray that our present separations will disappear and that we may celebrate our common calling to be the Church of Jesus Christ in our world.'

Secularisation challenges all these churches. In Quebec, for example, the attitudes characteristic of contemporary France are becoming more common although almost half the Christians in Canada are still Roman Catholics, at least nominally. In the 1950s approximately two in every three Canadians were going to church regularly; in the 1980s, approximately one in three. The time when a bestseller could be called *The Comfortable Pew* (by Pierre Berton in 1965) was over. 'Not since the days of the Clergy Reserves has Canada had anything resembling a legally established church,' says a shrewd observer, 'but the new experience is one of cultural disestablishment. By and large the mainline churches have ceased to be the glue of Canadian society.'[2] In South Africa churches of many varieties are far more prominent, for apartheid is attacked or defended through them. But if the day comes when the churches are no longer needed for these political purposes, something like the Canadian experience may be theirs. Certainly secularisation has been the experience of Australia. Although the Roman Catholic element in the population has been kept fairly steady through the arrival of immigrants from traditionally Catholic countries in Europe, the total figures for weekly church attendance went down from thirty per cent of the population in 1960 to nineteen per cent in 1980. In the 1981 census one Australian in every ten was bold enough to declare 'no religion'. In New Zealand in 1926 only 5.4 per cent of the population declined to state a religious allegiance in the census. Half a century later the refusal was being made by 18.5 per cent.

Not only secularists can be outspoken in Australia. In a bravely candid book an Australian Anglican bishop, Bruce Wilson, has referred to a series of programmes on Australian television in 1981 called *The Sunburnt Soul*. He wrote: 'The theory advocates "indigenisation", i.e. Australianising, of Christianity as the solution to declining beliefs and church participation. In detail it suggests that churches should be more informal (like pubs) as befits the Australian character, that religious language should be more Australian or ockerised, that Christianity should draw on symbols from the Australian bush in order to express its beliefs, that Christians should be more earthy and matey in their personal relationships, and that we should try to develop artistic images of an Australian Christ. There are certainly some grains of truth in this theory, but fundamentally . . . those who see indigenisation as the solution to decline are like ice chest salesmen. They imply that if you wish to sell ice chests in Australia, manufactured in Bethlehem and Nazareth and finished off in Canterbury and Rome, all you have to do is to paint them wattle yellow or Ayer's Rock red. The fact is that you will have great difficulty in selling even Australian-made ice chests today . . . For most Australians, God is an ice chest in a world that has invented the refrigerator.'[3]

But it seems improbable that the Christians involved in the future of these lands will always take the defeatist attitude that they have to market to a hostile public a cold or cooling religion. A European Christian looking at Australia, for example, cannot help noticing how widely it is held that the churches are less warm-hearted than the people. Public opinion tends to attribute this to the domination of the churches by European-minded clergy; and public opinion seems to be correct. The phenomenon which was so important in the history of the USA, of the denomination being a shelter to immigrants, has not been nearly so important in Australia. Although Australians resent jokes about their origins in convict settlements, the ethos of rebellion against all authority, including the feeling that authority-figures are hypocrites, has been specially strong in this nation. Why, then, has Australia done so little to produce its own version of Christianity – which Bishop Wilson speaks of as a mere possibility? One explanation is that its population has so far been too small. Influences from Britain or Ireland, and more recently from the USA, have seemed inescapable because those far-off lands were the sources of the culture; yet precisely the acceptance of those influences had helped to make Christianity appear to be a religion which rival authorities with roots outside Australia were seeking to impose. Only in the post-war years has the population become so multicultural, at least in the cities, and so sizeable that a real sense of positive Australian self-identification is growing. The situation in New Zealand seems to be essentially the same. A roughly similar analysis of Canada may also be true, although there the churches have been more popular than in Australia (and, if the expression may be forgiven by Canadians, more like the USA's). For many years 'Canada' seemed to be happily enough new Europe – Nova Scotia or New France or British North America. Only recently has a sense of Canadian nationhood begun to overwhelm these imported ethnic memories. It is symbolised in the new national flag, with the simplicity of the maple leaf replacing the previous combination of the flags of the British and French empires.

These churches in new nations will surely have great opportunities in a history which in the 1980s has scarcely begun. The societies around them will be proud of their material achievements but the history of humanity tells against any suggestion that a hardnosed materialism will permanently satisfy the spirit. On the contrary, there has been a ready response to distinctively Australian evangelists and pastors such as Alan Walker and John Smith; missionaries from Australia and New Zealand are going into Asia in considerable numbers; and the Canadian churches have been creative in stirring up their nation's conscience about the rights of the country's own 'Indians' and Eskimos, and about the Third World, specially Latin America. It seems likely that the participation of the churches in the dramatic struggles for justice between the races in South Africa – struggles in which most of the churches have in the end come out bravely on the side of justice – will show that religion remains a vitally important force in society. The 1985 award of the Nobel Peace Prize to Desmond Tutu, later to be elected as the Anglican archbishop of Cape Town, suggested the world's admiration. And Canada, Australia and New Zealand, where South Africa's tragic dramas are followed with special interest, will not be the last countries to see the point that the constitution by renewed churches, rooted in the life of the people, can be central and creative.

It is possible that a sign to the world will be raised by the victory in the Dutch Reformed Church of those who are prepared fully to accept coloured and blacks as fellow Christians and fellow citizens. Already in the mid-1980s many Dutch Reformed laymen and some ministers – led by the heroic veteran, Byers Naude, but mostly in the younger generation – see very clearly that apartheid must be abandoned. The theological defence of it was always on the defence of separation, not exploitation – and this defence has crumbled in many consciences as the fact has been accepted that races have to live and work together. These Afrikaners now know in their hearts that they belong to Africa and that no further trek into isolation is possible. The alternative to this acceptance of reality would make the Dutch Reformed Church a group rejected, condemned and despised both by almost the whole of the rest of the worldwide Christian church and by almost the whole of the rest of a multiracial nation under black rule. Similarly, it is possible that the churches in Canada, Australia and New Zealand, which in the past have been so widely regarded as the shrines of European colonisation, will fully accept the vision of a new nation to be built by many races. Indeed, in the mid-1980s that development looks likely. The alternative would make the churches into museums.

In all these nations the charismatic revival is powerful in the churches. It may encourage escapism. In South Africa, for example, among the whites it has sometimes degenerated into a cult of prosperity as God's blessing, avoiding the question of who is being exploited in order to make this prosperity possible. Or the independent churches in the black townships may escape from crushing social problems into emotionalism and Utopian dreams. In other countries the charismatic revival may be content to reproduce the styles of the USA without getting involved in the 'political' or 'cultural' problems which have to be faced by churches which really are about their own nations. But in South Africa and elsewhere the charismatic revival has also shown that it can give a new heart of courage to men and women who then throw themselves into the struggles for social justice, being passionate to build new Christian nations. If the future brings a crisis in which the whole of the old social order goes up in flames – and that looks horribly probable in South Africa in 1986 – this new spiritual power may prove to be essential to the capacity of Christians to endure and to hope.

Futures of peace?

So the churches on the islands of the Caribbean and the South Pacific, and in the vast territories of the old Commonwealth, seek their own new identity. Their searches are, although very varied, in essence typical of the most significant developments in Christianity in many other lands.

Everywhere, it seems probable, the period when Europe was decisive in the formulation of this originally Asian religion will disappear into history. But the Christian message which the Europeans took into all the world will not disappear. It will be spread not by preachers with European accents in churches which look like bits of Europe but by neighbours who are friendly. It will be communicated in stories and songs rather than in doctrines; in small communities rather than in large institutions. It will accept its religious or irreligious neighbours. And something will be seen that, tragically, not many Europeans saw in the years of their ascendancy. It will be understood that Christianity requires justice and mercy in the life of the society as well as purity and love in the life of the individual. Everywhere control by the clergy will be reduced as lay Christians work out their own ways of following their Lord and spreading his love to others of the laity. Everywhere the feeling for the unity of Christians will be expressed in ways not determined by any part of Europe's own divided heritage. Everywhere Christians will have to come to terms with the great non-Christian religions (Hinduism and Buddhism now belong to Canada and Australia as well as to South Africa). The challenge of secularisation will be even more piercing. Everywhere Christianity will have to reckon with modern or post-modern lifestyles, with the new science, the new politics, the new morality – challenges now specially acute in Europe itself. But after a history bursting with energy, it can be expected that Christianity will have its own futures.

Obviously these futures will be inseparable from the wider futures of humanity, and I must face the question whether in futures when nuclear weapons cannot be disinvented human life will be possible or worth living. The contrast between Christians who do, and those who do not, consider the possession of such weapons morally legitimate is one of the most striking examples of Christian diversity in our time. Many would think 'diversity' too kind a word. I do not, however, want to burden the reader by any lengthy reminder of the nuclear threat. I have contributed a little to the discussion, as any thinking person must. I wrote a pamphlet called *Withdrawing from the Brink in 1963*; I wrote a chapter surveying recent Christian debates in a book called *Dropping the Bomb* (1985); I could write much more here. All I need write is that the long discussion has left me absolutely convinced that the Christian church must be a church of peace-makers, with never-ending prayer and thought about this threat. But I am totally unsure that the church ought to be committed to the advocacy of complete, unilateral and unverified disarmament. Since politics is the art of the possible, policies are questionable which stand no chance at all of being adopted by peoples and governments. In this field, while lesser national 'deterrents' such as Britain's or France's could certainly be renounced without increasing any real danger, both the American and the Soviet peoples and governments are clearly unwilling to trust each other sufficiently to abandon their entire nuclear stockpiles. The ugly truth is that these satanic instruments of death, when kept by both 'sides' to deter each other, are widely believed to be the pillars of peace. Such is the mistrust of the superpowers for each other: in any previous period there would have been war. What I think could happen, and what I believe will happen, is the reduction of those absurdly expensive and unnecessary mountains of horror (for, to deter aggression, it is only necessary to threaten to obliterate Moscow or New York once), the development of non-nuclear alternatives and of anti-nuclear devices, and a gradual movement away from this great evil (for there is evil in the threat, let alone in the use, of these weapons) as the supreme means of keeping the peace. In other words, I believe that civilisation has a future since the terror of these weapons will prove greater than the mutual hatred of the superpowers. One day a world government may be able to insist on a monopoly of these weapons – a development which would itself be dangerous to freedom. But I am aware that Christian faith is one of the grounds on which I base this hope and I am glad that many Christians have a simpler faith, virtually amounting to pacifism. This debate between Christians who do not break off fellowship with each other seems to be the most significant contemporary example of the diversity which is possible and legitimate as Christians work out the gospel in situations for which the Lord did not legislate. And the international fellowship of the deeply perplexed and frightened disciples of Jesus is in this situation very precious.

Many discussions have made me aware of how deep is the sorrow with which many Christians, specially young Christians, hear the spokesmen of Christianity expressing 'realistic' views such as those which I have just summarised. But I reply that when a danger is very terrible realism is loving – and can be courageous if unrealistic proposals are more attractive emotionally. And I also reply that both 'realists' and pacifists can be united in attention to the message of peace which the Bible proclaims. In poetry which has never been forgotten, the prophets of ancient Israel longed for peace (*shalom*). The New Testament records an answer to that prayer as the announcement of the Christmas angels. Jesus called the peacemakers blessed, for 'God shall call them his sons'. Paul and John, the theological giants among the early followers of Jesus, both encapsulated the gospel as 'grace and peace'. Luke described the Christian way as 'the way of peace' (Luke 1:79). I acknowledge fully and gladly that it is the vocation of Christian pacifists to concentrate on this message rather than on political considerations. Their purity keeps clean the conversation which Christian 'realists' attempt to hold with the leaders of an armed world.

The poor and the women

When I gladly observe that around the world the church is becoming the church of the poor and the church of women, I am specially conscious of my limitations, for I am a white man who has enjoyed many privileges within a system which is unjust to the poor and to women. But I have a few qualifications for offering a few comments. For seven years I was the chairman of Christian Aid, the largest of the agencies through which British Christians educate themselves in economics and channel their giving to world development. More recently I have been a priest in a church in a mostly poor district of London. In my family life I have not lived in a world different from the world of feminism. And as a student of the Bible I have meditated on its teaching. Indeed, I now want to make a good many biblical references – partly as a case study in the wider problem of the contemporary authority of the Bible, which will occupy us later.

As the emphasis shifts to the poor and the women, a return is being made to the origins of Christianity. The Hebrew scriptures reflect a society where strong men were to the fore, as they have been in almost all societies – but far more distinctive is the scriptures' constant reiteration that the God of Israel demands justice and blesses love. He is the God who makes a free people out of broken-spirited slaves, who demands fairness to foreigners because 'you were once foreigners in the land of Egypt', who is hotly against the oppression of the poor, who raises up prophets to denounce the rich and the powerful (Amos compares rich women with fat cows), who destroys Samaria and its kingdom because of its injustice as well as its idolatry, who is infuriated because poor people are enslaved for the price of a pair of shoes. In the psalms the 'poor' patiently pray to God – and are heard. In the legislation is enshrined the ideal that every fiftieth year (the year of jubilee) all land which had been sold should be returned to its original owner. Slavery, too, should never be permanent. Also distinctive is the tenderness with which many marriages are described; in the Song of Songs the erotic poetry is spoken by the bride as well as the bridegroom. Here is a blessing on what must always be the chief delight of the poor. But in their own right women can become prophets (beginning with Miriam who dances to the sound of her tambourine at Exodus 15:20) and judges (including Deborah who administers justice under a palm tree at Judges 4:5). The New Testament reflects a society where the poor are still exploited, slavery is accepted and male Jews, if devout, are not allowed to speak with women outside the home – but far more distinctive is the song of the mother of Jesus that the 'Mighty One' has lifted the humble and satisfied the hungry, sending the rich empty away. Paul accepts most of the customs of his time, but his deepest insight is that now 'there is no such thing as Jew and Greek, slave and freeman, male and female; you are all one person in Christ Jesus' (Galatians 3:28). No other attitude was ultimately possible for a person who followed Jesus.

It can be said that the Bible is ambiguous on social issues; that realists as well as pacifists, chauvinists as well as feminists, can quote it. But if we sincerely want to know where the Bible's emphasis lies, we have only to look at the practice of Jesus and of the first Christians.

The practice of Jesus with regard to the poor was to become one of them. His own background was, it seems, far from destitute. A 'carpenter' was skilled and the Galilee depicted in the parables enjoyed parties and knew about merchants, bankers, farmers who prospered and fishermen who hired help. But he became convinced that he had been sent to announce good news to the poor. His sympathy lay with the unemployed who needed a day's wage however little they could work and with Lazarus who begged at the rich man's gate – and he did more than sympathise. His own lifestyle as a teacher and healer was described by him as more homeless than the foxes and the birds, and finally as the way trodden by criminals. He changed his class in addition to any descent from his eternal dignity; there is this double meaning in Paul's 'he was rich, yet for your sake he became poor' (2 Corinthians 8:9). And many were challenged to abandon everything in order to follow him. A rich man could do this by a miracle, but a camel would find it easier to pass through the eye of a needle. It seems probable that Luke (Luke 6:20–26) has preserved the original emphasis in the Beatitudes – the pronouncement that 'you who are in need . . . you who now go hungry' are the truly blessed – rather than Matthew (Matthew 5:3–12), who interprets this as a blessing on those who 'know their need of God' and who 'hunger and thirst to see right prevail'. For many passages in the gospels report that Jesus taught that those who had like him embraced poverty in order to announce the kingdom of God to the poor would soon be satisfied by the coming of that kingdom. And many passages in the rest of the New Testament witness that when the church came as a foretaste of the kingdom, its leaders and most of its members were, like the Son of Man, not secure economically. Initially the community lived off the capital produced by the sale of any possessions, in the expectation that 'the kingdom' was imminent – but the Jerusalem church was soon reduced to poverty, having to accept the aid which Paul organised in the Gentile churches. ('All they asked was that we should keep their poor in mind' was Paul's boast to the Galatians.) These churches included some well-off and well-connected people: in Corinth some Christians had too much to drink while others had not enough to eat, and the letter to the Philippians could end with a reference to Christians working in the emperor's palace in Rome. But Paul seems to have been describing the usual situation when in his first letter to them he reminded the Christians in Corinth that 'few of you are men of wisdom, by any human standard; few are powerful or highly born' (1 Corinthians 1:26). Other letters in the New Testament show that many Christians were slaves. The letter of James attacks employers with a vigour worthy of the Hebrew prophets. The gospel for the poor is a favourite theme of Luke's, but in Matthew's gospel, too, the Christians and the poor are not two distinct categories. The promise of a reward to anyone who 'gives so much as a cup of cold water to one of these little ones, because he is a disciple of mine' (Matthew 10:42) is expanded into a blessing on those who have befriended the poor. Without knowing it, they have given Jesus food, drink, a home and clothing and have visited him when sick or in prison (Matthew 25:31–46).

In the first century AD only a man could lead the public life that Jesus led – and one without wife or children needing his daily care. But Jesus' identification with women was as complete as it could be without becoming one or being married. Matthew's gospel has a clear hint of this unconventionality when it defiantly lists among the ancestors of Jesus Tamar, Rahab, Ruth and Bathsheba – a woman who tricked a man by pretending to be a prostitute, a woman who was one, an Arab woman and a woman guilty of adultery. Luke reports that Jesus and his twelve chosen men were accompanied by a number of women who had been set free from evil spirits and infirmities and who provided for them out of their own resources – a group including Mary of Magdala (a woman never named with a husband) and the wife of a highly placed civil servant (Luke 8:2–3). Named women went with Jesus to the death and the burial. Such loyalty responded to his unconventionality in holding religious discussions with women – even (according to John 4:8–30) with a Samaritan woman who had 'no husband' but plenty of confidence in her theological ability.

Jesus noticed a widow putting all she had into the collecting box (Mark 12:41–44). To a Pharisee on another occasion he said: 'You see this woman? . . . this woman has made my feet wet with her tears and wiped them with her hair . . . she has been kissing my feet ever since I came in . . . she has anointed my feet with myrrh' (Luke

7:44–46). Another woman poured very expensive perfume over his head, probably intending to greet him as a king although he took it as 'anointing my body for burial'. He is said to have predicted: 'wherever in all the world the Gospel is proclaimed, what she has done will be told as her memorial' – although the male evangelist tells us the name of the host, Simon the leper, but not her name (Mark 14:3–9). And this recognition of Jesus by women continued after his death. The fourth gospel includes a tradition that Mary of Magdala was the first to see him alive. 'Some women of our company have astounded us,' say the men walking to Emmaus on the day of the resurrection (Luke 24:13–32) – or are the 'two of them' on that road husband and wife? In Acts we meet the prominent 'disciple' in Joppa named Tabitha or Gazelle; Lydia the businesswoman who was Paul's first convert in Europe and who had her whole household baptised; and the four unmarried daughters of Philip the deacon who 'possessed the gift of prophecy'. Paul also mentions that women can 'prophesy' – that is, speak 'as from God' (1 Corinthians 11:5). Phoebe was a deaconess (Romans 16:1). Priscilla, the wife of Aquila, is shown as teaching a learned Jew (Acts 18:2,26). This husband-and-wife team is greeted in Rome (Romans 16:3), as are women who 'toil'. Euodia and Syntyche share Paul's struggles in the cause of the gospel (Philippians 4:2–3). There are a number of references to congregations meeting in the houses of the richer women among the Christians. One group is mentioned as 'Chloe's people' (1 Corinthians 1:11). Such tributes to women deserve to be weighed alongside Paul's instructions to the Corinthians that women should keep their heads covered while praying, and should not address congregations, since 'man is the image of God, and the mirror of his glory, whereas woman reflects the glory of man'. Later in the New Testament, the ordering of a patriarchal society is echoed in the teaching of Ephesians 5:23 that 'the man is the head of the woman'. But with more originality husbands are told to 'love your wives, as Christ also loved the church' and the new love glows in the exhortation: 'Be subject to one another out of reverence for Christ.' In the letters to Timothy that measure of originality seems to have been abandoned. There, women are told to keep quiet although they can be 'saved through motherhood'.

The vision of equality between poor and rich, women and men, marked heretics in the Middle Ages, the left wing of the Reformation, the Quakers in seventeenth-century England, and marginal groups such as the Shakers in the nineteenth-century USA. More effectively, the social conventions were defied by movements within Catholicism such as the Benedictines whose early ideal was one of hard-working poverty, the Franciscans who caught a saint's vision of Christ among the poor, and the whole vast monastic movement. Although it acquired corporate property on an enormous scale (as did the Benedictines and even the Franciscans), the great network of monasteries, friaries and convents was always a protest against self-enrichment. It always gave unmarried women an outlet for self-fulfilment, not excluding the possibility of ruling a convent as an abbess. The church history of the Middle Ages shines with the names of women who were teachers of the spiritual life. And during the nineteenth century the energy of the original Christian gospel poured out in movements of social reform. The work of women who identified themselves with the poor was conspicuous in many countries. But, worldwide, it has been the special glory of the church in the twentieth century to become again not only the church *for* the poor and the women but also visibly the church *of* the poor and women. And no Christian body has done more to encourage this development than the World Council of Churches, because that international fellowship has repeatedly chosen women and other speakers close to the poor to raise their voices in its meetings and has continuously put the concerns thus voiced at the top of the agenda.

The statistics of distress are various, and in detail unreliable or fast-changing, but some figures say something of the agony and the anger. According to a significantly uncertain estimate by the World Bank in 1986, 'between 340 million and 730 million' people excluding China suffer from malnutrition. Each year at least thirty-six million new jobs are needed to meet the hunger for paid work. More than fifteen million children die of preventable diseases each year under the age of five and less than a quarter of young people of the appropriate age are in secondary education. Women constitute one third of those seeking jobs outside the home and perform two thirds of the hours worked by humanity; yet they receive only a tenth of the world's income and own only one per cent of the world's property. It is not to be expected that in such a world those who inherit the Hebrew scriptures and the Christian gospels should confine their energies to devotional exercises. For it is a world which could make sure that all its population expected within this century had basic needs supplied. But considerably more is spent on arms than on all forms of education and health care. More than a quarter of all high-level scientists are employed in military research. It is a mad and bad world, man-made, and it echoes with the voice of God: 'Let my people go!'

Christian bodies such as the World Council of Churches are surely right when they are penitent for the role played by 'Christian' nations in the creation of such a world. The colonial powers or the transnational corporations controlled by 'Christians' suppressed industries in other countries (for example, the textile industry in India). They reserved the best jobs – or, as in Kenya, the best land – to Europeans. They turned the emphasis in agriculture away from the centuries-old subsistence farming to the production of crops for export – often at low prices and with fluctuating markets (for example, cocoa in West Africa). They have ripped out natural assets without replacing them or paying good prices for them (for example, timber in Brazil). They have paid miserably low wages. Transnational corporations have attracted capital from local banks as well as from their own sources and transnational banks have demanded crippling rates of interest on their loans; and these foreign investors have often retained very large profits in the countries of their headquarters. Moreover, 'Christian' nations have dominated the international arms trade which has so disastrously diverted the developing nations' scarce resources. These are terrible indictments and each one of them points to a major reform that is morally imperative. It can be expected that future generations will look back with amazement at the years when the exploitation of the poorer by the richer nations was largely accepted by the churches and when the right of the poor close at hand to receive justice rather than charity was largely ignored. In church after church, 'church life' has marginalised the poor.

The churches' attitude to women has often been similar. 'Christian' men have often been among those who have bullied and exploited women. The churches, which ought to have been models of human unity and equality 'in Christ', have tragically often been not only middle class but also masculine in their ethos. Women have, on the whole, been welcome only to admire and to assist, although they have normally made up the majority in the congregation. Even in the 1980s their position is discussed in some gatherings of men – for example, in all-male conferences of bishops – in a manner which boils down to the assertion of their inferiority. But with differences of speed reflecting the different positions of women in the different cultures, it can be expected that in many churches women will be allowed and encouraged to preside at the eucharist, as the supreme Christian symbol of their equality with men. The position of women in the first century AD was not such as to make it at all likely that they presided. But in many societies in the mid-1980s the position is already different and women in the rest of the world can look forward to further progress. Since it is very widely agreed that Paul's insistence that women should not go bareheaded or teach in the congregation is not permanently authoritative, in the future the question 'Who can preside at the eucharist?' – a question not handled at all in the New Testament – is not likely to be answered by 'Men only.' The suggestion that women are unable to 'represent' Christ, in so far as the president of the eucharist represents him, is not likely to find widespread favour among those who remember the women saints and who know the quality of the women clergy where they exist. The suggestion that women ought not to exercise authority will seem unconvincing to people who know that a woman can be a highly competent and much-feared prime minister even during the twentieth century and even in a country as conservative as India, Sri Lanka, Norway or Britain. And the suggestion that if they are ordained women will betray the truth represented by the image of God as 'Father' in favour of some new cult of a fertility goddess will not impress those who remember how much solidly Christian teaching women give and have given in all the Christian centuries. Arguments against the equality of women and men in the church which can still be heard in the 1980s are likely to sound very strange in the centuries to come.

Realism demands an answer to world poverty which is more complex than simply blaming the rich nations. The answer to the population explosion – which was caused not by the evils of colonialism but by the progress which has reduced infant mortality – involves, on a massive scale, the addition of contraceptives to the spread of hygiene and medicine. Although as people become more prosperous they tend to have smaller families (as has been dramatically demonstrated in newly industrialised countries such as South Korea), it is not safe to rely on 'restraint' or on 'nature' to control births. How can that be safe, when the world population in the 1980s is almost five times what it was in the 1880s and is expected to double by the 2080s? At the fourth UN-sponsored population conference, in Mexico City in 1984, representatives of the developing nations, previously hard to convince, answered that question decisively. And a realistic answer to the dismaying problem of the poverty now afflicting overgrown populations is also clear – although hard. It involves the addition of appropriate government and of appropriate technology in agriculture and industry to the impact already made by modernisation.

The voices from the poorer nations which are realistically hopeful are voices which call for self-reliance. The local society needs to be restructured politically so that peasants and workers have far more of a stake in its development. The local culture needs to encourage hard and enterprising work. The local government needs to practise honest and efficient administration and to put the welfare of the people, specially food production, above the elitism of what often passes for 'modern progress' and above the militarism of 'national security'. Above all, education in many shapes – through the media and the religious bodies as well as through classes in colleges or schools or out among the people – needs to awaken the people to a sense of their own dignity and ability, producing tough adults who will organise, campaign, strike and vote. Those who are privileged, inside and outside the poorer countries, are rightly challenged to make an 'option for the poor'. They have a moral obligation to allow the poor a fair chance in life – which in developing countries means higher taxes for the rich and tighter controls for foreigners, and which in industrial nations means the lowering of the tariff and quota walls which keep out food and manufactures produced by poorer nations. But the 'option' most needed by the poor is an option in their own favour. To be liberated, they must first believe in their own capacity for freedom. To prosper, they must believe that they can earn their own prosperity. Despite much suffering and many mistakes, the people of China have begun to show the world how a nation can save itself. The best contribution which Christians in rich countries can make is to applaud this development – and to encourage it by urging the acceptance of the economic consequences in the shape of changed international trade. The negative plea that rich countries should consume less, often heard in the churches, is moral only on the surface. Normally, the truly moral action is to consume what is healthy, what one can pay for and what fits into the prosperity of all nations. When in the recession of the 1970s industrial production was cut back world-wide, world food prices fell because there was less demand. The results were that the richer nations' farmers had to be subsidised and protected against international competition at the expense of the taxpayers – and exporters in the poorer nations experienced disaster. In the tough world which economists analyse, the poor need the rich who can pay well in free trade between the nations.

Realism seems to say something essentially similar about the poor in those countries where (for the first time in history) they are the minority, perhaps a quarter instead of three quarters as still in the Third World. Fearful losses have been inflicted on the poor of the industrial nations by the succession of the industrial revolutions. Sucked into the cities as cheap labour, they have been spewed out of the industrial system when it has been more profitable to use machines. Kept alive by modern medicine, they have been made lonely and unhappy by the modern breakdown of family life. Made aware by TV of the world's luxuries and glories, they have been imprisoned in a decaying ghetto. Rightly it is often argued that their plight needs government action, which means public expenditure out of taxation. But short-term handouts cannot be the main answer. Not only are they often hard to argue for against the short-term self-interest of the taxpayer. More important is the self-respect of the poor. What is needed is a whole vision of a postmodern society which, knowing that it has no real alternative if it is to be reasonably harmonious, will discover an economically secure and a psychologically strong place for those who do not have the skills needed by the current industrial processes. There are many things which such people can do to help themselves and to help their communities. Once such a vision is accepted as the public philosophy, solutions in the terms of economics can be found – for example, in the use of taxes to create jobs or to pay wages. If the economics of the future is to be the economics of machine-made abundance, a society with that wealth must surely be able to afford to restore work to the working class.

All that seems to be realism about poverty. It needs to be admitted by those who make their protests on behalf of the poor. But how much more needs to be admitted by those, including many Christians, who have willingly or unwillingly been citizens of nations conspicuous for indifference to the poor! Here is the value of the movement for a radically simpler lifestyle as a sign of identification with the poor. It is not sensible to advocate that any whole nation should become poorer. But individual self-denial as a sign is a different matter. It seems probable that future generations will compare it with the older discipline of fasting and with the vocations of monks, nuns or missionaries to embrace poverty. Christians who deny themselves luxuries in order to express a vision are not arguing in terms of what nations ought to do in their trading relationships. They witness in a style which goes deeper and further than any discussion of economics. They signal the hope that humanity can combine to build a world without the present flagrantly unjust contrasts between the poor and the privileged, between the nations and within every nation. Their protest against selfishness is needed as the vision arises of a world in which the priority is given not to short-term profits but to poor people's self-reliance, self-respect and self-fulfilment.[4]

Sincere Christians concerned to secure justice for women can agree with the realists that there are limits to what can be done by legislation or by the pressure of opinion favouring 'equality' – limits caused by

biology and psychology. For it is true that many women are happy to
make the loving care of a man and of children the chief interest in
their lives. Because of this they are willing to sacrifice careers and
inconvenience employers. The love which rewards them in their
families means more to them than any money. They are not fully
represented by women who are eager to compete in the marketplace,
to argue in conferences and to rise to the top of professions. In their
view, the man-hatred expressed by a few feminists is itself a sign of the
sickness of North American or European society. Women who are
glad to be women are often also glad to put a lot of their love into
unpaid work – which is likely to become increasingly the experience
of men. And all that needs to be admitted by feminists, if the aim is
women with self-respect. But how much more needs to be admitted
by Christians who cling to a male-dominated church and even to a
masculine God in a world where women, flattered in songs, are in
reality exploited like cattle! And how important is the vocation of
another creative minority, the Christian feminist movement! In many
nations in the 1980s women are almost always restricted by male
employers to low-paid jobs, are not given equal opportunities for
education, and are expected by men to take care of all the menial
chores. Women have too little personal status, in law and in public
opinion. They are not given the freedom to own property or even to
own their bodies; the number of children they are to rear is decided
for them. Their marriages are often arranged for them and are
sometimes hellishly loveless. And the vision arises of an alternative: a
society in which women are not flattered but treated seriously and
equally.

Towards the end of the twentieth century we are living in a time
when, longing to make a world of justice for all women and men but
by his own choice depending on human cooperation, God cries 'like a
woman in labour, whimpering, panting and gasping' (Isaiah 42:14) –
and when the Son of Mary, longing to gather them 'as a hen gathers
her brood under her wings' (Matthew 23:37), again announces good
news to the poor and to women. In our time the divine patience still
resembles a housewife's as she sweeps a whole floor to find a coin, or a
cook's as she uses a little yeast to leaven a great quantity of flour. But
ours is an age when a liberation from many forms of oppression is
being inspired by the wisdom of the Spirit of God – and the fact that
'wisdom' and 'spirit' are feminine nouns in Hebrew is a little reminder
of the infinitely more important fact that the feminine half of humanity reflects the Motherly Father's character of patient love. In such a
time there is no real option for the church if the church is to pursue its

own often expressed ambition to serve God. After many centuries when it was something very different, the Christian church has to become more and more fully the church of the poor and the church of women.[5]

Two types of faith

As I attempt to offer 'educated guesses' about Christianity in the years ahead, I find myself compelled to acknowledge that there is a difference between two types of faith. These two types may be seen in the Bible and in the first centuries of the church; in Christianity's American popularity; in its encounters with Africa and Asia; in its responses to the secularisation of Europe; in all the islands and territories where it has begun to be rooted. The difference has been expressed by historians, sociologists and theologians in a variety of ways. Here faith delights to be different; there it takes on the colour of the environment. Here it is totally committed; there it includes doubts and hesitations. Here it is static; there it is ready for an experiment and pleasantly excited by a novelty. Here it bows down before a mystery; there it tries to solve a problem. Here it is a closed system; there it is still open to many influences from the surrounding culture, whether Hindu, tribal, secular or other. Here it relies ultimately on divine revelation; there it relies ultimately on human experience. Here it is obedient to an institution; there it knows no court of appeal higher than the individual's conscience. Here it appeals to written authorities, whether in the Bible or in the church's tradition (Kant's 'heteronomy'); there it acknowledges no authority greater than truth or goodness as perceived by the individual (Kant's 'autonomy'). Here it deduces consequences from a system of doctrine; there it seeks to understand situations which are often felt to be unprecedented and ambiguous. Here Christianity is a creed accepted or rejected as a whole; there it is a way of life slowly discovered by personal exploration. Here it offers peace of mind, and from that springs the will and the energy to pass this peace to others in evangelism; there it restlessly and tentatively seeks truth and is shy in intruding on the searches which others must make for themselves. And these two types of faith inspire two ways of hearing the teaching of Jesus himself. To some Christians he is the Lord, the founder of the church, the lawgiver, the teacher with a total authority. But as others hear him, he is a man of mysteries and sorrows who teaches in parables which – like his life as a whole – provoke either uncomprehending hostility or a profoundly personal insight; so that he leaves behind not dogmas but disciples, not a new code of belief and behaviour but a vision, a hunger, a thirst and a rebellion.

Similar types exist in other religious traditions. In my short studies I have mentioned the contrast between Hinduism as a complete civilisation with many divinities, temples, myths and rituals and Hinduism as a mysticism beyond all 'names and forms'; between Buddhism as an elaborate tradition and the repudiation of all authorities in Zen; between the rigours of Islamic law and the charismatic informality of the Sufis; between Orthodox Judaism and the unorthodox searches of individual Jews. But in the churches and other Christian movements, both types are specially strong. On the one hand, Christianity has shown itself to be capable of developing a particularly formidable institutionalism and systematisation. Although there have been frequent splits and clashes between the churches and other movements because of disagreements about what is the right institution or system, it has been normal for most of the most loyal adherents of the different churches to share a common character. They all need to depend on clear and confident guidance and they all believe that the only effective style of evangelism is one where the proclamation of the true religion and the true church is unhesitating and uncomplicated. What they want, and what they think others want, is certainty. On the other hand, Christianity has from its beginnings nurtured an uncommon number of people who have rebelled against the external authorities which seemed to threaten their own integrity. These Christians have usually not seen any need to attend the clergy's ceremonies very often or to take much notice of the clergy's teaching; or if they have themselves been clergy, they have made loud protests against any notion that true religion could be imposed from above.

It seems certain that for many years to come each of the main faiths of humanity will retain a hard conservative core which will successfully resist 'absorption' or 'compromise'. But I have given some reasons for expecting that each of these faiths will have to rely more on experienced reality and less on inherited tradition – a change which will increase the possibilities of dialogues with Christians, possibly resulting in the revision of convictions. And now as I consider the main forms of Christianity, I find it difficult to believe either that conservatism will disappear or that it will stop a ferment of rethinking.

In the 1980s it often seems that only conservative religion prospers. That is obviously the appearance of, for example, Islam. Among Christians, Catholicism and Protestantism alike seem to be rejecting 'liberalism', and Eastern Orthodoxy is apparently content to conserve. I need not repeat the explanation that in a time of change and confusion this kind of stability including an element of nostalgia is attractive. Nor need I restate the well known fact that religion makes a suitable rallying point for conservatives since an attitude of humble dependence on some stability must always be present whenever anyone worships any reality believed to be divine, holy and eternal. All religion has such changelessness at its heart. Nor need I stress the strengthening of the position of an unchanging religion in a society by the use which can be made of it in the backward-looking causes of racism (anti-Western as well as anti-black, anti-Arab as well as anti-Jew), nationalism, provincialism and tribalism. Many psychological and sociological factors help to explain why strong religion is often conservative. But there is also a religious reason for this. Conservative religion, precisely because it encourages an attitude of awestruck dependence on God (or sometimes on the ultimate reality understood impersonally), appeals to people in whom the religious sense is particularly strong. Sensing the presence of the eternal and all-holy reality in whom (or in which) are the depth of truth and the height of beauty, the combination (it is often believed) of sovereign power with compassionate love, such people do not wish to question or to argue. They 'take off their shoes'. They 'repent in dust and ashes'. They are content to adore and when they rise from their worship their wish is to obey the command which they have heard: the command to be pure with that purity. Essentially that is what 'revelation' means to the best of those who are conservative in religion. That is why they submit to 'authority' with a devout 'faith' and that is why they love the 'tradition' through which they have been granted this glimpse of a transcendent glory. In brief, conservative religion can be a religion for those who, feeling acutely that they are sinful, ignorant and mortal, become saints in the eyes of their contemporaries.

I have observed – and read in history – how this type of religion can feed not only psychological and social attitudes which I regard as unhealthy, and not only a fundamentalism which I think is plainly untrue, but also minds and lives which seem to me worthy of great respect (and in my case envy). A concern for peace, for example, or a concern for the poor, if inspired by this kind of faith, may well be more courageous and more enduring than a concern which depends merely on a fashionable trend among those who think of themselves as being 'progressive'. Even conservative Christians in Latin America, whether Catholic or Protestant, although they seem to be tragically wrong in opposing progress, may be making a contribution to Christianity by preventing its shallow identification with 'socialism'. Even fundamentalists in the USA may have a value in that they draw attention to elements in the Bible which are not easily packaged into the *Reader's Digest* consensus about the American way of life. Christian conservatives in Africa or Asia may be the ones who preserve something in Christianity which would get lost if there were to be too quick an agreement with another religious tradition. And as Christians respond to the challenge of secularisation felt so painfully both in 'liberal' Western Europe and in Communist Europe or China, there may be a need of the insistence that the God whom Christians have seen in the face of Jesus is not merely the God seen in the processes of nature as described by science – and is not merely the God seen in the triumphs of the revolution of the proletariat when under the 'correct' Marxist leadership.

However, other pressures are also to be seen as the twentieth century of the Christian era draws towards its close. The many pressures which make for change are not leaving the great religious traditions unaffected. People who look to meditation, worship and a strong moral tradition to provide an island of stability in an ocean of change also have to swim in that ocean; they cannot always be isolated from modernity. And people who are devout in the exercise of their religious instincts are also becoming educated in the modern disciplines of science and history, just as they are becoming liberated in the modern freedoms of political, economic or sexual life; they cannot always escape thinking and deciding for themselves. Knowledge and the liberty to apply it to religion are in the air which modern people breathe, whether or not secularisation results. An American sociologist, Peter Berger, put his finger on it in the title of his book of 1979: *The Heretical Imperative.* I have pointed out these 'liberal' tendencies when briefly describing various powerful movements in contemporary religion. Now I want to watch these tendencies at work in the discussion about what constitutes essential Christianity – and at work also in the changing characters of contemporary Christianity's two most powerful embodiments, Catholicism and Evangelicalism.[6]

The apostolic faith and its expressions

Everywhere it is, and will remain, a question for Christians how they can restate their message in a new context of life and thought without falling into 'syncretism' – the surrender of the heart of Christianity in order to please non-Christians. How can the folk religion of Latin America, which has been analysed as 'Christopaganism', be brought back to the Bible? How can the religion of the USA be also the religion of Jesus Christ? How can the liberation theology of Latin America, or the new Chinese Christianity, avoid sprinkling holy water on Marxism? How can an African Christianity be more Christian than is Voodoo in Haiti or Umbanda in Brazil? How can an Indian or Muslim or Jewish Christianity preserve the unique claims of Christ? How can Christianity in Japan, if it is to be renewed, be more than one of the new religions? How can Christians in a secular Europe be more faithful to the gospel than were the 'German Christians' who welcomed Nazism?

It is surely not surprising that Christians have found this question of syncretism, with its many sub-questions, so very difficult. Nor is it surprising that the answer has so often come by hardening the particular form of Christianity which has a Christian's allegiance. In all the contexts which I have briefly looked at in this book there has been a conservative response among Christians who are sensitive to the great danger of syncretism. In modern as in ancient times, many Christians have believed it to be their duty to prefer the narrow road – and they have felt no great shame when accused of a narrow mind. Basically that explains why there are fundamentalists in the USA, why the devout in Latin America often think liberation theology too political, why Chinese Catholics have retained the Latin language, why many African Evangelicals persist in rejecting most of their own tribal inheritance, why most Indian Christians are far from eager to continue or to adopt Hindu customs, why Japanese Christians are suspicious of Shinto and Buddhism or Egyptian Christians of Islam, and why the confrontation with Western secularism has so often been thought to demand a faith and a courage no less persistently inflexible than the defiance of the martyrs under the persecutions in the Soviet Union.

Yet the conservative response is not the only response which seeks to be faithful to the gospel – and many conservative Christians are among those who recognise that the gospel itself demands a degree of flexibility when a new culture becomes the context within which the good news of Christ must be told. Since the gospel is good *news*, there is built into the very idea of 'the gospel' the need to communicate. Evangelists have to understand the people who are being invited to understand what is new. If they speak or live in a way that does not communicate, they do not pass on the news.

A conference on 'Salvation Today' convened by the World Council of Churches at Bangkok in 1973 faced the challenge of 'culture', meaning a people's style of life. 'Culture,' it was said, 'shapes the human voice that answers the voice of Christ.' And it was asked: 'How can we responsibly answer the voice of Christ instead of copying foreign models of conversion . . . imposed, not accepted?' It was seen that different peoples had different ideas of what mattered in 'salvation'. At about the same time a roughly similar recognition of the importance and variety of humanity's cultures came from Pope Paul VI (in *Evangelii Nuntiandi*) and from an international congress of Evangelicals in Lausanne. But continuing reflection has persuaded many Christians that *all* 'models of conversion' are shaped by cultures which are foreign to the peoples being reached. No evangelist can leave behind his own culture any more than he can step out of his skin. He will try to echo the 'voice of Christ' as faithfully as possible – but he will do so in his own accent, so that the 'voice of Christ' is mingled with, say, the voice of America (or the voice of Rome or of Byzantium). The motto of the Lausanne Congress, 'Let all the earth hear his voice,' must always result in the world hearing many voices from many cultures as the gospel is transmitted from place to place and from generation to generation. So the question is inescapable: What binds all Christians together? What is essential to the gospel?

The simplest answer is to say that only comparatively unimportant details of the life and teaching of the church need be, or can be, adjusted to a particular place or time. That answer is found at its purest and deepest in Eastern Orthodoxy – and not only within the Soviet Union. In response to Roman Catholicism as defined in the 1870s the Eastern patriarchs robustly declared: 'Among us novelties cannot be introduced by patriarchs or councils, for the guardian of religion is the whole body of the Church, that is, the people who desire to conserve its faith unchanged.' In 1973–81 representatives of the Orthodox church met with the theologians representing the Old Catholics (a much smaller body which had split from the Roman Catholics, protesting against innovations about a hundred years previously). These delegates based a strongly conservative agreement about the nature of the church on some words spoken by a saint, Cyril of Jerusalem, in the fourth century: 'The church is called catholic because it extends all over the world; because it teaches universally and completely one and all of those doctrines which ought to come to the knowledge of humanity, concerning things both visible and invisible, heavenly and earthly; because it brings into subjection to godliness the entire human race, governors and governed, learned and unlearned.' The meeting also agreed that it was 'false and unacceptable' to believe that none of the present divided churches can be regarded as 'a genuine and essentially complete representation of the true Church'. On the contrary, 'from the day it was founded right down to our own days, the true Church, the one, holy, catholic and apostolic Church, has gone on existing without any discontinuity wherever the true faith, worship and order of the ancient undivided Church are preserved unimpaired as they are reflected in the definitions and canons of the seven Ecumenical Councils and the acknowledged local synods, and in the Church Fathers'. Elsewhere it is said that the unity of the church is not abolished 'so long as the local churches maintain pure and undefiled the faith transmitted to them from the Lord through the apostles'. This joint Orthodox/Old Catholic Commission 'gives heresy and schism the appropriate significance and regards communities which continue in heresy and schism as in no sense workshops of salvation parallel to the true visible Church' – while also believing that 'the divine omnipotence and grace are present and operative wherever the departure from the fulness of truth in the one Church is not complete'.[7]

But such an answer does not convince all thoughtful Christians. The picture of the Catholic church painted long ago by the eloquence of Cyril of Jerusalem is hard to reconcile with the realities of churches divided and deeply influenced by different cultures. For example, in Jerusalem patriarchs, archbishops and bishops preside over communities each of which has its own merits and limitations. To say that the representation of 'the true Church' in one of these churches is 'genuine' is not necessarily to say that it is 'complete'. To say that 'heresy and schism' are evil is not necessarily to condemn churches which have thought it right to develop their teaching and their organisation after the date of the last of the seven ecumenical councils acknowledged by the Orthodox (787). And to admire those councils is not necessarily to agree that they maintained without any change the teaching of Jesus and his apostles 'pure and undefiled'.

It is no accident that much of the reassessment of 'Catholic' orthodoxy in the twentieth century has been expressed in a dialogue with a theologian of the nineteenth, John Henry Newman. In his *Essay on the Development of Christian Doctrine* (1845), Newman put his finger on the decisive point that development of a certain kind is necessary to Christianity's vigour. 'It is indeed sometimes said that the stream is clearest nearest the spring,' he wrote. 'Whatever use may be made of this image, it does not apply to the history of philosophy or belief, which on the contrary is more equable, and purer, and stronger when its bed has become deep, and broad, and full . . . In a higher world it is otherwise, but here below to live is to change, and to be perfect is to have changed often.' While an Anglican, Newman had come to see that what was then the standard Anglican appeal to the teaching of 'the Primitive Church' was nothing but a 'paper religion'. A living faith could not be sustained solely by what had been agreed in the first few centuries: that was too insubstantial. Primitive Christianity had been developed by the seven ecumenical councils – but not even those councils could provide adequate nourishment in the nineteenth century. This conviction led Newman to become a Roman Catholic, for it seemed to be only the Church of Rome that convincingly claimed to be a school of holiness (always Newman's supreme concern), to have had a relationship with the whole Christian world (and Newman was ahead of his time in rejecting the dominance of religion by nationalism), and to have come down on the right side in all the controversies aroused by heretics. He was well aware of criticisms that the Church of Rome had itself erred by innovating; he had made many such criticisms himself. But he now concluded that the doctrinal developments in Rome had been only 'consolidations or adaptations'. 'Doctrine', he now maintained, 'is where it was, and usage, and precedence, and principle, and policy.' For the Church of Rome had never contradicted its own previous teaching – one test of a true development of doctrine. And its 'consolidations or adaptations' had exhibited other essential 'notes', defined by him as 'preservation of type, continuity of principle, power of assimilation, logical sequence, anticipation of the future, conservative action on the past, chronic vigour'. It had been the 'infallible expounder' needed by a Christianity which must develop and which, in the wrong hands, could develop wrongly.

So Newman thought, on the eve of his submission to the Church of Rome. But he and others continued to ponder the question: What is Christianity's right and healthy development? Newman came to feel many reservations about the Vatican's performance in his time and many later Roman Catholic theologians have more openly voiced dissatisfaction, sharing to some extent the objections traditionally made by the Eastern Orthodox, the Protestants and the Anglicans. In 1845 Newman, it seems clear, had put his finger on the essential question – but not his hand on the complete answer.

In 1975 the World Council of Churches (with Orthodox and Old Catholic participation) embarked on a study programme considering 'Apostolic Faith Today'. The starting point has been the Nicene-Constantinopolitan creed of 381, well described (by J. N. D. Kelly) as 'one of the few threads by which the tattered fragments of the divided robe of Christendom are held together'. In recent international theological dialogues, the representatives of many churches – not only Orthodox and Roman or Old Catholic, but also Anglican, Lutheran, Methodist and Reformed churches – have stated that their churches 'accept' this venerable creed. My own position, if I may mention it, is one of acceptance. On many hundreds of occasions I have gladly led a congregation in the recital of the creed in order to express our commitment to the 'one holy, Catholic and apostolic Church' and to its faith. It is surely understandable that there should be an alarmed reaction to any line of thought believed to be suggesting that the creed should be revised or replaced. Certainly no new creed could have a similar authority unless it were to be endorsed by a council as widely representative of Christians as the councils of Nicaea and Constantinople were in 325 and 381.

But there are great difficulties also in any suggestion that the creed of 381 can provide the basis for the common 'confession' of the 'apostolic faith' in the twentieth century and in the ages to come. Some of the problems surfaced in a 1982 report which the Faith and Order Commission of the World Council of Churches has adopted, setting out the questions to be tackled in any 'explication' of the old creed. Others have appeared in the course of the commission's other work up to August 1985.

Not all the questions debated by modern theologians were included in this report. In a world full of disorder and suffering, in what sense is God 'almighty'? (The difficulty of this question is partly eased if the better translation 'sovereign' is used for the Greek *Pantokrator*, 'All-Ruler' for 'Almighty' suggests that God could do anything.) Can God the Father be known outside Christianity? Can God also be called the Mother? What is the real relationship between the Father and the Son, indicated in the creed by the philosophical term 'of one substance' (or 'Being')? Is the ultimate principle of unity in the trinity to be found in the 'substance' or 'person' of the Father or in the relationship of the three? What, indeed, do these terms 'substance' and 'person' mean now? What is indicated by the picture-language 'begotten from the Father before all ages' and 'sits on the right hand of the Father'? Is it meaningful to say that 'all things came into existence' not only through the Father's self-expression or Word but through 'one Lord, Jesus Christ', the human form of the Word? How literally need a Christian understand the statement that 'he came down from heaven'? Is birth without a human father necessarily believed if it is held that 'he was incarnate from the Holy Spirit and the Virgin Mary'? Is belief in the empty tomb vital to the belief that 'he rose again'? What is the nature of the salvation achieved by Christ 'for us men'? What must be believed about the glory in which 'he will come again' – or about 'the resurrection of the dead and the life of the world to come'? How 'charismatic' or dramatic are the gifts of the Holy Spirit?

The 1982 report did not notice the absence from the creed of 381 of any reference to the Old Testament – apart from the belief that the Holy Spirit 'spoke through the prophets' – and of any reference at all to the life of Jesus between 'he became man' and 'he was crucified for us under Pontius Pilate'. And the report can be said to have been too diplomatic when dealing with the controversies which did preoccupy those who accepted the creed in ancient times. It did not argue theologically for the abandonment of the *filioque* clause (that the Holy Spirit 'proceeds from the Father and the Son'), which was added in the West to the indignation of the East. Instead the report tamely 'proposed to use the original Greek text of the Nicene Creed, without thereby prejudging in any way the theological views of the churches on this issue'. It was also timid when glancing at the excommunications and anathemas which the churches have hurled at each other in breach of the spirit of the Christian gospel. It suggested merely: 'Without necessarily dissociating themselves from those judgements as such, the churches might perhaps discover that they do not apply to those other churches as they are at present. Perhaps particular condemnations never applied to the basic intentions of the positions that occasioned them.'

But despite this avoidance of many necessary theological tasks, the 1982 report produced a formidable list of agenda showing where current discussion is lively. 'How shall we understand the relation of scripture and the creed?' The creeds of the early Christian centuries 'intended to convey a summary of the central teaching of the scriptures' but were 'dependent on the culture, the needs and the situations of the time' – so that 'not everything is said explicitly' in the creed of 381, where 'certain affirmations came into focus for historical reasons'. In the twentieth century some Christian traditions give a 'central and decisive role' to this creed, 'not only in its substantial content but even in its wording', but others 'might value the creed above all as a procedural model for a task which needs to be accomplished even anew, namely the confession of the faith in particular circumstances and with the conceptual and linguistic tools available at the time'.

The report then outlined the kind of questions which a 'contemporary explication of the Nicene faith' would need to address. 'What does faith in one God mean for human community torn by poverty, militarism, racism?' How do Christians explain the creed to those who 'charge us with having surrendered the unity of God' – or to those who 'consider God to be a human creation' – or to those who, 'venerating Jesus, consider him to be a mere human being'? 'How are we to explicate to present-day men and women in the many relationships of their lives that it is this incarnation that provides meaning for human life? . . . How do we proclaim God's coming into human suffering on the cross, strengthening and empowering as well as consoling those who are oppressed by sin and evil? . . . How do we make clear in our twentieth-century world that this cross and this resurrection lie at the roots of a new life? . . . By what means do we recognise that the same Spirit is speaking today who spoke through the prophets? . . . How can we bear witness to this community of faith as a liberating and reconciling people of God, confessing one faith and one baptism, sharing one table, and hospitable to all, especially to each other's members and ministers? . . . How can we today share in a reconciliation and redemption among women and men, among persons of all races and classes, which is appropriate to the costliness of God's forgiveness of us all in Christ? . . . How can we explicate a Christian hope, rooted and grounded in eternal life with God, which addresses urgent human problems, which illumines human suffering and persecution, which clarifies and judges human utopias in the light of God's coming kingdom?'[8]

All these questions – those which the 1982 report stated, and those which it avoided – are as tough as they are important. It is greatly to the credit of the World Council of Churches that its Faith and Order Commission has been tackling them with courage and competence. Light may be expected from this source. But it seems improbable that Christians will ever be able to agree completely about the right answers and it is also to the credit of the commission that it shows no sign of attempting to achieve this. A problem can look very different when it is viewed inside a situation where it seems a matter of life or death and when it is viewed from a distant shelter; when it is viewed through the spectacles of an adventurous temperament and when it reaches the vision through the dark glasses of habitual conservatism. Thus there will be some Christians to whom science matters almost supremely, and others who think little of it; some who are at home in a world of traditional religion and others who find great difficulty in understanding it. Equally sincere Christians will differ in their convictions about the extent to which 'reinterpretation' is needed in order to make sense in one or other of these contexts: some will hold that the only 'restatement' needed is not interpretation but proclamation.

This disagreement need not be regarded as a disaster. Unless one is able to believe that the theology of one place and one time has captured the mystery of God in a formulation which now has to be made compulsory everywhere, it makes no sense to expect all the theologies of Christians to be uniform. Unless one is able to believe in a God who excludes from eternal life any of his children who before dying were unable in endorse a theological formula, 'salvation' does not depend on belief in any creed. So the Christian can accept without dismay the fact that the theologians have failed to find a completely and permanently adequate formulation of the 'essence' of Christianity – the foundation to which all the rest is superstructure, the centre to which all the rest is circumference, the spirit to which all the rest is body. Amid the battles waged by Protestants against Catholics and against each other during the sixteenth and seventeenth centuries, the distinction was often made between the 'fundamental articles' of Christian faith and minor or 'indifferent' matters (Melanchthon's *adiaphora*), and some attempts were made to get Christians to agree on the fundamentals, leaving other matters to be regulated locally. In 1626 Peter Mederlin produced a phrase which has deserved its modern fame: 'Unity in what is necessary, liberty in what is doubtful, love in everything.' But it was never possible to reach agreement as to precisely which 'articles' in the faith were necessary because fundamental. There were fierce disputes between Protestants. Even leading theologians working on this theme in one place, Western Europe, and in one time, the 'early modern' period of 1800–1950, have failed to reach agreement or even contact. Thus the quest of Schleiermacher produced results very different from the quest of Newman; and Karl Barth's theology of the 'Word of God' was again different. The differences were not due merely to problems of communication (although it was a loss that Newman knew no German and therefore was not familiar with the thought of Schleiermacher, while Barth did not care to read much English and therefore ignored Newman). When the liberal Protestant, Adolf Harnack, produced a famous 'essence of Christianity' in lectures delivered in Berlin as 1899 turned into 1900, a Catholic writer (George Tyrrell) compared him with a man who looked for the face of Jesus down a deep well and saw reflected in the water a liberal Protestant face. That has often been quoted as if it were a devastating comment. Actually, it was a statement of what happens in all theologies. As I attempted to outline in my first chapter, already in the first century there was a diversity in perceptions of Jesus. When Paul looked into the depth of his experience he saw the Christ who met his own needs, not the needs of the Jewish Christians of Jerusalem. When John looked into his own deep well, he saw the Jesus of the fourth gospel.

This diversity disappoints many. People who enthusiastically embrace one or other of the interpretations of the gospel often wish that all other Christians would do the same – and they find it difficult to see how with integrity other Christians can fail to do this. People who are unfamiliar with theology often assume that it is a simple business which has been made complicated by the faults of the theologians – and they advocate simple solutions which echo the opinions of those theologians who are regarded by them, however vaguely, as 'authoritative'. Even the World Council of Churches sometimes seems to nurse the illusion that a comprehensive theological consensus is possible, in the same optimistic spirit that has inspired many dreams of a united church. Thus the Vancouver Assembly of the WCC in 1983 was persuaded to approve a statement that 'any common attempt by the churches to express that faith which unites all contemporary churches and all believers of all ages with the apostolic Church would need to be conceived along three lines: first, a common *recognition* of the apostolic faith as expressed in creeds of the undivided Church such as the Apostolic Symbol and especially the Nicene Creed; second, a common *explication* of the faith so recognised in terms understandable today; and third, a common *confession* by the churches today of that same apostolic faith in relation to contemporary challenges to the Gospel'. But in the light of history it is inconceivable that the Nicene Creed will ever be 'recognised' as apostolic, 'explained' as meaningful and 'confessed' in practice by 'all contemporary churches and all believers' without very great diversity. Nor does there appear to be any need to believe that a degree of 'common' agreement greater than the Bible's is the will of the God revealed in the Bible. To some extent the Vancouver report just cited recognised the difficulties. 'Such an achievement,' it said after recording its unrealistic dream, 'is obviously beyond the reach of any commission document or WCC action. It could only be an event given by God and received by the churches themselves.' And the work so far done in the WCC's project wisely recognises the legitimacy of many theological alternatives.

The truth that emerges out of the argumentative history of theology is that disagreements are both inevitable and comparatively unimportant. The heart of Christianity is an experience through which God's reality is apprehended personally. 'I know who it is in whom I have trusted' precedes 'the sound teaching . . . the treasure put into our charge' (2 Timothy 1:12–14) – and it survives the fresh expression of the teaching and the new arrangement of the treasure. Although it is difficult to put into a large number of intellectual propositions which all Christians will accept as a detailed creed, Christianity is a definite experience. Its power can be felt when it receives expression in the realm of art rather than in the realm of law – as in a canticle such as *Te Deum Laudamus*, or in the holy mystery of the Orthodox Liturgy, or in a great Protestant hymn, or in the music of Bach, or in a painting by a master. Best of all, it can be felt in the life of a saint – for example, a martyr in Africa or Latin America. Here is the experience, in the power of God the Spirit, of God's love embodied in Jesus, through whom God is near as Father and every other human being is near as neighbour. That is the 'event' which God has already given and Christians do not need any better event. This experience gives rise to the Jesus prayer, the most dearly loved of all single-sentence prayers in the Orthodox churches, a prayer repeated countless times: 'Lord Jesus Christ, Son of God, have mercy on me a sinner!' The belief that this prayer is in touch with the ultimate reality is the faith that is believed everywhere, always, and by all Christians. And from that belief a great diversity develops healthily.[9]

The emerging Catholicism

What, then, will be the shape of the Christian community which for Christ's sake will honour the poor and the women – and which for the sake of Christian evangelism will welcome a diversity of theologies interpreting the gospel of Christ in many contexts? What will Catholicism be?

To answer, we must first attempt to understand the riddle of Roman Catholicism. With about 850 million baptised members according to the statistics which some prefer, the Roman Catholic Church has about 550 million more members than Protestantism, almost seven hundred million more than the Orthodox and 'Oriental' churches, about 750 million more than the 'non-white indigenous' congregations and about eight hundred million more than Anglicanism. Even if we prefer the more cautious *Britannica World Data*, which counts some 627.5 million nominal or practising Roman Catholics, this church is still the largest. The futures of the smaller churches must to a large extent depend on their relations with this mother or very big sister. And futures thinking in this sphere has the advantage that the Roman Catholic Church has been a highly centralised body. It was transformed by a single conference in Rome, the Second Vatican Council, changing many teachings and practices with a speed and thoroughness inconceivable in any institution with a less tightly organised structure; and although this church is no longer so mono-lithic as it was before the 1960s, it still largely depends for its identity throughout the world on its reactions, totally or partially submissive, to one man. The pope personalises living Catholicism. Although recent popes have repeatedly – and no doubt sincerely – spoken of their 'service', they serve an institution which is still in many ways an absolute monarchy. The Vatican's bureaucracy describes itself as the mere instrument of the pope. The Synod of Bishops is chosen by him and advises him and he has the power to appoint almost all the bishops. Yet to a surprising extent the future of Roman Catholicism is in the 1980s still a riddle. This is because the Second Vatican Council was so ambiguous. After it, the church was no longer a fortress, static, defensive, defiant and isolated – but not yet an army marching in one direction. Twenty years of post-conciliar controversy have shown that both radicals and conservatives can appeal to their favourite passages in the council's teachings. Its constitutions, decrees and declarations amounted to over a hundred thousand words, with almost a thousand footnotes. The contradictions which they con-tained, explicitly or implicitly, have guaranteed an uncertainty which can be expected to last until the Third Vatican Council – if and when that is convened.

The ambiguity was present from the moment when Pope John XXIII conceived the idea of a council. The idea was, as he said, 'completely unexpected'. His own piety was happily traditional and 'obedience and peace' was his motto. As papal nuncio (ambassador) in France he had done his duty in suppressing the experiment of 'worker-priests', agreeing with his masters in the Vatican that the attempt to deploy priests with full-time jobs within a secularised working class was making the priests too unconventional. His appeal for prayer for his council in 1959 ended with an offer of an 'indulgence of ten years to be gained by the faithful who recite the above prayer devoutly and with a contrite heart' – and he never contradicted the traditional doctrine that this meant a remission of ten years from the pains of purgatory after death. His opening speech to the council in 1962 placed it under the auspices of the Virgin Mother of God, and asserted the church's 'unfailing' *magisterium* (teaching authority). The only unusual note was a complaint about 'prophets of doom'. 'We sometimes have to listen, much to our regret, to voices of persons who, though burning with zeal, are not endowed with too much sense of discretion or measure. In these modern times they can see nothing but prevarication and ruin.' But in his optimism Pope John never advocated a revolution. On the contrary, the church's doctrine was taken for granted as 'familiar to all'. All that the council might consider was 'the way in which it is presented' in order that the church might 'show herself to be the loving mother of all, benign, patient, full of mercy and goodness towards the brethren who are separated from her'. So there was calm. But it was the calm before the storm. The reforms which Pope John's council either made explicitly or was understood as encouraging caused more changes to take place in the Roman Catholic Church in the next ten years than in the previous three hundred. The confusion which resulted made the next pope refer to his troubles as a crucifixion and the strain seems to have contributed to the death of Pope John Paul I thirty-three days after his election in 1978.

The assembled bishops, who unintentionally brought about this confusion, thought of themselves in a highly traditional manner. In practice they neither insisted that the papacy and its officials should be reduced in their power over them nor that their own power over priests and laity should be limited. Their Dogmatic Constitution on the Divine Revelation claimed that 'the task of authentically interpreting the word of God, whether written or handed on, has been entrusted exclusively to the teaching office of the Church'. About the Bible, the council said that 'everything asserted by the inspired authors must be held to be asserted by the Holy Spirit'. In particular, 'Holy Mother Church has firmly and with absolute confidence held, and continues to hold, that the four gospels, whose historical character the Church unhesitatingly asserts, faithfully hand on what Jesus Christ, while living among men, really did and taught for their eternal salvation'. The Decree on Ecumenism stated that 'it is through Christ's Catholic Church alone that the fullness of the means of salvation can be obtained'. In the Dogmatic Constitution on the church it was taught that the bishops presided 'in place of God over the flock . . . Just as the role that the Lord gave individually to Peter, the first of the apostles, is permanent and was meant to be transmitted to his successors, so also the apostles' office of nurturing the Church is permanent, and was meant to be experienced without interruption by the sacred order of bishops'. The Decree on Bishops claimed that 'in this Church of Christ the Roman Pontiff . . . by divine institution enjoys supreme, full, immediate and universal authority over the care of souls. Since he is the pastor of all the faithful . . . he holds a primacy of ordinary power over all the churches.' ('Immediate' here means 'direct from Christ' and 'ordinary' means 'by reason of his own office'.) Under the pope, the bishop also has very extensive powers in his diocese; for example, all other men's rights to appoint priests to parishes 'are to be suppressed'.

It was in keeping with this emphasis on tradition and power that during the twenty years after the council the pope personally, or the Vatican acting on his behalf, censored as too liberal the *New Catechism* blessed by the Dutch bishops (1967); rejected the advice of the majority of an expert advisory commission and repeated the prohibition of all artifical contraception (1968); brushed aside pleas from bishops and many others that priests might be allowed a free choice between celibacy and marriage (1969); issued a Declaration on Sexual Ethics which peremptorily dismissed all possible exceptions to the rule that sexual activity must be confined to marriage (1974); declared that the questioning of the idea of 'infallibility' by Europe's most popular theologian, Hans Küng, had made him no longer a teacher of the Catholic faith (1979); issued a warning 'instruction' to Latin Americans using Marxist categories of thought and silenced Brazil's most popular theologian, Leonardo Boff, for a period which might have been longer than a year had he not received such strong local support (1985); and declared one of the most distinguished and well supported theologians in the USA, Charles Curran, to be 'not competent or eligible' to teach Catholic theology because of his views on abortion and divorce (1986). The Vatican discouraged, vetoed or dismissed African and Asian church leaders who wanted to move faster in making Catholicism more thoroughly local in its style. It did very little to give effective authority to the national Bishops' Conferences or to the international Synod of Bishops chosen by the pope to advise him from 1965 onwards without participation by theologians. It took care that, in the appointment of bishops, preference should usually be given to men whom it could trust over men of a type that would probably have been elected had there been a local election. Sometimes the two categories of men coincided – but in the Netherlands, for example, in the USA or often in Latin America, they emphatically did not. Thus selected and instructed the hierarchy became distinctly more conservative than the clergy or laity.

This conservative reaction to change was noticeable at the Synod of Bishops summoned to Rome in 1985 to review the period since 1965, although radical voices were raised there and the final document left many conservatives dissatisfied. Next year, a further 'instruction' about the Latin American theology of liberation was issued. This document was rightly acclaimed as more positive than its predecessor. But it avoided all the sharpness of these theologians' identification with the angry poor. Indeed, it avoided any quotation of the theologians, confining its discussion of Christian freedom to quotations from the Bible, a few European theologians and the Vatican's own previous pronouncements. It was a document many miles away from any Latin American library – or slum.

The most effective expression of the conservative mood was in the addresses delivered by Pope John Paul II in many parts of the world. He was not a man who owed his power entirely to his office. A Pole strong in mind and body, a poet and an actor, a theologian but also a pastor with a human touch, he would have been outstanding had he never been elected to the throne of St Peter. But thanks to his charismatic personality, conveyed by a brave and skilled use of modern methods of travel and communication, the papacy became the focus of Roman Catholicism to a degree not expected when all the publicity surrounded the council and its new thoughts. The council, it now seemed, had been called into being by the optimism of one pope and could easily be eclipsed by the populist conservatism of another.

Yet the new thoughts of 1962–65 remained on record. They had an authority all the greater because never before in the history of the Roman Catholic Church had there been an assembly of bishops so large, so well advised by theological experts and ecumenical observers, so well supported by a worldwide interest in their debates, and so willing to handle a wide range of subjects. (The council even issued a 'decree on the instruments of social communication'.) The riddle of Roman Catholicism is constituted by the impossibility of restoring the pre-1962 status quo after this outburst of creative energy at the council. Indeed, the future Pope John Paul II, who played little part in the council but learnt much from it, wrote a book in Polish in 1972 in order to interpret it to his compatriots. When translated into English in 1980, his book was called *Sources of Renewal*.

He had picked on the theme from the council which had meant the most to him as a bishop called to hold together a church under communism. The council's decree on religious freedom was significant as a proclamation of the rights of man, with an essential part of human dignity consisting in the freedom to seek and worship God with the person's conscience. The council's definition of the church was welcome as a clarification of the importance of the mission or 'apostolate' of each member of the 'People of God': pope, bishop, priest, layman. The leaders of the church must always act together, in 'collegiality' – and its members must always behave acceptably, in 'responsibility'. They must be loyal to the leaders, whose authority rested not on any worldly status but solely on their willingness to serve the people in imitation of the good shepherd and by his commission. And this corporate action by the 'missionary community' must be inspired by the eagerly active participation of the laity in its worship. The need was to 'enrich' the people's faith, to increase their 'consciousness' of redemption, to help them to more 'mature' attitudes through a holiness which would be a kingly self-rule. Not only in the mind of the future pope, but also in the daily life of the Polish church, all these themes were entirely compatible with the support of a strong hierarchy, with a firm doctrinal and moral traditionalism (for example, a devotion to Mary), and with a delight in the 'solidarity' of corporate worship. And it was natural that many other leaders and members of the Roman Catholic Church should be attracted to this understanding of the council's intentions. They have wanted a church renewed but not changed basically. With that in mind the cardinals elected John Paul II as the first non-Italian pope since 1523; and his pontificate shows that his strategy of renewal without radical change has been what is wanted by many bishops, priests and laity dismayed by the disorder unleashed by the council.

But many Catholics, including some bishops, have interpreted the council in a much more radical sense. I have already indicated something of the impact of Vatican II on the USA and Canada. There, the emphasis on the laity as being the Spirit-guided presence of the church in the world produced a rejection of dependence on the clergy, made all the sharper because it coincided with a rejection of American-Irish or French-Canadian conservatism. In many nations the interpretation of the religious life of monks, friars and sisters as a 'sign' to the world, erasing the false distraction between higher and lower levels of holiness, resulted in the religious orders abandoning many customs which had cut them off from the world. The generally positive attitude to the values of the modern world including married sexuality led to the abandonment of the priesthood, or of thoughts of preparation for it, by considerable numbers of men who were now convinced that they could do God's will better as married laymen. The crisis of confidence came over the question of contraception. The council's emphasis that in marriage sex was for love as well as for procreation seemed to hold out hopes that the ban would be relaxed. Many expected it to be – and they included many bishops. When Pope Paul VI refused to relax the ban, many of the laity were in no mood to obey. The clergy, with their morale and prestige already lowered, were left with the unenviable task of dealing with the problem pastorally. In practice that usually meant accepting the lay decision to defy the pope in bed – a decision which hastened the decline of the practice of regularly confessing sins to a priest with a request for moral guidance. About the effects of the council on North America, Western Europe and some other areas between 1965 and 1985, it seems true to say that the destruction of the church's old strength was more conspicuous than any constructive renewal of the kind advocated by John Paul II. John XXIII would have been horrified. Paul VI, who did see the rebellion of clergy and laity, was heartbroken. But more eloquent than the distress in the Vatican was the departure of leading theologians from the priesthood – among the English-writers, Charles Davis in England, John McKenzie in the USA, Gregory Baum in Canada and Peter Kelly in Australia.

In some parts of the world the immediate influence of the council was more conspicuously constructive – although there, too, the necessary abandonment of attitudes which for centuries had been regarded as essential to Catholicism brought confusion and pain. In Latin America the endorsement of social justice by the council and the popes seems to have been intended as backing for the optimistic idea of peaceful cooperation under US economic leadership and without any revolutionary disturbance of the class structure – the idea which the Pearson Commission encapsulated in its 1967 report, *Partners in Development.* But the blessing on social justice could also be interpreted as a cry of angry identification with the poor and as a summons to the involvement urged by a movement such as Christians for Socialism. In Africa and Asia the politeness of the council to the non-Christian religions and the acceptance of non-Western cultural forms in the expression of doctrine and worship were not intended to lead to a 'diversity of theologies': so Paul VI emphasised to the Synod of Bishops in 1974. On the contrary, the decree on the missionary activity of the church affirmed that 'the whole Church is missionary'; that the evangelism of those as yet unreached by the gospel was 'the greatest and holiest work of the Church'; that it was God's plan that the whole human race should form 'one People of God, joined in one Body of Christ'. But the result of the council was the end of the vision of the Catholic church as an island of European-style piety set in a sea of 'native' evil. Africa and Asia could get to heaven without joining the church – and Catholic Africans and Asians at worship could use much of their pre-Christian religious heritage. At the council the bishops who had been born in the Third World were, on the whole, prepared to listen to the articulate Europeans. They were overawed by the proceedings and often uncertain in their command of the Latin which had to be used to speak in public. When they returned to their own countries, most of them showed that their loyalty to Rome and their sense of the universal church had been increased, not diminished, by their experience. But the council had opened itself sufficiently to the sounds and smells of the poverty and piety of the Third World to mean that the control of the church by Europe was broken for ever.

The paradox is that this end to European control was brought about largely through the influence of West European theologians on the council. A number of them had been warned, or had been stopped as teachers, by the Vatican under Pius XII, but the theology which they had persisted in writing was now given access to the minds of some two thousand bishops. Early in the council these bishops realised, mostly to their surprise, that the drafts of statements prepared by the officials of the Vatican were theologically inadequate: they merely repeated dogmatic positions relying on the Vatican's authority and they concentrated on questions of jurisdiction and organisation. The senior bishops who defended the Vatican's conservatism turned out to be too elderly to be effective. Pope John, although an old man, had spent almost all his life outside Rome and was now impatient with the inertia of the bureaucracy over which he had been called to preside against all expectations; and Pope Paul, although a cautious man who had served Pius XII, was highly intelligent, well able to appreciate that the world was bigger and more important than the bureaucracy. But if a comparatively fresh theology was needed, it could not yet be supplied from the Third World. So the gap was filled by the thinking of the European theologians – Chenu, Congar, Daniélou and de Lubac, the Frenchmen anxious to get the church into contact with the world of the laity and with scholarly knowledge; Karl and Hugo Rahner and Hans Küng, the Germans determined that Christian doctrine should measure up to the challenges of educated humanism; the many theologians who were convinced that 'moral theology' must take love, not law, as its basis; the monks and others who had pioneered the liturgical renewal by stressing that Christian worship was the response of the people of God to the word of God. Theirs was the theology which now permeated the council's documents although it did not exclude conservatism.

It was a Bible-based theology. Not only was the Bible quoted plentifully. It was also allowed to shape the council's thought. Thus the Dogmatic Constitution on the Church began with a vision of God's purpose for humanity revealed in the creation and in the Old

Testament, as well as in Christ, making the church 'like a pilgrim in a foreign land' (Augustine of Hippo's phrase) until the 'total splendour' of the end of history. This idea of a pilgrim people was different from the previously frequent glorification of the church as the 'perfect' and even 'divine' society. There were many references to the mystery of God which is dispelled only by his revelation – an approach unlike the neat dogmatism of the textbooks which had been instilled into generations of priests. 'The teaching office of the Church is not above the word of God but serves it, teaching only what has been handed on.' Although the council of Trent had decreed that scripture and tradition deserved equal reverence, this council pointedly refused to say that the tradition of the church was a source of revelation separate from the Bible. Even the authority of the Bible was limited, for the infallible truth to be acknowledged in it is 'the truth which God wanted put into the sacred writings for the sake of our salvation' – a truth proposed and expressed in a variety of ways, depending on whether a text is history of one kind or another, or whether its form is that of prophecy, poetry or some other kind of speech. 'The interpreter must investigate what meaning the sacred writer intended to express and actually expressed in particular circumstances as he used contemporary literary forms.' Thus a charter was given to Catholic biblical scholarship, which since the modernist crisis at the beginning of the century had languished under censorship. And that blessing on the biblical scholars was typical of the council's recognition of what could be contributed to the worship, life and mission of the church by many who were not bishops or not clergy, according to their own free consciences. Symbolically, the 'index' of prohibited books maintained by the Vatican was abolished and the 'Holy Office' which had been the successor to the Inquisition was replaced by a Congregation for the Doctrine of the Faith charged with the duty to encourage sound teaching rather than to seek out error. Even those who were not Catholics or not Christians were now welcomed as collaborators in the church's service to humanity. There was no condemnation even of the communists, who at this time were being invited to dialogues symbolised by Pope John's reception of Soviet leaders in the Vatican.

Two of the most prominent consequences of the council were the disuse of Latin and the recognition of other churches. Both moves were made with many hesitations and qualifications, for they signalled the end of the Counter-Reformation which had been the main movement in Roman Catholicism since the 1560s – but they were made. Although John XXIII strongly defended the use of Latin in an 'apostolic constitution' in 1962, the first 'constitution' published by the council (in 1963) was on the liturgy and it allowed the use of local languages in place of Latin. At first it was envisaged that the central part of the eucharist (the 'canon') would remain in Latin, but it was not long before that restriction was left behind. Indeed, in many parts of the church official enthusiasm for new forms of worship became such that bishops insisted on the exclusive use of the 'vernacular' mass although many worshippers preferred the Latin to which they had become accustomed and ridiculed the clumsiness of the new words, while many priests further shocked traditionalists by their zest in informality, particularly in the use of the guitar and the folk song. The face of Catholicism, as encountered by the laity Sunday by Sunday, had changed almost beyond recognition.

Another dramatic change was the official entry of the Roman Catholic Church into the ecumenical movement. In 1863 Pope Pius IX had condemned 'the very serious error into which some Catholics miserably fall, who think that men who live in error and are strangers to Catholic faith and unity can reach eternal life. This is of course contrary to Catholic faith in an extreme degree (*maxime*).' Such Christians were far worse off than any pagans 'who are affected by invincible ignorance about our most holy religion'. The steps leading up to the formation of the World Council of Churches aroused no sympathy in the Vatican. It was the characteristic stance of Pius XII to call for the 'return' of the Catholic church's 'children' since that church was 'the whole Christ, Head and Body'. Now the churches represented officially by ecumenical observers at the Second Vatican Council found themselves being addressed with 'respect and affection' as 'ecclesial communities'. The decree on ecumenism announced that those 'who believe in Christ and have been properly baptized are brought into a certain, although imperfect, communion with the Catholic Church'. They are 'incorporated into Christ' and are 'brothers in the Lord'. 'Moreover some, even very many, of the most significant elements or endowments which together go to build up and give life to the Church herself can exist outside the visible boundaries of the Catholic Church.' Detailed tributes were paid to the traditions of the Eastern churches not in communion with Rome and in 1965 the pope and the patriarch of Constantinople jointly declared that they 'regret and remove from memory' the mutual excommunications of 1054. But respectful mention was also made of other 'separated brethren'. 'Among those in which some Catholic traditions and institutions continue to exist, the Anglican Communion occupies a special place.' Committing themselves to the ecumenical movement 'under the inspiring grace of the Holy Spirit . . . to attain that fullness of unity which Jesus Christ desires', the bishops exhorted 'all the Catholic faithful to recognise the signs of the times and to participate skillfully' – a participation which was already 'growing daily'. 'There can be no ecumenism worthy of the name,' they said, 'without a change of heart. For it is from newness of attitudes, from self-denial and unstinted love, that yearnings for unity take their rise and grow toward maturity.'

In the twenty years after the council a number of conversations at the world level were held between representatives of the Roman Catholic Church and of other churches. These explored the implications for the churches in their official relationships of what seemed to be a growing 'convergence' or even 'consensus' between the theologians. And as one reviews the conversations together, one sees that a bridge has indeed been built over divisions and even over (as the Methodist-Roman Catholic dialogue noted) 'deep crevasses'. This has proved possible because these fellow Christians have been prepared to listen to each other, asking themselves whether they could not discern behind statements or customs which seemed strange or offensive an intention close to their own or identical with it. But another major influence has been the common willingness to base Christian theology on the Bible interpreted with realistic admissions that the Bible is itself coloured by historical conditions and leads into developments of church life and doctrine as history continues. The importance of the Christian tradition has been acknowledged, particularly by consulting the early centuries before Christianity was divided – but there has been no slavish copying of antique models. It has been seen that the message of the Bible is restated by new generations and new cultures in forms which deserve respect – but which may need to be reformulated in due course for they are human rather than perfect. Such influences have made for careful scholarship, biblical and historical. But they have also encouraged the 'newness of attitudes' which the council advocated. A deeper appreciation of the culturebound realities of the biblical world and of the human facts of history has liberated Christians. They have dared to think out for themselves what it means for them to be loyal in their own day to the teaching of the Bible as a whole and to the experience of the church as a whole.

By going to the Bible together, Roman Catholics and others have been able to find much common ground on which to stand – and it has given them a base for a mission to a world where Christianity as such is increasingly compared both with the non-Christian religions and with the secular ideologies. The church is seen essentially not as an organisation similar to secular governments or corporations but as an organism made by God the Holy Spirit to be *koinonia*, the New Testament's untranslatable Greek word which indicates partnership, fellowship and communion; and leadership in the church is seen not as denomination but as a service to this communion. Faith is seen essentially not as an emotion similar to the feelings about ourselves or other people which psychologists analyse but as a response, corporate as well as individual, to the self-revelation and the saving acts of the perpetually mysterious because transcendent God. These new emphases are to be seen throughout the life and teaching of the Roman Catholic Church since the 1960s. For example, they influenced the radical revision in 1983 of the code of canon law last revised in 1917.

Sharing this approach, Roman Catholic, Lutheran and Anglican representatives have been able to achieve a far-reaching consensus in the understanding of 'justification'. They have, in effect, buried the quarrel of the Reformation about whether a sinner is justified by faith alone or by his works (including his assent to the church's doctrines and practices) which are meritorious. Their 1972 report stated: 'Catholic theologians also emphasize that God's gift of salvation to the believer is unconditional as far as human accomplishments are concerned. Lutheran theologians emphasize that the event of justification is not limited to individual forgiveness of sins, and they do not see in it a purely external declaration of the justification of the sinner. Rather the righteousness of God actualized in the Christ event is conveyed to the sinner through the message of justification as an encompassing reality basic to the new life of the believer.' So the stress is on God's grace, received by faith, demonstrated by love. When in a book of 1957 Hans Küng had argued that there was no need to maintain Protestant objections to Catholic teaching if that teaching were not confined to some polemical phrases adopted by the council of Trent, his theological brilliance had been widely admired – but it had been suspected that it would prove impossible to reconcile the two positions, now as during the sixteenth century. However, the synthesis which he had outlined proved sound when examined suspiciously.

The emergence of agreement can also be seen in the text on *Baptism, Eucharist and Ministry* agreed by the Faith and Order Commission of the World Council of Churches in 1982. The Christian believer is baptised and the meaning of that is, at bottom, what unites him or her with all other Christians – for the meaning is that the believer is united with Christ by the grace of God. Baptism is the sacrament of participation in the life, death, resurrection and mission of Jesus, because it is the recognition of the gracious God coming in Jesus. It is not primarily the naming of an individual. Nor is it primarily the testimony by an individual that he or she has been 'saved' or 'born again'. It is the sign of belonging to the body of Christ, God's 'new creation'. This agreement leaves unanswered the question whether young members of the families of believers can rightly be baptised – but so does the New Testament, and various dialogues and joint congregations involving Baptists have left the question to the conscience of the believer.

The most characteristic act of the baptised is to celebrate the eucharist together and the meaning of the eucharist has been explored in various interchurch dialogues. It is not primarily the devotion of an individual. Nor is it merely a common meal. It is nothing less than the memorial of Christ's self-sacrifice – and in the Bible 'memorial' (*anamnesis*) means nothing less than 'the making effective in the present of an event in the past', a definition endorsed by Roman Catholics and Lutherans. Anglicans and Roman Catholics in dialogue have agreed that 'the Eucharistic memorial is no mere calling to mind of a past event or of its significance, but the Church's effectual proclamation of God's mighty acts'. That does not mean that Calvary can be repeated; this sacrifice was 'offered once for all by Christ and accepted once for all by the Father'. But 'Christ in the Holy Spirit unites his people with himself in a sacramental way so that the Church enters into the movement of his self-offering'. In this context 'the elements are not mere signs; Christ's body and blood become really present and are really given' although this 'does not imply material change'. Many Protestants would hesitate over the use of the word 'become' in that formula because they fear a claim that there is a material change, and in his *Credo of the People of God* (1968) Pope Paul VI reaffirmed traditional doctrine. 'In this sacrament,' he declared, 'there is no other way in which Christ can be present except through the conversion of the entire substance of bread into his Body and through the conversion of the entire substance of wine into his Blood, leaving unchanged only those properties of bread and wine which are open to our senses . . . In the order of reality which exists independently of the human mind, the bread and wine cease to exist after the consecration.' But the Roman Catholic theologians conversing with the Anglicans have agreed that the word 'transubstantiation' indicates that 'God effects a change in the inner reality of the elements' but does not explain 'how the change takes place'. In the 'mystery of the Eucharist' there is, they say, 'an indissoluble unity: Christ giving his body and blood, and the communicants feeding upon them in their hearts by faith'. Methodists conversing with Roman Catholics have reached other agreements. 'Christ, in the fullness of his being, is present in the Eucharist; this presence does not depend on the experience of the communicant, but it is only by faith that we become aware of it. This is a distinctive mode of the presence of Christ; it is mediated through the sacred elements of bread and wine, which within the Eucharist are efficacious signs of the body and blood of Christ.'

Since the most prominent function of the work of the 'presbyter' or 'priest' (the shortened Anglo-Saxon version of the same word) is to preside at the eucharist, agreement about the ordained ministry is greatly eased by agreement about the eucharist. The nature of this ministry is not usually regarded by theologians as a topic very high in what the Second Vatican Council called the 'hierarchy of truths' for the Christian, since the New Testament gives no clear teaching about it. But in these conversations it has generally been agreed that, because so many Christians are convinced that the development of the threefold ministry of bishop, presbyter and deacon was under the guidance of the Holy Spirit, this must be the pattern to be accepted in a future reunion. It is, for example, recommended in *Baptism, Eucharist and Ministry*. But there are no extravagant claims about the 'apostolic succession' of bishops or about the 'character' of the priests and bishops ordained by them.

The claim that bishops as distinct from presbyters were instituted by the apostles is found in the documents of the Second Vatican Council. It was reiterated by the Sacred Congregation for the Doctrine of the Faith, with papal approval, in 1983, as the basis of the doctrine that 'when the Catholic Church imposes hands on those to be ordained and invokes upon them the Holy Spirit, she is conscious of handing on the power of the Lord, who makes the bishops, as successors of the apostles, partakers in a special way of his threefold priestly, prophetic and royal mission. In turn, the bishops impart, in varying degrees, the office of their ministry to various persons in the Church' (*Sacerdotium Ministeriale*). But the claim that the apostles started this way of organising the church has not been pressed in the dialogues with theologians of other churches, because there is no historical evidence for it. Instead it is acknowledged that in later times as in the New Testament 'oversight' (in Greek, *episkope*) can be exercised in churches which do not have bishops, and that in churches which do have them their 'succession' or continuity depends far more on what they teach than on who ordained them. As Roman Catholics have freely granted in their dialogues with Anglicans, Lutherans and Methodists, only these acknowledgements make sense of the complexities and ambiguities of history.

Priesthood, too, has been interpreted with restraint. For example, 'Lutherans and Catholics start from the common conviction that the trend towards the emergence of the special ministry which finds expression in the New Testament is of normative significance for the post-apostolic church'; yet 'when ministers are described as priests in the Catholic tradition, this is to be understood only in the sense that in the Holy Spirit they share in and manifest the one priesthood of Jesus Christ'. The Anglican-Roman Catholic conversations made it clear that although the priest is called by Christ and not merely by the local congregation, he (like the bishop who ordains him) serves 'the word of God' and functions humbly within the total mission of the church which is the body of Christ. And these dialogues have also made it clear that, although it is generally agreed that a threefold 'special ministry' is desirable, no church has yet worked out satisfactorily, either in theology or in practice, an answer to the question: What are bishops, priests and deacons meant to be? The continuing uncertainties come to a head in passionate disagreement about the further question: Is it right to ordain women to these offices?

It has not proved easy to unite or reconcile churches which have this threefold ministry with those which do not. But it has become apparent in interchurch conversations (for example, in the talks held by the Lutherans with Anglicans and Roman Catholics) that there is no longer the old strength in all the old convictions. It used to be taken for granted by episcopalians that there should be no communion with non-episcopal churches, whose ministry was thought to be 'invalid'. That is no longer said with conviction. (The Orthodox churches have not yet moved to a new position, but the main explanation seems to be that they have not yet felt under great ecumenical pressure.) And if it is granted that essentially the same eucharist is celebrated in episcopal and non-episcopal churches, a fuller reconciliation becomes easier to imagine. As *Baptism, Eucharist and Ministry* said, 'today churches are expressing willingness to accept episcopal succession as a sign of the apostolicity of the life of the whole Church. Yet, at the same time, they cannot accept any suggestion that the ministry exercised in their own tradition should be invalid until the moment that it enters into an existing line of episcopal succession. Their acceptance of episcopal succession will best further the unity of the whole Church if it is part of a wider process by which the episcopal churches themselves also regain their lost unity.'

What, then, are the prospects for the reunion of the Roman Catholic Church with other episcopal churches? The Second Vatican Council radically changed the atmosphere in which this question is asked. For example, in his first address to the council as pope, Paul VI referred to the ecumenical observers and to 'the deep sadness we feel at their prolonged separation. If we are in any way to blame for that separation, we humbly beg God's forgiveness and ask pardon of our brethren who feel themselves to have been injured by us. For our part, we willingly forgive the injuries which the Catholic Church has suffered . . .' But it has become clear that the problem of papal authority remains at the centre of the riddle of the future.

The key question confronting the leadership is whether a principle applies to the church which papal encyclicals have repeatedly said applies to the state. This is the principle called 'subsidiarity'. In the teaching of popes since Pius XI, it means that the state should offer help (in Latin *subsidium*) to the family and other associations, and should leave them free in their own spheres, since 'it is an injustice and also a grave evil and a disturbance of right order to assign to a greater and higher association what lesser and subordinate organisations can do' (*Quadragesimo Anno*). Here is an assertion of democracy, or at least of popular participation, against the centralisation of power under Fascism or communism. But this principle has not been matched by much willingness to decentralise within the church. There, the papacy remains in theory an absolute monarchy although in practice it has of course been unable to keep a tight control on a church of between 625 and 850 million people. And for all its talk about 'collegiality' under the headship of 'Peter', the Second Vatican Council did not secure any administrative changes which would thoroughly apply 'subsidiarity' to the life of the church. Crucially, the status of the national episcopal conferences was left ill-defined in relation both to individual diocesan bishops and to the Vatican. Episcopal conferences have been allowed to deal with minor ecclesiastical affairs and also to pronounce on social problems, but Rome has reserved to itself decision-making on questions regarded as crucial, such as marriage for priests or contraception for the married. And powerful voices have continued to assert that no theologically significant body lies between the bishop of Rome and the local bishop.

So in what sense is the church 'infallible'?

The Second Vatican Council limited 'the infallibility with which the Redeemer willed his Church to be endowed in defining a doctrine of faith and morals' to 'the deposit of divine revelation which must be religiously guarded and faithfully expounded'. Since what is authentically revealed by the true God must be true, all Christians can agree that the church when it faithfully receives and expounds the divine revelation is free from error. But when Roman Catholic theologians such as Hans Küng restricted the church's infallibility to this, they were authoritatively disowned because the council went far beyond this. It repeated the teaching of the First Vatican Council (1870) that 'the Roman Pontiff, when he proclaims by a definitive act some doctrine of faith and morals' issues definitions which 'of themselves, and not from the consent of the Church, are justly styled irreformable, for they are pronounced with the assistance of the Holy Spirit, an assistance promised to him in the blessed Peter. Therefore they need no approval of others, nor do they allow an appeal to any other judgement.' This seems a clear repudiation of, for example, the *Declaration du Clergé de France* which in 1682 stated that the judgement of the pope, unless it has received the assent of the church, is not beyond correction. (This position, at the time endorsed by thirty-four French bishops including the indefatigably traditionalist Bossuet, is known as Gallicanism.) The contribution made by the Second Vatican Council was to stress that 'the infallibility promised to the Church resides also in the body of bishops when that body exercises supreme teaching authority with the successor of Peter. To the resultant definitions the assent of the Church can never be wanting, on account of the activity of the same Holy Spirit, whereby the whole flock of Christ is preserved and progresses in unity of faith. But when either the Roman Pontiff or the body of bishops together with him defines a judgement, they pronounce it in accord with revelation itself. All are obliged to maintain and be ruled by this revelation, which, as written or preserved by tradition, is transmitted in its entirety through the legitimate succession of bishops and especially through the care of the Roman Pontiff himself.'

On the face of it this claim about the church's infallibility covers all the definitions of doctrines of faith and morals by popes and by the twenty-one 'ecumenical councils' of bishops recognised by the Roman Catholic Church. Apparently it restricts the church ('the whole flock of Christ') to those who are 'ruled by' these definitions, thus excluding all Christians who are not Roman Catholics; and it excludes the possibility that the popes or bishops will ever be disloyal to the divine revelation, since they alone transmit it and they have access to it even when it is not 'written'. However, in practice the claim is neither so comprehensive nor so exclusive. It has seldom been argued that none of the teaching of the popes or of the councils is reformable.

The Second Vatican Council did not claim infallibility for its own work. It contradicted the teachings of many previous popes, although it did not point this out. It taught that even the writers of the Bible used 'contemporary literary forms' which expressed their meaning 'in particular circumstances'. It also made many positive statements about, for example, the Orthodox churches, which have vigorously rejected claims made by the papacy and by the Roman Catholic councils from time to time in particular circumstances. Thus dogmas were no longer 'truths fallen from heaven' as they had seemed to the papacy in 1907 (*Lamentabili*). The council opened the door to the possibility of reinterpreting the Roman Catholic doctrinal tradition in the context of its historical development – and since 1965 many theologians have entered a realm of uncertainty through that door.

The Anglican-Roman Catholic theological commission propounded ideals for the papacy and for other 'primates' or senior archbishops. 'Primacy fulfils its purpose by helping the churches to listen to one another, to grow in love and unity, and to strive together towards the fullness of Christian life and witness; it respects and promotes Christian freedom and spontaneity; it does not seek uniformity where diversity is legitimate, or centralize administration to the detriment of local churches.' But these theologians acknowledged that 'neither theory nor practice has ever fully reflected these ideals. Sometimes functions assumed by the see of Rome were not necessarily linked to the primacy: sometimes the conduct of the occupant of this see has been unworthy of his office: sometimes the image of this office has been obscured by interpretations placed on it: and sometimes external pressures have made its proper exercise almost impossible.' This commission also affirmed that 'when the Church meets in ecumenical council its decisions on fundamental matters of faith exclude what is erroneous'. But it explained that only the decrees in which the ecumenical councils of the first centuries formulated 'central truths of salvation faithful to Scripture and consistent with Tradition' possessed this authority in both the Roman Catholic and the Anglican traditions; and it explained why. 'The creed which we call Nicene,' it said, 'has been received by the Church because in it the Church has recognised the apostolic faith.'

The commission concluded that through 'universal councils' and 'a universal primate who, presiding over the *koinonia*, can speak with authority in the name of the Church', the church can make a decisive judgement in matters of faith, and so 'exclude error'. But this was qualified. 'The purpose of this service cannot be to add to the content of revelation, but is to recall and emphasize some important truth; to expound the faith more lucidly; to expose error; to draw out implications not sufficiently recognized; and to show how Christian truth applies to contemporary issues.' Even a purpose so restricted is still very wide, so it is stressed that 'all such definitions are provoked by specific historical situations and are always made in terms of the understanding and framework of their age' and that 'neither general councils nor universal primates are invariably preserved from error even in official declarations'. And the commission's final verdict on definitions of doctrine was modest: 'in the continuing life of the Church they retain a lasting significance if they are safeguarding the substance of the faith'.

Unfortunately it is necessary to ask, as other Christians converse with Roman Catholics about the possibilities of agreement and union, whether the 'substance' of the 'apostolic' faith is 'safeguarded' by the only two definitions which have been made by popes in modern times with an explicit claim to infallibility. These definitions concern the Virgin Mary. Previously loved and honoured greatly, during the century and a quarter before the 1960s she came to occupy a place at or near the centre of the devotional life of many Roman Catholics. Her motherly humanity was a relief amid a religion which tended to emphasise the supernatural, the moral and the masculine; and her 'appearances', usually to illiterate girls, were considerably more popular than the dry dogmas of theologians. Her shrines attracted popular enthusiasm and could be the scenes of faith-healing or of fervent patriotism. In European religion she filled a gap left by the flight of the female divinities; at Guadalupe in Mexico her shrine was on the site of a temple to a pagan goddess. But the ecclesiastical authorities had always maintained a certain reserve. The Second Vatican Council declared that the 'Blessed Virgin is invoked by the Church under the titles of Advocate, *Auxiliatrix*, *Adjutrix* and *Mediatrix*. These, however, are to be so understood that they neither take away from, nor add anything to, the dignity and office of Christ the one Mediator.' And the council decided to include its teaching about her in its Dogmatic Constitution on the Church, not making it a separate document as originally recommended.

Later, the Anglican-Roman Catholic commission agreed 'in recognising the unique grace and vocation of Mary, Mother of God Incarnate (*Theotokos*), in observing her festivals and in according her honour in the communion of saints. We agree that she was prepared by divine grace to be the mother of our Redeemer, by whom she herself was redeemed and received into glory.' Many other Christians, for example the Orthodox, would agree with that. Many textbooks and encyclopaedias of doctrine published by Roman Catholics since 1965 show that these careful words, or words very similar to them, are widely thought to be the best way of teaching the faithful, for the words which popes used in days past are thought to have belonged to 'the understanding and framework of their age' rather than to 'the substance of the faith'. This attitude is in sharp contrast with the teaching of Pope Pius XI in 1928 that 'true Christians give exactly the same belief to the dogma of the Immaculate Conception as to that of the Holy Trinity, and to that of the Infallibility of the Chief Pontiff as the Vatican Council defined it as to the Incarnation of our Lord Jesus Christ' (*Mortalium Animos*).

In 1854 Pope Pius IX declared 'that the doctrine which holds that the most blessed Virgin Mary, in the first instant of her conception, by a singular grace and privilege granted by Almighty God in view of the merits of Jesus Christ, the Saviour of the human race, was preserved free from all stain of original sin, is a doctrine revealed by God and therefore to be believed firmly and constantly by all the faithful'. This dogma of the immaculate conception can be understood as an expression of the faith that Mary was 'prepared by divine grace to be the mother of our Redeemer' in terms of a particular understanding of 'original' sin. A century later, human sinfulness was still being described by Pope Pius XII in traditional terms. 'Original sin is the result of a sin committed, in actual historical fact, by an individual named Adam, and it is a quality native to all of us, only because it has been handed down by descent from him' (*Humani Generis*, 1950). 'As a consequence of the fall of Adam the lower faculties of human nature are no longer obedient to right reason, and may involve man in dishonourable actions' (*Sacra Virginitas*, 1954). And it can be understood that when human nature is thus interpreted it seems necessary to believe that the mother of Jesus, who was 'full of grace' or 'most favoured' (Luke 1:28), was 'preserved from all stain of original sin'.

In 1950 Pope Pius XII declared it to be a divinely revealed dogma 'that the Immaculate Mother of God, the ever Virgin Mary, having completed the course of her earthly life, was assumed body and soul into heavenly glory. Hence if anyone, which God forbid, should dare wilfully to deny or call into doubt that which we have defined, let him know that he has fallen completely from the divine and Catholic faith.' This dogma of the 'assumption' (including the perpetual virginity) of Mary can be understood as an expression of the faith that she was 'received into glory'. It was so expressed by a pope who believed that virginity is 'preferable to marriage because it is a very efficacious means for devoting oneself wholly to the service of God'

(*Sacra Virginitas*) and who understood Christ's own glory as the continuation of 'his physical body which, born of the Virgin Mary, now sits at the right hand of the Father' (*Mystici Corporis*). When virginity and resurrection are thus interpreted, it seems necessary, or at any rate natural, to believe that the mother of Jesus experienced neither sexual intercourse nor physical death.

If it is allowed that theologies now largely belonging to history did shape the words used in 1854 and 1870, the way may be open for the Roman Catholic Church to cease to condemn those Christians who cannot believe that those words were revealed by God – or who, if they accept those words, cannot believe that they are essential to Christian faith. ('In ecumenical dialogue,' the council declared, 'Catholic theologians standing fast by the teaching of the Church and investigating the sacred mysteries with the separated brethren must proceed with love for the truth, with charity and with humility. When comparing doctrines with one another, they should remember that in Catholic doctrine there exists an order or "hierarchy" of truths, since they vary in their relationship to the foundation of the Christian faith.') Christians who take this attitude have many respectable predecessors. It has often been noticed that the gospels refer to the brothers and sisters of Jesus without any suggestion that their mother was always a virgin. Thomas Aquinas was among the theologians who, because it seemed to them incompatible with Mary's humanity, resolutely opposed the doctrine connected with the festival of the Conception. It was not until the fifteenth century that the festival was authorised by a pope and the doctrine declared a 'pious opinion' by a council. In the next century the council of Trent refused to make the doctrine more than that. There is no evidence that the story that Mary's body was either assumed into heaven during her natural life, or assumed on the way to the burial, or raised from the tomb three days later, was known before the fourth century. The Orthodox churches still observe the festival of the death of Mary as her 'Falling Asleep' (*koimesis*), deploring the papacy's attempt to enforce definitions of its physical aspect. Rome's formal involvement in the doctrinal question began in the eighteenth century, when belief in the physical assumption of Mary was declared 'probable'.

These theological issues must be of interest to Christians who ask how far the service of the papacy to the church's unity must be tied to the acceptance of particular formulations of doctrine. Other questions seem, however, more urgent to most Christians. How far has the papacy the right to discipline theologians of whose work it disapproves? How far has it the right to appoint bishops whose opinions are far more conservative than those prevailing in their dioceses? How far has it the right to insist on the celibacy of priests (with small exceptions in favour of the clergy of the Uniate churches which adhere to most of the customs of the Orthodox churches and in favour of some married men previously ordained in other churches) – at a time when an acute shortage of priests often means that the faithful cannot receive the sacraments? How far has it the right to condemn artificial birth control – at a time when most married Catholics with easy access to contraceptive devices use them, and when the growth of the population condemns many regions of the world to degrading and killing poverty? How far has it the right to maintain a structure which still makes the church for many practical purposes an absolute monarchy, where the pope is under no obligation to consult with anyone about anything and where many policy decisions which are wide open to criticism – for example, about the investment and use of the Vatican's large financial resources – are still taken in secret?

In the mid-1980s deeply convinced and very powerful forces in the Roman Catholic Church press for a conservative answer to all these questions. But many Catholics give another answer. To quote only one example: in December 1985, in the very week when the Synod of Bishops in Rome was hearing about the dangers of changes in the church, the Institut für Demoskopie published the results of a survey of Catholics in West Germany, traditionally one of the world's most conservative Catholic communities. It showed that under a quarter regarded papal decisions as binding on them, under forty per cent went to mass every Sunday, and about sixty per cent were in favour of intercommunion with Protestants. At the same time it was made very clear that the world's largest Catholic community – the church in Brazil, with a baptised membership of over a hundred million – was irritated by uncomprehending criticism from Vatican officials although it had cordially welcomed the pope's long and sensitive visit in 1980. The conclusion may be drawn that the papacy, if it would limit its attempted jurisdiction and aim instead at the articulation of the conscience of the worldwide Christian community while leaving much more to local decisions, would greatly increase its actual influence – to a point higher than any other in its stormy history. Instead of being 'undoubtedly the gravest obstacle in the path of ecumenism' (the words are those of Pope Paul VI, in 1976), it would become the focus of the unity of most Christians. Instead of issuing orders which have been widely ignored even by Catholics who applaud his public appearances, the pope could be seriously honoured in accordance with his most profoundly Christian title, 'servant of the servants of God'. In the middle of the nineteenth century there was the illusion that the integrity and power of the papacy depended on the possession of the papal states. But when stripped of its political status in Italy, the papacy conquered a new kingdom – of hearts. The pope became the 'prisoner in the Vatican', surrounded by a hostile Italian republic; but to millions around the world he was sacred, the infallible Holy Father. And now modern methods of communication offer a new opportunity to a pope of the future. If he could cease to claim to be infallible when defining compulsory dogmas for which there is no biblical evidence, he could be acknowledged in the leadership of the preaching and living of the gospel in all the world. If stripped of his claim to universal jurisdiction over all the world's dioceses, the bishop of Rome could have a solid claim to universal love.[10]

The Evangelical future

It also seems probable that even if a reformed Roman Catholicism gradually broadens out to include the Eastern Orthodox, the Anglicans and some mainline Protestant denominations, there will still be a large place in worldwide Christianity for the tradition which can be called Evangelical. Like Roman Catholicism, it changes because it lives. But it is perpetually marked by an impatience with the institutions and regulations of the churches because it gives such high priority to the personal knowledge of Jesus the Lord and Saviour, to private prayer, to Bible study and to evangelism.

I have a personal reason to acknowledge the spiritual power of this movement. I spent some ten years of my life in the service of the Student Christian Movement, mainly as the editor of its publishing house, and fully shared its commitment to liberal scholarship, social relevance and Christian reunion. But the SCM became increasingly preoccupied with the politics of the left and with the morality of progressive humanism and seemed to have lost its Christian basis, at least in the eyes of those students who were prepared to join a society with 'Christian' in its title. Its numbers declined sharply in comparison with those of the Christian Unions or Evangelical Unions, which were based firmly on the Bible and prayer. The process which I witnessed in Britain was matched in the USA (where the University Christian Movement ceased to exist) and in many other countries. So I learnt in my own experience how the Evangelical emphasis has apparently proved stronger than 'liberalism', creating its own denominations or 'parachurch' movements as well as large groups within the historic churches. In Latin America the Pentecostal churches are dynamic; many African Christians express their vigour in this way, inside or outside missionary-founded churches; all over Asia alert young people are responding to this approach; Evangelical groups are strong in many places in Europe and the Commonwealth countries; revivals which are Evangelical in some sense have influenced churches as historic as the Coptic Church in Egypt; the charismatic movement is said to include about thirty million Roman Catholics. There is no organ of unity comparable with the papacy or the World Council of Churches, but clearly here is a 'third force' to be seen clearly enough on occasions such as the 1974 Congress on World Evangelisation in Lausanne. Then about 2,700 leading Evangelicals from more than 150 countries gathered at Billy Graham's invitation. Yet *The New Face of Evangelicalism* was the brave title of a book of essays reflecting on that experience (edited by C. Rene Padilla). For the Lausanne Congress announced a change comparable with the Roman Catholic change registered by the Second Vatican Council – and later Evangelical meetings heard that 'new face' talking.

In 1980 the World Evangelical Fellowship held its seventh General Assembly in London. The preparatory volume was introduced by the General Secretary, Waldron Scott, with an essay entitled 'Evangelical Ambiguity'. He claimed that 'Evangelicals hold in common a central core of doctrine and experience' and that 'not since the first decade of this century has there been such a high level of Evangelical self-awareness and self-confidence'. But he noted that this contemporary movement was in 'ferment' – as well he might: not long afterwards, he was asked to resign because his sympathies were too wide.

In one of these essays the Director of the Mexican Bible Institute faced the challenge of economics and politics in turbulent Latin America, quoted the renewed activity of the Catholic Church and reported Evangelical support for the formation of a Latin American Council of Churches. The General Secretary of the Association of Evangelicals of Africa and Madagascar wrote that 'our first assignment as Evangelicals should be that of making Christianity at home in Africa . . . The Church should develop a theology and philosophy of self-reliance . . . We cannot afford to continue fighting the war in strange armour.' He recognised that 'we need to make disciples' but hoped that 'the art of discipleship will help us to rediscover the traditional African community system of living'. The Executive

Secretary of the Asia Theological Association said bluntly: 'it is now vital to dissociate Christianity from the West'. Evangelicals should join with other Christians in dialogues with local non-Christians and in the vigorous defence of human rights. The General Secretary of the Indian Evangelical Mission hoped that Asian missionaries would be effective within Asia, because they would know what poverty and suffering meant. An expert on communications criticised many attempts to penetrate Asia by Christian broadcasting because they ignored the plunder of Asia in the years of Christian colonialism. 'Never before have so many voices been communicating the Gospel to so many people', yet 'never before has the Gospel message been communicated to so little effect'. One leader praised the recent concentration of missionary thinkers on the need to 'contextualise' the gospel within the culture to which it was being addressed: only so could Asia's peoples be persuaded. Others praised the recent spread of Evangelical agencies relieving the world's hunger. From Yugoslavia there was rejoicing that under communism strong Evangelical elements were to be found in Orthodox and Catholic revivals. It was added that 'Christianity should no longer be identified with anti-communism'. From the USA and from Western Europe it was said that Evangelicals were throwing themselves both into the concern for the poor on the margins of capitalism and into the intellectual integration of faith and knowledge. A woman wrote about the contribution which women could make. A Nigerian who belonged to a Pentecostal church wrote: 'I seriously question if the Evangelical movement can survive if there is complete polarization between it and the Pentecostal movement.' An American Catholic involved in the charismatic movement in Western Europe declared: 'To be a good Catholic one must be a good Evangelical.' In many of these essays there was emphasis that good Evangelicals could be found in the main denominations as well as in the American-style 'parachurch' movements. But it was also stressed repeatedly that the church is mainly a lay movement, not entirely dependent on buildings or professional preachers – and that 'church growth' must be a spiritual movement. There was no enthusiasm for numerical growth without spiritual deepening.[11]

In 1982 a conference was held in Bangkok. As a Kenyan leader, Bishop David Gitari, explained, 'it was the first time that theologians of Evangelical conviction from the Two Thirds World had met at their own initiative to focus attention on what Jesus of Galilee means in their own contexts and in their attempt to fulfil his mission'. Rene Padilla of Argentina contributed a detailed and sympathetic summary of the Christology of the radical Jesuit, Jon Sobrino, concluding that 'Two Thirds World Christology stresses the humanity of Jesus Christ and challenges us to rediscover the social dimensions of the Gospel. It stresses the fact that Jesus's death was the historical outcome of his life and challenges us to suffer because of righteousness. It stresses the historical nature of the Christian life and challenges us to commitment to Jesus Christ for the transformation of the world.' A fellow Argentinian dwelt on the option of Jesus for the poor of Galilee in opposition to the priests and the other rich men of Jerusalem. A Brazilian spoke with great sensitivity of the religiosity of the Latin American poor, particularly of the submerged Indians – a cult of the Earth, of the Woman and of protecting saints and other spirits amid 'an ethos of being abandoned, being orphaned, living in solitude, fatalism and death'. A black American, George Cummings, spoke of the 'Black Christ', the suffering servant, met in the experience of generations of the oppressed in the USA – and he protested at the failure of fellow Evangelicals with whiter skins and larger incomes to understand. From Ghana Kwame Bediako spoke of African tribal religion – and was scarifying about the missionaries' record of misunderstanding. In this context the gospel has to be heard first as a message about the mightiest 'spirit power', about the greatest 'ancestor' and about the 'chief' who is now available to all tribes. Two Indians criticised the lack of appreciation of non-Christian cultures. They blamed Western missionaries and fellow Evangelicals who had recently developed into a 'younger church version of the same Western missionary enterprise'. They issued a bold, although also careful, plea for dialogue between Asia's faiths. 'Can we not say not just that God has left himself a witness in these religions, but that he is actually at work in them?' Other Evangelical theologians, from the Philippines and Thailand, spoke with great appreciation of Buddhist ethics and of the belief in a Buddha-to-come as providing 'points of contact' for the gospel. Bishop Michael Nazir Ali of Pakistan outlined the possibilities of a dialogue with Muslims about the doctrine of the trinity – rejecting the temptation to minimise Christ ('Muslims rightly claim affinity between their own view and that of "radical" theologians in the West') but searching for ways of expressing orthodoxy in terms familiar to Muslims. 'In my experience,' he said, 'there are two kinds of Muslim who are open to the Gospel. One is the ethically motivated Muslim who is seeking for justice. The other is the person who has had an overwhelming religious experience.' And Wayan Mastra of Indonesia spoke of the gospel in the context of Bali, where ninety-eight per cent of the people are Hindus with many 'animist' beliefs. The Christ of Bali is the liberator from oppression by landlords – and, in religious experience, the 'Spirit of God' who is ever present like the wind, the fire and the water worshipped in animism.[12]

Three books of essays preparing for Britain's Second Evangelical Congress at Nottingham in 1977 handled many cultural and social questions sensitively. Its methodology was explained by Bruce Kaye: 'An issue in the present situation has been taken, and then analysed in depth to see what is at stake in it and how Christian truth may be related to it.' Definitions of 'Christian truth' were not made with any simple-minded desire to indoctrinate or with any hatred of Catholicism. At this congress Michael Green, one of the Church of England's leading Evangelicals, was to hope that 'soon it will become too expensive, mercifully, to send local leaders to theological college', and another, David Watson, was to acknowledge that in many ways 'the Reformation was one of the greatest tragedies that ever happened to the Church'. Introducing the preparatory studies John Stott, whose mind was behind this conference as it had been behind the 'covenant' produced by the Lausanne Congress, wrote about 'the Lord Christ who calls his people in every generation to a fresh obedience . . . Christian obedience must be earthed in the contemporary world'. But 'we Evangelicals have been slow to give our minds to these problems. We confess that we have a lot of catching up to do.' In answer to the question 'Who is Christ?' John Stott declared that 'theological formulation is indispensable'. In answer to the question 'What is the authority of Scripture?' he confessed that 'we are sometimes slovenly, sometimes simplistic, sometimes highly selective and sometimes downright dishonest'. A better approach 'asks how much culture conditioned the way God spoke his Word and conditions the way we hear it'. Although 'our Evangelical righteousness has sometimes been more pharisaic than Christian, for we have made up, or received and handed on, a tradition of dos and don'ts, obligations and taboos', Christian maturity 'is found neither in blind obedience to statutes and ordinances, nor in a contrived conformity to a party discipline, but in a humble and joyful acceptance of our Father's revelation, a thoughtful and responsible application of it to the complexities of modern life, and a readiness to respect those whose applications do not entirely coincide with our own'.[13]

An essentially similar call came from a much smaller conference of Evangelical leaders in the USA, near Chicago in 1977. It bravely criticised much of the legacy of American fundamentalism, although its language was guarded because that legacy was still a powerful factor in the religious scene. 'We dare not move beyond the biblical limits of the Gospel,' this conference declared reassuringly – 'but we cannot be fully Evangelical without recognising our need to learn from other times and movements concerning the whole meaning of the Gospel.' Accordingly this meeting dared to criticise an American tradition which was, it said, individualistic, sectarian and anarchic. This tradition claimed to be independent of the past but in effect that made it creedless, poor in sacramental understanding and undisciplined in spirituality.[14]

What accounts for this recognition of contemporary realities – an openness which has alarmed many who regard themselves as the custodians of the Evangelical tradition?

The basic explanation is, surely, that many Evangelicals have realised that the Bible itself embodies and demands a certain flexibility in the statement of the gospel. Addressing a Consultation on World Evangelisation (at Pattaya in Thailand in 1980) John Stott made this clear: 'There is only one Gospel, on which all the apostles agreed . . . Yet the apostles expressed this one Gospel in various ways – now sacrificial (the shedding and sprinkling of Christ's blood), now Messianic (the breaking in of God's promised rule), now legal (the Judge pronouncing the unrighteous righteous), now personal (the Father reconciling his wayward children), now salvific (the heavenly Liberator coming to rescue the helpless), now cosmic (the universal Lord claiming universal dominion); and this is only a selection. The Gospel is thus seen to be one, yet diverse. It is "given", yet culturally adapted to its audience.' The right Evangelical and missionary approach, he declared, 'combines commitment to the fact of revelation with commitment to the task of contextualisation. It accepts that only biblical formulations of the Gospel are permanently normative, and that every attempt to proclaim the Gospel in modern idiom must justify itself as an authentic expression of the biblical Gospel. But if it refuses to jettison the biblical formulations, it also refuses to recite them in a wooden and unimaginative way.'[15]

The Lausanne Congress, like the Second Vatican Council, seemed in some passages to endorse a very conservative understanding of the authority of the Bible. Thus we read in the Lausanne Covenant: 'We affirm the divine inspiration, truthfulness and authority of both Old and New Testament Scriptures in their entirety as the only written word of God, without error in all that it affirms and as the only infallible rule of faith and practice.' But like the council, the congress also recognised the difference between the Bible's permanently authoritative message and the culturally conditioned forms in which it has been expressed. In his opening address Billy Graham confessed that he had often failed to separate the gospel from its American cultural wrapper – and he urged the congress to do better. At many points, it did. Graham was not the only prominent evangelist to seek greater sensitivity to the relationships between the world's cultures and the one gospel. And the question of the human, culturally conditioned, elements in the Bible was not entirely shirked. The Lausanne Covenant can be interpreted – and has been, by some of its own architects – as saying that not everything affirmed *in* the Bible is affirmed *by* it in the sense of being endorsed as vital to its message.

Many Evangelicals, like many Roman Catholics, have felt perfectly free in recent years to accept and use any soundly based literary and historical 'criticism' of scripture. Many would say that what the Bible 'affirms' without error is not any one detail but its message understood as a whole. That is the 'word of God' or 'the gospel', which can and must be applied to new historical or cultural situations and expressed within them. For example, C. Rene Padilla interprets biblical authority in a way which would have seemed strange to fundamentalists as well as to liberals in a previous generation. 'From one point of view,' he has written, 'the Bible must be read "like any other book". This means that the interpreters have to take seriously that they face an ancient text with its own historical horizons. Their task is to let the text speak, whether they agree with it or not, this demands that they understand what the text meant in its original situation.' But he continued: 'To read the Bible "like any other book" is not only to take seriously the literary and historical aspects of Scripture but also to read it from the perspective of faith. That is, since any book should be read in the light of the purpose for which it was written, and since the Bible was written that God may speak in it and through it, it follows that the Bible should be read with an attitude of openness to God's Word, with a view to conscientious response.' And he concluded: 'the urgent need everywhere is for a new reading of the Gospel *from within* each particular historical situation, under the guidance of the Holy Spirit . . . It is only as the word of God "becomes flesh" in the people of God that the Gospel takes shape within culture.'[16]

Many books have been written, and many conferences held, in the twentieth-century attempt of Evangelicals to defend and commend the essential Christian gospel without claiming that every word in the Bible fulfils the same purpose or possesses the same authority. It is widely granted in Evangelical circles that it is not the purpose of the Bible to teach science. Thus the two accounts of the creation at the beginning of Genesis can be treated as poetry and compared with other creation myths. The statement that 'the sun stayed in mid heaven and made no haste to set for almost a whole day' (Joshua 10:13) was never meant to be quoted against modern astronomers. Nor, it is generally agreed, is the Bible concerned to teach politics; the two accounts of the institution of the Israelite monarchy in the middle of 2 Samuel, one favourable, the other hostile, can be regarded as rival stories from rival schools of thought. In a time when every seriously moral person in the world must be concerned about overpopulation, pollution and the exhaustion of this planet's resources, it is fully acknowledged that the commandment to 'be fruitful and increase, fill the earth and subdue it' (Genesis 1:28) is not God's only command. Nor is it the will of God that 'native' peoples should be slaughtered or subjugated as the Canaanites were in Israel's promised land. Nor are all biblical rulings about social customs held to be permanently authoritative. The freedom of Christians to ignore most of the detailed commandments in the Hebrew scriptures has been recognised almost universally. Such freedom is often held to include (for example) the instructions in the New Testament that women in the congregations must be veiled and silent. To imitate Christ it is not necessary to be homeless and defenceless or to wash feet. Naturally Evangelicals have approached all the teaching of Jesus with a special reverence, but in recent years it has often been agreed that it was no part of the purpose of those who recorded this teaching to settle literary or historical questions asked by modern 'critics'. The attribution of a psalm to King David in the New Testament is not enough to decide the question of authorship. The mention of 'Zechariah son of Berachiah, whom you murdered between the sanctuary and the altar' (Matthew 23:35) is not enough to assure us that the prophet Zechariah, whose father was Berachiah but about whose death nothing is known, met the same fate as Zechariah son of Jehoida (2 Chronicles 24:21). It has often also been recognised that there are editorial touches in the gospels. Every Evangelical treasures Christ's 'great commission': 'Go forth therefore and make all nations my disciples; baptize men everywhere in the name of the Father and the Son and the Holy Spirit' (Matthew 28:19). But not every Evangelical need believe that the trinitarian formula of baptism, shown by the rest of the New Testament to have evolved gradually, was spoken by Jesus on that day. It is not essential to Evangelical faith to hold that Methuselah did actually live 969 years – or that every detail is historically accurate in the gospels. Every Evangelical will gladly agree that 'every inspired scripture has its use for teaching the truth and refuting error, or for reformation of manners and discipline in right living, so that the man who belongs to God may be efficient and equipped for good work of every kind' (2 Timothy 3:16–17) – but it has not been found necessary always to agree as to what this 'use' is. Timothy presumably had to struggle in order to understand the 'use' to a Christian of the Hebrew scriptures. Jesus is himself represented as wrestling with the scriptures, in order to discern their 'use' to him. In the wilderness, it is reported, he had to subordinate scriptural promises of miraculous food and protection to other passages with a higher authority. Those who seek to apply the gospel to twentieth-century problems often have to use their minds in order to discriminate between biblical texts. A wealth of Evangelical and other scholarship is now available to assist them and there has been much learned discussion of the principles involved ('hermeneutics', the science or art of interpretation).

Questions about the Holy Spirit are inseparable from such questions about the Bible. Does the Holy Spirit blot out differences of culture and personality – or are these differences accepted, used and transfigured gloriously? There was a time when that question was answered in practice by bringing great pressure on converts to conform to models admired by English-speaking Evangelicals or by the pietists of Germany and Scandinavia. But that rigidity has now become a minority attitude in the worldwide Evangelical movement. Bible-heroes, Bible-writers and Bible-readers are enjoyed in their variety. Are the gifts of the Holy Spirit always given in the manner of the day of Pentecost as described in the Acts of the Apostles? Are all Christians entitled to a dramatically experienced 'second baptism' followed by ecstatic 'tongue-speaking'? Comparatively few Evangelicals have insisted on it. Many in this movement have, indeed, been hostile to the claims of the Pentecostal churches and the wider charismatic movement, believing either that 'tongue-speaking' ceased at the end of the period of the New Testament or that it no longer deserves prominence in the Christian message. And Pentecostal and charismatic Christians have themselves had to admit that many who are attracted by these dramatic phenomena have not experienced them for themselves with any spectacular intensity. Any apparent insistence on 'tongue-speaking' in Acts has been subordinated to the Bible's message as a whole – which in the conviction of most Evangelicals, including most Pentecostals and charismatics, celebrates 'varieties of gifts' and gives pride of place to the quiet gifts of love, joy and peace, the gifts which, as Paul taught the Corinthians, make possible 'the best way of all'.

If that much at least must be said about the Evangelical reconsideration of the nature of the authority of the Bible, it should also be noted that many Evangelicals have rethought the nature of the Christian mission, transmitting the message of the Bible as a whole. They have seen that it is not enough to go for the individual's decision to accept Christ and thus to be saved from hell. That, indeed, is an understanding of evangelism which is still very common. But it has been widely seen to belong to a culture, West European or North American, which stresses the individual and minimises the significance of the community. The spread of Christianity in Latin America, Africa and Asia has been one factor in teaching the Christians around the North Atlantic that the most important human attitudes are usually derived from membership of a group. Many Evangelicals have therefore urgently stressed the need of every Christian to belong to a congregation or at least to a branch of a 'parachurch' movement. Evangelicalism has rediscovered the church.

It has also rediscovered the gospel as a message about God's righteousness having radical implications for the whole life of society including economics and politics while not offering any detailed blueprint for a 'Christian society'. It is seen that Christians from overseas can often make themselves useful by being technical experts and educators, not by 'running' churches in a poorer country – and it is seen that the Christians of the country must commend themselves by their down-to-earth contributions to the welfare of village, city or nation. The pietism which avoids all entanglement in such 'worldly' concerns is generally rejected, whether the politics espoused are of the left or the right and whether the pressure comes from first-hand experience of poverty or from the conscience of the relatively rich. In keeping with this awareness of the realities of human experience, many Evangelicals have also acknowledged that Christian conversion is not exactly the same as the once-for-all decision which in this tradition is called 'regeneration'. It is a series of responses to the demand and offer of Christ in all the changing scenes of life. The change and mobility of modern life have taught evangelists that 'disciple-making' inaugurates a process of lifelong learning. And it has been seen that it is difficult to reconcile belief in God as 'love' with the doctrine that God condemns all who have not accepted Christ as saviour before death to hell. Evangelicals, almost to the same extent as Catholics, have been among those Christians who have openly sought ways of expressing the 'wider hope' for the salvation of non-Christians. While pure 'universalism' (the belief that all *must* be saved in the end) has usually been seen to be incompatible with the

God-given freedom of the will, at the very least it has been affirmed that God, so far from predestinating some to eternal damnation, wills 'that all men should find salvation and come to know the truth' (1 Timothy 2:4). While Evangelicals have always refused to be as negative as many other Christians have been about personal evangelism or overseas missionary work, they have in many cases ceased to be as negative as their predecessors were about non-Christian religion and ethics. Their emphasis has been on the positive gospel of salvation and joy – and, supremely, on the person of Jesus.

After the 1968 Assembly of the World Council of Churches, in Uppsala, some Evangelicals were deeply concerned that the traditional challenge to evangelism and missionary work was being obliterated by the concentration on revolutionary and other 'social action'. The reaction included a fresh and powerful call to Evangelicals to withdraw from denominations affiliated to the WCC. It came from the influential London preacher, Martyn Lloyd-Jones. It was echoed by another internationally prominent Evangelical, Francis Schaeffer, who in the USA had been one of the founders of the Bible Presbyterian Church. Under the leadership of Professor Peter Beyerhaus, the Frankfurt Declaration was drawn up in 1970. But the new call aroused less response than had been expected. Most Evangelicals from the Third World refused to endorse this declaration, while also being unhappy about the WCC's apparent lack of conviction about the necessity of evangelism. To them, the words from Frankfurt seemed too individualist, escapist and, in general, negative. Their refusal stimulated the agreements about evangelism from which I have already quoted.[17]

To this rethinking of the aim of the Christian mission has been added a reconsideration of its strategy. Up to the middle of the twentieth century the Evangelical vision was, in the main, one of rescuing 'saved' converts from societies which were condemned as thoroughly evil. These converts acknowledged their 'sin' and 'guilt' and accepted the 'atonement' accomplished by Christ as 'salvation' from 'hell' – or they said they did, although there was usually no ready equivalent to these biblical ideas in their own cultures. The 'mission compound' on the outskirts of a town or village, a place where a new Christian might take refuge from the hostility of family and neighbours, symbolised this one-by-one strategy. There was little or no hesitation in saying that a Christian must adopt a new name (often a name which complimented the foreign missionary's home country) and by baptism must cease really to belong to family, caste, village, tribe and people. But more recently it has been seen that in many places this strategy was failing to build a church which was more than a small minority, largely hereditary and static. The Lausanne Congress was eloquently reminded that most Christians were failing to convert their neighbours and that many millions of 'non-Christians' (it was said, some 2,700 million) lived beyond the reach of 'near-neighbour evangelism' because they lived in places where no church at all existed.

The answer is advocated that the church must be planted within every one of the world's cultures. Thus a movement called 'Jews for Jesus' is active in the USA; under Evangelical sponsorship, it consists of Christians who retain Jewish customs in addition to their new beliefs and practices. Experiments have been made in gathering 'Hindus for Jesus' or 'Muslims for Jesus'. Already in the story of the modern missionaries it can be seen that their greatest successes have come when peoples have responded but have kept many of their traditions – such as the Nagas in India, the Bataks in Indonesia or many tribesmen in Papua New Guinea.

The Lausanne Congress was impressed by speakers who developed the point which had been made by an eminent missionary, Donald McGavran, in his *Bridges of God* twenty years previously. Family and kinship ties are ready-made, divinely ordained, 'bridges' over which an individual or preferably a whole group can cross into the Christian church. Most people prefer to become Christians without leaving family, caste, class, tribe or people. But if the unreached peoples of the world are to be invited to use such bridges into the church, Christians on their side of the bridges must study far more carefully the people's culture. For example, before very long in its encounter with Christianity a people needs the Bible, or at least the New Testament, in its own tongue – which often has first to be reduced to writing. Heroic work has been done by agencies such as the Bible Societies or the Wycliffe Bible Translators. By 1980 the scriptures had been translated into more than 1,800 languages. But the best translators know that true translation often means finding the 'dynamic equivalent' for a term in the original language, instead of being content with a formally corresponding word. Just as Paul and others who first interpreted the gospel in Greek had to find equivalents for 'Son of Man' and 'kingdom of God', so it is necessary to translate imaginatively 'Lamb of God' for a people without sheep or 'Christ' for a people without a messianic expectation – and to find equivalents for countless other biblical terms if the Bible's message is to have a powerful meaning in a new culture. As a title, *Bridges of God* would not have been understood in a Palestine where bridges were unknown. After his first ten years as Secretary for Translations with the American Bible Society, Dr Eugene Nida summed up the message which he has often repeated to his fellow Evangelicals. He has not been afraid to say that the gospel should be related to many cultures – a procedure which is safe provided only that it is related primarily to God in Christ. 'The Christian position is not one of static conformity to dead rules, but of dynamic obedience to a living God,' he wrote. 'While the Qur'an attempts to fix for all time the behaviour of Muslims, the Bible clearly establishes the principle of relative relativism, which permits growth, adaptation and freedom under the Lordship of Jesus Christ.'[18]

Many of Donald McGavran's original ideas about church growth have been revised by him, his associates and his critics. It has been questioned whether a whole group can be deeply converted (is it not best to think of 'multi-individual conversions'?). It has been asked whether a congregation can be deeply Christian if it is deliberately exclusive (is it not best to teach every congregation to ignore differences of caste, tribe, class and nation?). The enthusiasm for statistics seems very American. So far young American Evangelicals are the only people who have offered themselves as overseas missionaries in large numbers in response to the new call to reach all the earth's peoples. They have often been considered naive and insensitive and a number of governments have done their best to keep them out as troublemakers. So these 'bridges of God' need further study. But it is widely agreed that the recognition of the importance of 'cultures' in the spread of Christianity needs to be made more sensitive not abandoned. Attention has been drawn to a very important issue.

Missionary enthusiasm in its old or new form has driven many thousands of Evangelicals into countries where they have to struggle to become familiar with the language and the culture. Among missionaries from the USA, those happy to be sponsored by exclusively Evangelical organisations greatly outnumber those sent by denominations belonging to the National Council of Churches (in 1980, by about ten to one). Broadcasts and books often suggest that this Protestant, North American, emphasis – often with a conservative tone which in practice finds it difficult to enter any other language or culture – is going to predominate in years to come. But reflection about the Christian futures suggests other considerations. If what is being discussed is the Christian mission, it is very striking that there is so often a conspiracy of silence about the Roman Catholic Church, which greatly outnumbers Protestantism. The number of Roman Catholic missionaries in the world seems to be almost the same as the

Protestants' numbers (about sixty-five thousand). In Latin America converts to Protestant churches are almost certain to have been nominal Roman Catholics and it must be a serious question whether the main prayer of Protestants should not be for the renewal of Catholicism itself. In Africa, Asia, the Pacific islands and Europe the Roman Catholic Church seems to be, on the whole, at least as able as the Protestants to bring Christ's message to the peoples with imagination and self-sacrifice. Protestants who do not rejoice over this have a clear duty to ask themselves whether there is prejudice or jealousy in their hearts. What if the bridge provided by God has on it a very popular statue of the Holy Mother and Child? What if incense, candles and flowers are chosen by people who want to acknowledge the gospel at the Christian end of the bridge? And if it is the case that the best hopes for the Christian mission lie in the movements of peoples into the church, it seems obvious that the most acceptable ambassadors of the church are likely to be evangelists who already have many points of contact with the peoples being invited to cross the bridges. Latin America does not welcome 'Yankee' or 'Gringo' religious imports; the best evangelists in Africa are Africans; India, whose government severely restricts its visas to missionaries from overseas, will become more massively Christian only if the Indian churches become more keenly missionary; Asia's future must lie in Asia's hands; and Europe feels that it knows its own problems best, without being told by its American cousins that it ought to be more positive and efficient. The small movements of Third World missionaries already arising in the 1980s may therefore be of more significance than the much larger numbers sent out from the USA, because they may be pointers to the most promising future – to the 'spontaneous expansion of the church' (a phrase much used by a prophetic twentieth-century missionary, Roland Allan). Much the same may be true of the small experiments in mission being made by the European churches in their depressing situation. And in the future these local evangelists may, or may not, find it helpful to make use of the Evangelical movement's traditional terminology. In the 1980s all that can be said is that within this movement there is an active debate similar to the Catholic debate about whether the existing official theology merely needs to be 'adapted' to the new situation or whether a more radical restatement is needed.

Traditionally the principles of Evangelicalism have seemed clear enough, from the days before the formation of the Evangelical Alliance in London in 1846 to the Lausanne Congress and beyond. With phraseology differing only slightly, the 'fundamentals' have been thought of as being: the infallibility, inerrancy or 'verbal' or 'plenary' inspiration of scripture; the salvation of those who believe in the one saviour, whose self-offering on Calvary satisfied the just wrath of the Father against sin by providing a sacrifice as a substitute for our punishment; the 'justification' of a sinner in God's eyes by this faith, not by any 'good works'; the virginal conception and physical resurrection of the saviour; his second coming to earth in visible glory. Only on this basis, it was believed, did the Holy Spirit work in 'regeneration' and 'sanctification'. But in the light of the ongoing debate it must now be questioned whether these 'fundamentals' in their traditional formulations are any more sacrosanct than the medieval or Counter-Reformation or nineteenth-century formulations of Roman Catholic doctrine. If Evangelicals want to say that the gospel affirmed by the Bible is true, is it necessary to invite criticism on historical and literary grounds by saying that the whole Bible is without error? If what is desired is the statement that in Christ God reconciles people to himself by the manifestation of his holy love and by his own self-surrender, accepting the burdens and pains of humanity in order to end humanity's alienation, is it necessary to talk exclusively or primarily in the language of the 'penal-substitutionary' theory of the atonement? That theory is easily intelligible in a culture where the demands of 'justice' can be met whether or not the particular individual being punished is guilty. Even there, however, it is a dangerous theory, as many Evangelicals have felt – for if crudely expounded it can fail to teach that God was in the crucified Christ. The intention of the theologians who used this theory was to stress that God's love provided the sacrifice, but this intention was not always perfectly fulfilled in popular expositions, which left behind the image of the angry God. And the theory is less effective in cultures with a more refined system of justice. It seems unnecessary to insist on this particular theory since most cultures are familiar with all the ideas which seem to be really essential. The costliness of righting wrong, including the forgiveness of wrong; the self-sacrifice of a good, heroic person such as a mother or a rescue worker; the courage of one who mediates between two groups or individuals at variance – such ideas seldom seem either strange or less than sacred. If what is desired is the communication of the truths of the incarnation and resurrection to minds which have been shaped by science, is it necessary to insist that Jesus had no human father and that he appeared after his death in a 'physical' body? If what is desired is to say that Jesus will win because God will win, is it necessary to picture the triumph of God by the image of Jesus returning like an astronaut through the clouds? And if what is desired is to proclaim Jesus as Lord and saviour, is it necessary to be much harsher about 'natural' or 'non-Christian' human goodness than he was in his parables?

It will be for further generations of Evangelicals to answer these questions. But at the beginning of the 1980s a Presbyterian church bureaucrat in the USA, Richard Hutchenson, summarised impressions derived from a study of the literature of a movement which was causing him to think by its success in enlisting adults and the young. 'I was surprised at the insistence and the consistency with which contemporary Evangelical writers are separating themselves from the fundamentalists . . . They consider themselves far removed from the narrowness, closed-mindedness and hostility of the fundamentalist spirit. The second surprise was the level of social concern expressed in the writings of the new Evangelicals . . . The final surprise was the level of willingness to enter into dialogue with the liberals, the acceptance of the reality and even necessity of certain kinds of biblical criticism, and the desire to move beyond the present outdated polarization of Protestant Christianity. One cannot estimate how influential these new Evangelical writers are with the great mass of American religious conservatives . . . This openness, however, is not incompatible with what I have observed in my contacts with Evangelicals in my own denomination.'[19]

My own expectation is like Richard Hutchenson's. It is that the Evangelical future will include many Christians who are very simple in their interpretations of the experience of accepting Jesus as saviour – but the leadership and the theology will be increasingly open to a changing world. And I can point to a document which seems to catch the music of this future.

In 1982 the Central Committee of the World Council of Churches adopted an 'affirmation' about *Mission and Evangelism* which had been in the making since 1976. This statement begins: 'The biblical promise of a new earth and a new heaven where love, peace and justice prevail invites our actions as Christians in history.' But wisely it does not pause to unpack the theoretical meaning of the Bible's symbolism. (Is this planet going to be replaced? Is this universe? Is humanity perfectible?) It proceeds immediately to consider Christian action against sin, for it takes seriously the 'monstrosity' of sin. 'Sin, alienating persons from God, neighbour and nature, is found both in individual and corporate forms, both in slavery of the human will and in social, political and economic structures of denomination and dependence.' Confronting sin, Christ 'took upon himself the guilt even of those who crucified him' – and in so doing 'revealed the immeasurable depth of God's love for the world'. The gospel is accordingly 'an invitation to recognise and accept in a personal decision the saving Lordship of Christ', but 'we cannot limit our witness to a supposedly private area of life' because the gospel also summons us 'to accept responsibilities in terms of God's love for our neighbour'. So the church is needed. The churches' 'common witness should be the natural consequence of this unity in Christ' and the sowing of the seed of church life 'needs to be continued until there is, in every human community, a cell of the kingdom, a church confessing Jesus Christ and in his name serving his people'. Priority must be given to the poor. 'A growing consensus among Christians today speaks of God's perpetual option for the poor' and 'God is working through the poor of the earth to awaken the consciousness of humanity to his call for repentance, for justice and for love'. The church must undertake 'mission in and to six continents' – and a dialogue with people of other religious convictions and ideological persuasions in order 'to discern the unsearchable riches of God and the way he deals with humanity'. Here is a call to Christians to 'express their faith in the symbols and images of their respective cultures', in particular by participating in 'the struggle of the less privileged for their liberation'. It is a call to convey by actions more than by words an invitation which people can understand.

What is the ecumenical goal?

It is therefore evident that Christians are entering an age of disunity if 'disunity' is defined as the refusal to agree about the details of doctrine and organisation. It is plainly impossible that the tone of the religion of North America should be identical with the tone of the religion of Latin America, or that Indian Christians should think (or act) the same as African Christians, or that in Asia there should be one church achieving uniformity, or that Christians among Muslims should be the same as Christians among Jews, or Christians in capitalist societies the same as Christians in the 'socialist camp', or that the response to European secularisation should be the same as the response to tribal paganism, or that the poor and the rich (or the women and the men) should be indistinguishable, or that Evangelicals should agree in every matter with Catholics, or (in each of these two great traditions) that liberals should see eye to eye with conservatives. It is also highly unlikely that all the historic denominations will consent to disappear completely within the next hundred years in order to be united totally with each other. Similarly, the Pentecostal or charismatic groups which abound in many countries will maintain their own enthusiastic witness. And the 'non-white indigenous churches' such as Africa's independent churches – a category which may include a hundred million people in the 1980s – will not be absorbed into a tidy union.

This coming age of diversity will not be an innovation, whatever may be claimed by those who seek to impose their tradition on others. I have, I hope, shown that diversity was characteristic of Christianity right from the Galilean days when an ex-taxgatherer sat at supper with an ex-guerrilla. The New Testament contains four gospels, not one, and the letters preserved in it come from different traditions which may be called Pauline, Jewish and Early Catholic. Christianity later became more organised, but to restrict the true membership of the church to those who accepted the dogmatic definitions of its councils would be to ignore large numbers of ardent Christians. To identify Christianity with the development of Catholicism is, similarly, to ignore both Western deviations (such as the Donatist or Celtic churches) and Eastern Orthodoxy as it maintained its own worship and witness after 1054. The age of the Reformation shattered irretrievably such unity as Western Catholicism had possessed – and the churches of the Reformation could never agree among themselves or even preserve their internal unity. Substantial movements broke away in order to assert the believer's freedom against state control or in order to assert the believer's conservatism against the critical scholarship or the 'social gospel' of nineteenth-century liberals. There is no way of tidying up all this history except a method which admittedly has been much practised: the closing of the eyes and of the mind to everything that does not fit in with the prejudices of the favoured group.

As I look back over this history of disputes, I find myself compelled to disagree with the easy judgement (which I used to accept) that it has all been the product of sin. Often these disagreements were conducted in a very sinful manner: the disputants exhibited arrogance and cruelty and they disastrously used the power of the state to enforce points of theology. But disunity is not the only sin. People can conform to religious institutions, keep the peace and maintain unity for sinful reasons including a preference for a quiet life (and, for clergymen, a steady income). Had the leadership of the Christian church been able to count on the conformity of the entire membership, its pride, idleness and corruption would probably have been greater than the sum total of the sins to be observed in the history that did occur. And the history of disunity has had its bright spots. Disputes which arise out of deeply conscientious differences of opinion, and which are conducted with some awareness that God's love is being talked about, have often brought salt into an insipid religion and have thrown light on problems which the lazy had found too difficult. Diversity, inevitably resulting in controversies, has on the whole been a strength.

Against the contemporary and traditional fact of diversity, however, has to be set the fact that Christians have always been convinced that *some* unity is their duty. The best Christians have always seen that some unity was commanded by the common Lord. And in the twentieth century the ecumenical movement has been seen by many Christians – probably by steadily increasing numbers around the world – as nothing less than an attempt to obey the Lord's command. The passages in Paul's letters which speak of the church as the body of the Christ who cannot be divided have been taken to heart and the 'high priestly' prayer for the disciples' unity (John 17) has been heard as a cry from Christ's own heart. An immense effort, spiritual and intellectual, has been put into the search for a unity which would answer that prayer. At the centre of Christian history in the twentieth century it has been seen that competition in missionary work could not commend the gospel of peace and love; that it was not enough to reach 'comity' agreements between missionaries, or cooperation between missionary-led churches; that the churches which had sent out Protestant missionaries were themselves challenged to unite; that the Orthodox and Oriental churches should be included; that the Roman Catholic Church must recognise the brotherhood of the baptised and move towards a fuller recognition of 'separated brethren'; that the churches must have serious and patient dialogues about their agreements and differences; that attempts must be made at unions between churches at the national level; that locally there must be fellowship. All along the road Christians have felt that they have been lured or driven by the Holy Spirit – from the World Missionary Conference at Edinburgh in 1910, through the formation of the World Council of Churches in 1948 and the equally exciting promises of the Second Vatican Council, and also in the small steps which have had to be taken in innumerable neighbourhoods if the grand gestures were to make for genuine progress. And during this ecumenical pilgrimage many Christians have discovered that they are no longer divided by deeply conscientious convictions; that, in truth, they are divided by mere habits reinforced by social and economic factors; that their disputes are no longer salt and light but are burdens inherited from the past, impeding the progress of the body of Christ.

A large part of the problem confronting the modern ecumenical movement has been found to lie in the incompatibility of the visions of unity already held by the main Christian traditions. Thus the Roman Catholic Church and the Orthodox churches have both asserted the claim to be the only true church of Christ – although since the 1960s the Roman Catholics have modified that claim by various formulae and the Orthodox, while holding on to it in theory, have exposed themselves to other traditions by their participation in the life of councils of churches. The Evangelicals, in their international associations, have also claimed that the only truly Christian unity is to be found in submission to the scriptures interpreted by them – although often they, too, have struggled to formulate a more generous inclusiveness. It seems that the chief merit in these rival claims is their agreement that it is not right for Christians to be completely and complacently divided. Against all the tendencies to be comfortable in familiar divisions, these claims restlessly assert that the church is meant to be not a collection of fragments but the body of the Lord; not a street full of clubs but an army of love with the gospel as its marching orders. Thus even divisive theologies bear their witness to the insistence on a certain unity which is to be found in the Bible and in some of the deepest Christian experience.

Does this mean the disappearance of every denomination into 'one church'? *God's Reign and Our Unity*, the 1984 report of a commission of Anglican and Reformed churchmen, said that 'if we are as realistic about Baptism as the apostolic writers are, then we are already by our baptism one body, and the continued separation of our two communions is a public denial of what we are already in Christ'. One of the architects of that report, Bishop Lesslie Newbigin, has written that 'sociologists have pointed out that the denomination (which is essentially a product of the North American experience in the past two hundred years) is the form taken by a privatised religion in a secularised society, a religion which no longer makes total claims on the life of society. A denomination is a voluntary association of like-minded people who have joined together to practise and propagate some form of Christian religion. It does not claim to be the Catholic Church, but only to be one possible and partial manifestation of it. But the Church of the New Testament, which is always a visible body of people who can be named, is something for which a much more awesome claim is made. It is the assembly of actual men and women whom the living God is gathering in each place and in all places. It is both local and Catholic, but it cannot be denominational.'[20] In a similar vein Karl Barth wrote: 'There is no justification, theological, spiritual or biblical, for the existence of a plurality of churches genuinely separated and mutually excluding one another . . . A plurality of churches in this sense means a plurality of lords, a plurality of spirits, a plurality of gods. There is no doubt that to the extent that Christendom does consist of actually different and opposing Churches, to that extent it denies practically what it confesses theoretically – the unity and the singularity of God, of Jesus Christ, of the Holy Spirit.'[21]

The most influential modern statement of the ideal of Christian unity was adopted by the World Council of Churches at its Assembly in New Delhi in 1961 and has been repeatedly reaffirmed in later meetings of that richly representative fellowship. The statement reads: 'We believe that the unity which is both God's will and his gift to his Church is being made visible as all in each place who are baptized into Jesus Christ and confess him as Lord and Saviour are brought by the Holy Spirit into one fully committed fellowship, holding the one apostolic faith, preaching the one Gospel, breaking the one bread, joining in common prayer, and having a corporate life reaching out in witness and service to all and who at the same time are united with the whole Christian fellowship in all places and all ages in such wise that ministry and members are accepted by all, and that all can act and speak together as occasion requires for the tasks to which God calls his people.'

This statement was elaborated by the World Council of Churches Assembly in Nairobi in 1975 when it defined the unity being sought beyond the local level. It said: 'The one church is to be envisioned as a conciliar fellowship of local churches which are themselves truly united. In this conciliar fellowship each local church possesses, in communion with the others, the fullness of catholicity, witness to the same apostolic faith, and therefore recognises the others as belonging to the same Church of Christ and guided by the same Spirit.' Nairobi then summarised the New Delhi statement, which it described as a sketch of 'full organic unity'. Its own vision was, it said, 'not different' – for 'in it, each church aims at maintaining sustained and sustaining relationships with her sister churches, expressed in conciliar gatherings whenever required for the fulfilment of their common calling'. In harmony with this vision, the constitution of the WCC was amended, making it clear that the council calls the churches 'to the goal of visible unity in one faith and in one Eucharistic fellowship expressed in worship and in common life in Christ'.

That Nairobi statement made no reference to the role of bishops and the next WCC Assembly (in Vancouver) failed to add anything of substance to the words of 1961 and 1975. But as we have seen, the *Baptism, Eucharist and Ministry* text of 1982 reflects what seems to be a growing acceptance of the necessity of 'oversight' (*episkope*) including personal oversight of the kind exercised by bishops – although among Protestants this acceptance is made in guarded terms. Recent theological conversations between Roman Catholics, Orthodox, Anglicans and Lutherans have also produced an agreement in outline that it is proper and useful for some bishops, the 'primates' including the pope, to be given a special responsibility for strengthening the unity between the churches in a region or at the world level – although at this last point the Orthodox, Anglicans and Lutherans hesitate.

Thus recent statements record a considerable advance on earlier and vaguer ideas of unity. But further advance is plainly needed if the ecumenical goal is to be reached – and is to be found to be more than an illusory mirage in the desert of ecclesiastical rhetoric. In 1978 the National Ecumenical Consultation of the Episcopal Church in the USA endorsed a vision of 'the visible unity we seek' set forth in some words from the Faith and Order Commission of the World Council of Churches: 'They will share the bread and the cup of their Lord; they will acknowledge each other as belonging to the body of Christ at all places and at all times; they will proclaim the Gospel to the world with one mind and purpose; they will serve the needs of humankind with mutual trust and dedication. And for these ends they will plan and decide together in assemblies constituted by authorised representatives whenever that is required.' But this meeting added: 'We do not yet see the shape of the collegiality, conciliarity, authority and primacy which need to be present and active in the diocese with its parishes as well as nationally, regionally, universally. We do not yet know how the particular traditions of each of the communions will be maintained and developed for the enrichment of the whole Church. We do not yet see how the Church will be shaped by the particular histories and cultures within which she is called to fulfil her mission.' It was a brave confession of agnosticism – but in the 1980s the thoughtful members of many other churches have a roughly similar attitude of questioning in the movement for Christian reunion.[22]

Questions which need to be answered include these. Is 'one fully committed fellowship' of the local church in the New Delhi statement necessarily expressed by all the Christians in a neighbourhood worshipping together Sunday by Sunday? This appears to be the implication and is in accord with the ideal behind the formation of the united Church of South India (CSI), which is known to have been in the minds of those who drafted the statement. But even in such a 'united' church as the CSI different styles of worship and teaching are accepted and are on offer Sunday by Sunday, at least in many towns. And this 'united' church is likely to be outnumbered by the Christians who worship at the Roman Catholic mass – or by Protestants who worship more informally. Is it therefore acceptable that a 'local church' should be understood as Roman Catholics and Orthodox usually understand the term – as a diocese? And is it acceptable that within this diocese there should be congregations which draw adherents from outside the immediate neighbourhood because they are edified by particular ways of worship and teaching? Can there legitimately be working class congregations, or high caste congregations, or homosexual congregations, or (as in Latin America) 'communities' which meet regularly outside church buildings? Is it even proper to have a diocese made up of specialist congregations? For example, was it proper for the Anglican church in New Zealand to create a diocese for its Maori members? Is the Christian pluralism in the church of the Holy Sepulchre in Jerusalem entirely a scandal?

If diversity is to be permitted and even encouraged at the local level, is it right for those congregations which adhere to a particular emphasis to seek not only fellowship with other churches in their immediate neighbourhood but also a different kind of fellowship with other congregations also adhering to this tradition? In short, may denominations continue in some shape? They have a bad name in ecumenical circles. But it can be replied that they safeguard the freedom of the Spirit against the tendency of powerful church leadership to impose uniformity. And it may be asked whether even so sensitive an ecumenist as Bishop Newbigin is fully aware of the dangers of attempts to impose uniformity when he writes with favour of a religion which makes 'total claims on the life of society' and of a church which 'claims to be more than a partial manifestation of the Catholic Church'. At any rate, the millions who go to the world's churches have in practice given more support to denominationalism than the theologians have. In the early 1970s there was, therefore, a move in some circles associated with the World Council of Churches to secure a fuller recognition of the denominations in the ecumenical movement. Dr Eugene Carson Blake, formerly the chief executive of an American denomination and then General Secretary of the World Council of Churches, proposed that the international denominational bodies should be represented formally in the structure of the WCC – although the proposal was rejected. The 1977 Assembly of the Lutheran World Federation agreed that the goal was 'reconciled diversity', a phrase which was understood as being a code-word for the permanence of a modified denominationalism – although the Nairobi statement was intended as a counterblast. When such provocative talk died down, the idea of a continuing diversity between congregations was revived in the widespread proposal that denominations should 'covenant to unite' by the recognition of the essential faith in each other, by the mutual recognition of ministers and members, by joint ordinations and by some joint decision-making, rather than by a merger in one step. It is along these lines that the Consultation on Church Union in the USA, involving ten denominations, has been working.

Such ideas had much in common with the Roman Catholic practice of allowing clergy and congregations adhering to a particular tradition in worship and church life to combine in a 'uniate' church with its own bishops. These bishops are distinct from bishops of 'the Latin rite' in the same area, as well as from Orthodox or Anglican bishops who do not accept the superior authority of the pope. In Egypt the Catholics, fewer than seventy thousand in full membership, are divided into no fewer than seven communities, each cherishing its own rite. The Second Vatican Council's decree on 'the Eastern churches' mentioned the interim nature of such arrangements, preferring as the ideal the reconciliation of all the churches so that there could be one bishop in one place; but at present the arrangement satisfies those who wish to combine the Orthodox style (for example, married parish priests) with papal authority. It has often been suggested that Anglicans, if reconciled to Rome, might also be accorded 'uniate' status. This seems to have been in the mind of Pope Paul VI, who in 1970 greeted the Anglican communion as 'an ever-beloved sister' and assured it that in any 'embrace in the one authentic communion of the family of Christ' 'there will be no seeking to lessen the legitimate prestige and worthy patrimony of piety and usage proper to the Anglican Church'. The 'uniate' arrangement exists within Orthodox life. Their congregations (for example, in the USA) can be grouped on ethnic lines and ministered to by ethnic bishops and priests although Orthodox doctrine insists that in each diocese there is only one bishop to be reckoned Orthodox (with, of course, the possibility of episcopal assistants). So is the goal only the reconciliation, not the merger, of denominations? Is it enough to aim at a 'communion of communions'?

Such questions lead back into the problem of the papacy. It is not a problem which can be evaded in any realistic assessment of the ecumenical goal of Christians, since more Christians obey the pope (at least in theory) than do not. Therefore it directly challenges the World Council of Churches. In the 1960s there was talk that the Roman Catholic Church might join the WCC. Roman Catholic hierarchies have joined many national councils of churches and at the world level there has been some effective cooperation between agencies of the Vatican and of the WCC, for example in relief work or in theological study. But it was soon realised that membership would mean major upheavals for both bodies. The Roman Catholic understanding of ecumenism would have to be developed to allow its bishops to be seen consulting regularly with other church leaders, and with lay men and women, apparently on terms of equality. The entire style of the WCC would have to be adjusted to the entry of a church far larger than any other, with far higher claims for itself and with far greater hesitations about the radical commentary on contemporary politics and economics which has become one of the WCC's chief concerns. Although the WCC has kept the door open, there is understandable relief that in the 1980s the Roman Catholic Church seems very unlikely to walk through it in the near future. Already the WCC has often felt compelled to refrain from applying to the governments of traditionally Orthodox countries, most notably the Soviet Union, the standards which it applies to other nations – for it is well aware that its Orthodox members belong only by the permission of the governments. Roman Catholic membership would pose greater problems, not least because of the Vatican's record of anti-communism. Yet what is the World Council of Churches without the world's largest church?

The Orthodox churches are challenged very painfully by the problem of the papacy. In the happy ceremonies accompanying the end of the lifting of the excommunications in 1965, both Pope Paul VI and the ecumenical patriarch of Constantinople seemed to be saying that their churches were on the verge of 'full communion' or even 'union'. Since then renewed attempts have been made to prepare for a 'great and holy synod' of the Orthodox churches, which would no doubt have the relationship with Rome high on its agenda. But the problem of the papacy remains insoluble in Orthodox eyes while the papacy retains its claims to infallibility and to universal jurisdiction in the church. The Orthodox are not even able to agree about the powers of the primates of their own churches. The ecumenical patriarchate is a focus of unity but its status has inevitably fallen since its links with the Byzantine empire were severed and since Istanbul became a Muslim or secular city. Thus when he learnt of the lifting of the excommunications in 1965, the archbishop of Athens protested.

'The Church of Greece,' he wrote, 'has learned with great disappointment of the initiative of the Ecumenical Patriarch. No individual has
the right to undertake acts of such importance on his own. The right
belongs to the whole of Orthodoxy.' The ancient patriarchates of
Jerusalem, Antioch and Alexandria are also shadows of their former
selves. The churches of Greece, of the Balkan countries, of Russia
and of the other republics in the Soviet Union view all these ancient
centres of Orthodox life, as they view each other, with a determination not to allow effective power to any primate outside the nation.
Part of the reason is that they depend on the good will of their
governments, which are strongly nationalist. The consequence is that
great difficulties are experienced in planning for any international
gathering which would do for Orthodoxy something like what the
Second Vatican Council did for Roman Catholicism. Another consequence is the humiliating disarray of Orthodoxy in the USA.[23]

Evangelicalism has yet to come to terms fully with any of the
Christian forces just discussed – the Roman Catholic Church, the
Orthodox churches or the WCC. Yet worldwide, Evangelicalism is
itself a great and growing force. Most of the most active Protestant
Christians are far more interested in what are perceived to be its
agenda – conversion, the healing of the person, deep and joyful
prayer, Bible study, evangelism, church growth – than in what is
perceived to be the ecumenical task: patient collaboration between
Christians in theological study, in ecclesiastical reorganisation, in
charitable relief and in political action. But I have already given
reasons for believing that this task is beginning to concern many
Evangelicals. It also seems evident that the ecumenical movement,
with its focus in the WCC, gradually became during the 1970s far
more sensitive to Evangelical concerns, which must always be important for anyone involved in a really vigorous local church. That
sensitivity lies behind the many declarations to the effect that the
faithful proclamation of the gospel includes church membership and
social responsibility as well as the individual's conversion. There has
also been much more awareness in the leadership of the Roman
Catholic Church of the contribution which can be made by Evangelicals with enthusiasm for the Bible and with experience of the gifts of
the Holy Spirit. It is a contribution wider than the widespread
cooperation in Bible translation, publication and distribution – and
wider than the extensive participation by Catholics as well as Protestants in the charismatic movement. In the Orthodox and Oriental
churches, too, there are renewal movements which share many of the
Evangelical values. But it remains to be seen how much willingness

there is to cross the barriers which have in so much history so deeply separated Evangelicals from the rest. Will more Evangelicals profoundly acknowledge the Christianity of their fellow Christians – and believe that they can learn from it? Will the Roman Catholic Church officially relax some of its insistence on tradition, organisation and discipline in order that the new wine of the Spirit can be put into new bottles? Will Orthodoxy modify its concentration on the historic liturgy in order to emphasise the activities which the Evangelicals hold dear? And in a world where non-Christian movements are often dominant, will Orthodoxy cease to think that 'evangelism' mainly means a threat to draw its members into other churches? Will the World Council of Churches truly honour, and give a hearing to, Christians whose radicalism is shown chiefly by the simple holiness of their Bible-based lives? To none of these questions is the obvious answer 'yes'.

I am not going to produce an Anglican answer to all these questions about Christianity's futures. I am an Anglican and I am very thankful that the history which I have summed up was allowed to unfold, so as to enrich me as well as large numbers of better Anglicans. This tradition has moulded me – even while I criticise it or discuss matters apparently remote from it. But it has also helped to give me sympathy with the loyalties of other Christians to other traditions. In particular I am fascinated by the way in which the combination of riches which I think of as being 'Anglican' can be found in other traditions although without the wrappings put on them by the English or English-thinking culture in its historical development. For example the Catholicism of the Second Vatican Council may be regarded as a struggle to accept the message of the Bible, the message of tradition and the lesson of contemporary experience – which is the combination of sources of authority which I revere as an Anglican. I welcome that, especially since Anglicanism was born in a devoutly Catholic England. I have also been impressed by the strong spirituality of Orthodoxy, which insists on fellowship and on wholeness and balance in the faith which spirituality (so to speak) breathes out. My life would have been inspired by the Orthodox liturgy had I been born in Russia, say, or Greece or Romania – or so I hope, knowing that Orthodoxy has so often meant the courage of martyrs. I can recognise in Lutheranism things treasured by Anglicans – the Bible and its offer of God's justifying grace, the sacraments and their comfort, the common creed, the piety of the heart and the passion for truth – although the history of Lutheranism has had almost nothing to do with the influences radiating out from England.[24] Similarly I recognise much of the heritage that I love in Methodism although the Anglican authorities made the separate identity of Methodism inevitable within John Wesley's lifetime and although the worldwide denomination now has a non-Anglican ethos. I have longed for Anglican-Methodist reunion. And although the Calvinism in the Reformed tradition does not attract me theologically, I know both that many Anglicans have been Calvinists and that many pioneers of the ecumenical movement have been Reformed churchmen. Indeed, I have learnt from the Anglican teachers whom I most revere that Anglicanism must be sacrificed (not rejected and abandoned) in order that a more deeply and comprehensively Christian church may arise. As I contemplate the prospects of Christianity in the Americas, Africa or Asia, or even in a secularised Europe or in the 'white' Commonwealth, and when I think about the size and vitality of Catholicism and Evangelicalism, it seems to me improbable that the English religious tradition to which I have attached myself with all my mind and heart will provide the world's sole or central illumination in the years which lie ahead. In brief, I am – I trust – a modest Anglican.

But I believe that through an experience which was certainly not planned or expected in the sixteenth century Anglicans have learnt something about authority and something about comprehensiveness. I cannot do better than to quote words on these subjects which came from two Lambeth Conferences of Anglican bishops. In 1948 it was said: 'Authority, as inherited by the Anglican Communion from the undivided Church of the early centuries of the Christian era, is single in that it is derived from a single divine source, and reflects within itself the richness and historicity of the divine Revelation, the authority of the eternal Father, the incarnate Son, and the life-giving Spirit. It is distributed among Scripture, Tradition, Creeds, the Ministry of the Word and Sacraments, the witness of the saints, and the *consensus fidelium* [agreement of the faithful], which is the continuing experience of the Holy Spirit through his faithful people in the Church. It is thus a dispersed rather than a centralised authority, having many elements which combine, interact with, and check each other; these elements together contributing by a process of mutual support, mutual checking and redressing of errors or exaggerations to the many-sided fulness of the authority which Christ has committed to his Church.'

About comprehensiveness, it was said in 1968 that 'it demands agreement on fundamentals, while tolerating disagreement on matters in which Christians may differ without feeling the necessity of breaking communion. In the mind of an Anglican, comprehensive-

ness is not compromise. Nor is it to bargain one truth for another . . .
Rather it implies that the apprehension of truth is a growing thing: we
only gradually succeed in "knowing the truth". It has been the
tradition of Anglicanism to contain within one body both Protestant
and Catholic elements. But there is a continuing search for the whole
truth in which these elements will find complete reconciliation.
Comprehensiveness implies a willingness to allow liberty of interpretation, with a certain slowness in arresting or restraining explora-
tory thinking. We tend to applaud the wisdom of the rabbi Gamaliel's
dictum that if a thing is not of God it will not last very long (Acts
5:38–9). Moreover we are alarmed by the sad experience of too hasty
condemnation in the past (as in the case of Galileo). For we believe
that in leading us into all the truth the Holy Spirit may have some
surprises in store for us in the future, as he had in the past.'

Communion in diversity

So I end with the conviction that communion in diversity is the key
idea which can be drawn from the Anglican tradition – and from many
other sources also, supremely the Bible. It can provide guidance as
future generations of Christians seek to strengthen their unity amid
many differences and controversies.

As has often been noted in recent theological discussion, it is
possible to understand much of the New Testament through the word
'communion'. Communion (in Greek, *koinonia*) is what Jesus the
Son has with the heavenly Father in the Spirit, and it is what the Spirit
spreads. Communion is what Christians have with each other in the
power of the Spirit and it is what humanity is offered by the gospel. It
is what Catholics find in the holy church and Evangelicals in the small
group. It is what makes the traditional 'religious community' or the
modern Christian commune. It is what makes the local church a
church, supremely as the baptised celebrate the eucharist. The sexes,
the generations and the classes can then commune together. Communion can be sustained where there is very little agreement about
theology or politics and where differences of temperament are acute.
It is what makes a religion popular, as in the Americas – and Africa
seems to possess its secret. Communion with God and with the
neighbour is what many Indians and other Asians have sought
through many centuries although often it has seemed a goal forever
beyond the reach of the self. Secularised Europeans can open their
eyes when they see it lived. The evidence of communion, the 'high

priestly' prayer of John 17 says, is what would make the world believe. And communism is a secular alternative to it in which a third of the world does believe, at least to the extent of being governed by communists.

Inevitably an idea so rich is applied to problems of church life in many different ways. My own experience has led me to believe that communion must grow before there can be an end to the separation of denominations or even the real beginning of a widespread welcome to changes in denominations for the sake of unity. I have been an active member (and chairman) of a pressure group supporting two schemes to reconcile churches in England. The group, now called Christians Together, was refounded after the defeat of the second scheme in 1982, but the experience of that defeat taught me painfully how it is easy to criticise the details of any scheme. Only if there is a basic will to unite can the difficulties be overcome – and that determination can arise only out of communion, a process in which some detailed questions will be answered and others forgotten. It may take many years of a developing communion to reach the point where a complete union, or a 'covenant' for it, stands a chance of obtaining adequate support. That is why it is now so widely recognised that local communion is absolutely essential. Conversations between experts who represent divided churches can also be important. Their agreements can show those willing to be shown how comparatively trivial are the issues on which these churches still disagree. But the possibility of action will depend on the local communion of churches.

Communion is an idea which can be applied to many problems of church order through episcopacy. And the link can be made without falling into the trap of saying that bishops are essential to the life of the Christian church, a proposition for which there is no biblical or historical evidence. Nor am I hinting that a bishop should have powers unfettered by any synod or committee. There is no sound theological or practical reason why he should be allowed to be a dictator. On the contrary, much experience shows that an episcopal church is governed best when there is a balance between a bishop's initiatives and a group's collective (and often more cautious) wisdom. But without constitutional or synodical episcopacy – something very different from a dictatorship – the tension between diversity and unity seems to be an insoluble riddle. The bishop, when properly functioning, is not only the father-in-God of an area but also a representative of the wider church to that area. Communion with the bishop indicates a will to be 'catholic' (*kata holon*, 'according to the whole'), for it declares that one wishes to be in communion outside the group

which one specially favours. It should not be a merely formal
connection. It can be all the more valuable for being a relationship
with a human being to be gossiped and grumbled about, and where
possible loved, rather than the acceptance of the opinions of a
committee. Indeed, if this personal relationship is taken as the model
of the unity being sought, there need be no attempt to achieve
uniformity of opinions apart from the few essential agreements about
the 'apostolic faith' – the gospel known in Christian experience.
Room can be found for many varieties of life and thought in a diocese
or region whose bishop or bishops practise and encourage communion. A Methodist theologian who presided over the final revision of
the ecumenical text on *Baptism, Eucharist and Ministry* has wisely
imagined 'a national web of "dioceses" (probably much smaller than
the diocese, or equivalents, of any existing denomination), each
containing "congregations" in various liturgical, spiritual and cultural styles with free interchange of affiliation among individual
members, and each diocese being in conciliar communion with all
other dioceses in the land and indeed in every part of the world where
unity among Christians had progressed thus far.'[25]
In many circumstances it could be right for congregations or
communities sharing a special emphasis to be associated together.
They could be ministered to by specialist bishops. Thus Anglicans,
for example, could remain associated within dioceses which also
include many Roman Catholics, Lutherans, Methodists and others;
in relationship with those fellow Christians, they could be 'united not
absorbed' (to use a phrase which survived from the premature
Anglican-Roman Catholic conversations in Malines in the 1920s). A
glimpse of such a future seemed to be given when the pope and the
archbishop of Canterbury stood side by side in Canterbury Cathedral
in 1984. A variety of 'rites' could remain in dioceses where there are
now Orthodox, Oriental and Uniate churches, but their bishops
would all be in communion with each other. These associations of
like-minded Christians could be expressed in international fellowships if that should be wanted by their supporting congregations.
But their ministers and members would all be welcomed to officiate
or belong in any other congregation in the diocese. Although in time
the desire to be identified as a denomination or other movement
might wither away (as it seems to have done in China), there would be
no need to provoke reactions by making post-denominationalism
immediately compulsory. Such a policy of slow growth into unity
would no doubt involve many oddities. But it is right to recall the
point made by Karl Barth that denominations 'mutually excluding

each other' are a great and scandalous oddity. And it is right to remember how resistant almost every denomination has been to any invitation to attend its own funeral. 'Reconciled diversity', although not ideal, would be better than a situation in which denominationalism is deplored on ecumenical occasions but, in practice, maintained vigorously.

Unity could be expected to grow out of the experience of deliberation and decision-making with people who share not a special emphasis (denominational or other) but a faith in Christ and a commitment to a neighbourhood. National and regional synods could be elected. They could make decisions where decisions need to be made on practical questions in church life, particularly in the appointment and oversight of the bishops and the clergy. Normally when religious, moral or social questions are discussed in response to pressure from the congregations, the guidance which the synod issues would be persuasive rather than legislative. It could commend itself – or fail to commend itself – to the conscience of the Christian. If this principle could be understood by everyone, it would surely reduce the damage done by attempts to legislate about theological thought, sexual morality or political voting. But occasionally the members of a synod could be convinced that obedience to the gospel about communion demands a very stern warning to Christians whose opinions would, if accepted, destroy communion. An example is the witness of the German Confessing Church in the 1930s against the Nazis. Another is the series of pronouncements in the 1970s and 1980s that the doctrine of racial supremacy, known in South Africa as apartheid, is an evil heresy. In a few extreme cases, such as the rise of another Hitler or Stalin, there could be excommunication.

These national or regional synods would need to be kept outward-looking. They could welcome as observers and collaborators representatives of fellow Christians in the neighbourhood who are not yet ready to accept the Catholic structure of the church as just outlined. And to express their Catholicism they would need to be in communion with other synods around the world – particularly through their bishops, for bishops are traditionally expected to be travellers. At the world level, presumably with headquarters in Rome and New York, there could be a staff of experts facilitating such a communion. This staff would serve international councils and conferences developing work which has exposed Christians to each other, to the world around them and to their Lord. The pattern of these councils and conferences would have to be worked out. It has been assumed too easily that the model is provided by the councils of bishops in the early Christian centuries. But at the council of Nicaea about 230 bishops were present. In the 1980s there are almost 4,500 Roman Catholic bishops in the world; in Brazil alone, the Episcopal Conference numbers 289. The number of bishops who would have to be included in any council representing world Christianity would be very much larger – and presumably the council could not be confined to bishops. Effective work will, it seems likely, demand that any world council will consist of episcopal, clerical and lay representatives, elected by the continents. And to be effective this national, regional and global work would need to be overseen by experienced pastors – the patriarchs, archbishops, presiding bishops or primates. The only primate likely to be nominated seriously for the presidency of the college of bishops and of the Christian world headquarters is the bishop of Rome.

Of course the road to such a goal is full of obstacles. Innumerable warnings against false hopes of an easy progress could be quoted. A reality is that individuals, groups and large institutions, being human, are bound to be tempted to cling to the prominence and the power which they have inherited or acquired in the age of denominationalism. The expectation that these temptations will be overcome easily is folly. But with the 'folly' of the gospel, it is possible to hope. Indeed, 'to be baptised into Christ is to be baptised into hope' – as Pope Paul VI and Archbishop Coggan of Canterbury jointly declared in Rome in 1977, when they said that many were asking themselves 'whether they have a common faith sufficient to be translated into communion of life, worship and mission'. If it is believed that the greatest reality is the God who sends his Spirit to give Christians both unity and courage, hope may even be regarded as a realistic assessment of current trends.

Those who predict that the Christian idea of communion in diversity will fail because all religious motivation must fail ought to ponder a comment by Paul Johnson, an independent journalist and controversialist of distinction. Towards the end of his *A History of the Modern World* (1983) he wrote: 'What is important in history is not only the events that occur but the events that obstinately do not occur. The outstanding non-event of modern times was the failure of religious belief to disappear.'[26] From this observation he drew a conservative lesson, defending a traditional style of Roman Catholicism. But I conclude that belief in God through Jesus, which certainly has failed to disappear, is likely to inspire future Christians both to respect the diversity which God blesses and to seek the communion which is commanded by love.

APPENDIX
ANGLICAN PRINCIPLES OF UNITY

A resolution of the General Convention of the Episcopal Church, USA, in 1982.

Resolved, the House of Deputies concurring, That the 67th General Convention of the Episcopal Church re-affirm the Chicago-Lambeth Quadrilateral as found on pages of 876–878 of the Book of Common Prayer as a statement of basic principles which express our own unity, and as a statement of essential principles for organic unity with other churches, and affirm the following as an explication of that basic document without denying anything contained therein: that

1. The Holy Scriptures of the Old and New Testament are the word of God as they are witness to God's action in Jesus Christ and the continuing presence of his Holy Spirit in the Church, that they are the authoritative norm for catholic faith in Jesus Christ and for the doctrinal and moral tradition of the Gospel, and that they contain all things necessary for salvation.

2. The Apostles' and Nicene Creeds are the forms through which the Christian Church, early in its history under the guidance of the Holy Spirit, understood, interpreted and expressed its faith in the Triune God. The continuing doctrinal tradition is the form through which the Church seeks to understand, interpret and express its faith in continuity with these ancient creeds and in its awareness of the world to which the Word of God must be preached.

3. The Church is the sacrament of God's presence to the world and the sign of the Kingdom for which we hope. That presence and hope are made active and real in the Church and in the individual lives of Christian men and women through the preaching of the Word of God, through the Gospel sacraments of Baptism and Eucharist, as well as other sacramental rites, and through our apostolate to the world in order that it may become the Kingdom of our God and of his Christ.

4.   Apostolicity is evidenced in continuity with the teaching, the ministry, and the mission of the apostles. Apostolic teaching must, under the guidance of the Holy Spirit, be founded upon the Holy Scriptures and the ancient fathers and creeds, making its proclamation of Jesus Christ and his Gospel for each new age consistent with those sources, not merely reproducing them in a transmission of verbal identity. Apostolic ministry exists to promote, safeguard and serve apostolic teaching. All Christians are called to this ministry by their Baptism. In order to serve, lead and enable this ministry, some are set apart and ordained in the historic orders of Bishop, Presbyter, and Deacon. We understand the historic episcopate as central to this apostolic ministry and essential to the reunion of the Church, even as we acknowledge 'the spiritual reality of the ministries of those Communions which do not possess the Episcopate' (Lambeth Appeal 1920, Section 7). Apostolic mission is itself a succession of apostolic teaching and ministry inherited from the past and carried into the present and future. Bishops in apostolic succession are, therefore, the focus and personal symbols of this inheritance and mission as they preach and teach the Gospel and summon the people of God to their mission of worship and service.

NOTES

Chapter one

1 Summaries of theological history include from the USA Hans Schwarz, *On the Way to the Future* (revised, 1979), and from England Brian Hebblethwaite, *Christian Hope* (1984). John Macquarrie's essay on *Christian Hope* (1978) was of special value and the best big book is Jürgen Moltmann, *Theology of Hope* (in English, 1967). My own *A Reason to Hope* (1978) may be found relevant. Far more factual and statistical – in the opinion of most other experts, too optimistically statistical – is that treasure-house of information, *World Christian Encyclopaedia* (1982), edited by David B. Barrett, revised annually in the *International Bulletin of Missionary Research*. A good recent discussion of the wider scene is Barry B. Hughes, *World Futures: A Critical Analysis of Alternatives* (1985).

2 The list of books recommended in my *A Key to the Old Testament* (1976) may be supplemented by, e.g., W. H. Schmidt, *An Introduction to the Old Testament* (1984). Norman Gottwald, *The Tribes of Yahweh: A Sociology of Liberated Israel* (1979) was a powerfully relevant interpretation.

3 Emil Brunner, *The Christian Doctrine of God* (1949), pp. 206–7.

4 C. H. Dodd, *The Founder of Christianity* (1970) is the best introduction, to be supplemented by Norman Perrin, *Rediscovering the Teaching of Jesus* (1967) and *Jesus and the Language of the Kingdom* (1976); Geza Vermes, *Jesus the Jew* (1973); James D. G. Dunn, *The Evidence for Jesus* (1985). I suggested many other books for further study in my *Jesus for Modern Man* (1975). Among later publications Michael Grant, *Jesus* (1977), James P. Mackey, *Jesus the Man and the Myth* (1979) and E. P. Sanders, *Jesus and Judaism* (1985) are of exceptional interest as history. The religious problems were exhaustively covered by Edward Schillebeeckx's two studies, *Jesus: An Experiment in Christology* (in English, 1979) and *Christ: The Christian Experience in the Modern World* (in English, 1980). Shorter, but also by a Roman Catholic scholar, was Ben F. Meyer, *The Aims of Jesus* (1979).

5 Stephen Neill, *A History of Christian Missions* (1964), pp. 17, 28. This book contains a valuable bibliography.

6 Michael Grant, *St Paul* (1976) was a historian's portrait. Two studies by James D. G. Dunn, *Unity and Diversity in the New Testament* (1977) and

Christology in the Making (1980), are of special importance among recent contributions by biblical scholars. They include extensive bibliographies. A basic book is W. G. Kummel, *The New Testament: The History of the Investigation of its Problems* (1972).

7 Lesslie Newbigin, *Foolishness to the Greeks* (Geneva, 1986), p. 56. Jack Rogers and Donald McKim showed that 'inerrancy' in its modern sense has little solid support in the history of theology, in *The Authority and Interpretation of the Bible* (1981). Roman Catholic and Evangelical approaches are discussed in chapter seven. Other recent scholarship and theology were summed up by James Barr, *The Scope and Authority of the Bible* (1980), *Holy Scripture: Canon, Authority, Criticism* (1983) and *Escaping from Fundamentalism* (1984), and by Anthony Thiselton, *The Two Horizons* (1980). Ellen Flesseman-van Leer edited *The Bible: Its Authority and Interpretation in the Ecumenical Movement* (Geneva, 1980).

8 V. C. Samuel, *The Council of Chalcedon Re-examined* (Madras, 1977), p. 295.

9 W. H. C. Frend, *The Rise of Christianity* (1984) was a history of the first six hundred years, listing many more specialised studies. Aloys Grillmeier, *Christ in Christian Tradition: From the Apostolic Age to Chalcedon* (²1975), was another comprehensive work, on doctrine. Charles Cochrane, *Christianity and Classical Culture* (1940) is a classic. The best recent defence of patristic orthodoxy is Walter Kasper, *The God of Jesus Christ* (1984), and the best recent outline of an alternative is James P. Mackey, *The Christian Experience of God as Trinity* (1983). Anglican theological studies have included G. W. H. Lampe, *God as Spirit* (1977) and the less radical David Brown, *The Divine Trinity* (1985). Historical studies have included J. N. D. Kelly, *Early Christian Creeds* (revised, 1972) and *Early Christian Doctrines* (revised, 1977) and R. P. C. Hanson, *Tradition in the Early Church* (1962). The World Council of Churches has published the results of informal conversations between historians of the creeds in *The Roots of Our Common Faith* (Geneva, 1984) and between 'Eastern' and 'Oriental' Orthodox theologians in *Does Chalcedon Divide or Unite?* (Geneva, 1981). Truthful histories of the origins of the Catholic ministry have included William Telfer, *The Office of a Bishop* (1962) and Edward Schillebeeckx, *The Church with a Human Face* (1985). J. M. R. Tillard has studied the evolution of the papacy in *The Bishop of Rome* (1983) and J. N. D. Kelly its personalities in the *Oxford Dictionary of Popes* (1986).

Chapter two

1 Introductions include Paul Johnson, *A History of Christianity* (1976) and Ninian Smart, *The Phenomenon of Christianity* (1979).

2 I suggested books for further study in the three volumes of my history of

Christian England (1981–84). See also C. J. Stranks, *Anglican Devotion* (1961); Martin Thornton, *English Spirituality* (1963); *Anglican Spirituality*, edited by W. J. Wolf (1982); John R. H. Moorman, *The Anglican Spiritual Tradition* (1983).

3 Recent studies include A. M. Ramsey, *From Gore to Temple* (1960); Leslie Paul, *A Church by Daylight: A Reappraisement of the Church of England and its Future* (1973); Geoffrey Rowell, *The Vision Glorious: Themes and Personalities of the Catholic Revival in Anglicanism* (1983); Alan M. G. Stephenson, *The Rise and Decline of English Modernism* (1984); Paul Welsby, *A History of the Church of England 1945–80* (1984); Adrian Hastings, *A History of English Christianity 1920–85* (1986). My *Leaders of the Church of England 1828–1944* (1971) contained many suggestions for further reading.

4 The commission's report was *For the Sake of the Kingdom* (1986).

5 In *The Anglican Tradition*, edited by Richard Holloway (1984), p. 71.

6 A. M. Ramsey, *The Gospel and the Catholic Church* (1936), p. 220. Recent studies include *The Anglican Communion: A Survey*, ed. J. W. C. Wand (1948); J. W. C. Wand, *Anglicanism in History and Today* (1961); Dewi Morgan, *Agenda for Anglicans* (1963); Stephen Bayne, *An Anglican Turning Point* (1964); Stephen Neill, *Anglicanism* ([4]1977); Alan M. G. Stephenson, *Anglicanism and the Lambeth Conferences* (1978); Stephen W. Sykes, *The Integrity of Anglicanism* (1978); Urban T. Holmes, *What is Anglicanism?* (1982); Mary Tanner, *Anglicans in Dialogue* (1984). The Anglican Consultative Council has published John Howe, *Highways and Hedges: A Study of Developments in the Anglican Communion 1958–82* (1985) and a study of *The Chicago-Lambeth Quadrilateral* (1984). Philip Turner and Frank Sugeno edited *Crossroads are for Meeting* (1986). *The Study of Anglicanism* edited by John Booty and Stephen Sykes is in preparation.

Chapter three

1 Jon Sobrino, *The True Church and the Poor* (1984), p. 28.

2 Robert McAfee Brown, introducing *The Power of the Poor in History* by Gustavo Gutierrez (1984). He also wrote *Theology in a New Key: Responding to Liberation Themes* (1978) and *Unexpected News* (1984).

3 Good introductions are Eugene Nida, *Understanding Latin Americans* (revised, 1976); José Miguez Bonino, *Revolutionary Theology Comes of Age*, published in the USA as *Doing Theology in a Revolutionary Situation* (1975); Alfred T. Hennelly, *Theologies in Conflict* (1979); Enriques Dussel, *The History of the Church in Latin America* (in English, 1982); Thomas C. Bruneau, *The Church in Brazil: The Politics of Religion* (1984); Gustavo Gutierrez, *We Drink from our Own Wells* (in English, 1984); Juan Luis Segundo, *Theology and the Church* (1985), a reply to the first 'Instruction' of the Congregation for the Doctrine of the

Faith (1984); Edward L. Cleary, *The Church in Latin America Today* (1985). Alain Gheerbrant, *The Rebel Church in Latin America* (in English, 1974), Joseph Gremillion, *The Gospel of Peace and Justice* (1976) and Penny Lernoux, *Cry of the People* (1982) documented rebel and official developments in Catholicism, and John Eagleson and Philip Scharper edited *Puebla and Beyond* (1979). Of special value for writings up to 1975 is *Frontiers of Theology in Latin America*, edited by Rosino Gibellini (in English, 1979). Trevor Beeson and Jenny Pearce compiled *A Vision of Hope: The Churches and Change in Latin America* for the British Council (1984) and included suggestions for further reading. Philip Berryman, *The Religious Roots of Rebellion* (1984), documented Christian participation in social change in Central America. Sergio Torres and John Eagleson edited *The Challenge of Basic Christian Communities* (1981). Other assessments include Alvaro Barriero, *Basic Ecclesial Communities* (in English, 1982); Guillermo Cook, *The Expectation of the Poor* (1985); and Leonardo Boff, *Ecclesiogenesis* (in English, 1986).

4 Edmund Fawcett and Tony Thomas, *America and the Americans* (1983), p. 400. This excellent survey by two journalists of the London-edited *Economist* was published in the USA as *The American Condition*. A convenient recent summary of religious statistics is *All Faithful People* by Theodore Caplow and others (1983).

5 Robert T. Handy, *A Christian America* (1971), p. 213. H. Richard Niebuhr, *The Kingdom of God in America* (1937) still deserves study, as does his theological analysis of *Christ and Culture* (1951).

6 An excellent history of 'five hundred years of religion in America' has been provided by Martin E. Marty, *Pilgrims in Their Own Land* (1984). *Christianity in America: A Handbook* (1983), edited by Mark A. Noll and others, was a popular Evangelical presentation which included lists of books for further reading, as did the more scholarly Sydney E. Ahlstrom, *A Religious History of the American People* (revised, 1975) and Robert T. Handy, *A History of the Churches in the United States and Canada* (1977). Commentaries by reliable scholars have included Peter L. Berger, *Facing up to Modernity* (1978); Andrew M. Greeley, *The Denominational Society* (1972) and *The American Catholic: A Social Portrait* (1977); Martin E. Marty, *The Modern Schism* (1969) and *A Nation of Behavers* (1976); Sidney E. Mead, *The Lively Experiment* (1963); Gayraud S. Wilmore, *Black Religion and Black Radicalism* (revised, 1983). More recent studies include Peter Clecak, *America's Quest for the Ideal Self* (1983); Jay P. Dolan, *The American Catholic Experience* (1985); William Halsey, *The Survival of American Innocence* (1980); James J. Hennessey, *American Catholicism* (1982); Dean R. Hodge and David A. Rozen, *Understanding Church Growth and Decline 1950–1978* (1979); James D. Hunter, *American Evangelicalism: Conservative Religion and the Quandary of Modernity* (1983); George Marsden, *Fundamentalism and American Culture* (1980); Rodney Stark and

William S. Bainbridge, *The Future of Religion* (1984); John F. Wilson, *Public Religion in American Culture* (1979). Richard Quebedeaux produced a number of books on the Evangelicals in the 1970s and in *By What Authority?* (1982) he assessed the 'electronic church'. Paul A. Crow, *Christian Unity: Matrix for Mission* (1982), was a good summary. *Religion in America* (1982), edited by George C. Bedell and others, collected key documents and extracts. *The Sacred in a Secular Age* (1985), edited by Phillip E. Hammond, collected studies by sociologists participating in the Society for the Scientific Study of Religion. George Gallup, Jr., and David Poling analysed public opinion in *The Search for America's Faith* (1980).

7 The most brilliant, and very far from naive, expression of Latin American Utopianism is Rubem Alves, *A Theology of Human Hope* (in English, 1969). He also wrote *Tomorrow's Child* (1972) and *Protestantism and Repression* (1985). He once described the 'Christian realism' associated with Reinhold Niebuhr in the USA as an 'ideology of the Establishment', but the discussion was more subtle in Dennis P. McCann, *Christian Realism and Liberation Theology* (1981) and José Miguez Bonino, *Toward a Christian Political Ethic* (1983). *Theology in the Americas* (1976), edited by Sergio Torres and John Eagleson, documented a seminal conference. Frederick Herzog presented *Justice Church: The New Function of the Church in North American Christianity* (1980) and Richard Shaull presented the poor of South and North America as *Heralds of a New Reformation* (1984). In *Unexpected News* a US theologian, Robert McAfee Brown, celebrated the fresh insights which come through 'reading the Bible with Third World eyes', mainly Latin American (1984). In *Distant Neighbours: A Portrait of the Mexicans* (1985) Alan Riding looked over the frontier. A good economic survey has been provided by Ronald H. Chilcote and Joel C. Edelstein, *Latin America: Capitalist and Socialist Perspectives of Development and Underdevelopment* (1986). The best Christian defence of the economic philosophy prevailing in the USA has been offered by Michael Novak, *The Spirit of Democratic Capitalism* (1982).

8 This symposium was edited by Pablo Richard (in English, 1983).

9 Robert N. Bellah and others, *Habits of the Heart: Individualism and Commitment in American Life* (1985), pp. 22–55. Prof. Bellah also collaborated with Charles Y. Glock to collect essays on the upheaval of the 1960s in *The New Religious Consciousness* (1976) and with Phillip Hammond to give some of the background in the more recent and more sedate *Varieties of Civil Religion* (1980).

10 The classic statement of intellectual seriousness in futures thinking was Bertrand de Jouvenal, *The Art of Conjecture* (in English, 1967). A history of the future was provided by I. F. Clarke, *Patterns of Expectation 1644–2001* (1979). Alvin Toffler's stimulating journalism in *Future Shock* (1970) and his more optimistic *The Third Wave* (1980) summed up much informed discussion and achieved immense popularity. So did

John Naisbitt's *Megatrends* (1982), with its confidence that the USA could 'avoid the prospect of becoming a Great Britain' (1984 ed., p. 280). But this line of thinking, of which the most authoritative example was Daniel Bell, *The Coming of Post-Industrial Society* (1973), was put in its historical and sociological context by, e.g., Krishan Kumar, *Prophecy and Progress* (1978). Certainly some trends provide little ground for the Toffler-Naisbitt optimism. *Faith, Science and the Future* (1978), edited by Paul Abrecht, was prepared for a world conference of the World Council of Churches with a vocally critical contingent from Latin America. *The Global 2000 Report to the President* (1982), commissioned by the doomed President Carter, was full of warnings about the USA as well as about the world, although it was attacked as pessimistic by Julian Simon and Herman Kahn in *The Resourceful Earth* (1984). The annual *World Development Report* compiled by the staff of the World Bank is valuably factual. In *The Naked Public Square* (1984) Richard J. Neuhaus urged the US churches to influence public policy and so shape the future. He pleaded for understanding between 'mainline' liberals and Evangelical conservatives. In *The Public Church: Mainline–Evangelical–Catholic* (1981), Martin E. Marty saw the beginnings of a closer collaboration but excluded the fundamentalists. A constructive Catholic approach was made by John A. Coleman in *An American Strategic Theology* (1982). Earlier approaches were analysed by Charles E. Curran, *American Catholic Social Ethics* (1982), before the Vatican disowned him.

Chapter four

1 *Irruption of the Third World*, ed. Virginia Fabella and Sergio Torres (1983), p. 72.
2 Good summaries with bibliographies, admittedly by Englishmen, were C. P. Groves, *The Planting of Christianity in Africa*, in four volumes (1948–58); T. A. Beetham, *Christianity and the New Africa* (1967); Adrian Hastings, *A History of African Christianity 1950–1975* (1979); Peter Falk, *The Growth of the Church in Africa* (1979). Other important histories include E. A. Ayandele, *The Missionary Impact on Modern Nigeria 1842–1914* (1966); *Christianity in Tropical Africa*, ed. C. G. Baeta (1968); David B. Barrett, *Schism and Renewal in Africa* (1968), a study of the independent churches; *Christianity in Independent Africa*, ed. Richard Gray (1978); N. J. Ndiokwere, *Prophecy and Revolution* (1981); Roland Oliver, *The Missionary Factor in East Africa* (revised, 1965); Lamin Sanneh, *West African Christianity: The Religious Impact* (1983); Bengt Sundkler, *The Christian Ministry in Africa* (1960). Lloyd Timberlake, *Africa in Crisis* (1985), illuminated the 'causes and cures of environmental bankruptcy'.
3 Recent scholarly contributions include F. E. Boulaga, *Christianity without Fetishes* (1984); Kwesi Dickson, *Theology in Africa* (1984); Joseph

Donders, *Non-Bourgeois Theology: An African Experience of Jesus* (1985); Adrian Hastings, *Christian Marriage in Africa* (1973) and *African Christianity* (1976); Eugene Hillman, *Polygamy Reconsidered* (1979); Bolaji Idowu, *African Traditional Religion: A Definition* (1973); John S. Mbiti, *African Religions and Philosophy* (1969), *Concepts of God in Africa* (1970) and *New Testament Eschatology in an African Background* (1973); G. H. Muzorewa, *The Origins and Development of African Theology* (1985); Henry Okullu, *Church and State in Nation Building and Human Development* (Nairobi, 1984); Lamin Sanneh, *West African Christianity* (1983); Aylward Shorter, *African Culture and the Christian Church* (1973), *African Christian Theology* (1975) and *African Christian Spirituality* (1978); Monica Wilson, *Natural Symbols* (1970) and *Religion and the Transformation of Society* (1971). *Biblical Revelation and African Beliefs*, edited by Kwesi Dickson (1969), *The Emergent Gospel*, edited by Sergio Torres and Virginia Fabella (1978), and *African Theology en Route*, edited by Kofi Appiah-Kubi and Sergio Torres (1979), were important symposia. Self-revealing writings by Africans include Jomo Kenyatta, *Facing Mount Kenya* (1938); Kenneth Kaunda, *A Humanist in Africa* (1966); Julius Nyerere, *Ujamaa: Essays on Socialism* (1968); and the novels by China Achebe, *Things Fall Apart* (1958) and *No Longer at Ease* (1960), and by Ngugi wa Theiongo, *Petals of Blood* (1977), are outstanding in a wealth of creative writing. Accounts by missionaries who have lived close to the people include Vincent J. Donovan, *Christianity Rediscovered* (1978); Aylward Shorter, *Priest in the Village* (1980); Joseph G. Healey, *A Fifth Gospel* (1981). John V. Taylor, *The Primal Vision* (1963), was a pioneer's plea for sympathy with African traditional religion, but warnings against over-hasty 'Africanisation' have included, from Evangelicals, Tokunboh Adeyemo, *Salvation in African Tradition* (Nairobi, 1979) and Byang Kato, *Theological Pitfalls in Africa* (Kisumu, 1975); and from a Catholic, Charles Nyamiti, *African Theology: Its Nature, Problems and Methods* (Kampala, 1971) and *The Scope of African Theology* (Kampala, 1973). G. C. Oosthuizen criticised the independent churches in *Post-Christianity in Africa* (1968).

4 The Church History Association of India is publishing an ecumenical *History of Christianity in India*, edited by F. S. Downs and others (Bangalore, 1982–) which is superseding all earlier surveys. For the non-Christian background, *Hinduism in the Village Setting* and *Hindu Patterns of Liberation*, published by the Open University Press (1978), are good introductions with bibliographies. The political background was surveyed by M. J. Akbar, *India: The Siege Within* (1985), and Christian responses were illustrated by Catholic and Syrian/Protestant symposia: *The Indian Church in the Struggle for a New Society*, ed. D. S. Amalorpavadass (Bangalore, 1982) and *Religion and Society: The First Twenty-five Years*, ed. Richard W. Taylor (Bangalore, 1983). An interesting symposium on *The Influence of Hinduism on Christianity* was edited by Gnana Robinson (Madurai, 1980). John A. T. Robinson listed

many earlier books in his discussion of Christianity and Hinduism, *Truth is Two-eyed* (1979). Specially useful are M. Azariah, *Witnessing in India Today* (Madras, 1983); R. H. S. Boyd, *India and the Latin Captivity of the Church* (1974) and *An Introduction to Indian Christian Theology* (revised, Madras, 1975); Bede Griffiths, *Return to the Centre* (1976) and *The Marriage of East and West* (1982); Klaus Klostermaier, *Hindu and Christian in Vrindaban* (1969), entitled *In the Paradise of Krishna* in the USA; *Searching for an Indian Ecclesiology*, ed. Gerwin van Leewen (Bangalore, 1984); Donald McGavran, *Understanding the Church in India* (Bombay, 1979); Raymond Panikkar, *The Unknown Christ of Hinduism* (revised, 1968) and *The Vedic Experience* (Pondicherry, 1983); S. J. Samartha, *The Hindu Response to the Unbound Christ* (Madras, 1974); E. J. Sharpe, *Faith Meets Faith* (1977); William Stewart, *India's Religious Frontier* (1964); M. M. Thomas, *The Acknowledged Christ of the Indian Renaissance* (1969), *Salvation and Humanisation* (Madras, 1971) and *The Secular Ideologies of India and the Secular Meaning of Christ* (Madras, 1976); Ben Wati, *Whither Evangelicals?* (New Delhi, 1975). F. Houtat and G. Lemercinière studied *The Genesis and Institutionalisation of Indian Catholicism* (Louvain, 1981) and F. E. Keay provided *A History of the Syrian Church in India* (New Delhi, 1960). Evaluations of the Church of South India have been made in the Paul Report on *Renewal and Advance* (Madras, 1963) and the Abel Report on *Thirty Years* (Madras, 1978). In *Men and Gods in a Changing World* (1980), Judith Brown compared religious experience in India and in Britain. V. S. Naipul, *India: A Wounded Civilization* (1977), was brilliantly despairing about the country, whose vitality was celebrated in Salman Rushdie's *Midnight's Children* (1981), a novel which is a comedy and more, and in Dominique Lapierre's moving account of life in Calcutta, *The City of Joy* (in English, 1986).

Chapter five

1 Walbert Bühlmann, *The Coming of the Third Church* (in English, 1974), pp. 160–1. His other books – *The Search for God: An Encounter with the Peoples and Religions of Asia*, *All Have the Same God*, *God's Chosen Peoples* and *The Future of the Church* (in English, 1979–86) – show that he is far better qualified than I am to make the point I am making.

2 Bede Griffiths, *The Marriage of East and West* (1982), p. 201. His other books include *Return to the Centre* (1976).

3 *Irruption of the Third World*, ed. Virginia Fabella and Sergio Torres (1983), p. 68.

4 *Living Theology in Asia*, edited by John C. England (1981), p. 175.

5 The most vivid introduction was provided by Masao Takenaka, *Christian Art in Asia* (Kyoto, 1985). *World Christian Encyclopaedia* (1982), edited by David B. Barrett, is invaluable. Sketches of the theological task have

been offered by Choan-Seng Song in *Christian Mission in Reconstruction* (Madras, 1975), *Third-Eye Theology* (1979), *The Compassionate God* (1982), *Tell Us Our Names* (1984) and *Theology from the Womb of Asia* (1986); and Tissa Balasuriya in *Jesus Christ and Human Liberation* (1976), *The Eucharist and Human Liberation* (1979) and *Planetary Theology* (1984). International collections of articles include *Asian Voices in Christian Theology* (Manila, 1976), edited by Gerald H. Anderson; *Asian Christian Theology: Emerging Themes* (1980), edited by D. J. Elwood; *The Human and the Holy* (1980), edited by E. P. Nacpil and D. J. Elwood; *Asia's Struggle for a New Humanity* (1980), edited by Virginia Fabella; *Doing Theology in a Divided World* (1985), edited by Virginia Fabella and Sergio Torres. The conference report *Irruption of the Third World*, cited above, contains a good bibliography, as does John England's collection, *Living Theology in Asia*. More local collections include *Households of God on China's Soil* (1982), edited by Raymond Fung; *Minjung Theology* (1981), edited by Kim Young Bock, about Korea; a special number of the *International Review of Mission* on Korea (January 1985); *Church, State and People: The Philippines in the 80s* (Manila, 1981), edited by F. V. Carino. Some of Kim Chi-Ha's writings were translated as *The Gold-Crowned Jesus* (1978). Parig Digan analysed 'social protest' with a bibliography in *Churches in Contestation* (1984). Histories include Robert C. Orr, *Religion in China* (1980); Allen J. Swanson, *The Church in Taiwan* (1981); Avery T. Willis, *Indonesian Revival* (1977); R. and L. R. Constantino, *The Philippines: The Continuing Past* (Manila, 1978); D. K. Wilson, *The Christian Church in Sri Lanka* (Colombo, 1975). Leslie Lyall, *God Reigns in China* (1985), told that story from a firmly Evangelical viewpoint and G. Thompson Brown, *Christianity in the People's Republic of China* (1983), told it more cautiously. *Faith in Modernisation* (Singapore, 1985), the record of a visit sponsored by the Christian Conference of Asia, was of special value. Angelo S. Lazzarotto studied *The Catholic Church in Post-Mao China* (Hong Kong, 1982). In contrast, Keith Hinton described a free market for religion in *Growing Churches: Singapore Style* (1985). *The Asian Journal of Thomas Merton* (1968) was a moving record of an American Catholic monk's discoveries, well interpreted in Monica Furlong, *Merton: A Biography* (1980). Gabriel Kolko, *Vietnam: Anatomy of a War 1940–75* (1986), analysed a nightmare which still disturbs Christianity's Asian mission.

6 Frederick Franck, *Pilgrimage to Now/Here* (1974), pp. 88–9.

7 Nancy Wilson Ross, an American convert, presented *Buddhism: A Way of Life* (1981) with a bibliography. Anthony Fernando, *Buddhism Made Plain* (1985), was a sympathetic view from Sri Lanka. Melford Spiro, *Buddhism and Society* (1980) was sociological, as were Richard Gombrich, *Precept and Practice* (1971), about Sri Lanka, Jane Bunnag, *Buddhist Monk, Buddhist Layman* (1973), about Burma, and Robert Ekvall, *Religious Observances in Tibet* (1964). Sympathetic interpret-

ations by Christians have included George Appleton, *On the Eightfold Path* (1961); Frederick J. Streng, *Emptiness: A Study in Religious Meaning* (1967); Heinrich Dumoulin, *Christianity Meets Buddhism* (1974); Richard H. Drummond, *Gautama the Buddha* (1974); Lynn de Silva, *The Problem of the Self in Buddhism and Christianity* (Colombo, 1975); Hans Waldenfels, *Absolute Nothingness* (1980); John B. Cobb, *Beyond Dialogue* (1982).

8 Leslie Howard, *The Expansion of God*, pp. 358–9 (slightly abbreviated).

9 Kosuke Koyama has published in English essays on *Waterbuffalo Theology* (1974) and an autobiographical meditation on *Mount Fuji and Mount Sinai* (1984). Masao Takenaka, *God is Rice* (1986), was suggestive. For the background to Japanese Christianity Fujio Ikado, *The Religious Background of Japanese Culture* (Tokyo, 1973), and the novels by Shasaku Endo, <u>*Silence*</u> and *The Samurai* (in English, 1969–82), are important. Perceptive reports by foreign observers include Carl Michalson, *Japanese Contributions to Christian Theology* (1960); Raymond Hammer, *Japan's Religious Ferment* (1961); Robert Lee, *Stranger in the Land: A Study of the Church in Japan* (1967); Richard H. Drummond, *A History of Christianity in Japan* (1971); H. B. Earhart, *Religion in the Japanese Experience* (1974); James M. Phillips, *From the Rising of the Sun* (1981). Aelred Graham pioneered in *Zen Catholicism: A Suggestion* and *Conversations: Christian and Buddhist Encounters in Japan* (1967–69), and William Johnston interpreted Zen Buddhism on the basis of experience in Japan in *Silent Music* (1974), *The Inner Eye of Love* (1978) and *The Mirror Mind* (1981).

10 W. Cantwell Smith, *Islam in Modern History* (1959), pp. 72–3.

11 Fazlur Rahman has provided a modern presentation of *Islam* (1966) and a discussion of *Islam and Modernity* (1982) which is courageously honest. John L. Esposito edited *Voices of Resurgent Islam* (1983), about many countries. Good accounts by journalists include V. S. Naipaul, *Among the Believers* (1981) and Malise Ruthven, *Islam in the World* (1984). Ernest Gellner analysed *Muslim Society* (1981) and Edward Mortimer *Faith and Power: The Politics of Islam* (1982). W. Montgomery Watt summed up forty years of study in *Islam and Christianity Today* (1983) and Kenneth Cragg's illuminating books include *The Call of the Minaret* (1956), *Sandals at the Mosque* (1959), *Counsels in Contemporary Islam* (1965), *The Event of the Quran* (1971), *The Mind of the Quran* (1973), *The Wisdom of the Sufis* (1974) and *Muhammad and the Christian* (1984). Geoffrey Parrinder studied *Jesus in the Quran* (1965). Michael Nazir Ali, *Islam: A Christian Perspective* (1983), reflected experience in Pakistan. In *The Gospel and Islam* (1979), edited by Dan M. Curry, missionaries usefully exchanged experiences. The World Council of Churches published *Christians Meeting Muslims* (Geneva, 1977) and *Christian Presence and Witness in Relation to Muslim Neighbours* (1981), and an American Jesuit, Richard Rousseau, has collected documents illustrating *Christianity and Islam: The Struggling Dialogue* (4 vols, 1981–85).

Robert B. Betts surveyed *Christians in the Arab East* (revised, 1978).

12 Gershom Scholem, *Of Jews and Judaism in Crisis* (1976), p. 22.

13 The best recent expositions of Judaism seem to be Abba Hillel Silver, *Where Judaism Differed* (1956); Abraham Joshua Hisch, *God in Search of Man* (1956); Isidore Epstein, *Judaism: A Historical Presentation* (1959); Louis Jacobs, *Principles of the Jewish Faith* (1964) and *A Tree of Life* (1984); Nicholas de Lange, *Judaism* (1986). Lionel Blue, *To Heaven with Scribes and Pharisees* (1975), was warmly human, and Samuel Sandmel, *We Jews and Jesus* (1965), was a scholarly and powerful presentation of some of the central problems. Martin Gilbert told the story of *The Holocaust* (1985) and Ignaz Maybaum discerned *The Face of God after Auschwitz* (Amsterdam, 1965). Dow Marmur offered brave reflections on the future of Judaism in *Beyond Survival* (1982). Christian responses were outlined in Peter Schneider, *Sweeter than Honey* (1966); Ignaz Maybaum, *Trilogue between Jew, Christian and Muslim* (1973); Rosemary Ruether, *Faith and Fratricide* (1974); Kenneth Cragg, *This Year in Jerusalem* (1980); John T. Pawlikowski, *Christ in the Light of Christian-Jewish Dialogue* (1982); Alan Ecclestone, *The Night Sky of the Lord* (1984). The World Council of Churches published *Jewish-Christian Dialogue* (Geneva, 1975). Conor Cruise O'Brien, *The Siege* (1986), analysed 'the saga of Israel and Zionism' gloomily. Larry Ekin, *Enduring Witness: The Churches and the Palestinians* (Geneva, 1985), accounted for part of the gloom.

14 W. Cantwell Smith, *The Faith of Other Men* (1962), p. 133. Edward J. Hughes has assessed *Wilfred Cantwell Smith: A Theology for the World* (1986).

15 Raymond Panikkar, *The Unknown Christ of Hinduism* (1968), pp. 27, 48.

16 Paul Tillich, *Christianity and the Encounter of the World Religions* (1963), p. 53.

17 Alan Race, *Christians and Religious Pluralism* (1983), Arnulf Camps, *Partners in Dialogue* (in English, 1983), Paul E. Knitler, *No Other Name?* (1985) and Richard H. Drummond, *Toward a New Age in Christian Theology* (1985) surveyed the theological debate. *Attitudes Toward Other Religions* (1969), edited by Owen C. Thomas, and *Christianity and Other Religions*, edited by John Hick and Brian Hebblethwaite (1980), presented its chief participants. Significant recent pleas for 'dialogue' by eminent scholars include Ninian Smart, *Beyond Ideology* (1979); John Hick, *God Has Many Names* (1980) and *Problems of Religious Pluralism* (1985); W. Cantwell Smith, *The Meaning and End of Religion* (^{2}1978) and *Toward a World Theology* (1981). John R. Cobb, Jr., *Christ in a Pluralistic Age* (1975), was a distinguished example of the use of 'Christ' in a loose sense, and W. A. Visser't Hooft, *No Other Name* (1963), summed up the protest against 'syncretism'. Differences between Christians which emerged at a 1976 conference in the USA, recorded in *Christian Faith in a Religiously Pluralist World* (1978), edited

by Donald Dawe and John Carman, were explored helpfully in a 1979 conference, published as *Christ's Lordship and Religious Pluralism* (1981), edited by Gerald H. Anderson and Thomas F. Stansky. Stanley Samartha edited collections of essays including *Living Faiths and Ultimate Goals* (Geneva, 1974) while at the World Council of Churches, and his own writings include *Courage for Dialogue* (1982). Christopher Lamb, *Belief in a Mixed Society* (1985), was wise about practical problems illustrated in Britain's experience, and with the same background Kenneth Cracknell, *Towards a New Relationship* (1986), was wise about principles.

Chapter six

1 Bertrand Russell, *A History of Western Philosophy* (1946), p. 515.
2 Bryan Wilson summed up the challenges in *Religion in Secular Society* (1966), *Contemporary Transformations of Religion* (1976) and *Religion in Sociological Perspective* (1982). Among the many illuminating writings of David Martin his *General Theory of Secularisation* (1978) and *The Breaking of the Image* (1980) are the most comprehensive. The older literature on European secularisation was surveyed and compared with evidence about the USA by Martin E. Marty, *The Modern Schism* (1969). Hans Mohl edited *Western Religion: A Country by Country Sociological Inquiry* (The Hague, 1972) and sketched a 'new social-scientific theory of religion' in *Identity and the Sacred* (1976). The historical background was outlined by Owen Chadwick, *The Secularisation of the European Mind in the Nineteenth Century* (1978) and *The Popes and European Revolution* (1981), and by Hugh McLeod in *Religion and the People of Western Europe 1789–1950* (1981). The intellectual background was outlined by L. Kolakowski, *Positivist Philosophy: From Hume to the Vienna Circle* (1968), H. Stuart Hughes, *Consciousness and Society 1890–1930* (1974) and Hans Küng, *Does God Exist?* (1980). Historical studies in greater depth were collected in *The Enlightenment in National Context* (1981), edited by Roy Porter and Mikulas Teich and in *Nineteenth-Century Religious Thought in the West* (3 vols, 1985), edited by Ninian Smart, John Clayton, Patrick Sherry and Steven T. Katz. Reading about one country was suggested by A. D. Gilbert, *The Making of Post-Christian Britain* (1980) and Adrian Hastings, *A History of Christianity in England 1920–85* (1986), with my own *Christian England*, vol. 3 (1984). Maurice Cowling analysed the intellectual debate in *Religion and Public Doctrine in Modern England* (1980–85) of which two volumes have so far appeared. On other nations the literature includes David Kertzer's study of *Comrades and Christians* (1980), in Italy; Peader Kirby, *Is Irish Catholicism Dying?* (Dublin, 1984); B. Szajkowski, *Next to God, Poland* (1984); and *The Church and Civil Religion in the Nordic Countries of Europe* (Geneva, 1984), edited

by Bela Harmati. Volumes nine and ten in the *History of the Church* (in English, 1981), edited by Hubert Jedin, Konrad Repgen and John Dolan, recounted developments in Catholicism, and Wayne A. Detzler, *The Changing Church in Europe* (1979), held out hope of some Evangelical warmth in the 'deep freeze of secularism'.

3 *K. Marx and F. Engels on Religion* (Moscow, 1972) is one of the convenient collections. Trevor Beeson surveyed *Discretion and Valour: Religious Conditions in Russia and Eastern Europe* (revised, 1982). To his bibliography should be added Dimitry Pospielovsky, *The Russian Church under the Soviet Regime* (2 vols, 1983), Michael Bourdeaux, *Risen Indeed: Lessons in Faith from the USSR* (1983) and Sir John Lawrence, *The Hammer and the Cross* (1986). *Light through the Curtain*, edited by Philip Walters and Jane Balagarth (1985), was a collection of brief testimonies by Christians under communist regimes. Roger Garaudy's writing, e.g., *Marxism in the Twentieth Century* and *The Alternative Future* (in English, 1970–76), recorded the pilgrimage of a French communist into religion in order to preserve his idealism. Jan Lochman, *Encountering Marx* (in English, 1977), was a Czech Christian's emphasis that Marx, too, had ideals. More substantial studies of the theory include Nicholas Lash, *A Matter of Hope: A Theologian's Reflections on the Thought of Karl Marx* (1981) and *Marxism and Christianity* by Denys Turner, who believes that 'morality, under capitalism, is Marxism' (p. 83). Harsher glimpses of morality under communism were provided by, e.g., Alexander Solzhenitsyn, *The Gulag Archipelago* (in English, 3 vols, 1974–78). *A Dictionary of Marxist Thought* has been edited by Thomas Bottomore (1983).

4 Sabino Acquaviva, *The Decline of the Sacred in Industrial Society* (in English, 1979), pp. 201–2.

5 Bryan Wilson, *Religion in Sociological Perspective* (1982), pp. 46, 51, 179. Alasdair MacIntyre commented on the intellectual background in *Secularisation and Moral Change* (1967) and *After Virtue* (1981), in a roughly similar vein.

6 David Martin, *A Sociology of English Religion* (1967), Thomas Luckmann, *The Invisible Religion* (in English, 1967) and Robert Bocock, *Ritual in Industrial Society* (1974) explored religion outside the churches. Roy Wallis edited *Sectarianism* (1975) and wrote *Salvation and Protest* (1979) and *The Elementary Forms of the New Religious Life* (1983). W. J. Hollenweger described *The Pentecostals* (1972) worldwide. David Clarke, *The Liberation of the Church* (1984), surveyed the ideals and experiences of radical groups, mainly but not exclusively in Britain.

7 Bryan Wilson, *Religion in Sociological Perspective* (1982), pp. 139–40.

8 Michael Biddiss, *The Age of the Masses* (1977), p. 349. This is volume six in the Pelican History of European Thought.

9 The declaration of the 'Third Ecumenical Encounter' was reprinted in *Apostolic Faith Today*, edited by Hans-Georg Link (Geneva, 1985), pp. 201–11.

10 A. N. Whitehead, *Religion in the Making* (1926), p. 57, was quoted with approval in, for example, John Polkinghorne, FRS, *One World: The Interaction of Science and Theology* (1986). I offered suggestions for reading in my *Religion and Change* (1969) and *What is Real in Christianity?* (1972). Since then the most helpful book in this field known to me is Hans Küng, *On Being a Christian* (1974). John Hick and Michael Goulder debated *Why Believe in God?* (1983). Richard Swinburne defended belief in God in *The Concept of Miracle* (1970), *The Coherence of Theism* (1977), *The Existence of God* (1979) and *Faith and Reason* (1981). Among the literature suggesting how the religious spirit survives in the age of science, A. R. Peacocke's *Creation and the World of Science* (1979), Sir Alister Hardy's *The Spiritual Nature of Man* (1980) and *Darwin and the Spirit of Man* (1984), and Hugh Montefiore's *The Probability of God* (1985) stand out. More detailed literature includes Paul Davies, *God and the New Physics* (1983) and A. R. Peacocke, *God and the New Biology* (1986). John Macquarrie magisterially surveyed the frontiers of philosophy and theology in the European world of thought, 1900–80, in *Twentieth Century Religious Thought* (revised, 1983). A useful short list of other recent books on religion and science may be found in *How to Read the World: Creation in Evolution* by three French scientists – Christian Montenat, Luc Plateaux and Pascal Roux (in English, 1985). A thoughtful outline of a completely non-miraculous form of Christianity was provided by Maurice Wiles, *God's Action in the World* (1986).

11 Lesslie Newbigin, *Foolishness to the Greeks* (1986), p. 118. Peter Hall edited *Europe 2000* (1977) and in *Making Sense of Europe* (1986) Christopher Tugendhat made sense of the Community. English theologians recently commenting knowledgeably on politics include Ronald H. Preston, *Religion and the Persistence of Capitalism* (1979) and *Church and Society in the Late Twentieth Century: The Economic and Political Task* (1983); Charles Davis, *Theology and Political Society* (1980); Peter Hinchliff, *Holiness and Politics* (1982). A well-informed Evangelical contribution was John Stott, *Issues Facing Christians Today* (1984). James Robertson, *Future Work* (1985), was illuminating about emerging economic trends, and the Church of England report on *Faith in the City* (1985) penetrated into areas being left behind. An international discussion on *Will the Future Work?* was edited for the WCC by Howard Davis and David Gosling (1986). Paul Mojzes expertly analysed *Christian-Marxist Dialogue in Eastern Europe* (1981) and Nicholas Piediscalzi and Robert C. Thobaben collected essays from many other parts of the world in *Three Worlds of Christian-Marxist Encounters* (1985). René Coste surveyed *Marxist Analysis and Christian Faith* (in English, 1985). In this dialogue, the most important book so far has been Milan Machovec, *A Marxist Looks at Jesus* (in English, 1976). Peter Hebblethwaite, *The Christian-Marxist Dialogue and Beyond* (1977), Ans van der Brent, *Christians and Communists: An Ecumenical Perspective* (Geneva, 1983)

and W. J. Milligan, *The New Nomads: Challenges Facing Christians in Western Europe* (Geneva, 1984) were suggestive.

12 *A New Dictionary of Christian Ethics* (1986), edited by John Macquarrie and James Childress, is a comprehensive introduction. Recent substantial studies include the two Church of England reports on *Marriage and the Church's Task* (1978) and *Homosexual Relations* (1979). The best commentary on the realities known by me has been supplied unofficially by a Roman Catholic expert, Jack Dominian, in *Proposals for A New Sexual Ethic* (1977) and *Marriage, Faith and Love* (1981). Some may prefer the more official and theoretical Karol Wojtyla, *Love and Responsibility* (in English, 1981). A comparison of Roman Catholic and Protestant teachings on marriage, after a careful dialogue, may be found in *Growth in Agreement*, ed. Harding Meyer and Lukas Vischer (1984), pp. 278–306. Sensitive Evangelical discussion of sexual morality may be found in John Stott, *Issues Facing Christians Today*, pp. 234–340. Also helpful is J. B. Nelson, *Embodiment: An Approach to Sexuality and Christian Theology* (1978).

Chapter seven

1 Hints about the future may be found in *New Mission for a New People* (1977), edited by David Mitchell; William Watty, *From Shore to Shore: Soundings in Caribbean Theology* (Kingston, 1981); Noel Leo Erskine, *Decolonizing Theology: A Caribbean Perspective* (1981); Charles W. Forman, *The Island Churches of the South Pacific* (1982); and John Garrett's two books about the South Pacific churches, *To Live among the Stars* (Geneva, 1982) and *A Way in the Sea* (Melbourne, 1982). *Tides of Change: Pacific Christians Review Their Problems and Hopes* (Melbourne, 1981) was edited by Vaughan Hinton. A symposium on *Religious Co-operation in the Pacific Islands* (Suva, 1983) was edited by F. Afeaki, R. Croncombe and J. McClaren. The best study of the inheritance is Alan R. Tippett, *Solomon Islands Christianity* (1967). The quotation is from an address by Dr Watty to the Methodist Conference in England in 1985.

2 Rodney M. Booth, *The Winds of God: The Canadian Church Faces the 1980s* (Geneva, 1982), p. 90. The historical background was presented by John Webster Grant, *The Church in the Canadian Era* (Toronto, 1972).

3 Bruce Wilson, *Can God Survive in Australia?* (Sutherland, NSW, 1983), pp. 29–33. The history was illuminated by Frank Engel, *Australian Christians in Conflict and Unity* (Melbourne, 1984). Sociological studies have included Hans Mohl's analysis of *Religion in Australia* (Melbourne, 1971) and Ian Black and Peter Glasner, *Practice and Belief* (Sydney, 1983). Brian Colless and Peter Donovan edited *Religion in New Zealand Society* (1980). Philip Slater edited *Religion and Culture in Canada* (Waterloo, Ont., 1976), Stewart Crysdale and Les Wheatcroft *Religion*

in Canadian Society (Toronto, 1976) and John R. Williams *The Canadian Churches and Social Justice* (Toronto, 1984). The *International Review of Mission* had special numbers on Australia in January 1979 and Canada in July 1982. The literature about an incomplete drama includes Marjorie Hope and James Young, *The South African Churches in a Revolutionary Situation* (1981), and *Whose Rubicon?*, published after a visit by the British Council of Churches (1986).

4 Richard Dickinson, *Poor Yet Making Many Rich* (Geneva, 1983), pp. 6, 37. This was a summary of the recent thinking of the World Council of Churches, which sponsored two memorable collections of essays: *Towards a Church of the Poor* (Geneva, 1979), edited by Julio de Santa Ana, and *The Community of Women and Men in the Church* (Geneva, 1983), edited by Constance F. Parvey. *Essays on The Bible and Liberation: Political and Social Hermeneutics* (1983) were edited by Norman K. Gottwald. An American scholar, Wayne Meeks, has surveyed *The First Urban Christians: The Social World of the Apostle Paul* (1983). Theo Whitvleit, *A Place in the Sun: Liberation Theology in the Third World* (in English, 1985) and Deane William Ferm, *Third World Liberation Theologies* (1986) were good introductions by scholars in the Netherlands and the USA. Donal Dorr, *Spirituality and Justice* (1984), an impressive Roman Catholic approach, was from an Irish as well as African background. Also helpful are two Anglican contributions: David Sheppard, *Bias to the Poor* (1983) and Charles Elliott, *Praying the Kingdom* (1985), with the report to the archbishop of Canterbury, *Faith in the City* (1985). Ronald J. Sider, *Rich Christians in an Age of Hunger* (1977), raised an eloquent and influential voice from the USA. Willy Brandt has prophesied about *World Armament and World Hunger* (1986) and Kenneth Greet about this and other crises in *What Shall I Cry?* (1986).

5 Elaine Storkey, *What's Right with Feminism* (1985) was a balanced introduction with a good bibliography. Feminist theology includes Elizabeth Schussler Fiorenza, *In Memory of Her: A Feminist Reconstruction of Christian Origins* (1983); Patricia Wilson Kastner, *Faith, Feminism and the Christ* (1983); Rosemary Radford Ruether, *New Woman, New Earth* (1975) and *Sexism and God-Talk* (1983); Phyllis Trible, *God and the Rhetoric of Sexuality* (1978) and *Texts of Terror* (1984); Elizabeth Moltmann-Wendel, *A Land Flowing with Milk and Honey* (in English, 1986). There is no need to go with Mary Daly *Beyond God the Father* (1973).

6 A classic study of the different types was H. Richard Niebuhr, *Christ and Culture* (1952). Recent studies include from the USA Lonnie D. Cleaver, *The Shattered Spectrum* (1981) and from Britain Ruth Page, *Ambiguity and the Presence of God* (1985). A penetrating discussion of dependence and independence may be found in Bruce Reed, *The Dynamics of Religion* (1978). Robin Gill explored *The Social Context of Theology* (1975) and *Theology and Social Structure* (1978).

7 *Growth in Agreement*, ed. Harding Meyer and Lukas Vischer, pp. 390–419.

8 Hans-Georg Link, *Apostolic Faith Today*, pp. 216–27.

9 Stephen Sykes, *The Identity of Christianity* (1984) and Paul Avis, *Ecumenical Theology and the Elusiveness of Doctrine* (1986), were illuminating Anglican essays in this field. Hans-Georg Link has edited for the WCC four books on *Confessing Our Faith around the World* (Geneva, 1984–85).

10 The Second Vatican Council whose *Documents* were edited by Walter M. Abbott with commentaries (1966) unleashed a flood of literature on Roman Catholicism, its leadership and its crisis. The permanently valuable contributions include Peter Hebblethwaite's books, the most substantial of which is his biography of *John XXIII* (1984) and the latest his *Synod Extraordinary* and *In the Vatican* (both 1986). Bishop B. C. Butler's *The Theology of Vatican II* (1967) and *The Church and Unity* (1979) recorded the mature and moderate reflections of one of the council's principal theologians. *Toward Vatican III: The Work that Needs to be Done* (1978), edited by David Tracy with Hans Küng and J. B. Metz, was a symposium by scholars associated with the international journal *Concilium*, which maintains an independent commentary (its conservative rival being *Communio*). Outstandingly clear and courageous in the world of *Concilium* is Hans Küng, whose thought has developed since *The Council and Reunion* (in English, 1964) through *Infallible?* (1971) to *The Church Maintained in Truth* (1980). *The Jerome Bible Commentary* (1968) showed the strength of Roman Catholic biblical scholarship. *The Encyclopaedia of Theology* (in English, 1975), edited by Karl Rahner, made available the cream of European Catholic thought. Robert J. Schreiter, *Constructing Local Theologies* (1985), began to move outside Europe. Three books by Avery Dulles, *Models of the Church* (1978), *Models of Revelation* (1983) and the *Catholicity of the Church* (1985), were seminal contributions from the USA. Yves Congar, *Diversity and Communion* (in English, 1984), was a reflection by a veteran French ecumenist, crowning a labour first made public by his *Chrétiens désunis* (1937). Bill McSweeney, a sociologist, analysed *Roman Catholicism: The Search For Relevance* (1975), and Michael Winter asked *What Ever Happened To Vatican II?* (1986), answering that 'the quality of the conciliar documents is so good, that it is unbelievable the results have been so poor' (p. 11). Peter Nichols, *The Pope's Divisions* (1981), presented a shrewd outsider's view of the Vatican and the worldwide church which it has been trying to control. John A. Coleman, *The Evolution of Dutch Catholicism 1958–1974* (1978), was an American scholar's study of an area of particularly lively experimentation before the Vatican largely succeeded in reasserting control, at least over the bishops. Francis A. Sullivan, *Magisterium: Teaching Authority in the Catholic Church* (1983), was a scholarly assessment of old and new discussions. One of the last and best pieces of theological work done by

W. A. Visser't Hooft, the first General Secretary of the WCC, was a study of 'Teachers and the Teaching Authority' printed in the *Ecumenical Review* (April 1986). Thomas S. Derr, *Barriers to Ecumenism: The Holy See and the World Council on Social Questions* (1983), warned against optimism about cooperation at the top but was more hopeful about local collaboration. Sympathetic Anglican responses were edited by Mark Santer in *Their Lord and Ours* (1982), but Hugh Montefiore expressed many Anglican anxieties in *So Near and Yet So Far* (1986).

11 *Serving our Generation* (1980) was edited by Waldron Scott. Essays on *The Future of World Evangelization: The Lausanne Movement* (1984) were edited by E. R. Dayton and Stephen Wilson. The Lausanne addresses, *Let the Earth Hear His Voice* (1975), were edited by J. D. Douglas.

12 *Sharing Jesus in the Two Thirds World* (1984) was edited by Vinay Samuel and Chris Sugden.

13 *Obeying Christ in a Changing World* (3 vols, 1977) was edited by John Stott, who also edited *The Year 2000 AD* (1983). The background was studied by Christopher Catherwood, *Five Evangelical Leaders* (1984), and Randle Manwaring, *From Controversy to Co-existence: Evangelicals in the Church of England 1914–80* (1985).

14 Robert F. Webber and Donald Bloesch edited *The Orthodox Evangelicals* (1978).

15 This address begins *Perspectives on the World Christian Movement: A Reader*, ed. Ralph D. Winter and Steven C. Hawthorne (1981). David J. Hesselgrave offered an Evangelical interpretation of 'Contextualisation' in *Communicating Christ Cross-Culturally* (1978), *Planting Churches Cross-Culturally* (1980) and *Counselling Cross-Culturally* (1984).

16 *Down to Earth: Studies in Christianity and Culture*, ed. John Stott and Robert Coote (1978), pp. 71–8.

17 The documents were edited by Donald McGavran in *The Conciliar–Evangelical Debate* (1977). Commentators include Orlando E. Costas in *The Church and its Mission: A Shattering Critique from the Third World* (1974), *Integrity of Mission* (1979) and *Christ outside the Gate* (1982). More hostile were Harvey Hoekstra, *The World Council of Churches and the Demise of Evangelism* (1979) and Francis Schaeffer, *The Great Evangelical Disaster* (1984). The present General Secretary of the WCC, Emilio Castro, has published wise reflections on *Freedom in Mission* (1985).

18 Eugene Nida, *Customs, Culture and Christianity* (1954), p. 52.

19 Richard G. Hutchenson, Jr., *Mainline Churches and the Evangelicals* (1981), pp. 25–6. Examples of 'inclusive' Evangelicalism in the USA have included Donald G. Bloesch, *The Future of Evangelical Christianity* (1983) and Bernard Ramm, *Beyond Fundamentalism: The Future of Evangelical Theology* (1984).

20 *Faith and Faithfulness*, edited by Pauline Webb (Geneva, 1984), p. 3.

21 Karl Barth, *Church Dogmatics*, vol. IV/1 (in English, 1956) p. 675.

22 *A Communion of Communions: One Eucharistic Fellowship*, edited by
   J. Robert Wright (1979), recorded this discussion.
23 The best Orthodox discussions known to me are Vladimir Lossky, *The
   Mystical Theology of the Eastern Church* (in English, 1957); Kallistos
   Ware, *The Orthodox Church* (1964) and *The Orthodox Way* (1979); John
   Meyendorff, *Orthodoxy and Catholicity* (1966) and *Catholicity and the
   Church* (1983); John Zizioulas, *Being as Communion* (1985). *Orthodox
   Thought* (1983) was a recent report on consultations sponsored by the
   WCC. A. M. Allchin, in *The Kingdom of Love and Knowledge* (1979),
   collected essays on the encounter between Orthodoxy and the West.
   Archbishop Methodios Fouyas summed up the relationship of *Ortho-
   doxy, Roman Catholicism and Anglicanism* (1972).
24 Ulrich Duchrow, *Conflict over the Ecumenical Movement* (in English,
   Geneva, 1981), was a study by a former staff member of the Lutheran
   World Federation. Similarly searching self-examinations from within
   other traditions are much to be desired. A useful summary of the work of
   the World Council of Churches since 1948 has been provided by Ans van
   der Brent, *Vital Ecumenical Concerns* (Geneva, 1986). The Faith and
   Order Commission's report of its Salamanca consultation on *What Kind
   of Unity?* (Geneva, 1974) was of permanent value.
25 Geoffrey Wainwright, *The Ecumenical Movement* (1983), p. 12.
26 Paul Johnson, *A History of the Modern World* (1983), p. 698. The US
   edition was entitled *Modern Times*.

INDEX

Abraham, 18, 260, 274
Action Française, 309
Acquaviva, S., 321, 322
Acts of the Apostles, 31–3, 37, 40, 46, 278
Adventists, 134, 181, 330–1
Africa and Christianity, 172–201
Africa Evangelical Fellowship, 181
African independent churches, 181–3, 192
Africa Inland Mission, 181
African traditional religion, 172–5, 180, 191–201
Agnosticism, 311
Ahimsa, 213
Aids, 160, 354
Albania, 288, 319
Albigensians, 303
Alcuin, 79
Alexander VI, 116
Alexandria, 45, 53, 65
Alfred, 79
Algeria, 258
All Africa Conference of Churches, 189
India Seminar, 204
Union Council, 317
Allan, R., 429
Allende, Pres., 126, 152
Alliance for Progress, 120
Alternative Service Book, 91
Alves, R., 124
Ambedkar, B. R., 208, 242
Ambrose, 53, 54
Amida, 244
Amin, I., 187
Amos, 23, 371
Andronicus, 29
Anglican Consultative Council, 99, 108
Anglicanism, 75–8, 99, 179, 204, 403, 405, 406–7, 408, 411, 412, 442–4 and see Episcopal Church

Anglo-Catholics, 84–5
Anglo-Saxon Christianity, 77–9
Anicetus, 46
Anti-Semitism, 265–7
Antioch, 38, 39, 46, 53, 66, 67
Apocalyptic, 25–6
Apostles, 28–9, 38, 67
Apostles' Creed, 67, 88, 102
Apostolic Faith Today, 388–394
Apollinarius, 64–5
Arabic, use of, 257–8
Arabs, 72, 257–8
Arians, 62–3, 66
Armenia, 68
Armininians, 83, 88
Arusha Declaration, 187
Ashkenazim, 270
Ashoka, 242
Asia and Christianity, 226–52
Asia Theological Association, 418
Assemblies of God, 118, 135
Assman, H., 124
Association of Evangelicals of Africa, 417
Assumption of BVM, 413–4
Athanasian Creed, 67
Atonement, 430
Augustine of Canterbury, 77–8
Augustine of Hippo, 58–9, 65, 83, 402
Australia, 95, 98, 102, 286, 361–8
Authority for Anglicans, 443
Azariah, Bp., 202
Azariah, M., 207–8, 219

Balfour Declaration, 269
Bandaranaike, Mrs, 239

Bangkok Conference of Evangelicals, 418–20
Bangladesh, 240
Baptism, 18, 33, 47, 191, 405–6
Baptism, Eucharist and Ministry, 405–8, 437, 446
Baptists, 76, 96, 131, 133, 181, 205, 316
Barrett, D., 174, 182, 227
Barth, K., 14, 276, 280, 301, 392, 436, 446–7
Basil, 53
Basques, 287, 311
Baum, G., 400
Bavaria, 287
Bayne, S., 110
BCMS, 96
Becket, T., 80
Bede, 79
Bediako, K., 419
Belgium, 287
Bellah, R. N., 169
Benevolent Empire, 132
Berger, P., 384
Berlin Conference, 179
Berton, P., 365
Beyerhaus, R., 426
Bhagavad Gita, 214, 216, 223–4, 275
Biafra, 184
Biblical authority, 41–3, 102, 396, 402, 421–4
Biblical translation, 427–8
Biddiss, M., 332
Birth control, 141, 159, 163, 349, 350, 354, 397, 399–400, 415
Bishops, 51, 57–8, 100, 192–4, 401, 407–8, 410, 436–7, 445–6
Bismarck, Count v., 308, 312
Blacks in USA, 114, 138, 142, 149
Blake, E. C., 164, 438
Bodhisattva, 244

P. 274   Gen. 1–11 : material to grasp the dialogue of God with humanity.